ROMAN JAKOBSON
SELECTED WRITINGS
VII

ROMAN JAKOBSON

SELECTED WRITINGS

VII

Contributions to Comparative Mythology. Studies in Linguistics and Philology, 1972–1982.

Edited by Stephen Rudy, with a preface by Linda R. Waugh

1985
MOUTON PUBLISHERS
BERLIN · NEW YORK · AMSTERDAM

CIP-Kurztitelaufnahme der Deutschen Bibliothek

Jakobson, Roman:
Selected writings / Roman Jakobson. – Berlin ; New York ; Amsterdam : Mouton
NE: Jakobson, Roman: [Sammlung]
7. Jakobson, Roman: Contributions to comparative mythology. – 1985

Jakobson, Roman:
Contributions to comparative mythology. Studies in linguistics and philology, 1972 – 1982 / Roman Jakobson. Ed. by Stephen Rudy. With a pref. by Linda R. Waugh. – Berlin ; New York ; Amsterdam : Mouton, 1985.
    (Selected writings / Roman Jakobson; 7)
    ISBN 3-11-010617-5
NE: Jakobson, Roman: [Sammlung]

Library of Congress Cataloging in Publication Data

Jakobson, Roman, 1896–1982
    Contributions to comparative mythology.
    (Selected writings / Roman Jakobson ; 7)
    English, French, and Russian.
    Includes bibliographies and indexes.
    1. Linguistics – Addresses, essays, lectures. 2. Philology – Addresses, essays, lectures. 3. Mythology, Indo-European – Addresses, essays, lectures. I. Rudy, Stephen. II. Jakobson, Roman, 1896–1982. Studies in linguistics and philology, 1972–1982. 1985. III. Title. IV. Title: Studies in linguistics and philology, 1972–1982. V. Series: Jakobson, Roman, 1896–1982. Selections. 1962 ; 7.
P217.J3 vol. 7   [P49]   410   84–20713
ISBN 0-89925-051-3

Printed on acid free paper

© Copyright 1985 by Walter de Gruyter & Co., Berlin. All rights reserved, including those of translation into foreign languages. No part of this book may be reproduced in any form — by photoprint, microfilm, or any other means — nor transmitted nor translated into a machine language without written permission from the publisher. Typesetting: H Charlesworth & Co. Ltd., Huddersfield, England. — Printing: Druckerei Gerike GmbH, Berlin. — Binding: Lüderitz & Bauer Buchgewerbe GmbH, Berlin.
Printed in Germany.

CONTENTS

Preface (*Linda R. Waugh*) IX

PART ONE
CONTRIBUTIONS TO COMPARATIVE MYTHOLOGY

Slavic Gods and Demons 3

Linguistic Evidence in Comparative Mythology 12
I. State and Program of Comparative Mythology, 12. — II. Russian Perun and his Slavic and Indo-European Kin, 16. — III. The Slavic Velesъ and his Indo-European Cognates, 24. — IV. Svarogъ and his Iranian Prototype. Slavic Gods of Iranian Background, 25. — V. Slavic Gods and their Semantic Namesakes in the Indo-European World, 30.

The Slavic God Velesъ and His Indo-European Cognates . . 33
I. Russian *Volosъ* and *Velesъ*, 33. — II. *Veles* in South Slavic Toponymy and Czech Demonology, 36. — III. The *Vel-* Family of Baltic Spirits, 37. — IV. Vedic *Varuṇa*, 39. — V. The Root *Wel-* in Celtic Lore; The "People of *Varuṇa*", "The Son of *Fel*", and "The Grandson of *Velesъ*", 40. — VI. *Velesъ/Volosъ* — *Vēlinas* — *Varuṇa*, 41. — VII. Vedic *Varuṇa*, Avestan *Ahura-Mazdā*, and Celtic *Esus*, 42. — VIII. *Velesъ* and *Volosъ* as Compounds, 43. — IX. Gaulish *Vellaunus*, 43. — X. Anatolian *Wališ-* and Old Norse *Ullr* or *Ullinn*, 44. — XI. A Summarized Comparison of the Cognates, 44. — XII. Slavic *Vъlxvъ* "Magician" and North Russian *Jols* "Devil", 45. — XIII. Vedic *Vala* — Lithuanian *Vēlė* — Czech *Vele*, 46. — XIV. Supreme Deities of the I.-E. Pantheon and their Degradation, 47.

Древнеармянский Вахагн в свете сравнительной мифологии 49

PART TWO
STUDIES IN LINGUISTICS AND PHILOLOGY, 1972–1982

A. PHONOLOGICAL AND MORPHOLOGICAL STUDIES

(*with L. R. Waugh*) An Instance of Interconnection between the Distinctive Features 59

Mutual Assimilation of Russian Voiced and Voiceless Consonants 62

The Primary Syntactic Split and Its Corollary 66

Spatial Relationships in Slavic Adjectives 68

Notes on the Declension of Pronouns in Contemporary Russian 73

B. CRUCIAL QUESTIONS OF LINGUISTIC THEORY

Verbal Communication 81

The Fundamental and Specific Characteristics of Human Language 93

Communication and Society 98

Language and Culture 101

Metalanguage as a Linguistic Problem 113

Mark and Feature 122

Structuralisme et Téléologie 125

On Aphasic Disorders from a Linguistic Angle 128

The Grammatical Buildup of Child Language 141

On the Linguistic Approach to the Problem of Consciousness and the Unconscious 148

Brain and Language: Cerebral Hemispheres and Linguistic Structure in Mutual Light 163

The Evasive Initial 181

C. TOWARDS A NOMOTHETIC SCIENCE OF LANGUAGE

Glosses on the Medieval Insight into the Science of Language 185

A Glance at the Development of Semiotics 199

The World Response to Whitney's Principles of Linguistic Science 219

La première lettre de Ferdinand de Saussure à Antoine Meillet sur les anagrammes 237

A Few Remarks on Peirce, Pathfinder in the Science of Language 248

Einstein and the Science of Language 254

The Twentieth Century in European and American Linguistics: Movements and Continuity 265

CONTENTS VII

Toward the History of the Moscow Linguistic Circle . . . 279
Очередные задачи общей лингвистики 283
Pëtr Bogatyrëv (29.I.93–18.VIII.71): Expert in Transfiguration 293
По поводу книги Н. С. Трубецкого "Европа и человечество". 305
The Immediate Quests and Accomplishments of Comparative Linguistics 314

D. PHILOLOGICAL GLEANINGS

When a Falcon has Molted 321
Goroun's Urn 332
The Etymology of *Grib* (E. Sl. Fungus, W. Sl. Boletus). . . 336

E. POETICS

Andrew Marvell's Poem *To His Coy Mistress* 341
Deržavin's Last Poem and M. Halle's First Literary Essay . 349
Игра в Аду у Пушкина и Хлебникова 353
From Aljagrov's Letters 357
Из комментария к стихам Маяковского "Товарищу Нетте — пароходу и человеку" 362

PART THREE
RETROSPECTIONS

My Favorite Topics 371
On the Dialectics of Language 377

List of Illustrations 379
Index of Names 380
Index of Languages Discussed 390
Index of Subjects 392
Index of Mythological Names 401
Index of Mythological Motifs 404

PREFACE

I. Volume VII of Roman Jakobson's *Selected Writings: Contributions to Comparative Mythology; Studies in Linguistics and Philology, 1972–1982*, contains 33 studies, all written during Jakobson's American period. It incorporates 4 works on comparative mythology (Part One of the volume), 27 on linguistics, philology, and poetics (Part Two), and 2 of a more retrospective bent (Part Three). Two of the contributions are published here for the first time: "Očerednye zadači obščej lingvistiki" [Current tasks of general linguistics], and "Andrew Marvell's Poem *To His Coy Mistress*"; and three are available here for the first time in their original English version, having been published previously only in a translated version: "The Fundamental and Specific Characteristics of Human Language", "Communication and Society", and "My Favorite Topics". Five others were translated into English especially for this volume: "Linguistic Evidence in Comparative Mythology", "The Immediate Quests and Accomplishments of Comparative Linguistics", "When a Falcon has Molted", "Goroun's Urn", and "The Grammatical Buildup of Child Language".

This volume has been in preparation for several years. The author established the list of entries, and at the time of his death in July 1982 was working on the revision of various studies which were to have been included had he been able to finish them. Other than these omissions, the contents of the volume are as he envisaged them. However, the editor decided to establish for Part Two, not a chronological order as originally set out by Jakobson, but a breakdown into topical sections which correspond to previous volumes of his *Selected Writings*. Moreover, it was felt that "My Favorite Topics" and "On the Dialectics of Language", which originally figured in the chronological list, could, because of their nature as self-characterizations, serve in the guise of a retrospect, since the author had planned to write a retrospect, just as for the previous six volumes, but did not have the time to do so. These two essays have thus been established as Part Three by the editor.

Perhaps more than any other of Jakobson's *Selected Writings*, Volume *VII* must be viewed in conjunction with the previous volumes[1], since the extraordinarily broad range of topics presented here has ties with all the rest of his work. But what perhaps is even more Jakobsonian about this volume is that, just as Jakobson here continues his previous work in domains such as phonology, grammatical morphology, linguistic theory, comparative linguistics, history of linguistics, child language and aphasia, philology, poetics, mythology — at the same time he pushes this work further and he even ventures into new areas: Slavic gods and their counterparts in other Indo-European cultures, grammar and syntax in child language acquisition, adjectival lexical meaning, Russian pronominal morphology, metalanguage, the unconscious, anagrams, medieval linguistic theory, language and the brain, Einstein and linguistics, to name a few. And while all of these contributions are those of the mature Jakobson, always with an eye to future research[2], some, Janus-faced, mark a return to and a contextualization of his early Russian experience — Aljagrov (Jakobson's pseudonym as a young poet), the Moscow Linguistic Circle, Bogatyrëv, Trubetzkoy, and Majakovskij. We also find here a characteristic of Jakobson's later period: studies of a more autobiographical stamp, a tradition which began with his "Retrospects", continues here in "The Evasive Initial" and "From Aljagrov's Letters", and culminates in the *Dialogues* (1982, to be incorporated in *SW VIII*). This volume is, thus, an example of the "dynamic synchrony" — continuity with the past (a return to past themes) and preparation of the future (delineation of new topics) — which Jakobson was prone to point to as the necessary stamp of any system which will survive and which attests to the vitality of its creative potential.

* * *

Part One of this volume contains four of Jakobson's contributions to the study of comparative mythology. At the time of his death, he was working on the revision of other, unpublished materials intended to be included in this section, based on courses and lectures he had given in

---

[1] The *Selected Writings* (henceforth abbreviated as *SW*) contain the following volumes: *I, Phonological Studies* (1962; 2nd, expanded ed. 1971); *II, Word and Language* (1971); *III, Poetry of Grammar and Grammar of Poetry* (1981); *IV, Slavic Epic Studies* (1966); *V, On Verse, its Masters and Explorers* (1979); *VI, Early Slavic Pathways and Crossroads* (1985); *VIII, Major Works, 1976–1980* (in preparation).
[2] See Vjačeslav V. Ivanov, "Roman Jakobson: the Future", in *A Tribute to Roman Jakobson* (Berlin: Mouton, 1983).

the areas of Slavic and Indo-European mythology and paganism. But unfortunately, he was unable to finish them: thus, Part One is considerably shorter than Jakobson had envisaged[3].

While these mythological studies may be read as an integral whole, they also provide material which is germane to and is illuminated by an understanding of other parts of Jakobson's work, in particular his contributions to Slavic epic studies, including his masterful works on the Igor' Tale contained in *SW IV*, his studies on Slavic medieval questions reprinted in *SW VI*, and his articles on philological questions included in section C of the present volume and in the corresponding section of *SW II*.

Jakobson's contributions to comparative mythology are densely textured, reflecting the diversity of his interests and the breadth of his intellectual scope. As a whole, these writings may be characterized, as Riccardo Picchio has said of the third study reprinted here[4], as "outstanding example[s] of [Jakobson's] erudite versatility and masterly combination of the techniques of textual criticism, formal analysis, etymology, comparative philology and linguistics, as well as religious and literary history, all leading toward a new critical synthesis".

All of the articles given here show the results of Jakobson's fascination with Russian oral culture — proverbs, legends, riddles, children's counting-out rhymes, *byliny* (heroic epic verse), spoken verse, recitatives, sung verse, spirituals, fairy tales, folk tales, and the like — in addition to his interest in written culture and literature. And while his work in the mid to late 1940's on Russian fairy tales, the Igor' Tale, the Vseslav Epos, and Slavic epic verse[5] provided an obvious link to his interest in Slavic and more widely in Indo-European mythology, it was his concern with structural linguistics and especially his own apprenticeship in comparative linguistics which provided the methodological and theoretical underpinning. In fact, his characterization of comparative linguistics is particularly precise as a discussion of the methodology he followed in his comparative mythological work as well: "Comparative linguistics brings out 1) intrinsic typological parallels, 2) analogical

---

[3] They are, however, contained in the Roman Jakobson archive and are now part of the Massachusetts Institute of Technology Archives and Special Collections, in Cambridge, Massachusetts.
[4] Riccardo Picchio, "Roman Jakobson on Russian Epics and Old Russian Literature", in *Roman Jakobson: Echoes of his Scholarship*", ed. by D. Armstrong and C. H. van Schooneveld (Lisse: The Peter de Ridder Press, 1977), p. 331.
[5] See, for example, "La Geste du Prince Igor'", *SW IV*: 106–300, "The Vseslav Epos" (with Marc Szeftel), *SW IV*: 301–368, "Slavic Epic Verse: Studies in Comparative Metrics", *SW IV*: 414–465.

developmental traits due to similar social and cultural preconditions, 3) correspondences based on common ancestry, and 4) points of likeness caused by diffusion. Finally etymologists trace the connection of the vocabulary and phraseology of a given language with historical events, morals and manners"[6]. This formulation could profitably be compared with "The Immediate Quests and Accomplishments of Comparative Linguistics", reprinted in section C of the present volume, which, though written as a preface to the book *Indoevropejskij jazyk i indoevropejcy* [Indo-European and the Indo-Europeans] by T. V. Gamkrelidze and V. V. Ivanov, is also a sketch of Jakobson's own attitude toward reconstruction and historical-typological analysis.

"Slavic Gods and Demons", the first of the studies in this volume, was originally published in 1950 as a contribution to the Funk and Wagnall's *Standard Dictionary of Folklore, Mythology, and Legend*. It is, in Calvert Watkins' characterization, "one of the most remarkable publications of Jakobson's entire career .... Perhaps never before or since has an entire field been so deftly and so surely delineated and defined, and so many fertile suggestions for future exploration been so lightly tossed out, in so few pages."[7] "Linguistic Evidence in Comparative Mythology", a more specific discussion and exemplification of Jakobson's linguistic technique in mythological work, "The Slavic God Velesъ and his Indo-European Cognates", which had received the characterization of Picchio cited above, and "Drevnearmjanskij Vaxagn v svete sravnitel'noj mifologii" ["Old Armenian Vahagn in the Light of Comparative Mythology"], drafted in April/May 1982 in the Massachusetts General Hospital and presented posthumously to the International Conference on Armenian Studies in Erevan in September 1982 by his widow Krystyna Pomorska — all provide eloquent testimony to Jakobson's skills as a comparatist and mythologist.

* * *

Part Two of this volume — "Studies in Linguistics and Philology, 1972–1982" — contains Jakobson's last, shorter works around the themes central to *SW I, II, III,* and *V*. The longer writings of this same period will be published in *SW VIII*. The first two articles in Part A, Phonological and Morphological Studies, expand upon Jakobson's

---

[6] "Retrospect", *SW IV*, p. 648.
[7] Calvert Watkins, "Slavic Mythology and Folklore", in *Roman Jakobson: What He Taught Us*, ed. by M. Halle (Columbus, Ohio: Slavica Publishers, Inc., 1983), p. 38 and in *A Tribute to Roman Jakobson, op. cit.*, p. 39.

work in phonology (see as well *SW I* and *SW VIII*). "An Instance of Interconnection between the Distinctive Features"[8], based on principles outlined in Jakobson and Waugh's *The Sound Shape of Language*[9] and written after the book was in press, explores further the questions of phonological opposition and markedness. In particular, it discusses the reversibility of markedness when a given feature is linked concurrently with other features and the relation of such reverses with universal and implicational laws as evidenced by phonological systems of the linguistic world.[10] In "Mutual Assimilation of Russian Voiced and Voiceless Consonants"[11], what is at issue is not only the question of markedness but also dynamic synchrony, the fact that a system or a subsystem (here, the relation between obstruents and sonorants of Russian coupled with that between voiced and voiceless pairs) may be characterized by intermediate units, borrowings and other foreignisms, as well as by closer vs. further correlations — *i.e.*, by different weightings of the units. Here is the specific application of Jakobson's tenet that no system can be seen as static or as the mechanical aggregate of its parts.

The two following studies in this section — one on syntax and the other on the lexicon — are particularly interesting because they contain a discussion of areas which Jakobson generally only alluded to in previous work and for the study of which one is obliged to peruse carefully *SW II* and *SW III* in particular. "The Primary Syntactic Split and its Corollary" continues Jakobson's concern with child language acquisition and would most profitably be read in

---

[8] Written in collaboration with L. R. Waugh. Interestingly, this is the only co-authored paper in the volume, in contrast with the other volumes of *Selected Writings*, which contain many co-authored works.
[9] Roman Jakobson and Linda R. Waugh, *The Sound Shape of Language* (Bloomington, Ind.: Indiana University Press and Hassocks, England: Harvester Press, 1979. Second edition, Berlin: Mouton, forthcoming).
[10] This may profitably be read in conjunction with "Mark and Feature", incorporated in Part Two, Section B of this volume.
[11] An earlier discussion of similar questions may be found in "Die Verteilung der stimmhaften und stimmlosen Geräuschlaute im Russischen" (*SW I*: 505–509) and "K voprosu o gluxosti i zvonkosti russkix ščelinnyx gubnyx" [On the question of voicelessness and voicing in Russian labials] (*SW I*: 728–733).
[12] "Kindersprache, Aphasie, und allgemeine Lautgesetze", *SW I*: 328–401 (translated as *Child Language, Aphasia, and Phonological Universals*, the Hague: Mouton, 1968); "Les Lois phoniques du langage enfantin et leur place dans la phonologie générale", *SW I*: 317–327 (translated as "The Sound Laws of Child Language and their Place in General Phonology", *Studies in Child Language and Aphasia*, the Hague: Mouton, 1971: 7–20); "Anthony's Contribution to Linguistic Theory", *SW II*: 285–288 *(Studies...*: 31–37); "Why 'Mama' and 'Papa'?" *SW II*: 21–30 (*Studies...*: 21–30); "Phonology and Phonetics", *SW I*: 464–504, especially 491–504 (also published as the first part of *Fundamentals of Language*, the Hague: Mouton, 1956).

conjunction with his previous work on that topic[12], as well as with his study "Shifters, Verbal Categories, and the Russian Verb" (*SW II*: 130–147), in addition to the various writings on child language included in this volume. What is particularly of interest here is his insistence on the importance of the syntactic notions of subject vs. predicate in correlation with the liberation of language from the *hic et nunc* of the speech event through the emergence of the verb vs. the noun and shifters vs. non-shifters.

"Spatial Relationships in Slavic Adjectives" contains one of the few synchronic studies of lexical meaning in Jakobson's published oeuvre, as against grammatical meaning, which received much of his scholarly attention[13]. Aside from his philological studies, contained in *SW II* and this volume, and various allusions to lexical meaning embedded in particular in Part B: Crucial Questions of Linguistic Theory (*SW II*) as well as in his writings on poetics (*SW III*), there is a fairly long discussion of lexical meaning to be found for example in *Aspects of the theories of Roman Jakobson*, based on lectures he gave at Louvain[14]; however, the latter volume was not approved by Jakobson since he was unable to correct the text. In addition, there are very suggestive remarks on lexical meaning in the unpublished notes contained in his "La Théorie saussurienne en rétrospection"[15]. While lexical meaning is, according to Jakobson, to be differentiated from grammatical meaning by its non-obligatoriness and its less tightly constrained structure[16], the same methodological and theoretical preliminaries are followed: the presence of various formal elements (here, derivational suffixes) is used as a means of delimiting the items to be studied, the pairs of adjectives are seen in relation one to another and in particular with respect to the concept of opposition and markedness, and data from child language acquisition is brought in to support the analysis.

"Notes on the Declension of Pronouns in Contemporary Russian" continues the tradition exemplified by Jakobson's work on the verbal

---

[13] See for example the works collected in *SW II*, Part A: Morphological Studies and *SW III*, Part One: Principles and Part Two: Readings.
[14] M. van Ballaer, *Aspects of the Theories of Roman Jakobson* (Memoir, Katholieke Universiteit te Leuven, 1972).
[15] The first part of that article, which is a general discussion, will appear in *Linguistics Vol. 22* (1984), 161–196; the section dealing with lexical meaning was, however, too fragmentary for publication and will be included in the Jakobson archives.
[16] See "Boas' View of Grammatical Meaning" in *SW II*: 489–496. See also, Linda R. Waugh "Introduction", in Roman Jakobson, *Russian and Slavic Grammar, Studies 1931–1981*, ed. by L. R. Waugh and M. Halle (Berlin: Mouton, 1984), pp. ix–xvi.

and nominal systems of Russian.[17] This is a terse study aimed at showing the special place of pronouns in the grammatical system by correlating their meaning with their formal properties while establishing the invariants which underlie their declensional pattern.

Section B, Crucial Questions of Linguistic Theory, contains 12 articles which significantly expand upon themes found in the same-named part of *SW II*. "Verbal Communication", first written for a special issue of *Scientific American* on communication and thus destined for the wider public, is a new departure for Jakobson since it provides a synthetic, encyclopedic approach to the question of the nature of language: relational invariance vs. contextual variation, markedness and opposition, dynamic synchrony and diversity of codes, context-sensitivity, syntax as grammatical forms and processes, written vs. oral language, and the history of linguistics — especially the mutual relation between relativity theory and the growth of phonology. "The Fundamental and Specific Characteristics of Human Language", written for a Salk Institute Conference on the Biological Foundations of Language, provides an integrated discussion, highly accessible to the non-specialist, of Jakobson's views on child language acquisition and the importance of child language for our understanding of the nature of human language and its differentiation from animal communication. Both "Communication and Society" and "Language and Culture" — the only synthetic statements by Jakobson about the relation between linguistic and cultural systems[18] — envisage language as a communicative, a semiotic, and a cultural phenomenon and argue on the one hand for both nature and culture, both inheritance and acculturation as the foundations for language, and on the other hand for the importance that linguistic (especially grammatical) categories have for our cognitive and "mythological" patterns. Here, as elsewhere, Jakobson argues against the absolutization of our understanding of the nature and foundation of language and culture.

"Metalanguage as a Linguistic Problem", first presented at the Presidential Address to the Linguistic Society of America in 1956 but

---

[17] "Zur Struktur des russischen Verbums" (*SW II*: 3–15), "Beitrag zur allgemeinen Kasuslehre: Gesambedeutungen der russischen Kasus" (*SW II*: 23–71), "Shifters, Verbal Categories, and the Russian Verb" (*SW II*: 130–147), and "Morfologičeskie nabljudenija nad slavjanskim skloneniem" [Morphological Observations on Slavic Declension] (*SW II*: 154–183). These articles are also published in English translation (where relevant) in *Russian and Slavic Grammar, Studies 1931–1981*, *op. cit.* See also Igor Mel'čuk, "Three Main Features, Seven Basic Principles, and Eleven Most Important Results of Roman Jakobson's Morphological Research", in Roman Jakobson, *Verbal Art, Verbal Sign, Verbal Time*, ed. by Krystyna Pomorska and Stephen Rudy (Minneapolis: Univ. of Minnesota Press, 1985).

[18] But see also "Language in Relation to other Communication Systems", *op. cit.*

not published until 1976, brought for the first time to the attention of modern linguistics the importance of metalanguage in our everyday linguistic life and in child language acquisition as well as its self-evident importance for linguistic methodology. The general schema for the study of metalanguage outlined in the first few pages was also the basis for Jakobson's path-breaking delineation of the poetic vs. other functions of language usage (in "Linguistics and Poetics" [*SW III*: 19–51]). "Mark and Feature", a terminological paper dealing with the differentiation of two technical terms, argues that any phonological or grammatical opposition (whatever may be the underlying feature) is to be seen as a correlation of a marked pole or mark (*n.b.*, 'pole' or 'mark', not 'feature') with an unmarked pole; however, which pole is the marked one may depend upon the simultaneous and sequential contexts which the feature is contained in[19]. "Structuralisme et téléologie" contains Jakobson's mature reflections on the fundamental components of the teleological nature of language in all its functions as intertwined with his concepts of structure, opposition and markedness, communicative value, and signification.[20]

The remaining five studies in this section: "On Aphasic Disorders from a Linguistic Angle", "The Grammatical Buildup of Child Language", "On the Linguistic Approach to the Problem of Consciousness and the Unconscious", "Brain and Language: Cerebral Hemispheres and Linguistic Structure in Mutual Light", and "The Evasive Initial" (in addition to the already mentioned "The Primary Syntactic Split and its Corollary" and "The Fundamental and Specific Characteristics of Human Language"), on the one hand expand on the discussion of themes contained in his studies of child language and aphasia[21] and on the other hand explore in depth new areas: language in relation to consciousness and the unconscious, and hemispheric specialization in the brain. What binds these studies together is their plea for the recognition that all of these questions must be approached from an

---

[19] See also "An Instance of Interconnection between the Distinctive Features", discussed above.
[20] See also his earlier sketches: "The Concept of the Sound Law and the Teleological Criterion" (*SW I*: 1–2); "Proposition au Premier Congrès International de Linguistes. Quelles sont les méthodes les mieux appropriées à un exposé complet et pratique de la phonolologie d'une langue quelconque?" (*SW I*: 3–6); "Retrospect" (*SW II*: 711–712).
[21] For child language, see the studies listed in footnote 12 above. For aphasia, see "Aphasia as a Linguistic Topic" (*SW II*: 229–238); "Two Types of Aphasia and Two Types of Aphasic Disturbances" (*SW II*: 239–259); "Toward a Linguistic Classification of Aphasic Impairments" (*SW II*: 289–306); "Linguistic Types of Aphasia" (*SW II*: 307–333). (These are all reprinted as well in *Studies on Child Language and Aphasia*, op. cit.)

eminently linguistic point of view since they concern language, that the search for general laws must underlie any discussion of data, and that neither in the analysis of specific data nor in questions of interdisciplinary work should there be isolationism, i.e., the divorcing of the phenomena from their context, or colonialism, i.e., the unwarranted mixing of various domains, but rather autonomy and integration.

"On Aphasic Disorders from a Linguistic Angle" provides a retrospective and prospective view by Jakobson of his own and other's work on aphasia and thus may serve as a general introduction to this area. "The Grammatical Buildup of Child Language" affords for the first time a synthesis of Jakobson's work on the child's learning of grammar, since most of his previous studies on child language were centered on phonology. "On the Linguistic Approach to the Problem of Consciousness and the Unconscious" provides Jakobson's first general discussion of this question[22]. The historical point of view in this study centers on the early work of J. Baudouin de Courtenay and M. Kruszewski[23] (stressing in particular the question of "unconscious generalization" or "apperception"), as well as on the later work of F. de Saussure, F. Boas, and E. Sapir ("unconscious patterning"), in the light of recent research concerning metalanguage and child language, in addition to the hitherto unknown concept of "set" in the process of development by the Georgian school of psychology.

"Brain and Language", first published as a pamphlet in 1980, grew out of corresponding material in *The Sound Shape of Language* (pp. 28–36) and represents one of Jakobson's preoccupations in the last period of his life. In fact he confessed once that if he were to be a young linguist now he would study language and the brain, and language and schizophrenia; moreover, one of my last conversations with him had to do with the latest research on the relation between distinctive features and the brain. Jakobson saw that the work on hemispheric specialization and on the localization of various functions within the hemispheres

---

[22] The role of the unconscious was already alluded to in previous work — see for example "Subliminal Verbal Patterning in Poetry", *SW III*: 136–147, and "La Théorie saussurienne en rétrospection", *op. cit.* See in addition, Elmar Holenstein, *Roman Jakobson's Approach to Language* (Bloomington, Ind.: Indiana Univ. Press, 1976), 64–69.

[23] For further discussion of these two scholars, see "Jan Baudouin de Courtenay" (*SW II*: 389–393), "The Kazan' School of Polish Linguistics and its Place in the International Development of Phonology" (*SW II*: 394–428), "Značenie Kruševskogo v razvitii nauki o jazyke" [The Significance of Kruszewski for the Development of the Science of Language] (*SW II*: 429–450), and "Polish–Russian Cooperation in the Science of Language" (*SW II*: 451–455). And for an appraisal of Jakobson's work in this area, see Edward Stankiewicz, "Roman Jakobson's Work on the History of Linguistics", in Armstrong & van Schooneveld, *op. cit.*, pp. 435–452.

correlated with findings in linguistics. In particular, it has corroborated the differentiation of linguistic from other auditory phenomena, including music. Furthermore, Jakobson felt vindicated that, in the investigation of the localization of linguistic phenomena, the division between on the one hand the phonemic, especially the distinctive (and their ancillary redundant) features — *i.e.*, those features which exhibit mediacy, an indirect tie with meaning — and on the other hand the expressive and physiognomic features and intonations — *i.e.*, those which exhibit immediacy, a direct tie with meaning — was reflected in hemispheric specialization.[24] Those features which evidence mediacy seem to be associated with the left hemisphere and those evidencing immediacy with the right hemisphere. In addition, the propensity of the left hemisphere for future time and abstract cognition as against that of the right hemisphere for past time and sensitive/sensible cognition (pertaining to the senses and thus concrete) is correlated with the work of the great semiotician C. S. Peirce.

"The Evasive Initial" is an unusual event in Jakobson's publishing life, comprising his keen and playful observations of his own disabilities after suffering a mild stroke. It is uncharacteristic of Jakobson that the discussion should be couched in the form of a report in the first person[25] about some other unnamed person (who happens to be himself), a self-observation differentiating the scholar from the man. What *is* characteristic is that he used the occasion to make further generalizations on the dichotomies: reading/writing, left-/right-handedness, and left-to-right-/right-to-left systems of writing (in view of their relation to hemispheric specialization).

Section C, Toward a Nomothetic Science of Language, the longest section of the volume, centers on questions of the history of linguistics and of semiotics. Jakobson's interest in the history of linguistics dates from his earliest writings and indeed references to this topic are at the core of his scholarly oeuvre[26]. It is typical of his approach that, as Edward Stankiewicz has said, "Jakobson's historical interests are far from antiquarian: he probes the past for its relevance to the present and traces the growth of the ideas which have made linguistics into a pivotal

---

[24] See *The Sound Shape of Language, op. cit.*, 13–18, 36–47.
[25] Jakobson seldom used the first person, except in his more autobiographical writings: Roman Jakobson and Krystyna Pomorska, *Dialogues* (Cambridge, Mass: MIT Press, 1983); "Retrospect" (in all the *Selected Writings*); and interviews. For a discussion, see Krystyna Pomorska, "The Autobiography of a Scholar", *Proceedings of the First Roman Jakobson Colloquium, 1984* (Berlin: Mouton, forthcoming).
[26] The bulk of his work in the history of linguistics is contained in the section, Toward a Nomothetic Science of Language, in *SW II*: 369–602.

science of man, a science which now bears the decisive imprint of his thought."[27] In "Glosses on the Medieval Insight into the Science of Language" — in a departure from the tendency evidenced by *SW II* to focus on 19th and 20th century figures and schools — Jakobson restores, for the linguistic community, the nearly forgotten but highly original theory *de modi significandi* and demonstrates its validity for current inquiry into the nature of grammatical and lexical meaning and into *ars poetica*.

"Glance at the Development of Semiotics", written in 1975, is Jakobson's first truly synthetic study of semiotics, *sensu stricto*[28]. In fact, one can say that he was never as devoted to semiotics as in the last period of his life. Here, he rehabilitates the lost thinking of Jean Henri Lambert, Joseph Marie Hoene-Wronski, and Bernard Bolzano, and treats as well the semiotic contributions of Edmund Husserl, Charles Sanders Peirce, and Ferdinand de Saussure. The article closes with Jakobson's own characterization of vital questions of semiotic (and hence, linguistic) inquiry.

"La première lettre de Ferdinand de Saussure à Antoine Meillet sur les anagrammes" is a contribution to the history of poetics, linguistics, and semiotics, since it is here that Jakobson endorses Saussure's interest in anagrams, judged by Jakobson (in contradistinction to many other scholars) to be among Saussure's most interesting insights. In Jakobson's estimation, it is this work which allowed Saussure to overcome his own formulation of the strict linearity of the *signifiant* (against the absolute definition of which in the *Cours de linguistique générale* Jakobson was to argue in a variety of different publications[29]), and at the same time to explore the nature of the poetic text as exhibiting inner laws of structure in its own right.

"Einstein and the Science of Language" explores in greater depth issues already hinted elsewhere: the influence of relativity theory on Jakobson's own development (see "Retrospect", *SW I*: 632), the development of Einstein's thoughts on relativity theory in conjunction with his stay in the household of the linguist Jost Winteler (also discussed in "Verbal Communication"), and the importance of relations and equivalence for modern linguistics. In addition, what emerges here for the first time is a discussion of thinking as a semiotic, but not necessarily

---

[27] See Edward Stankiewicz, *op. cit.*, p. 435.
[28] Cf. his general discussions: "Linguistics in Relation to Other Sciences" (*SW II*: 655–696), "Language in Relation to Other Communication Systems" (*SW II*: 697–710), and "Retrospect" (*SW II*: 711–724).
[29] See for example the "Retrospects" to *SW I* and *SW II*.

linguistic, activity: thinking can take place in other than linguistic symbols.

Three of the studies in this section — "The World Response to Whitney's Principles of Linguistic Science", "A Few Remarks on Peirce, Pathfinder in the Science of Language", and "The Twentieth Century in European and American Linguistics: Movements and Continuity" — attest to those late 19th and 20th century American figures who most influenced Jakobson's thinking in linguistics and semiotics since his arrival in America in 1941. The first study underlines Whitney's influence upon and strong reputation in European linguistic circles, and explores especially Saussure's unpublished reflections on the American's work. Both the article on Peirce — whom Jakobson had virtually rediscovered for the American linguistic and semiotic community not long after his arrival in America and who was to have a decisive impact on Jakobson's work — and the pages devoted to the semiotician in "A Glance at the Development of Semiotics" (and elsewhere[30]) center on those areas which bind his own work to that of the semiotician: duality and dyads, translation and interpretation as semiotic questions, invariance and structure, iconicity as a counterpart to the arbitrariness of the sign, and time in relation to signs.[31] Perhaps most notably, his commentary on Peirce contains a binarization of Peirce's tripartite division of the sign (icon, index, and symbol): Jakobson adds a fourth sign, the 'artifice' (in which imputed similarity, such as parallelism[32], plays a chief role) and analyses this four-fold system with two dichotomies: similarity/contiguity (already known through Jakobson's work on aphasia and on poetics[33]), and factual/imputed. Jakobson also speaks, tellingly and knowingly, of Peirce's heroic and painful struggle to have his ideas accepted or even known. This is but one of several examples of Jakobson's interest in the lives of innovative scholars who were misunderstood and thus, like himself, had met with various difficulties and often even hostility. "The Twentieth Century in European and American Linguistics: Movements and Continuity" includes Jakobson's

---

[30] See "A Glance at the Development of Semiotics", discussed above, as well as "Linguistics in Relation to Other Sciences", *op. cit.*, and "Language in Relation to Other Communication Systems", *op. cit.*
[31] The question of the unity of time and of its semiotic/conceptual nature was always of concern to Jakobson. Cf. his discussion of Einstein's concept of relativity alluded to above. See also Krystyna Pomorska, "The Autobiography of a Scholar", *op. cit.*
[32] See also "Grammatical Parallelism and its Russian Facet", *SW III*: 98–135.
[33] See his seminal work, "Two Aspects of Language and Two Types of Aphasic Disturbances", *SW II*: 239–259.

own evaluation of the importance of such American linguistic figures as Leonard Bloomfield, Franz Boas[34], and Edward Sapir[35].

The next four articles in this section mark a return by the mature Jakobson to his Russian roots and in particular to his very early growth as a scholar. "Toward the History of the Moscow Linguistic Circle", is a precious document, informed by his own, central activity in this group. "Očerednye zadači obščej lingvistiki" [Current Tasks for General Linguistics], the last public lecture (in 1979) that he delivered at Moscow University where he himself had heard lectures about the same subjects as a student, is a summing up of the Russian contributions to linguistics, and a delineation of those pressing tasks which remain on the agenda for world linguistic science and which were already anticipated by the Moscow Linguistic Circle. "Pëtr Bogatyrëv (29.I.93–18.VIII.71): Expert in Transfiguration" is an affectionate appraisal of Jakobson's first collaborator, with whom he conducted field work during his undergraduate days (see "Preface", *SW IV*: vii–viii and "Retrospect", *SW IV*: 635–706) and then later wrote two fundamental studies on the question of folk poetry and literature[36], in which they argued that folklore is a collective, social phenomenon, and thus is analogous to the linguistic concept of *langue*, while literature is an individual, personal phenomenon, and thus is analogous to the linguistic concept of *parole*. Jakobson's appraisal of Bogatyrëv's work delineates, in a few lines, the structuralist and semiotic elements in the latter's studies of folk theatre, religious ritual, and folklore. "Po povodu knigi N. S. Trubeckogo 'Evropa i Celovečestvo'" [About N. S. Trubetskoy's book *Europe and Mankind*], written as a preface, presents the consistency and continuation of Trubetzkoy's thoughts concerning fundamental anthropological issues[37].

Section D., Philological Gleanings, adding to his earlier contributions in this same area, provides an eloquent example of Jakobson's breadth and depth of scholarly range, and brings together his own knowledge of

---

[34] Also explored in his "Franz Boas' Approach to Language" (*SW II*: 477–488) and "Boas' View of Grammatical Meaning", *op. cit.*

[35] It is curious, as Edward Stankiewicz has pointed out (*op. cit.*, p. 448ff), that despite Jakobson's deep admiration for Sapir and despite the evident influence of Sapir's work on his own, Jakobson never published a full-scale study of Sapir's work, although there are, in these three contributions, in his studies on the history of linguistics, and in other work (see e.g., *The Sound Shape of Language*), many highly positive references to Sapir.

[36] "Die Folklore als eine Besondere Form des Schaffens", *SW IV*: 1–15, "K probleme razmeževanija fol'kloristiki i literaturovedenija" [On the problem of the differentiation of folkloristics and literary analysis], *SW IV*: 16–18.

[37] See also Roman Jakobson, ed., *N. S. Trubetzkoy's Letters and Notes* (the Hague: Mouton, 1975).

Russian language and culture, cultural history, comparative philology and linguistics, etymology, textual analysis, poetic analysis, and the history of word meaning. "When a Falcon has Molted" continues his in-depth study of certain verses in the *Igor' Tale*, while "Goroun's Urn" unravels a 10th century Eastern Slavic inscription. "The Etymology of *Grib* (E. Sl. Fungus, W. Sl. Boletus)" conforms brilliantly to the principles set forth above for the study of etymology.

Section E, Poetics, is a continuation of Jakobson's life-work, specifically his later preoccupation with the poetry of grammar and grammar of poetry (*SW III*; see also *SW V*). Significantly, "Deržavin's Last Poem and M. Halle's First Literary Essay", written in 1982, is very different in its conception from the very early (1959) study, "Andrew Marvell's Poem *To his Coy Mistress*": one can see here the development of Jakobson's own technique in this area, which he himself created. "Igra v Adu u Puškina i Xlebnikova" [A Game in Hell in Puškin and Xlebnikov] discusses the relation between the literary text and the illustrated subtext in the popular edition of Puškin which was an inspiration to Xlebnikov. It thus provides, as does indeed Jakobson's work on poetics as a whole, a methodology for further intertextual analysis. "Iz kommentarija k stixam Majakovskogo 'Tovariščju Nette — paroxodu i čeloveku'" [From the commentary on Majakovsky's poem "To Comrad Nette — steamship and man"], a recounting of the factual background to the poem[38], has an autobiographical admixture, since it touches on Jakobson's own role in introducing Nette to Majakovskij and since he himself is alluded to in the poem. "From Aljagrov's Letters" is even more notably autobiographical, for it is, like "The Evasive Initial" mentioned above, a playful allusion to Jakobson himself; but unlike that other article, "I" here is only allowed when he quotes his own letter to the experimental poet, A. E. Kručenyx. Far from being the ailing octogenarian of that other study, he is here the seventeen-year-old supraconscious poet, full of energy, writing his theoretical musings about the ultimate goal of poetry. Linked with the earlier studies on poetics contained in *SW III* and *SW V*, it gives valuable insight into Jakobson's own development as a poet and poetician.

* * *

Part Three, Retrospections, contains two remarkable documents: "My Favorite Topics", presented in January 1981 by Jakobson on the

---

[38] For more discussion the reader is referred to Krystyna Pomorska, "A Semiotic Approach to the 'Literature of Fact': Majakovskij's Poem 'To Comrade Nette'", *American Journal of Semiotics* 2: 71–88, 1983.

occasion of his having been awarded the Premio Internazionale per la Filologia e Linguistica, and "On the Dialectics of Language", written shortly before his death, on the occasion of his having been awarded the Hegel-Preis of the city of Stuttgart. These are both retrospects which serve to give a global overview by Jakobson not only of the writings contained in this volume, but also of his scholarly method and ideology. They are a sort of supercommentary meant to encapsulate all of his Retrospects to *SW I* through *VI*. It is characteristic that here recurs the topic which Jakobson already announced in his first "Retrospect": "The RETROSPECT ... is focused upon the constants which unify the writer's inquiry. Thus the concluding essay recurs to the same principle of invariance which is the keystone of the entire volume"[39]. Twenty years later, in these meta-retrospects, Jakobson asserts again that the common denominator of his work is the relation between and "interplay of invariance and variation" since, in his view, "the inseparability between invariance and variability [is] the *conditio sine qua non* of scientific analysis".

III. The editorial work for this volume, including the excellent indexes, was done by Stephen Rudy of New York University. He was aided by Dr. Brent Vine, who during his tenure as Assistant to the Estate of Roman Jakobson helped prepare the entire manuscript for typesetting. Professor Calvert Watkins of Harvard University was kind enough to check the mythological part. The Massachusetts Institute of Technology contributed both indirectly and directly to the final preparation of the volume by supporting the Jakobson Archives and Publications Project and by facilitating the editor's work there as a research associate in spring 1983. We are all indebted to the editor himself for his enormous and sustained work on the *Selected Writings* project as a whole; his dedication and skill have been essential to the publication of the oeuvre of Roman Jakobson.

Linda R. Waugh
Cornell University

---

[39] *SW I*, finished Feb. 1962, p. 658. See also Elmar Holenstein, *Roman Jakobson's Approach to Language, op. cit.*, pp. 95–103; and Linda R. Waugh, *Roman Jakobson's Science of Language* (Lisse: Peter de Ridder Press, 1976), pp. 68–89, for a further discussion of the role of invariance in Jakobson's work.

PART ONE

CONTRIBUTIONS TO COMPARATIVE MYTHOLOGY

SLAVIC GODS AND DEMONS

The Christianization of the Slavs expanded gradually from the 8th until the 13th century, now and then provoking local pagan revolts (in Bohemia soon after its baptism, which dates from the late 9th century, and among the Poles and Eastern Slavs throughout the 11th century), or creating those whimsical combinations of paganism and Christianity labeled in Church Slavonic vocabulary as "double faith" (*dvoevĕrie*).

The conversion of the Kievan court belongs to the end of the 10th century and the pagan tradition is still fresh in the minds of the earliest Russian annalists. Both the *Primary Russian Chronicle*, compiled about 1111, and the *First Novgorod Chronicle* reproduce many records of the 11th century which contain a detailed report on the annihilation of the official paganism in Kiev and Novgorod and various reflections of the subsequent double faith. Moreover, the *Primary Chronicle* includes the authentic text of Russian-Greek treaties (945, 971) with native pagan oaths. From the 11th century many allusions to the old deities and pre-Christian beliefs occur also in the various Russian writings against the pagan survivals. Former Russian gods are occasionally interpolated into translated literary works (*Malalas Chronicle*; *Alexandreis*) or in accord with the Byzantine pattern, appear as rhetorical adornments in the original epos (*Igor' Tale*).

The Northwestern (Maritime) Slavs from the Vistula to the Elbe stubbornly resisted German crusades, and the history of this struggle is told (a) in the Latin Chronicles of three German clergymen — two from the 11th century (Thietmar of Merseburg; Adam of Bremen), and one from the 12th century (Helmold); (b) in three biographies of Otto of Bamberg compiled in the 12th century; (c) in the *Gesta Danorum* by Saxo Grammaticus (about 1188). These sources, supplemented by some less important German documents and by the Icelandic *Knytlinga Saga* (around 1265), exhibit a rich picture of the Northwestern Slavic idolatry; and their authors, in spite of their Roman bias and insufficient acquaintance with the Slavic people and language, have proved to be, in the light of recent archeological research, noticeably more accurate in their reports than was usually assumed.

The literary data on the beliefs of the other Slavs are much scantier, partly because of their early Christianization (particularly in the case of Czechs and Bulgars) or because of the late origin of documents relating to the pagan past (e.g., most of the mythological testimonies in the *Polish Chronicle* of the 15th century have been found to be mere inventions). Marginal residues of Slavic heathenism as recorded in 1331 from the Slovenes on the Isonzo are rather exceptional, but the folklore of all the Slavic peoples — notwithstanding the various superstrata, borrowings from abroad, and modifications — offers to the careful investigator many striking survivals, especially in demonology and in calendrical and family rites. From the times preceding the Christianization of the Western and Southern Slavs, a few Greek and Latin writings give scrappy indications of single Slavic religious concepts or terms; in the 6th century the Byzantine historian Prokopios briefly refers to the Slavic faith and the Gothic chronicler Jordanes cites the Slavic *strava* (funeral meal); a Latin document of the 8th century mentions *treba* (sacrifice).

The relative linguistic unity and negligible dialectal differentiation of the Slavic world until the end of the first millennium A.D., and particularly the considerable lexical uniformity of Slavic pre-Christian beliefs, corroborate the supposition of a substantial unity for the cult of the Primitive Slavs. In the vocabulary originally connected with worship, the Slavs and partly the Baltic peoples, their closest linguistic neighbors, present striking similarities with Indo-Iranian as well as with Thraco-Phrygian nomenclature. The fund linking the Primitive Slavs with the Iranians is particularly important. The proximity in the religious pattern and terminology finds its expression both in the features which they preserved jointly from the Indo-European heritage or which they modified in one and the same way. In some cases where we are authorized to presume a direct borrowing, the direction is from Iranian to Slavic. These Slavic-Iranian affinities are all the more indicative in that Indo-European languages are mostly divergent in their religious vocabulary.

Slavs and Iranians nearly eliminated the Indo-European name of the worshipped sky (**dyēus*). They agree 1) in substituting the name of the cloud (Slavic *nebo*) for that of the sky, 2) in converting the derivative "celestial" (**deiwos*), used by Indo-Europeans to denote gods, into the word for "hostile demonic being" (compare the term *divъ* attested in the demonology of various Slavic peoples and the corresponding she-demon *divii, diva, divožena*), 3) in assigning the general meaning "god" to a term which originally signified both wealth and its giver (*bogъ*). Thus the Slavs participated in the Iranian evolution into a clear-cut dualism and, according to Helmold's accurate testimony, they were wont to worship divinities of good and those of evil, "being convinced that happiness comes from the god of good while misfortune is dispensed by the deity of evil". And the Slavic term for faith (*věra*) coincides with the Iranian term for religious choice between good and evil. The Slavs (and the Balts too) share with the Iranians the use of the same term for holy (originally "provided by supernatural beneficial power", Slavic *svętъ*). The Slavic term for "peace agreement" and for "community agreeing" (*mirъ*) is connected with the Iranian Mithra. In Slavic and Iranian similar verbs express the various processes originally pertaining to the religious pattern, as: worshipping (*žrěti*), wailing (*vъpiti*), invocation (*zъvati*), divination (*gatati*), proclamation (*věštati*), drawing (*pьsati*), chastising (*kajati*), fearing (*bojati sę*), protecting (*xraniti*), etc. Such fundamental spiritual terms as word (*slovo*) and deed (*dělo*) are common to Slavic and Iranian, as are also such designations of the basic ritual implements as "fire" (*vatra*), "chalice" (*čaša*), "burial (literally 'magian') mound" (*mogyla*), and such curative terms as "cure" (*goiti*), "healthy" (*sъdravъ*), and "sick" (*xvorъ*). There are several common expressions for ill-omened concepts: "evil" (*zъlo*), "shame" (*sramъ*), "guilt" (*vina*), "sinister" (*šui*); moreover the Slavic stem **kostjun-* (literally "osseous"), denoting "profane, temporal", seems to be a loan translation. The Common Slavic *rai* "paradise" has been acknowledged as a direct borrowing from Iranian *rāy-* "heavenly radiance, beatitude".

Like the religious terminology, the pantheon of the Slavs offers more Common Slavic than tribal features and partly points to Indo-European roots, or at least shows Indo-Iranian, especially Iranian, and perhaps Thraco-Phrygian, connections. It was hinted by Prokopios, and six centuries later observed by Helmold, that among the multiform divine powers worshipped by the Slavs, one is believed to rule over the others in heaven and to care for celestial things, "whereas the rest, obeying the duties assigned them, have sprung from his blood and enjoy distinction in proportion to their nearness to that god of gods". The scattered data we possess on the Slavic deities, and in particular on their mutual kinship and hierarchy, do not permit us to reconstruct this whole system. Nevertheless there are indications arguing for kinship and hierarchy.

The storm god Perunъ is closely connected by name and functions with the Vedic Parjánya, with the Lithuanian (as a matter of fact,

Common Baltic) Perkúnas (replaceable under tabu by Perúnas), with the Norse Fjǫrgynn (supposed to be the archaic designation for the Thunderer) and with the Albanian Perëndi, now denoting both "god" and "sky". It is probable that Greek *Keraunós* "thunderbolt" (used also in epithets of the thunder-god) is a rhyme-word substituted for a tabued *Peraunós. The Indo-European name for this hypostasis of a sky divinity contains, beside a nasal suffix, the alternating verbal root *per-/perk^w-* (or *perg-*), signifying "to strike, to splinter", and used particularly of lightning. This root appears, e.g. in Latin and Germanic, as a substitute name for the oak, a tree favored by the thunderstorm and devoted to the thunder god; and in the Indo-European tradition the same root with a nasal suffix denotes the "oak-wooded hill" — Celtic-Latin *Hercynia* (*Silva*), Gothic *fairguni*, Slavic *pergynja (Old Church Slavonic *prěgynja*, Old Russian *peregynja*, Polish *przeginia*). The leading role of Perun in Russian heathenism, the connection of the oak with this god, and the veneration of the *peregynja* are clearly attested by Russian sources. Perun was identified with Thor by the Varangians, with Zeus by the Russian bookmen, and with Elijah in Christianized folklore. Outside Russia, the god Perun, distorted to Prone and worshipped in oak-groves, appears in Helmold's *Chronicle*; Perun's son Porenutius figures in the mythological records of Saxo Grammaticus; Perun's name is echoed in Slovak maledictions (Peron, Parom), in the Polabian word for Thursday (*perŭndan*), in such appellatives for thunder and lightning as the Polish *piorun* and the Bulgarian folklore form *perušan*, as well as in West and South Slavic proper names, both personal and local, these mostly linked with oak-forest or hill. The ritual of the rain charm, widespread among Bulgars and Serbs and thence in Greece and Rumania, assigns the paramount role to a vigorously chaste girl (as yet unable to conceive and born of a mother who since has become unable to conceive). Nude and draped with flowers, she whirls ecstatically in the middle of a ring, invoking in song the sky or Elijah to moisten and fructify the earth. She bears the reduplicated name of Perun, either unchanged (Perperuna) or with hypocoristic modifications. This couple Perunъ-Perperuna recalls the Germanic Fjǫrgynn-Fjǫrgyn and the Lithuanian Perkúnas-Percuna tete. In another variant of the South Slavic ritual, the main role was performed by a boy assuming Perun's name, reduplicated and altered: the people, whirling and drinking, besought him for rain. To the same cycle refer the old Russian reminiscences of Pereplut, worshipped by whirling and libations, as well as the Magdeburg epistle of 1008 damning the "impudent" god Pripegala. In some areas of Serbia and Bulgaria the name Perperuna is replaced by Dodola or Dudula, and a similar form *du(n)dulis* (tied with an onomatopœic verb for thunder) is currently substituted by Lithuanians for the tabued Perkunas. Thus, in the Balkan Slavic rain charms, one not only finds archaic features reminiscent of Jupiter Elicius and *aquælicium*, of Zeus, Naios and Dodona, as well as of the Vedic hymns to Parjánya, but even the tabu name itself, together with its substitute, reveals a prehistoric origin.

The Slavic Svarogъ is recorded and identified with Hephaistos by an old Russian glossator of the *Malalas Chronicle*. Svarogъ's son was venerated by Russians as Svarožičь and by the Northwestern Slavs as Svarožicь. The name survives in Rumanian *sfaróg* "torrid", and in the names of hills along the Slavic-German border (Kashubian Swarożyn, elsewhere with a tabu substitution Tvarog, Tvarožic, etc.). Under another substitute name (Rarog, further modified to Rarach, Jarog) this spirit continues to live in Western Slavic (particularly Czech and Slovak) demonology as a supernatural falcon and fiery dwarf who beams and turns into a whirlwind and various animals. The name and the characteristic traits of this Slavic deity are obviously connected with the Iranian Vrthragna and his main incarnation Vāragna, the supernatural falcon, and with the cognate figures in Indic (Indra Vr̥trahan) and Armenian mythology (Vahagn). The other incarnations of Vrthragna — wind, gold-horned aurochs, horse, boar — as well as his close ties with fire and smithery are reflected by Slavic tradition as well. Indra, the virility epithet of this deity, lost its mythological connotation in the Slavic adjective *jędrъ* "virile, vigorous, fast" (in the same way as Slavic secularizes the adjective *svobodь* "free", corresponding to the Phrygian Sabadios). But the various aspects of this divine virility find their expression in the conjoined names recorded from the Northwestern Slavs, Svętovitъ (overlapped by St. Vitus after Christianization but still figuring in toponymy), Jarovitъ (surviving as Jarilo in the folk-Russian phallic spring ritual), Porovitъ (with the same first root as Perunъ), and Ruevitъ. These four manifestations of the military deity were apparently symbolized by the polycephalic form of the Northwestern Slavic idols, and could be compared to the Iranian four-faced warrior god Vrthragna, with such attributes as "making bright" and "making virile". At least two of the mentioned designations had a calendrical connotation: 1) *jaro* ("spring") is connected with *jarъ* ("young, ardent, bright, rash"), and Jarovitъ's priest proclaims in his name, "I am your god who covers the plains with grass and the woods with leaves"; 2) *ruenъ* is the autumnal month named for the ruts and mating calls of newly matured animals. The whole ritual, focusing upon the annual cycle and on predestination, displays associations with Vrthragna's cult. The prophetic role of the horse in the divination ceremonies of the Northwestern Slavs is confirmed by its magic functions in Russian popular tradition, particularly by the traditional horse epithet — *věščij* "seer" — which has an exact correspondence in the *Avesta*. And the Common Slavic term for "time" (**vermę*) conceives of it as a wheel-track (compare Old Indic *vartman-*).

Like the Vedic Vṛtrahan, the Slavic Svarogъ generated the sun, Хърсъ Dažьbogъ, according to the Old Russian records. These designations survive among old personal names, Dadzbog in Polish, Hrs in Serbian. Helmold's "ydolum *** Podaga" is perhaps a distortion of Dabog. For the bookmen, Dažьbogъ was identical with Helios. In old Russian tradition both celestial fire and the fire of the hearth are said to be Svarogъ's son. Хърсъ is an obvious borrowing from the Iranian expression for the personified radiant sun (*Xursīd* in Persian). Dažьbogъ means "the giver of wealth", like the Vedic Bhaga. Stribogъ, the neighbor of Dažьbogъ on the Kievan hill before Russia's conversion, means literally "the apportioner of wealth", like Bhaga's partner Aṁśa, and Palmer detects a striking parallel to this couple in the mythological references of the oldest Greek poets. Větrъ "wind", personified in Primitive Slavic (compare Indo-Iranian Vāta-), is quite naturally termed "Stribogъ's descendant" in the *Igor' Tale*.

The Russian peace treaties with the Greeks do not mention Svarogъ probably because of his bellicose connotation, but after the sovereign Perunъ, the oath of 971 invoked Volosъ as "the god of cattle". Also, another Russian form, Velesъ, is attested, and the Czech tradition of the 15th and 16th centuries remembers a demon Veles. The alternation of the two variants **velesъ* and **velsъ* (whence Volosъ), seems to stem from Primitive Slavic. (The etymology is still controversial.) Volosъ was identified with Apollo in the Old Russian literary pattern and replaced by St. Blasius (Vlas) in Christianized folklore. Beside Volosъ, Russian tradition knows another god of the cultivators, with the characteristic name Rodъ (literally "kin"), thus corresponding to such deities as the Celtic Teutates, Latin Quirinus, Umbrian Vofionus. Among the Kievan court idols neither Volosъ nor Rodъ was admitted, although the Old Russian literary tradition presents the latter as the primordial god. His feminine counterpart Rožanica (in Serbocroatian and Slovenian popular tradition Rodjenica, Rojenica), literally meaning "genitrix" and mostly named in the plural, was identified by Russian bookmen with Artemis. The only goddess of the Kievan official pantheon, Mokošь, literally "moist", and represented by some vestiges in Russian folklore and in

Slavic toponymy, is probably nothing but another name for the slightly personified "Mother moist earth" (*Mati syra zemlja*), still adored in Slavic, chiefly Russian, popular tradition, and closely related to similar female deities in Baltic, Phrygian, and Indo-Iranian mythology. The Iranian Ardvī ("moist") Sūrā Anāhitā is particularly close to Mokošь: both of them protect semen, child-bearing, and sheep-breeding.

It is noteworthy that one of the Iranian demonic beings, the winged monster Sīmorg, was adopted under the name Simarglъ in the Kievan official pantheon on the eve of Russia's Christianization, and that the Persian poet Khaqani at the end of the 12th century symbolizes the Russian intruders precisely as Sīmorgs. However the whole of Slavic demonology still awaits an attentive comparative analysis both of its peculiarities and of the multifarious ties linking it with its environment.

Originally published in *Funk and Wagnalls Standard Dictionary of Folklore, Mythology and Legend*, volume II (New York, 1950), under the title "Slavic Mythology".

BIBLIOGRAPHY

For a survey and reproduction of the medieval records on Slavic mythology see:
Mansikka, V. J., *Die Religion der Ostslaven* 1, *FFC* 43 (1922);
Gal'kovskij, N., "Drevnerusskie slova i poučenija, napravlennye protiv ostatkov jazyčestva v narode", *Moscow Archaeological Institute, Zapiski* 18 (1913);
Meyer, K. H., *Fontes historiae religionis slavicae* (Berlin, 1931);
Zíbrt, Č., *Indiculus superstitionum et paganiarum* (Prague, 1894);
Brückner, A. *Mitologia Polska* (Warsaw, 1924);
Beševliev, I., "Gr"cki i latinski izvori za vjarata na prab"lgarite", National Museum of Ethnography of Sofia, *Bulletin* 8–9 (1929);
Leicht, P.-S., "Tracce di paganesimo fra gli Sclavi dell' Isonzo nel secolo XIV", *Studi e materiali di storia della religioni* 1 (1925).

The best summary work is still:
Niederle, L., *Život starých Slovanů*, part II, vol. I, first edition 1916, second edition 1924 (condensed in *Manuel de l'antiquité slave* 2, Paris, 1926).

Some corrections and supplements:
Sobolevskij, A., "Zametki po slavjanskoj mifologii", *Slavia* 7 (1928);
Brückner, A., *Mitologia slava* (Bologna, 1923);
Urbańczyk, S., *Religia pogańskich Słowian* (Cracow, 1947).

Archeological additions:
Palm, T., *Wendische Kultstätten* (Lund, 1937);
Albrecht, C. "Slavische Bildwerke", *Mainzer Zeitschrift* 23 (1928).

Valuable but in many respects antiquated is the latest English survey:
Máchal, J., "Slavic Mythology", *Mythology of All Races* 3 (Boston, 1918; abstract of his Czech outline of 1891).

Dilettantic and chauvinistic:
Wienecke, E., *Untersuchungen zur Religion der Westslaven* (Leipzig, 1940).

Insufficient material used and avoidance of comparative method harm the newest compilation:
Unbegaun, B., "La religion des anciens Slaves", *Mana*, tome 2, no. 3 (Paris, 1948).

Most stimulating linguistic contributions are offered by:
Rozwadowski, J., in *Rocznik oryentalistyczny* 1 (1914);
Meillet, A., in *Revue des Études Slaves* 6 (1926);
Máchek, V., in *Linguistica Slovaca* 3 (1941).

On Slavic popular beliefs see particularly:
Moszyński, K., *Kultura ludowa Słowian* 2, no. 1 (Cracow, 1934);
Bystron, J., *Słowiańskie obrzędy rodzinne* (Cracow, 1916).

For single Slavic peoples:
Haase, F., *Volksglaube und Brauchtum der Ostslaven* (Breslau, 1939);
Zelenin, D., *Očerki slavjanskij mifologii* (Petersburg, 1916);
Bogatyrev, P., *Actes magiques, rites et croyances en Russie Subcarpathique* (Paris, 1929);
Seržputovskij, A., *Prymxi i zababoni belarusaw paljašukow* (Minsk, 1930);

Nikol'skij, N., *Živěly w zvyčajax, abradax i verannjax belaruskaha sjalanstva* (Minsk, 1933);
Biegeleisen, H., *Matka i dziecko w obrzędach, wierzeniach i zwyczajach ludu polskiego* (Lwow, 1927);
idem, Wesele (Lwow, 1928);
idem, U kolebki — przed ołtarzem — nad mogiłą (Lwow, 1929);
Bystroń, J., *Słowiańskie zwyczaje żniwiarskie w Polsce* (Cracow, 1916);
Schneeweis, E., *Feste und Volksbräuche der Lausitzer Wenden* (Leipzig, 1931);
Zíbrt, Č., *Staročeské výroční obyčeje, pověry, slavnosti a zábavy prostonárodní* (Prague, 1889);
Schneeweis, E., *Grundriss des Volksglaubens und Volksbrauches der Serbokroaten* (Celje, 1935);
Marinov, D., *Narodna vjara i religiozni narodni običai* (Sofia, 1914);
Kemp, P., *Healing Ritual: Studies in the Technique and Tradition of the Southern Slavs* (London, 1935).
On mythological motives in folk art, see:
Gorodcov, V., "Dako-Sarmatskie religioznye èlementy v russkom narodnom tvorčestve", *Trudy Gos. Ist. Muzeja* 1 (Moscow, 1926).

LINGUISTIC EVIDENCE IN COMPARATIVE MYTHOLOGY

I. STATE AND PROGRAM OF COMPARATIVE SLAVIC MYTHOLOGY

Although the steady growth of comparative Indo-European linguistics during the last century was accompanied by parallel efforts at the elaboration of comparative mythology, the development of the latter was retarded by several factors. The methodological shortcomings of the new discipline had a pernicious effect on its concrete results. The shakiness and doubtfulness of its conclusions naturally provoked a negative reaction, but the sound criticism of dubious hypotheses threatened to degenerate into a devastating, even more unfounded hypercriticism, a doctrine of fruitless skepticism. Side by side with the brilliant and promising ventures into the domain of comparative Indo-European mythology that have been made over the past few decades in international (especially French and Italian) science and that developed in close association with contemporary linguistic thought, there continue to appear influential works on the mythology of diverse Indo-European peoples that deliberately reject the comparative method and the use of linguistic comparison and reconstruction in the study of ancient religions. As a result, the facts under study are forcibly taken out of context and thus become meaningless. The historical perspective disappears, and the image of the whole is lost behind the scattered and isolated fragments.

Let us examine the theses that are consistently defended in several characteristic postwar outlines of Slavic mythology.[1] We shall answer their a priori skepticism by presenting a few clear illustrations of the application of linguistic devices and criteria in examining the available evidence about the native Slavic gods.

We find particularly unacceptable in the works under discussion the

[1] Typical "skeptical" surveys include: B. Unbegaun, "La religion des anciens Slaves", *Mana: Introduction à l'histoire des religions* 2 (Paris, 1948), 387–445; A. Schmaus, "Zur altslavischen Religionsgeschichte", *Saeculum* 4 (1953), 206–230; A. Stender-Petersen, "Russian Paganism", in his *Russian Studies = Acta Jutlandica* 28, 2 (Copenhagen, 1956), 44–53; Z. R. Dittrich, "Zur religiösen Ur- und Frühgeschichte der Slaven", *Jahrbücher für Geschichte Osteuropas*, N.F. 9 (1961); F. Vyncke, *De Godsdienst der Slaven* (Roermond, 1969).

refusal to use the allegedly bankrupt etymological method. In actuality, prominent international linguists of several generations have done a great deal for the comparative analysis of the roots of Indo-European, and particularly Slavic, mythological names. These successful experiments demand a systematic continuation. The shakiness of certain etymologies demands greater precision, but certainly not the termination of the inquiry.

The fruitful investigations on the part of Zelenin, Bonfante, Havers, Specht, Èrdedi, and others into the role of verbal interdictions eloquently discredit the skeptics' warnings against references to taboo in etymological comparisons.[2] It suffices to recollect such substitutes for religious names in American English as "gosh" (< god), "golly" (< holy), "gee" (< Jesus), "tarnal" (< eternal), "goldarned" (< goddamned), "great Scott" (< great god),[3] or in Serbian *bora mi, broda mi, gloga mi* (in place of *boga mi* "my God"), in order to pay proper attention to sound replacements and metatheses, as well as to morphological and lexical changes, in ancient sacral nomenclature.

The doubts of the skeptics concerning toponymic vestiges of mythological names are no less arbitrary. The place of worship often stubbornly preserves its name despite the disappearance of the cult itself. One cannot artificially divorce observations about the names of the gods either from pagan relics in toponymics or from ancient religious terminology. However deep are the divergences in this sort of vocabulary among the Indo-European peoples, the Slavs nevertheless retained a number of strikingly archaic elements. Correspondingly, we can reasonably expect to find ancient survivals in mythology and in mythological names. The richness of the pre-Christian layer in Common Slavic religious terminology, especially the presence of a series of terms relating to a highly developed sacrificial worship, decisively refutes the assertions that there is no evidence of the existence of liturgical ritual in the Slavic pagan tradition; cf. the pre-Christian Church Sl. term žьrьcь "priest" (lit. "sacrificer"; cf. *žrьtva* "sacrificial offering, victim"), inherited from Common Slavic.

---

[2] D. Zelenin, "Tabu slov u narodov vostočnoj Evropy i severnoj Azii", 1–2, *Sbornik Muzeja Antropologii i Ètnografii* 8–9 (1929–1930); G. Bonfante, "Études sur le tabou dans les langues indo-européennes", *Mélanges de linguistique offerts à Charles Bally* (Geneva, 1939); W. Havers, "Neuere Literatur zum Sprachtabu", *Akademie der Wissenschaften in Wien, Phil.-hist. Klasse, Sitzungsberichte*, 223, no. 5 (1946); I. Èrdedi, "Jazykovye tabu v ural'skix jazykax", *Annales Universitatis Scientiarum Budapestinensis de Rolando Eötvös Nominatae*, Sectio Philologica 5 (1964), 95–117.
[3] Cf. H. L. Mencken, *The American Language* (New York, 1937, 4th ed.), 316f.; E. C. Hills, "Exclamations in American English", *Dialect Notes* 5, 7 (1924).

Among the books published under Hitler during the years of his offensive against the Slavs were the chauvinistic publications of Erwin Wienecke and Leonhard Franz.[4] These works employed all possible contrivances in an effort to convince readers that Common Slavic beliefs remained on the level of primitive demonology and did not evolve into a faith in individual gods — "die arteigene Kultur der Slawen war so unentwickelt"[5] — until, according to the authors, the Slavic peoples on the threshhold of their historical existence finally underwent the religious influence of the Germans. Unfortunately, both of these theses — the first a naive notion of a barbaric state of "godless" faith in demons which ignores worldwide anthropological research, the second a blind confidence in the Germanic importation of worship of gods to the Baltic and Eastern Slavs — have filtered into several works of scholarship in the postwar period as well. Everything that Wienecke and Franz ascribed to Germanic influence — for example, the sanctuaries, the sculptural images of gods, and the cult of a sacred, prophesying horse at Retra, Szczecin, and Arkona, — all are found to have ever new and convincing correspondences in archeological finds and folkloric survivals throughout the entire Slavic world.

Were the beliefs of the Slavs to have undergone a Germanic influence, this would naturally be reflected in the religious vocabulary of Slavic paganism as well. Yet, whereas the material culture of the Slavs absorbed numerous lexical Germanisms, such phenomena are totally absent from the language of the primitive Slavs' spiritual culture. Moreover, a series of studies, beginning with the fundamental writings of Jan Rozwadowski and Antoine Meillet,[6] brought to light the numerous Iranian reflections in the ethico-religious terminology of the early Slavs. These consist partly of direct borrowings and partly of primordial Indo-European words that underwent an Iranian modification in their meanings. Thus, for instance, even the distinctive religious revolution reflected in the Iranian lexical pattern expanded to Common Slavic, which, together with Iranian, changed the original designation of the heavenly deity (*$deiwos$) into the name of the evil demon hostile to gods (Av. $daēva$-, Church Slav. $divъ$); on the other hand, the general meaning of "deity" was assigned to the term "giver" (Av. $baga$-, Church

---

[4] E. Wienecke, *Untersuchungen zur Religion der Westslaven* (Leipzig, 1940), Leonhard Franz, *Falsche Slawengötter* (Brno, 1943, 2nd ed.).
[5] L. Franz, *op. cit.*, p. 9.
[6] J. Rozwadowski, "Stosunki leksikalne między językami słowiańskimi a irańskimi", *Wybór pism* 2 (Warsaw, 1961); A. Meillet, "Le vocabulaire slave et le vocabulaire indo-iranien", *Revue des Études Slaves* 6 (1926).

Slav. *bogъ*). Furthermore, the original noun for the worshipped heaven (*dyēus) was replaced by the original word for "cloud" (Av. *nabah-*, Church Slav. *nebo*). Finally, according to the observation of Vittore Pisani, the Indo-European term *ĝhemōn "human being", closely linked to the noun for earth, *ĝhōm, was eliminated.[7] The closeness of the Slavic religious vocabulary to the Iranian, exposing the communality of both faith and ritual, also finds a striking parallel in the names and functions of individual gods. Yet the skeptics either ignore this connection or construct unsubstantiated surmises about purely literary secular borrowings, proper merely to a narrow social elite.

Hostility toward the comparative method, that effective instrument of historical linguistics, inevitably leads investigators of Slavic pagan antiquity to an impoverishment and distortion of the mythological data. Despite the vital continuity of the Slavic oral tradition, the skeptics put in doubt the historical instructiveness of the folk rituals, legends, and beliefs of the recent past. When separated from the folkloric names and motifs, the written sources inevitably lose their informative value. The fruitful slogan of the perspicacious builder of comparative mythology, Georges Dumézil — "Il faut étudier les dieux les uns par rapport aux autres"[8] — is obstinately opposed by the skeptics, who instead promote a devastating isolationism: each god is studied exclusively in isolation, without taking into account ancient testimony concerning his place in the divine hierarchy, such as the instructive order of the list of Kievan idols found in the early chronicles (cf. the Russian *Primary Chronicle* for the year 980). The genealogy of the gods is denied, in spite of their traditional patronymics and the genealogical indications in the Old Russian texts. The local cult is examined without considering its connections with tribal gods, and the tribal gods are viewed as unconnected with those of the other Slavs; in particular, the gods of the Baltic Slavs are artificially isolated from the Russian deities. Finally, the kinship between the gods of the Slavic peoples and those of other Indo-European groups is denied. Naturally, when all comparison is forbidden the literary documents of the eleventh and twelfth centuries lose their value as evidence, and in the end — with all sorts of deliberate motivations — even their exactness and veracity are thrown into doubt. As a matter of fact, the comparison of written and folkloric sources and the collation of the information of contemporaries about the gods of the

---

[7] V. Pisani, "Il paganesimo Balto-Slavo", in *Storia delle Religioni*, ed. P. T. Venturi (Turin, 1949), p. 63.
[8] G. Dumézil, *Tarpeia* (Paris, 1947), p. 11.

Slavic East and Northwest, combined with a widening of the framework of Slavic mythology so as to include a constant regard for the linguistic data, confirm the authenticity of the bookish sources on the pre-Christian beliefs of Old Russia and the Polabian-Pomeranian region and make it possible to fill in many of the gaps. Attempts at viewing the responses of the Old Russian bookmen to the eradicated pagan religion and its survivals as mere prejudiced fabrications prove unwarranted. Their accounts can be verified by comparison with reliable evidence contained in the work of the Germans who fought West Slavic polytheism. The basis of the latter's reports are by no means the stereotyped *interpretatio ecclesiastica*, as the German scholars of the World War II period would have one believe, but a completely realistic informational account.

In order to show by means of concrete examples the applicability of the techniques of comparative linguistics to the Slavic mythological data, it is necessary to revise, complete, summarize, and reinterpret the observations and notions that have been accumulated in the scholarship on the subject.

II. RUSSIAN PERUNЪ AND HIS SLAVIC AND INDO-EUROPEAN KIN

In scholarly surveys of Slavic paganism, efforts continue to be made to explain the worship of Perun as a local Russian innovation, a late mythological personification of the "roaring thunder" referred to as "Perun" in the Common Slavic language.[9] Meanwhile, the suffix *-unъ* undoubtedly designated from the earliest times precisely an agent or subject. Next to ancient personal names known among the Western and Baltic Slavs (*Perun, Peruničić*, etc.), the names of South Slavic heights, villages, forests, and streams are also highly significative. These names, attested since the early Middle Ages and collected by Iordan Ivanov, S. Trojanović, and M. S. Filipović, include *Perun, Perunac, Perunovac, Perunike, Perunička Glava, Peruni Vrx, Perunja Ves, Peruna Dubrava* (the possessive form *Perunjь is particularly indicative here).[10] In Istria by the slope of the mountain *Perun* there is a natural boundary which goes by the ancient ritual name of *Trebišče* (the Slavic pagan term *treba*

---

[9] E.g., A. Stender-Petersen, *op. cit.*, p. 49f.
[10] I. Ivanov, "Kul't Peruna u južnyx slavjan", *Izvestia Otdelenija slov. i jazyka Akademii Nauk* 8, No. 4 (1903), 140–174; M. S. Filipović, "Tragovi Perunova kul'ta kod Južnih Slovena", *Glasnik Zemaljshog Muzeja u Sarajevu*, Nova Serija, 3 (1948), 63–80; S. Trojanović, "Glavni srpski žrtveni običaji", *Srpski Etnografski Zbornik* 17 (1911), 114f.; cf., more recently, I. Duridanov, "Urslaw. *Perynъ und seine Spuren in der Toponymie", *Studia Slavica Academiae Scientiarum Hungaricae* 12 (1966), 99–102.

"sacrifice" is mentioned as early as a Latin manuscript of 758).[11] Among these geographic names, such folkloric formations as *Perunuša*, *Peruščice*, *Perudina*, *Peratobac* should be juxtaposed to emotional and god-fearing substitutions of phonemes and entire suffixes in sacred tabooed names: cf. the following formula, full of paronomasias, ascribed to the potter Pidьbljanin, a participant in the "drowning" of the idol of Perun in the first Novgorod Chronicle (989) — "Ty, reče, *Perušice*, dosyti esi *pi*lъ i ja*lъ*, a nyne *po*plovi *pro*cь" "Thou, Perušice," he said, "thou hast eaten and drunk thy fill, and now swim away!"[12] The form *Porunъ* replaced the name of Zeus in the Old Russian manuscript of the *Alexandreis*.[13] In the incantatory formulae and songs of Slovakia and Moravia the name *Parom*, contaminated with *hrom*, and the Slovak variant *Peron* still serve as a substitute for Perun, according to the testimony of A. Václavík.[14] The Bulgarian folk riddle, the answer to which is "thunder" (*gъrmotevica*), reads: "Skokna *perušan*, podskokna, vsičkata zemja potърsi" "*Perušan* jumped and jumped again and shook the whole world".[15] These substitutions show the god of the Baltic Slavs, attested by Saxo Grammaticus as *Porenutius*, to be a Lekhitic affective variant, possibly a designation of Perun's descendant: *Poruniec*, *Pioruniec*, or rather *Piorunic*.

Helmold's "Chronicon Slavorum" tells about the holy oaks near Stargard dedicated to the god *Prone* (with a distorted variant *Prove*).[16] This is clearly connected with Perun Dubnjak. Perun's oak figures in the Galician *gramota* of 1302 as well.[17] To the form *Prone* correspond the names of the Pomeranian villages *Prohn* and *Pronstorf*, with the variants *Pyron*, *Peron*, and *Perone* (cf. the noun for thunder in one of its Slovak alterations, *Peron*).[18]

In the pantheon of the Baltic Slavs names with the attributive suffix -*ovit*/-*evit* were epithets,[19] and each of them designated one of the forms

---

[11] Filipović, *op. cit.*, p. 66.
[12] *Novgorodskaja pervaja letopis' staršego i mladšego izvodov*, ed. A. N. Nasonov (Moscow-Leningrad, 1950), p. 160.
[13] Cf. L. Niederle, *Život starých slovanů. Základy kulturních starožitností slovanských* = *Slovanské starožitnosti. Oddíl kulturní* vol. 2, part 1 (Prague, 1924, 2nd ed.), p. 99, fn. 4.
[14] A. Václavík, "Slovanské prvky v české lidové kultuře", *Slovanství v české národné životě*, ed. J. Macůrek (Brno, 1947), p. 197.
[15] S. Mladenov, *Etimologičeski i pravopisen rečnik na b"lgarskija knižoven ezik* (Sofia, 1941), p. 419.
[16] Cf. P. Diels, "*Prove*", *Archiv für slavische Philologie* 40 (1925), p. 156.
[17] Cf. Bulaxovskij, Review of L. P. Jakubinskij's *Istorija drevnerusskogo jazyka*, in *Izvestija AN SSSR, Otdel literatury i jazyka* 12, 6 (1953), p. 558.
[18] Cf. V. Pisani, *op. cit.*, p. 66.
[19] Cf. A. Sobolevskij, "Zametki po slavjanskoj mifologii. Po povodu truda prof. L. Niederle: *Slovanské starožitnosti*", *Slavia* 7 (1920), p. 17.

or phases of the masculine force, one of the seasons of the year and, correspondingly, one of the hypostases of the multifaceted deity, or perhaps one of a close-knit group of gods. The names mentioned include: *Porovit* (in the sources *Porevith, Puruvit*); *Rjujevit* (*Rugievith, Riuvit*; cf. Old Russian *rjuti* "to roar, howl", the fall month *rjuenъ* "September"); *Svętovit* (*Zvantevith, Sventevic*), worshipped, according to Helmold's testimony, as the "most powerful in foretelling the future" of all the Slavic gods (cf. *svęt-* in the original pagan meaning "endowed with a miraculous and beneficial power" and *svjatki*, the winter festival that features ritual fortune-telling); *Jarovit* (*Gerovit, Herovith*; cf. Russ. *jaryj, jarkij* "bright", Ch. Sl. *jarъ* "violent", Russ. *jarovoj* "spring, summer (adj.)", and in the Russian and Serbian spring rituals *Jarilo*).[20] The root **por-/per-*, which links Porovit with Perun, appears in Slavic with the meaning of an aggressive, robust and strong power and ripe, stormy summertime (cf. Russian *porá* "the appointed time", *pórnyj* "virile, ripe, strong, in one's prime", *poráto* "strongly", Church Slavonic *pora* "strength").[21]

The stubbornly repeated conjecture that the Russian Perun might be the Slavic name for the Varangian Thor, which arose through a "mechanical transfer of Nordic ideas to the Slavic lands", lacks any foundation.[22] First, the erection of Perun's idols in Kiev and Novgorod in 980 is expressed in the Russian Primary Chronicle as the immediate result of the prince's victory over the Varangian warriors — "se gradъ našь i my prijaxomъ i" "This city is ours and we took it over"; just after having overcome the foreigners, "nača knjažiti Volodimirъ vъ Kievě odinъ i postavi kumiry na xolmu vně dvora teremnogo — Peruna derevjana *** Posadi Dobrynju uja svoego vъ Nověgorodě, i prišedъ Dobrynja Novugorodu postavi Peruna kumirъ nadъ rěkoju Volxovomъ" "Vladimir began to rule solely in Kiev and set up idols on a hill outside the palace — one of Perun, made of wood *** Vladimir had appointed his uncle Dobrynja to rule over Novgorod and after coming to Novgorod he set up an idol of Perun overlooking the river Volxov."[23] Secondly, in the testimonies on Perun there is nothing decisive that links

---

[20] A. Brückner, *Mitologia Slava* (Bologna, 1923); idem, *Mitologja polska* (Warsaw, 1924).

[21] Cf. V. Dal', *Tolkovyj slovar' živogo velikorusskogo jazyka* 3 (St. Petersburg-Moscow, 2nd ed., 1882), 310f.

[22] A. Stender-Petersen, *op. cit.*, p. 53.

[23] *Polnoe sobranie russkix letopisej, izdavaemoe postojannoju istoriko-arxeografičeskoj komissieju Akademii Nauk SSSR* 1: *Lavrent'evskaja letopis'*; vyp. 1: *Povest' vremennyx let* (Leningrad, 2nd ed., 1926), col. 78f.; cf. *The Russian Primary Chronicle*, trans. and ed. S. H. Cross and O. P. Sherbowitz-Wetzor (Cambridge, Mass., 1954), p. 93f.

him specifically with Thor: the image of the thunder-god belongs to the pantheon of almost all Indo-European peoples,[24] and more importantly, linguists have explicitly uncovered, step by step, the link between the name and functions of Perun and the names and functions of a whole series of gods of other tribes. It is true that even the evident kinship of the Slavic Perun and the Lithuanian *Perkūnas* and Latvian *Pę̄rkuôns* (in both cases the name refers at once to the god and to thunder) has been put in doubt more than once, since a Slavic *-yn-* should have corresponded to the Baltic suffix *-ūn-* and, moreover, a final *k* is missing in the root of the Slavic name. However, A. Meillet convincingly showed the unusual alternation of the root **per-* with the velar enlargement in the present tense of the Armenian verb *harkanem* "I beat, I cut, I chop wood, I kill" (cf. Old Irish *orgaid* "he kills", both based on a stem **per-g-*), and without enlargement the aorist *hari* (cf. Old Church Slavonic *perǫ*, Lithuanian *periù*, *peřti* "strike").[25] This verb is closely linked to the terms for thunderstorms and storms in Armenian, where it often signifies a clap of thunder (cf. also *orot* "thunder", *orotam* "I rumble", < I-E **por-*),[26] and likewise in Slavic lexical use (I. Ivanov cites the Bulgarian expression "Dъždъ́t peré li peré" "The rain pours and pours").[27] The Lithuanian ethnographer Jonas Balys, in a list of indigenous substantives, cites the peculiar form *Perúnas*, with omitted enlargement, in place of the prohibited form *Perkúnas*.[28] As for the vowel in the suffix, the Slavic linguistic world displays a characteristic tendency to separate the masculine suffix *-un-ъ* from the feminine *-yn-ь*: *Xot-un-ъ* — *Xot-yn-ь*, *Gor-un-ъ* — *Gor-yn-ь*, *Pol-un-ъ* — *Pol-yn-ь*. Correspondingly, the Novgorod pagan temple of Perun was called *Perynь*, and the same basic form is preserved in Balto-Slavic toponymy: *Perin* (< *Perynь*) *planina*.[29] Compare also the dialectal alternation *perínь-perunika* or *peruníga* in the Bulgarian name for the plant *Iris germanica* (Serbian *perùnika* and *bògiša*).[30]

Perunъ and *Perkúnas* belong, as is especially clearly shown in the remarks of V. V. Ivanov, to the family of mythological names endowed

---

[24] Cf., *i.a.*, H. M. Chadwick, "The Oak and the Thunder-God", *The Journal of the Anthropological Institute of Great Britain and Ireland* 30, New Series 3 (1900), p. 38.
[25] A. Meillet, *op. cit.*
[26] E. Lidén, *Armenische Studien* (Göteborg, 1906), p. 88.
[27] I. Ivanov, *op. cit.*, p. 145.
[28] J. Balys, "Perkūnas lietuvių liaudies tikėjmuose" ("Der Donner im litauischen Volksglauben"), *Tautosakos Darbai* 3 (Kaunas, 1937), 149–238.
[29] Cf. H. Máchal, *Nákres slovanského bájesloví* (Prague, 1891), p. 22f.
[30] N. Gerov, *Rečnik na b"lgarskyj jazyk*, supplementary volume (Plovdiv, 1908), p. 249.

with regular reflexes of the same root *per- and an -n- suffix.[31] This suffix, low-pitched or high-pitched, adheres either directly to the root or to the root extended by a voiced or voiceless velar enlargement (a variation natural to mythological onomastics). One finds the unenlarged root in the Albanian complex form *Perëndi, Perudi* "god, heaven", in the Hittite name for the deity and the holy cliff *Peruna-*, in the name of a god of war *Perun* among the Pamirian Kafirs, cognate with the name for the Pleiades in Pashto, *Pērūne* (cf. Av. *paoiriiaēinī-*), and finally, in Ancient Greek κεραυνός "thunderbolt", which also appears as an epithet of Zeus, and in Hesiod's *Theogony* as the name of a separate deity, where it may have served as a synonymic substitution for the prohibited form *περαυνός.[32] Velar enlargements occur in the Old Indic form *Parjánya-*, which figures in the *Rigveda* as the name of the god of storm and rain and as the word for a storm cloud and likewise in the name of the similar Norse god *Fjǫrgynn*.[33] These gods are viewed by Indologists and Germanists as archaic survivals which were thrust into the background in the Indian and Scandinavian worlds when the classical pantheons were elaborated.

In the Indo-European languages taboo supplants the ancient names for the oak tree and necessitates a whole series of consistent substitutes. One of these substitutes preserves the meaning "oak" but has apparently undergone a change in the initial consonant, again as a result of taboo: Latin *quercus* originates in the root *perkʷ- and, as was shown by J. Vendryes,[34] belongs to "the ancient stock of religious concepts" and is related by a primary or secondary connection to the extended alternant of the above-mentioned root *per-. The name of the deity is simultaneously tied to the splintering thunder and the splintered oak (cf. the alternating epithets of Zeus Κεραυνός and Φηγωναῖος; for the latter,

---

[31] V. V. Ivanov, "K ètimologii baltijskogo i slavjanskogo nazvanij boga groma", *Voprosy slavjanskogo jazykoznanija* 8 (Moscow, 1958).
[32] Cf. V. Ivanov, *op. cit.*; C. Bartholomae, "Der indogermanische Name der Plejaden", *Indogermanische Forschungen* 31 (1912/13), 35–48; A. Walde and J. Pokorny, *Vergleichendes Wörterbuch der indogermanischen Sprachen* 2 (Berlin-Leipzig, 1927), p. 42f.
[33] Cf. G. Bühler, "Zur Mythologie des Rig-Veda, I. Parjanya", *Orient und Occident* 1 (1862), 214–229; L. von Schroeder, "Der siebente Āditya", *Indogermanische Forschungen* 31 (1912/13); G. Kleinschmidt, "Perkūnas und Parjanya", *Zeitschrift der Altertumsgesellschaft Insterburg* 2 (1888), 163–185; A. Ludwig, *Die Mantralitteratur und das alte Indien* = *Der Rigveda oder die heiligen Hymnen der Brāhmana* 3 (Prague, 1878), 322f.; A. Kaegi, *Der Rigveda* (Leipzig, 2nd ed., 1881), p. 57 and fn. 139; J. Wackernagel, *Altindische Grammatik* 1: *Lautlehre* (Göttingen, 1896), §52a (p. 57); A. A. Macdonell, *Vedic Mythology* (Strassburg, 1897), pp. 84f., 127 (with references to J. Schmidt and Leskien); H. Hirt, "Die Urheimat der Indogermanen", *Indogermanische Forschungen* 1 (1892), p. 480f.
[34] J. Vendryes, "Sur un nom ancien de l'arbre", *Revue celtique* 44 (1927), p. 313ff.

compare Greek φηγός "oak"). The names of wooded hills, especially heights, covered with forests of oak, are associated with the name of the thunder-god and with the oak as an inseparable part of his worship (cf. the Celtic designation of those performing the rites as "tree-experts": *druid* < *dru-vid among the Irish and *derwydd* among the Welsh). Others include Celtic-Latin *Hercynia silva*, Gothic *fairguni*, Old High Germ. *Fergunna*, Old Church Slavonic *prěgyni*, and the Polish toponymic *Przeginia*. From the forgotten archaic forms *prěgyni* and *peregyni* in later Russian copies of the older texts, and through reinterpretation of *bregynja* and *beregynja* (from *breg*, *bereg* "shore"), there arise in the commentaries to Slavic mythology fantastic speculations about otherwise unknown female water-sprites,[35] more accurately river-spirits, whereas the Old Russian scribe simply condemned all those who participated in the worship of holy trees ("trebu kladutь i tvorjatь *** *peregynjam*").[36] The neglect of the methods of comparative linguistics on the part of textual criticism leads to the creation of arbitrary fictions not just in this case alone. The variation of velar enlargement in the roots of the cited sacral terms negates the stubbornly advanced hypotheses about Germanic borrowing from Celtic and Slavic from Germanic.

Closely echoing the ritual prayers preserved in the *Rigveda* appealing to the god *Parjánya* for the rain essential to the harvest are the South Slavic sung prayers about the opening of the sky and the sending down of the vital rain.[37] In a ritual dance, children raise their voices in incantational songs to the selected virgin, a girl who has not yet experienced menstruation and who is the last daughter of a post-menopausal woman. While the youngsters circle around, old women pour water over the chosen girl, who is naked except for a covering of leaves and grass. Bulgarians and Macedonians praise her as either

---

[35] E.g., B. Unbegaun, *op. cit.*, p. 427; more recently, N. V. Čurmaeva, "Bereginja", *Russkaja reč'*, 1969, No. 5, p. 424f.
[36] As eloquently proved by M. Durnovo, "Starosłowiańskie *Prěgyni*", *Prace Filologiczne* 10 (1926), 105ff.
[37] On this South Slavic ritual see: G. Eckert and P. E. Formozis, *Regenzauber in Mazedonien = Volkskündliche Beobachtungen und Materialen aus Zentralmazedonien und der Chalkidike* 3 (Thessaloniki, 1943); E. Schneeweis, *Grundriss des Volksglaubens und Volksbrauchs der Serbokroaten* (Celje, 1935), 219ff.; M. Arnaudov, *Studii v"rxy b"lgarskite obredi i legendi* (Sofia, 1924); D. Marinov, "Narodna věra i religiozni narodni običai", *Sbornik za narodni umotvorenija i narodopis* 28 (1914); Z. Ujváry, "Une coutume des Slaves du Sud: la 'dodola'", *Slavica* 3 (Debrecen, 1963); H. Barić, "Dodole" in his *Prilozi za književnost, jezik, istoriju i folklor* 1 (1921); V. Čulinović-Konstantinović, "Dodole i prporuše", *Narodna Umjetnost*, 1963, no. 2, 73–96; M. Filipović, "Tragovi Perunova kul'ta kod Južnix Slovena", *Zemal'ski muzej u Bosni i Xercegovini. Glasnik Zemal'skogo muzeja u Sarajevu. Društvena nauka*, N.S., 3 (1948, 1954); A. P. Stoilov, "Molba za d"žd"", *Sbornik za narodni umotvorenija i narodopis* 18 (1901).

Preperuna — this name figures centrally in the sung appeals — or, with a regressive dissimilatory loss of the first liquid, *Peperuna*, or, with the substitution of other suffixes, *Preperuda/Peperuda, Pepereda*, or *Preperuga/Peperuga*, and the crossing of the suffixes *-una* and *-uga* yields the peculiar form *Peperunga* or, with the nasal transposed, *Pemperuga*. Mythological associations linked with the butterfly (cf. her Serbian name *Vještica*) also explain the Bulgarian entomological names *peperuda, peperuga*.

The ritual call for rain was transmitted long ago from the Balkan Slavs to neighboring peoples, who evidently preserved the original form of the mythological name: besides the modified forms, partly of Slavic and partly of local origin, one finds in Greek ritual the basic form Περπεροῦνα, in Albanian *Perperona*, in Arumanian *Pirpirúnă*.[38] The Slavic prototype of all these forms can only be *Perperuna (with the later regular transition to *Prěperuna*), i.e., the derived feminine form of the name *Perunъ* with a reduplicated root. Cf. in this ritual such double incantations for rain to "strike" as the Serbian "Udar, Udar, rosna kišo" "Thunder, thunder, dewy rain!",[39] and also the reduplication of the root in the ritual appeals which changed *Mars* into *Marmar, Mamers, Mamercus, Mamurius*, Bacchus into βακχέβακχον, and the Old Armenian *Vahagn* into *Vahēvahē*. The pair *Perun* and *Perperuna* correspond to the Germanic (Norse) god *Fjǫrgynn*, with the matching goddess *Fjǫrgyn*, the mother of thunder; likewise in Lithuanian mythology *Perkúnas* is given a female companion: he was accompanied, if Johan Lazicius is correct, by *Perkúna*, "mater fulminis atque tonitrui".[40]

Perperuna appears in Bulgaria and Macedonia also under the name *Dodola, Dudola, Dudula*, and in Serbia such is her sole sobriquet in the majority of instances: *Dodola, Dudulejka*, and so on. Hence in Greek Ντουντουλέ, in Albanian *Dudule*, in Rumanian *Dodólă, Dudolă, Dudulă* (cf. the Russian dialectal forms *dúdala, dúdolka, dúdolica* "one who drinks or sucks much").[41]

The Bulgarian palatal variant *Didjulja, Didjul, Djudjul* should be

---

[38] Cf. T. Kind, *Sammlung neugriechischen Volkslieder* (Leipzig, 1833), p. 13; G. F. Abbott, *Macedonian Folklore* (Cambridge, 1903), p. 119; I. Dalametra, *Dicționar macedoromîn* (Bucharest, 1906), p. 170.
[39] Vuk Karačić, *Život i običaji naroda srpskoga* (Beč, 1867), p. 62.
[40] Johan Lasicius, *De Diis Samagitarum* (1580), as cited by W. Mannhardt, *Letto-Preussische Götterlehre = Magazin der Lettisch-Literärischen Gesellschaft* 31 (Riga, 1936), p. 356.
[41] Cf. S. Mladenov, *op. cit.*, p. 418; P. Skok, *Etimologijski rječnik* ... 1 (Zagreb, 1971), p. 421; G. F. Abbott, *op. cit.*, p. 119; I. Candrea, *op. cit.*, p. 425; *Dicționarul limbii romîne* ..., "dódolă"; *Slovar' russkix narodnyx govorov*, ed. F. P. Filin, 8 (Leningrad, 1972), pp. 247, 250.

compared to the form *Dzidziela* in the Polish mythological evidence gathered by Długosz.[42] Related to *Dodola* or *Dudula*, the synonymic variant of *Perperuna*, are the substitute synonyms used throughout Lithuania to avoid naming thunder by its direct, tabooed name *Perkúnas*, namely *Dundùlis* "rumbling, peals of thunder" (*dundĕti* "to thunder") and the diminutives *Dundusėlis*, *Dundutis* or *Dudutis* (*dudénti* "to thunder a bit").[43] Cf. Latvian *dudina pḗrkuoniṅš* "thunder is thundering a bit".[44] Interestingly enough, in Polish one finds two coexisting forms — the verb *dudnić* "to thunder" alongside the common noun *piorun* "thunder". It would be difficult to explain the correspondences between these two — South Slavic and Lithuanian — sacral synonymous pairs without appealing to the legacy of Balto-Slavic antiquity. One should not exclude the possibility that Ζεὺς Νάϊος (*Jupiter elicius* or *pluvius*) and Δωδώνη[45] originate in one and the same cycle of Indo-European myths as does the concubine of stormy Perun, *Perperuna Dodola*.

In Dalmatia Perperuna has the name *Pr̃poruša* with the substitution *per* > *por* in the second part of the reduplicated root and with zero grade in the first part. The identical composition of the reduplicated root *per*- "to beat" is observed in the Serbo-Croatian noun *pr̃por* "coitus piscium" and in the verb *pr̃poriti se*, synonymous with *biti se* (*biju se ribe* "coeunt pisces").[46] Apparently the reduplication of the same root, but with a reverse order of the two modifications, took place in a verb applied to demons by the Old Russian author of the anti-pagan glosses to the Discourse of Gregory the Theologian, published by N. M. Gal'kovskij: "поръпрјутьсја (variant поропръščјutsja) въ попелѣ томъ".[47]

Old Russian sermons condemn the worshippers of *Pereplut*, who "vertjačesja emu pijutъ vъ rozěxъ".[48] Whirling is a characteristic feature accompanying the Balkan rain incantation. Both Peperuda and her retinue "skača na edno město i se vъrti v kolelo".[49] Water was poured over her and in certain places over a youth playing the role of Peperuda, or wine was drunk in praise of the deliveress or deliverer from drought.

[42] Cf. Niederle, *op. cit.*, p. 176.
[43] Cf. J. Balys, *op. cit.*, p. 218f.; M. Niedermann, A. Senn, F. Brender, *Wörterbuch der litauischen Schriftsprache* 1 (Heidelberg, 1932), p. 136ff.
[44] Cf. *Russkij Filologičeskij Vestnik* 70 (1913), p. 105.
[45] On Δωδώνη cf. J. Friedrich, *Dodonaica. Beiträge zur Religions- und Kulturgeschichte Dodonas* (Freiburg, 1935).
[46] P. Skok, *Etimologijski rječnik*. ... 3 (Zagreb, 1973), p. 55f.
[47] N. M. Gal'kovskij, "Drevnerusskie slova i poučenija, napravlennye protiv ostatkov jazyčestva v narode", *Zapiski Imp. Moskovskogo Arxeologičeskogo Instituta* 18 (1913), p. 34.
[48] Cf. A. Sobolevskij, *op. cit.*, p. 177.
[49] Marinov, *op. cit.*, p. 517.

One easily recognizes in the name *Pereplut* the reduplicated root *per-*, with the pleophonic form (*per-* > *pere-*) in the first component and zero grade in the second. The second *r* became *l* as a result of progressive dissimilation (Filipović noted the formula *Prepelice* — *Preperuše*; cf. the Rumanian variants *Papalúgă*, *Papalúdă*).[50] The suffix *-ut-* is among the series of suffixes which replace the consonant of the original *-un-* (*-ud-*, *-ug-*, *-uš-*): cf. the Rumanian variant *Băbărútă*, as well as such names as *Bogut*, *Borut*, *Milut*.[51] It is possible that the turns of phrase "doždь *prapruden*ъ" (First Novgorod Chronicle) and "doždь *praprudoju* neiskazaemo silen*ъ*" (First Pskov Chronicle), which puzzled Sreznevskij, are an East Slavic trace of Peperuda calling forth the rain.[52]

The name of the divinity *Pripegala*, who is cursed four times in the appeal of 1108 for a crusade against the Slavic pagans, is undoubtedly an incorrect rendering by the Archbishop of Magdeburg.[53] There is, nevertheless, a form close to that given in this document, *Prepeluga*, which is once again a variant of the name *Perperuna*. But even if one leaves aside the late, conjectural echoes of Perun's name, one is still forced to conclude that his cult had wide dissemination and deep roots in Slavic paganism, a fact that is clearly reflected not only in the texts, but also in onomastics, as well as in the folklore of the Slavs and their neighbors. Moreover, the comparative study of the names and functions of the pagan gods of the Indo-European world supplies Perun with diverse kinsmen and forces one to raise the question of their common ancestor in Indo-European antiquity.

III. THE SLAVIC VELESЪ AND HIS INDO-EUROPEAN COGNATES

In the treaty with the Greeks of 971 the Russians swear an oath in the name of Perunъ and Volosъ, "god of cattle" (*skotii bogъ*).[54] In referring to the seer Bojan, who combines the features of poet and guslar-player with those of magician and predicter of the future, the *Igor' Tale* calls him *Velesovъ vnuče* "grandson of Veles". In this connection a series of Old Irish words comes to mind: *fili*, gen. *filed* "seer: poet, musician,

---

[50] Tiktin, *op. cit.*, 3, p. 1117; *Dicţionarul limbii romîne* ..., 3, p. 316; Candrea, *op. cit.*, p. 896.
[51] Cf. F. Miklosich, *Vergleichende Grammatik der slavischen Sprachen*, vol. 2 (Vienna, 1875), p. 200f.
[52] I. Sreznevskij, *Materialy dlja slovarja drevnerusskogo jazyka* 2 (Petersburg, 1902), p. 1371.
[53] Cf. Niederle, *op. cit.*, p. 155.
[54] The section on Velesъ/Volosъ was elaborated in the article "The Slavic God Velesъ and His Indo-European Cognates", reprinted below, pp. 33–48. See the references there.

magus and soothsayer" (*welēts from I-E *wel-/ul- "to see"); cf. felmac "son of musical, poetic or prophetic power" (mac "son"); in Tacitus Veleda, a prophetess deified by the Celts. As J. Pokorny notes, Ullr (*Wulþuz), the Norse god of well-being, is called by a name formed from the zero grade of the same root; skot "cattle", which were under the protection of the clairvoyant Volos, simultaneously signified in Old Russian both a herd of cattle and wealth in general.

The form Velesъ, which repeatedly occurs in Old Russian texts together with the vocable Volosъ, coincides with the demonic name Veles in Czech formulaic curses, evidenced by texts of the fifteenth-sixteenth centuries. Cf. in Macedonian toponymics Veles, Greek Βελεσσός, Albanian Veles. If the first member of the sequence, vel, here originates in the I-E root *wel-, then the second member -es-, in all likelihood, is a reflex of I-E *esu-, which is found in the name of the ancient Celtic divinity Esus, in Latin erus "master" (< esus, cf. Old Latin esa "mistress"), in Iranian ahu- "genius, chief" and in derivative sacral forms, Avestan ahura- "lord" and Old Indic asura- "lord; demon", as well as in Greek ἐύς and Hittite aššuš "good, suitable". If one can interpret Old Russian Velesъ and Old Czech Veles as *wel-esu-, then the Old Russian Volosъ probably reflects the zero grade of the second member, i.e. *wel-su-, with the regular East Slavic change of the diphthong -el- to -olo- (for the zero grade cf. Old Indic su- "good" in compounds).

Deserving of further elaboration is A. Brückner's surmise of the relationship of the root *wel-s- with the group of words vlъšьba "magic" (< *ulk-s-), vъlxvъ "magus", vlъsnuti "to conjure" and so on, but the connection with Lithuanian mythological vocabulary — Vėlės "spirits of the dead", Vėlinas "spectre, demon", Veliuonà "goddess of the forefathers' shadows" — remains in question, even though it is quite natural to widen the theme of keen surveillance and insight to include the all-seeing eye's embrace of the other world.

Despite the significantly smaller number of parallels to Veles-Volos in Slavic and other languages compared with the whole chain of correspondences to Perun, nevertheless both the phonological and semantic shape of this mythological name permits one to advance the hypothesis that its prototype is Indo-European.

IV. SVAROGЪ AND HIS IRANIAN PROTOTYPE. SLAVIC GODS OF IRANIAN BACKGROUND

If the common Slavic Perun and, in all likelihood, Volos go back directly to the Indo-European system of beliefs, then in Slavic Svarog one discovers an interlingual filiation of another, somewhat distinctive type. The bookmen of Kievan Russia replaced the name of Zeus by Perun, while the Russian gloss in Malala's Chronicle, repeated in the Hypatian Chronicle under the year 1114, identifies the Slavic Svarog, the first to forge weapons, with the god of fire Hephaestus and calls the kingly sun "Svarog's son".[55] The "Sermon of a Lover of Christ" (*Slovo Xristoljubca*), directed against the survivals of Russian paganism, contains a condemnation of fire worshippers, who call it Svarožič and play to a fire lit where the crops are dried.[56] The West Slavic equivalent *Svarožic* (*Zuarasici, Zuarasiz diabolus*), according to eleventh-century sources, "*a cunctis gentilibus honoratur et colitur*".[57]

Together with Russian *Svaruževyj* and *Svaryže*, the toponymics of the western outskirts of the Slavic world, particularly in the names of mountains, preserve traces of the worship of Svarog and Svarožič: for example, among the Kashubians *Swarożyno siodło* is adjacent to *Deiwelsberg* and *Twarożna góra*, the latter with a substitution of the initial consonant as a result of taboo; similar names of heights in Bohemia and Moravia — *Tvarožna*; and in documents of the fourteenth-fifteenth centuries the names of mountains in lower Styria — *Twarog* and *Tbaraschitzberg*.[58] Another relic of Svarog is to be found in a Rumanian word borrowed from the Slavs, *sfarόg*, designating everything burnt through, charred, scorched, dried up by intense heat, in general any sort of dry object.[59]

Contemporary Slavic languages preserve a proper name which differs from the form *Svarog* only in its initial consonantism and, in certain regions, in the substitution of the ending *-och* or *-ach* for the original *-og*. The Czech linguists J. Kořínek and V. Máchek collected extremely instructive observations about this name and its bearer.[60] In Czech and Slovak folk beliefs there is a miniature demonic being called *Rároh* or *Raroh, Rároch* or *Raroch, Rarách* or *Rarach, Rarášek, Raraš*, and finally — with a dissimilatory modification of the intervocalic liquid — *Radášek*; in Polish demonology it is named *Rarόg*, and in Ukrainian — *Papir*. According to Czech and Slovak beliefs it is at once generous and

---

[55] Cf. L. Niederle, *op. cit.*, p. 105, fn. 2.
[56] Cf. L. Niederle, *op. cit.*, p. 106, fn. 2.
[57] Cf. Niederle, *op. cit.*, p. 106, 133.
[58] A. Brückner, "Fantazje Mitologiczne", *Slavia* 8 (1929), 340ff.
[59] I. Candrea, *op. cit.*, p. 1140; H. Tiktin, *op. cit.*, 3, p. 1413; *Dicţionarul limbii romîne ...*, 4, p. 108.
[60] J. M. Kořínek, "K čes. rarach", *Listy filologické* 60 (1933), 28–37; V. Máchek, "Slav. rarogъ 'Würgfalke' und sein mythologischer Zusammenhang", *Linguistica Slovaca* 3 (1941), 84–88.

vindictive, an unusually mobile spirit who assumes the shape of birds, animals, and dragons, and who is closely linked to the fire on the hearth; its body sparkles, its hair blazes, a radiance emerges from its mouth. It flies through the chimney and is carried off by the night in a fiery swirl or is transformed into a whirlwind. A. Hajný, an expert on the folklore of the Poděbradsk region, gives a characteristic example of the beliefs about the miraculous appearance of this gnome on earth: it hatches if the first egg of the first laying of a purely black hen is sheltered in the bosom of a man who has sat on a stove for nine days and nights without praying or washing.[61]

Some forms of the above, including Czech *jarášek*, Slovenian *rárog*, *rárožica* and *járog*, Croatian *rarov*, Lithuanian *ràragas* or *vãnagas*, designate one of the mighty varieties of falcons, often with the connotation of sorcery.[62] Rumanian *sfaróg* should also be compared with Czech and Slovak *rárož* "brushwood" and *rárohy, rarohy* "refuse".[63]

Dumézil, whose views are supported by the observations of S. Wikander, P. J. de Menasce, and J. Duchesne-Guillemin,[64] reconstructed the Indo-Iranian myth that forms the basis of the Old Indic and Iranian legends: the hero of the former is *Indra Vṛtrahan* "Vṛtra-slayer", in the Iranian version *Vərəθrayna* — with the corresponding adjective *vārəθrayna* — and *Vahagn, Vahram, Vram* in the Armenian mythological echoes of the Iranian tradition and in their most important relic, a fragment of an ancient song about Vahagn, copied by Moses of Xoren probably at the end of the fifth century and attentively investigated by Dumézil.[65]

E. Benveniste established the immediate Iranian prototype of the Armenian form: *varhrayn > varhayn > vahagn*.[66] To all appearances *svarogъ* originates from the same Middle Iranian form *varhayn*. It is significant that precisely the seventh of the nine metamorphoses of the

---

[61] A. Hajný, "Rarášek. Z bájesloví lidu na Poděbradsku", *Věstník. Rozhledy historické, topografické, statistické, národopisné, školské po okresním hejtmanství Poděbradském* 1898, no. 2, 20–22.
[62] "Falco cinereus" or "falco lanarius", cf. Kořínek, *op. cit.*, p. 35.
[63] P. Syrku, "Rumynskij *sfarog* i slavjanskij *Svarog*", *Žurnal Ministerstva Narodnogo Prosveščenija* 251 (1881), 21ff.
[64] G. Dumézil, "Vahagn", *Revue de l'histoire des religions* 117 (1938), 152–170; S. Wikander, *Vayu* (Uppsala, 1941), p. 133; P. J. de Menasce, "La promotion de Vahrām", *Revue de l'histoire des religions* 133 (1947–1948), 5ff.; J. Duchesne-Guillemin, *Zoroastre* (Paris, 1948), 43ff.
[65] G. Dumézil, *op. cit.*, p. 161ff; cf. also N. O. Èmin, *Issledovanija i stat'i po armjanskoj mifologii, arxeologii, istorii i istorii literatury* (Moscow, 1896), 61ff.
[66] E. Benveniste and L. Renou, *Vṛtra et Vṛθragna: Étude de mythologie indo-iranienne* = *Cahiers de la Société Asiatique* 3 (Paris, 1934), p. 31ff.

god-like *Vərəθrayna* was his transformation into the mighty, fast-flying falcon *vārəyna-* (*mərəyō mərəyanąm* "bird of birds", as the *Avesta* defines him). Both compound words — *vərəθrayna* and *vārəyna* — are similar in their etymological composition, and both are endowed with one and the same initial root **wer-*; furthermore, their literal meaning coincides — "smasher of resistance, victor over opposition". In all likelihood, besides the direct name of the Iranian hero (*varhayn*), his similar-sounding, figurative appellation (*vārayn*) in turn influenced the Slavic transmission. Or rather the Slavic *a*, which speaks in favor of a long vowel in its Iranian model, may be related also on account of the adjectival form *vārəθrayna-* (< *vārhayn*). As far as the initial *s* in the name *Svarogъ* is concerned, it is understandable that the Iranian root, designating "opposition, repulse", was conveyed by the similar-sounding and synonymous Slavic root *svar-* (cf. *svarъ* "quarrel, fight, opposition"). One cannot exclude the possibility that this Slavic root, usually linked to the Indo-European **swer-* "to speak" by etymologists, belongs rather to the same word family as Indo-Iranian **vāra-* and **vṛtra-*, etc., originating in an alternant **swer-* of the root **wer-* "to close, defend, offer resistance". Of course, one can ascribe to the influence of taboo the deviations in the initial consonantism of the names *rarog* and *jarog*, but if, at the same time, one compares these two Slavic forms to Iranian *varhrayn* and takes into account the widely attested loss of the initial *v* in this name, then the resulting Slavic form *orrogъ* would have shared the fate of the combination **per-rovъ* > *pēr-rovъ*, which yielded two doublets in Old Slavonic, *pěrovъ* with a reduction of the double liquid and *prěrovъ*, with the change *tērt* > *trět*. Thus, from **orrogъ*, **arrogъ* either changes into **arogъ* and further into *jarogъ* with the inevitable prothetic *j*, or by means of metathesis — but again quite regularly — into *rarogъ*.

Both fundamental and semantically closely linked names for the image of the Iranian mythological hero — man-shaped and bird-shaped — are clearly reflected in the Slavic *Rarog*. His transformations into birds and animals are similar to the metamorphoses which Vərəθrayna undergoes, and the first of the nine incarnations enumerated in the *Avesta*, his identification with the wind, is likewise characteristic of Rarog. The thematics of the myth of the second birth of the Indo-Iranian dragon-slayer who hid in the stalk of a lotus flower were also refracted uniquely on Slavic soil. The motifs assumed by the Armenian gnome, — his being enveloped in flames, his speed and flightiness, his fiery curls and burning eyes — coincide with the image of Rarog, and the ties of the latter with the fire of the hearth echo the image of *Varhran* in

Zoroastrian cosmology, which H. S. Nyberg demonstrated.[67] Cognate to the mentioned hero of the Indo-Iranian world is the divine *Agni*, who controls celestial as well as terrestrial fire and the sun together with sacrificial flame.[68] *Agni* leads us back to Svarog, who was equated with Hercules. The sun was born of Svarog, according to an Old Russian gloss, and of *Indra Vṛtrahan*, according to the *Rigveda*.[69] In the latter it is *Indra Vṛtrahan* who is connected with the first forging of weapons, while in the Russian gloss the same feat is ascribed to Svarog.

The connection of the mythological name *Svarogъ* and its folkloric echoes *Rarog*, *Jarog* with the Iranian models and their simultaneous semantic similarity make it possible to widen the already striking inventory of Slavic-Iranian correspondences in religious vocabulary.

Both Rarog and Vərəθrayna are closely linked to Av. xʽarənah- "radiance, halo".[70] It is not surprising that "sъlnьce-car' synъ Svarogov eže est' Dažьbogъ" ("the sun-king, son of Svarog, who is Dažьbog") carries the additional name *Xъrsъ*, from Iranian *Xursīd* < *Hvarəxšaēta*- (hence also the medieval Serbian personal name Hrs).[71] Cf. in the chronicle under the year 980 the indicative combination *Xъrsъ Dažьbogъ*, as well as the correspondence of two synonymous formulae: *Xrъsovi* *** *putь* in the *Igor' Tale* and the combination *hvarə*- "sun" and *paθ*- "path" in the *Avesta*.[72]

It is not hard to answer V. Jagić's perplexed question as to why Dažbog is not named Svarožič in the Russian gloss later inserted in the Hypatian Chronicle.[73] As was often the case in Old Russian practice, here a combination with a possessive form, *synъ Svarogovъ* "Svarog's son", corresponds to the patronymic. Russian *Dažьbogъ* and Church Slavonic *Daždьbogъ* (cf. also Dažbogovičь in a Ukrainian *gramota* of the fourteenth century) find their echo in the Old Polish personal name *Dadzbog*, and, in Serbian, in the appellation of the folklore demon *Dabog*, *Daba*, in analogous forms of personal names attested in medieval texts, *Daba*, *Dabić*, *Dabović*, as well as in the name of a

---

[67] H. S. Nyberg, "Questions de cosmogonie et de cosmologie mazdéennes", *Journal asiatique* 219 (1931), p. 1ff.; idem, *Religionen des alten Iran* (Berlin, 1938), p. 70.
[68] Cf. Macdonell, *op. cit.*, 88ff.
[69] Cf. Niederle, *op. cit.*, p. 106; Macdonell, *op. cit.*, p. 60.
[70] E. Benveniste and L. Renou, *op. cit.*, p. 7; J. Duchesne-Guillemin, "Le xʽarənah", *Annali*, Instituto Orientale di Napoli, 1963.
[71] Cf. Niederle, *op. cit.*, p. 109f., 120f.; R. Jakobson, *Selected Writings* IV: *Slavic Epic Studies* (The Hague-Paris, 1966), pp. 291f., 701f.
[72] Line 159 of the *Igor' Tale* — cf. Jakobson's edition in *Selected Writings* IV, pp. 145, 184, 185, and the discussion on p. 291; *Avesta*, Yašt XIII, 16, 57.
[73] V. Jagić, "Zur slavischen Mythologie" (review of A. Brückner, *Mitologja słowiańska*), *Archiv für slavische Philologie* 37 (1920), p. 498.

mountain, *Dajbog*, connected with folk beliefs (cf. in relation to the form *Dabog* the whimsical metathesis *Podaga* in Helmold's testimony about the Vagrian gods).[74] The morphological composition of these compounds with two roots, with the imperative as the first member, is clear, as is the original meaning of the entire name — "giver of riches".

The direct coupling of "Dažьbog and Stribog" in the chronicle list of Vladimir's gods under the year 980 alludes to the parallel external and inner form of the two names. *Stri* is the imperative mood of the Common Slavic verb **sterti* (I-E **ster-*, whence Greek στόρνυμι "spread", Latin *sternō* "id.") "to extend, spread, widen, scatter" (cf. *Strzyboga* in Polish toponymics). Besides the usual Slavic forms with the prefix *pro-*, the unprefixed forms of this verb are preserved in medieval Czech and Russian texts: *nepokoj střieti* in the Old Czech *Alexandreis*, *sterlisja* "were dispersed" in the First Pskov Chronicle.[75] Next to *Dažbog* "giver of riches", *Stribog* meant "disperser, apportioner of riches", and the connection of the former with the sun and the latter with the wind is evident. Let us recall the *Yašt* of the *Avesta* (XV. 46) in which *Vayu*, the Iranian god of winds, proclaims: "Hupairitå nąma ahmi" "I am called he who spreads." In the formula of the *Igor' Tale* — "Se větri, Striboži vnuci, vějutъ sъ morja strělami na xrabryě pъlki Igorevy" "It is the winds, Stribog's grandsons, that blow from the sea with arrows on Igor's brave troops"[76] — Stribog and the dispersed arrows (*strělami*) are linked, one would think, not only by alliteration, but by a genuine etymological figure, being, in N. Kruszewski's legitimate notion, "words of one and the same root".[77]

V. SLAVIC GODS AND THEIR SEMANTIC NAMESAKES IN THE INDO-EUROPEAN WORLD

Comparison with the morphological relics of other branches of the Indo-European world reveals kinsmen of Dažbog and Stribog, related not only by the external but by the inner, semantic form of their names.

---

[74] Cf. Niederle, *op. cit.*, p. 110; W. Taszychi, "Najdawniejsze polskie imiona osobowe", *Polska Akademja Umiejętności, Wydział filologiczny, Rosprawy* 62, no. 3 (1925), p. 19; V. Čajkanović, *op. cit.*, 93ff.; E. Dickenmann, "Serbokroatisch *Dabog*", *Zeitschrift für slavische Philologie* 20 (1950), 323–346.

[75] Cf. R. Trautmann, *Die alttschechische Alexandreis* (Heidelberg, 1916), p. 19, l. 1490, p. 134; I. Sreznevskij, *Materialy ...*, 3, p. 848.

[76] Line 48 of the *Igor' Tale*: cf. Jakobson's edition in *Selected Writings* IV, pp. 137, 170, 171, and the note on Stribog on p. 290ff.

[77] N. Kruszewski, "Zagovory kak vid russkoj narodnoj poèzii", *Izvestija Imp. Varšavskogo Universiteta*, 1876, No. 3.

The two interconnected Slavic gods may be added to the mythological pairs investigated by Palmer: such, according to the testimony of the poet Alcman, are the oldest of the Greek gods — Αἶσα "lot" and Πόρος "apportionment" [allotment] — or, correspondingly, the δαίμονες πλουτοδόται "wealth-bestowing spirits" in Hesiod, and in the Old Indic circle of gods the "giver" *Bhaga-* and the "apportioner" *Aṁśa-*.[78]

The semantic structure of names in turn permits one to unite in one a gallery of gods belonging to different tribes: Celtic *Teutates* (derived from **teutā* "stock, tribe"), Latin *Quirinus*, god of the community and of procreation (from **coviria, cūria*), Umbrian *Vofionus* (from **leudh-*; cf. Anglo-Saxon *lēod* "people", Old Ch. Sl. *ljudie* "id."), in E. Benveniste's definition, "soit un dieu de la 'croissance' *** soit, ce qui revient au même, un dieu de la nation, de la communauté",[79] and correspondingly the Old Russian *Rodъ* (cf. in contemporary dialects *rodá* "apparition, ghost", *rodímec* "demon"), mixing the two meanings of the common noun *rod*, i.e. "procreation" and "tribe". As Kalima showed, the spirits *šüntü* in Karelian and *sünd* in Vepse demonology, lit. "birth", are calques of Old Russian *Rodъ*.[80] Here in place of relative homonymy, which makes it possible to reconstruct the original etymological composition of such lexemes as Perun and related Indo-European hieratic names, synonymy should be subjected to comparative analysis. In this and in several other examples descriptive names of similar semantic structure, perhaps as a result of taboo, replaced along similar lines the original general name of a functionally identical divinity.

The firm bond between the different Slavic tribes, preserved until the beginning of the first millenium, the protracted epoch of paganism in connection with the late penetration of Christianity to the Slavic people, and the subsequent long drawn-out period of double faith, — all these factors permit one to use widely the valuable evidence of eye-witnesses of the last stages of Slavic traditional beliefs and to reconstruct the basic traits of Common Slavic religion. Such an initiative is successful only if one does not surrender to the risky speculations of the skeptics about solitary gods without kith or kin, with which, supposedly, only the social élite of individual Slavic tribes provided itself not long before their

---

[78] L. R. Palmer, "The Indo-European Origins of Greek Justice", *Transactions of the Philological Society* 1950[1951], 149–168; G. Dumézil, *Naissance d'archanges* (Paris, 1945), p. 83; idem, *Lex dieux des indo-européens* (Paris, 1952), pp. 51ff., 55ff.
[79] E. Benveniste, "Symbolisme social dans les cultes gréco-italiques", *Revue de l'histoire des religions* 129 (1945), p. 8; cf. G. Dumézil, *Tarpeia: Essais de philologie comparative indo-européenne* (Paris, 1947), p. 112f.
[80] J. Kalima, "Karjalais-vepsäläisestä Vapahtajan nimityksestä", *Mémoires de la Société Finno-Ougrienne* 63 (1928), 257–272.

baptism. It is noteworthy that practically all the Old Russian gods named in the texts are attested as well in the onomastics of the other Slavic languages.

As far as the significance of the Slavic data for the comparative-historical mythology of Indo-European peoples is concerned, the thesis, repeated often in recent years, that ascribes a more folkloric character to Slavic and Baltic mythology in comparison with the more cultivated and retouched mythological systems of the Indic, Iranian, Greek, Roman, Celtic and Germanic worlds becomes ever more convincing. It was precisely the absence of a scholarly, literary reworking that made it possible for the more conservative Slavic and Baltic beliefs to hold on to their prehistoric survivals, which are only with difficulty deciphered in the mythological tradition of other Indo-European peoples.

The synchronic approach to language, which replaced the one-sided genetic conception, cast new light on the fundamental problems of comparative-historical linguistics as well. In turn the structural analysis of myths and mythological systems, which has creatively mastered the methods of contemporary linguistics and which, following the courageous initiative of V. Ja. Propp, advances newer and newer tasks in the latest works of C. Lévi-Strauss, A. J. Greimas and the recent Moscow Symposium on the Structural Study of Sign Systems, will undoubtedly make possible a more integral and systematic approach to the religions of the distant past. Typological comparison, which is being practiced ever more widely in contemporary linguistics, shows mythology the way to reconstruct the whole on the basis of its fragmentary remains.

First presented as a report to the Seventh International Congress of Anthropological and Ethnological Sciences, Moscow, 6 August 1964, and published in the proceedings of the Congress ("Rol' lingvističeskix pokazanij v sravnitel'noj mifologii", *VII Meždunarodnyj kongress antropologičeskix i ètnografičeskix nauk, Trudy* 5 [Moscow, 1970], 608–619). The article was translated from Russian by Stephen Rudy for the present volume. The editor has added subtitles and references on the basis of materials prepared by the author.

THE SLAVIC GOD VELESЪ AND HIS INDO-EUROPEAN COGNATES

> Ci dobbiamo quindi aspettare che il paganesimo balto e slavo conservi almeno dei tratti essenziali della religione indoeuropea; e avremo qua e là occasione di accennare ad analogie fra la religione baltica o slava, e quella indiana o greca o romana, analogie le quali risalgono senza dubbio al periodo della unità originaria.
>
> Vittore Pisani[1]

I. RUSSIAN *VOLOSЪ* AND *VELESЪ*

Two forms — *Volosъ* and *Velesъ* — occur in the ancient Russian texts as designations of a pagan deity. The hazardous assumptions of two different gods, one, *Volosъ*, and the other, *Velesъ*, and the attempts to interpret *Volosъ* as a Russian artificial hypervernacular alteration of the Saint's name Βλάσιος, Church Slavonic *Vlasъ*, and, on the other hand, to derive *Velesъ* from the devil's designation Βελίας, Βῆλος must be discarded as totally untenable.

The Russian *Primary Chronicle* cites three peace treaties with the Greeks, Oleg's of 907, Igor''s of 945, and Svjatoslav's of 971. According to all three treaties, the representatives of Rus' swore by their god *Perunъ*, but in the oaths of 907 and 971 the god *Volosъ*, in turn, is invoked immediately after *Perunъ*. The *Legend of Vladimir's Baptism* describes the smashing and sinking of two idols — first *Volosъ*, and, thereupon, *Perunъ*.[2] A preacher against survivals of Russian paganism lists the objects of lasting worship, among them *Perunъ*, followed by *Volosъ* (*Slovo nekoego Xristoljubca* in one of its versions).[3] As for the variant *Velesъ*, the ancient Russian legend *Xoždenie Bogorodicy po mukam* offers a list of pagan deities with the sequence *Velesъ*, *Perunъ*,[4] while, in the *Vita of St. Avraamij of Rostov*, *Velesъ* is the only pagan god

---

[1] V. Pisani, "Il paganesimo balto-slavo", *Storia delle Religioni*, ed. by P. T. Venturi, 2 (Torino, 1949), p. 61.

[2] See A. Šaxmatov, "Korsunskaja legenda o kreščenii Vladimira", *Sbornik statej, posvjaščennyx V. I. Lamanskomu* 2 (Petersburg, 1908), p. 1143.

[3] See E. Aničkov, *Jazyčestvo i drevnjaja Rus'* (Petersburg, 1914), p. 377: *moljatsja *** Perunu, Volosu skotъju bogu.*

[4] See I. Sreznevskij, *Drevnie pamjatniki russkogo pis'ma i jazyka* (Petersburg, 1863), p. 205; N. Tixonravov, *Pamjatniki otrečennoj russkoj literatury* 2 (Moscow, 1863), p. 23: *Velesa, Peruna na bogy obratiša.*

to appear.⁵ The possessive adjective *Velesovъ* is attested in the *Igor' Tale*, v. *17*. The same form in both of its variants — *Velesov* and *Volosov* — occurs in North Russian toponymy, while among the Old Russian personal names, only the form *Volos* is known.⁶

In the Old Russian texts a few traits may contribute to the portrayal of the deity in question.

1) If some other gods are named jointly with *Velesъ/Volosъ*, then *Perunъ*, the chief figure of the ancient Russian pantheon, appears as his immediate neighbor.

2) If only one god is mentioned jointly with *Perunъ*, it is necessarily *Velesъ/Volosъ*. Thus, in the Russian-Greek treaties, *Perunъ* is named either alone or together with *Volosъ*, and the old accounts of Russia's Christianization deal either with the destruction of *Perunъ*'s idol only or also with the similar end of the sculptured *Volosъ*.⁷

3) The report of the *Primary Chronicle* assigned to 980 on the expulsion of Varangians by Vladimir, the subsequent inauguration of his sovereignty and its symbolic expression — graven images of indigenous gods erected on that Kievan hill near his court where *Perunъ* was standing during the reign of Vladimir's grandfather (*Prim. Chron.*, year 945) — omits *Volosъ*, and, most probably, his Kievan idol stood elsewhere.

4) The form *Volosъ* figures only with the apposition *bogъ* "god", and the latter noun is accompanied by the attribute *skotii*, while in the absence of such an apposition, the doublet *Velesъ* is the only one attested.⁸

5) The expression *skotii bogъ* with the unambiguously possessive form of its adjective can mean nothing else than "the cattle god". According to the treaty of 907, as cited by the *Primary Chronicle*, the representatives of Rus' who took their oath *po ruskomu zakonu* swore "both by *Perunъ*, their own god (*Perunъmь bogъmь svoimь*), and by *Volosъ*, the

---

⁵ See A. Ponomarev, *Pamjatniki drevnerusskoj cerkovno-učitel'noj literatury* 1 (Petersburg, 1894), p. 221f.: *čto radi skorbja sědiši bliz strastnago sego idola Velesa?* *** *razoriti mnogostrastnogo sego idola Velesa*.

⁶ *Velesovo rebro, Volosova gora, selo Velesovo, derevnja Volosovo* and, apparently with a taboo substitution of the initial labial, *Bolosovo*: see, e.g., V. Vinogradova, *Slovar'-spravočnik "Slova o polku Igoreve"* 1 (Moscow-Leningrad, 1965), p. 96f.; V. Miller, "K voprosu o Slove o polku Igoreve", *Kritičeskoe Obozrenie* (1879), No. 3; A. Sobolevskij, "Volosij Vlasij", *Russkij Filologičeskij Vestnik*, 16 (1886), pp. 185–187; A. Pogodin, "Neskol'ko dannyx dlja russkoj mifologii v XV. veke", *Živaja Starina* 20 (1911), p. 426f.; V. V. Ivanov and V. N. Toporov, *Slavjanskie jazykovye modelirujuščie semiotičeskie sistemy* (Moscow, 1965), p. 22.

⁷ See Ivanov and Toporov, *op. cit.*, p. 21.

⁸ Cf. V. Toporov, "Fragment slavjanskoj mifologii", *Kratkie soobščenija Instituta slavjanovedenija AN SSSR*, 30 (1961), p. 21.

god of cattle (*Volosъmь, skotьemь bogъmь*)": the opposition *svoimь* and *skotьemь*, underscored by a contrastive word order, reveals a difference in the immediate spheres of the two gods — the human and the animal realms. It is probable that the pagan oaths underwent some alteration under the pen of the pious chronicler, who was disinclined to use the term "god" for heathen deities. Thus, in the *Primary Chronicle*, the oath of the unbaptized (*nekrъščeni*) warriors of 945 is said to declare that its violators would be "accursed of God and of *Perunъ*", but the words *ot Boga i ot Peruna* may have supplanted an earlier, much more probable formulation: "of the god *Perunъ*" (*otъ boga Peruna* or with a reiterated preposition *otъ boga otъ Peruna*). Correspondingly, the oath of 971 must have sounded originally "may we be accursed of *Perunъ*, the god whom we worship, and of *Volosъ*, the cattle god" (*da iměemъ kljatvu otъ boga, vъ nьže věruemъ, — Peruna, i Volosa, boga skotьja*). Here again the chronicler apparently endeavored to disjoin the god and *Perunъ*, since he professed that the objects of pagan worship "are not gods, but only wooden idols which exist today but tomorrow will rot away, whereas there is only one God, that whom the Greeks serve and worship and who has created heaven and earth ***".[9] Therefore, an inappropriate preposition was inserted before the names of *Perunъ* and *Volosъ* by false analogy with the antecedent *vъ nьže*: according to the Laurentian codex, *ot boga v neže věruem v* [!] *Peruna i v* [!] *Volosa boga skotьja* (but Hypatian *skotьja boga*). Thus, once more, *Perunъ*, "the god whom we ourselves venerate", i.e. "our own god" (*svoi*), turns out to be opposed to the "cattle god", with emphatic support by a contrastive word order: apposition plus its attribute plus the head word, as opposed to the head word plus the attribute of the apposition plus the apposition itself.

6) The oath of 945 refers to *Perunъ* only: its violators, accursed of this god, will be slain by their own weapons. On the other hand, the oath of 971 invokes not only *Perunъ* but also *Volosъ*: and, correspondingly, it adds to the death from one's own weapons another punishment: "May we become golden as gold" (*da budemъ zoloti jako zoloto*). This image already puzzled the scribe responsible for the Laurentian copy, and he substituted *koloti* for *zoloti*, while all other manuscripts reproducing the *Primary Chronicle* preserve the vocable *zoloti, zolotě, zlati*. The sense of the strange punishment inflicted by *Volosъ* has remained obscure[10] and will be reinterpreted below (III).

---

[9] Cf. S. H. Cross and O. P. Sherbowitz-Wetzor, *The Russian Primary Chronicle* (Cambridge, Mass., 1953), p. 95.
[10] Cf., e.g., V. Istrin, "Dogovory russkix s grekami X veka", *Izvestija Otd. rus. jaz. i slov. RAN* 29 (1924), p. 390.

7) The legendary "Seer Bojan", repeatedly invoked in the *Igor' Tale* as a miraculous poet, musician and divinatory wizard, is declared in a solemn apostrophe to be the grandson (or offspring) of *Velesъ*: *Věščij Bojane, Velesov vnuče!* It is particularly significant that in the introduction to the narrative this designation is used to evoke Bojan's metaphoric, esoteric, patently zoomorphic style and to reply to these supernatural tropes and visions cherished by the grandson of *Velesъ*, god of flocks, with a much more earthly and topical manner of narration.[11]

II. *VELES* IN SOUTH SLAVIC TOPONYMY AND CZECH DEMONOLOGY

Outside of the Eastern Slavic area such Southern Slavic toponyms as *Veles* in Macedonia (Alb. *Vɛlɛs*, Greek Βελεσσός) and *Velesovo* in Krajina still await closer examination. Several Czech sources of the fifteenth and sixteenth centuries name a demonic being, *Veles*. *Tkadleček*, the famous Czech novel written on the threshold of the fifteenth century, puts the following exclamation into the mouth of its angry hero: *Ký jest črt, aneb ký veles, aneb ký zmek tě proti mně zbudil?* ("What devil or what veles or what dragon incited you against me?"). This text indicates that together with the devil and the fabulous dragon of Czech folklore, *Veles* also belongs to the gang of traditional evil spirits. A Hussite sermon of 1472 calls the parishioners to leave their sins with this spirit (*u Velesa*). A byword recorded in 1598 by T. Hájek depicts *Veles* as a sly whisperer: "*Ký Veles jim jich našepce!*". A German story about a malicious wife whose husband dreamed she *wer ein Ganß, und flüge über Meer, und keme nimmermehr heim* (K. Huberin, *Spiegel der Haussucht, Jesus Syrach genandt*, Nuremberg, 1554), appeared seventeen years later in a Czech translation which adds "she should fly somewhere beyond the sea to *Veles*": *někam k Velesu za moře* (T. Rešel, *Kniha Jezusa Siracha*, Prague, 1571). M. Zámrský's sermon of 1590 presents a noteworthy modification: *někam k Velesu pryč na moře* ("somewhere away upon the sea to *Veles*"). The question raised by J. Jireček and supported by Anučin as to whether sea and *Veles* were not associated in the Czech tradition, so that one of the two images could have attracted the other, remains valid.[12]

---

[11] On Bojan see R. Jakobson, *Selected Writings*, IV (1966), pp. 278ff., 346f., 607ff.
[12] Cf. J. Jireček, "O slovanském bohu Velesu", *Časopis Musea Království českého* 49 (1875), p. 408f.; Č. Zíbrt, "Něco o bohu Velesu", *Slovanský sborník* 5 (1886), p. 318f.; D. Anučin, "Sani, laďja i koni, kak prinadležnosti poxoronnogo obrjada", *Drevnosti — Trudy Moskovskogo Arxeologičeskogo Obščestva* 14 (1890). p. 180; Z. V. Tobolka, "O Velesovi", *Český lid* 3 (1894), p. 530f.

Veles is not the sole deity to evolve into a demonic creature in Czech popular tradition.[13] The surmise of a single borrowing from Russian language and beliefs is obviously groundless. The Czech and Russian homophonic forms must go back to a common mythological name, *Velesъ*. Consequently, such isolationist attempts to confine the question of *Velesъ/Volosъ* to the Eastern Slavic area as the shaky explanation of the Russian form *Velesъ* by pleophony lose any trace of probability.

III. THE *VEL-* FAMILY OF BALTIC SPIRITS

The Baltic heathen survivals display the root *vel-* in a whole family of mythological names: Lithuanian *Vēlinas*, *Vélnias*, *Vėls* — a demon identified with the devil under the pressure of the ecclesiastical pattern; Old Lithuanian *Velionìs* or *Veliónis* — "deus animarum", *Veliuonà* — goddess of the forefathers' shadows; *Vẽles* or *Vẽlės* — spirits of the dead, *Vėlė* — specter, spook; Latvian *Vęĩns*, *Vęĩls* — demon, devil; according to Lange-Stender's *Latvian Mythology* of the eighteenth century, *Vels* — god of the dead; *Velis*, plur. *Veļi* — sprites of the dead.[14] After J. Dobrovský's ingenious surmise, these names were often brought together with the Slavic *Velesъ/Volosъ*,[15] and Lithuanian folklore reveals certain features of *Vēlinas/Vélnias* and *Vẽlės* which link these supernatural beings with their assumed Slavic correlatives.[16] Lithuanian folk legends stress the close connection both of *Vẽlės* and *Vēlinas* with the animal kingdom. *Vēlinas* figures as a skillful hunter (*egeris*) and sharpsighted teacher of the chase, who is famous as well as *Vẽlės* for the wild pursuit of game (*laukine medžiokle*).[17] On the other hand, cattle is protected by *Vēlinas*; he subjects bovines to magical

---

[13] On the Czech demon *Rarach* as a folklore survival of the Slavic god *Svarogъ* see R. Jakobson, "Rol' lingvističeskix pokazanij v sravnitel'noj mifologii"; cf. the English translation, *supra*, p. 26ff.

[14] See E. Fraenkel, *Litauisches etymologisches Wörterbuch* (Heidelberg-Göttingen), p. 1218f.; A. Mažiulis, "Vėlė lietuvių tikėjime", and R. Sealey, "Velnias i lietuvių tautosakoje", *Lietuvių Enciklopedija* 33 (1965), pp. 301, 335f.; A. Leskien, "Litauisches vėlės", *Indogermanische Forschungen* 34 (1914), pp. 333–336; J. W. E. Mannhardt, *Letto-preussische Götterlehre* (Riga, 1936), p. 626.

[15] See V. Jagić, *Istočniki dlja istorii slavjanskoj filologii*, II: *Novye pis'ma Dobrovskogo*, etc. (Petersburg, 1897), p. 600; Jireček, *op. cit.*, p. 416; L. Niederle, *Slovanské starožitnosti*, II:I² (Prague, 1924), p. 113; A. Brückner, *Mitologia Slava* (Bologna, 1923), p. 133f.; V. Pisani, *op. cit.*, p. 73. In his letter of May 5, 1793 Dobrovský states: "Mit weles kommt das Litauische welnas, welinas Teufel überein. Jetzt heisst alles Teufel nach den Grundsätzen des Christenthums, weil nach Gott kein anderes Wesen gelten kann. Man muss aber die alte Mythologie und Daemonologie herstellen, wie sie war und seyn musste."

[16] J. Basanavičius, *Vėlės ir Velniai lietuvių tautosakoje* (Shenandoah, Pa., 1902) and *Iš gyvenimo Vėlių bei Velnių* (Chicago, 1903).

[17] Basanavičius, *Iš gyvenimo ...*, pp. 120f., 283, 377, 380.

performances and punishes those which disobey his orders. *Vēlinas* himself assumes the shape of a bull.[18] A bond between cows and *Veļi* appears in the ritual Latvian folk song:

> *Kas tur skaņi gavilēja*
> *Kapu kalnu galiņā?*
> *Mūs māsiņa gavilēja*
> *Veļu govis ganīdama.*[19]

("Who worships so loudly/on the top of the graveyard hill?/Our little sister worships/tending the cows of *Veļi*"). The entire quatrain is saturated with alliterations: the syllable *ga* which inaugurates the second hemistich of all four lines; the four *ka* permeating the uneven syllables in the first hemistich of both initial lines (*kas-ska-ka-kal*); and the intra-linear alliterations in both final lines (*mūs-mās, go-ga*). Against this copious background, the reiterated verb *gavilēja* "celebrates, worships" acts as a significant paronomastic blend (*g.v.l*) of the two key words *Veļu* (*v.l*) and *govis* (*g.v*) "Veli's cows".

The Lithuanian popular tradition asserts that if someone is punished and bitten by *Vėlės*, "the man turns yellow and comes to naught" (*žmogus pagelsta ir ima nykti*).[20] This survival throws light on the menacing punishment by *Volosъ* evoked in the Russian-Greek treaty of 971 (*da budemъ zoloti jako zoloto*). Cf. such names for wasting diseases as Russian *zolotúxa* "scrofula"; Old Czech variants *zlatenicě* and *žlutenicě* "jaundice"; Czechomoravian and Slovak dialectal *zlátenica, zlatnica, zlátka*; Serbocroatian *zlàtenica* "idem".[21]

The Russian exorcism against scrofula orders *zolotúxa-krasnúxa* to go out from the man, from his head and eyes and away into the open fields, into the blue seas, upon the deep swamps, etc.[22] This evocation of the seas may be confronted with the Old Czech incantational call for the expulsion of the evil wife "somewhere away upon the sea to Veles",

---

[18] *Iš gyvenimo ...*, pp. 348, 363, 380f.
[19] K. Barons, *Latvju Dajnas* (Jelgava, 1894).
[20] *Iš gyvenimo ...*, p. 134.
[21] See V. Flajšhans, *Klaret a jeho družina* 2 (Prague, 1928), pp. 521, 532; V. Machek, *Etymologický slovník jazyka českého a slovenského* (Prague, 1957), p. 586.
[22] *Zolotuxa-krasnuxa, podi iz raba* (by name), *iz bujnoj golovy, iz jasnyx očej, u čistye polja, u sinie morja, na rostani, povoroty, na glubokie bolota* (L. Majkov, *Velikorusskie zaklinanija*, Petersburg, 1869, p. 42). Prof. F. B. J. Kuiper (Leiden) commented on my study in a letter of July 30, 1968: "In the Vedic ritual the god Váruṇa is represented by a man who has yellow eyes (*piṅgākṣa-*). The Avestan epithet of Miθra, viz. *zairi.dōiθra-*, may express the same meaning. The same word *zairi-* occurs in its Sanskrit form *hári-* as an epithet of *Váruṇa* in Ath. [*Atharvaveda*] V.V.II.I. This reminds one of the *Zolotúxa-krasnúxa* which is asked to go away *iz jasnyx očej*". Cf. note 37.

while the "deep swamps", as waters in general, are believed, in Lithuanian oral tradition, to be the favorite abode of *Vēlinas*, who easily rides over marshes inaccessible to human beings.[23]

IV. VEDIC *VARUṆA*

Ferdinand de Saussure was apparently the first to suppose a genetic connection between *Vēlinas* and the Vedic *Varuṇa*. In a letter of December 1907 to A. Meillet[24] he responded to the latter's study on Mitra,[25] agreed with its skeptical attitude "au rapport de *Varuṇas* avec οὐρανός" and suggested a new etymology: "je me suis plus d'une fois demandé si un réflexe européen de ce vieil Āditya ne se trouvait pas dans le *vélnias* des Lituaniens, ou plutôt dans leur *vēlinas* (dont *vélnias* me paraît un *dérivé*). Comme c'est justement le groupe des Ādityas qui paraît, par le *bogŭ* slave, avoir joui des faveurs de ce rameau des populations indo-européennes, il ne serait pas très surprenant qu'un *vēlinas* baltique ait existé comme dieu des châtiments pour une faute morale, et ait laissé, ensuite, le diable pour héritier de son nom, tout en se trouvant, par les origines, identique au Varuṇas hindou."

This ingenious and phonetically impeccable hypothesis makes it necessary to interpret the morphological components of the nouns in question. The *n*-suffixes with variable vowels in their onset (*Varuṇas, Vēlinas, Veliónis, Veliuonà*)[26] are typical of Indo-European mythological names. Cf. Lat. *Fortūna*; Lith. *Žvoruna*; the family of cognate theophoric names: Slav. *Perunъ* (derivative *Perynь*), *Perperuna*, Lith. *Perkúnas, Perkuna tete*, Latv. *Perkuôns*, Alb. *Perɛndï*, Ved. *Parjánya*, Old Norse *Fjǫrgynn, Fjǫrgyn*, Greek Κεραυνός, Hitt. *Peruna-*;[27] cf. also the Anittaš text of the seventeenth century B.C., which designates the storm-god, head of the Hittite pantheon, by an ideogram with the subsequent suffix *-unni* in dat.-loc. and which has been deciphered *Tarḫunnaš* "vanquisher, smasher" with the root *tarḫ-* "vanquish, smash" and the suffix *-ŭnas*.[28]

The Indo-European root **wel-* may be identified easily, if we take into account the "huge eyes" (*dideles akys*) and the piercing look of the hunter *Vēlinas*, who beholds all flesh as well as the netherworld behind "the little gate of *Vẽlės*" (*Velių varteliai*) and if, on the other hand, we

---

[23] *Iš gyvenimo* ..., p. 380.
[24] "Lettres de Ferdinand de Saussure à Antoine Meillet" published by E. Benveniste, *Cahiers Ferdinand de Saussure* 21 (1964), p. 115f.
[25] A. Meillet, "Le dieu indo-iranien Mitra", *Journal Asiatique* (1907), p. 143ff.
[26] Cf. K. Būga, *Priesagos -ūnas ir dvibalsio uo kilmė* (Kaunas, 1921).
[27] Cf. Jakobson, "Rol'..." (*supra*, p. 19f.).
[28] See J. Friedrich, *Hethitisches Wörterbuch*, Ergänzungsheft 2 (Heidelberg, 1952), p. 24.

elicit the salient feature of *Varuṇa*. This Vedic god is depicted repeatedly as farsighted, all-seeing, clairvoyant, thousand-eyed; he never closes his eyes and watchfully surveys the realms of life and death which he governs with the assistance of undeceived thousand-eyed spies — messengers who look across the whole world so that nothing in the universe, no action, no thought, and no device, remains invisible to the omniscient deity; no sin can be kept hidden from him.[29] Hence, the root **wel-*, which signifies "sight, insight, foresight, observance, vigilance", underlies the Vedic names of the divine seer.[30]

V. THE ROOT **WEL-* IN CELTIC LORE; THE "PEOPLE OF *VARUṆA*", "THE SON OF *FEL*", AND "THE GRANDSON OF *VELESЪ*"

The same root **wel-* plays a substantial part in the archaic religious terminology of the Celts. Cf. *Veleda*, the Celtic name of a prophetess reported by Tacitus; Old Irish *fili* "seer, poet, magician", plur. *filid* "the official custodians and transmitters of the mythological tradition", displaying the ancient interdependence of poetry, divination and music.[31] A similar interlacement is observable in the cult of the mysterious thaumaturge *Varuṇa*.[32] His devotees, *Gandharva*, surname of "the people of *Varuṇa*", eager to communicate with the other world, were wizards, marvelous musicians, singers and dancers in contradistinction to *Brāhmaṇas*, deprived of the right to practice all these arts.[33]

According to the Irish gloss in O'Davoren 880, "*fel* (**wel*) is poetic and musical power, whence *felmac* is the son of musical and poetic power". This term, designating a seer, inspired poet and musician, is applicable not only to "the people of *Varuṇa*" but presents, moreover, a remarkably close correspondence to the formula "grandson or descendant of *Velesъ*", used in the *Igor' Tale* to apostrophize "the seer Bojan", performer on *gusli*, magician and prophetic poet of the early times.

---

[29] Cf. A. A. Macdonell, *Vedic Mythology* (Strassburg, 1897), p. 23f.; A. Hillebrandt, *Varuṇa und Mitra* (Breslau, 1877), p. 79ff.; R. Pettazzoni, "Le corps parsemé d'yeux", *Zalmoxis* 1 (1938), p. 8f. The diverse attempts to interpret the name *Váruṇaḥ* have been surveyed in M. Mayrhofer's *Kurzgefasstes etymologisches Wörterbuch des Altindischen*, Lieferung 19 (Heidelberg, 1967), pp. 151–153.
[30] Cf. J. Pokorny, *Indogermanisches etymologisches Wörterbuch* (Bern-Munich, 1959).
[31] Cf. J. de Vries, *Keltische Religion* (Stuttgart, 1961); A. and B. Rees, *Celtic Heritage* (London, 1961); T. F. O'Rahilly, *Early Irish History and Mythology* (Dublin, 1946).
[32] Cf. J. Gonda, *Epithets in the Ṛgveda* (The Hague, 1959), p. 114.
[33] See G. Dumézil, *Mitra-Varuṇa* (Paris, 1940). A comparison of the Gandharvas and Brahmaṇas with the Filids and Druids, respectively, would be instructive; cf. J. Vendryes, "La religion des Celtes", *"Mana" — Introduction à l'histoire des religions*, 2: *Les religions de l'Europe ancienne* 3 (Paris, 1948), p. 290ff.

VI. *VELESЪ/VOLOSЪ* — *VĚLINAS* — *VARUṆA*

Despite the relative scarcity of our data about *Velesъ/Volosъ*, we discover a few additional features that link him with *Varuṇa*. The formulaic designation of *Volosъ* as "the god of cattle", as well as the connection between *Vělinas* and cattle in Lithuanian folklore finds a striking correspondence in the weighty role assigned to cattle by the myths surrounding *Varuṇa*. In his monograph *Varuṇa and Mitra*, Hillebrandt devoted special chapters to "Varuṇa und die Kuh" and "Varuṇa und der Schaf" and broached the still-pending question, "warum die Kuh zu Varuṇa in näherer Beziehung steht". The cow and the sheep emerge as god's relatives. He is the protector and holder of neat, a cheerful donor of good milk cows, calved again and again. The cow permeates Varuṇa's body. A herd of one hundred cows conceals and saves the god's virility.[34] Varuṇa knows "the secret hidden names of the cows" and proclaims that the clairvoyant poet, initiated into the thrice seven names borne by the cow, will prosper the poetic art by transmitting them as secrets to a later generation (RV VII.87.4 and VII.41.5).[35]

In the Rigveda hymns to *Varuṇa*, "bucolic imagery" holds a conspicuous place: thoughts which crave for the wide-eyed god are compared to cows going into the pasture-fields; "the cow-like dawns" are evoked in connection with the daily praises for *Varuṇa*, who is asked to free us from evil "as a calf from halter" (II); the divine king is implored to free the supplicant from the fetter as a cow-thief unties a young calf (VII); "*Varuṇa* guards the thoughts of men, just as herds of cows are shepherded", he is strong "like a herdsman", and all wisdom has its home in him "like cows together in the stall" (VIII). The relation of this deity to cattle is a current topic in the Rigveda as well as in ritual literature.[36]

Both *Volosъ* and *Varuṇa* act as guardians of right and guarantors of human treaties who severely punish the infringement of vows by afflicting the violators with a disease.[37] Perhaps the connection of

---

[34] See Hillebrandt, *op. cit.*, pp. 16. 77f., 88ff.; G. Dumézil, *Ouranós-Váruṇa* (Paris, 1934), p. 72.
[35] Cf. C. Watkins, "Language of gods and language of men: Remarks on some Indo-European metalinguistic traditions", *Myth and Law among the Indo-Europeans*, ed. by J. Puhvel (Berkeley and Los Angeles, 1970).
[36] Cf. H. D. Griswold, *The God Varuna in the Rig-Veda* (Ithaca, N.Y., 1910), p. 8; A. Hillebrandt, *Vedische Mythologie* 3 (Breslau, 1902), p. 30.
[37] Cf. H. Oldenberg, *Die Religion der Veda* (Berlin, 1894), pp. 203, 293. Hillebrandt, *Varuṇa und Mitra*, p. 63ff., and *Vedische Mythologie* 3, p. 27: "Seine oft genannte Fessel ist nicht nur die Wassersucht; Krankheit aller Art und selbst der Tod suchen den heim, der Varuṇa's Zorn verfällt". Cf. note 22.

Varuṇa with waters, discussed over and over by Indologists,[38] could be associated with the aquatic bent of *Vēlinas* and with the bond between the sea and *Veles* in Czech sources. Also, the sovereignty over the other world draws the Vedic god together with *Vēlinas* and his Baltic correlatives.[39]

VII. VEDIC *VARUṆA*, AVESTAN *AHURA-MAZDĀ*, AND CELTIC *ESUS*

In the Rigveda, the apposition *Asura* "mighty, lord" was connected primarily with *Varuṇa*, though it extended occasionally first to other gods and then, to demons.[40] *Ahura-Mazdā*, the Avestan deity corresponding exactly to the Vedic *Varuṇa Asura*, has preserved only the second part of the latter's double name. Yet, like the divine seer, ostensibly nicknamed *Varuṇa*, his Iranian double displays miraculous eyesight and vigilance, a far-flung network of reconnaissance and a supernatural omniscience; he stands guard over peace treaties (*miϑra*) and chastises their transgressors[41] (cf. the Russian-Greek pact cited under 907: "kljašasja Volosъmь skotьemь bogъmь i utvьrdiša *mirъ*"[42]). Beasts are under his care and control.

In these names the Indic *asu-* and Iranian *ahu-* "genius, chief" go back to I.E. *$es\underset{\sim}{}$-os/es-u*, literally "existent, essential", derived from the verb **es-* "to be" and reflected as well in Latin *erus* < *esus* "master", Greek ἐύς and Hittite *aššuš* "good, suitable". The name of the ancient Celtic god *Esus* belongs to the same family.[43] The bullhead ornamenting the famous Trier bas-relief dedicated to *Esus* prompts us to confront him with such divine patrons of cattle as *Varuṇa Asura* and *Velesъ/Volosъ*. It

---

[38] See, e.g., H. Lüders, *Varuṇa* 1: *Varuṇa und die Wasser* (Göttingen, 1951).
[39] On Varuṇa as "Herrscher im Totenreich" see Hillebrandt, *Vedische Mythologie* 3, p. 36, and on the corresponding survivals in Lithuanian mythology and ritual, cf. A. Brückner, "Osteuropäische Götternamen", *Zeitschrift für vergleichende Sprachforschung* 50 (1922), p. 180f.
[40] Cf. Macdonell, *op. cit.*, p. 24; P. von Bradke, *Dyâus Asura, Ahura Mazdâ und die Asuras* (Halle, 1885), p. 120f.; Oldenberg, *op. cit.*, p. 163; Dumézil, *Mitra-Varuṇa*.
[41] Cf. Oldenberg, "Varuṇa und die Adityas", *Zeitschrift der deutschen morgenländischen Gesellschaft* 50 (1896), p. 43ff., M. Eliade, *Traité d'histoire des religions* (Paris, 1964), p. 72ff.
[42] Cf. Meillet, *op. cit.*, p. 144f.
[43] Cf. J. Wackernagel, *Altindische Grammatik* 2, 2 (Göttingen, 1954), p. 857; A. Walde, *Vergleichendes Wörterbuch der indogermanischen Sprachen* 1 (Berlin-Leipzig, 1930), p. 161; A. Ernout & A. Meillet, *Dictionnaire étymologique de la langue latine* (Paris, 1951³), p. 359; E. Boisacq, *Dictionnaire étymologique de la langue grecque* (Heidelberg-Paris, 1938³), p. 298; O. Szemerényi, "The Greek Nouns in -εύς", *Gedenkschrift Paul Kretschmer* 2 (Vienna, 1957), p. 175; E. Laroche, *Les noms des Hittites* (Paris, 1966), p. 321; Vendryes, *op. cit.*, p. 263; V. Pisani, *Le religioni dei Celti e dei Baltoslavi nell'Europa precristiana* (Milan, 1950), p. 35.

is noteworthy that the same sculpture represents *Esus* axing a tree, and the ritual sacrifice to him was *homo in arbore suspenditus*; it may be significant that the sacrifices offered to *Varuṇa* had to be cut with an ax.[44]

VIII. *VELESЪ* AND *VOLOSЪ* AS COMPOUNDS

The same pair of constituents which serve as two autonomous words in *Varuṇa Asura* has merged into one compound in the corresponding Slavic name *Velesъ*. It is one of the Slavic archaic compounds with an initial athematic constituent like **čel-věkъ* "man", i.e. "tribesman" (cf. Rus. *čeljad'* "body of menials", Lith. *keltis* "clan", *vaĩkas* "boy, fellow"), *gu-mьno* "threshing floor", i.e. "tread of bulls", *skor-lupa* "shell", i.e. "crusty peel", **četver-nogъ* (OChSl *četvrěnogъ*, Old Russ. *četverenogъ*), etc.[45] The proper meaning of *Velesъ* would be "master, genius of vision" or "good in vision".

As for the Russian doublet *Volosъ* (occurring — nota bene — only in concatenation with the following apposition *bogъ*), its most probable prototype had been **Vel-sъ* with the subsequent Eastern Slavic change of the diphthong /el/ into /ol/ and, further, into /olo/; cf. /melko/ > /molko/ > /moloko/. The component *sъ* goes back to the zero-grade variant **sǝ-os/su* of the form **esǝ-os/esu*. Cf., e.g., Skt. *su-* "good"; the epithet of *Taranis*, the Celtic thunder-god, *Su-cellos* "striking well"; and Slavic **sъ-čęstije* "good fortune", **sъ-dorvъ* "healthy, robust".[46]

IX. GAULISH *VELLAUNUS*

Apparently, *Vellaunus*, one of the ancient bynames of *Esus*, attested in the epigraphic texts of continental Gallia,[47] contains the habitual *n*-suffix and the same compound **Vel-s-* as in the Slavic **Velsъ*, with the regular Celtic change /ls/ > /ll/; this form reappears also in the tribal name *Vellauni*. The juxtaposed Celtic deities — *Taranis*, with the two mutually synonymous substitutes *Sucellos* and *Bussumarus*, and *Esus*,

---

[44] See de Vries, *op. cit.*, p. 97; G. Dumézil, *La Saga de Hadingus* (Paris, 1953), p. 156, and *Mitra-Varuṇa*, p. 49. Cf. the Western Slavic *by-* "to be": *bydlo* "domicile, husbandry, cattle", *bydlec, bydlič* "resident, householder".
[45] See A. Pogodin, *Sledy kornej-osnov v slavjanskix jazykax* (Warsaw, 1903); G. Il'inskij, *Praslavjanskaja grammatika* (Nežin, 1916), pp. 303–305. Cf. A. Meillet, *Introduction à l'étude comparative des langues indoeuropéennes* (Paris, 1934), p. 254ff.
[46] See J. Baudouin de Courtenay, "Próby zestawień etymologicznych, II", *Studja staropolskie, Księga ku czci A. Brücknera* (Cracow, 1928), pp. 220–224.
[47] Cf. Pisani, *Le Religioni ...*, p. 35.

with the substitutes *Vellaunus* and *Canetonessis* "singer" — like their Slavic, traditionally joint relatives *Perunъ* and *Velesъ/Volosъ*, present an integral couple of the divine striker and the melodious seer.

X. ANATOLIAN *WALIŠ-* AND OLD NORSE *ULLR* OR *ULLINN*

The Slavic god *Velesъ/Volosъ* finds his cognates in the Baltic, Indo-Iranian and Celtic areas. In ancient Anatolian onomastics, where *Peruna-*, the equivalent of Slavic *Perunъ*, emerges among the theophoric Hittite names, V. V. Ivanov has detected the stem *Wališ-* as a possible parallel to Velesъ.[48] Pokorny recognizes the same root **wel* in the Old Norse name of the god *Ullr* (**Wulþuz*) or, in other ancient variants, *Ull* and *Ullinn* (with an *n*-suffix; cf. *Óðr* and *Óðinn*). This god, like *Vēlinas*, was conversant with animals and renowned as an alert, sharp-sighted, unerring hunter; Scandinavian toponymics reveals his close connection with pastures. The fragmentary mythological data on *Ullr* depict him as a wise magician, miraculous seafarer and steady protector of peace and order. Similar to the vows consecrated by *Volosъ* or *Varuṇa*, solemn oaths used to be sworn *at hringi Ullar*, and this ring is interpreted as a symbol of binding or fettering.[49]

XI. A SUMMARIZED COMPARISON OF THE COGNATES

The relative variety in the treatment, combination and use of the two constituents within the bipartite name of the Supreme Seer in the diverse Indo-European languages and, in particular, a free choice of allomorphs is quite a typical feature of mythological nomenclature, prompted in part by the severe rules of taboo and partly by the vital needs of ecstatic expressivity. A rigorous, pedantic application of current phonetic and grammatical rules to such a highly specialized field of language as

---

[48] V. V. Ivanov, *Obščeindoevropejskaja, praslavjanskaja i anatolijskaja jazykovye sistemy* (Moscow, 1965), p. 285; A. Goetze, "Some Groups of Ancient Anatolian Proper Names", *Language* 30 (1954), pp. 354, 358.

[49] J. Pokorny, *Indogermanisches etymologisches Wörterbuch* (Bern-Munich, 1959), p. 1136f.; J. Hoops, *Reallexikon der germanischen Altertumskunde* 4 (Strassburg, 1918–19), p. 372f.; E. Wessén, "Studier till Sveriges hedna mytologi och fornhistoria", *Uppsala Universitets Årsskrift* (1924), §6; J. de Vries, *Altgermanische Religionsgeschichte* 2 (Berlin, 1957), §§ 443–447: Ullr und Ullinn, and "Over enkele godennamen", *Tijdschrift voor Nederlandse Taal en Letterkunde* 53 (1934), p. 193ff.; K. F. Johansson, "Über die altindische Dhiṣaṇā und Verwandtes", *Skrifter utg. av Kgl. hum. vetenskapssamfundet i Uppsala* 20 (1918), p. 137, confronts the names *Ullr* and *Varuṇa*.

hieratic onomastics would be sheer fallacy.⁵⁰ Licenses characteristic of hypocorisms appear also in theophoric names.

In the bipartite divine name, its constituents *wel- and *es₂os function either as autonomous words — Varuṇa Asura — or as members of a compound — Veles, Volos, Wališ-, Vellaunus- or, finally, only one of these parts is uttered: the first in Vēlinas, Vę̄lns, Ullr, and the second in Esus and Ahura. The n-suffix at the end of the 1) simple or 2) compound stem appears in 1) Varuṇa, Vēlinas, Vę̄lns, Ullinn and in 2) Vellaunus.

The widespread occurrence of both roots in the theonymy of the Indo-European world, their prevalent merger into one divine name, and the striking resemblance in mythological functions tied to this onomastics enable us to look for the same ancestry of all historically attested variants.

The common prototype of these mythological beings apparently displayed a supernatural acumen and a control over spheres alien and recondite to ordinary mortals, namely over the animal world, the hereafter, and the magic art; for mankind, the all-seeing god was principally a steadfast protector of peaceful settlements and a stern chastiser of their violators.

XII. SLAVIC *VЬLXVЪ "MAGICIAN" AND NORTH RUSSIAN JOLS "DEVIL"

We leave open the intriguing question⁵¹ whether there exists some etymological connection between Velesъ/Volosъ and the Old Church Slavonic vlьxvъ or vlъxvъ (Old. Rus. vъlxvъ, borrowed by Finnish as velho, Veps völh, Estonian võlhu), pl. vlьsvi, vlъsvi, "vates, magus, incantator", vlьšьba, vlьšьstvo "magia", vlьšьskъ "magicus", vlъsnovati, vlъsnǫti "balbutire", vlьsьnъ "cui impedita est lingua" ("tongue-tied", literally "bewitched").⁵² In the pagan tradition of Kievan Rus' vъlxvъ

---

⁵⁰ Cf. Jakobson, "Rol' ..." (cf. supra, p. 13); de Vries, Altgermanische ..., §514: "Die Forschung der letzten Jahre hat gezeigt, dass gerade in religiösen Benennungen die Lautgesetze nicht in ihrer unbedingten Strenge befolgt werden müssen".
⁵¹ See Brückner, Mitologia Slava, p. 135f.; Pisani, Le religioni ..., p. 61.
⁵² See A. Dostál et al., Slovník jazyka staroslověnského (Prague, 1962), p. 203; F. Miklosich, Lexicon palaeoslovenico-graeco-latinum (Vienna, 1862–5), p. 69f.; I. Sreznevskij, Materialy dlja slovarja drevnerusskogo jazyka 1 (Petersburg, 1893), pp. 381–384; J. J. Mikkola, Berührungen zwischen den westfinnischen und slavischen Sprachen (Helsinki, 1894), p. 103f.; the Old Czech gloss in "Mater Verborum" (see A. Patera, "České glosy v Mater Verborum", Časopis Musea Království Českého, 51/1877, p. 388) — vlichvec (vlchvec) "pithones" — might be confronted with Old Church Slavonic vlъxvujǫšti — imǫšti duxъ pithonьskъ (Dostál, loc. cit.). For other words related with *vlъxvъ in Slavic languages see J. Schütz, "Věščii Bojane, Velesovъ vъnuče", Slavistische Studien zum Internationalen Slavistenkongress in Prag 1968 (München, 1968), p. 546.

occupied a significant place and, according to the testimonies of the chronicler, the first two centuries of Russian Christianity witnessed a number of popular movements and heathenish uprisings led by "sorcerers" of this name and mould.

Zelenin's surmise, which traces the sobriquet *Jols* "devil", recorded in the Kostroma dialect, to the name of *Volosъ* seems plausible:[53] by virtue of an ancient taboo, **Vъlsъ*, the reduced grade of **Volsъ*, could have been introduced with further substitution of /j/ for the initial /v/.

XIII. VEDIC VALA — LITHUANIAN VĖ̃LĖ — CZECH VELE

One may assume an etymological kinship between *Varuṇa* and the Vedic demon *Vala*, who in turn was a proprietor and guardian of cows (*govapus*) and who burst into a colorful lament at their sudden loss. The lack of change *l > r* may indicate a dialectal variant.[54] The relation between the names *Varuṇa* and *Vala* is comparable to that between Lith. *Vėlinas* and *Vė̃lė* or Latvian *Vęlns* and *Velis*. The Slavic folk songs for Christmas Eve are rich in heathenish survivals; around 1400 an inquisitive writer and learned monk of the Břevnov monastery, Jan z Holešova, recorded the exordium of such a Czech Christmas carol ("in vulgari: Koleda") — *Vele vele dubec stojí prostřed dvora*.[55] If, in accordance with Niederle's apposite suggestion, one interprets the introductory *Vele* as a vocative designation of *Veles*,[56] it would be the sole Slavic instance in which the component **wel-* is used without the other constituent part

---

[53] See D. Zelenin, "Tabu slov u narodov vostočnoj Evropy i severnoj Azii", *Sbornik Muzeja Antropologii i Ėtnografii* 9 (1930), p. 178.

[54] Cf. Hillebrandt, *Vedic Mythology* 3, p. 265: "Bei dem geringen Umfang unseres Materials können wir daraus Folgerungen nicht ziehen; es kann sein, dass die Bezeichnung vala aus einem anderen Dialekt herübergenommen ist und mit ihm auch die verhältnismässig grosse Anzahl seltener Worte, auf die wir in diesem Sagenkreise stossen."

[55] The best critical edition of this treatise is by A. Brückner, "Largum Sero Jana Holeszowskiego", *Rozprawy Akademii Umiejętności*, Wydz. filol., 54 (1916), pp. 308–351; cf. also H. Usener, *Christlicher Festbrauch. Schriften des ausgehenden Mittelalters* (Bonn, 1889): Z. Nejedlý, *Dějiny předhusitského zpěvu* (Prague, 1904), p. 233, republished as *Dějiny husitského zpěvu* 1: *Zpěv předhusitský* (Prague, 1954), p. 311f.; the same exordium with the reverse order of the subject and predicate and with a brief recapitulation of the comment made by Jan z Holešova, entered into a manuscript sermon of 1436 from the pen of *Frater Mathias, Canonicus Monasterii Gradicensis*, has been reproduced by F. Černý, "Kázání kněze Matěje s českými glosami", *Vestník České Akademie* 9 (1900), p. 296. Prof. A. Frinta of Charles University has prepared for publication an apparent variant of the same song detected by him in recent Czech oral tradition.

[56] Niederle, *op. cit.*, p. 114.

and, at the same time, without any derivational suffixes.[57] Brückner's interpretation of *Vele* as a mere exclamation similar to the occurrence of *ole* in Slavic folk songs is unpersuasive, since the latter presents a natural combination of the interjectional *o* with the enclitic particle *le*. The fragment under discussion agrees with the habitual verse form (6 + 6) and imagery of the traditional *koleda* pattern (the ritual oak standing in the middle of the yard).[58] The Břevnov treatise discloses that the same apostrophe was repeated "per singulos versus huius satis longi cantici" which promised people of firm faith "fortunam et bonam gubernacionem rerum et vite".[59] As we know from later Slavic carols, the heralded abundance is embodied chiefly in the increasing strength, splendor and fertility of cattle.[60] By the magic influence of the miraculous tree, the yard is suddenly flooded with extraordinary cows and their countless calves. An ancient, vanishing allusion to "the god of cattle" hidden in the appeal *Vele Vele* seems to be quite verisimilar within such a framework.

XIV. SUPREME DEITIES OF THE I.-E. PANTHEON AND THEIR DEGRADATION

The myth of *Indra*'s having rent *Vala* may be confronted with the inveterate views on the original Indo-Iranian preeminence of *Varuṇa*,[61] his supersession by *Indra* throughout the Rigvedic period, and the gradual change of his traditional second name *Asura* into a designation

---

[57] However, an Old Russian *hapax legomenon*, "*Vela* the goddess", awaits closer examination. The Čudov version of the "Slovo kako pervye poganii verovali v idoly", a homily against pagan survivals, cited by V. J. Mansikka, "Die Religion der Ostslaven", *FF Communications* 43 (Helsinki, 1922), p. 177ff., and rich in archaic vestiges, states that some people, baptized yet ignorant of what Christianity is, still address their prayers *kutnu bogu* ("to the house god") *i velě bogyni* ("and to *Vela* the goddess"), *i jadrěju* (a *hapax* apparently connected with *jadro* "kernel, testicle", *jadret'* "to ripen, mature, grow virile and strong", probably cognate with the Vedic *Indra*; cf. V. Machek, "Name und Herkunft des Gottes Indra", *Archiv Orientální*, 12/1941, p. 143), *i obiluxě* (a *hapax* related to *obil'e* "abundance", Old Rus. *obilъ* "plenty"), *i skotnu bogu* ("and to the god of cattle"). On *-ěj* and *-uxa* as suffixes of personal names see F. Miklosich, *Die Bildung der slavischen Personen- und Ortsnamen* (Heidelberg, 1927), pp. 6, 15.
[58] Numerous examples are adduced by A. Potebnja, "Obzor poětičeskix motivov koljadok i ščedrovok", ch. 15: Čudesnoe derevo, *Russkij Filologičeskij Vestnik* 13 (1885), p. 315ff. (for metrics, cf. *RFV* 11/1884, p. 16); Brückner, *op. cit.*, p. 349f.; Č. Zíbrt, "Ohlas staročeské koledy v koledách moravských", *Český lid* 25 (1925), p. 83f.
[59] Brückner, *op. cit.*, p. 341.
[60] Cf. P. Caraman, *Obrzęd kolędowania u Słowian i u Rumunów* (Cracow, 1933), p. 32ff.; see p. 40, the Polish *kolęda* with the joyful news of the cow which bore two calves endowed with fairy names; "Krowisia się omnożeyła,/Parę wołków położyła./ — A jakież im miano damy?/ — A jednemu złotorożek/A drugiemu srebrny rożek ... . " Cf. *Varuṇa*'s concern with the sublime names of the cows.
[61] Evidenced as *u-ru-wa-na* in the Mitannian treaty of the XIV c. B.C.

of demons.⁶² This change actually prefigures a similar metamorphosis of the pristine divine magician into such demonical apparitions of the Christian age (*Götterdämmerung*) as the Lithuanian *Vẽlinas*, the Latvian *Vę̃lns*, the Czech *Veles* and perhaps also the North Russian *Jols*.

This alleged degradation of *Varuṇa* finds a certain analogue in the historical fate of *Ullr*, who must have been the earliest Norse mythological god of wealth, peace and victory and who played a leading role, or even "*die* führende Rolle", as experts assert. "Zahlreiche Ortsnamen, ganz besonders in Schweden, zeigen, dass im nordgermanischen Kult Ullr eine viel grössere Bedeutung gehabt hat, als aus den wenigen Zeugnissen, die wir von diesem Gotte haben, hervorgeht."⁶³ As the great investigator of Norse antiquities, Magnus Olsen, concluded, this ancient god seems to have yielded his superior rank to Thor, "en yngre dublet til Ullinn-Ull".⁶⁴ Quite parallel opinions were expressed repeatedly about two cognates of the Slavic *Perunъ*, the gods *Parjanya* and *Fjǫrgynn*, on the question of their displacement in Vedic and Germanic mythology. The pre-Christian lore of Slavs did not undergo such *profonde modificazioni* as one observes in the seriously remolded mythological patterns of those Indo-European peoples who exhibit a much earlier and stronger mobility and cultural intercourse.⁶⁵ In particular, *Perunъ* and *Velesъ/Volosъ*, appearing as the supreme divine patrons in Russian pacts of the tenth century, turn out to reflect two initially prominent deities of the common Indo-European pantheon.

First published in *Studi linguistici in onore Vittore Pisani* (Brescia, 1969), with the following authorial note: "This paper, drafted in December 1967, develops a few theses of two lectures on comparative mythology presented by the author in the Harvard Philological Club, January 14, 1968 and in the Università degli Studi di Roma, January 28 of the same year. For friendly help and inspiring suggestions, thanks are due to Marija Gimbutas, Daniel Henry Holmes Ingalls, and Calvert Ward Watkins."

⁶² See R. Roth, "Die höchsten Götter der arischen Völker", *Zeitschrift der Deutschen Morgenländischen Gesellschaft* 6 (1852), p. 67ff.; W. D. Whitney, "On the Main Results of the Later Vedic Researches in Germany", *Journal of the American Oriental Society* 3 (1853), p. 327; cf. Macdonell, *op. cit.*, pp. 28, 65f., 156f.; K. Bohnenberger, *Der altindische Gott Varuṇa nach den Liedern des Ṛgveda* (Tübingen, 1893), p. 88.
⁶³ See Hoops, *loc. cit.*
⁶⁴ M. Olsen, *Hedenske kultminder i nordiske stedsnavne = Skrifter utgit av Videnskapsselskapet i Kristiania*, Hist.-filos. kl., 1914, #4 (1915), esp. Ch. 16. De Vries, *Altgermanische ...*, §447, recounts the fate of *Ullr*: "Seine Wechselbeziehung zu Odin hat ihn an Bedeutung verlieren lassen, nachdem dieser in seinem Siegeszuge fast die gesamte Königsmacht in seiner Person zusammengezogen hatte. Denn sein Kult war zu Anfang der Zeit, von der die schriftlichen Überlieferungen uns berichten, schon erloschen; wie lange vorher, das wissen wir nicht." Various vestiges, however, testify that this god "zu einer uralten Schicht der germanischen Religion gehört" (446).
⁶⁵ Pisani, "Il paganesimo ...", p. 61.

ДРЕВНЕАРМЯНСКИЙ ВАХАГН В СВЕТЕ СРАВНИТЕЛЬНОЙ МИФОЛОГИИ

Книгу *VRTRA et VRΘRAGNA*, совместную работу Э. Бенвениста и Л. Рену (Париж, 1934), открывает мудрый завет первого соавтора: "Мифологический факт является в первую очередь языковым фактом." В силу названного методологического принципа два этимологически родственных образа — иранский VRΘRAGNA и индийский VRTRAHAN — поддались более точному учету. Однако тот же, но шире примененный языковедческий подход позволил монографии Ж. Дюмезиля, "VAHAGN" (*Revue de l'histoire des religions*, CXVII, 1938), внести несколько коррективов, а именно пристальный учет экспансии индоиранского мифа из Ирана в Армению и внимательный разбор девяти стихов о VAHAGNE в армянском памятнике пятого века дал возможность восстановить пропуск в иранских текстах, пробел, объяснимый глубоким стилистическим различием между авестийским перечнем репертуара чудодейственных воплощений героя и сохранившимися в индийской и армянской литературе прославлениями одного, основоположного чуда, дошедшими до нас в индийской и в армянской письменности.

Ирано-славянская диффузия мифа в свою очередь требует расследования. Мифологические показания древнерусской письменности называют в числе богов СВАРОГА и его сына СВАРОЖИЧА, отожествленного с солнцем и делящего свой патроним с главным идолом полабского храма в Ретре, согласно описанию очевидца. В пограничных, частью онемеченных округах ляхитских и словенских корней, наблюдатели, по свидетельству чешского историка Яна Пейскера, обнаруживают "многочисленные" примеры возвышенностей с названиями, таящими имена Сварога и Сварожича, в единичных случаях с сохранением начального *s*, но чаще с табуированным *t*: таковы *Swarożyno Siodło*, *Twarożna góra*, *Twaraschitzberg*.

Наиболее вероятным источником славянского, явно заимствованного имени SVAROGЪ, надо считать иранское мифологическое имя VRΘRAGNA с его задним открытым гласным между вибрантом и велярным согласным. Если непосредственным образцом для армянского имени VAHAGN послужил исторический вариант VARHRAGN, то славянская форма наиболее тесно связана с диалектным среднеиранским обликом VARAGN, на который в 1950 году обратил наше внимание ученый иранист П. Тедеско.

Начальный согласный славянской формы — либо новый пример беглого *s*, либо контаминация с ходовым славянским корнем *svar*-, означающим "отповедь, распрю" и созвучным семантически с иранским VṚθRA, "сопротивление," т.е. первой частью составного имени VṚθRAGNA.

В числе десяти перевоплощений авестийского VṚθRAGNA седьмое, выделенное магией число, занимает особливо значимое место в характеристике героя, превращая последнего в наивысшей породы сокола, VĀRAGNA. Бенвенист (стр. 34) справедливо усматривает увлекательную возможность предположить, что в основе формы VĀRAGNA- лежит значение "сокрушитель обороны," и таким образом "подлинное этимологическое родство сблизило бы бога VṚθRAGNA с птицей, раскрывающей его сущность." Однако тот же исследователь предусматривает равно и вероятие обратного хода вещей, т.е. применение этимологии народной, основанной на прославленном сходстве сокола и божества в зоркости, в стремительности полета и в боевом натиске.

Каков бы ни был исторический порядок соотношения между божеством и его седьмым перевоплощением, несомненен факт славянского размежевания обоих аспектов, т.е. божества VṚθRAGNA и его воплощения VĀRAGNA. Самый бог и его порождение развернуты в вертикальную двоицу, а именно семейство — СВАРОГЪ и его сын под патронимом СВАРОЖИЧЬ, собственным именем ДАЖЬБОГЪ, а также нарицательным и ласкательным среднего рода СЪЛНЬЦЕ, чему в Ведах соответствует VṚTRAHAN с его новосозданным светилом, а в армянском мифе VAHAGN выходит из пламени с огнем волос, огнистой бородой и глазами- солнышками. В восточнославянской *Повести временных лет* ДАЖЬБОГЪ сочетается с грамматическим приложением ХЪРСЪ, т.е. с эпитетом "лучезарный", словообразовательным сородичем авестийского XVARƏNAH- "священное озарение," "лучистое благо". XVARƏNAH- увенчивает два воплощения, седьмое, т.е. XVARƏNAH-, и первое- воплощение VAHA (слав. ВѢТР с активным одушевленным суффиксом).

Горизонтальный параллелизм сближает в древнерусской литературной традиции ДАЖЬБОГА с его собратом СТРИБОГОМ, по закону импликации требующим в перечнях богов соприсутствия ДАЖЬБОГА.

Оба божества сцеплены тождеством второй части своих сложных имен (-бог), а также императивом и реальным значением первой части: "податель благосостояния" — солнце, и "раздатчик" — ветер (ср. ст. чеш. *strieti* и др. рус. *strěti*). Недаром потомки СТРИБОГА зовутся "вѣтри" и формулы посвященные ДАЖЬБОГУ и СТРИБОГУ объединены сомкнутой сетью выразительных параномазий: вѣ*три*, стрибожи *стрѣ*лами; о*би*да дажьбожа у*буди*. Ветер в Ведах провозглашает "Меня зовут тем, кто рассевает." Схожие функциональные двоицы обиходны в индоевропейских мифологических системах; ср. вед. BHAGA-AMÇA, др. гр. ΑΗΣΗΠΌΡΟΣ (L. R. Palmer).

Усвоение иранской формы VĀRAGNA- обозначавшей воплощение бога VR̥θRAGNA в высшую разновидность сокола (*Würgfalke, cinereus*) и распад связи между обоими именами характерны для славянского языкового мира, где название сокола приобрело языковую окраску существенно отличную от божеского имени. Это название сокола частью сохранило свое орнитологическое значение, частью распространилось и на другие виды соколов или хищных птиц вообще, большей частью же сохранило идею демонического характера иранской мифологической птицы. Образ демонической птицы получил широкое распространение в западнославянских языках и в западной окраине южнославянского языкового круга, как свидетельствуют краеведческие показания двух последних веков. Лабиальный приступ формы VĀRAGNA- сменился предвокальным йотом, или же иранское сочетание начального *a* с долгим *p* дало ход метатезе: *ap < pa*. Оба перехода распространены во всех перечисленных языках, причем формы на *X*- особенно привычны в языках с переходом конечных звонких мгновенных велярных в соответствующие длительные. Несколько примеров: словенские JÁROG, JÁROŽICA, RÁROH, RÁROG; польские JAROG, RARÓG; силезский JARÁŠEK; чешские RÁRACH, RARÁCH, RARÁŠ, RARÁŠEK, RADÁŠEK (ю. чеш., формы с расподоблением внутренних согласных), RARAŠIK, RARÁŠČATA, RÁROŽ, RÁROHY, RAROH, RAROCH; словацкие RÁROH, RARÁŠIK. Подробные обзоры чешских поименных мифических существ разработали языковеды Ján Kořínek (*Listy filologické* LX, 1933) и Václav Machek (*Linguistica slovaca* III, 1941).

Machek в своих соображениях о связи форм славянских обозначений сокола вообще и демонической птицы частности с иранским VĀRAGNA- и поставил рассудительный вопрос о зависимости славянского, преимущественно фольклорного слова от иранского источника.

Мифологическое сходство обоих имен не подлежит сомнению. Чешский Рарах, которому краевед А. Hajný посвятил обстоятельный очерк, отличается теми же чертами ("Rarášek", *Věstník: Rozhledy historické, topografické, statistické, národopisné, školské po okresním hejtmanství Poděbradském*, 1898, No. 2, стр. 20–22).

В своих демонических характеристиках и функциях, вся эта славянская словесная семья проявляет целый ряд ярких сходств с иранскими образцами, особенно с именем, данным в Авесте седьмому (из основных) воплощению бога VRΘRAGNA и другому из его главных воплощений, т.е. первому. Ветер и огонь, краеположные стихии характеризующие Рараха, как свидетельствует Hajný:

"Люди у нас представляют себе 'Рарашка' в виде летящего над горизонтом огня. Портной возращался поздней ночью домой. Внезапно он увидел над собою на небе огонь, будто огненную пулю. Он испугался и пошел быстрее домой. Но огонь непрерывно шел за ним до самой деревни. Устрашенный бедняк прибежал домой и созвал домочадцев посмотреть на огонь. Все еще видели, как тот влетел в соседнюю деревню и там опал. Это был несомненно Рарашек. Следует напомнить, что бурный ветер у нас тоже носил имя Рарашек. В сильном вихре, который подымает пыль и мусор и уносит все это столбом ввысь, люди усматривают Рарашка, и всячески его избегают."

Если Рарашек враждебен человеку, он разносит и обращает в прах весь его несжатый хлеб. Способность превращаться в различных птиц и зверей повсеместно приписывается Рарашку. Это демон огненного тела и, превращаясь в змею, днем и ночью испускающий искры. Рарашек все чаще представляется вольшебной птицей, перья которой обладают магической силой. Из зоба этой чудодейственной птицы вылетает зной, подлинное дыхание Рарашка.

Чудотворный характер приписываемый рождению, точнее перерождению, которое переживают ведийский VRTRAHAN и армянский VAHAGN, находит себе параллель в чешском фольклорном предании о том, как создается, точнее воссоздается, Рарах. Девять мифологически изысканных условий необходимы для создания Рарашка. Он должен быть первым птенцом из первого яйца первого сноса, и курица должна быть вся черная без единного перышка иного цвета. На этом яйце не может сидеть курица, а высидеть его может только мужчина, охраняя его подмышкой и на припечьи в течение девяти дней и девяти ночей, не молясь и не моясь.

Любопытны примеры скрещения обеих славянских разновидностей *svar-* и *jar-* в разнообразном применении к суши *non-plus ultra* по выражению П. Сырку, исследовавшему румынский диалектизм *сфарог* восточнославянского происхождения (*Ж.М.Н.П.*, CCLI, май, 1887) и, с другой же стороны, в чешских диалектах RÁROŽ ("дотла иссушенный хворост") и в словацких RÁROHY ("валежник").

Written in Cambridge, Mass., May 1982, for the International Symposium on Armenian Linguistics, Erevan, September 1982, and published in *Istoriko-filologičeskij žurnal*, Armenian Academy of Sciences, 4 (99), 1982.

PART TWO

RECENT STUDIES IN LINGUISTICS AND PHILOLOGY

A
PHONOLOGICAL AND MORPHOLOGICAL STUDIES

AN INSTANCE OF INTERCONNECTION BETWEEN THE DISTINCTIVE FEATURES

R. JAKOBSON AND L. R. WAUGH

"The invariance is generally relative rather than absolute." Gunnar Fant, *Speech Sounds and Features* (Cambridge, Mass., 1973), p. 163.

The focal task faced by the investigator of distinctive features is the diligent insight into the inner logic of their mutual relationship. Comparative analysis gradually widens the scope of implicational laws which establish the relative order of linkage between different features within single phonemes and sequences, as well as within entire phonological systems, and this relative order embraces a broad range of associations spreading from compulsory copresence to strict incompatibility. The development of such an inquiry, with a consistent search for invariants, is the only reliable way toward a typology of those systems, a way which enables us to view and to interpret multifarious linguistic universals, some of them devoid of exceptions and others endowed with a probability near-to-one.

The minimal display of a hierarchical structure, namely the division of any distinctive feature into a pair of opposites, one marked and the other void of mark, calls for the analyst's vigilant attention to the interplay of concurrent features, and especially to the context-sensitive reversibility of the relative order between the marked and unmarked opposites within any feature in regard to the other concurrent features.[1]

In our work on *The Sound Shape of Language*[2] we tried to trace the interconnection of the diverse distinctive features and noted that feature systems reflect neurological encoding and decoding, as it has been revealed by the new, remarkable experimental data on the connections between speech and the brain.[3] Our present note is a complementary draft of certain universal relations between obstruents and two of their

---

[1] Cf. V. V. Ivanov, "On Antisymmetrical and Symmetrical Relations in Natural Sciences and Other Semiotic Systems", *Linguistics* 119 (1974), pp. 35–40.
[2] R. Jakobson and L. R. Waugh, *The Sound Shape of Language* (Bloomington, Ind. and London, 1979).
[3] See especially L. J. Balonov and V. L. Deglin, *Slux i reč' dominantnogo i nedominantnogo polušarij* (Leningrad, 1976).

characteristic features labelled "abrupt–continuant" and "strident–nonstrident or mellow".[4]

The comparative study of vowels and consonants gives clear evidence for their two-faced mutual relation.[5] We may also refer to the tentative summary of this status in our book of 1979. While consonants are opposed to vowels by a distinct noise element, as Hugo Pipping noted,[6] at the same time vowels are opposed to consonants through the latters' pronounced "sonority" (*Schallfülle*), a concept enrooted in speech analysis since the renowned *Grundzüge der Phonetik zur Einführung in das Studium der Lautlehre der indogermanischen Sprachen* by Edward Sievers[7] and Otto Jespersen's *Lehrbuch der Phonetik*.[8]

Sonority as the common and basic property of the vowels proves to be their only mark as long as the initial step of language acquisition does not endow the vowel with any distinctive subdivision, whereas consonants are already bifurcated into grave and acute opposites, with a sense-discriminative task of the new opposition. At this stage distinctive consonants such as [p] and [t] form sequences with a mere "supporting vowel" (voyelle d'appui). Only in rare instances can the order of the alternates be inverted in their information-bearing role, as, for instance, [ap] "leap" ~ [pa] "repose" in the holophrastic phase of one American-English infant.

The maximum contrast to the sonority mark of vowels is implemented by plosive consonants. Thus the stops appear to be the optimal nonvocalic phonemes. With respect to the opposition vocalic ~ nonvocalic, the continuants exhibit a noticeable attenuation: the reduction of sonority is lessened. Thus in the contraposition of stops and constrictives it is the latter which function as the marked opposites.

Accordingly, in those languages of the world which have no phonological opposition of abrupt and continuant obstruents, only stops are used or at least only stops occur as basic variants, those which show but a minimum dependence on the sequential environment.

The noise element which specifies the consonants and sets them off against the nonconsonantal phonemes is particularly appreciable in the intense noisiness, generated by the use of a supplementary impediment

---

[4] Cf. R. Jakobson and M. Halle, "Phonology in Relation to Phonetics", in *Manual of Phonetics*, ed. by B. Malmberg, (Amsterdam, 1968), pp. 411–449.
[5] See in particular C. G. M. Fant, "Auditory Patterns of Speech", *Proc. Symposium on Models for the Perception of Speech and Visual Form* (Cambridge, 1967), pp. 111–125.
[6] See his *Inledning till studiet av de nordiska språkens ljudlära* (Helsinki, 1922).
[7] Leipzig, 1901; pp. 528–535.
[8] Leipzig, 1904; pp. 196ff.

accompanying the production of strident obstruents as compared with their nonstrident (mellow) counterparts. While the optimal damping of the sound is achieved by the abrupt obstruents, it is the strident constrictives which exert a maximum turbulence.

The distribution of mark and unmarkedness between stridency and mellowness is diametrically opposite in abrupt and in continuant consonants. Mellowness for the abrupts and stridency for the continuants are exemplifications of the unmarked status, in contradistinction to the marked concurrence of abruptness and stridency, evidenced by the affricates, as well as to the likewise marked concurrence of continuity and mellowness, displayed by constrictives of reduced friction, such as the interdental θ or the bilateral ϙ.[9]

Hence, in the languages of the world, the concurrence of abruptness and stridency (the existence of affricates) as well as the concurrence of continuance and mellowness (in constrictives of reduced friction) necessarily implies the copresence of mellow stops and of strident continuants in the same phonological pattern.

Analogous examinations have to be continued and extended as to the mutual cohesions of all other distinctive features, consonantal and vocalic as well. This research should unveil the general rules which underlie the framework of the extant languages and which are assumed to delimit the universal repertory of distinctive features and of their bundles.

Written in Cambridge, Mass., spring of 1978, for the Gunnar Fant Festschrift, *Frontiers of Speech Communication Research*, ed. B. Lindblom and S. Öhman (London, 1979).

---

[9] Cf. R. Jakobson, C. G. M. Fant, and M. Halle, *Preliminaries to Speech Analysis* (Cambridge, Mass., 1963), §§2.32–2.323.

MUTUAL ASSIMILATION OF RUSSIAN VOICED AND VOICELESS CONSONANTS

To sum up the two-decade exchange of insights into the title topic, let us state that the Standard Russian *V* (whether palatalized or not) occupies an obviously intermediate position between the obstruents and the sonorants. With all the obstruents it shares the passive property of losing voicedness before the subsequent voiceless obstruents of the same cluster. Cf. *koróva* "cow" — dimin. *koróvka* [fk] with *berëza* "birch" — *berëzka* [sk]. The devoicing of the final voiced obstruent leads to a similar change of the antecedent [v]: *krivda* [vd] "falsehood" — gen. pl. *krivd* [ft]. But while assimilable to the following voiceless consonants, the voiced *V*, in contradistinction to all the obstruents, lacks their active power of imposing voicedness upon the antecedent voiceless consonants.

If a pre- or intervocalic cluster contains more than one obstruent, the last of them imposes its voicedness or voicelessness upon all the antecedent obstruents whether they are contiguous or separated by some interjacent members of the cluster, namely by sonorants or by *V* (*k vdové* [gvd] "to the widow").

Thus within a pre- or intervocalic cluster voiced and voiceless obstruents are mutually incompatible. However, the voiced *V*, while it cannot be followed, may be preceded by voiceless consonants: cf. on the one hand the adjective *lóvkij* [fk] "adroit", derived from *lovít'* "to catch", and on the other hand *v skváẑine* [fskv] "in the chink".

Such prepositions or prefixes as *pod* "under", *nad* "over", *bez* "without", *iz* "out of", *v* "in", *pred* "before", the preposition *pered* "before", the prefix *raz-* and on the other hand the prepositions or prefixes *ot* "from", *s* "with" and the preposition *k* "to" lose the original, independent voicedness and voicelessness of their final or sole consonant at the beginning of those clusters which contain obstruents endowed with an active assimilative power.

Cf. the following clusters formed by the preposition *ot*, by the prefix *vz*, and by the initial consonant of diverse roots: *ot vzlóma* [dvzl] "from breaking in", *ot vzrýva* [dvzr] "from an explosion", *ot vzvízga* [dvzv'] "from a scream", *ot vzbúčki* [dvzb] "from a scolding", *ot vzdóxa* [dvzd] "from a sigh", *ot vspléska* [tfspl'] "from a splash", *ot vstrjáski* [tfstr'] "from a shaking", *ot vsxódov* [tfsx] "from shoots".

Examples of prepositions and prefixes with independent voicedness and voicelessness at their end: *pod r'jánym* [dr'j] *konëm* "under a spirited horse" — *ot r'jánogo konjá* [tr'j] "from a spirited horse"; *nad Mléčnym* [dml'] *Putëm* "over the Milky Way" — *ot Mléčnogo* [tml'] *Puti* "from the Milky Way"; *beznravstven* [znr] "immoral" — *s nravoučeniem* [snr] "with a moral admonition"; *v mnóžestve* [vmn] "in the multitude".

Such an independent voicedness or voicelessness also remains before a *V* which is not followed by any additional obstruent: *iz vas* [zv] "from you" — *s vámi* [sv] "with you"; *bez v'júgi* [zv'j] "without a blizzard" — *s v'júžnym* [sv'j] *vétrom* "with a snow storm"; *pod vlást'ju* [dvl] "under the authority" — *ot vlastéj* [tvl] "from the authorities"; *iz l'vínoj* [zl'v'] *pásti* "from the lion's mouth" — *s l'vínoj dólej* [sl'v'] "with a lion's share"; *nad vragóm* [dvr] "over the enemy" — *ot vragá* [tvr] "from the enemy"; *iz vnučát* [zvn] "of grandchildren" — *s vnučátami* [svn] "with grandchildren"; *nad vran'ëm* [dvr] *i nad rvan'ëm* [drv] "over lies and over rags" — *ot vran'já* [tvr] *i ot rvan'já* [trv] "from lies and from rags"; *bez vvóza* [zvv] "without import" — *s vvózom* [svv] "with import".

When in its concluding part a cluster introduced by one of the prepositions or prefixes cited above contains no *V*, the first obstruents of the cluster take on the last one's voicedness or voicelessness: 1) *ot lgún'i* [dlg] *slýšal* "heard from a liar (fem.)"; *k lžívym* [glž] *slovám* "to the mendacious words"; *ot l'gótnyx* [dl'g] *uslóvij* "from favorable terms"; *k l'dístomu* [gl'd'] *béregu* "to the icy coast"; *s rdéjuščim* [zrd] *rumjáncem* "with a glowing color"; *ot ržávčiny* [drž] "from rust"; *k ržanój* [grž] *muke* "to the rye flour"; *ot mzdy* [dmzd] *ne otkázyvajsja* "don't give up the recompense"; *s mglístogo* [zmgl'] *véčera* "from the hazy evening"; *s mgnovénnym* [zmgn] *porývom* "with a momentary fit"; 2) *pered l'stívymi* [tl's't'] *slovámi* "in the face of flattering words"; *nad rtut'ju* [trt] "over mercury"; *v mšístom* [fmš] *krajú* "in a mossy land"; *pod mčaščujusja* [tmč] *mašinu* "under a speeding car"; *iz Mcénska* [smc] "from (the town of) Mcensk"; *v mstítel'nom* [fms't'] *tóne* "in a vindictive tone"; *v mšístom* [fmš] (but *v mglístom* [vmgl']) *bolóte* "in a mossy (hazy) swamp". Some of the examples cited also allow another, optional implementation in Russian speech, namely a syllabic consonant (cf. Reformatskij, 1971).

It is again to A. A. Reformatskij (1975) that we owe the neat observation that the prefinal obstruent keeps its voicedness before the devoiced reflex of *V* in such seemingly uncommon sound combinations as the predicative adjectives *rezv* [zf] "frisky", *trezv* [zf] "sober", and the genitive plural *jazv* [zf] from *jázva* "ulcer"; to these forms the noun *xorúgv'* [gf'] "gonfalon" could also be added. Hence it appears that in the postvocalic clusters, just as in the prevocalic position, the distinction of voiced and voiceless obstruents before *V* has been preserved: cf. *vetv'* [tf'] "branch", *mërtv* [rtf] "dead", and such gen. plur. forms as *bitv* [tf] "battles", *kljatv* [tf] "vows", *jastv* [stf] "viands".

In the Russian sound pattern the phonemes /v/ and /f/ do not constitute as strict a pair as the other oppositions of voiced and voiceless consonants. Beside the still foreign tinge of /f/, particularly when in a final position, it is the inadmissibility of the distinction voiced/voiceless before /f/ that separates the latter from /v/: cf. *bez vórsa* [zv] "without nap" — *s vórsom* [sv] "with nap" and *bez fórsa* [sf] "without swagger" — *s fórsom* [sf] "with a swagger". The devoiced reflex of the final /v/ can be, in Sapir's terms (Mandelbaum, 1949:53), characterized as a consonant with a voicing "latency": voicedness disappears in the absolute form of the word but reappears when the word is followed by an enclitic with an initial sonorant or vowel: *ot jázv mol* [zvm], *trézv li* [zvl'], *rézv už* [zv]. In general, in Russian the external sandhi displays striking differences between the reflexes of /v/ and /f/. In a close collocation the initial obstruent of the second, especially enclitic, word imposes its voicedness or voicelessness upon the final /v/ of the first word, whereas a final /f/ tends to avoid assimilation; cf. the nouns *Petróv* and *graf* "count" followed by the same enclitics: *Petróv že* [vž], *Petróv by* [vb], *Petróv to* [ft] — *gráf že* [fž], *gráf by* [fb], *gráf to* [ft].

Written in Cambridge, Mass., March 1977, for *Sign and Sound: Studies Presented to Bertil Malmberg on the Occasion of His 65th Birthday* (= *Studia Linguistica* 32, 1–2, 1978).

REFERENCES

Anderson, H., 1969. "The phonological status of the Russian 'labial fricatives'", *Journal of Linguistics* V: 121–7.
Baranovskaja, S. A., 1968. "Pozicionnoe vlijanie na var'irovanie soglasnyx po zvonkosti — gluxosti v sovremennom russkom literaturnom jazyke", *Trudy Universiteta družby narodov im. Patrisa Lumumby* XXIX: 28–29.
Barinova, G. A., Ševoroškin, V. V., 1972. "Reguljarnye i nereguljarnye sočetanija soglasnyx v russkom jazyke", *Problemy strukturnoj lingvistiki 1971* (Moscow), 334–341.
Es'kova, N. A., 1971. "K voprosu o svojstvax sonornyx soglasnyx v russkom jazyke", *Razvitie fonetiki sovremennogo russkoga jazyka* (Moscow), 243–247.
Jakobson, R., 1956. "Die Verteilung der stimmhaften und stimmlosen Geräusch-

laute im Russischen", *Festschrift für Max Vasmer* (Berlin, 1956); reprinted in *Selected Writings* I (The Hague-Paris, 1962 and 1971), 505–509.

—"K voprosu o gluxosti i zvonkosti russkix ščelinnyx gubnyx", *Slavia Orientalis*, XVII (1968); reprinted in *Selected Writings* I (The Hague-Paris, 1971), 728–733.

Mandelbaum, D. G., ed., 1949. *The Selected Writings of Edward Sapir* (Berkeley).

Panov, M. V., 1967. *Russkaja fonetika* (Moscow), 86f.

Reformatskij, A. A., 1971. "Slogovye soglasnye v russkom jazyke", *Razvitie fonetiki sovremennogo russkogo jazyka* (Moscow), 200–208.

—"[zf] iz ⟨zv⟩", idem, *Fonologičeskie ètjudy* (Moscow), 129–133.

Shapiro, S., 1966. "On Non-distinctive Voicing in Russian", *Journal of Linguistics* II, 189f.

Ševoroškin, V. V. 1963. "O structure zvukovyx cepej", *Problemy strukturnoj lingvistiki* (Moscow), 174f.

—1971. "O dvux [v] v russkom jazyke", *Razvitie fonetiki sovremennogo russkogo jazyka* (Moscow), 279–287.

—1973. "K issledovaniju struktury fonetičeskix slov v russkom jazyke", *Problemy strukturnoj lingvistiki 1972* (Moscow), 564–574.

—"Distributivnaja fonetika russkogo jazyka v sravnitel'no-tipologičeskom aspekte", ibidem, 575–585.

Zaliznjak, A. A., 1975. "Razmyšlenija po povodu *jazv* A. A. Reformatskogo", Institut russkogo jazyka AN SSR, Predvaritel'nye publikacii 71 (Moscow), 13–23.

THE PRIMARY SYNTACTIC SPLIT AND ITS COROLLARY

A child's acquisition of two-term sentences "is as a matter of fact a verbal and mental revolution", as I have repeatedly ventured to bring out.[1] Only at this stage does a real language, independent of the *hic et nunc*, come into being. The child begins to realize his ability and right to assign different predicates to the same subject and, conversely, to combine different subjects with one and the same predicate. As long as the subject and the predicate cannot be expressed in their interrelation, the speaker remains completely dependent on the immediate temporal and spatial environment, but with the emergence of dichotomous constructions, he obtains the possibility both to denote phenomena of permanent validity and to talk of events or objects distant in time and/or in space, particularly of events belonging to the remote past or supposed to occur in the future. Moreover, he is in a position to build entire fictions, consisting of events which neither took nor will take place anywhere. Hence, one may quote typical misuses of this verbal and mental liberation, such as the childish assertion "dog meow(s)".

When observing the difference between the two gradual viewpoints, first of the sentenceless infant and then of the child who has mastered the twofold utterances, one is inclined to compare such a difference with the divergence between theater and cinema experiences, the latter ones consistently changing the visual angle as well as the temporal and spatial perceptions of the spectator.

If at the holophrastic stage the baby's talk was confined to his immediate simultaneous outlook and thus represented a peculiar unity of time, space, and interlocutors, the subject/predicate speech diversifies the narrated events in their relation to the speech event and to the latter's participants. In this connection there arises a necessity for a grammatical designation of the narrated event with reference to the

---

[1] See, most recently, "Aphasic Disorders from a Linguistic Angle", *Nordisk Tidsskrift for Logopedi og Foniatri* 2 (1977), p. 101.

speech event and to its addresser and addressee. Thus the development of child's language into binomial "full-fledged sentences", according to Laguna's parlance,[2] demands the elaboration of grammatical implements, namely specifically grammatical words (pronouns) and conjugational devices. Classes such as person, tense, mood, and "source of speaker's evidence" belong to a particular kind of formal units termed "shifters" and specified by the fact that the general meaning of such a category "cannot be defined without a reference to the message".[3] For instance, the first person designates the addresser of the message to which the given expression (whether pronominal or verbal) pertains. It is in the presence and absence of shifters that the basic difference between verbs and nouns consists. The inner relation between the construction of an explicit subject/predicate sentence and of the development of shifters in children's language and, on the other hand, the interrelation between the disturbances of these two grammatical phenomena in aphasics demand the systematic attention of observers and inquirers.

Written in Cambridge, Mass., June, 1979, for the Hansjakob Seiler Festschrift, *Wege zur Universalienforschung* (Tübingen, 1980).

---

[2] Grace Andrus de Laguna, *Speech: Its Function and Development* (Bloomington, Ind., 1963), p. 99.
[3] Cf. this author's survey, "Shifters, Verbal Categories, and the Russian Verb", *Selected Writings*, II (The Hague-Paris, 1971), pp. 130–147.

SPATIAL RELATIONSHIPS IN SLAVIC ADJECTIVES

Four Russian adjectives display the derivational suffix -*ok*- with an alternation of a stressed and correspondent pretonic vowel; these adjectives designate an optimal extension of four fundamental spatial relationships, as opposed to a reduced extension. This reduction is designated by correlate adjectives whose suffix differs from the former one by an alternation of the posttonic vowel in the word end with a zero vowel in all other positions. Cf. *vysókij, vysók, vysókó, vysoká* "high, tall" v. *nízkij, nízok, nízko, nizká* "low", a full-scale upward extension and a decreased one; *glubókij, glubók, glubókó, gluboká* "deep" v. *mélkij, mélok, mélko, melká* "shallow"; the two likewise opposite levels of a downward extension; *širókij, širók, širókó, široká* "broad, wide" v. *úzkij, úzok, úzko, uzká* "narrow", an extension from side to side in its large-scale and curtailed varieties; *daljókij, daljók, daljóko/dalekó, daleká,* "far, distant" v. *blízkij, blízok, blízko, blizká* "near, close", a complete and a diminished moving off.

This pattern goes back to a common Slavic configuration distinctly reflected in the vocabulary of the early Church Slavonic writings with its pairs: *vysok*- v. *nizъk*-, *glǫbok*- v. *mělъk*-, *širok*- v. *ǫzъk*-, and *dalek*- v. *blizъk*-. The other Slavic languages offer close parallels to the Russian system, while showing dialectal fluctuations between the semantically correlate stems *mělъk*- and *plytъk*-, a later substitution for *plъtъk*-, according to Vaillant's assumption.[1] Cf. S.-Cr. *vìsok* v. *nìzak, dùbok* v. *plìtak, šìrok* v. *ùzak, dàlek* v. *blìzak*; Pol. *wysoki* v. *nizki, głęboki* v. *płytki/mialki, szeroki* v. *wązki, daleki* v. *blizki*.

Beside these four spatial evaluations of an immovable onlooker (ascensional, descensional, bilateral, and frontal prospect), there are no other examples of the derivational suffix -*ok*-/-*ek*- among Slavic adjectives, with the only exception of two Old Church Slavonic tactile

---

[1] A. Vaillant, "Les adjectifs slaves en -ŭkŭ", *Bulletin de la Société de Linguistique de Paris* 31, n. 93 (1931), 43–46.

vocables, the very rare *grǫstokъ* "heavy" v. *lьgъkъ* "light", and *žestokъ* "hard" as opposed to *mękъkъ* "soft"; John Exarch of Bulgaria underscored this antithesis: *Teplo i studeno, mękъko že i žestoko*. The latter adjective penetrated into Old Russian chiefly with the figurative meaning of an antonym to *krotъkъ* "gentle, meek" and without accentual alternation which is typical of the native Russian adjective with the same suffix.

As pointed out by Trubetzkoy, those Slavic adjectives in *-u-* which carried a connotation of "somewhat little" or "undersized" attracted a secondary diminutive suffix *-ko-* "sans modifier essentiellement leur sens primitif, tout comme en russe moderne l'ancien *malyj* 'petit' a été remplacé par son diminutif *malen'kij* qui signifie cependant non pas 'tout petit', mais 'petit' tout simplement".[2] The gradual effacement of the difference between the declension of stems in *-u-* and in *-o-* raised the value of the double suffixes *-uko-* and favored their productivity. Their diminutive and correspondingly emotive tint of endearment supplied them with a mark, in contradistinction to the unmarked adjectives without suffix, as, for instance, *tьnъkъ* "thin" v. *tъlstъ* "thick", *kortъkъ* "short, brief" v. *dьlgъ* "long, lasting", or *rědъkъ* "sparse, rare" v. *čęstъ* "dense, frequent".

Any of the four common Slavic pairs of adjectives which designated two grades of strictly spatial, linear extension apparently required a particularly clear-cut formal contraposition, signaled by the difference between the thematic suffixes *-o-* and *-u-*, while the secondary suffix was extended to the *-o-* stems as well, *niz-ъ-kъ → vys-o-kъ*, and so forth. The distinction between *-u-* and *-o-* in these compound suffixes was sufficient to carry the mark of diminutiveness, whereas the use of the same component *-ko-* in both members of each pair merely stressed their correlativity. "C'est sur le modèle de la coexistence de **onzŭ-* avec **onzŭkos* qu'on a pu créer à côté de **ūpso- *ūpsokos*",[3] but the new compound suffix *-o-ko-* had its definitely limited range of application and was not designed for further expansion.

It is notable that in the comparative degree these adjectives retained their root free of suffix, as attested most clearly in S.-Cr. *vȋšī, dȕbljī, šȋrī, dȃljī*. Cf. such Rus. nouns as *vys', glub', šir', dal'*, and, correspondingly, four far-flung directional adverbs *vvys', vglub', všir', vdal'*. The aberrant *-e-* in *dalekъ* has not yet found a satisfactory explanation, and the origin

---

[2] N. S. Trubetzkoy, "Les adjectifs slaves en -ъkъ", *Bulletin de la Société de Linguistique de Paris* 24, n. 73 (1923), 130–137.
[3] *Ibid.*, p. 133.

of this adjective still remains controversial (as acknowledged by Vaillant).[4]

There is a palpable and tenacious relationship between the two members of each pair and between the four pairs discussed above. Humorous discourse and oral tradition offer countless examples. A dialogue of Gogol''s *Revizor* in its early version reads: "*Dlja čego ž blizko, vsjo ravno i daleko. Otčego ž daleko, ved' vsjo ravno i blizko. Èto ved' vsjo tol'ko v voobraženii kažetsja, čto blizko, ono vsjo ravno, čto daleko.*" Cf. in Russian adages or bywords such current antitheses as: *Vyše lesa stojačego, niže oblaka xodjačego; Vysoko zamaxnulsja, da nizko stegnul; Melka reka, da omuty gluboki; Ložka uzka, taskaet po dva kuska: nado razvesti pošire, čtob taskala po četyre; Tuda široka doroga, da ottol' uzka; Dal'še polož', bliže voz'mjoš'*.

Parallel or polar members of cognate pairs appear in expressive confrontations. Kirša Danilov's collection of epic poems begins with the lines: *Vysota li vysota podnebesnaja,/gluboa glubota akijan more,/široko razdol'e po vsej zemli,/gluboki omoty dneprovskija/*; according to the popular folk song, *Ty leti, leti, sokolik, vysokó i dalekó,/i vysóko, i daljóko, na čužuju storonu/*; in proverbial sayings: *Do neba vysoko, do carja daleko; Sidi vysoko, da pljuj daleko; Nizko, tak blizko, a vysoko, tak daljoko; Čto klanjaeš'sja nizko, al' prazdnik blizko?; Bej čelom niže: do neba vysoko, do lica zemli bliže; I ne vysok, da v plečax širok*. Cf. such Czech locutions as *daleko široko* or "*výhled měkam daleko, vysoko i hluboko*". Perhaps the extension *niz-* of the original root **ni* in such forms as *nizъ, nizъkъ* is due to the influence of the homologous terms **ǫzъ-kъ*, **blizъ-kъ*.

Since the adjectives designating a reduced extent are the marked members opposed to their unmarked counterparts devoid of diminutive value, it is quite natural that as a rule only such unmarked adjectives, but not their marked antonyms, underlie the formation of substantives "to name the entire parameter";[5] cf. Rus. *vyšiná/vysotá, glubiná, širiná*; Czech *výše/výšina/výška, hlubina/hloubka, šíře/šířka, dálka*. The inappropriateness of marked adjectives for this end is emphasized by a jocular equation of opposites in the verses of a traditional children's chant to a ritual loaf: *Kák na Vániny imeníny ispeklí my karaváj/Vót takój vyšiný, vót takój nižiný,/Vót takój širiný, vót takój užiný/*.

---

[4] A. Vaillant, *Grammaire comparée des langues slaves* 2 (Paris: Les langues du monde, 1958), 575.
[5] See particularly V. V. Ivanov, "Semantičeskaja kategorija malosti-veličiny v nekotoryx jazykax Afriki i tipologičeskie paralleli v drugix jazykax mira", in *Problemy afrikanskogo jazykoznanija* (Moscow: AN SSSR, Institut jazykoznanija, 1972), 50–96, esp. 55.

In some languages the meaning of the parameter "height, depth, width, distance" may be extended to the underlying adjectives as well, as long as they are used with a quantifier, as, for instance, in the English phrase "two meters high",[6] or quite similarly in German "zwei Meter hoch", Czech "dva metry vysoký", and Serbo-Croatian "dva metri visok", whereas in some other languages, such as Russian or Polish, adjectives do not admit substantival quantifiers, and the latter are used as modifiers of spatial abstract nouns: Rus. *vyšinoj* or *glubinoj* or *širinoj v dva metra*, Pol. *o wysokości* or *głębokości* or *szerokości dwóch metrów* "two meters in height, depth, width". Also the "neutral" questions of measure, according to Clark's terminology, in such languages as Russian operate preferently with nouns: *kakoj vyšiny, glubiny, širiny*? Nevertheless, the adjectives *vysok, glubok,* etc., share the unmarkedness of the abstract nouns they underlie.

Another typical manifestation of unmarked adjectives is their ability to supplement the marked contraries also by a category of marked contradictories: Rus. *nevysokij, neglubokij, neširokij, nedaljokij*. In the current lexical use analogous negative formations from the marked diminutive adjectives, such as *nenizkij, neuzkij*, etc., are unusual.[7]

Linguistic data collected and analyzed by Ivanov disclose the widespread, in all probability universal tendency of languages to superpose the grammatical meaning "less" as a marked category upon the simpler, unmarked, primary concept of increase. One is tempted to confront this phylogenetic evidence with ontogeny and, in particular, with the revealing study devoted by Margaret Donaldson and Roger Wales to "the development of cognitive and linguistic skills in children between the ages of three-and-a-half and five".[8] According to this research, children initially use the words *more* and *less* indiscriminately; originally, and for many children even persistently, both of these terms are understood as signifying "more". Subtraction proves to be for these children a far less feasible task than addition. The markedness of subtractive devices, in contraposition to the additive operations, both verbal and cognitive, has been definitely brought to light; and — in Sapir's terms[9] — the various lesses of languages turn out to be a superstructure upon the correlate

---

[6] Cf. H. H. Clark, "The Primitive Nature of Children's Relational Concepts", in *Cognition and the Development of Language*, ed. J. R. Hayes (N.Y.: Wiley, 1970), Ch. 8.
[7] Cf. the observations of I. I. Mel'čuk, "K poznaniju slovoobrazovanija", *Izvestija Akademii Nauk SSSR, Serija lit. i jaz.* 26, 4 (1967), 359.
[8] M. Donaldson and R. Wales, "On the Acquisition of Some Relational Terms", in *Cognition and the Development of Language*, ed. J. R. Hayes (N.Y.: Wiley, 1970), Ch. 7.
[9] E. Sapir, "Grading: A Study of Semantics", in his *Selected Writings*, ed. D. G. Mandelbaum (Berkeley-L.A.: Univ. of California, 1949), 122–149.

mores, the restriction of a measurable property is opposed as a marked antonym to its unmarked full-fledged display.

Written in Cambridge, Mass., October 1973, for *Scritti in onore di Giuliano Bonfante* (Brescia, 1976).

NOTES ON THE DECLENSION OF PRONOUNS IN CONTEMPORARY RUSSIAN

In pronouns not only affixes, but, in contradistinction to all other inflected parts of speech, also the root morphemes carry a formal, grammatical meaning.

The Russian declinable pronouns offer two syntactic varieties: those which function primarily as syntactic subjects or objects, and those primarily invested with the grammatical role of attributes.

Russian pronouns fall into two declensional types: on the one hand, a specifically pronominal variety of declensional paradigm, and on the other hand, a transitional type of declension.

The paradigm of the latter type contains two varieties of grammatical desinences, one "concise" and the other "expanded." The concise desinences consist either of a mere zero sign or maximally of a single actual phoneme, and they serve to build the nominative sg. or plur. and the accusative sg. or plur., insofar as this case has not merged with the genitive. All other case forms of the transitional declension are supplied with expanded desinences, each containing at least two phonemes. The expanded pronominal desinences of the transitional declension encompass a similar number of phonemes as the corresponding desinences of the full adjectival declension, whereas in the choice of constituent phonemes there appear several differences between the transitional declension of pronouns and the full adjectival declension, e.g., instr. *vse(ě)m* versus *zlym*.

Only some of the subject-object pronouns display a specifically pronominal declension, whereas a few other pronouns of the same syntactic variety, and moreover, all the attributive pronouns belong to the transitional declension.

The specifically pronominal declension singles out either the properly personal pronouns (namely the 1. and the 2. persons based on the distinction of the addresser and addressee), or the reflexive pronominal forms confined to the sg. oblique cases. The solely grammatical meaning, carried, as mentioned above, by the pronominal roots, finds its characteristic expression in the wide use of full or partial suppletion by paradigms of the specifically pronominal declension, and on the other hand, in a formation of tautologically underscored, close morphological subclasses.

Thus, suppletion separates the nominative sg. of the 1. person pronoun "ja" from the rest of its case forms, and furthermore, all the plural forms of the 2. person from all of its singular forms.

The single paradigms of the specifically pronominal declension are denoted merely by the initial consonant of the pronoun.

The oblique cases of 2. person pronouns share their initial consonant with the nominative forms of the same person and number: sg. "t" — plur. "v".

The oblique cases of the 1. person sg. pronouns (*menja, mne, mnoj*) share the basic distinctive feature of their initial consonant, namely nasality, with the oblique plur. cases of the same person (*nas, nam*) and the grave (labial) variety of the initial nasal with the plural (*my*).

In the plur. oblique cases of the 1. and 2. person pronouns the initial consonant is invariably followed by the formative "a" and diverse desinences according to the cases: the joint form of accusative, genitive, and locative displays a final "s" (*nas, vas*), otherwise unfamiliar to Rus. affixes; whereas, the dative "m" and the instrumental "mi" are common especially to the plural desinences of all the Russian declinable words (*starym, starymi, gorodam, gorodami*).

The oblique cases in their specifically pronominal declensional paradigm undergo common structural rules. Each of these systems presents an oxytone: its accent falls on the last or single syllable of the word. The instrumental in "-oj" admits an optional stylistic variant in "óju" (*tobóju*). Each of these systems is confined to three mutually differing case forms, all three disyllabic, unless there appears between interaccentual, atonic vowels a pair of nasals which favors an abbreviation and subsequent abolishment of syllabic intervals between the accented vowels.

In the specifically pronominal declension each of the oblique case forms from its beginning to the accented vowel contains two consonants. The tonality opposition of acute and grave consonants underlies the treatment of all these case forms. Acute—grave is the order regularly followed by the two obstruents within the three oblique case forms differing from each other in the 2. person pronoun singular declension. See, e.g., the acute (dental) "t" which precedes the grave (labial) "b" in *tebjá* etc. Easily explainable is the tendency to accompany the direction from a plain to a flat (rounded) vowel with a parallel shift of the neighboring consonant from sharpness (palatalization) to plainness. In comparison with the obstruents of the 2. person sg. pronouns, 1. person sg. pronouns follow the opposite direction in the tonality feature of their nasal consonants, namely grave—acute. See, e.g. *menja*, etc.

A single distinctive feature, the presence of nasality, unifies all the nominative 1. person pronominal forms, the "m" of *my* and of the possessive *moj*, the "n" of the plural oblique cases and the possessive *naš*, as well as the immediate or mediated group of "m" and "n" of the singular oblique forms.

Beside the specifically pronominal declension of the 2. and 1. person pronouns, the former dealing with the addressee and the latter with the addresser of the speech event referred to, the specifically pronominal type of declension singles out the reflexive pronouns which, however, in contradistinction to the personal pronouns are deprived of nominative and of plural forms.

Of the personal pronouns, those of the 2. person designate the addressee of the speech event, and hence, stand nearer to the reflexive pronouns which designate the addressee of the narrated event. The reflexives share with the 2. person pronouns the acute—grave order of the two obstruents, while demanding the sole replacement of the voiceless "t" by the equally voiceless "s". See, e.g. *tebja* and *sebja*.

The transitional type of declension shows several variations in desinence phonemes. There is an alternation between "i" and "e" (< ě). The alternant appears as "e" when both of two conditions are met: namely, there is no antecedent "yod", and the syllable of the desinential vowel is at the same time the initial syllable of the word. The alternant is "i" when neither of these two conditions is present: instr. sg. *vsem, kem* but *čjim, samím, étim*; nom. plur. *vse, te* but *čji, sámi, éti*; gen. plur. *vsex, tex* but *étix, samíx*; instr. plur. *čjimi, étimi* but *vsémi, témi, odními*.

Pronouns invested with a double stem before a zero desinence (*to-t, k-to, č-to*), preserve only the shorter of the two doublets when followed by real (non-zero) desinential suffixes (*t-ogó, té; k-ogó, k-em, č-egó*).

The strong tendency of the pronouns to move the stress to the last vowel of the word is near to a general law: *kogó, čegó, togó, komú, samogó, samíx, samím,* etc.

This removal of the accent to the final syllable does not involve pronouns with prefixed stems: in *étot* the interjectional "e" is used as an affective prefix which signals a closer spatial relation between the narrated content and the participants of the speech event (cf. gen. *étogo*, instr. *étim* and *togó, tem*).

The plural instrumental desinence, regularly preceded by the dative desinence, is conceived as a double desinence, and the stress remains on the vowel of the dative. See, e.g., *samím — samími, vsém — vsémi,* etc.

The possessive adjectives which relate to pronouns (viz. are "motivated by pronouns" according to N. Švedova's terminology[1]) are treated as belonging to the transitional declension of pronouns, and in particular, they shift the accent to the word end: *moegó, svoemú, čjemú.* Cf. the similar modifications of the possessive forms of the sg. 2. person *tvoj* and of the reflexive *svoj,* as well as the initial "m" common to the sg. 1. person pronoun and to the possessive *moj* "mine", and to the sg. oblique cases of the 1. person pronominal forms such as *mnoj* as well as the nominative plural *my.* But no removal of stress takes place in possessives which relate to adjectives: cf. *čjegó, tvoegó,* with such forms *božij(žej), ptičij(-ej)* with a zero desinence, *bóžjego, ptíčjego.* Among the possessives relating to pronouns, the formal *naš, vaš* retain the initial accent (*nášego, vášemu,* etc.) perhaps even prompted by the sibilant desinences of gen. plur. *nas, vas.*

The paradigm of the so-called "3. person" pronoun (see its explicit logical analysis by E. Padučeva)[2] occupies an intermediate position between two varieties of declension — one specifically pronominal and the other transitional. With the 3. person pronoun the 1. person paradigm shares a radical suppletion between the nominative sg. form and the other, oblique forms of the same pronoun: cf. the postvocalic "n" of the nominative *on* with the prevocalic "yod" of *ja* and the initial glide "yod" of all the 3. person forms different from the nominative: gen.-acc. *ego* and *eë, emú, im* (< *jim*) etc. The reverse distribution of "yod" and "n" in the two oppositions of the twofold kinds of case forms must be noted: the "yod" of the *ja* and the "n" of the *on* in the nominative as well as the nasals of the oblique other 1. person cases contrast with the initial "yod" of the 3. person oblique cases. Yet after prepositions the initial "yod" of all the 3. person pronouns changes into a palatalized "n," and even Russian repetitive constructions of 3. person pronouns in locative forms demand an explicit reference to that locative frame and subsequently a substitution of the prefixal nasal for the initial "yod." Hence a steadfast commutation of the initial "yod" to the prefixal palatalized "n" becomes a compulsory feature of the 3. person

---

[1] N. Ju. Švedova (chief ed.), *Russkaja grammatika,* by the Institute of Russian Language at the USSR Academy of Sciences, Moscow, 1980.
[2] E. V. Padučeva, "Problemy logičeskogo analiza mestoimenij", *Semiotika i informatika* XV (Moscow, 1980), pp. 125–153.

locative in all its grammatical contexts and remains the sole formulation admissible, whereas such readings as *pri nëm, nej, nix and such ones as *pri nëm, ej, ix are rejected. Meanwhile, the elliptic variants such as "*pri otce, syne i vnukax*", as well as "*pri mne, tebe i vas*" remain valid.

The chief difference between the declension of the 3. person and that of the 1. and 2. persons lies in the formal rendering of grammatical genders in the sg. facet of the former's paradigm and no distinction of genders in the latter.

First published in the *International Journal of Slavic Linguistics and Poetics* 23 (1981–1982).

B

CRUCIAL QUESTIONS OF LINGUISTIC THEORY

VERBAL COMMUNICATION

For all human beings, and only for human beings, language is the vehicle of mental life and communication. It is natural that the study of this explicit and effective instrument, together with the rudiments of mathematics, is among the oldest sciences. The earliest linguistic work we possess, a Sumerian grammar of nearly 4,000 years ago, was succeeded by continuous efforts in various countries to interpret the makeup of the locally privileged language and the verbal network in general, as well as by speculations on the mysterious gift and confusion of tongues. If we concentrate our attention on the Indic and Greco-Latin tradition, beginning with the pre-Christian centuries, we can hardly find a single period without persistent inquiries into some facet of language. In many cases discoveries were made only to be temporarily swept away. Thus, for instance, the historic attainments of the Schoolmen's linguistic (particularly semantic) theory were dismissed after, as Charles Sanders Peirce used to say, "a barbarous rage against medieval thought broke out".

The variety of languages in space and time was the focal point of investigatory interest throughout the 19th century. Linguistics was held to be exclusively comparative, and the genetic relationship of kindred languages going back to a supposedly uniform parent language was considered the chief or only goal of linguistic comparison. The regularity of changes undergone by each of these languages at any given time was the acknowledged theoretical prerequisite for a conversion of the observed diversity of languages into their conjectured original unity.

This tenet was worked out meticulously by the Neogrammarian trend that dominated European (primarily German) linguistics during the last third of the 19th century. The "linguistic philosophy" of the Neogrammarians was viewed by their champion Karl Brugmann (1849–1919) as an antidote to "the arbitrariness and error to which a crude empiricism is everywhere exposed". This philosophy implied the acceptance of two uniformities, each concerned with successive stages:

(1) the antecedent uniformity and subsequent plurality and (2) a uniform, "exceptionless" mutation from an earlier stage to a later one within any given speech community. Thus the question of likeness and divergence was applied primarily or even solely to the temporal sequence of linguistic phenomena, whereas the coexistence and simultaneous interplay of invariance and variation within any given state of language remained unnoticed.

The same epoch that brought the rise of this influential school saw the emergence of several geographically scattered investigators and theoreticians of language who had outgrown the standard beliefs of their time and environment. These bold precursors of the present-day linguistic quest were born in the middle decades of the century; their remarkably original and mutually independent but basically convergent theses appeared in the 1870's and at the beginning of the 1880's. Methodological and philosophical preconditions for an immediate implementation of their novel ideas were still lacking, yet the vital problems they raised show a remarkable parallelism in time and essence with the ideas that underlie the development of modern mathematics and physics.

It was in the 1870's that both in mathematics and in the research work of the *avant-garde* linguists the conjugate notions of invariance and variation assumed ever greater importance and brought forward the corollary task of eliciting relational invariants from a flux of variables. The historic proposal "to study the constituents of a multiplicity with regard to those properties which are not affected by the transformations of the given group" in Felix Klein's (1849–1925) Erlanger Programm of 1872 was aimed at developing a generalized geometry. A similar principle inspired the linguistic outposts of the same age, in particular the few initial publications of Henry Sweet (1845–1912), Jan Baudouin de Courtenay (1845–1929), Jost Winteler (1846–1929), Mikolaj Kruszewski (1851–1887) and Ferdinand de Saussure (1857–1913). All of them considered the Neogrammarian doctrine either unsuitable or insufficient for a more general and immanent science of language, as Kruszewski wrote to Baudouin in a sagacious letter of 1882. To quote the conclusion of my own survey of Sweet's arduous struggle, each of these spirited trailblazers who ventured to look far ahead "bears a stamp of tragedy on his whole life", owing to the resistance of a conservative milieu and perhaps even more to the ideological tenor of the Victorian era, which impeded the concrete application and further development of daring designs and unwonted approaches.

At the beginning of the 1930's N. S. Trubetzkoy (1890–1938), a wise, inquisitive linguist of the era between the world wars, came by pure chance on Winteler's dissertation. In a letter of January, 1931, Trubetzkoy extolled the remarkable foresight of Winteler, whose unprecedented vistas and methods had met with a disappointing lack of comprehension and had doomed him to the lot of a mere schoolteacher. Winteler's book *Die Kerenzer Mundart des Kantons Glarus in ihren Grundzügen dargestellt*, completed in 1875 and published a year later in Leipzig, contains an analysis of his native Swiss-German dialect "outlined in its fundamentals" and shows a rare depth and insight into the essentials of linguistic structure, particularly in cardinal questions of sound-patterning.

The memoirs of the septuagenarian Winteler written for the Zurich fortnightly *Wissen und Leben* in 1916 quote a judgment he heard four years after the appearance of his dissertation: "If only one would have started differently, then one could have become a university professor, while now one has to stay a lifelong schoolmaster." The retired instructor of the cantonal school in Aarau confesses how often he grieved over his cruel fate. Even Winteler's modest career was clouded by incomprehension and endangered by accusations of his being "redder than the socialists".

The adolescent Albert Einstein, who had left the regimented gymnasium in Munich he so deeply detested, sought admission to the Federal Institute of Technology in Zurich but failed the entrance examination and in 1895 took refuge in the liberal cantonal school at Aarau, some 25 miles from Zurich. A recent essay by Gerald Holton in *American Scholar* (Vol. 41, No. 1, Winter, 1971–72) indicates that the Aarau days were "a crucial turning point" in Einstein's development, and Einstein repeatedly acknowledged their beneficial import. Adopted as a boarder and treated as a member of the family in Jost Winteler's household, Einstein met, as his biographers say, his "lucky star". Even when he moved to Zurich for graduate studies, he missed no opportunity to call on his dear old friend in Aarau. Forty years later, during Einstein's stay at the Institute for Advanced Study in Princeton, he still remembered and praised "the clairvoyant Papa Winteler".

It was in the relaxed atmosphere of the Aarau school that the young Einstein recovered his repressed bent for science. When we read about the "thought experiment" that was performed there by the prodigious teen-ager and that gradually led him to his theory of relativity, the question of what influence was exerted on him by his daily conversations with the lucid scholar suggests itself. Winteler remained true to the principle of "configurational relativity" (*Relativität der Verhältnisse*) that had been disclosed in his dissertation with special reference to the sound pattern of language. In particular, his theory required a consistent distinction between the relational invariants and variables within language, respectively termed "essential" and "accidental" properties. According to Winteler's insight, speech sounds cannot be evaluated in isolation but only in their relation to all other sound units of the given language and to the linguistic functions assigned to them in such a manifold. Correspondingly, the symmetry properties of the whole pattern were explicitly recognized and examined by the audacious "autodidact", as the author of the *Kerenzer Mundart* introduced himself.

Einstein, the future proponent of "empathy [*Einfühlung*] into external experience", obviously felt a spiritual affinity with such an ardent devotee of science as Winteler, who had dared in 1875 to preface his book with the farsighted declaration: "My work in its essence is addressed solely to those who are able to grasp verbal form as a revelation of the human mind that stands to the mind in much more inner and sweeping relations than even the best products of a most consummate literature. Thus the addressees of my work must conceive the inquiry into the latent powers which determine the continual motion of verbal form as a task which, in its interest and relevance, competes with any other field of knowledge."

Reports about the free and spirited exchange of opinions that reigned in Winteler's family circle enhance the certainty of the deep imprint left by his exciting ideas on Einstein's responsive mind. Hence the parable of a seed doomed "to die without having borne any fruit", the gloomy vision that haunted Winteler's imagination from his youth, seems to have met with a luminous refutation.

The story of Winteler and Einstein provides us with a new and significant example of the suggestive interconnections between linguistics and mathematics, of their historical parallelism and, particularly, of an equally radical difference between two stages in the development undergone by each of these sciences. As historians of mathematical ideas have repeatedly stated, the concept of invariance has found a wide scientific application only in our century, after "the reverse side of invariance", the idea of relativity and its corollaries, had been gradually disclosed and mastered. The emergence of Einstein's theory and the advances in the analysis of purely topological relations indeed find striking correspondences in the simultaneous unfolding of similar linguistic conceptions and methods. The present manifestly constructive period in the history of linguistic science has ensued as a sequel to anticipations raised by Winteler and other pioneers.

In the Neogrammarian tradition the notions and labels "comparative" and "general" linguistics nearly merged, and the comparative method was confined to a merely historical or, strictly speaking, genealogical study of cognate dialects and languages. Today virtually any linguistic problem whatever has received a thoroughly comparative treatment. Any question of language and languages is conceived of as being a comparative operation in search of the equivalent relations that underlie the structure of a given language, and that furthermore allow us to interpret the structural affinities and divergences between languages, however distant they may be in origin and location. The decisive procedure for scientific inquiry into the different levels of linguistic structure is a consistent elicitation and identification of relational invariants amid the multitude of variations. The variables are investigated with reference to the set of diverse transformations that they undergo and that can and must be specified.

Whatever level of language we deal with, two integral properties of linguistic structure force us to use strictly relational, topological definitions. First, every single constituent of any linguistic system is built on an opposition of two logical contradictories: the presence of an attribute ("markedness") in contraposition to its absence ("unmarkedness"). The entire network of language displays a hierarchical arrangement that within each level of the system follows the same dichotomous principle of marked terms superposed on the corresponding unmarked terms. And second, the continual, all-embracing, purposeful interplay of invariants and variations proves to be an essential, innermost property of language at each of its levels.

These two dyads — markedness/unmarkedness and variation/invariance — are indissolubly tied to the be-all and end-all of language, to the fact, as Edward Sapir (1884–1939) put it, that "language is the communicative process par excellence in every known society". Everything language can and does communicate stands first and foremost in a necessary, intimate connection with meaning and always carries semantic information. The promotion of meaning to a pivotal point of structural analysis has been an ever stronger claim of international linguistic endeavors during the past five decades. Thus, for instance, 20 years ago the French linguist Émile Benveniste, one of the leading figures of the structural trend, declared in a programmatic study that in the final account careful reflection on the makeup of any language points to the "central question of meaning", and that a deepening insight into this problem will open the way to the future discovery of "transformational laws in linguistic structures".

True, various reductionist experiments were conducted in America. At first repeated efforts were made "to analyze linguistic structure without reference to meaning". Some later tests confined the removal of meaning to the study of grammatical structures under such slogans as "Linguistic description minus grammar equals semantics". All these tentative operations were undoubtedly of considerable interest, particularly since they succeeded in providing us with a graphic demonstration of the omnipresent semantic criterion, no matter what level and constituent of language is examined. One can no longer continue to play hide-and-seek with meaning and to evaluate linguistic structures independently of semantic problems. Whatever end of the linguistic spectrum we deal with, from the phonic components of verbal signs to the discourse as a whole, we are compelled to bear in mind that everything in language is endowed with a certain significative and transmissible value.

Thus in approaching speech sounds we must take into account the fact that they are cardinally different from all other audible phenomena. An astounding discovery of the recent past is that when two sounds are presented simultaneously to both ears, any verbal signals such as words, nonsense syllables and even separate speech sounds are better discerned and identified by the right ear and all other acoustical stimuli such as music and environmental noises are better recognized by the left ear. The phonic components of language owe their particular position in the cortical area, and correspondingly in the aural area, solely to their verbal functions, and henceforth a constant regard for these functions must guide any fruitful study of speech sounds.

In its sound pattern any language contains a certain limited number of "distinctive features", discrete and ultimate relational invariants that can, under a set of transformations, endure even drastic alterations in every respect save their defining attributes. "The categorial nature of perceptual identification", pointed out by the psychologist Jerome S. Bruner in his memorable study "Neural Mechanisms in Perception" (1956), maintains the constancy and validity of these features in verbal communication, where they exercise the fundamental faculty of semantic discrimination.

The pattern of distinctive features is a powerful and economical code: each feature is a binary opposition of a present mark and a missing mark. The selection and interconnection of distinctive features within any given language reveal a remarkable congruity. A comparison of the existing phonological structures with the laws underlying the development of children's language enables us to outline the typology of feature systems and the rules of their internal hierarchical arrangement. The communicative relevance of distinctive features, which is based on their semantic value, brings to naught any chance occurrence and contingency in their patterning. The list of distinctive features that exist in the languages of the world is supremely restricted, and the coexistence of features within one language is restrained by implicational laws.

The most plausible explanation of these either totally or nearly universal principles in regard to the admissibility and interconnection of features apparently lies in the internal logic of communication systems that are endowed with a self-regulating and self-steering capacity. The quest for a universal table of distinctive features must certainly apply the same method of extracting invariants that has been used with respect to single languages: in the context of different languages the same feature with unaltered categorial attributes may vary in its physical implementation.

Transformations that provide the invariants with diverse concomitant variations can be roughly divided into two kinds of alteration: contextual and stylistic. Contextual variants point to the concurrent or consecutive neighborhood of the given feature, whereas stylistic variants add a marked — emotive or poetic — annex to the neutral, purely cognitive information of the distinctive feature. Both of these invariants and variations belong to the common verbal code that endows interlocutors with the competence to understand one another.

For the study of verbal communication it is necessary to face the fact that any speech community and any existing verbal code lack uniformity; everyone belongs simultaneously to several speech communities of different extent; he diversifies his code and blends distinct codes. At each level of the verbal code we observe a scale of transitions that range from maximum explicitness to the briefest elliptic structure, and this scale is subject to a set of rigorous transformational rules. The cardinal property of language noted by the initiator of semiotics, Charles Sanders Peirce (1839–1914), namely the translatability of any verbal sign into another, more explicit one, renders an effective service to communication in that it counteracts ambiguities caused by lexical and grammatical homonymy or by the overlapping of elliptic forms.

People usually display a narrower competence as senders of verbal messages and a wider competence as receivers. The differences in patterning and extent between the codes of the addresser and the addressee attract ever closer attention from students and teachers of language. The core of this divergence was grasped by St. Augustine: "In me it is the word which takes precedence over the sound [*In me prius est verbum, posterior vox*], but for thee who looks to understand me, it is first the sound that comes to thine ear in order to insinuate the word into thy mind." The two-way transformations that make it possible to determine the state of the outputs from that of the inputs and vice versa are an essential prerequisite for all genuine intercommunication.

Both spatial and temporal factors play a significant role in the structure of our verbal code. Various forms of interdialectal code-switchings are among the daily devices in our verbal intercourse. Bilingualism or multilingualism, which allows total or partial shifts from one language to another, cannot be rigidly separated from interdialectal fluctuations. The interaction and interpenetration of single languages in a polyglot's use follow the same rules that apply in the case of translations from one language into another.

As for the time factor, I refer to my earlier objections to the tenacious belief in the static character of the verbal code: Any change first appears in linguistic synchrony as a coexistence and purposive alternation of more archaic and new-fashioned dictions. Thus linguistic synchrony proves to be dynamic; any verbal code at all its levels is convertible, and in any conversion one of the competing alternants is endowed with a supplementary informational value and hence displays a marked status, in contradistinction to the neutral, unmarked character of the other. A historical phonology and grammar, for example the millennial history of the English sound, word and sentence pattern, develop into a study of extractable constants and temporal transformations that both demand an adequate explanation.

The unparalleled expediency of language is rooted in a consistent superposition of several interconnected levels, each of which is differently structured. The system of a few distinctive features serves to build a more differentiated morphological code of entities endowed with inherent meaning, namely words and, in those languages where words are decomposable, their minimal meaningful constituents (roots and affixes), termed morphemes. The analysis of the morphological units once again reveals a system of relational invariants — binary oppositions of marked and unmarked grammatical categories — but there is a difference of basic importance between a phonological and a grammatical opposition: in the former case the coupled contradictories reside in the perceptible side of language (*signans*, or "signifier"), whereas in the latter they lie in its intelligible side (*signatum*, or "signified").

To illustrate this difference let us first cite an opposition of a phonological mark and its absence: nasalized/non-nasalized implemented by such pairs of consonants as *m/b* and *n/d* or the French nasal vowel in *bon* as opposed to *beau*. On the other hand, in a grammatical opposition such as preterit/present the first, marked tense signals the precedence of the narrated event over the speech act, whereas the general meaning of the unmarked present tense carries no information about the relation between the narrated event and the speech act. This relation varies and its specification depends on the context. Compare the diverse contextual meanings of the same present-tense form in the four sentences "Spring begins today"; "A year from today he begins a new trip"; "With the death of Caesar a new era begins for Rome"; "Life begins at 50."

Here, again, as when treating the sound pattern, we come across the momentous property of natural languages, namely their context-sensitivity. Precisely this property sets them apart from their formalized, artificial superstructures, which tend to a context-freedom. The significant difference between context-free and context-sensitive sign systems had been perspicuously noted by Noam Chomsky, but as Daniel A. Walters complains in *Information and Control* (1970), the specific properties of context-sensitive grammar still receive much less attention than context-free grammars. It is the context-sensitivity of a natural language at *all* levels that provides it with a unique abundance of free variations. The dialectical tension between invariants and variables, which in their own way also appear to be pertinent, ensures the creativity of language.

Morphology answers the phonological pattern of *distinctive* features with an equally coherent and step-like organization of equally binary *conceptual* features; they remain invariant while undergoing a set of transformations that convert the general meanings of grammatical categories into varied contextual (including situational) meanings. In this way we proceed from one grammatical area to a superior one, namely from morphology as a study of totally coded units to the analysis of syntactic structures that combine coded matrices with a free or, as is always the case in verbal communication, *relatively* free selection of words that fill them up.

Words display two patently distinct kinds of semantic value. Their compulsory *grammatical* meaning, a categorial relational concept or group of concepts that words constantly carry, is supplemented in all autonomous words by a *lexical* meaning. Like grammatical meanings, any general lexical meaning is in turn an invariant that under diverse contextual and situational transformations generates what Leonard Bloomfield (1887–1949) precisely defined as "marginal, transferred" meanings. They are sensed as derivative of the unmarked general meaning, and these tropes either stand in agreement with the verbal code or they are an *ad hoc* digression from it.

The rules of syntax are ordered, and these rules and their order itself determine a "grammatical process" that never fails to impart a "grammatical concept", in accordance with the subtle terms introduced by Sapir. Any syntactic structure is a member of a transformational chain and any two partially synonymous constructions display an interrelation of markedness and unmarkedness. For example, in English the passive is marked in relation to the unmarked active mood. Hence an expression such as "Lions are hunted by natives", similar to but not identical in meaning with the sentence "Natives hunt lions", marks a shift in semantic perspective from the agent to the goal by focusing on "lions" and allowing the omission of the agent, namely "lions are hunted".

In its general meaning any noun is a generic term relating to all members of a class or to all stages of a dynamic whole. The contextual as well as situational application of these characteristics to particulars is a transformation of the widest range. This interplay of universals and particulars, which is often underrated by linguists, has for ages been discussed among logicians and philosophers of language, such as the 12th-century Schoolman John of Salisbury, to whose formula — *Nominantur singularia sed universalia significantur* ("Particulars are named but universals are signified") — Peirce repeatedly refers.

When we observe the highly instructive process of a child's gradual advance in the acquisition of language, we see how decisively important the emergence of the subject-predicate sentence is. It liberates speech from the here and now and enables the child to treat events distant in time and space or even fictitious. This capacity, which mechanists sometimes label "displaced speech", is in fact the first affirmation of language's autonomy. In sign systems other than natural or artificial languages there are no parallels to the formulation of general and particularly equational propositions, no capacity for building logical judgments.

The progress of a child's language depends on his ability to develop a metalanguage, that is, to compare verbal signs and to talk about language. Metalanguage as a part of language is, again, a structural trait that has no analogues in other sign systems. The founder of the Moscow linguistic school, F. F. Fortunatov (1848–1914), stressed that "the phenomena of language themselves appertain to the phenomena of thought". Interpersonal communication, which is one of the indispensable preconditions for the infant's access to speech, is gradually supplemented by an internalization of language. Inner speech, one's dialogue with oneself, is a powerful superstructure on our verbal intercourse. As the study of language disturbances shows, impairments of inner speech take a conspicuous place among verbal disorders. A lesser dependence on the environmental censorship contributes to the active role of inner speech in the rise and shaping of new ideas.

The equivalence relation that under various names — transformation, transference, translation and transposition — has since the interwar era been gradually approached by linguists at different ends of the world proves to be the mainspring of language. In the light of this relation several controversial questions of verbal communication may receive a more exact and explicit treatment.

Written language is an evident transform of oral speech. All sane human beings talk, but almost half of the world's people are totally illiterate, and the actual use of reading and writing is an asset of a scarce minority. Yet even then literacy is a secondary acquisition. Whatever script is employed, as a rule it refers to the spoken word. Along with invariants common to the oral and written language, each of the two systems in its constitution and use shows a number of pertinent peculiarities. In particular, those properties that depend on the spatiality of written texts separate them from the purely temporal structure of oral utterances. The comparative study both of verbal patterns and of their roles in social communication is an urgent task that can no longer be neglected. Many hasty generalizations will be dismissed. Thus, for instance, the role of schooling and continual transmission, far from being confined to the world of letters, is attested as well in oral traditions and rhetorical art. The wider diffusion of the written word in the recent past is now being matched by such technical devices of oral messages "to whom it may concern" as radio, television and instruments for recording speech.

In my study "Linguistics and Poetics" (cf. *Selected Writings* III [The Hague-Paris-New York, 1981], pp. 18–51) I attempted to outline the six basic functions of verbal communication: referential, emotive, conative, poetic, phatic and metalingual. The interaction of these functions and, in particular, the consequent grammatical transformations cannot receive an adequate linguistic treatment unless survivals of mechanistic views are discarded. For example, the extension of the referential (alias ideational) function at the expense of the conative function leads our language from secondary, obviously marked translations of imperative primary forms such as "Go!" into circumlocutions such as "I wish you would go", "I order you to go", "You must go" or "You should go", with a truth-value forcibly imposed on the conative expression. Efforts to interpret imperatives as transforms of declarative propositions falsely overturn the natural hierarchy of linguistic structures.

Finally, the analysis of grammatical transformations and of their import should include the poetic function of language, since the core of this function is to push transformations into the foreground. It is the purposeful poetic use of lexical and grammatical tropes and figures that brings the creative power of language to its summit. Such a marked innovation as the inverse temporal perspective recently used by three Russian poets independently of one another is hardly fortuitous. "The future for you is trustworthy and definite. You say: Tomorrow we went to the forest." (A. Voznesenskij); "It happened that I found myself tomorrow." (S. Kirsanov); "It was tomorrow." (G. Glinka). In a letter dated March 21, 1955, four weeks before his death, Einstein wrote: "The separation between past, present, and future has only the meaning of an illusion, albeit a tenacious one."

Written in Cambridge, Mass., June 1972, for a special issue of *Scientific American* on communication (vol. 227, no. 3, Sept. 1972).

THE FUNDAMENTAL AND SPECIFIC CHARACTERISTICS OF HUMAN LANGUAGE

1.0. In order to outline and discuss the specific and integral characteristics of human language, perhaps the most suitable way is to trace the young child's verbal development from its first steps until the acquisition of a full-fledged language, at least in its fundamental architectonic properties.
1.01. In confronting the ontogeny of language with diverse varieties of animal communication, our attention shall be focused on mammals and birds in view of the closer propinquity of those species to humans.
1.1. The first stage of the child's initiation to language produces only single-word constructions or, to use a terser terminology, mere holophrases. Their functions, originally syncretic, — simultaneously emotive, conative, and referential — gradually branch off and give rise to a prevalently or purely referential subclass of holophrastic utterances which are used chiefly or solely to designate and identify certain environmental items.
1.11. So far no messages confined to an identifying, referential (or in other terms, cognitive) function and free from any emotive and conative function (particularly from any role of exclamation, call, instruction, summon, order) have been detected in the intercommunication of animals; only in relations between certain tamed animals and their tamer, the former may be trained by the latter to respond to a limited number of outer stimuli in producing specific signals imparted by the trainer to his trainees.
1.2. The successive multiplication of holophrases indispensably multiplies the repertoire of their perceptible differential components which are necessary for the recognition and distinction of these messages. Strict implicational laws determine the gradual selection and assimilation of these discrete and ultimate "distinctive features", and in his speech production and perception the child is constrained to observe the significant invariants of his evolving phonemic system. Hence certain rudiments of phonological analysis and synthesis necessarily belong to the earliest subliminal operations in children's linguistic life.

1.21. Thus any human language, beginning with the holophrastic stage of children's speech, is endowed with two kinds of discrete constituents: carriers of meanings, on the one hand, and mere differentials of meaningful units, on the other hand, build two interrelated yet still autonomous systems. This universal duality of levels has no analogue whatever in animal communication. Only human language begets multiple semantic differences by commuting and/or permuting one and the same pair of distinctive features.

2.1. In the child's linguistic development the first, holophrastic stage is followed by a stage of single phrases. Children develop a joint use of word pairs where one of the two components appears to be subordinated to the other and serves as its modifier (determinant). In this stage of children's linguistic development the repertoire of units used solely or chiefly as modifiers is naturally smaller than the number of independent units.

This stage endows the child with the primaries of his subliminal grammar: the difference between part and whole, viz. word and phrase; the syntactical principle of dependence; the morphological principle of two word-classes, viz. words able and words unable to serve as modifiers. The difference between the word-class and its diverse members prompts a discrimination between grammatical and lexical concepts.

2.11. The primary syntactical notion of subordinative dependence between two meaningful units is alien to animal communication. The casual accumulation of different signals within one animal, especially avian performance, may be compared with the optionally early appearance of a string of two or more phrases within one children's utterance, but such combinations do not display any intrinsic structural hierarchy.

3.1. The third and, definitely, the most decisive stage on the path from infancy (*infantia* = speechlessness) to a command of language generates an aptitude for building independent clauses, syntactical constructions which comprise both an explicit grammatical subject and an explicit grammatical predicate. Any referential holophrase or two-word phrase of both previous stages acted as a verbal appendage to the immediate situation and was correspondingly interpreted and labeled in the centenary scholarly tradition as a "psychological predicate" to an outward, *hic et nunc* observable and nonverbalized stimulus. But as soon as predication obtains its grammatical counterpart in a subjection, and herewith a mutual attachment of subject and predicate takes place in the clause itself, then and only then does referential speech cease to be a mere apprehension of the child's synchronous percepts and changes into a free and variable, mutable assignment of subjects and predicates to each other, with a detachment of his verbal performances from local and momentary circumstances. The young child acquires the ability to speak of things and events distant in space and/or time, or fictitious, irreal, perhaps even inconceivable. He gradually develops an intuitive insight into the significant difference between words as wholly and utterly coded units, on the one hand, and on the other hand, the syntactical code. The latter superimposes definite matrices upon combinations of words into groups of diverse hierarchy, but the speaker retains a considerable freedom in selecting words with which he may fill these matrices in his actual speech. Often this relative freedom appears to be sensed quite patently by two- and three-year-old children.

The establishment and development of self-contained independent clauses enriches the child's linguistic competence with several indispensable novelties. All the referential phrases of the previous stage had a deictic ingredient and, namely, they merely pointed at the given state of affairs, whereas the newborn clauses of the subsequent stage are free of any compulsory pointing at some environmental stimuli.

The child's clauses are his primary propositions, and in order to clarify the constitutive role played by the rise of independent clauses in children's linguistic development, one might refer to Hughlings Jackson's attempt at defining speech as the "power to propositionize".

Naturally, the appearance and development of propositions entails the three forms of truth testing: affirmation, negation and question enter into the child's thought and language.

The emancipation of verbal symbols from compulsory deictic bonds with the *hic et nunc* enables the speaker to vary the semantic capacity of the same word by using it in its widest, generic sense or in its narrowest, particular application, or in some intermediary extent prompted by the context. Judgment, the supreme achievement of the same developmental stage, enables the child to construct clauses with mere generic meanings.

Children's freedom to diversify the context of one and the same word creates a difference between the proper, nuclear meaning of this word and its marginal, figurative (metaphoric or metonymic) meanings; two interlinked properties of human language, its context sensitivity and its creativeness, become apparent.

It is during this stage of linguistic growth that the cleavage between verbal design and token or, in a somewhat different formulation, the tension between code and message, is either latently or even patently realized by the child. Such realization is a corollary of that developmental advance which behaviorist psychologists and linguists call "relayed" or "displaced" speech, i.e., speech no longer confined to events experienced in the present by the speaker himself. The act of pointing at the given non-verbalized situation is complemented or replaced by pointing at the verbal context of one's own or interlocutor's message. Inner linguistic duplex structures, a further necessary and prompt consequence of this process, enter into children's use.

Notwithstanding the pertinent and indispensable part which the four types of these duplex structures take in the buildup of any human language, here they can be but briefly enumerated. Two of them are circular: (1) "reported speech" = message referring to another message; (2) "proper name", as opposed to appellatives, is a coded unit whose meaning implies a reference to the code ("Jerry" means someone *named* Jerry). In the two other types of duplex structures, code and message overlap: (1) "metalinguistic" (or "autonymous") mode of speech = messages referring to the code; (2) "shifters" (such as personal pronouns and tenses) = coded units whose general meaning implies a reference to the message.

The superposition of subordinating and subordinate clauses within a new, higher grammatical unity termed "complex sentence" marks the further, fourth stage in the acquisition of language. This stage usually displays a still clearer discernment of the main factors constituting any speech event — such as addresser, addressee, referent, code, and message — and a higher differentiation of verbal functions oriented toward each of the above mentioned factors: emotive, conative, referential, metalingual, and poetic. The autonomy of these basic functions increases along with their higher integration. Their relative hierarchy exhibits a greater variability, and the alternation of distinct hierarchical patterns underlies the formation and diversification of verbal styles.

3.11. Neither spontaneous animal communication nor responses of experimental animals to human trainers show even slight correspondences to the fundamental notion of clause or to any other linguistic devices acquired by two- and three-year-old children together with the use of clauses. None of the numerous studies devoted to animal communication, and in particular to the patterns used by mammals and birds, has shown a genuine, even if rudimental, parallel to such early and essential linguistic acquisitions as the ability to propositionize, to separate messages from surrounding situations, and to invent novel messages. In animal communication the code is tantamount to the corpus of signals, and neither directional changes in deictic signals nor the gradation of emotional force could be equated with creative freedom, the essense of human language. Hierarchy, the manifold and fundamental principle of any linguistic structure, is alien to animal communication.

The latter is devoid of all those dichotomies which underlie human language, and lacks, e.g., such oppositions as general and particular, nuclear and transferred, and the four "duplex structures" which are of paramount importance in any exchange of verbal messages.

4.0. The manifold and instructive universals which linguistics has gradually traced in the patterning of numerous contemporary languages and of older languages documented or scientifically reconstructed, show such a high degree of verbal sophistication that, as G. G. Simpson states, the "tens or hundreds of thousands of years" which must separate all these "already modern" and "complete" languages from the rise of human speech obviously inhibit the efforts "to determine the evolutionary origin of language" (*Science*, CLII/1966, p. 477). One may add, however, that the universal or nearly-universal laws of implication which prove to underlie the linguistic structure in its statics and dynamics may be with a high probability extended also to glottogony.

Simpson's critical remarks on the phylogenetic references to the acquisition of language by children cannot be passed over: "In fact the child is not evolving or inventing primitive language but is learning a particular modern language, already complete and unrecognizably [?] different from any possible primitive language. Moreover, the child is doing this with a modern brain already genetically constructed (through the long, long action of natural selection) for the use of complete, wholly nonprimitive language." However, the usual sequence of children's acquisitions apparently points to an intrinsically motivated and therefore most probably perpetual order.

Anyway, the chasm between the highest "zoosemiotic" patterns and even the earliest stages of transition from infancy to the gift of tongue is so deep that the cardinal dissimilarities widely outweigh the scanty correspondences. Human language, to quote G. G. Simpson (p. 476) once more, "is absolutely distinct from any system of communication in other animals". It may be added that even the utilization of signals learned by an experimental animal from its trainer differs totally from children's acquirement and use of verbal communication. None the less, despite all the intricacy of questions involved, the genesis of language as the principal event in the metamorphosis of the actually prehuman *Homo alalus* into a true human being, *Homo loquens*, must undergo a joint interdisciplinary search by linguists, biologists and neurologists, as well as anthropologists and archeologists.

Written in the summer of 1969 in La Jolla, California, for the Salk Institute Conference on the Biological Foundations of Language.

COMMUNICATION AND SOCIETY

Edward Sapir, the great linguist of our century, characterized communication as the dynamic aspect of human society. There is no society without "a highly intricate network of partial or complete understandings between the members of organizational units of every degree of size and complexity". According to the precise judgment of the same scholar, language, "the most explicit type of communicative behavior", appears to be "the communicative process par excellence in every known society, and it is exceedingly important to observe that whatever may be the shortcomings of a primitive society judged from the vantage point of civilization, its language inevitably forms as sure, complete, and potentially creative an apparatus of referential symbolism as the most sophisticated language that we know of".

Language is the fundamental but not at all the only system of communication. The science of signs, repeatedly set forth and programmed by philosophers and linguists and labelled *semiotics* (or *semiology*) is now rapidly developing and investigates the common features of all sign systems, their interrrelation, and their specifics. Of course, language, its structure, and its influence on the other systems of signs are substantial questions of semiotics, but it would be a fallacy to neglect or underestimate all the other systems of human signs and to impose upon them properties characteristic of language but foreign to the other sign systems.

When speaking of language as a communicative tool, one must remember that its primary role, interpersonal communication, which bridges space, is supplemented by a no less important function which may be characterized as intrapersonal communication. The latter gradually develops in children's acquisition of language and creates such important mental procedures as inner speech with its internal dialogues. While interpersonal communication bridges space, intrapersonal communication proves to be the chief vehicle for bridging time.

I would like to refer to the penetrating statement of another prominent linguist of our century, Émile Benveniste: "Si nous posons qu'à défaut du langage, il n'y aurait ni possibilité de société, ni possibilité d'humanité, c'est bien parce que le propre du langage est d'abord de signifier." It's more than obvious that signs in general and verbal signs in particular cannot be treated without persistent regard to their signification. Consequently, the study of signification, the inquiry into the various types of meanings in their interrelations, briefly, that series of tasks which is usually labelled *semantics*, is a decisive component of the science of verbal signs, i.e. linguistics, and of the science of all possible signs, i.e. semiotics.

The aptest explorers of verbal signs since ancient times saw the essence of their structure in the relation between the *signans* and the *signatum*, according to St. Augustine's translation of the Greek terms introduced by the Stoics (*signifiant* and *signifié* in Ferdinand de Saussure's French adaptation). *Signans* meant the perceptible and *signatum* the intelligible, translatable aspect of the *signum* (sign). The science of language, on all of its levels, inevitably implies semantics. In other words, a linguistics that discards meaning would be meaningless.

Poetry is focussed upon the verbal sign as such. This characteristic of poetry implies the focus upon sound, meaning, and their interplay. Semantics is a vital constituent of poetry and, correspondingly, of its scientific analysis, termed poetics.

Any part of linguistics is preoccupied by a search for invariants in their relation to variations. All the applications of this principle deal primarily with the semantic value of verbal signs, whatever the rank of these signs in the system of language. Thus semantic attitude must be strictly respected in regard to phonemic components, morphemes, words, syntactic structures, particularly sentences, and finally discourse in its segmentation. The essential difference between grammatical and lexical meanings, which was grasped by the medieval science of language, must undergo a wide development in linguistics.

Questions of the relation between the general meaning of a verbal sign and its context is at present the vital task of linguistics on all its levels, because "context sensitivity" is the decisive property of our languages, which underlies their creativeness. The difference between the context-sensitive natural languages and the context-free formalized languages is an important source for comparative semantic investigation.

The utilization of the criterion "context sensitivity" opens the way to a linguistic reinterpretation of the age-long experience contained in traditional rhetorics with its doctrine of tropes and figures.

In the light of verbal semantics many domains until recently overlooked by linguistic theory and methodology, namely metalanguage, paraphrase, circumlocution, translation, bilingualism, multilingualism, and amalgamation of languages, promise and begin to yield a rich harvest for a comprehensive analysis of speech in all its varieties.

The semantic inquiry into grammar and vocabulary may still make effective use of the legacy bequeathed by one of the most ingenious linguists, Sánchez de las Brozas, "Cathedratico de Rhetorica en Salamanca", whose *Minerva: seu de causis linguae Latinae commentarius* of 1562 and 1587 abounds in remarkable anticipatory insights into the innermost problem of linguistic dialectics: the tension between two polar bents — explicitness and ellipsis.

Written in Cambridge, Mass., December 1973, for the volume *Lingüística y significación* (Barcelona, 1974), where it appeared in Spanish translation.

LANGUAGE AND CULTURE

The two speeches which have just been delivered[1] are the first lectures in Japanese which I have heard in my life, and I shall tell you exactly what my feeling was. Around 1910, in my Moscow high-school years, I saw and heard a remarkable Japanese actress from Tokyo, Hanako. She ravished the Russian audience, was extolled by avant-garde writers and sketched by modern painters. I was deeply impressed by her performance and recounted to my parents her talks and monologues. Surprised by their question — "But what was her language?" — I answered, "Of course, it was Japanese, but we did understand it." This is exactly what I can add to the clear-cut assertion of Professor Tsurumi.

What is needed in order to grasp the language of another? — One must have a keen feeling of intelligibility, an intuition of solidarity between the speaker and listener, and their joint belief in the capability of the message to go through, a capability which, in Russian, has found a felicitous label, *doxodčivost'*. If one longs for communication with his fellow man, the first step toward mutual comprehension is ensured. Because what is language? Language is overcoming of isolation in space and time. Language is a struggle against isolationism. And this fight occurs not only within the limits of an ethnic language, where people try to adjust to each other, and to understand each other within the bounds of family, town, or country; a similar striving also takes place on a bilingual or multilingual, international scale. One feels a powerful desire to understand each other. A palpable specimen is the example of neighboring Norwegian and Russian fishermen, who, during decades, or perhaps even centuries, met together for joint work and thus elaborated a common language which was called — Russians thought the label is Norwegian, and Norwegians, that this term is Russian — briefly, the common verbal code was named *moyapåtvoya*, which, in a Scandinavian

---

[1] "The Japanese Language and the International Language" by Shunsuke Tsurumi and remarks concerning Roman Jakobson by Shirô Hattori.

shaping of Russian, means "mine in your way". This may serve as a foreword to the topic of my paper.

Four decades ago, when the First International Congress of Linguists met in The Hague, all of us were struggling for the autonomy of linguistics, namely for the elaboration of its own specific methods and devices, and the very important task was to find out and to show where are the boundaries of linguistic science and what are the questions to which linguists must, and only linguists actually can, give an answer. Now, when we are near to the Tenth Congress of Linguists, which will begin in Bucharest at the end of this August, we stand before a completely different problem. At present, it is no longer the slogan of autonomy, but a program of integration, a plan of interdisciplinary relations, the problem of creative cooperation between diverse sciences. It is the problem of harmonious coordination for constructing a joint scientific domain, a science of mankind, and — in a far wider scope — a general science of life. Of course, integration implies autonomy, but, as it was once more neatly emphasized here by my dear friend, Professor Shirô Hattori, integration implies autonomy and excludes isolationism, because any isolationism harms our cultural life and our life in general. Obviously, there is no real integration without an autonomy which takes into account the necessity of intrinsic laws for every partial field and every discipline. There is another foe of these two creative ideas, autonomy and integration. The other dread enemy beside isolationism is heteronomy, or — if you permit me to translate this somewhat technical term into the vocabulary currently used by the newspapers — it is "colonialism" that we have to combat. Autonomy and integration: always welcome; isolationism and colonialism: henceforth inadmissible.

Now, what is the problem of language and culture? These two concepts are to be viewed in their interconnection. Then, first and foremost, what should we have in mind: language *and* culture or language *in* culture? Can we consider language as a part, as a constituent of culture, or is language something different, separate from culture? I know, many in the audience would like to ask: well, but how would one define culture? There are so many definitions, and an entire voluminous book was devoted by two outstanding American anthropologists, Kluckhohn and Kroeber, to the multifarious definitions of culture, their detailed list and discussion.[2] We may choose a very simple, operational definition, proposed in the instructive book *Human Evolution* by the

---

[2] C. Kluckhohn and A. L. Kroeber, *Culture = Papers of the Peabody Museum* 47 (I), 1952.

biologist Campbell: "Culture is the totality of behavior patterns that are passed between generations by learning, socially determined behavior learned by imitation and instruction."[3] I think, one can agree with this emphasis on imitation and instruction as the basic cultural devices. But there is one gap in the passage cited and Professor Tsurumi's lecture showed what the gap is: the diffusion of culture takes place not only in time but also in space. Learned solidarity of contemporaries cannot be disregarded. Yet if we accept the standpoint that cultural values are transmitted by learning, then what is to be said about language? Is it a cultural fact? Evidently language is transmitted by learning, and of course the acquisition of the child's first language implies a learning contact between the infant and his parents or adults in general. If, moreover, one has to learn a second or further language, it requires a relation between people who learn one from the other. Among the definitions of culture current in anthropological literature, we also find an assertion that the principal way of diffusion for cultural goods is through the word, through the medium of language. Does this statement apply also to language itself? Of course, language is learned through the medium of language, and the child learns new words by comparing them with other words, by identifying and differentiating the new and previously acquired verbal constituents. According to the precise formula of the great American thinker Charles Sanders Peirce, verbal symbol originates from verbal symbol. Such is the way of language development.

If we define language as a cultural phenomenon, a very serious question immediately arises. In culture, we deal with the relevant notion of progress. I hardly need to add that any idea of straightforward progress is a bewildering oversimplification. We find most various and whimsical curves, and if we confront, for instance, the poetry of Dante and the pictorial masterpieces of the Italian 14th and 15th centuries with Italy's poetry or art of the recent epochs, we could hardly view the 19th century as thoroughly advanced in comparison with works of the trecento. Many other striking examples could be adduced. When contemplating the fascinating Franco-Cantabrian cave paintings of beasts and hunters produced in the paleolithic period, sometimes we cannot but state how much more impressive and monumental they are than the so-called realistic canvases of modern Europe, and, in particular, the official art of its authoritarian powers. These observations,

---

[3] B. G. Campbell, *Human Evolution — An Introduction to Man's Adaptations* (Chicago, 1967, second ed.).

however, do not imply any denial of progress. In the history of art, we deal with a progressively developing differentiation, technical innovations, etc. Similar conclusions on gradual sophistication may be made in the history of sciences, where, likewise, no straightforward line of development can be admitted. For instance, I recollect what was said to me by the greatest specialist of our time in questions of hearing, Professor G. von Békésy, who experienced a lively pleasure when reading Latin acoustical treatises of the 16th and 17th centuries where, despite the immense technical progress of modern acoustics, he used to detect some ideas of a higher refinement; with an affable smile he added: "It is not at all surprising; Stradivarius was made, not today, but just then." Similar things could be stated on diverse scientific, for example, linguistic problems; certain branches, especially semantics, were in some respects more deeply conceived and elaborated during the Middle Ages than at present. Nonetheless, we must not forget those general lines of development which lead us still farther and farther and open ever new vistas.

Now let us approach language itself. Vocabulary may become richer and more adapted to the newer and more complex culture. The same with phraseology and with the diversity and variability of verbal styles. But in the grammatical system, morphological and syntactic, and in the whole sound pattern, no progress whatever has been detected. We can compare languages of the most cultivated nations with those of the so-called primitive peoples and we observe analogies and parallels between the former and the latter both in their grammatical processes and concepts: morphological categories and subclasses; structure of phrases, clauses, and sentences. All attempts of diverse linguists to find here traces of progress, and divergences between peoples of different cultural levels in the grammatical and phonological structure of their languages remained vain.

Occasionally, the question was raised whether that Samoyed language which has only one conjunction, in correspondence with our two conjunctions "and" and "or", does not reflect a more primitive ethnic mind. However, a written variety of American English has recently developed a synthetic conjunction "and/or", which is often considered a quite useful cultural tool. Now let us discuss whether a language which has merely one conjunction "and/or" instead of our two conjunctions "and" and "or" is impoverished in its communicative means. Not at all! Everything can be expressed. If in this type of Samoyed language one says that "father and/or mother, one of them, will come", we know that *or* is meant. If, however, the native says that "father and/or mother, both of them, will come", then obviously *and* is the key: again, there is no annoying ambiguity in the message. The grammatical structure never does prevent the speaker from conveying the most complex and most exact information. If we venture to translate Albert Einstein's or Bertrand Russell's books into Bushmen or Gilyak languages, this task is perfectly achievable, whatever the grammatical structure of the given vernacular. Only its vocabulary must be enriched and adapted to the needs of a new scientific terminology. However, any new scientific or technical branch requires similar terminological reforms, adjustments, and innovations in languages of our civilization as well. Thus, for instance, such new fields as molecular genetics or quantum theory have generated their own, completely new dictionary, whereas the phonology, morphology, and syntax are pliable to any cultural need, with no request for modifications.

Still, there is the problem of explaining why no progress is seen in the phonological and grammatical structure of languages. The penetrating linguist Nikolaj Trubetzkoy told me once: "We should not forget that, in the age between two and five years, when we acquire the fundamentals of phonology and grammar, we do not belong to any adult culture, and the cultural level of the children's environment plays no substantial role." The primary orientation of infants tending to acquire the environmental language is directed towards linguistic universals. Here, we face the problem of universality in regard to languages. Yes, we search for a common language with our fellow men, and there is only one necessary prerequisite for finding a common language. Namely, we must apprehend that other human beings also speak a human language, and that, consequently, our languages are mutually translatable. Under these conditions, we may and must look for an actual accomplishment of the translation intended. Such a possibility vanishes only in the case when one of the virtual interlocutors does not realize that the other fellow is equally a human being. According to an old legendary story, after a shipwreck, the only white man who managed to reach a remote island was regarded by the natives as some kind of ape or demonic being. In either case, he was not suspected of mastering any intelligible language, and perished, unable to convince the aborigines that he, too, was a human being, and that, therefore, mutual comprehension was achievable.

We are faced with the fundamental fact and problem of the universally human, and only human, command of language. Except in obviously pathological cases, all human beings, from their childhood, speak and understand speech. Nothing similar to human intercommunication exists outside mankind. This unique endowment must have some biological premises, namely, certain particular properties in the structure of the human brain. A further pertinent phenomenon has come to light. We observe a set of universal features in the structure of languages. Thus, all languages exhibit the same architectonic pattern: the same hierarchy of constituents from the smallest units to the widest, viz. from distinctive features and phonemes to morphemes, and from words to sentences. Any language whatever displays the same rules of implication and superposition, the same order alien to other sign systems. This structure of language turns it into an indispensable tool of thought and endows it with an imaginative and creative power. Language enables us to build ever new sentences and utterances, and to speak about things and events which are absent and remote in space and in time; to evoke nonexistent fictitious entities as well. The humane essence of language lies in the liberation of sayers and sayees from a confinement to the *hic et nunc*.

Now, when taking into account the universally human, and only human, nature of language, we must approach the question of boundaries between culture and nature; between cultural adaptation and learning on the one hand, and heredity, innateness on the other — briefly, to delimit nurture from nature. Once again, we are faced with one of the most intricate questions of present scholarship. It is necessary to realize and to remember that the absolute boundary which our forebears saw between culture and nature does not exist. Both nature and culture intervene significantly in the behavior of animals, and also in that of human beings. A leading expert in problems of animal behavior, the English zoologist W. H. Thorpe, showed us, on the basis of his own observations and experiments which were supported by the research of other specialists, that birds, for instance, finches, if totally isolated from all other birds even before emerging from the egg, and moreover, if they are deafened after being hatched, still perform the inborn blueprint of the song proper to the habit of their species, or even to the "dialect" of the subspecies.[4] This is a really inborn inheritance. If these artificially isolated fledgelings, (on the condition that their hearing has not been injured), are introduced into the society of other finches, they find and imitate their tutors. No equality exists even in the song of finches: there are better and worse performances, and the fledgelings try to follow the best singers. They learn, and their song improves.

---

[4] W. H. Thorpe, *Bird Song* (Cambridge, 1961); *Learning and Instinct in Animals* (London, 1963, second ed.).

In my adolescence, I had the opportunity to observe nightingales of the Tula region. If there was a master nightingale in the surroundings, all other neighboring nightingales sought to imitate him and to sing the habitual song with its customary variations in the best and most expanded way. But, whatever happens, a nightingale performs nothing else than the nightingale's native song, and if you put a nightingale nestling among birds of another species, he will still cling to his inborn pattern without any adaptation to the environment. It is quite different with human children. If deprived of the adults' model, they will remain speechless, without any traces of ancestral verbal habits. What they received as a biological endowment from their ancestors is the ability to learn a language as soon as there is a model at their disposal. Any of the extant human languages may serve them as an efficient cultural model. I knew a Nordic girl who spent her early childhood in South Africa, surrounded by aborigines, whom her father, a Norwegian anthropologist, was investigating. She spoke Bantu so well that students of Bantu could use her as a perfect native informant. After the family's return to Norway, if she at any time felt insulted by her parents, she retorted in the purest Bantu language.

We conclude that both components — nature and culture, inheritance and acculturation — are present, but that the hierarchy of both factors is different. It is primarily nature in animals; primarily culture, ergo learning, in human beings. Accordingly, how will we define the place of language? We must say that language is situated between nature and culture, and that it serves as a foundation of culture. We may go even further and state that language is THE necessary and substantial foundation of human culture.

When we hear the exact translation of these statements into Japanese by such a connoisseur of the two languages involved as Professor Shigeo Kawamoto, once more we ascertain the wonderful possibility of transposing scientific propositions and, in general, any statement of a purely cognitive character from one language into another. We learn again that the whole problem consists in a subtle, rational adjustment of the lexical and phraseological inventory. And what about the grammatical pattern? Here we enter into a question which had been repeatedly raised and, at the beginning of the 19th century, was clearly formulated by the prominent philosopher of language, Wilhelm von Humboldt. The most challenging approach to this question has been developed by the inquisitive linguist Benjamin Lee Whorf (1897–1941), plunged in a search as to whether and to what degree differences in the grammatical structure of languages reflect various attitudes toward the universe and dissimilarities in the thought of given ethnic groups.[5] Sometimes, such a quest for an interconnection between language and thought led to narrowly isolationist doctrines, claiming that divergences in linguistic structure predestine peoples to an inevitable failure to understand each other. It might be replied to these fallacies that in any intellectual, ideational, cognitive activities, we are always positively able to overcome the, so to speak, idiomatic character of grammatical structure and to reach a complete mutual comprehensibility.

However, beside strictly cognitive activities, there exists, and plays a great role in our life, a set of phenomena which might be labeled "everyday mythology", and which finds its expression in divagations, puns, jokes, chatter, jabber, slips of the tongue, dreams, reverie, superstitions, and, last but not least, in poetry. The grammatical patterning of language plays a significant and autonomous part in these various manifestations of such mythopoeia.

I shall limit myself to a few examples. Students whose native tongue has no grammatical division of nouns into those of feminine and those of masculine gender are inclined to believe that such a division is purely formal. They admit that in application to animates a concept of the two sexes seems to underlie and to justify the difference of the two classes in languages which distinguish the above-mentioned grammatical genders, and that in these cases, the grammatical distinction is understandable, although hardly necessary. But we are told that, in respect to inanimate nouns, the opposition of feminines and masculines loses any semantic pertinence. Let us illustrate the latent semantic value of these opposites in such a language as Russian, where the division of all nouns into genders is a relevant grammatical process. About 1915, an experiment was made in the Moscow Psychological Institute with the purpose of investigating how the ability to personify inanimate objects and abstract notions works. Fifty people were asked whether they could attribute such a personal nature to the days of the week. Five people said that to them the question made no sense, and were asked to leave the hall. The other forty-five had to write down how they visualized any week-day. The results were that all saw Monday, Tuesday, and Thursday as males, and Wednesday, Friday, and Saturday as females. Most of them did not realize that the reason for this division lies in the fact that in Russian these first three words are masculine, while the other three are feminine.

There is a superstitious or jocular foretoken that is widespread in Russia: when a knife (designated by a masculine noun) falls off the

---

[5] B. L. Whorf, *Language, Thought and Reality* (Cambridge, Mass.: M.I.T., 1956).

dining table, a male visitor is to be expected, but when it happens to be a fork or a spoon, then — in view of their feminine names — a female is supposed to come. In verbal art, the category of grammatical genders creates most peculiar situations. When, in my childhood, I read Grimms' folk tales in Russian translation, I asked my mother, "How is it possible that death is an old man while actually she is a woman?" In German, the word for death — *der Tod* — is masculine, whereas its Russian equivalent — *smert'* — is feminine. The association between sex and gender even filters into figurative art. The Russian painter I. Repin reacted to a German picture of "Sin" represented as a naked woman by an angry remark: "What a stupidity; sin (Russian masculine *grex*) must be virile." Yet for Germans, with their feminine *die Sünde*, a manlike image of sin looks perverted.

The question of genders causes trouble in the translation of poetry. A noted Czech poet and translator of Russian poetry, Josef Hora, once called me in Prague, and said, "I am going crazy. I have translated all the poems of Boris Pasternak's book *My Sister Life* (*Sestra moja žizn'*), but I am unable to reproduce its title." The word for life (*žizn'*) is feminine in Russian, but masculine in Czech (*život*). He felt that it was awkward to build an apposition between the feminine sister and the masculine name of life, or to substitute *Brother* for *Sister* in Pasternak's suggestive simile. I shall choose my last example from countless, equally embarassing, divergences. In the famous octet of one of the greatest German poets, Heinrich Heine, a fir tree, alone and surrounded by snow and darkness in the far north, dreams about a palm, also lonely in the parching heat of the south. In its German text, this succinct poem is full of lyrical, unquenchable longing and grief; the contrasting genders, the masculine *Fichtenbaum* and the feminine *Palme*, prompt an erotic symbolism. The latter vanishes upon translation into a language deprived of a similar grammatic division, and for instance, English renditions of these lines make an insipid, rhetorical impression. A different complication arises when the same poem is transposed into Russian, where the names of the two trees both belong to the feminine gender (*sosna, pal'ma*). Therefore, in the translation made even by such an artist of Russian verse as Lermontov, native readers feel a peculiar, let us say, sugary tinge. French readers and listeners are amused or bewildered by Heine's octet when translated into their mother tongue, which calls both trees by masculine nouns: *le pin, le palmier*.

Such grammatical categories as genders obviously find a wide and multiplex employment in those varieties of language where poetic or emotive function prevails over strictly cognitive aims. But what is the

role of grammatical categories in the ordinary, current language of our everyday life? How can we define the grammatical meanings which necessarily underlie those categories? The pathfinder of American linguistics and anthropology, Franz Boas (1858–1942), outlined the specific character of grammatical meanings, namely the fact that they are compulsory in our speech.[6] Speakers are obliged to make constant use of them. Russian distinguishes, for instance, the perfective aspect, which signalizes the completion of a given process, and the imperfective, which does not. Any time a Russian verb is used, one must state whether the completion is meant, or only the process, with no regard to completion. And when such a binary selection is incessantly repeated, almost in every sentence or even clause, one has to deal with a similar choice. This constant repetitiveness furthers a latent readiness (*Einstellung*) to respond to the given alternative and develops a specific subliminal orientation of the speakers' and listeners' attention. A similar focusing of attention takes place in regard to genders.

Grammatically, languages do not differ in what they *can* and cannot convey. Any language is able to convey everything. However, they differ in what a language *must* convey. If I say in English (or correspondingly in Japanese) that "I spent last evening with a neighbor", you may ask whether my companion was a male or a female, and I have the factual right to give you the impolite reply, "It is none of your business." But if we speak French or German or Russian, I am obliged to avoid ambiguity and to say: *voisin* or *voisine*; *Nachbar* or *Nachbarin*; *sosed* or *sosedka*. I am compelled to inform you about the sex of my companion not by virtue of a higher frankness, openness, and informativeness of the given languages, but only because of a different distribution of the focal points imparting information in the verbal codes of diverse languages. If you translate the mentioned sentence from Japanese into German, and the context of this sentence remains unknown to you, then three binary selections, compulsory in German, but deprived of equivalents in the grammatical pattern of Japanese, viz. a selection between masculine and feminine, between singular and plural, and between the definite and indefinite article, constrain you to choose one of eight semantically distinct possibilities: *mit dem Nachbar*; *mit einem Nachbar*; *mit den Nachbarn*; *mit Nachbarn*; *mit der Nachbarin*; *mit einer Nachbarin*; *mit den Nachbarinnen*; *mit Nachbarinnen*. Of course, if the verbal context or the nonverbalized situation of the given sentence does not supply its

---

[6] Cf. R. Jakobson, "Boas' View of Grammatical Meaning", *American Anthropologist*, Memoir 89, 1959; reprinted in *Selected Writings* II (The Hague-Paris, 1971), 489–496.

translator with sufficient cues, the latter faces certain dilemmas. They disappear when the same sentence has to be translated from German into Japanese, which is devoid of such grammatical distinctions. On the other hand, similar complications arise also for a translator of a German or Russian text into Japanese, which, in turn, is rich in grammatical distinctions without equivalents in Western languages. The outlined difficulties almost come to naught when translating a scientific work written clearly, unambiguously, and with lucid contextual meanings of all its verbal constituents.

The case of poetic language is quite different. One might even say that a close, faithful translation of poetry is a contradiction in terms. What remains possible is a congenial transposition — a free, creative response of an English poet to a Russian or Japanese author, and vice versa — a performance essentially similar to an artful, ingenious transposition of a poem or novel into a painting, motion-picture, ballet, or a piece of music. On the futility of any literal translation of poetic works into another language, we find a charming Russian story recounted by the linguist A. Potebnja: when a Greek was weeping over a native song, and curious Russians asked him to translate it, he replied that it was about a tree with leaves on its branches and a singing bird among the leaves; he added, "It's nothing when translated, but as long as I hear it in Greek, it makes me cry."

Our discussion of language and culture would remain incomplete without a few concluding remarks on the culture of language. With the general development, growth, and differentiation of culture, a consistent and active attention to the culture of language in its various aspects becomes an ever more intricate, responsible, and pressing task, on which linguists must cooperate deliberately and systematically with creative writers and other efficient carriers of cultural activities. In particular, the manifold problems of language teaching and learning on its different levels demand a wise and influential intervention from linguistic science. Various questions of standardization also acquire a heightened significance, and we linguists are prompted by colleagues from diverse fields of science, for instance, physics, who realize the great instrumental role of language in scientific operations, and who envisage and welcome the decisive contribution to be brought by the science of language to an overall checking inquiry into the language of science. In this connection it is, indeed, appropriate once more to recollect Niels Bohr's insistence on the complementarity between the formalized or semiformalized language of sciences, particularly physics, and the usual, natural language which is the final foundation, the root of such artificial superstructures. This interrelation necessitates a durable interdisciplinary work. People primarily involved in the science of language, in other words linguists, must undertake it in collaboration with those representatives of diverse sciences who pay careful attention to the make-up of the formalized languages used by the given disciplines.

As to the question of the first paper delivered today, the need and task of an international auxiliary language, we must state that this question, or rather bundle of questions, which had been deliberately disregarded by most linguists and linguistic institutions of the late nineteenth century, are presently more and more discussed. Linguists see now, with an ever greater clarity, that the study of a language cannot stop at its limits, and that we are faced with the vital phenomenon of languages in contact. The further experience of linguistic science reveals that interlingual ties are not confined to a territorial contact, since, furthermore, there exists a cultural contact between languages, independent of geographical contiguity. Such contact becomes an ever stronger international and universalistic bent and force, both in cultural and in linguistic aspects.

First presented as a public lecture in Tokyo on July 27, 1967 and published in *Sciences of Language* (Tokyo), vol. 2, no. 3 (May 1972).

METALANGUAGE AS A LINGUISTIC PROBLEM

Language must be investigated in all the variety of its functions. An outline of these functions demands a concise survey of the constitutive factors in any speech event, in any act of verbal communication. The ADDRESSER sends a MESSAGE to the ADDRESSEE. To be operative the message requires a CONTEXT referred to ("referent" in another, somewhat ambiguous nomenclature), seizable by the addressee, and either verbal or capable of being verbalized; a CODE fully, or at least partially, common to the addresser and addressee (or in other words, to the encoder and decoder of the message); and, finally, a CONTACT, a physical channel and psychological connection between the addresser and the addressee, enabling both of them to enter and stay in communication. The six different functions determined by these six factors may be schematized as follows:

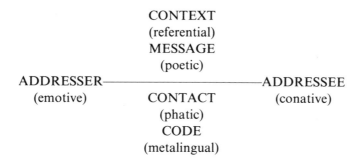

```
                    CONTEXT
                  (referential)
                    MESSAGE
                    (poetic)
ADDRESSER─────────────────────────ADDRESSEE
(emotive)           CONTACT           (conative)
                    (phatic)
                     CODE
                 (metalingual)
```

Although we distinguish six basic aspects of language, we could, however, hardly find verbal messages that would fulfill only one function. The diversity lies not in a monopoly of some one of these several functions but in their different hierarchical order. The verbal structure of a message depends primarily on the predominant function. But even though a set (*Einstellung*) toward the referent, an orientation toward the CONTEXT — briefly the so-called REFERENTIAL, "denotative", "cognitive" function — is the leading task of numerous messages, the accessory participation of the other functions in such messages must be taken into account by the observant linguist.

The so-called EMOTIVE or "expressive" function, focused on the ADDRESSER, aims a direct expression of the speaker's attitude toward what he is speaking about. It tends to produce an impression of a certain emotion whether true of feigned; therefore, the term "emotive", launched and advocated by Marty, has proved to be preferable to "emotional". The purely emotive stratum in language is presented by the interjections. They differ from the means of referential language both by their sound pattern (peculiar sound sequences or even sounds elsewhere unusual) and by their syntactic role (they are not components but equivalents of sentences). "*'Tut! Tut!'* said McGinty"; the complete utterance of Conan Doyle's character consists of two suction clicks. The emotive function, laid bare in the interjections, flavors to some extent all our utterances, on their phonic, grammatical, and lexical level. If we analyze language from the standpoint of the information it carries, we cannot restrict the notion of information to the cognitive, ideational aspect of language. A man, using expressive features to indicate his angry or ironic attitude, conveys ostensible information. The difference between [yɛs] "yes" and the emphatic prolongation of the vowel [yɛ:s] is a conventional, coded linguistic feature like the difference between the short and long vowel in such Czech pairs as [vi] "you" and [vi:] "knows", but in the latter pair the differential information is phonemic and in the former emotive. As long as we are interested in phonemic invariants, the English [ɛ] and [ɛ:] appear to be mere variants of one and the same phoneme, but if we are concerned with emotive units, the relation between the invariant and variants is reversed: length and shortness are invariants implemented by variable phonemes.

Orientation toward the ADDRESSEE, the CONATIVE function, finds its purest grammatical expression in the vocative and imperative, which syntactically, morphologically, and often even phonemically deviate from other nominal and verbal categories. Imperative sentences cardinally differ from declarative sentences: the latter are and the former are not liable to a truth test. When in O'Neill's play *The Fountain* Nano, "(in a fierce tone of command)", says "Drink!" — the imperative cannot be challenged by the question, "Is it true or not?" which may be, however, perfectly well asked after such sentences as "one drank", "one will drink", "one would drink", or after such conversions of the imperative sentences into declarative sentences: "you will drink", "you have to drink", "I order you to drink." In contradistinction to imperative sentences, declarative sentences are convertible into interrogative sentences: "did one drink?", "will one drink?", "would one drink?", "do I order you to drink?"

The traditional model of language as elucidated in particular by Karl Bühler was confined to these three functions — emotive, conative, and referential — and to the three apexes of this model — the first person of the addresser, the second person of the addressee, and the "third person" proper — someone or something spoken of. Certain additional verbal functions can be easily inferred from this triadic model. Thus the magic, incantatory function is chiefly some kind of conversion of an absent or inanimate "third person" into an addressee of a conative message. "May this sty dry up, *tfu, tfu, tfu, tfu*" (Lithuanian spell). "Water, queen river, daybreak! Send grief beyond the blue sea, to the sea-bottom, like a grey stone never to rise from the sea-bottom, may grief never come to burden the light heart of God's servant, may grief be removed and sink away." (North Russian incantation). "Sun, stand thou still upon Gibeon; and thou, Moon, in the valley of Aj-a-lon. And the sun stood still, and the moon stayed ***" (Josh. 10:12). We observe, however, three further constitutive factors of verbal communication and three corresponding functions of language.

There are messages primarily serving to establish, to prolong, or to discontinue communication, to check whether the channel works ("Hello, do you hear me?"), to attract the attention of the interlocutor or to confirm his continued attention ("Are you listening?" or in Shakespearean diction, "Lend me your ears!" — and on the other end of the wire "Um-hum!"). This set for CONTACT, or in B. Malinowski's terms PHATIC function, may be displayed by a profuse exchange of ritualized formulas, by entire dialogues with the mere purport of prolonging communication. Dorothy Parker caught eloquent examples: "'Well!' she said. 'Well, here we are', he said. 'Here we are', she said, 'Aren't we?' 'I should say we were', he said, 'Eeyop! Here we are.' 'Well!' she said. 'Well!' he said, 'well.'" The endeavor to start and sustain communication is typical of talking birds; thus the phatic function of language is the only one they share with human beings when conversing with them. It is also the first verbal function acquired by infants; they are prone to communication before being able to send or receive informative communication.

The set (*Einstellung*) toward the MESSAGE as such, focus on the message for its own sake, is the POETIC function of language. This function cannot be productively studied out of touch with the general problems of language, and, on the other hand, the scrutiny of language requires a thorough consideration of its poetic function. Any attempt to reduce the sphere of poetic function to poetry or to confine poetry to poetic function would be a delusive oversimplification. Poetic function is not the sole function of verbal art but only its dominant, determining function, whereas in other verbal activities it acts as a subsidiary, accessory constituent. This function, by promoting the palpability of signs, deepens the fundamental dichotomy of signs and objects. Hence, when dealing with poetic function, linguistics cannot limit itself to the field of poetry.

"Why do you always say *Joan and Margery*, yet never *Margery and Joan*? Do you prefer Joan to her twin sister?" "Not at all, it just sounds smoother." In a sequence of two coordinate names, as far as no rank problems interfere, the precedence of the shorter name suits the speaker, unaccountably for him, as a well-ordered shape of the message.

A girl used to talk about "that horrible Harry." "Why horrible?" "Because I hate him." But why not *dreadful, terrible, frightful, disgusting*?" "I don't know why, but *horrible* fits him better." Without realizing it, she clung to the poetic device of paronomasia.

Two alliterative clusters must have favored the coalescence of "French fries" into a habitual phrase-word.

The political slogan "I like Ike" [ay layk ayk], succinctly structured, consists of three monosyllables and counts three dipthongs [ay], each of them symmetrically followed by one consonantal phoneme [..l..k..k]. The setup of the three words shows a variation: no consonantal phonemes in the first word, two around the dipthong in the second, and one final consonant in the third. Both cola of the trisyllabic formula "I like/Ike" rhyme with each other, and the second of the two rhyming words is fully included in the first one (echo rhyme), [layk] — [ayk], a paronomastic image of a feeling which totally envelops its object. Both cola alliterate with each other, and the first of the two alliterating words is included in the second: [ay] — [ayk], a paronomastic image of the loving subject enveloped by the beloved object. The secondary, poetic function of this electional catchphrase reinforces its impressiveness and efficacy.

A discrimination clearly anticipated by the Ancient Greek and Indic tradition and pushed forward by the medieval treatises *de suppositionibus* has been advocated in modern logic as a need to distinguish between two levels of language, namely the "object language" speaking of items extraneous to language as such, and on the other hand a language in which we speak about the verbal code itself. The latter aspect of language is called "metalanguage", a loan-translation of the Polish term launched in the 1930's by Alfred Tarski. On these two different levels of language the same verbal stock may be used; thus we may speak in English (as metalanguage) about English (as object language) and interpret English words and sentences by means of English synonyms and circumlocutions. Jeremy Bentham respectively delineates "expositions by translation and by paraphrasis". Like Molière's Jourdain, who used prose without knowing that it was prose, we practice metalanguage without realizing the metalingual character of our statements. Far from being confined to the sphere of science, metalingual operations prove to be an integral part of our verbal activities. Whenever the addresser and/or the addressee need to check up whether they use the same code, speech is focused upon the CODE and thus performs a METALINGUAL (or glossing) function. "I don't follow you — what do you mean?" asks the addressee, or in Shakespearean diction, "What is't thou say'st?" And the addresser in anticipation of such recapturing questions inquires: "Do you know what I mean?" Then, by replacing the questionable sign with another sign or a whole group of signs from the same or another linguistic code, the encoder of the message seeks to make it more accessible to the decoder.

— I eagerly brought out: "But not to the degree to contaminate." "To contaminate?" — my big word left her at a loss. I explained it. "To corrupt." She stared, taking my meaning in. (Henry James, *The Turn of the Screw*.)

— It done her in ... — What does doing her in mean? — Oh, that's the new small talk. To do a person in means to kill them. — You surely don't believe that your aunt was killed? — Do I no! (G. B. Shaw, *Pygmalion*.)

Or imagine such an exasperating dialogue. — "The sophomore was plucked." "But what is *plucked*?" "*Plucked* means the same as flunked." "To be *flunked* is *to fail in an exam*." "And what is *sophomore*?" persists the interrogator innocent of school vocabulary. "A *sophomore* is (or means) a *second-year student*."

Such equational propositions ordinarily used by interlocutors nullify the idea of verbal meanings as "subjective intangibles" and become particularly conspicuous in cases of their reversibility: "A second-year student is (called) a sophomore"; "A gander is an adult male goose", but also conversely "An adult male goose is a gander." The former proposition is an example of C. S. Peirce's thesis that any sign translates itself into other signs in which it is more fully developed, whereas the reverse translation from a more explicit to a terser way of expression is exemplified by the latter proposition.

Signs are viewed by Peirce as equivalent "when either might have been an interpretant of the other". It must be emphasized again and again that the basic, immediate, "selective" interpretant of any sign is "all that is explicit in the sign itself apart from its context and circumstance of utterance", or in more unified terms: apart from its context either verbal or only verbalizable but not actually verbalized. Peirce's semiotic doctrine is the only sound basis for a strictly linguistic semantics. One can't help but agree with his view of meaning as translatability of a sign into a network of other signs and with his reiterated emphasis on the inherence of a "general meaning" in any "genuine symbol", as well as with the sequel of the quoted assertion: A symbol "cannot indicate any particular thing: it denotes a kind of thing. Not only that, but it is itself a kind and not a single thing." (*Collected Papers*, 2.301.) The contextual meanings which particularize, specify, or even modify such a general meaning are dealt with in Peirce's speculative grammar as secondary, "environmental" interpretants.

In spite of some students' objections, it is clear that the "selective interpretant" of a proper name, too, necessarily has a more general character than any single "environmental interpretant". The context indicates whether we speak about Napoleon in his infancy, the hero of Austerlitz, the loser at Waterloo, the prisoner on his deathbed, or a hero in posthumous tradition, whereas his name in its general meaning encompasses all these stages of his life and fate. Like the metabolic insect in the sequence *caterpillar-pupa-butterfly*, a person may even acquire different names for consecutive temporal segments, "momentary objects" in W. V. Quine's terminology. Married name is substituted for maiden name, monastic for secular. Of course, each of these named stages could be further segmented.

Metalingual operations with words or syntactic constructions permit us to overcome Leonard Bloomfield's forebodings in his endeavors to incorporate meaning into the science of language. Thus, for instance, the alleged difficulty of describing meanings in the case "of words like *but, if, because*" has been disproved by the treatment of conjunctions in symbolic logic, and such anthropological studies as *Les structures élémentaires de la parenté* by Claude Lévi-Strauss have proved the groundlessness of assumptions that the various terminologies of kinship "are extremely hard to analyze". Yet on the whole Bloomfield's justified view of "one of the meanings as *normal* (or *central*) and the others as *marginal* (*metaphoric* or *transferred*)" requires a consistent application in semantic analysis: "The central meaning is favored in the sense that we understand a form (that is, respond to it) in the central meaning unless some feature of the practical situation forces us to look to a transferred meaning." Such is the contextual metaphoric use of *gander* or *goose* in application to a person who resembles the bird in stupidity. The same word in the contextual meaning "look, glance" is a metonymic transfer from the goose to its outstretched neck and goggling eyes in a metaphoric application to a human being. *Goose* is a designation of a bird species with no reference to sex but in contexts opposing *goose* to *gander*, the narrowed meaning of the former vocable is confined to the females. The opposite transfer, Bloomfield's "widened meanings", may be exemplified by the use of the phrase-word *morning-star* to designate the planet Venus without reference to the time of its appearance. The literal, untransferred meaning of the two phrase-words *morning-star* and *evening-star* becomes apparent, for example, if during an evening stroll, by a casual slip of the tongue one would bring to the attention of his perplexed partner the bright emergence of the *morning-star*. In contradistinction to the indiscriminate label *Venus*, the two phrase words, discussed by G. Frege, are actually suitable to define and to *name* two different spatio-temporal phases of one planet in relation to another one.

A relational divergence underlies the semantic variance of near-synonyms. Thus, the adjectives *half-full* and *half-empty* refer to quantitatively the same status of the bottle, but the former attribute used by the anecdotal optimist and the latter one substituted by the pessimist betray two opposite frames of reference, the full and the empty bottle. Two slightly deviant frames of reference separate the anticipatory *twenty minutes to six* from the retrospective *five forty*.

The constant use of metalingual commutations within the actual corpus of any given language offers a groundwork for a description and analysis of lexical and grammatical meanings which complies even with the platform of those inquirers who still believe that "the determining criteria will always have to be stated in distributional terms". Let us cite such pairs of reversible propositions as "hermaphrodites are individuals combining the sex organs of both male and female" — "individuals combining the sex organs of both male and female are hermaphrodites", or such pairs as "centaurs are individuals combining the human head, arms, and trunk with the body and legs of a horse" — "individuals combining the human head, arms, and trunk with the body and legs of a horse are centaurs." In those two pairs we are faced with metalingual statements which impart information about the meaning assigned to the word *hermaphrodite* and *centaur* in the English vocabulary, but which say nothing about the ontological status of the individuals named. We apperceive the semantic difference between the nouns *ambrosia* and *nectar* or between *centaur* and *sphinx* and we can, for instance, transmute the two latter words into pictures or sculptures, despite the absence of such kinds of individuals in our experience. The words in question may even be used not only in a literal but also in a deliberately figurative meaning: *ambrosia* as a food which gives us divine delight; *sphinx* as a designation of an enigmatic person.

Statements of existence or nonexistence in regard to such fictional entities gave rise to lengthy philosophical controversies, but from a linguistic point of view the verb of existence remains elliptic as far as it is not accompanied by a locative modifier: "unicorns do not exist in the fauna of the globe"; "unicorns exist in Greco-Roman and Chinese mythology", "in the tapestry tradition", "in poetry", "in our dreams", etc. Here we observe the linguistic relevance of the notion *Universe of Discourse*, introduced by A. De Morgan and applied by Peirce: "At one time it may be the physical universe, at another it may be the imaginary 'world' of some play or novel, at another a range of possibilities." Whether directly referred to or merely implied in an exchange of messages between interlocutors, this notion remains the relevant one for a linguistic approach to semantics.

When the universe of discourse prompts a technological nomenclature, *dog* is sensed as a name of various gripping and holding tools, while *horse* designates various supportive devices. In Russian *kon'ki* "little horses" became a name of skates. Two contiguous stanzas of Pushkin's *Eugene Onegin* (Fourth Chapter, XLII–XLIII) depict the country in early winter, and the gaiety of the little peasant boys cutting the new ice with their skates (little horses) is confronted with the tedious time of the landlord whose helpless saddle horse stumbles over the ice. The poet's clearcut contrastive parallelism of *kon'ki* and *kon'* "horse" gets lost in translation into languages without the equine image of the skates. The conversion of *kon'ki* from animals into inanimate tools of locomotion, with a corresponding change in the declensional paradigm, has been effected under a metalingual control.

Metalanguage is the vital factor of any verbal development. The interpretation of one linguistic sign through other, in some respects homogeneous, signs of the same language, is a metalingual operation which plays an essential role in child language learning. Observations made during recent decades, in particular by the Russian inquirers A. N. Gvozdev and K. I. Čukovskij, have disclosed what an enormous place talk about language occupies in the verbal behavior of preschool children, who are prone to compare new acquisitions with earlier ones and their own way of speaking with the diverse forms of speech used by the older and younger people surrounding them; the makeup and choice of words and sentences, their sound, shape and meaning, synonymy and homonymy are vividly discussed. A constant recourse to metalanguage is indispensable both for a creative assimilation of the mother tongue and for its final mastery.

Metalanguage is deficient in aphasics with a similarity disorder, labeled "sensory impairment"; despite instructions, they cannot respond to the stimulus word of the examiner with an equivalent word or expression and lack the capacity for building equational propositions. Any aptitude for translation, either intralingual or interlingual, is lost by these patients.

The buildup of the first language implies an aptitude for metalingual operations, and no familiarization with further languages is possible without the development of this aptitude; the breakdown of metalanguage plays a substantial part in verbal disturbances. Finally, the urgent task which faces the science of language, a systematic analysis of lexical and grammatical meanings, must begin by approaching metalanguage as an innermost linguistic problem.

We realize ever more clearly that any verbal message in the selection and combination of its constituents involves a recourse to the given code and that a set of latent metalingual operations underlies this perpetual framework.

First presented as the Presidential Address at the Annual Meeting of the Linguistic Society of America, December 27, 1956, and published in *Különlenyomat a Nyelvtudományi Közlemënyek* 76. Kötetének 2. Számából (1976), where it is dedicated "to the memory of his true friend and the courageous champion of linguistic truth, Gyula Laziczius".

MARK AND FEATURE

The concept of opposition underlies both the phonological and the grammatical pattern of language. In contradistinction to any pair of mere contingents that carry no predictive information about each other, opposition is an intuitive logical operation which implies the mental copresence of the two opposites. As was pointed out by the perspicacious Dutch analyst of language, Hendrik Pos,[1] the presence of one term necessarily educes the other, opposite one: thus in such couples of abstracts as mobility-immobility, remoteness-proximity, expensiveness-cheapness, the members of each pair are inseparably linked with each other in our minds.

With respect to the phonological framework of language, any among its constituent oppositions displays a particular, supplementary item sensed as present in one and absent in the other of the two opposites. In the terminology elaborated and discussed in the Prague international phonological conference of 1930, any entity opposed to its absence was named *priznak* in Russian, *Merkmal* in German, and *marque* in French, later transposed into English as *mark*. The *principium divisionis*, underlying any given opposition and conceived as the latter's property, acquired the following labels: Rus. *različitel'noe svojstvo*, Germ. *distinktive Eigenschaft*, Fr. *propriété distinctive* (or in Saussure's footsteps, *élément différentiel*). In English, Sapir's and Bloomfield's term *distinctive feature* was adopted for the same concept by the phonological research of the forties and contributed to the acceptance and dissemination of the wording *trait distinctif* in French linguistics.

Let us illustrate the conceptual and terminological discrimination outlined above by the example of vocalic quantity (relative duration) functioning as the "distinctive feature" of the long/short phonological

---

[1] "La notion d'opposition en linguistique", *Onzième Congrés International de Psychologie* (Paris, 1938), 245; "Perspectives du structuralisme", *Travaux du Cercle Linguistique de Prague*, VIII (1939), 71ff.

opposition. The mark of this feature is length opposed to shortness, viz to the lack of prolongability. The two opposites, in the given case long versus short, have been provided with the Germ. attributes *merkmalhaft* (or *merkmalhaltig, merkmaltragend*) versus *merkmallos*, Rus. *priznakovyj–bespriznakovyj*, Fr. *marqué–non-marqué*, and therefrom Engl. *marked–unmarked*. Thus the *principium divisionis* of long and short vowels, or, in other words, the distinctive feature of the "quantitative" opposition, bifurcates into the "marked feature" of longs and the "unmarked feature" of shorts.

The diffusion and literary translation of linguistic studies written in English and French led to the mechanical transposition of the terms *marked–unmarked* (or *marqué–non-marqué*) into German *markiert–unmarkiert* and Russian *markirovannyj–nemarkirovannyj* and to the obliteration of the original attributes, Germ. *merkmalhaft–merkmallos* and Rus. *priznakovyj–bespriznakovyj*, notwithstanding the priority of these Russian and German concepts and terms, which first emerged in Trubetzkoy's correspondence of 1930 with the present author.[2]

What, however, became a bewildering and obviously erroneous innovation, was the widespread use of the German term *Merkmal* and Russian *priznak* in a broadened sense which adds to the meaning of "mark" also that of "distinctive feature". The Russian palatalized /t'/ differs from the phoneme /z/ by three features, namely by the presence of the sharpness mark (versus the non-sharp /t/) and, on the other hand, by the absence of two marks: /t'/ and /t/ are 1) discontinuous (abrupt) in contradistinction to the marked continuants /s'/, /s/ and 2) voiceless in contradistinction to the marked voicing of /d'/ and /d/. Thus /t'/ and /t/ are doubly unmarked versus the markedly continuant and voiced /z/.[3] The homonymous use of one and the same name for "mark" and "feature" leads inevitably to such incongruous designations as *unmarkiertes Merkmal* or *nemarkirovannyj priznak* for any unmarked feature like voicelessness or discontinuity.

The confusion of two distinct terms and concepts — "mark" and "feature" — in German and Russian linguistic praxis finds its probable historical explanation in a kind of repugnance toward the vagueness and objectlessness of the noun "property" favored by Trubetzkoy — *Eigenschaft, svojstvo* — and, on the other hand, in an unwillingness to assign a precise technical meaning to such indeterminate lexical equivalents of "feature" as Germ. *Zug* and Rus. *čerta*. Be it as it may, in this

---

[2] See R. Jakobson, *Selected Writings*, I (second edition, The Hague, 1971), 734ff.
[3] Cf. *ibid.*, 738ff.

point both Russian and German linguistic terminology asks to be revised, both with respect to the sound pattern of language and to its grammatical categories.

Written in Cambridge, Mass., August 1974, for *World Papers in Phonetics: Festschrift for Dr. Onishi's Kiju* (Tokyo: The Phonetic Society of Japan, 1974).

STRUCTURALISME ET TÉLÉOLOGIE

C'est à force d'analyser des poèmes que j'ai commencé à travailler sur la phonologie. Les sons du langage ne sont pas seulement un fait d'expérience externe, acoustique et motrice, mais on y découvre des éléments qui jouent un rôle premier dans le système significatif du langage, et si l'on pousse l'analyse jusqu'au bout, ce sont les traits distinctifs que soustendent la langue et la texture de la poésie. Ce qui m'a guidé dans ces recherches, ce fut l'expérience de la nouvelle poésie, le mouvement quantique de la science de l'époque et les idées phénoménologiques dont nous avons pris connaissance à l'Université de Moscou vers 1915.

C'est en 1915 que ce groupe d'étudiants qui venait de former le Cercle Linguistique de Moscou a pris la décision d'étudier la *structure* linguistique et poétique du folklore russe et le terme *structure* a déjà acquis pour nous sa connotation relationnelle, bien que le *Cours* de Saussure paru pendant la guerre restait encore inconnu à Moscou.

Arrivé à Prague en 1920, je me suis procuré le *Cours de linguistique générale* et c'est précisément l'insistance, dans le *Cours* de Saussure, sur la question des relations qui m'a surtout impressionnée: elle correspond de manière frappante avec l'accent particulier des peintres cubistes tels que Braque et Picasso non pas sur les choses elles-mêmes, mais sur leurs rapports. La même attitude topologique qui nous hantait en linguistique se manifestait simultanément dans les arts et dans les sciences. Il y a un terme dans le *Cours* de Saussure qui me donnait à penser: c'est celui d'*opposition* qui suggérait inévitablement l'idée d'une opération logique latente.

Mais quand nous nous sommes mis à travailler sur la phonologie, ou en d'autres mots, sur l'étude strictement linguistique de la matière phonique du langage, c'est plutôt l'exposé fait par l'élève de Saussure, Albert Sechehaye, dans son livre *Programme et méthodes de la linguistique théorique* (1908) qui m'a orienté vers les entités fondamentales de cette discipline: "Chaque langue suppose un *système phonologique*, c'està-dire une collection d'idées *** de sons ***. En dernière analyse, ce système est porteur de toute pensée dans le langage, puisque les symboles n'existent et n'ont de caractère propre que par son secours. Il constitue, lui aussi, une 'forme' ***, car on peut concevoir le système phonologique sous son aspect algébrique et remplacer les trente, cinquante ou cent éléments qui le composent dans une langue donnée, par autant de symboles généraux qui fixent leur individualité, mais non pas leur caractère matériel".[1] Et c'est à Sechehaye que je renvoie en parlant de la phonologie dans mon livre sur le vers tchèque terminé en 1922. Egalement, lorsqu'en 1919 j'ai affirmé, dans mon étude sur Xlebnikov,[2] que la poésie se sert plutôt des phonèmes que des sons, l'influence des élèves tels que Ščerba et Polivanov a dépassé, une fois de plus, celle du maître, Baudouin de Courtenay.

Dans le langage poétique, ce qui attirait le plus mon attention de chercheur, c'est son caractère *téléologique*: il y a là une finalité mais je me suis tout de suite trouvé en désaccord avec ceux qui affirmaient que ce n'est que la poésie qui, à la différence du langage usuel, est munie d'un but. J'objectais que le langage usuel à son tour a un but, mais un but différent.

L'orientation générale de Saussure fut antitéléologique, ainsi que celle de Baudouin de Courtenay qui prêchait que la science doit répondre à la question des causes et non des buts: telle fut l'idéologie de l'époque dont on trouve encore pas mal de survivances. Même aujourd'hui, il y a des gens pour lesquels la téléologie est synonyme de théologie. Or, il faut dire que l'intuition obligeait ces deux grands précurseurs de la linguistique moderne à s'écarter de ce dogme dans leurs recherches.

Dès le début, j'ai cherché à renoncer aux définitions extrinsèques, non linguistiques qu'on donnait d'habitude aux entités phonologiques et j'ai combattu les tentatives d'imposer aux *valeurs* de communication telles que le phonème des définitions premièrement psychologiques, acoustiques ou motrices. Aussi, dès le début de mes recherches phonologiques, j'ai assigné au phonème le rang d'une notion secondaire par rapport au réseau d'oppositions qui détermine la constitution de chaque phonème du système donné.

C'est ce que j'exprimais, dès 1928, dans mes *Remarques sur l'évolution phonologique du russe comparée à celle des autres langues slaves*[3] : "Nous appelons système phonologique d'une langue le répertoire, propre à cette langue, des 'différences significatives' existant entre les idées des

---

[1] Cf. R. Jakobson, *Selected Writings* I (The Hague-Paris, 1971), 311–316.
[2] R. Jakobson, *Novejšaja russkaja poèzija* (Prague, 1921); cf. *Selected Writings* V (The Hague-Paris-N.Y., 1979), 299–354.
[3] *Selected Writings* I, 7–116.

unités acoustico-motrices, c'est-à-dire le répertoire des oppositions auxquelles peut être attachée, dans une langue donnée, une différence des significations". Mais le même chapitre, "Notions fondamentales", reste encore coupable d'une contradiction interne: j'affirmais à l'époque que "tous termes d'opposition phonologique *non susceptibles d'être dissociés en sous-oppositions phonologiques* plus menues sont appelés phonèmes". Or, un peu plus loin, en introduisant le concept de corrélations, je dis que les phonèmes corrélatifs sont dissociables, car on peut abstraire d'un côté leur *principium divisionis*, et de l'autre, "l'élément commun qui les unit".[4] Il a fallu évidemment poursuivre l'analyse, et en 1931 j'ai posé la question du phonème comme faisceau de traits distinctifs, d'abord dans mon étude sur la phonologie du slovaque et ensuite dans une note sur le phonème pour l'Encyclopédie tchèque.[5] Ma communication au Troisième Congrès International des Sciences Phonétiques (Gand, 1938) a dressé le bilan de cette dissociation systématique des phonèmes, entités complexes, en des éléments différentiels indécomposables.[6]

Ces éléments oppositifs sont réellement perçus par les sujets parlants et on peut démontrer les corrélats physiques et moteurs des oppositions en question. Méfions-nous des modèles abstraits en dehors de la réalité perceptive. C'est une autre question que de savoir si ces rapports sont conçus par nous de façon consciente ou subliminale; en tout cas le métalangage les met en relief. Si nous reconnaissons ces rapports malgré toutes les distorsions possibles, c'est parce qu'ils existent et restent valides: on peut définir en quoi consiste l'invariance du rapport. L'idée d'une invariance topologique est incontestablement réaliste. Les deux éléments qui s'opposent l'un à l'autre ne sont jamais équipollents: l'un d'eux, hiérarchiquement supérieur, fait contrepoids au partenaire non marqué. C'est un point essentiel de la linguistique structurale telle que je la définis à la suite de Troubetzkoy.

Written in Cambridge, Mass., 1974, for *L'Arc* 60 (1975), devoted to Jakobson.

---

[4] *Ibid.*, 8ff.
[5] *Ibid.*, 224ff., 231.
[6] Cf. R. Jakobson, *Essais de linguistique générale* 2 (Paris, 1973), ch. VI.

ON APHASIC DISORDERS FROM A LINGUISTIC ANGLE

Après tout, c'est ainsi que nous communiquons, par des phrases, même tronquées, embryonnaires, incomplètes, mais toujours par des phrases. C'est ici, dans notre analyse, un point crucial.

— Émile Benveniste
3 septembre 1966[1]

Over three decades ago, in 1941, when I was about to publish my first study dealing with aphasia, *Child Language, Aphasia, and Phonological Universals*,[2] I was surprised at the extent to which linguists neglected questions concerning children's acquisition and pathological disruptions of language. In particular, the field of aphasia was usually disregarded. There were, however, a few neurologists and psychologists who insisted on the important role that linguistics can play in this domain. They realized that aphasia is first and foremost a disintegration of *language*, and as linguists deal with language, it is linguists who have to tell us what the exact nature of these diverse disintegrations is. Such were the questions raised, for instance, by A. Pick, A. Gelb, K. Goldstein, and M. Isserlin.[3] But among linguists themselves there reigned a total indifference to problems of aphasia. Of course, as always, one can find exceptions.

Thus from the early 1870's, one of the greatest precursors of modern linguistics, Jan Baudouin de Courtenay, consistently observed and investigated cases of aphasia and in 1885 devoted to one of them a detailed Polish monograph, *From the Pathology and Embryology of Language*,[4] which was supposed to be followed by further papers. This study combines a rich and careful collection of data with an emphasis on

---

[1] É Benveniste, "La forme et le sens dans le langage", *Problèmes de linguistique générale* 2 (Paris, 1974), 121.
[2] R. Jakobson, *Child Language, Aphasia and Phonological Universals* (The Hague: Mouton, 1968), translated from the German original of 1941 (cf. *Selected Writings* I, 328–401).
[3] Cf. A. Pick, "Aphasie und Linguistik", *Germanisch-romanische Monatsschrift* 8 (1920); A. Gelb and K. Goldstein, "Über Farbennamenamnesie nebst Bemerkungen über das Wesen der amnestischen Aphasie überhaupt und die Beziehung zwischen Sprache und dem Verhalten zur Umwelt", *Psychologische Forschung* 6 (1924); K. Goldstein, "Die pathologischen Tatsachen in ihrer Bedeutung für das Problem der Sprache", *Bericht über den XII Kongress der Deutschen Gesellschaft für Psychologie in Hamburg* (Jena, 1932); M. Isserlin, "Über Agrammatismus", *Zeitschrift für die gesamte Neurologie und Psychiatrie* 75 (1922).
[4] Jan Baudouin de Courtenay, "Z patologii i embryologii języka", in his *Prace filologiczne* 1 (1885–86).

the vital necessity of inquiring into child language and aphasia for linguistic theory and phonetics. The prospects of finding general laws based on the comparison of aphasic syndromes with systems of ethnic languages was anticipated. A few decades later, Ferdinand de Saussure, in sketching a review of A. Sechehaye's *Programme et méthodes de la linguistique théorique* (1908), underscored the relevance of Broca's discoveries and of pathological observations on the diverse forms of aphasia, which have especial interest for the relations between psychology and grammar: "Je rappelle par exemple les cas d'aphasie où la catégorie des substantifs tout entière manque, alors que les autres catégories établies du point de vue de la logique restent à la disposition du sujet."[5]

These significant calls remained, however, as most of Baudouin's and Saussure's exhortations, without any immediate response. But at present, beginning with the forties and early fifties, one observes a substantial change. It becomes ever clearer "à quel point l'approche linguistique peut renouveler l'étude de l'aphasie", as has been pointed out by H. Hécaen and R. Angelergues: "Il faut, en effet, que toutes les utilisations du langage libre et conditionné soient analysées à tous les niveaux du système linguistique."[6]

The question of levels is relevant indeed. Too often, attempts to treat the linguistic aspect of aphasia suffer from inadequate delimitation of the linguistic levels. One could even say that today the most important task in linguistics is to learn how to delimit the levels. The various levels of language are autonomous. Autonomy doesn't mean isolationism; all levels are interrelated. Autonomy does not exclude integration, and even more — autonomy and integration are closely linked phenomena. But in all linguistic questions and especially in the case of aphasia, it is important to approach language and its disruption in the framework of a given level, while remembering at the same time that any level is what the Germans call *das Teilganze* and that the totality and the interrelation between the different parts of the totality have to be taken into account. Here very often linguists commit a dangerous error, namely, they approach certain levels of language with an attitude of heteronomy (colonialism), rather than of autonomy. They treat one level only from the point of view of another level. In particular, when dealing with

---

[5] R. Godel, *Les sources manuscrites du Cours de linguistique générale de F. de Saussure* (Geneva-Paris, 1957), 51ff.; F. de Saussure, *Cours de linguistique générale*, critical edition by R. Engler (Wiesbaden, 1967), 35.
[6] H. Hécaen and R. Angelergues, *Pathologie du langage — l'aphasie* (Paris: Larousse, 1965).

aphasia, we must immediately recognize that the phonological level, though of course it is not isolated, maintains its autonomy and cannot be viewed as a simple colony of the grammatical level.

One must take into account the interplay of *variety* and *unity*. As Hécaen states, "l'aphasie est en même temps une et multiple".[7] The multiple forms of linguistic disintegration must be distinguished, and it would be erroneous to study this multiplicity from a merely quantitative point of view, as if we were merely dealing with different degrees of disintegration, whereas in fact we face a significant qualitative diversity as well.

Furthermore, when we discuss those forms of aphasia in which disruption of the sound-pattern of language is a relevant factor, we must remember that for contemporary linguistics there is no such field as sounds for themselves only. For the speaker and listener speech sounds necessarily act as carriers of meaning. Sound and meaning are, both for language and for linguistics, an indissoluble duality. Neither of these factors can be considered as a simple colony of the other: the duality of sound and meaning must be studied both from the angle of sound and from that of meaning. The degree to which speech sounds are a completely peculiar phenomenon among auditory events has been made clear by the remarkable experiments conducted in diverse countries during the last decade: these investigations have proved the privileged position of the right ear, connected with the left hemisphere, in perceiving speech sounds. Is it not a remarkable fact that the right ear is a better receptor of speech components, in contradistinction to the superiority of the left ear for all non-verbal sounds, whether musical tones or noises? This shows that from the beginning speech sounds appear as a particular category to which the human brain reacts in a specific way, and this peculiarity is due precisely to the fact that speech sounds fulfill a quite distinct and multifarious role: in different ways they function as carriers of meaning.

When we study the diverse linguistic syndromes of aphasia, we must pay consistent attention to the hierarchy of linguistic constituents and their combinations. We begin with the ultimate discrete units of language, "distinctive features", or *mérismes*, as Benveniste proposed to call them.[8] The fundamental role played by the identification and discrimination of these linguistic quanta in speech perception and in its

---

[7] *Ibid.*
[8] É. Benveniste, "Les niveaux de l'analyse linguistique", in his *Problèmes de linguistique générale* 1 (Paris, 1966), 223f.

aphasic disruptions has been exhaustively investigated and convincingly shown by Sheila Blumstein, who combines a thorough training in linguistics and neurology.[9] The French equivalent of "distinctive feature" is *trait distinctif* or, in Saussure's occasional nomenclature, *élément différentiel*, whereas the term *trait pertinent*, sometimes used by French linguists, is misleading, since any constituent of language proves to be pertinent in some respect and the notions of distinctiveness and pertinence do not coincide.

The bundle of concurrent distinctive features is labeled "phoneme", according to the French term *phonème*, introduced in the 1870's and gradually redefined. It is an important and useful concept on the condition that one realizes its derived, from the viewpoint of linguistic structure, secondary character in relation to its components, the distinctive features. The exaggerated attempts to abolish the concept of the phoneme are as equally unfounded as the opposite retrograde efforts to minimize or even to discard the concept of distinctive features in favor of phonemes. In the summary of her monograph, S. Blumstein points out that "the notion *distinctive feature* has provided a principled explanation for the frequency of the different types of substitution errors made by aphasics" and that "moreover, the strategies for speech production demonstrated by aphasic patients suggested that the binary values ascribed to features in phonological theory may be an intrinsic part of the phonological system of the speaker". The basic structural principle of these values, namely the opposition of marked and unmarked entities, proves to be "an essential aspect of phonological analyses", since "the notion markedness characterised the direction of substitution and simplification errors made by aphasics".

The smallest unit that carries its own meaning is the "morpheme", a concept and term introduced by Baudouin de Courtenay. Unfortunately, French linguistic terminology, according to Meillet's testimony, adopted and utilized this term in a narrowed sense in order to translate Brugmann's German label *Formant*, applicable to affixes but not to the root, and certain annoying vacillations resulted in French grammatical nomenclature.

About the highest morphological unit, the "word" (*mot*), one can repeat what was said in reference to the phoneme: it is a substantial

---

[9] Sheila E. Blumstein, *A Phonological Investigation of Aphasic Speech* (The Hague: Mouton, 1973); cf. A. R. Lecours and F. Lhermitte, "Phonemic Paraphasias", in H. Goodglass and S. E. Blumstein, eds., *Psycholinguistics and Aphasia* (Baltimore: Johns Hopkins University Press, 1973).

concept that can be neither discarded nor considered as the ultimate grammatical unit instead of the morpheme.

The usual English hierarchy of syntactic structures — "phrase", "clause", "sentence" — proves useful in the analysis of spontaneous and conditioned aphasic speech. The French terminology is less stable. Perhaps Lucien Tesnière's *nœud* for the English "phrase"[10] and the traditional French names *proposition* and *phrase* for "clause" and "sentence" would be appropriate.

When I worked on a linguistic interpretation of aphasic data and then ventured to systematize the analysed material in the light of strictly linguistic criteria, step by step I observed salient correspondences between the linguistic types of aphasia and the topographic syndromes discovered by experts in studies of the cortex, especially by A. R. Luria,[11] and I outlined these manifest parallels in my papers of 1963 and 1966.[12] I prefer, however, to avoid making equations without having submitted them to a systematic interdisciplinary control, and my own work remains concentrated upon the verbal aspect of aphasia in its manifold ramifications. But I feel deeply impressed and inspired when reading the recent synthetic study of A. R. Luria, the great inquirer into cerebral mechanisms and their lesions as factors of the different kinds of aphasic disorders.[13] When this creator of neurolinguistics,[14] in developing his unwearying research of speech disturbances, expresses his "full agreement with the basic concepts proposed" in my linguistic attempts to detect and classify the linguistic syndromes of aphasia and offers further, decisive references to the "physiological mechanisms underlying these impairments", the cardinal conclusion one may draw is the necessity of an ever closer cooperation between linguists and neurologists, a joint and consistent scrutiny which promises to open a deeper insight into the still unexplored mysteries both of the brain and of language.

We must not only correlate but also consistently discriminate two basically different phenomena, emission and reception. To use the terms

---

[10] L. Tesnière, *Éléments de syntaxe structurale* (Paris, 1959).
[11] A. R. Luria, "Factors and Forms of Aphasia", *Ciba Foundation Symposium: Disorders of Language* (London, 1964); idem, *Higher Cortical Functions in Man* (N.Y.: Basic Books, 1966) — translated from the Russian original of 1962.
[12] See R. Jakobson, "Toward a Linguistic Typology of Aphasic Impairments" (1963) and "Linguistic Types of Aphasia" (1966), in *Selected Writings* II (The Hague: Mouton, 1971), 289–306, 307–333, reprinted in *Studies on Child Language and Aphasia* (The Hague: Mouton, 1971), 75–94, 95–125.
[13] A. R. Luria, "Two Basic Kinds of Aphasic Disorders", *Linguistics* 115 (1973).
[14] Cf. A. R. Luria, "Basic Problems of Neurolinguistics", in *Current Trends in Linguistics* 12.4 (The Hague: Mouton, 1974).

of Charles Sanders Peirce, there are two distinct *dramatis personae* in the "sayer" and the "sayee". Their attitudes toward code and message are quite different, and in particular, ambiguity, especially homonymy, is a problem faced only by the "sayee". Without the help of the context or situation, upon hearing "sun", he does not know whether "sun" or "son" is meant, whereas the "sayer" is innerly free of the "sayee's" probabilistic attitude, although he obviously may take account of the sayee's attitude and prevent some of the latter's homonymic handicaps. To illustrate the difference between the pattern of the sayer and that of the sayee, may I confess that although I succeed in following clear-cut Italian speech, I am almost unable to produce a single sentence in that language. Thus, in respect to Italian I cannot act as an addresser but only as an addressee, either silent or replying in a different language. In studying aphasia, we must keep in mind the possibility of a radical separation between these two *competences* and the quite usual privileged position of reception over emission. Such is the status of infants who have learned to understand the language of adults but are themselves unable to say anything. The capability of decoding can arise before and, in the case of aphasics, separately from the ability to encode.

I prefer to reserve for another occasion discussion of the newer aspects of linguistic research on aphasic disruptions of sound structure, despite the fascinating outlook these questions open at present to phonology. If one limits oneself, in moving to a higher and purely grammatical level of aphasia, and applying the principle of explanatory adequacy, to a rigorously linguistic analysis of verbal impairments at that level alone, one is led to obtain a clear and simple picture of them. Yet to grasp the linguistic syndrome of a given type of aphasia, we must follow several guidelines.

First, a zoologist would not begin to study the difference between plants and animals by examining such transitional species as sponges and corals. One would hardly begin to study sexes by concentrating one's attention on hermaphrodites. Of course there are many hybrid, complex, mixed cases of aphasia, but we are unaware of the existence of clearly polarized types, and these strictly distinct, so to say, "pure" cases, as neurologists call them, should underlie our study and classification of aphasics and subsequently guide us also in our inquiry into borderline occurrences, whatever their frequency may be.

Secondly, the significant difference between spontaneous and conditioned speech, a fact well known to linguists, must be carefully applied to the study of aphasia as well. In addition to the answers a patient makes to the doctor's questions, we have to observe the aphasic's totally spontaneous speech, especially in his familiar surroundings, and compare these two structurally distinct types of utterances. When approaching the question of required reproduction and repetition, one must remember that these processes occupy a very particular place in our verbal behavior. At the London Symposium on Disorders of Language held in 1963 at the Ciba Foundation, the linguist A. S. C. Ross spoke about the need for corpora of aphasic texts, published or mimeographed, with utterances emitted in various types of discourse and with different interlocutors.[15] Such material is absolutely indispensable for obtaining a linguistic description and classification of aphasic syndromes. Reliable linguistic conclusions cannot be made on the basis of a mere collection of patients' answers to the doctor's questions, posed, moreover, under the quite artificial conditions of medical interrogation.

From a linguistic point of view perhaps the clearest forms of aphasia were obtained in cases of outright agrammatism. We possess the remarkable insights into such cases by experts in aphasia like A. Pick, M. Isserlin, and E. Salomon in the past,[16] or at present, H. Hécaen and H. Goodglass and their linguistic collaborators.[17] It was Goodglass who found a consistent and revealing order in aphasics' treatment of an English inflectional suffix, a triple homonym carrying three completely different grammatical functions, namely the suffix /-z/, with its two positional variants /-iz/ and /-s/. This suffix with the same positional variants is used in the plural of nouns, e.g. "dreams", in the possessive form, e.g. "John's dream", and in the third person of the present, e.g. "John dreams", while the last form to survive is the nominal plural, "dreams".[18] In children's acquisition of language we find just the opposite order, a mirror image: the plural "dreams" is the first form to appear, the subsequent acquisition is "John's dream", followed finally, by the third person "John dreams".[19] The actual explanation lies in the hierarchy of levels: the plural form, "dreams", is one *word*, which

---

[15] A. S. C. Ross et al., "Edition of Text from a Dysphasic Patient", *Ciba Foundation Symposium: Disorders of Language* (London, 1964).
[16] A. Pick, *Die agrammatischen Sprachstörungen* (Berlin, 1913); M. Isserlin, *op. cit.*; E. Salomon, "Motorische Aphasie mit Agrammatismus", *Monatsschrift für Psychologie* 1 (1914).
[17] H. Hécaen, ed., *Neurolinguistique* ...; H. Goodglass, "Studies on the Grammar of Aphasics", *Journal of Speech and Hearing Research* 11 (1968); cf. D. Cohen and H. Hécaen, "Remarques neurolinguistiques sur un cas d'agrammatisme", *Journal de psychologie normal et pathologique* 62 (1965); H. Goodglass and J. Hunt, "Grammatical Complexity and Aphasic Speech", *Word* 14 (1958).
[18] H. Goodglass and J. Berko, "Agrammatism and Inflectional Morphology in English", *Journal of Speech and Hearing Research* 11 (1968).
[19] J. Berko, "The Child's Learning of English Morphology", *Word* 14 (1958).

implies no syntactic sequence, whereas the possessive, "John's", implies the *phrase* level, where "John's" is a modifier dependent on some headword like "dream", and finally, the third person, "dreams", requires a *clause* with a subject and predicate.

It is completely clear that more complex syntactic structures are the first to be discarded, and the first to be lost in the cases of agrammatism is the relation between the subject and predicate. Children begin with one-word phrases (holophrases), then they reach the actual phrase level — "little boy", "black cat", "John's hat", etc. — and the last to emerge is the construction of subject and predicate. The acquisition of such constructions is, as a matter of fact, a verbal and mental revolution. Only at this stage does a real language, independent of the *hic et nunc*, appear. Scholars used to speak about a "psychological predicate" in the case of a child who sees a cat and says "cat". This holophrase was interpreted as a predicate appended to the animal which is seen by the infant. But only when the child gains the ability to express both the subject and the predicate in their interrelation, only at this dichotomous stage, does language come into its own. Observers of children's language in various countries have witnessed diverse variants of one and the same event. A boy of perhaps two or three years comes to his father and says "dog meow" (or "meows"), and the parent corrects him by saying, "No, the cat meows and the dog barks." The child gets angry and cries. If, however, the father is ready to take part in the game and say, "Yes, the dog meows, and Peter meows, and Mommy also meows, but the cat and uncle bark", the child is usually happy. However, it may happen that the little speaker gets angry precisely at such a responsive father, because he believes that talking about meowing dogs is his childish privilege, which adults have no right to assume. The story reflects an important linguistic fact: in learning his mother tongue, the child realizes that he has the right to impose different predicates on the same subject, "dog" ("the dog ... runs, sleeps, eats, barks") just as he may combine different subjects ("dog, cat, Peter, Mommy") with one and the same predicate (e.g. "runs"). Then why not extend this freedom to assign new predicates and say "the dog meows"? The abuse of freedom is a typical side-effect of the child's verbal and mental liberation from the given situation. As long as he merely says "runs", or "cat", or "dog", he is totally dependent on the present temporal and spatial environment, but with the appearance of subject-predicate clauses, he suddenly can speak of things distant in time or space, events belonging to the remote past or to the future, and, furthermore, he can build entire fictions. It is this ability that gets lost in cases of outright agrammatical aphasia.

Observations about imperatives in the acquisition and dissolution of language are most instructive. Imperative structures do not imply the existence of the clause pattern, with its interplay of subject and predicate. Surmises that the imperative is a mere transform of a declarative verbal structure are without any foundation whatsoever. The imperative is the most elementary verbal form. For this very reason the imperative, which appears in the earliest stratum of children's language, is the most resistent in agrammatical aphasia, and the frequent tendency in inflectional languages to confine the imperative form to the bare root is in turn a convincing illustration of its primitive essence.

The absence of personal pronouns, which surprised investigators of agrammatism, is parallel to the disappearance of relational spatio-temporal markers. These phenomena enter into the category of "shifters", viz. those grammatical classes which imply in their general meaning a reference to that message in which they appear.[20] These duplex, overlapping classes are typical marked superstructures in the grammatical system, and this fact explains their late emergence in children's language and their early disappearance in classical cases of agrammatical aphasia.

When we approach the type of disturbance that was recently outlined by J. Dubois, H. Hécaen and their collaborators,[21] so-called "sensory" aphasia, and compare it with agrammatism, the linguistic polarity between these two types of aphasia becomes particularly clear. Point by point one is able to show a pure, genuine opposition between the two syndromes. The central point of divergence lies in the fact that in sensory aphasia the nuclear elements of the grammatical structure, nouns, tend to disappear, whereas for agrammatical patients it is precisely nouns which form the basic stock of their vocabulary. Sensory aphasia shows the diverse ways in which nouns are affected: they are simply omitted or replaced by pronouns, by different near-homonyms, by figurative expressions, etc. Briefly, what is under attack are nouns as the morphological units which are least dependent on the context, and among such morphological units, not necessarily, but first and foremost, one observes a disappearance of grammatical subjects as the most independent constituents of the sentence and the least conditioned by the context. It is just such self-contained entities that cause the greatest difficulties for

---

[20] Cf. R. Jakobson, "Shifters, Verbal Categories, and the Russian Verb", in *Selected Writings* II (The Hague: Mouton, 1971), 130–147.
[21] J. Dubois, H. Hécaen et al., "Analyse linguistique d'énoncés d'aphasiques sensoriels", *Journal de psychologie normal et pathologique* 67 (1970); cf. E. S. Beyn, "Osnovnye zakony struktury slova i grammatičeskogo stroenija reči pri afazijax", *Voprosy psixologii*, 1957.

this type of patient. Once, in Paris, Dr. Th. Alajouanine showed us a patient who suffered from a typical sensory aphasia as the result of an accident in the truck he drove. The greatest difficulty for him was to begin a sentence and, even more, a whole utterance with a nominal or pronominal subject. When I asked him, while he was writing, what he was doing, he answered, "J'écris". When we repeated the same question in referring to a student present, the answer was "Il écrit". But when I asked him, "What am I doing?", he had inhibitions before saying "Vous écrivez", and the same thing happened when a similar question was asked about a nurse who was writing something. This curious difference is easily explainable: in French *vous* and *elle* are independent pronouns and act as grammatical subjects even in elliptic sentences ("Qui écrit!" — "Elle!"), whereas *je, tu, il* are mere preverbs.

One cannot help but agree with the insistence upon the fact that the main loss in sensory aphasia afflicts not just subjects but nouns in general, since in contradistinction to agrammatism, which is primarily a syntactic disintegration, sensory aphasia, as a matter of fact, preserves syntax and affects primarily independent, indeed autosemantic morphological categories.

The relation between the treatment of nouns and verbs is one of the most cardinal questions for the study of language and language disturbances. The predominance of nouns over verbs in agrammatical patients has been demonstrated by J. Wepman.[22] A collaborator of Luria, L. S. Cvetkova, in her interesting Russian paper "Toward the Neuropsychological Analysis of So-Called Dynamic Aphasia",[23] showed how much more difficult the task of naming various verbs was for patients compared to listing concrete nouns. At best two or three verbs were produced. Permit me to tentatively confront these data with the new, still preliminary studies of R. W. Sperry and M. S. Gazzaniga on language comprehension in patients who have undergone split-brain operations.[24] The comprehension of nouns flashed to the right hemisphere proved to be high with the exception of verbal nouns, whether unsuffixed *nomina actionis* or *nomina actoris* with the suffix *-er* (like "locker", "teller", etc.). Also, adjectives "were easily identified by the

---

[22] J. M. Wepman et al., "Psycholinguistic Study of Aphasia", in *Psycholinguistics and Aphasia*, ed. H. Goodglass and S. E. Blumstein (Baltimore: Johns Hopkins University Press, 1973).
[23] L. S. Cvetkova, "K nejropsixologičeskomu analizu tak nazyvaemoj dinamičeskoj afazii", in *Psixologičeskie issledovanija* (Moscow: MGU, 1968); cf. A. R. Luria and L. S. Cvetkova, "The Mechanisms of 'Dynamic Aphasia'", *Foundations of Language* 4 (1968).
[24] M. S. Gazzaniga, *The Bisected Brain* (N.Y.: Appleton Century Crofts, 1970).

right hemisphere", with the exception of those derived from verbs, such as "shiny", "dried" and the like. With verbs "the performance level was poor". These data deserve to be compared with the relevant essay on the classification of language by the topologist René Thom.[25]

Thom posits a hierarchy of grammatical categories with the noun as the most stable and opposed in this respect to the verb, while verbal nouns are on the same level as verbs, and the adjective occupies an intermediate position between noun and verb. From the comparison of all these observations and insights it follows that the verb is a marked category, a superstructure in relation to the noun, and both the acquisition and disruption of language confirm this order. The confinement of "language comprehension in the right hemisphere" to pure nouns finds an explanation in their unmarked nature. The semantic mark of the verb, in contradistinction to the unmarkedness of the noun, is its reference to the time axis. Thus the immunity of the verb and of the syntactical sequence deployed in time are two natural and interconnected features of "temporal aphasias".

Many syntactic problems faced by the study of aphasia can be explained with reference to the hierarchy of linguistic structures, namely to the relation between the derived, marked, and the primary, unmarked variety. The examples often quoted from the speech of children or aphasics in languages which have different endings for the nominative and accusative cases are most instructive. Thus, in Russian, "*Papa* (nom.) *ljubit mamu* (acc.)" "Dad loves mom" may be inverted without a change in the relation between the grammatical agent and the patient, which are signaled by two different inflectional suffixes, but aphasics and little children erroneously understand the inverted sentence, "*Mamu* (acc.) *ljubit papa* (nom.)", as "Mom loves dad", since the former word order is neutral, unmarked, while the latter is marked as expressive, and only the unmarked order is grasped by such listeners. Dr. Goodglass' example, "the lion was killed by the tiger", tends to be interpreted by aphasics as "the lion killed the tiger", since in the usual, most normal word order the subject functions as an agent, whereas here it becomes the victim, and moreover, because the passive is a superstructure upon the active.

We cannot but agree with Dr. Goodglass in his rejection of the recent assumptions according to which aphasic losses affect only performance,

---

[25] R. Thom, "Sur la typologie des langues naturelles: essai d'interprétation psycholinguistique", in *The Formal Analysis of Natural Languages*, ed. M. Gross, M. Halle, and M.-P. Schützenberger (The Hague: Mouton, 1973).

but not competence.[26] These surmises are built on a very narrowed and arbitrary conception of what competence is. Competence is far from being a static and uniform phenomenon. Every speech community and each of its members dispose of a multiform competence, and the competence for speech production is quite different from that for speech perception; moreover, there is a substantial difference between competence in spoken and written language, again with a crucial subdivision into reading and writing. It would be an oversimplification to view these differences as mere varieties of performance. The codes themselves differ. Our competence for the explicit style of language is to be distinguished from our competence for different degrees of ellipsis. We must distinguish the verbal losses of an aphasic as speaker and as listener, and they can hardly be reduced by the scientific interpreter to questions of performance. The changes in an aphasic's speech are not mere losses, but also replacements,[27] and these replacements may be systematic, as for instance, the regularization of irregular verbs in the standard language, a phenomenon akin to the successive competences of a child in his approach to the mother tongue. The peculiar forms of interrelation between the explicit and elliptic codes either in children or in aphasics are an intricate and imminent problem for the inquirer.

Although linguists have wide possibilities of describing and interpreting aphasic facts within the frame of language, without going beyond the linguistic level, let us recall that one of the great forerunners of aphasiology and, one may add, of modern linguistics, the neurologist John Hughlings Jackson, viewed aphasia as one of the possible semiotic disruptions that can occur either singly or concomitantly with other losses. He preferred the term "asemasia" proposed by Allan McLane Hamilton as a generic name.[28] Of course, quite often the disruption may be limited solely to language, but we must consistently discuss the problems of language with regard to other problems of signs, such as gestures, graphics, music, etc., and their interrelations. Although we have significant research work on alexia and agraphia, studies of aphasia often neglect questions about the relation and difference between speech and writing. When, for instance, aphasia is discussed only or primarily on the basis of the patient's oral reactions to written words, the problem of the significant difference between written and spoken words is not

---

[26] Cf. E. Weigl and M. Bierwisch, "Neuropsychology and Linguistics", in *Psycholinguistics and Aphasia*, ed. H. Goodglass and S. E. Blumstein (Baltimore, 1973).
[27] Cf. John Hughlings Jackson, *Selected Writings* 2 (New York, 1958).
[28] J. H. Jackson, *op. cit.*; Allan McLane Hamilton, *Nervous Diseases: Their Description and Treatment* (Philadelphia, 1878).

taken into account. There is also a noteworthy difference between how patients react in their utterances to objects and to pictures of objects, for pictures enter into the field of signs, they are semiotic facts. Such questions as the chasm between aphasia and amusia, clearly stated by E. Feuchtwanger in the early thirties,[29] could and should be connected with the amazingly frequent lack of ear and sense for music among the greatest poets extolled for the "musicality" of their verses, which here appears to be a mere metaphor.

Briefly, the further development of linguistic inquiry into aphasia requires a greater concentration on the description and classification of the purely verbal syndromes,[30] but with a constant regard for the whole semiotic framework. The progress of any linguistic study and of neurolinguistic research in particular depends on investigators taking more and more into account than the fact that the difference between the patterns examined lies not only in the presence or absence of certain properties, but also — and even chiefly — in the difference between the predominant features, in short, in the different hierarchization of these properties.

First published in French translation, under the title "Les règles des dégâts grammaticaux", in *Langue, Discours, Société*, ed. J. Kristeva, J.-C. Milner and N. Ruwet (Paris, 1975), with the following dedication: "C'est à Émile Benveniste qui fut l'un des premiers à soutenir l'importance des études strictement linguistiques sur les syndromes de l'aphasie que je tiens à dédier en hommage d'admiration et d'affection cette étude basée sur mes rapports au Troisième Symposion International d'Aphasiologie à Oaxtepec, Mexique, novembre 1971, et au Congreso Peruano de Patologia del Lenguaje à Lima, Peru, octobre 1973." The English version published here first appeared in the author's book *The Framework of Language* (Ann Arbor, 1980).

---

[29] E. Feuchtwanger, "Das Musische in der Sprache und seine Pathologie", *Proceedings of the International Congress of Phonetic Sciences* (Amsterdam, 1932).
[30] Cf. such recent studies as M. Zarębina, *Disintegration of the Linguistic System in Aphasia* — Polish text with English summary (Warsaw: Polish Academy of Sciences, 1973).

THE GRAMMATICAL BUILDUP OF CHILD LANGUAGE

It is a great honor for me to speak in the Rhenish-Westphalian Academy of Sciences. I look forward to the discussion period with some impatience, since the problems touched upon in my presentation are closely connected with my entire linguistic work over several decades. I would like to return here to the essential questions of child language.

At the end of the 1930's, the work of the French-Belgian linguist Antoine Grégoire in particular made a fruitful impression on me, namely his monograph *L'apprentissage du langage* (Liège, 1937); it is actually a journal, which presents a comprehensive, painstaking picture of the speech activity of his two small sons. I marvel at the way this distinguished scholar was able to observe and record every moment of the linguistic development of his children with such perfect attentiveness.

Works such as the books of Grégoire or of the zealous and keen-sighted investigator of Russian child language acquisition Aleksandr Nikolaevič Gvozdev might best be compared to continuous film presentations in order to do justice to their precise results, and to their wealth of linguistic and psychological data, their abundance and thoroughness. In sharp contrast are today's ever-increasing snapshots of linguistic behavior and current linguistic ability, taken of the child a few times weekly or even monthly by the learned visitor, which chop up and destroy the total picture. The latter conceal the individual mainsprings of the changes and their order of succession, and thus make it impossible for us to draw conclusions regarding the dynamic laws of language acquisition.

To be sure, important new observations have been made concerning children's beginning attempts and efforts to learn to communicate at the pre-verbal age, and at the threshold of verbal exchange with their teacher, in particular their mother. Much new material has also been observed and clarified regarding the sequence of children's phonological acquisitions, but the grammatical buildup of child language still remains unexplained in many, or perhaps even in most, respects.

The question which from the very beginning interested me in particular was that of the relative role of imitation and of the child's creative gift in the acquisition of his first language. While certain investigators stress the importance of replication, others emphasize that of creative ability. It appears that a synthesis would be preferable. What does take place is neither a mechanical appropriation nor a miraculous creation out of the void. Imitation offers broad possibilities for the beginner's creative powers. The existing model permits a selection from the completed acquisitions and their proper sequence, thanks to which the child can acquire first one thing and only then the next. Universal laws of one-sided implication (or foundation) are at work here: no "B" could arise as long as "A" had not developed, whereas in the linguistic system "A" can exist independently of "B".

The investigation and explanation of the strict lawfulness observable in the development of child language progress only slowly. The Neogrammarian, unilaterally diachronic tradition, which was prominent in linguistics only a short time ago, showed no appreciation whatever either for the pure description of language structure or for the search for universal laws of structuring and restructuring. On the other hand, the Geneva school and its numerous epigones preached a strict and narrowly static version of synchrony and, as a matter of fact, of linguistic analysis as a whole, and concealed the means of comprehending child language, the nature and structure of which are subject to the laws of synchrony applied dynamically.

If, in spite of the residue of protracted skepticism, one now finally observes the wealth and meaning of universals in the structure of the world's languages and in the buildup of child language, many strikingly dynamic laws manifest themselves, especially in the development of the phonological inventory. These laws show either a general validity or at least a nearly universal probability. Two kinds of monopolistic attempts to explain this wide-ranging uniformity in the fundamentals of human language are apparent. On the one hand, slogans of a fanatical nativism issue forth and multiply; on the other hand, a persistent sociologism tries to convince us that all linguistic laws and tendencies toward uniformity are determined by the unswerving social usage and character of language.

As proof of the "innateness" of the fundamental laws of language, nativists adduce the relative ease and speed of language acquisition in small children the world over. As a matter of fact, however, children also learn, with the same naturalness, accuracy and ease, all of the external local particulars of the linguistic milieu to which they owe their first knowledge of language. The alleged rapidity of complete language acquisition likewise proves to be an exaggerated over-generalization. But the universally human and uniquely human desire and gift of mastering a language actively and passively from early childhood on is a capability embodied in the biological fact of being human, for, as Goethe says: "Each one learns only what he can."

Still, one must not forget — and it is forgotten, strangely enough, all too often — that, strictly speaking, what is acquired is a dialogue. For the child's speech and language two speech partners are necessary: on the one hand, the underage novice, and on the other, an older, more experienced companion, in particular the child's mother. Therefore, the development of language cannot be understood without bearing in mind, from the very first, two parties, two participants, of whom the one learns and the other in fact teaches. Today we often hear frivolous statements to the effect that the child requires no language instruction and quite independently gleans from what is heard whatever can be put to use for independent production. Critics who deny or belittle the role of learning or teaching in the child's acquisition of language are either laboring under the bureaucratic conception of an official educational establishment, or else are hypnotized by the once fashionable idea of a gap between parents and the younger generation. Close reciprocal accommodation remains an essential concomitant feature of language learning.

We are already in a position to establish the existence of numerous structural principles which languages hold in common, laws operating universally or nearly universally, among which the latter — widely distributed in space and time — tend toward exceptionlessness, without, to be sure, attaining it. Naturally, the biological basis plays a certain role, although one that remains indeterminate. On the other hand, one must never forget that language presents an essentially social totality, and that this dynamic whole, in the terms of the German philosophers, shows a constant *self-motion* (*Selbstbewegung*) — *self-stirring*, according to the terminology of cybernetics. The dynamic laws of language are furthered by the fact that an all-embracing collective system is involved, which its user comes to experience at the boundary between the conscious and the unconscious. To the subliminal domain belongs the striving after appropriate structures, which are followed by the linguistic community unconsciously, and partly also consciously, under more metalinguistic direction.

Language is first and foremost characterized by its essentially universal stratificational structure and is subject to a basically uniform principle of superimposed arrangement. Each level consists of internal relations exclusively its own, and of relations which bind each level with the others. The analysis of these relations, both the internal as well as the interlevel ones, is indispensable for understanding the system of language and its buildup.

Among the relations which the linguist deals with, true contrast, binary opposition, appears as the most typical and the most instructive. On the basis of numerous considerations, we know wherein the performance of such relations actually lies. Let me refer once more to the outstanding Dutch phenomenologist and theorist of language Henrik Pos, in order to discuss the precise nature of binary oppositions. As its designation implies, it is the simplest logical operation; and it differs from all other combinations and relations by virtue of the fact that in any procedure with a binary opposition, we necessarily have both of its members in mind, and utilize both for comparison. Thus it is impossible, for example, to judge largeness, without taking into consideration the idea of smallness; the meaning of the inexpensive is unthinkable without that of the expensive, etc. Therein lies the effective value of such oppositions. As child psychologists, especially Henri Wallon, have established, the child's early mental development is based directly on such binary contrasts.

My monograph *Kindersprache, Aphasie und allgemeine Lautgesetze*,[1] published in Sweden at the beginning of 1941, was an attempt to trace the gradual, step-like buildup of the phonological level in the early speech of the child, and if possible to interpret it. Step by step it became clear to me how extraordinarily important it is to keep constantly in view the complex interrelation between the parts and the whole, important not only in the area of child language acquisition, but in all questions of linguistic procedure as well. It has since become clear how useful the concept of the part-whole relation, introduced and developed by psychologists (in particular, Felix Krueger), proves for such research. If we wish to discuss and interpret the sound phenomena of child language, the various oppositions and their interrelations, we are evidently compelled to take the path of integration.

I must confess that at first it astonished me to perceive the child's developmental process through the analysis of its increasing phonetic capability. Particularly helpful for me in this respect was the preliminary work of two prominent scholars whose investigations were connected

---

[1] Cf. *Selected Writings* I (The Hague-Paris, 1971), 328–401, and the English translation, *Child Language, Aphasia and Phonological Universals* (The Hague-Paris, 1968).

with the progress of Gestalt psychology, Wolfgang Köhler and Carl Stumpf. In their consideration of speech sounds, both researchers managed to keep in mind, without confining themselves to details, the psychophysical basis of the vowel system as a whole. I realized that one must continue to work constantly in the direction of logical integration in order to understand the relation between the branches of the linguistic sound system, i.e. between vocalism and consonantism. Parallelism between these two systems had in fact been sought, but without allowing for the fundamental distinction in the distribution of the marked and unmarked member within an otherwise parallel opposition, and without taking into consideration the hierarchically different interrelation between the basic oppositions of both component systems.

We observe the same path from the single concept to the divided, and hence more complex concept in the sphere of grammar and its progress in the small beginner, with meaningful elements forming a focal point this early.

At first, each statement consists solely of a holophrase, a one-word sentence, to use an inexact expression which anticipates the future concepts of the word and the sentence and brings them into the discussion prematurely. In the state which follows, the holophrastic unity expands to comprise a second constituent. Thus, the first grammatical divisions arise simultaneously, on the one hand word and word-structure, on the other hand the main-word (open class) and the marked accessory-word ("pivot", according to the terminology of Martin Braine), e.g. *it ball, more ball, there ball, little ball*. Many observers have tried to find predication already in this stage, but the interpretation of such structures as individual, situationally-conditioned predicates represents a superfluous extension of the meaning of the term "predicate", which already in the course of the nineteenth century occasioned minute discussions that brought to light the special and critical role of the purely grammatical predicate. Moreover, the phrase *little ball* is still very remote from the clause *the (this, a) ball is little*. Neither *little doll* nor the diminutive *dolly* can be equated with the sentence *the doll is little*. The primary and unmarked function of the adjective is in no way predicative, but decidedly attributive, and it is only the subsequent, third stage of child language acquisition that brings into existence the elementary sentence — subject/predicate.

Let us take an interesting example to illustrate these chronological relationships. In English, there are three homonymous suffixes which have the sound -z, but which undergo fixed modifications (-əz, -s) under certain phonetic conditions. This suffix form has three distinct meanings:

first, that of the nominal plural (*cooks*); second, that of the possessive (*cook's hat*); and third, it is the inflectional form of the third person singular of the verb (*mummy cooks*). The child first utilizes this suffix for the plural ending, then for the possessive, and finally for the verb. According to analogous observations, aphasics follow a path which is directly the reverse, i.e. the elements lost display an exact mirror-image: of the three homonymous suffixes, the first to be lost is the verbal one, then the possessive, and finally the nominal plural. The reason is obvious: in differentiating between plural and singular, the word alone is involved, while in the use of the possessive form an entire phrase (*cook's hat*) comes into play. But when the person of the verb is involved, it is a question of the relationship between the predicate and the subject, and therefore the whole sentence is affected.

Thus we arrive at the sentence, and permit me to cite a truly typical occurrence, known from the speech activity of the child in many different countries. A two- or three-year-old boy comes to his father and announces: "Cat barks" (or "Kitty bowwow"). The father instructs his son: "No, no — dogs bark and cats meow." The child is in tears — his game has been ruined. Of course, there are more liberal parents, willing to acknowledge that cats bark and even to pursue the game: "Auntie barks, too, and Mama meows." The child is highly pleased. But certainly not always: there are some little ones who believe it to be their privilege as children to construct conjectures of this kind, and who are annoyed if adults claim such an advantage.

The above-mentioned dialogue, which is continually arising spontaneously, evidently has a deep linguistic foundation. When two-part (dyadic) sentences, whose subjects and predicates are both expressed, imprint themselves on a child's speech, then the little apprentice feels, either consciously or subliminally, that a totally new possibility has thus opened up for him. One can state at will about that very same cat, presenting itself as subject, that it runs, sleeps, eats, meows, etc.; then why shouldn't one also attempt to compose sentences like "Cat barks" and "Dog meows", if the same noun can be used with different verbs and the same verb is ascribed to different subjects? Here a typical by-product arises of the great linguistic and cognitive freedom which the child gains as a result of the two-part sentence-construction: attempts will of course be made to abuse this freedom. The annoyed child is, after all, ignorant of Catherine the Great's aphorism to the effect that freedom is merely the right to do what the laws permit. Such traditional children's jokes as "Birds ring, bells fly away" betray a similar temporary lack of restraint.

The syntactic innovation just pointed out represents a very important stage in the life of the child. Before this sudden change, he could only make himself understood about matters immediately at hand and directly accessible to his senses. Now, though, the little fellow feels equipped to converse about things far removed in space and time, or even imaginary. Only now does the actual creative power of human language appear, as well as the capacity for judgment rendered possible only through language. The extended transfer of the concept of predication from originally one-part, situationally-conditioned and subjectless utterances has exerted a bewildering influence on many psycholinguistic studies, where the importance of the linguistic duality of subject/predicate — which is decisive for the whole of human organization — has continued to be neglected.

In a friendly conversation with a highly respected behaviorist, my question as to whether communications exchanged between pigeons should be ascribed to a level analogous to human speech was answered in the affirmative. My further question, as to whether the distant past, the future or the imaginary could be the subject of communication among birds, elicited this reply: "No, but all of that should be regarded as 'displaced speech'!" I added that if this were the case, our disagreement proved to be purely terminological: what one of us designated as "displaced speech" was taken by the other as the true mark of human language.

We should note that the discovery of the sentence and the increasing freedom in its lexical filling out in the child's linguistic behavior is accompanied by a gradual freezing of word creation. Neologism is eclipsed by syntactic tasks. The period of freedom and productivity of words, which contrasts so strikingly with the fixed vocabulary of the adult, has been shrewdly recognized by the greatest observers of human language. "No one thinks up new words as often as children do", asserts L. N. Tolstoj, in order to show that the laws of linguistic structure are perceived better in childhood than in ripe old age. The American thinker Charles Sanders Peirce maintains that the child, "with his wonderful genius for language", loses this remarkable gift as time passes.

First presented at the 204th Session of the Rheinisch-Westfälische Akademie der Wissenschaften on May 28, 1975 in Düsseldorf and published in German, with the discussions following the report, in the *Vorträge* of the Academy (*Geisteswissenschaften*, G 218, 1977). Translated into English for the present volume by Brent Vine.

ON THE LINGUISTIC APPROACH TO THE PROBLEM OF CONSCIOUSNESS AND THE UNCONSCIOUS

In the second half of the 19th century the problem of "the unconscious", as the author of a critical survey has remarked, enjoyed a special popularity and was acknowledged as an important factor to be reckoned with when treating diverse topics in the theory of behavior.[1] Among the linguists of the time this issue was most distinctly and most insistently raised by the young Baudouin de Courtenay (1845–1929) and his brilliant disciple M. Kruszewski (1851–1887). When still in the final stage of his scholarly career, F. de Saussure (1857–1913), discussing a book published in 1908 by his student A. Sechehaye, declared that Baudouin de Courtenay and Kruszewski "have come closer than anyone else to a theoretical view of language without going outside purely linguistic considerations, yet they remain unknown to the majority of Western scholars".[2] Deplorable ignorance about the theoretical positions of these two scholars has been repeatedly attested to by Western linguists.

In Kruszewski's first scientific study, his Warsaw University thesis *Zagovory* ("Spells") — a work written on a broad ethnological theme (finished in January 1875 and published the next year) — the established view of language as "a product of man's conscious activity" was opposed by the author's own conviction that "human consciousness and will" exert "only little influence" on the development of language.[3]

Early in his Warsaw student years Kruszewski had attempted to peruse the text of Baudouin's first university lecture delivered in St. Petersburg in December 1870 and reproduced in *Žurnal Ministerstva Narodnogo Prosveščenija* in 1871 under the title, "Nekotorye obščie zamečanija o jazykovedenii i jazyke" ("Some General Remarks on

---

[1] F. B. Bassin, *Problema bessoznatel'nogo* (Moscow, 1968), 55.
[2] F. de Saussure, *Cours de linguistique générale*, critical edition, ed. R. Engler, 4 (Wiesbaden, 1974), 43.
[3] M. Kruszewski, "Zagovory kak vid russkoj narodnoj poèzii", *Izvestija Varšavskogo Universiteta*, 1876.

Linguistics and Language").[4] But on this first attempted acquaintance with Baudouin's text, the depth and breadth of its ideas proved beyond the novice's powers, as he himself acknowledged afterwards. However, five years later, while teaching school in the backwater town of Troick in Orenburg Province and amassing thereby the means for scholarly apprenticeship under Baudouin at the University of Kazan', Kruszewski once again, and this time with acute understanding, read that same lecture of 1870 and in a letter to Baudouin in September 1876 confirmed his "inclination toward a philosophical, or rather, logical outlook on linguistics". The letter makes allusion to Baudouin's list of "forces acting in language": "I must say, I know nothing that could exercise in me a more magnetic attraction to the science of languages than the unconscious character of linguistic forces which prompted you, as I have only now noticed, to adjoin the term *unconscious* consistently in your enumeration of those forces. Happily for me, this fits perfectly with a notion that has long stuck in my mind, — I mean, the idea of the unconscious process in general, an idea that radically departs from the point of view of Hartmann. Precisely in order to clarify the difference, I spent my vacation engaged in laborious and tedious study of Hartmann's philosophy in its version by Kozlov. At the moment, of course, my pupils' lesson assignments have taken Hartmann's place but I hope to get back to him again."[5]

Already in Baudouin's master's thesis of 1870 (printed in Leipzig under the title "O drevnepol'skom jazyke do XIV-go stoletija" ["On Old Polish Before the 14th Century"] and defended by him at the Historical-Philological Faculty of the University of St. Petersburg) among other major points there is one that declares: "When considering even the apparently simplest processes going on in language, it is necessary to keep in mind the force of unconscious generalization by the action of which a people subsumes all the phenomena of its mental life under certain general categories."[6] Baudouin's inaugural lecture in St. Petersburg, the one whose insistence on unconscious factors had so impressed Kruszewski, designates by the term *forces* "general factors which bring about the development of language and condition its structure and content". In the summary appended to this published

---

[4] See J. Baudouin de Courtenay, *Izbrannye trudy po obščemu jazykoznaniju* 1 (Moscow, 1963), 47–77.
[5] The Polish original of this letter was published by Baudouin in *Szkice językoznawcze* 1 (Warsaw, 1904), 134. The book by E. von Hartmann is his *Filosofija bessoznatel'nogo* 1–2 (Moscow, 1873–75).
[6] *Izbrannye trudy* ... 1, 46.

lecture the individual factors for the most part are marked with a reference to their unconscious character.[7] Among such factors most prominently figure "*habit*, i.e. unconscious memory" and on the other hand, "unconscious *oblivion* and incomprehension (forgetting of what was not consciously known and incomprehension of what could not be understood consciously); such forgetting and incomprehension constituting not something inconsequential and negative (as would be the case in conscious mental operations) but something productive, positive and conducive to the new by dint of its prompting unconscious generalization to move in new directions". This tendency to save the memory's labor and to relieve it from an excess of mutually unbound details Baudouin will later call (in his Derpt paper of 1888) "a special kind of unconscious (*nieświadoma*) mnemonics".[8]

By pointing to an analogy with biology, Kruszewski enlarged upon his teacher's idea of disappearance as an essential condition of development, and in his *Očerk nauki o jazyke* ("An Outline of the Science of Language")[9] he held consistently to the notion that "destructive factors" are exceedingly beneficial for language" (chapters VII, VIII). Some fifteen years later the issue of "oblivion" as a regular base of linguistic transformations, the issue courageously posed by Baudouin on the threshold of his scientific activities, was once again raised for discussion by Arsène Darmesteter (1846–1888) in the chapter "Oubli ou Catachrèse" of his probing semantic book.[10]

In Baudouin's lecture of 1870 "unconscious generalization" was characterized as "*apperception*, i.e. a force by the action of which people subsume all the phenomena of their mental life under certain general categories", and to this he added a comparison of the systems of categories in language, which are "joined together by the force of unconscious generalization", with "the systems of the celestial bodies which operate under the influence of the force of gravity".[11] If the connection between a given linguistic entity and related formations is "forgotten in the feeling of the people", it stands to the side until it falls under the influence of "a new family of words or category of forms". Baudouin insists that "people's feeling for language is no fiction, no subjective illusion but a real and positive category (function); it may be defined in terms of its properties and effects, as it can be verified

---

[7] *Ibid.*, 53.
[8] *Szkice* ..., 71.
[9] Kazan', 1883.
[10] A. Darmesteter, *La vie des mots étudiée dans leur significations* (Paris, 1886).
[11] *Izbrannye trudy* ... 1, 38.

objectively and proved by fact".[12] In the interest of terminological accuracy, Baudouin and, following him, Kruszewski preferred not to speak of "consciousness" of language but precisely of "a feeling for language", i.e. its unconscious, intuitive apprehension.

If "unconscious generalization, apperception", in accordance with Baudouin's classification, "represents the centripetal force in language", then, conversely, "unconscious *abstraction*, the unconscious tendency toward division and differentiation", allows of comparison with the "centrifugal force", and the "struggle of all the forces enumerated conditions the development of language".

Later, in Baudouin's "Obščij vzgljad na grammatiku" ("A General View of Grammar"), a section of his *Podrobnaja programma lekcij* ("Annotated Program of Lectures") given at the University of Kazan' during the academic year 1876–77,[13] their author returned to an examination of all the forces acting in language which he had previously identified, insisting anew on their unconscious character. This time laws and forces were subjected to parallel examination as "*static*, i.e. operating in a synchronic position (state) of language" and "dynamic, giving rise to the development of language". In connection with the question of the influence of books "on the language of people with a literary education", Baudouin, both in his Kazan' program of 1876–77 and in his lecture of 1870,[14] was prepared to acknowledge yet another of the forces acting in language but this time a force "comparatively not very powerful", namely "the influence on language of the human *consciousness*": "Although the influence of the consciousness on language makes a fully conscious appearance only among certain individuals, its effects are, nevertheless, imparted to the whole people, and in that way the influence of the consciousness can and does impede the development of a language; it counteracts the influence of unconscious forces — forces which by and large promote a more rapid development of language — and does so precisely for the purpose of making language a common instrument for the unification and mutual comprehension of all contemporary members of a nation, and its forebears and descendants, as well. What results from this is a certain degree of inertness in languages exposed to the influence of the human consciousness in contradistinction to the rapid natural movement of languages unaffected by that influence."

---

[12] *Ibid.*, 60.
[13] *Ibid.*, 102.
[14] *Ibid.*, 102, 58f.

In Kruszewski's theory "language is something that stands entirely by itself in nature" due to the co-participation of "unconscious-psychical phenomena" (*unbewusstpsychischer Erscheinungen*) which are governed by specific laws.[15] The attempt to characterize the laws underlying linguistic structure as well as its development was one of the most original and, at the same time, most fertile contributions made by the linguist during his all too brief career.

As for Baudouin, at the very start of the new century, he, in contrast to his own earlier insistent references to "unconscious factors", began attributing more and more significance to "the irrefutable fact of the intervention of consciousness in the life of language". In his words, "the tendency toward an ideal linguistic norm" is coupled with "the participation of human consciousness in the life of language", in particular, "any linguistic compromise occurring between peoples speaking different languages" inevitably involves "a certain portion of conscious creativity" (from an article of 1908, "Vspomogatel'nyj meždunarodnyj jazyk" ["An Auxilliary International Language"]).[16]

On the whole, Baudouin's view on the mental bases of linguistic phenomena evolved in the direction of bridging the gap between the conscious and the unconscious. At the end of his 1899 speech to the Copernicus Society of Cracow he likened consciousness to a flame that casts light on single stages of mental activity; unconscious (*nieświadome*) psychical processes also have the capability of becoming conscious (*uświadomianie*), but their potential consciousness is actually identifiable with the unconscious (*nieświadomość*).[17]

Statements on the subject in question made by Saussure during his tenure as professor in Geneva closely tally with the basic initial positions of Baudouin and Kruszewski. Saussure makes a clearcut distinction between the "unconscious activity" (*l'activité inconsciente*) of the participants in verbal communication and the "conscious operations" (*opérations conscientes*) of the linguist.[18] According to Saussure, "the terms a and b in and of themselves are incapable of reaching the sphere of consciousness, while at the same time the very difference between a and b is always perceived by it".[19] Drafts of his inaugural lecture in

---

[15] M. Kruszewski, "K voprosu o gune", *Russkij filologičeskij vestnik* 5 (1881), 5; *Über die Lautabwechslung* (Kazan', 1881), 6.

[16] See J. Baudouin de Courtenay, *Izbrannye trudy* ... 2 (Moscow, 1963), 152.

[17] See J. Baudouin de Courtenay, "O psychicznych podstawach zjawisk językowych", *Przegląd filozoficzny* 4 (Warsaw, 1903), 170–171.

[18] F. de Saussure, *Cours de linguistique générale*, critical edition, ed. R. Engler, 2 (Wiesbaden, 1967), 310.

[19] *Ibid.*, 266.

Geneva, which was delivered in November of 1891, contain discussion concerning the participation in language phenomena of the act of will, in the course of which discussion Saussure revealed a series of gradations in both the conscious and the unconscious will (*dans la volonté consciente ou inconsciente*). With respect to all other comparable acts, the character of the verbal act seems to Saussure "the least deliberative, the least premeditated and at the same time the most impersonal of all" (*le moins réfléchi, le moins prémédité, en même temps que le plus impersonnel de tous*). Despite the considerable range of the differences he discussed, Saussure at the time acknowledged only the quantitative ones (*différence de degrés*) as real, relegating the qualitative differences (*différence essentielle*) simply to a deep-seated illusion.[20]

Franz Boas (1858–1942), the founder of American anthropology and linguistics, devoted considerable attention to the topic of the unconscious factor in the life of language, principally within his extensive "Introduction" to Part I of the multi-volume series, *Handbook of American Indian Languages* (1911). A section in the second chapter of the "Introduction" is entitled "Unconsciousness of Phonetic Elements" and opens with the remark that "the single sound as such has no independent existence" and that it never enters into the consciousness of the speaker but exists only "as part of a sound complex which conveys a definite meaning". Phonetic elements "become conscious" only as a result of analysis. A comparison of words differing only in a single sound makes it clear that "the isolation of sounds is a result of a secondary analysis".[21]

To the "Unconscious Character of Linguistic Phenomena" Boas returns in a substantial section of the fourth chapter of the same "Introduction".[22] This chapter is devoted to the relation between linguistics and ethnology, and it closes with a discussion of general linguistic topics from which the fifth, and final, chapter turns directly to the "Characteristics of American Languages".[23] Saussure's already mentioned thesis about the "difference in degree of consciousness" between linguistic structure and parallel ethnological patterns is similar to Boas' thinking on "the relation of the unconscious character of linguistic phenomena to the more conscious ethnological phenomena". Boas believes that we are dealing here with a contrast that is "only

[20] *Cours* ..., 4, 6.
[21] F. Boas, "Introduction", *Handbook of American Indian Languages* 1 (Washington, D.C., 1911), 23–24.
[22] *Ibid.*, 67–73.
[23] *Ibid.*, 78–83.

apparent"and that "the very fact of the unconsciousness of linguistic processes helps us to gain a clearer understanding of the ethnological phenomena, a point the importance of which cannot be underrated. *** It would seem that the essential difference between linguistic classifications never rises into consciousness, while in other ethnological phenomena, although the same unconscious origin prevails, these often rise into consciousness, and thus give rise to secondary reasoning and to reinterpretations."[24] Among phenomena which are experienced "entirely subconsciously" by the individual and by the whole people, the author provides examples from the areas of beliefs, fashions, manners and the rules of modesty.[25]

Boas saw the great advantage of linguistics in the always constantly unconscious character of the categories formed in language, which makes it possible to investigate the processes underlying those categories without being misled by the "distorting factors of secondary explanations which *** generally obscure the real history of the development of ideas entirely".[26]

Precisely the unconscious formation of grammatical categories and their interrelations, which act in language without their having to emerge into consciousness, prompts Boas to bring the available forces of linguistics to bear on an objective analysis of the systematic grouping of grammatical concepts characteristic for a given language or a given territorial league: "The occurrence of the most fundamental grammatical categories in all languages must be considered as proof of the unity of the fundamental psychological processes."[27] At the same time, Boas warns investigators against repeated egocentric efforts to foist upon remote languages the system of one's own grammatical categories or the system of categories the scholar has become used to while working on languages close to his own.[28]

The problem of unconsciousness occupies a position of even greater importance in the work of Edward Sapir (1884–1939), the most prominent continuer of Boas' linguistic and anthropological vistas. In his frank review of the troubles faced by the science of language, "The Grammarian and his Language", Sapir advanced the thesis that the "psychological problem which most interests the linguist is the inner

---

[24] *Ibid.*, 67.
[25] *Ibid.*, 67–70.
[26] *Ibid.*, 71.
[27] *Ibid.*
[28] *Ibid.*, 35ff.

structure of language in terms of unconscious psychic processes".[29] If language possesses certain formal ways of expressing causal relations, the ability to receive and transmit them has nothing whatsoever to do with the ability to apprehend causality as such. Of these two abilities, the second bears a conscious, intellectual character and, like most conscious processes, requires a slower and more laborious development, whereas the former ability is unconscious and develops early without any intellectual efforts. In Sapir's judgment, the psychology that was available at the time his works were written did not seem altogether adequate to explain the formation and transmission of such submerged formal systems as are disclosed to us in the languages of the world. The language-learning process, "particularly the acquisition of a feeling for the formal set of the language", a process very largely unconscious, might possibly, "as psychological analysis becomes more refined", throw new light on the concept of "intuition", this intuition "being perhaps nothing more nor less than the 'feeling' for relations".[30]

In a work of the following year, "Sound Patterns in Language" (1925), in which he acutely posed the question of the speech sound systems, Sapir argued that an essential prerequisite for understanding phonetic processes is the recognition of a general patterning of speech sounds. An unconscious feeling for the relation between sounds in language promotes them to genuine elements of a self-contained "system of symbolically utilizable counters".[31] Further development in the study of the sound structure of language helped Sapir evolve a theory, in his 1933 article, "The Psychological Reality of Phonemes", regarding unconscious "phonological intuitions" and, in particular, to substantiate his own fruitful thesis, suggested by his years of fieldwork on the unwritten native languages of America and Africa, that not phonetic elements but phonemes are what the native member of the speech community hears.[32]

Of all Sapir's research works the one that most broadly covers the topic of the unconscious is the paper, "The Unconscious Patterning of Behavior in Society", which he prepared for the symposium "The Unconscious" held in Chicago during the spring of 1927. The author starts from the assumption that all human behavior, both individual and social, displays essentially the same types of mental functioning, both conscious and unconscious, and that the concepts of the social and the

---

[29] E. Sapir, *Selected Writings* (Berkeley-Los Angeles: Univ. of California, 1949), 152.
[30] *Ibid.*, 155-156.
[31] *Ibid.*, 35.
[32] *Ibid.*, 47ff.

unconscious are by no means mutually exclusive.[33] Sapir enquires why we are inclined to speak, "if only metaphorically", about forms of social behavior, of which the ordinary individual has no intelligible knowledge, as socially unconscious, and he answers his own question by pointing out that all those "relations between elements of experience which serve to give them their form and significance are more powerfully 'felt' or 'intuited' than consciously perceived". "It may well be", Sapir goes on to say, "that, owing to the limitations of the conscious life, any attempt to subject even the higher forms of social behavior to purely conscious control must result in disaster." Most instructive in Sapir's eyes is the ability of the child to master the most complex linguistic structure, whereas "it takes an unusually analytical type of mind to define the mere elements of that incredibly subtle linguistic mechanism which is but a plaything of the child's unconscious".[34]

Unconscious patterning covers the entire range of features of speech, including, along with the directly significant forms, the inventory of sound units and configurations; and unconscious patterning belongs to the practice of the ordinary members of the speech community or in Sapir's phrase, "the unconscious and magnificently loyal adherents of thoroughly socialized phonetic patterns".[35] The paper's final conclusion is noteworthy. Sapir believes that "in the normal business of life it is useless and even mischievous for the individual to carry the conscious analysis of his cultural patterns around with him. That should be left to the student whose business it is to understand those patterns. A healthy unconsciousness of the forms of socialized behavior to which we are subject is as necessary to society as is the mind's ignorance, or better unawareness, of the workings of the viscera to the health of the body."[36]

In the final third of the last century and the first third of the present one, the topic of the conscious and unconscious as two co-participating factors in language became the object of wide-ranging discussion in the works of the leading theorists of linguistics, as is evident even from our brief review of statements by Baudouin, Kruszewski, Saussure, Boas, and Sapir. Their considerable value notwithstanding, it can hardly be doubted that their primary assumptions need careful and penetrating reexamination.

Only in recent time has linguistics taken cognizance of the "metalingual function" as one of the basic verbal functions. In other

[33] *Ibid.*, 544.
[34] *Ibid.*, 548–549.
[35] *Ibid.*, 555.
[36] *Ibid.*, 558f.

words, utterances can have direct reference to the linguistic code and its constituents. F. F. Fortunatov (1848–1914), in a remarkable lecture delivered to a congress of teachers of Russian in 1903, argued with good reason that "the phenomena of language, in a certain respect, themselves belong to the phenomena of thought".[37] Metalingual operations constitute an important and indispensable part of our speech activity; through paraphrase, synonymy or via the explicit decoding of elliptical forms, they make it possible to assure full and accurate communication between speakers (see the present author's address of 1956 for the Linguistic Society of America, "Metalanguage as a Linguistic Problem", *supra*, 113–121). Instead of unconsciously automatized means of expression, the metalingual function brings into play the cognizance of verbal components and their relations, thereby significantly reducing the applicability of the inveterate idea, repeated by Boas, that, supposedly, "the use of language is so automatic that the opportunity never arises for the fundamental notions to emerge into consciousness" and for these notions to become a subject of our thought (*supra*, 153).

In 1929 Aleksandr Gvozdev, a dedicated investigator of infant speech, provided an engaging answer to the crucial but long neglected question as to "how preschool children see the phenomena of language";[38] and this answer has brought in its train a rich, although still far from complete, series of evidential materials on the subject such, for instance, as we find in the works of Čukovskij, Švačkin, Kaper, and Ruth Weir.[39] All these investigations and our own observations testify to a persistent "reflection about language on the part of children"; what is more, the child's initial language-acquisition is accompanied and secured by a parallel development of the metalingual function, which enables the child to delimit the verbal signs he masters and to elucidate for himself their semantic applicability. "Virtually every new word stimulates an effort in the child to interpret its meaning", Gvozdev declares and, with that declaration in mind, cites questions and thoughts typical for children. For example: "Are *sdoxla* and *okolela* the same?" (both verbs translate as "has died" with presumed reference to an animal and with different emotional shades); "It's people you say *tolstyj* ('fat') about, but about a

---

[37] F. F. Fortunatov, *Izbrannye trudy* 2 (Moscow, 1957), 435.
[38] A. N. Gvozdev, *Voprosy izučenija detskoj reči* (Moscow, 1961), 31–46.
[39] K. Čukovskij, *Ot dvux do pjati* (Moscow, 1966, 19th ed.); N. X. Švačkin, "Psixologičeskij analiz rannix suždenij rebenka. Voprosy psixologii reči i myšlenija", *Izvestija Akademii Pedagogičeskix Nauk* 6 (Moscow, 1954); W. Kaper, *Einige Erscheinungen der kindlichen Spracherwerbung im Lichte des vom Kinde gezeigten Interesses für Sprachliches* (Groningen, 1959); R. H. Weir, *Language in the Crib* (The Hague, 1962).

bridge you say *širokij* ('wide')"; "*Ubirajut* ('remove or dress up') means *ukrašajut* ('decorate'), doesn't it?" — asked in connection with the Christmas tree. Morphological analysis appears both in the making up of words by children and in their conscious translation of a newly created lexical item into the habitual language: "The stove's all seived up (*prorešetela*)." Father: "What?" — "It's gotten like a seive (*rešeto*)."[40]

Metalingual competence from the age of two turns the young child into a critic and corrector of the speech of surrounding people[41] and even arouses in him not merely "unconscious" but also "deliberate antagonism" toward "adult" speech: "Mamma, let's agree you can call them [sled runners] your way *poloz'ja* and I'll call them my way *povoz'ja*. After all, they *vozjat* (from the verb *vozit'* 'to carry by conveyance'), not *lozjat* (the child's ad hoc formation)."[42] Once they became aware of a pejorative tinge to the diminutive suffix *-ka*, the children whom Čukovskij observed were ready to protest against extensive use of this morpheme: "It's not nice to say bad words. You should say *igola s nitoj* (child's ad hoc formation), not *igolka s nitkoj* ('needle and thread')." Or: "She's a *koša* (child's ad hoc formation instead of the usual *koška* 'cat') because she's good. I'll call her *koška* only if she's bad." In the child's "conquest of grammar" his conscious awareness of linguistic categories generates creative experiments with such intricate morphological processes as aspectual opposition in verbs on the one hand — "*vyk, vyk i privyk* ('used, used and got used to'; *vyk* is the child's ad hoc formation of an imperfective past tense counterpart to the perfective past tense form *privyk*);[43] on the other hand, the child's effort to make a conscious connection between the form and the idea of grammatical gender may produce curious results: "*Luna* ('moon', feminine gender) is the wife of *mesjac* ('moon', masculine gender), while *mesjac* looks like a man"; "Is *stol* ('table', masculine gender) a daddy? *Tarelka* ('plate', feminine gender) — a mommy?"[44] A number of other typical examples of this same "linguistic consciousness" is given in Čukovskij's book: "Why is he *papa* ('daddy')? He should be *pap*, not *papa* (*pap* is the child's arbitrary application of masculine declension, 'daddy', in view of the papa's chiefly feminine declension)"; "You, Tanya (a girl's name), will be the *sluga* (interpreted as a female noun because of its prevalently feminine declension) and Vov (a boy's name) will be a *slug* (transposed

---

[40] Gvozdev, *op. cit.*, 40, 38.
[41] Cf. Švačkin, *op. cit.*, 127.
[42] Čukovskij, *op. cit.*, 62.
[43] Ibid., 42.
[44] Gvozdev, *op. cit.*, 44.

into a purely masculine paradigm)"; "You're a *muščin!*" (the child's ad hoc hyper-masculine version of *muščina* 'man', a masculine noun of chiefly feminine declension); "Maybe Musja (a girl's name) could have a *carapina* ('scratch', feminine noun), but I'm a boy — I'd have a *carap* (child's ad hoc masculine alteration of *carapina*)"; "*Pšenica* ('wheat', feminine noun) is the mommy and *pšeno* ('millet grain', neuter noun) is her baby" [compare the coercion of grammatical gender and the possessive adjectives in the folk nursery rhyme — "For the woman's rye (*rož'* 'rye', is a feminine noun), For the man's oats (*oves* 'oats', is a masculine noun), For the girl's buckwheat (*greča* 'buckwheat', is a feminine noun), For the kiddy's millet (*proso* 'millet', is a neuter noun) — with the similar childlike interpretation of the neuter gender].

Underlying a piece of humorous play described by Gvozdev resides a conscious awareness of the bare syntactic matrix: Mother is sitting and knitting. Papa asks: "Who's that?" Two-year-old Ženja, according to Gvozdev, obviously intentionally: "Papa." — "Doing what?" — "Writing." — "Writing what?" — "Apple", and he was quite pleased with his answers.[45] The minimal linguistic component follows suit, becoming the object of the child's conscious scrutiny: according to Gvozdev, a child, upon hearing the word *došlyj* ("clever") in a conversation, made the remark: "*Došlyj* — that's easy to mix up with *doxlyj* ('dead')", as if "warning himself against confusing two words of similar sound", differing only by a single distinctive feature.

There is evidence testifying to the conscious awareness on the part of small children to sounds and forms used by playmates who differ from them in age, in origin or who come from a different dialectal background. Finally, the references made by observers to the complex temporal aspect in the speech repertoire of young children are extremely instructive. Such children not infrequently display an amazing ability to remember stages they are about to pass through or have already passed through in their own language experience. Children reveal an ambivalent attitude toward the new verbal material they have barely just acquired. They reveal either eagerness to use the new material as widely as possible or, on the contrary, mistrust and reluctance. For example, a little four-year-old girl, when asked by her father why she favored saying *vov*, although she had learned to pronounce the word correctly as *volk* ("wolf"), replied, "It isn't so awful and mean that way."[46]

[45] *Ibid.*, 39.
[46] *Ibid.*, 36.

The active role of the metalingual function remains in force, undergoing considerable changes, to be sure, throughout our entire life and maintains the constant flux between the conscious and the unconscious in all our speech activity. Incidentally, an analogy, productive in this connection, between ontogenetic and phylogenetic relations makes possible a comparison of the concatenated stages of child speech development with the dynamics of the language community, in which successive changes experienced by the community allow of conscious awareness on the part of the speakers and do so inasmuch as the start and finish of any change inevitably undergo a stage of more or less prolonged coexistence, which relegates separate stylistic roles to the initial and to the terminal points of development. If, for example, a linguistic change consists in the loss of a phonological distinction, the verbal code will temporarily maintain both the explicit start of the development and its elliptical finish, each serving as a stylistic variant in the overall code and each, moreover, allowing for conscious awareness.

However, in our habitual use of language the deepest foundations of verbal structure remain inaccessible to the linguistic consciousness; the inner relations of the whole system of categories indisputably function, but they function without being brought to rational awareness by the participants in verbal communication, and only the intervention of experienced linguistic thought, equipped with a rigorous scientific methodology, is able to approach the innermost workings of linguistic structure consciously. Using a few graphic examples, we once demonstrated that the unconscious elaboration of the most hidden linguistic principles frequently constitutes the very essence of verbal art, however one gauges the differences between Schiller's belief that the poetic experience begins *"nur mit dem Bewusstlosen"* and Goethe's more radical thesis affirming the unconsciousness of all truly poetic creativity and casting doubt on the value of all authorial rational excogitations.[47]

The fact, observed by linguists, that the conscious and the unconscious factors form a constant bond in verbal experience needs the complementary interpretation of psychologists. We take the occasion of the Tbilisi International Symposium on the Unconscious to express the hope that the concept of "set" now in the process of development by the Georgian school of psychology will make it possible to define more closely the constant co-participation of the dual components in any kind of speech activity. As stated in the work of D. N. Uznadze (1886–1950),

---

[47] R. Jakobson, "Subliminal Verbal Patterning in Poetry", *Selected Writings* III (The Hague-Paris-N.Y., 1981), 136ff.

the eminent initiator of research on "the experimental bases of the psychology of set", conscious processes do not exhaust the content of our mind; aside from such processes, something else takes place in a human being which cannot be said to occur in the consciousness and yet exerts a decisive influence on the entire content of mental life. Such is what has been termed *set*, and Uznadze was inclined to think that without its participation "no processes as conscious phenomena could exist at all", and for the consciousness to start working in any particular direction, the presence of an active *set* was essential.[48]

A. S. Prangishvili, in his investigation of its governing principles, provided the concept of *set* with a new generalized definition: "Set invariably acts as an integral system with a constant group of characteristic features" — a formulation distinctly closer to the linguistic diagnosis.[49]

A. E. Sherozia, viewing conscious and unconscious experiences as colaterally subordinated and equally essential elements within "a single system of their relations", attaches to those experiences the "principle of complementarity" devised by Niels Bohr and insists on the necessity of a systematic confrontation of these two "correlative concepts" in view of the fact that "the concept of the unconscious is senseless taken independently of the concept of consciousness, and vice versa".[50] Following through on Uznadze's thoughts about "a specific set for language", Sherozia points the way to a psychological explanation and dialectical resolution of linguistic antinomies such as "the duality of the nature of the word — its individuality and its generality". An assertion of Sherozia's in particular, that our word "always bears a greater amount of information than our consciousness is able to extract from it, since at the basis of our words lie our unconscious linguistic sets",[51] corresponds with Sapir's supposition that to a large extent "the 'real world' is unconsciously built up on the verbal habits of the given group" and that not the same world "with different labels attached" but implicit differences of world outlook — "distinct worlds" — appear in the dissimilarity of languages.[52] This same principle was broadened and made more incisive by Sapir's perspicacious disciple, B. L. Whorf, who directed his efforts to inquiring into the effect of dissimilarities in the grammatical structure of languages on the difference in the perception

---

[48] D. N. Uznadze, *Psixologičeskie issledovanija* (Moscow, 1966), 179ff.
[49] A. S. Prangishvili, *Issledovanija po psixologii ustanovki* (Tbilisi, 1967), 56.
[50] A. E. Sherozia, *K probleme soznanija i bessoznatel'nogo psixičeskogo* 2 (Tbilisi, 1973), 8.
[51] *Ibid.*, 446.
[52] E. Sapir, *Selected Writings*, 162.

and appraisal of externally similar objects of observation.[53]

Sherozia comes close, in turn, to Sapir's thoughts on the necessity for restricting conscious analysis in the everyday practice of language (see above) with his persuasive surmise: "If we were to require our consciousness to have at its command everything that occurs in our language and speech *** it would have to reject such incessant labor."[54]

The theory of the integral system of connections between conscious and unconscious mental experiences now being erected on the "principle of relation" (*princip svjazi*) promises new vistas and unlooked-for finds in the domain of language, provided, of course, that psychologists and linguists engage in genuine and consistent collaboration directed toward eliminating two impediments — terminological disparity and oversimplified schematicism.

Presented as a lecture at the International Symposium on the Unconscious, Tbilisi, October 3, 1979, and published in Russian in *Bessoznatel'noe: Priroda, Funkcii, Metody, Issledovanija* 3, ed. A. S. Prangišvili, A. E. Šerozija, F. V. Bassin (Tbilisi, 1978). The English version reprinted here first appeared in the author's book *The Framework of Language* (Ann Arbor, 1980).

---

[53] B. L. Whorf, *Language, Thought, and Reality* (Cambridge, Mass.: M.I.T., 1956).
[54] *Op. cit.*, 453.

BRAIN AND LANGUAGE: CEREBRAL HEMISPHERES AND LINGUISTIC STRUCTURE IN MUTUAL LIGHT

I

Disruptions of language, and especially of its sound pattern, all provoked by diverse brain lesions, have posed a number of interdisciplinary questions point-blank and brought aphasia into the basic program of my studies in a manner parallel with the opposite, but nevertheless cognate, phenomena of language acquisition. The structural laws that govern the aphasic impairments of language were a problem cursorily pointed out in my address for the Fifth International Congress of Linguists which was to have been held in Brussels, September 1939 (see Jakobson, 1962, 317ff.).

In a paper presented at the Ciba Foundation Symposium on disorders of language (London, May 1963), I attempted to outline the linguistic viewpoint on aphasia and to defend the need for a classification of aphasic syndromes based on "thoroughly integrated medical and linguistic research". The study of aphasia could no longer bypass the pertinent fact that an intrinsically linguistic typology of aphasic detriments, drafted without regard to the anatomical data, yielded nonetheless a surprisingly coherent relational pattern remarkably close to the topography of those cerebral lesions which underlie the impairments. The three linguistic dichotomies of aphasic losses unwittingly approached the sixfold table of cerebral damages delineated by the prominent psychoneurologist A. R. Luria (cf. Jakobson, 1962, 289ff.). For the science of language these gradually emerging correspondences between the neural and linguistic fundamentals of an aphasic typology put an end to the randomly monistic "antilocalizationist theories" which strove to reduce the various types of aphasia to mere degrees of one single ailment (cf. Maruszewski, 35ff.; Luria, 1974). The question of the interconnection between the topography of the brain and the structure of language supplied the joint, coordinated research of the early sixties with new and wider outlooks.

II

As I pointed out in concluding remarks at the Symposium on Models for the Perception of Speech and Visual Form held in Boston, October 1964 (see Jakobson, 1971, 338), Donald Broadbent (1954) suggested and Doreen Kimura (1961) widely developed unusual experiments in dichotic hearing: a simultaneous two-channel reception of diverse auditory stimuli by the two ears. These tests proved that the right ear displays a better aptitude for a precise recognition of speech sounds, while the left differs from the right in exhibiting an efficient discrimination of all other acoustic units. (For references see Peuser, 250: Dichotomous Stimulation.) The privileged status of speech sounds in the right ear reveals the lateral pathway leading to the left hemisphere, as was vividly brought up in the discussion. We are faced with the substantial problem of assessing and explaining the difference between the speech components dependent on the left hemisphere and all other audible stimuli, tied exclusively to the right side of the brain. The discrimination between those central mechanisms controlling the linguistic sphere proper and those processing the perception and comprehension of all other sounds, whether produced by the human organs or of some extrinsic origin, was for a long time underestimated, disregarded, or even denied, whereas today the phonetic trend, preoccupied solely with speech sounds, becomes distinctly delimited from the nonspeech motor and acoustic domain.

At present, the gradually observed essential difference between the particular cerebral treatment of speech, on the one hand, and the remaining auditory phenomena, on the other hand, calls for further, much more comprehensive and specific scrutiny.

In addition to numerous medical examinations of patients "with stable, unilateral cortical lesions" (cf. Brenda Milner, 1975, 7), the ensuing progress in the investigation of the separate hemispheres profited from the split-brain experience connected with the section of the cerebral commissures, an operation performed on epileptics since the 1960's (cf. Gazzaniga & Sperry, 1967; Gazzaniga, 1970; Sperry, 1975). The conclusions drawn from these operations confirmed the intimate ties linking speech (and, also, at least certain varieties of writing and calculation) precisely with the left hemisphere — and what was particularly instructive — the connection between higher verbal processes and the left, dominant hemisphere. This connection proved instrumental in opening new insights into the structuration of language.

And now, unilateral electroconvulsive therapy (ECT), practiced on schizophrenic and on depressive patients, has been used in a most imaginative way to provide for the first time systematic data about brain and language in humans without fixed brain lesions. As the only preliminary effort in the same direction we may cite the Sodium Anytal injections reported by Milner (1975, 84f.), used to inactivate both hemispheres in turn. The fact that a unilateral ECT produces a short-term disruption of one hemisphere, a deficit followed by a gradual return to the normal state, permits comparisons never before feasible on such a scale. The procedure, developed since the late 1960's in some Russian medical centers, has been recently accompanied by minute and keen observations on changes in status and behavior after the unilateral shock.

Since the early 1960's the technique of unilateral electroconvulsive therapy underwent a considerable development (see e.g. Cannicott, 1963; Halliday et al., 1968), but the functional difference between the left- and right-sided shock lacked until recently any intense and systematic consideration. In the meanwhile, all we can say is that the temporal inactivation of one of the two hemispheres, depending upon the direction of the electric shock, results in opposite effects on the auditory as well as on the motor experiences of the patient.

For the preliminary evidence of this persistently progressing inquiry, see first and foremost the valuable publications sponsored by the Sečenov Institute of Evolutionary Physiology and Biochemistry at the Academy of Sciences (*Akademija Nauk* = AN) of the U.S.S.R.: the first, *Hearing and Speech of the Dominant and Nondominant Hemispheres*, written jointly by Balonov and Deglin (1976), and the second, *Unilateral Electroconvulsive Shock*, by the same authors and a few collaborators (1979). Substantial contributions to this research have been made by the eminent Russian expert in the science of language, Vjačeslav Ivanov, especially in his book *Even and Odd: the Asymmetry of the Brain and of Sign Systems* (1978) and in a later Tartu essay, "Semiotics of Oral Speech and the Functional Asymmetry of the Brain" (1979). Cf. also Bragina's and Dobroxotova's Russian book, *Functional Asymmetry and Psychopathology of the Focal Affections of the Brain* (1977), with its instructive perusal of the comparative inquiry into the relationship of the cerebral hemispheres.

Norman Geschwind's (1979) vigilant inquiry into the dependence of higher activities such as language "on specialized regions of the human brain" opens new vital questions for interdisciplinary research. While a linguist is obliged to stop at the functional asymmetry of the brain, Geschwind's rich neurological experience enables him to touch also on the arresting questions of the material, anatomic divergence between the two hemispheres (cf. Geschwind, 196; Galaburda et al., 1978).

III

After having outlined jointly with Linda Waugh a set of preliminary remarks and issues in *The Sound Shape of Language* (1979), the next step I would venture is a tentative answer to the question of the general criteria which separate the two spheres of auditory stimuli from each other — those processed by the left and those by the right hemisphere of the brain. The bifurcated cerebral localization of the two realms of constituents is so manifest that the question of those properties which encompass and unify each of the two varieties and discriminate them from each other inevitably arises.

First, the varied experiments with dichotic hearing; second, the evidence received from patients with split-brain operations; third, the examination of patients with one hemisphere damaged; and fourth and foremost, the comparative study of the temporary role played by the electroshocks when inactivating one of the hemispheres: all these sources agree in defining the exact range of the phenomena controlled by the left and those by the right hemisphere.

The disturbances of the sound pattern prove to be most rigorous in the abolishment of one-feature distinctions between phonemes (cf. Balonov, Baru & Deglin, 1975). The impoverishment and demolition of the phonemic, especially consonantal repertory sets in briefly after the shock, and the gradual reappearance of the former, habitual constitution takes from ten or twenty minutes to an hour-and-a-half (see *AN*, 1979, 70f. and 87). The relative chronology of this restitution should be thoroughly traced, as was suggested forty years ago at the Uppsala observations of the patients' verbal recovery from insulin shocks (see, now, Jakobson & Waugh, 34). In this way new data could be obtained for the ever timely question of similarities between the gradual restitution of ECT patients' speech and the progressive acquisition of children's language.

IV

The primary informative task of the ultimate components of language, the distinctive features and their phonemic bundles, requires that a mediate, even a multi-mediate relation be established before these elementary quanta, entities lacking by themselves "any singleness of reference" (see Sapir, *Selected Writings*, 34) and designating nothing but mere otherness, become organized into a cohesive referential complex. This network of language is under the full control of the left hemisphere.

As Balonov & Deglin conclude in the tenth, final chapter of their basic volume (*AN*, 1976, 182), "it appears evident that, as a rule, the left hemisphere carries out the classification of phonemes by proceeding from the distinctive features, supports the hierarchy of these features, and ensures herewith the stability of the language's phonological system". In turn, the process of inactivation undergone by the left hemisphere reveals a set of correspondences with the rules that underlie the ensuing disintegration of the given phonological system, on its auditory as well as motor level: cf. *AN*, 1976 (133, 136, 181f.) and *AN*, 1979 (103). As examples of symmetry between the dissolution of the vocalic and consonantal patterns, one may quote the relative stability of the poles of compactness — /a/ and /k/, as well as the parallel merger of tonality pairs like /u/ — /i/ and /p/ — /t/.

The even more mediate character of contextual, redundant features furthers the increase of their dependence on the left cerebral hemisphere. The frequently increasing scarcity of redundant variations in the speech of subjects with a temporal inactivation of the left hemisphere is a linguistic event that demands further attention.

V

In contradistinction to the multi-tiered involvement of the linguistic elements totally dependent on the intact activity of the left hemisphere, those sound phenomena which demand an unimpaired functioning of the right hemisphere all have in common one noticeable trait: they display a direct, immediate, ostensive relation between their external, material form and what is signaled. Our perception of speech sounds demands an apprehension of the sound pattern and of its cognitive functioning in a given language, whereas the identification of any nonspeech sound requires an immediate recognition of the stimulus perceived, its identification in form and meaning.

Both the experiments with dichotic hearing and the testimonies received from patients subjected to unilateral electroshocks have shown again and again the indispensable connection linking all these varied percepts, with the underlying activity of the right hemisphere. "Environmental noises such as a car starting, the sharpening of a pencil, water running, and oral emissions apart from speech — coughing, crying, laughing, humming, yawning, snoring, sniffling, sighing, panting or sobbing" were quoted as percepts controlled by the right hemisphere. Briefly, the latter processes any immediate audible manifestation of human and animal physiology and daily life, as well as motions stirred by the forces of nature (cf. Knox & Kimura, 1970; King & Kimura, 1972; Balonov & Deglin, 1977).

The allegiance of one, superficially similar sound to two different cerebral hemispheres is, one could say, prompted by Sapir's introductory discussion to his epochal "Sound Patterns of English" (see 33ff.), where he compares two physically more or less similar formations — the candle-blowing sound and the prevocalic *wh* of such words as *when* — the former "'a *directly* functional act', while the latter has *no direct* functional value, it is merely a link in the construction of a symbol": "in brief, the candle-blowing *wh* means business; the speech sound *wh* is stored-up play which can eventually fall in line in a game that merely refers to business." The former is obviously processed by the right, and the latter by the left hemisphere.

To return once more to the Russian observations made in unilateral shock therapy, "subjects with a temporarily inactivated right hemisphere were helpless when faced with a succession of distinct auditory stimuli which were perfectly recognizable as long as this hemisphere maintained its activity: the tinkling of bells, singing birds, splashing water, neighing horses, a howling snowstorm, a roaring lion, a crying child, a clatter of crockery, peals of thunder, a grunting pig, the clank of metal, the call of a rooster, a barking dog, a lowing cow, the sound of a furnace, a passerby's footsteps, a cooing dove, the rumble of a plane, cackling geese, a ringing telephone, the roar of waves at high tide. During the inactivation of the right hemisphere, the noise of applause was actually taken for the winnowing of grain, laughter for crying, a thunderstorm for an engine, the squeal of a pig for the noise of a Caterpillar tractor, the honking of geese for the croaking of frogs, a dog barking for the cackling of hens, the noise of a motorcycle for that of an animal" (see *AN*, 1976, Ch. 5; Jakobson & Waugh, 34f.).

VI

A peculiar place belongs to elements which permeate speech yet share the character of what one may call immediate signals. These particular ingredients of current discourse, listed loosely, without consistent delimitation, as interjections, exclamations, and ejaculations, stand outside the general syntactic patterning of language, and they are neither words nor sentences. They tend to differ from the phonological rules of usual vocabulary, and semantically they are reduced to stereotyped affective expressions.

As John Hughlings Jackson comments in his renowned essay of 1874 on the nature of brain duality (135), "the communist orator did not really make a blunder when he began his oration '*Thank God* I'm an atheist', for the expression *Thank God* is used by careless, vulgar people simply as an interjection, there being no thought at all about the primitive meaning". According to Jackson, "such ejaculations are verbal utterances more automatic than speech". It is characteristic that these zero parts of speech get easily misinterpreted or simply lost by subjects with a fully active left but simultaneously inactivated right hemisphere. The same situation frequently befalls violent swearing or cursing words and, on the other hand, endearments and other ritualized formulas of courtly etiquette. A similar plight embraces numerous parasitic elements such as "hem", and the slight, deliberate sound of a cough in the midst of an utterance (cf. Ivanov, 1979, 131).

The second section of the "Introduction" to Trubetzkoy's *Grundzüge der Phonologie* is entitled "Phonologie und Lautstilistik" and attempts to delineate the difference between phonological, sense-discriminating components proper and those stylistic modifications of speech sounds or of their sequences in discourse "by means of which emotionally tinged speech is distinguished from emotionally neutral, tranquil speech", either without any specification of the underlying emotion (e.g. German *schön* with a smaller or larger prolongation of the initial sibilant and with an additionally protracted vowel) or carrying a closer specification of the emotion meant, as for instance a tremor which is meant to render a feeling of fear. In both cases there is a thoroughly ostensive, immediate relation between the emotion and the means of signaling it. Such immediacy is a firm condition requiring the control of the right hemisphere, "mute" as well as "emoting" (Sperry, 11). A subject, without an activation of the right hemisphere, is liable to avoid any emotive ingredients, whereas the enactment of the right hemisphere makes the emotional shades of speech particularly apprehensible. Whatever common sound properties may be shared by the phonemic and emotive patterns of language, the dissimilar character of their use and their different cerebral location strikingly separate these two kinds of phenomena from each other.

When examining the role of the diverse emotives in speech, one must take into account Geschwind's judicious reminder (1979, 192) that the right hemisphere makes an important contribution to emotion and state of mind: "Lesions in the right hemisphere not only give rise to inappropriate emotional responses to the patient's own condition, but also impair his recognition of emotions in others. A patient with damage on the left side may not be able to comprehend a statement but in many cases he can still recognize the emotional tone with which it is pronounced. A patient with a disorder of the right hemisphere usually understands the meaning of what is said, but he often fails to recognize that it is spoken in an angry or a humorous way."

The inactivation of the right hemisphere imparts a monotonous, affectless character to the patient's utterances, and he loses the capacity of regulating his own voice in accordance with emotional situations. On the other hand, the reduction of the emotive ingredients leads the patient to a greater talkativeness. Thus the damping influence of the active right hemisphere moderates the verbal activity of the left hemisphere and increases the readability of the linguistic components. In this respect both hemispheres act in concert. One might recall that over one hundred years ago scientific intuition enabled the sagacious J. H. Jackson — especially in his essay of 1874 — to assign intellectual language to the left, and emotional to the right hemisphere (see 1958, p. 134). Already in 1866, the earliest of Jackson's notes on the physiology and pathology of language opens with the statement that "there are two modes of expression, the emotional and the intellectual" (see 1958, 121).

VII

The recent observations of speech in connection with unilateral electric shocks brought to light new, substantial proofs for the considerable independence of the sentential and, in particular, emotionally colored intonations. They emerge before children's acquisition of the sound pattern of their mother tongue, and in many aphasic instances we are faced with the mutual independence of such intonations and word phonology. The use of affirmative, interrogative, and avowedly emotional intonations outside of speech proper, or in mere mumbling sequences, provides additional proof for the autonomous occurrence of, so to say, extralinguistic intonational differences.

The experiments with dichotic hearing revealed the connection of such intonations solely with the right, yet by no means with the left hemisphere. Balonov's & Deglin's communications (*AN*, 1976, 171ff.) comprehensively show the independence of such kinds of intonations from the left hemisphere and place their appearance, clear perceptibility, and reproducibility under the normal activity of the right hemisphere: "In the period of the right hemisphere's inactivation the identification of intonations sharply worsens." All the data obtained find their obvious explanation in the immediacy of the signal value displayed by these intonations which serve, so to speak, as period, comma, question mark, exclamation point, or ellipsis.

The inactivation of the right hemisphere leads to a deficit in ostensive communication. In semiotic literature (see especially Osolsobĕ) this way of communication might be defined as "placing something at the disposal of the cognitive activity of a person". A couple of shorts and socks exposed in a window announces a haberdasher's shop. Ostension merges with synecdoche: the voice of a patient's wife, which he hears without seeing her, is her *pars pro toto*, just as the sound and/or grimace of yawning is an ostensive, synecdochic expression of the simulated or natural drowsiness of a fatigued or bored utterer. The presence of an emotive tinge in the speech sounds immediately introduces into the speaker's message information indicating his excitement.

VIII

In contradistinction to the left hemisphere, the right one secures the ability of the patient to identify such auditory signals as the voices of his acquaintances when he hears their speech without seeing them, whereas the subject with an inactivated right and active left hemisphere is unable to recognize the most familiar voices, even those of his wife and children, and he does not grasp the transition from one speaker to another. Briefly, all audible physiognomic symptoms cease to work for him, even such general ones as the recognition of the difference between male and female voices. Moreover, the question of the spatial source and direction of the voice heard remains unresolved: "Thus spatial hearing remains unaltered after left-sided shocks but appears disturbed after right-sided ones" (*AN*, 1979, 91).

The chief ability of the right hemisphere in the handling of auditory percepts consists in immediately changing them into a simple, concrete concept lying outside of language proper, disclosing the nearest contiguous source of the sound stimulus produced and heard.

The comparative analysis of speech samples generated and/or perceived during the inactivation of one of the hemispheres has been hitherto concentrated primarily on the phonic level of language. The no less important morphological, syntactical, and lexical levels of such a comparison have not yet yielded sufficient material for exact conclusions and have not yet attracted the systematic attention of investigators.

With the inactivation of the left hemisphere, the number of used and apprehended words and of their occurrences goes steadily down, as does the variety and length of their syntactic combinations and subordination levels: "After left-sided unilateral shocks one observes a shift toward a range of elementary, superficial formations, whereas the right-sided shocks are followed by a shift toward complex multi-leveled constructions." (*AN*, 1979, 75ff.)

The inactivation of the left hemisphere is particularly detrimental for verbs (except the simplest imperative formulas such as *stop* or *walk* or *help*) and for auxiliary words, while nominative forms of nouns, showing a much lower dependence on the context, are somewhat more under the control of the right hemisphere, especially when offering no complex word derivation, in particular no kinship with verbs. And finally, a higher resistability is exhibited by the most concrete and usual nouns (cf. Jakobson, 1980, 104f.; on the intricate question of verb-derived nouns see Wolf & Koff, 1970).

The immediacy of transition from the linguistic network to an extralinguistic reality makes a word less dependent upon the integrity of the left hemisphere. In this connection the extreme dependence of the so-called grammatical "shifters" (according to Jespersen's terminology) on the intact left hemisphere is most instructive, since the general meaning of a shifter comprises a simultaneous, double reference to the code and to the message (cf. Jakobson 1971, 130ff.). In contradistinction to the shifterless character of the noun, it is the compulsory participation of shifters in the structure of verbs which furthers an alienation between the verb and the right hemisphere. The disappearance of shifters from the range of grammatical categories and an atrophy of syntactic subordination are two characteristic effects called forth by the suppression of the left hemisphere.

Inactivation of the left hemisphere underlies the desemantization of words on their paradigmatic as well as syntagmatic axis. Ivanov (1978, 39ff., 45) has initiated a promising study of the distinctions and confusions between synonyms, antonyms, and homonyms that are committed by patients undergoing shock therapy. Changes in treatment of semantic similarities, contrasts, and contiguities in their relation to the withdrawal of single hemispheres promise to open new tempting outlooks.

The left hemisphere of the brain deals with categorization both in grammar and in the constructive operations of calculation (cf. Ivanov 1979, 126).

The captivating questions of the interconnection between script and cerebral hemispheres have been left aside in the present survey, in order not to embroil the discussion by including one more intricate, namely spatial factor.

The inquirers' find that, "after left-sided shocks, the entire scale of speech disturbances appears much more frequently among depressive patients than among schizophrenics" (*AN*, 1979, 69), requires further observations and analysis.

IX

The scrutiny of the varied sound stimuli remains incomplete as long as one has not intently compared the case of speech sounds with another system of auditory signs, namely with musical elements. The frequent lack of concurrence between aphasia and amusia has been repeatedly observed and described. The aphasic loss of speech is often combined with a preserved or even developed ability to sing.

Milner's observations of patients with temporal lobectomies for epilepsy evidenced the overwhelming connection of musical ability with the right hemisphere (1962), and Kimura's experiments in dichotic hearing support the same conclusion (1964). Kimura's "melodies test reconfirmed the finding, by then well established, of the left ear superiority/right hemisphere dominance" (Damásio, 146). The influence of unilateral shocks was keenly investigated by Balonov & Deglin (*AN*, 1976, Ch. 5 and Table 21; cf. Mindadze et al.). The inactivation of the right hemisphere hinders both the identification of short musical phrases and the recognition of familiar melodies, as well as the reproduction of motifs heard, whereas the inactivation of the left hemisphere favors and furthers all such accomplishments. Briefly, the situation with musical sounds creates a syndrome basically similar to the treatment of non-speech sounds and of the emotive ingredients in speech. The suppression of the right hemisphere may lead the patient as far as to a whimsical confusion between such dissimilar items as, for instance, the popular Russian song "Volga, Volga" and the melody of the rumba. The relative immediacy of musical perception explains the decisive role of the right hemisphere in the recognition, discrimination, and identification of phrases and melodies, as well as in their execution (Damásio, 151).

There is no doubt, however, that the question of musical perception still remains much less investigated than the various questions of verbal percepts, and that several fundamental musical problems await further and deeper inquiry. The partial deviations from the dominance of the right hemisphere in regard to musical perception, which have been incidentally noticed (see Bever & Chiarello; Gates & Bradshaw), must advance the search for their delineation and ultimate explanation. What must be particularly remembered is the variety of musical codes, which imposes an obligation upon the explorer to learn to discount from his questionnaire all those elements which are outside the basic musical perception of his examinees. More specifically, it is easy to comprehend why the similarity of accustomed, recalled melodies is more closely linked to the right hemisphere, in contradistinction to the recognition of unfamiliar pieces, a procedure which unwittingly opens the question of their underlying code and which may thus attract the left hemisphere, with its codifying specialization. The fundamental trait of musical signs, namely "*imputed similarity*", seems to be the true key to the unexpected, puzzling examples of their shift to the left hemisphere (cf. Jakobson, 1980, 22ff.).

In the confrontation of music with language the comparison must be confined solely to language in its poetic function.

One should also mention the frequent confusion examiners undergo between disability in perceiving music and in reading notes; sometimes such a mix-up embroils the task of assigning music to one of the two hemispheres.

At last, we are met with a peculiar analogy: the right hemisphere manifests a greater ability and concentration in identifying musical phrases and/or melodies precisely in the event that the left hemisphere remain inactivated (*AN*, 1979, 85ff.; Table 8.8), and this relation surprisingly corresponds to the greater talkativeness and verbal preciseness in speech of the left hemisphere when the right one is not working, as compared to the intact activity of both hemispheres.

x

In a stimulating paper devoted to "the functional asymmetry of the brain", Bragina & Dobroxotova have developed their view that the brain's hemispheres demonstrate different temporal orientations: "the right is turned into the past, the left into the future.*** The leftside hemisphere is responsible for supplying abstract cognition. Sensitive cognition leans on the right space and on the past, whereas abstract cognition leans on the left space and on future time" (pp. 137, 146). The authors underscore the fact that, in contradistinction to the past, the future "has not yet been given for the subject's sensible experience and cannot serve as support for the formation of sensitive images".

These considerations find an unexpected, memorable, and well-grounded correspondence in the philosophical writings of Charles Sanders Peirce (cf. *infra*, 248–253). In his contraposition of two kinds of signs, *icon* and *symbol*, the former is defined as "a representamen of what it represents and for the mind that interprets it as such, by virtue of its being as *immediate* image, that is to say by virtue of characters which belong to it in itself as a sensible object" (IV #447). The mode of being of the symbol is, in Peirce's conception of this term, different from that of the icon. While the icon has such being as belongs to *past* experience, the nature of a symbol, especially such as a verbal sign or the network of language, is the actually working *general* rule. According to Peirce, "whatever is truly general refers to the indefinite future.*** It is a potentiality; and its mode of being is *esse in futuro*." (II #148.) "The value of a symbol is that it serves to make thought and conduct rational and enables us to predict the future." (IV #448.)

Here lies the nucleus of an explanation for those "most surprising recent findings" which were pointed out by Geschwind (1979, 192): namely, "behaviors denoting a catastrophic reaction or indicating an anxious-depressive orientation of mood" are particularly frequent among left brain-damaged patients, "chiefly in subjects with severe aphasia". Such reactions "appear generally after repeated failures in verbal communication" (Gainotti, 53).

Likewise, the experience with unilateral electric shocks has confirmed the salient fact of "roughly expressed, negative emotions produced by the suppression of the left hemisphere" (Ivanov, 1978, 107), and hence by the atrophy of verbal symbols. "The negative emotional shift" stirred up by the left-sided shock can drive the grief and sorrow of a depressive patient to "a nightmarish terror" (*AN*, 1979, 96f.). The subject suffers from being deprived of the patterned symbols needed to program his future. It is with the functions of the "verbal hemisphere" that Ivanov connects "the realization of an individual as a single whole" (1979, 135).

The agnosia of symbolic rules and systems marks the inactivation of the left hemisphere. It occurs in an opposite sense if joined to the inactivation of the right hemisphere, and the consequent agnosia of ostension: when *res tota de parte* is no longer recognized by the subject.

The bipolar difference between these two opposite kinds of agnosia — in direct correspondence with the two contrary directions of the unilateral shocks — has found a telling illustration in the recent Russian report on the development of ECT (*AN*, 1979, 92ff.). During the inactivation of the left hemisphere the patient loses his "formal" orientation in time based on the conventional codes of watch and calendar symbols but is prone to maintain the direct, subjective evaluation of the time run, whereas the right-side inactivation preserves the formal responses while abolishing the immediate subjective chronology.

The question of the interrelation between an active hemisphere and an inactivated one opens the way to comparisons between joint active hemispheres with individual variations as to their functional hierarchy; the significance of these individual variations for characterological studies is beyond any doubt.

XI

Two sets of questions are brought up by progressing neurolinguistic research: first, the interhemispheric topics demand an ever closer linguistic, or to put it more exhaustively, semiotic approach; and secondly, we face a consistently interdisciplinary study of aphasic problems in connection with a difference in the affected zones of the left hemisphere. This inquiry, opened around the 1870's, most tangibly by the medical experts — Paul Broca, 1824–1880 (see 1888), J. H. Jackson, 1835–1911 (see now 1958), and Carl Wernicke, 1848–1905 (cf. Geschwind, 1967, Eggert, 1977) — still awaits new replies to the accumulated cruxes.

Experiments with unilateral electric shocks have already shown that this new technique can and will cast light not only on the interplay of both hemispheres, but also on the zonal subdivisions within the dominant (left) hemisphere, and on the correlative typology of aphasic impairments. As exemplified by Balonov & Deglin (*AN*, 1976, 191), the left-side electric shocks, with respect to the placement of convulsive electrodes more backwards or forwards, patently help to elucidate the substantial difference between postero-temporal and fronto-temporal lesions of the brain, a distinction which finds its expression in two opposite linguistic syndromes of aphasia. In connection with the continuous development of varied clinical observations and trials, such a leading explorer in the analysis of traumatic aphasia as A. R. Luria, in his studies of the seventies (see particularly 1973, 1974, and 1977), reached a final agreement with the earlier efforts on the linguistic side to delineate and explicate the dichotomous principles of aphasic disorders, even though "we don't yet know in detail the psychological features and physiological mechanisms underlying these impairments" (1973, 64).

Although at first glance these linguistic distinctions seemed to be "clinically insignificant" and although originally they found "no firm support in neurological characteristics", precisely the same linguistic distinctions have finally appeared to Luria as fundamental for the study of aphasia and at last "firmly supported by contemporary ideas of the functional organization of the human brain" (1977, 243). Thus the basic binary concepts viewed in the linguistic quest as the key to understanding the obvious dichotomy of aphasic disturbances, namely dyads such as Encoding/Decoding, Syntagmatic/Paradigmatic, and Contiguity/Similarity (cf. Jakobson, 1971, 229–259, 289–333; 1980, 93–111), gradually gained access in the advanced neuropsychological treatment of aphasic enigmas.

At present, those governing functions of the brain which are connected with the output of speech and with its input lend themselves to an attentive examination, and it seems as if the joint efforts of linguists and neurologists are summoned to suggest and open ever deeper insights both into the structure of language with reference to the brain and into the structure of the brain with the help of language. The necessary initial step on this path has been the delineation of the set of internal functional convergences which specify each of the cerebral hemispheres; these two heterogenous sets prove to form a cardinal dichotomous system of diametrically opposite, though complementary, properties, and such a state of affairs compels the maturing discipline of neurolinguistics to examine any display of one hemisphere with an unfailing reference to its counterpart on the other side of the brain.

It has been necessary to draw up a list of identifications and distinctions processed solely by the given hemisphere and inaccessible to the other hemisphere. The mutually exclusive stocks of the two hemispheres demand a clear delineation of the "many still rather ill-defined processes" which fall under the right hemisphere (cf. Milner, 1975, 83), but actually the immediacy of their signification offers us the sought-for definition. Thus, e.g., the *mediacy* of phonological devices, such as a distinction of higher and lower pitch in a polytonic language like Thai, explains the dependence of this distinctive feature on the left hemisphere, as has been proved by experiments with dichotic hearing and with unilateral shocks (cf. Jakobson & Waugh, 45). On the other hand, the *immediate* signification justifies the expected competence of the right hemisphere when, for instance, a higher pitch signals either an interrogative sentence or an emotive passage in the speaker's words, or finally, the presence of a female's voice in the discourse.

To conclude with a telling case (cf. Monrad-Krohn, 1947): A lesion of the left hemisphere, which was suffered by a Norwegian woman from a piece of shrapnel, cancelled the role of pitch in her native word pattern but released the latter's wider use in emotive variations to be processed by the right hemisphere. Each of the two signal systems — the immediate as well as the mediate one — is accessible to one single hemisphere: immediate signals can be processed only by the right hemisphere and mediate ones by the left.*

Completed in Cambridge, Mass. in April 1980 and first published as volume 4 of *New York University Slavic Papers* (Columbus, Ohio: Slavica Publishers, 1980).

---

* To my friends Norman Geschwind and Allan Keiler I am indebted for their enlightening suggestions and considerations.

REFERENCES

AN (1976) = Akademija Nauk SSSR — Institut Èvoljucionnoj Fiziologii i Bioximii Imeni I. N. Sečenova, *Slux i reč' dominantnogo i nedominantnogo polušarij* by Balonov, Lev & Vadim Deglin, Leningrad.
AN (1979) = Akademija Nauk etc., *Unilateral'nyj èlektrosudorožnyj pripadok* by Balonov, Lev, D. Barkan & V. Deglin, Leningrad.
Balonov, L., Baru, A. & Deglin, V. (1975), "Identifikacija sintezirovanyx glasnopodobnyx stimulov v uslovijax prexodjaščej inaktivacii dominantnogo i nedominantnogo polušarij", *Fiziologija čeloveka* 1, 395–404.
Balonov, L. & Deglin, V. (1977), "Vosprijatie zvukovyx nerečevyx obrazov (sluxovoj i muzykal'nyj gnozis) v uslovijax inaktivacii dominantnogo i nedominantnogo polušarij", *Fiziologija čeloveka* 3, 415–423.
Bever, T. G. & Chiarello, R. (1974), "Cerebral dominance in musicians and non-musicians", *Science* 185, 537–539.
Bragina, N. N. & Dobroxotova, T. A. (1977), *Funkcional'naja asimmetrija i psixopatologija očagovyx poraženij mozga*, Moscow.
Bragina, N. N. & Dobroxotova, T. A. (1977), "Problema funkcional'noj asimmetrii mozga", *Voprosy filosofii* 2, 135–150.
Broadbent, D. E. (1954), "The Role of Auditory Localization in Attention and Memory", *Journal of Experimental Psychology* 47, 191–196.
Broca, P. (1888), *Mémoires sur le cerveau de l'homme*, Paris.
Cannicott, S. M. (1963), "The Technique of unilateral electroconvulsive therapy", *American Journal of Psychiatry* 120, 477–380.
Damásio, A. R. & Damásio, Hanna (1977), "Musical Faculty and Cerebral Dominance", *Music and the Brain* ed. by M. Critchley et al., Springfield, 141–155.
Deglin, V. (1970), "O lateralizacii mexanizma èmocional'noj okraski povedenija", *Farmakologičeskie osnovy antidepressionogo povedenija*, Leningrad, 158–162.
Deglin, V. & Nikolaenko, N. (1975), "O roli dominantnogo polušarija v reguljacii èmocional'nyx sostojanij čeloveka", *Fiziologija čeloveka* 1, 418–426.
Eggert, G. H. (1977), *Wernicke's Works on Aphasia: A Sourcebook and Review*, The Hague.
Gainotti, Guido (1972), "Emotional behavior and hemispheric side of the lesion", *Cortex* 8, 41–55.
Galaburda, A. M., LeMay, M., Kemper, T. L. & Geschwind, Norman (1978), "Right-Left Asymmetries in the Brain", *Science* 199, 852–856.
Gates, Anne & Bradshaw, J. L. (1977), "Music Perception and Cerebral Asymmetries", *Cortex* 13, 390–401.
Gazzaniga, M. S. (1970), *The bisected brain*, New York.
Gazzaniga, M. S. & Sperry, R. W. (1967), "Language after Section of the Cerebral Commissures", *Brain* 90, 131–148.
Geschwind, N. (1967), "Wernicke's Contribution to the Study of Aphasia", *Cortex* 3, 449–463.
Geschwind, N. (1979), "Specializations of the Human Brain", *Scientific American* 3, 180–199.

Halliday, A. M., Davidson, K., Browne, M. W. & Kreeger, L. C. (1968), "Comparisons of the Effects on Depression and Memory of Lateral E.C.T. and Unilateral E.C.T. to the Dominant and Non-Dominant Hemispheres", *British Journal of Psychiatry* 114, 997–1012.

Ivanov, Vjačeslav V. (1978), *Čet i nečet; asimmetrija mozga i znakovyx sistem*, Moscow.

Ivanov, Vjačeslav V. (1979), "Nejrosemiotika ustnoj reči i funkcional'naja asimmetrija mozga", *Acta et Commentationes Universitatis Tartuensis* 481, 121–142.

Jackson, J. H. (1958), *Selected Writings*, ed. by J. Taylor, II, New York.

Jakobson, R. (1962), *Selected Writings* I, The Hague.

Jakobson, R. (1971), *Selected Writings* II, The Hague.

Jakobson, R. (1980), *The Framework of Language*, Ann Arbor.

Jakobson, R. & Waugh, L. (1979), *The Sound Shape of Language*, Bloomington, Ind. and London.

Kimura, D. (1961), "Cerebral Dominance and the Perception of Verbal Stimuli", *Canadian Journal of Psychology* 15, 166–171.

Kimura, D. (1964), "Left-Right Differences in the Perception of Melodies", *Quarterly Journal of Experimental Psychology* 16, 355–358.

King, F. L. & Kimura, D. (1972), "Left-Ear Superiority in Dichotic Perceptions of Vocal Nonverbal Sounds", *Canadian Journal for Psychology* 26, 111–116.

Knox, C. & Kimura, D. (1970), "Cerebral Processing of Nonverbal Sounds in Boys and Girls", *Neuropsychologia* 8, 227–237.

Luria, A. R. (1973), "Two Basic Kinds of Aphasic Disorders", *Linguistics* 115, 57–66.

Luria, A. R. (1974), "Language and Brain: Towards the Basic Problems of Neurolinguistics", *Brain and Language* 1, 1–14.

Luria, A. R. (1977), "The Contribution of Linguistics to the Theory of Aphasia", *Roman Jakobson — Echoes of His Scholarship*, ed. by D. Armstrong & C. H. van Schooneveld, Lisse, 237–251.

Maruszewski, M. (1975), *Language Communication and the Brain*, The Hague.

Milner, B. (1962), "Laterality Effects in Audition", *Interhemispheric Relations and Cerebral Dominance*, ed. by V. B. Mountcastle, Baltimore, 177–195.

Milner, B. (1975), "Hemispheric Specialization: Scope and Limits", *Hemispheric Specialization and Interaction*, ed. by B. Milner, Cambridge, Mass., 75–88.

Mindadze, A. A., Mosidze, V. M. & Kakuberi, T. D. (1975), "O muzykal'noj funkcii pravogo polušarija mozga čeloveka", *Communications of the Georgian Academy of Sciences* 79, 457–459.

Monrad-Krohn, G. M. (1947), "Dysprosody or Altered Prosody in Language", *Brain* 70, 405–415.

Osolsobě, I. (1967), "Ostension as the Limit Form of Communication and Its Significance in Art", *Estetika* 14, Prague, Czech paper 2–23 with an English summary.

Peirce, Charles Sanders (1958), *Collected Papers* II and IV, ed. by A. W. Burks, Cambridge, Mass.

Peuser, G. (1977), *Sprache und Gehirn: Eine Bibliographie zur Neurolinguistik*, Munich.

Sapir, Edward (1949), *Selected Writings*, Berkeley and Los Angeles.
Sperry, R. W. (1975), "Lateral Specialization in the Surgically Separated Hemispheres", *Hemispheric Specialization and Interaction*, ed. by B. Milner, Cambridge, Mass., 5–19.
Trubetzkoy, N. S. (1939), *Grundzüge der Phonologie = Travaux du Cercle Linguistique de Prague* 7; English translation by C. A. M. Bultaxe (1969), *Principles of Phonology*, U. of California Press.
Wolf, Catherine G. & Koff, Elissa (1978), "Memory for Pure and Verb-Derived Nouns: Implications for Hemispheric Specialization", *Brain and Language* 5, 36–41.

THE EVASIVE INITIAL

For decades, and especially since the end of the 1930's, I had under my observation the verbal behavior displayed by a polyglot of my generation. In his handwritten notes and blueprints for his own use he was repeatedly committed to one, single, unconscious deviation from current spelling usages; namely, he was inclined to omit the first letter of a word, whatever its length or make-up, and likewise, the first cipher of a number expressed by several figures. In the latter case, the initial figure was easily forgotten; hence, such a record as *311* would be erroneously interpreted as *eleven*, and thus would lead the writer to miscalculations. These evasions of the initial took place in any of the Western languages he used — English, French, German, Czech, and Polish, as well as in Russian, with its modified Cyrillic script. Such agraphic mishaps, although rare, have been well attested to in verbal pathology, and they demanded careful observation and explanation.

In the autumn of 1980, the man in question underwent a slight stroke with temporary left visual negligence as its chief effect. After a few days of hospitalization he was able to return to intellectual activities, but one behavioral feature emerged and continuously interfered with his reading. The initial letter of some words disappeared for this reader; it gave him the impression of sudden textual gaps which deliberately asked to be supplemented in his immediate memory. The supplementation of the omission would be necessary either because the gap created a sound combination nonexistent in the given language (e.g. the conversion of Engl. *imbecile* into *mbecile*); or, the sound pattern of the given language admitted the sound group in question but found no actual application for it in the proposed context; or, finally, the rules of patterning made it possible to fill the gap, but there remained a choice among more than one alternative (e.g. the group *ong* could have been preceded by *l, r, s, t, g*). One must note that such gaps arose independently of the degree and character of the distortion they created for the reader. But, of course, their restitution required different grades of tension for the perceiver's fresh memory in its corrective effort.

When, in the case observed, the propensity for dropping the initial entered into the perception of the ailing reader, the earlier tendency to omit the initial components in writing, strangely enough, disappeared.

Right-handers form the overwhelming majority of the readers and writers of the world. In cultures of left-right reading and writing, there is a powerful parallelism between the right-hander's approach toward the text he faces and the left-right (inside-outside) ordered system of script. The omission of the initial in the reader's perception is, in this bundle of related processes, a quite explainable elliptic operation. And there proved to be no place for any abolishment of initials when the patient described in this note was invited to exercise in reading a Hebrew text.

Written in Cambridge, Mass., Fall 1981, for *Voces Amicorum Sovijärvi: in honorem Antti Sovijärvi = Mémoires de la société finno-ougrienne* 181 (Helsinki: Suomalais-Ugrilainen Seura, 1982).

C

TOWARD A NOMOTHETIC SCIENCE OF LANGUAGE

GLOSSES ON THE MEDIEVAL INSIGHT INTO THE SCIENCE OF LANGUAGE

Si nous posons qu'à défaut du langage, il n'y aurait ni possibilité de société, ni possibilité d'humanité, c'est bien parce que le propre du langage est d'abord de signifier.
Émile Benveniste, "La forme et le sens dans le langage",
September 3, 1966.[1]

Dicendum quod in dictione duo sunt, scilicet vox et intellectus. Est enim vox principium materiale, significatio vero vel intellectus principium formale dictionis. Est autem dictio pars orationis ratione sue significationis et non ratione vocis.
Circa grammaticam, anonym. questiones, Ms. of Petrus de Limoges, s. XIII[2]

Benveniste's succinct survey of recent tendencies in general linguistics underscores "le caractère exclusivement historique qui marquait la linguistique pendant tout le XIXe siècle et le début du XXe".[3] One would think that this rigorously historical treatment of language, particularly stern in the leading linguistic current of the late nineteenth century, might have generated a thoroughly historical approach to the science of language as well. If, however, this school proved unable to produce a comprehensive history of linguistics, the reason lies in the erroneous reduction of linguistic science to historical or, properly speaking, genealogical questions and in the subsequent conclusion that the history of scientific linguistics begins only with the first scholarly endeavors to cope with such kinds of tasks.

The broad and durable popularity of the mentioned tenet has resulted in the ingrained and widespread belief that linguistics belongs to the young, even to the youngest sciences, whereas the very antithesis has to be expressly stated. The science of language is one of the oldest, perhaps

---

[1] *Le langage: Actes du XIIIe Congrès des sociétés de philosophie de langue française* 2 (Neuchâtel, 1967), 29–40; reprinted in Benveniste's *Problèmes de linguistique générale* 2 (Paris, 1974), 215–238.
[2] J. Pinborg, *Die Entwicklung der Sprachtheorie im Mittelalter = Beiträge zur Geschichte der Philosophie und Theologie des Mittelalters* 42 (1967), part 2, 42.
[3] E. Benveniste, "Tendances récentes en linguistique générale", *Journal de Psychologie* 47–51 (1954), 103–145 (reprinted in his *Problèmes de linguistique générale* 1 [Paris, 1966], 3–17).

even the oldest branch of systematic knowledge, or, according to the reiterated Scholastic adages, *scientia linguae est prima naturaliter* and *ceterarum omnium artium nutrix antiquissima*. Any pattern of writing, whether logographic, syllabic, or by and large alphabetic, is in itself a display of linguistic analysis. The earliest extant attempt toward a grammatical parsing and description, namely an outline of Sumerian grammar dating back almost four millennia that has been investigated by Thorkild Jacobsen,[4] is a remarkable Babylonian effort to cope with the knotty paradigm problem which, in fact, still pertains to the fundamentals of linguistic science.

The pristine origin of linguistic science is quite explicable. Language when used to talk about language is labeled metalanguage; linguists' discourse about language is an elaborate implementation of metalanguage, and since, moreover, any child's progressive acquisition of language is indispensibly joined with mastering the use of metalanguage, such primordial deliberations on language favor and further the emergence of a genuine inquiry into the verbal code.

Linguistics of today effectively combines and brings into concord innovations with an age-long and ever vital tradition of research and argumentation. Only a superstitious belief in the rectilinear progress of science would call into question the evident fact that any temporary current of linguistic thought is oriented toward certain angles of language and that in their investigation such a trend uses a restricted number of favorite contrivances. Under those circumstances, some targets and approaches remain in the shade, as long as the inquirer does not gain a widened scope and deeper insight by familiarizing himself with questions and working hypotheses raised in linguistics of the near and remote past and by testing them on the rich material gathered and accumulated since. One may quote the great musical reformer of our century: according to Igor Stravinsky, "a *renewal* is fruitful only when it goes hand in hand with *tradition*. Living dialectic wills that renewal and tradition shall develop and abet each other in a simultaneous process."[5]

A fancy kind of antitraditionalism is verily a traditional feature in the history of linguistic science. Jespersen's incisive remark on Neogrammarians of the eighties could be equally applied to various turns of time: while the ablest linguists of the new school "were taking up a great many questions of vast general importance that had not been treated by

---

[4] T. Jacobsen, "Very Ancient Linguistics", in *Studies in the History of Linguistics*, ed. Dell Hymes (Bloomington: Indiana University Press, 1974).
[5] I. Stravinsky, *Poetics of Music* (New York, 1947).

the older generation [or rather generations], on the other hand they were losing interest in some of the problems that had occupied their predecessors"; some of these issues went "out of fashion" and were "deprecated" as "futile and nebulous".[6] Discovery and forgetting go together, and some transient losses of memory may become an experimental asset. Beside the alternation of attractions and repulsions there exists, however, the beneficial phenomenon of synthesis, devoid of any miscarrying eclecticism, and our days seem to develop a particular aptitude for such a higher dialectic stage.

The use of preconceived and hackneyed schemes for the delineation of bygone epochs and schools proves to be the greatest stumbling block on the way to an objective historical view of linguistics from ancient times until recent decades. Too often, polemic slogans used by the younger scholarly teams in order to dissociate their aspirations from the precepts of the older generation are substituted for independent studies and unbiased interpretations of its bequest.

Thus, for instance, the still current allegation of linguistics manuals that the science of language did not advance in the Middle Ages is a mere groundless repetition of Humanist invectives *contra modos significandi*. In reality, one could easily assert, with particular reference to Jan Pinborg's expert compendium and several other historical surveys — by P. Rotta, R. H. Robins, P. A. Verburg, B. E. O'Mahony, E. Coseriu, G. L. Bursill-Hall, and J. Stéfanini — as well as to those, still too few, of the numerous manuscript treatises which so far have been published, that throughout the Middle Ages linguistic analysis was in the focus of acute scholarly attention, and especially the studies of the so-called *modistae* and of their precursors underwent in the period from the late twelfth till the early fourteenth century a strenuous and diversified development.[7]

The sphere of lexical meanings (*significata dictionum specialia*) was accurately discriminated from the system of grammatical meanings (*significata generalia*). The focal point of those Schoolmen's research,

---

[6] O. Jespersen, *Language, Its Nature, Development and Origin* (London, 1922).
[7] J. Pinborg, *Die Entwicklung* ...; P. Rotta, *La filosofia del linguaggio nella patristica e nella scolastica* (Turin, 1909); R. H. Robins, *Ancient and Mediaeval Grammatical Theory in Europe* (London, 1951); P. A. Verburg, *Taal en functionaliteit: een historisch-kritische studie over de opvattingen aangaande de functies der taal* (Wageningen, 1952); B. E. O'Mahony, "A Mediaeval Semantic", *Laurentinum* 5 (Rome, 1964); E. Coseriu, *Die Geschichte der Sprachphilosophie von der Antike bis zu Gegenwart* I (Stuttgart, 1969); G. L. Bursill-Hall, *Speculative Grammars in the Middle Ages* (The Hague-Paris, 1971); J. Stéfanini, "Les modistes et leur apport à la théorie de la grammaire et du signe linguistique", *Semiotica* 8 (1973).

modi significandi, or in modern, Sapirian terminology, "grammatical concepts",[8] were submitted to an ever stricter definition and examination of their specifics and hierarchical interrelation, with a particular attention paid to the parts of speech (*modi significandi essentiales*) and to their categorial modifications, such as cases or tenses (*modi significandi accidentales* with further subdivisions). Sapir's preliminaries to a classification of the parts of speech are reminiscent of the medieval endeavors to define them strictly *modaliter*.[9]

In the analysis into *modi significandi* and their *differentiae specificae*, every part of speech appears as a bundle of elementary features, and each of these minimal differential features is termed and interpreted by Simon Dacus[10] and Siger de Cortraco[11] as *modus significandi specificus*. Thus all *appellativa*, viz. substantive and adjective nouns jointly with substantive and adjective pronouns, signify *per modum entis*, in contradistinction to the *modus esse* of the verbal class. As was elucidated by Petrus Hispanus, *nomen est vox significativa ad placitum sine tempore*, in opposition to the temporal axis which marks the verb.[12] The adjective class of nouns and pronouns is separated from the substantive class of these two categories by the *modus adiacentis* opposed to the *modus per se stantis*, while the substantive and adjective nouns by their *modus determinatae apprehensionis* stand in opposition to the *apprehensio indeterminata* of the substantive and adjective pronouns. Authors of treatises *de modis significandi* may differ in terminological and definitional details, but in essence they follow the same principles of classification.

The corollary from such study of the *partes orationis in habitu*, viz. in the paradigmatic interrelation, was within the *Summa grammaticae* the systematic inquiry into *partes orationis in actu*, namely into the rules (*canones* or *regulae*) of their interconnection (*congruitas*) in binary syntactic structures, tersely defined as *congrua constructibilium unio ex modo significandi causata*.[13] The formation of such "unions" or *principia constructionis*, in terms of the "Questiones de modis significandi"

---

[8] E. Sapir, *Language: An Introduction to the Study of Speech* (N.Y., 1921), ch. 5.
[9] E. Sapir, *Totality* = Linguistic Society of America, *Language Monographs* 6 (1930).
[10] Cf. A. Otto, ed., *Johannis Daci Opera* = *Corpus philosophorum danicorum medii aevi* 1, parts 1, 2 (Copenhagen, 1955).
[11] Cf. G. Wallerand, *Les Oeuvres de Sigier de Courtrai* = *Les philosophes belges* 8 (Louvain, 1913), 10.
[12] Cf. J. M. Bocheński, *Summulae Logicales Petri Hispani* (Rome, 1947); J. P. Mullally, *The Summulae Logicales of Peter of Spain* (Notre Dame, 1945).
[13] See L. M. de Rijk, ed., *Petrus Abaelardus: Dialectica* = *Wijsgerige teksten en studies* 1 (Assen, 1956), 53, and C. Thurot, *Notices et extraits de divers manuscrits latins pour servir à l'histoire des doctrines grammaticales du Moyen Âge* (Paris, 1868), 219.

written by Nicolaus de Bohemia toward 1300,[14] underwent a close scrutiny and notable methodological deliberations. Consistent efforts to classify the diverse couples of *constructibilia*, as shown by Johannes de Rus in his *Tractatus de constructione* of the mid-thirteenth century,[15] mark a new stage of syntactic analysis.

The different levels of linguistic phenomena were clearly discerned. The sound of the word (*vox significativa audita*) and its meaning (*significatio vero vel intellectus*) are opposed to each other as *principium formale dictionis*. The notion of double articulation echoed nowadays in Russian and thereupon in Western linguistics may be traced back to the *doctrina de modis significandi* with its clear-cut idea of *articulatio prima et secunda*, which emerged perhaps under Greek incentives: one of these two articulations turns the sound matter (*vocis articulatio*) into words, while the other employs words to generate sentences.[16]

Each linguistic level obtains an adequate portrayal. Thus a proficient classifier of the thirteenth century, Guillelmus de Shyreswoode,[17] scrupulously delineates the speech sounds:

Sonus unus vox, alius non vox. Sonus vox est ut quod fit ab ore animalis; sonus non vox ut strepitus pedum, fragor arborum et similia.

Vox sic dividitur: alia significativa, alia non significativa. Vox significativa est, quo aliquid significat, non significativa, que nil significat ut buba blictrix.

Vox significativa quedam significat naturaliter, quedam ad placitum. Naturaliter, que natura agente aliquid significat ut gemitus infirmorum et similia; ad placitum, que ex humana institutione significationem recipit.

In a similar way *significatio* is defined by Petrus Hispanus: *rei per vocem secundum placitum repraesentatio*.[18]

On the threshold of our century the second volume of Husserl's *Logical Investigations*,[19] and especially its chapter "Der Unterschied der selbständigen und unselbständigen Bedeutungen und die Idee der reinen Grammatik" which soon became one of the milestones for the initial advance of structural linguistics, counterposed to the current, "exclusively empirical" grammar the early and once again timely "idea of a

---

[14] Cf. J. Pinborg, *Die Entwicklung* ..., 100.
[15] *Ibid.*, 52.
[16] Cf. M. Grabmann, "Der Kommentar des seligen Jordanes von Sachsen zum Priscianus minor", *Mittelalterliches Geistesleben* (Munich, 1956), 234, and J. Pinborg, *Die Entwicklung* ..., 44.
[17] M. Grabmann, "Die Introductiones in logicam des Wilhelm von Shyreswood", *Sitzungsberichte der Bayerischen Akademie der Wissenschaften* 10 (1937).
[18] J. M. Bocheński, *op. cit.*
[19] E. Husserl, *Logische Untersuchungen* 2 (Halle, 1901); see also the 1913 edition.

general and, particularly, a priori grammar". He proclaimed "the indubitably righteous design of a universal grammar as conceived by the rationalism of the seventeenth and eighteenth centuries". As Anton Marty, near to Husserl's train of thought, states in his lifework on the theory of language,[20] a "quite valuable contribution to general grammar" was made not only by Cartesians, but also by the third book of Locke's *Essay* and by the *Nouveaux essais* of Leibniz,[21] and the idea of a reasoned, general, universal grammar is to be traced even farther back, particularly to the Stoics and Scholastics. The connection of Husserl's acute insight into the phenomenology of language with the medieval philosophy of verbal signification has been pointed out.[22]

The pattern of grammar cherished, elaborated, and propagated by the *modistae* was *grammatica rationalis*, which they appraised as the purely and thoroughly scientific view of language, a *scientia speculativa*,[23] in contradistinction to the merely applied character of the so-called *grammatica positiva* or *practica*.

In his theory of verbal symbols and of signs in general Charles Sanders Peirce, as he himself acknowledges, "derived the greatest advantage from a deeply pondering perusal of some of the works of Medieval thinkers", and he refers expressly to Petrus Abaelardus and his younger ·contemporary Johannes de Salisbury, and to such eminent Schoolmen of the thirteenth century as Guillelmus de Shyreswoode and Petrus Hispanus.[24] But the chief scholastic impetus for Peirce and for later theoreticians of language[25] was *Grammatica speculativa*, long attributed to Johannes Duns Scotus, but actually written at the beginning of the fourteenth century by Thomas de Erfordia,[26] an astute and successful compiler of earlier theses *de modis significandi*.[27] Peirce, as he

---

[20] A. Marty, *Untersuchungen zur Grundlegung der allgemeinen Grammatik und Sprachphilosophie* 1 (Halle, 1908); see also S.-Y. Kuroda, "Anton Marty and the Transformational Theory of Language", *Foundations of Language* 9 (1972).

[21] J. Locke, *Essay Concerning Humane Understanding*, Book III: "Of Words or Language in General" (London, 1690); G. W. Leibniz, *Nouveaux essais sur l'entendement humain* (Berlin, 1703).

[22] L. Kukenheim, *Esquisse historique de la linguistique française et de ses rapports avec la linguistique générale* (Leiden, 1962).

[23] J. Pinborg, *Die Entwicklung* ..., 18.

[24] C. S. Peirce, *Collected Papers* 1 (Cambridge, Mass., 1931), 560; 2 (Cambridge, Mass., 1932), 317, 486.

[25] Cf. M. Heidegger, *Die Kategorien- und Bedeutungslehre des Duns Scotus* (Tübingen, 1916) and K. Werner, "Die Sprachlogik des Johannes Duns Scotus", *Sitzungsberichte der Wiener Akademie der Wissenschaften* 85, no. 3 (1877).

[26] Cf. G. L. Bursill-Hall, ed., *Thomas of Erfurt: Grammatica speculativa* (London, 1972).

[27] J. Pinborg, *Die Entwicklung* ..., 134.

himself says, shared the aim of this work from his own first steps in the late sixties toward a "general theory of the nature and meanings of signs", a science he even called "speculative grammar" before adopting Locke's term "semiotic".[28]

The medieval contributors to the development of scientific, rational grammar particularly insisted on the idea of *grammatica universalis*. The heightened interest in general rules and properties must have been spurred by the vehement sway of Arabic linguistic thought[29] and put a particular emphasis upon the invariants, for *in his impermutabilibus consistit grammatica regularis*, as it was taught since the early thirteenth century. Pursuit of universals met with mutually parallel problems on different levels of language, and the inquiry into those principles of syntactic constructions which *eadem sunt apud omnes* implied an intrinsic analysis of the *constructibilia* or, in other words, a search for the fundamentals (*generales virtutes*) of the *modi significandi* as such. Neither the question of general rules on the level of *voces significativae*, nor their essential affinity with the *principia generalia* on the higher levels of language were overlooked by the outliners of the *grammatica universalis*. One of the most sagacious medieval linguists, Robertus Kilwardby of the mid-thirteenth century, whose precious manuscripts still await publication and a comprehensive interpretation, expressly states that *modi pronuntiandi substantiales elementorum *** et similiter modi significandi et consignificandi generales* are identical *apud omnes*;[30] and the example both he and Nicolaus de Parisiis refer to, the "necessary" and world-wide functional distinction between vowels and consonants (*omnis vocalis per se sonat, consonans cum alio*), reappears in a quite analogous, rigorously distributional formulation used by the recent glossematic doctrine.

The oscillating attitudes observable among the adherents of universal grammar in regard to the diversity of linguistic structures and to their peculiarities *apud gentem illam cuius est lingua* led in the thirteenth century to a heated argument. In Kilwardby's creed, which enriches the long history of those adhesive ideas that recur again and again, the "deep structure", as it would be labeled today, can and must be abstracted by the grammarian *ab omni lingua*, and the elicited product of this operation, the universally compulsory *sermo significativus* may be

---

[28] C. S. Peirce, *Collected Papers* 1, 445; 2, 83, 332; cf. R. Jakobson, *Main Trends in the Science of Language* (London, 1973).
[29] J. Pinborg, *Die Entwicklung* ..., 25.
[30] Cf. C. Thurot, *op. cit.*, 125.

present *in mente* solely.[31] Or, in a somewhat later response of Boethius Dacus, *non enim omnia possibilia sunt in actu*.[32]

In accordance with patristic philosophy, medieval theoreticians of language paid rapt attention to internal speech, termed *verbum mentis sive interius* by Thomas Aquinas,[33] *sermo interior* by Occam, for whom *triplex est terminus: scriptus, prolatus*, and *conceptus*, more exactly defined as *intentio* and as *pars propositionis mentalis*.[34] Later this vital aspect of language remained underrated or unnoticed for a long span of time.

Boethius Dacus, who during the 1270's taught at the Faculty of Arts in the University of Paris,[35] is perhaps the most original and radical mind not only within the glorious group of Parisian scholars *de Dacia* in the late thirteenth century,[36] but also among all medieval inquirers into *modi significandi*. He was one of the greatest Danish contributors to the theory of language, and we do not forget that it was Denmark which throughout many centuries gave to international linguistics a long list of supreme thinkers. The consistently elaborated doctrine of Boethius faces us once more with those urgent themes and pointed claims which steadily recur on the winding paths of our science. Throughout the late twelfth and the following century we observe a gradual emancipation of linguistics. The first stage, as noted by Pinborg, was a progressive separation of grammar, concerned with *sermo congruus*, from logic, whose subject matter, *sermo verus*, was declared irrelevant for the science of language. The initial advances toward such a bifurcation were made in the twelfth century by Hugo de Sancto Victore[37] and consolidated by the *modistae* of the early thirteenth century. The next resolute step intended to free the science of grammar from all extraneous controlling influences was taken by Boethius Dacus. This scholar's methodological requirement for the elicitation of any scientific, and specifically grammatical theme always and solely *ex principis suae*

---

[31] J. Pinborg, *Die Entwicklung* ..., 29.
[32] J. Pinborg and H. Roos, eds., *Boethii Daci Opera* = *Corpus philosophorum danicorum medii aevi* 6, part 1 (Copenhagen, 1969), 160, 201.
[33] Cf. F. Manthey, *Die Sprachphilosophie des hl. Thomas von Aquin und ihre Anwendung auf Probleme der Theologie* (Paderborn, 1937).
[34] P. Boehner, ed., *Geuillelmus Ockham, Summa logicae* = *Franciscan Institute Publications*, Text series, 2.
[35] See S. S. Jensen, "On the National Origin of the Philosopher Boetius de Dacia", *Classica et Mediaevalia* 24 (1963).
[36] Cf. A. Otto, ed., *Johannis Daci Opera* = *Corpus philosophorum danicorum medii aevi* 1, parts 1 and 2 (Copenhagen, 1955) and *Simonis Daci Opera* = *Corpus* ..., 3 (Copenhagen, 1963), and H. Roos, ed., *Martini de Dacia Opera* = *Corpus* ..., 2 (Copenhagen, 1961).
[37] R. W. Hunt, "The Introduction to the 'Artes' in the Twelfth Century", in *Studia mediaevalia in honorem R. J. Martin* (Brugge, 1948).

THE MEDIEVAL INSIGHT INTO THE SCIENCE OF LANGUAGE 193

scientiae underlies and determines his whole treatment of grammatical concepts.

According to Boethius' doctrine,[38] the *modi significandi* pertain to the realm of *signa* or, in a closer view, linguistic signs, and nothing outside of this sphere — neither *res*, nor *modi essendi* — enters into the scope of the grammarian's competence. The combination of two meanings — one lexical, and the other grammatical — within a word is an inherent and creative capability of language. Thus, for example, a substantive does not name a substance but shows only that the given *conceptus mentis* is represented like a substance (*per modum substantiae*) yet could be actually represented by any other part of speech (*idem conceptus mentis per omnes partes orationis potest significari*), and on the other hand, everything, whether an actual entity or a negation or a pure figment, in its linguistic expression may obtain *modum significandi essentialem nominis*. Hence all such words become genuine substantives, irrespective of their lexical meanings (*significata lectionum*).

The insistence upon the creative power of language, which is peculiar to the whole movement of *modistae*, appears particularly outspoken in Boethius Dacus and somewhat differently in Raymundus Lullus with his conception of language as *ars inveniendi*.[39] This resolute emphasis shows homologous features with the powerful poetic trend which enveloped the various countries of Europe precisely through the late twelfth and most of the thirteenth century and which displayed an intent concentration on the inner creativity of verbal art. In a brief commentary to the so-called "parabolic-figurative style" cherished during that epoch in Russia, I was faced with such striking parallels as "the Golden Age of the French medieval literature" with its meridional *poésie recluse* (Provençal *trobar clus*) of Raimbaut d'Aurenga and Arnaud Daniel de Ribérac, or the German *blüemen* in Wolfram's epics. Among further "synchronic international correspondences", one had to evoke the subtle symbolism and hermetism cultivated in the skaldic poetry of the late twelfth century, similar tendencies in the Irish poetry of the same time, enigmatic speech (*significatio*) and *ornatus difficilis* advocated in the contemporaneous Latin manuals of *ars poetica*, especially by Ganfredus de Vinosalvo, and practiced in the international Latin poetry after the First Crusade, and finally the same epoch in the Byzantine literary mastery with its "multiplex semantic structures".[40]

[38] Cf. J. Pinborg, *Die Entwicklung* ..., 78–85.
[39] P. A. Verburg, *op. cit.*, 54ff.
[40] R. Jakobson, "The Puzzles of the Igor' Tale", *Selected Writings* IV (The Hague-Paris, 1966), 382ff.

Conspicuous affinities between verbal art and verbal theory are a noteworthy and periodically reemerging phenomenon. A historical confrontation of Old Indic poetry and equally subtle treatises on poetic form with the native science of language would undoubtedly throw a new light on many cruxes of Sanskrit poetics and linguistics. We recall Saussure's stirring suspicion of an influence which the traditional analytic devices practiced in Vedic carmina might have exerted upon the grammatical science of India, "au double point de vue *phonique* et *morphologique*".[41]

Returning to the deliberations of medieval linguists, I must confess that the more one plunges into their writings, the stronger is the impression of an unsurpassed skill in the arduous tasks of semantic theory. If Boethius Dacus and the other investigators of the *modi significandi* have taken the first place in unraveling the complexity of GRAMMATICAL meanings, the other influential course of medieval thought deeply concerned with language, namely the theory of *suppositiones*,[42] gives us the firmest outlook on multiple questions tied to LEXICAL meanings and especially on the cardinal problem of general and contextual meanings in their hierarchical relationship. The question of "congruous speech" plays a focal role in the study of the *modi significandi*, while problems of "intelligible speech" become primary in the analysis of the *suppositiones*.

In an effort to disentangle the intricate questions of lexical meaning and to find the way to their persuasive solution, K. O. Erdmann published a paper on the system of "suppositions" as one of the crucial topics of Scholastic preoccupations with thought and language in their interplay, and later, in 1900, changed this essay into a chapter of his book *Die Bedeutung des Wortes*:

Die Lehre der Supposition, die Jahrhunderte hindurch in unerhörter Breite ausgesponnen wurde, ist heute so gut wie vergessen. Der Begriff der Supposition selbst sollte nicht vergessen werden; er umfasst und kennzeichnet eine Gruppe wichtiger Tatsachen.[43]

Peirce insisted on reviving the concept and name of suppositions and

---

[41] J. Starobinski, *Les mots sous les mots. Les anagrammes de F. de Saussure* (Paris, 1971), 38.
[42] Surveyed by E. Arnold, "Zur Geschichte der Suppositionstheorie", *Symposion* 3 (Munich, 1952), but still awaiting a systematic linguistic interpretation and appraisal; cf. L. M. de Rijk, "The Development of Suppositio naturalis in Mediaeval Logic", *Vivarium* 9 (1971).
[43] K. O. Erdmann, *Die Bedeutung des Wortes* (Leipzig, 1900).

on pursuing the relevant distinction between "signification" and "supposition":[44] *Differunt autem significatio et suppositio* — as it has been stated by Petrus Hispanus — *unde significatio prior est suppositione.*[45] From the twelfth century on, the perplexing phenomenon of *univocatio* was defined and treated as *manente eadem significatione variata nominis suppositio.*[46]

According to Peirce, "nothing can be clearer" than the thesis he liked to quote from the *Metalogicon* II of Johannes de Salisbury:[47] *Aliud scilicet esse quod appellativa significant et aliud esse quod nominant. Nominantur singularia sed universalia significantur.*[48] The dialectical tension between the generic unity of the inherent meaning, on the one hand, and the multitude of contextual meanings, *suppositionum varietas*, on the other hand, or briefly, between intension (depth) and extension (breadth), was conceived as the fundamental *proprietas terminorum*. The manifold adaptations of inherent meanings to diverse types of verbalized or verbalizable contexts was turned by Schoolmen, from Petrus Abaelardus[49] and Petrus Helias[50] to Guillelmus Occam,[51] into shrewd stemmata ("trees") with dichotomously systematized types of suppositions.[52] The ways in which *per translationem* a *nomen* turns in discourse into a *terminus* were intently explored, with many still valid and suggestive linguistic finds, and with a rigid delimitation of *suppositio formalis* (object language) and different varieties of *suppositio materialis* (metalanguage), neatly discerned by Shyreswoode (see fn. 17 *supra*).

A shaken but nonetheless tenacious prejudice incessantly attributes to the Middle Ages a plain ignorance of linguistic science. This bias shows to how great an extent we remain ignorant even of the cornerstones of medieval thought which, as a matter of fact, obviously outdate some modern-day preliminaries to the theory and methodology of semantics.

Nevertheless, the abundant examples of gratuitous oblivion and presumptuous contempt cannot obliterate the fact of the latent and intermittent but still fertile continuity. On the one hand, the Schoolmen's linguistic tenets had been nursed by Greek and Latin antiquity, in

---

[44] C. S. Peirce, *Collected Papers* 5 (Cambridge, Mass., 1935), 320.
[45] Cf. Bocheński, *op. cit.*
[46] Cf. E. Arnold, *op. cit.*, 60.
[47] *Collected Papers* 2, 317, 364, 391, 434.
[48] Cf. C. C. J. Webb, ed., *John of Salisbury, Metalogicon libri* 3 (Oxford, 1929).
[49] L. M. de Rijk, *op. cit.*
[50] R. W. Hunt, "Studies on Priscian in the Twelfth Century", *Mediaeval and Renaissance Studies* 2 (1950).
[51] P. Boehner, ed., *Geuillelmus Ockham, Summa logicae* ...; E. A. Moody, *The Logic of William of Ockham* (London, 1935).
[52] Cf. E. Arnold, *op. cit.*, 102; G. L. Bursill-Hall, *Speculative Grammars* ..., 348ff.

particular by the Aristotelian and Stoic thought with the latter's Augustinian sequel, and by Donatus and Priscianus, the renowned transmitters of Alexandrian models. Patristic and Byzantine,[53] as well as Arabic cogitations, also seem to have impelled the Western medieval inquirers into language.

On the other hand, the Scholastic search left deep, though mostly hidden traces in the grammatical theories of later centuries. First and foremost one may cite such a landmark in the development of the *scientia linguae* as the greatest achievement of Renaissance linguistics, the book by Franciscus Sanctius Brocensis, *Minerva: seu de causis linguae Latinae* (or, according to another variant of the subtitle: *sive de proprietate sermonis Latini*),[54] with its leading principle — *syntaxis est finis grammaticae* — and with a stupendous series of conjugate chapters, "*De ellipsi*", "*De zeugmate*", and "*De vocibus homonymis*". All three of them were apparently stimulated by the *Syntaxis figurata* which Thomas Linacer had offered at the end of his renowned syntactic manual in accordance with a time-honored compositional pattern.[55] *Minerva*, imbued with the idea of ellipticity as the motive power of language, is firmly rooted in the foundations of the Schoolmen's *grammatica rationalis* and in the medieval manuals of rhetoric (which unfortunately remain even less explored than their grammatical counterparts). At the same time this bold "Cathedratico de Rhetorica en Salamanca", with his emphasis upon a strictly rational method (*ratio* opposed to *auctoritas*) and upon a critical approach to the ruling of *magni viri*, has been rightly considered a "precursor of rationalism" and a discoverer of novel linguistic paths and prospects.[56]

His work enjoyed a widespread popularity; between 1664 and the beginning of the nineteenth century it was printed, with retouches and additions by commentators, at least twelve times in various European

---

[53] J. M. Anderson, "Maximi Planudis in Memoriam", *Generative Grammar in Europe*, ed. F. Kiefer and N. Ruwet (Dordrecht, 1973).
[54] F. Sanctius Brocensis, *Minerva: seu de causis linguae Latinae commentarius* (Salamanca, 1562); see also the 2nd ed. of 1587. Cf. J. M. Liaño Pacheco, *Sanctius El Brocense* (Madrid, 1971).
[55] T. Linacer, *De emendata structura latini sermonis libri* 6 (London, 1524).
[56] See M. Barrado Sánchez, *La elipsis según el Brocense en relación con su sistema gramatical* (Segovia, 1919); A. F. G. Bel, *Francisco Sánchez el Brocense = Hispanic Notes and Monographs Issued by the Hispanic Society of America* 7 (London, 1925); A. Navarro Funes, "La teoría de las formas gramaticales según el Brocense", *Boletín de la Universidad de Granada* 1 (1929); C. Garcia, "Contribución a la historia de los conceptos gramaticales. La aportación del Brocense", *Revista de Filologia española*, 71 (Madrid, 1960); C. F. Lázaro Carreter, *Las ideas lingüísticas en España durante el siglo XVIII* (Madrid, 1949); E. del Estal Fuentes, *Francisco Sánchez de las Brozas y la doctrina de la elipsis. Introducción al estudio de la Minerva* (Salamanca: Facultad de Filosofia y Letras, 1973).

centers. As early as 1628, one of these enrapt commentators, Gasper Scioppius, published his own *Grammatica philosophica*, centered around ellipsis and opening the way to many successive samples of tentative "philosophical grammars".[57] In the nineteenth century, despite the hostility of sectarian historicism toward the fanatic seeker of ellipsis, rare instances of deserved recognition still emerged and Sanctus was even hailed as Humboldt's precursor by a grammarian of Humboldtian stamp.[58] Through the 1870's and 80's, in an international linguistic and philosophical discussion about the very essence of impersonal sentences, their three-centuries-old elliptic interpretation by Sánchez de las Brozas was still cited and reinterpreted.[59]

In the past century the distinguished Italian critic Francesco de Sanctis proclaimed Sánchez Brocense "the Descartes of Grammarians". Benedetto Croce recalls this appraisal and views the Spanish savant as the most profound among the Renaissance explorers of language.[60] Since the beginning of our century there has grown both in Spain and in international scholarship a new attraction toward *Minerva's* linguistic anticipations which are cognate both with the Schoolmen's legacy and with the modern scientific quest. Golling's "Introduction to the History of Latin Syntax" declared in 1903:

Die glänzendste Erscheinung unter den Grammatikern des 16. und der beiden folgenden Jahrhunderte ist Fr. Sanctius Brocensis. In seiner Minerva *sucht er *** die innere Notwendigkeit und logische Geschlossenheit der lateinischen Syntax nachzuweisen *** Der tiefe spekulative Blick verbunden mit logischer Schärfe und Konsequenz [hat] dem Sanctius eine Bedeutung verliehen, die seine Lehren noch in der Gegenwart als beachtenswert erscheinen lässt.*[61]

In the grammatical literature of the seventeenth century the place of prominence belongs to Arnauld's and Lancelot's *Grammaire générale et raisonnée*,[62] which aimed to explain, as the subtitle claims, "les raisons de ce qui est commun à toutes les langues et des principales différences qui s'y rencontrent". This significant work and its governing methods and principles, as it was clearly and decisively stated by Claude

---

[57] G. Sciopius, *Grammatica philosophica* (Milan, 1628).
[58] C. Michelsen, *Historische Übersicht des Studiums der lateinischen Grammatik seit der Widerherstellung der Wissenschaften* (Hamburg, 1837).
[59] F. Miklosich, *Subjektlose Sätze* (Vienna, 1883).
[60] B. Croce, *Estetica come scienza dell'espressione e linguistica generale* (Palermo, 1902).
[61] J. Golling, "Einleitung in die Geschichte der lateinischen Syntax", *Historische Grammatik der lateinischen Sprache*, ed. G. Landgraf, 3 (Leipzig, 1903).
[62] A. Arnauld and C. Lancelot, *Grammaire générale et raisonée*, avec les remarques de C. P. Duclos, préface de M. Foucault (Paris, 1969).

Lancelot, the experienced linguistic co-editor of the Port-Royal publication, obviously depend on the hundred-years older *Minerva*. The latter was the main, but certainly not the only guide through which Scholastic approaches to grammatical problems pervaded "les fondemens de l'art de parler" of the Port-Royal team. The diffusion of the *Grammaire générale et raisonnée*, whether direct or mediate, since its original edition of 1660, was enormous until the first half of the last century, a century which after 1846 put an end to its numerous republications. The temporary aversion and oblivion, linked to the one-sided historical bent which was particularly potent among linguists of the late nineteenth century, found, however, a severe retort in Saussure's *Course of General Linguistics*, recorded by his students:[63]

La base de la grammaire de Port Royal était beaucoup plus scientifique que celle de la linguistique postérieure. *** *Après avoir fait de l'histoire linguistique fort longtemps, il est certain qu'il faudra revenir sur la grammaire statique traditionnelle, mais y revenir avec un point de vue renouvelé .**** *Ce sera une des utilités de l'étude historique d'avoir fait comprendre ce qu'était un état. La grammaire traditionnelle ne s'est occupée que de faits statiques; "la linguistique historique" nous a fait connaître un* nouvel ordre de *faits, mais ce que nous disons: ce n'est que l'*opposition des deux ordres *qui est féconde comme point de vue.*

Saussure countered the Neogrammarian negative attitude toward the Port Royalists by a negation of negation, and his unerring flair for the dialectic of scientific advance confronts us with a predictable continuation of this development in the recent fierce discussions, reevaluations, and critical editions of this "traditional" textbook.[64] One could again recall Stravinsky's catchword on renewal and tradition, which "develop and abet each other in a simultaneous process".

Based on the author's concluding paper at the Newberry Conference on Historical Linguistics, February, 1968, and elaborated in Cambridge, Mass., Fall 1973 for *Mélanges linguistiques offerts à Émile Benveniste* (Paris, 1975).

---

[63] F. de Saussure, *Cours de linguistique générale*, éd. critique par R. Engler (Wiesbaden, 1967), 183ff.
[64] See N. Chomsky, *Cartesian Linguistics* (New York-London, 1966); H. Aarsleff, "The History of Linguistics and Professor Chomsky", *Language* 46 (1970); H. H. Brekle, ed., *Grammaire générale et raisonnée, ou La grammaire du Port Royal* 1–2 (Stuttgart, 1966); Robin Lakoff, review of Brekle's book in *Language* 45 (1969), 343–64; and for further bibliography R. A. Hall, Jr., "Some Recent Studies on Port-Royal and Vaugelas", *Acta Linguistica Hafniensia* 12 (1969).

A GLANCE AT THE DEVELOPMENT OF SEMIOTICS

I

Emile Benveniste in his "A Glance at the Development of Linguistics", the beautiful study whose heading I borrow for this presentation, brings to our attention that "linguistics has a double object: it is the science of language and the science of languages. *** It is on languages that the linguist works, and linguistics is first of all a theory of languages. But *** the infinitely diverse problems of languages have the following in common: at a certain degree of generality, they always put language into question."[1] We deal with language as a universal invariant with respect to varied local languages which are variable in time and space. In the same order of things, semiotics is called upon to study the diverse systems of signs and to bring out the problems which result from a methodical comparison of these varied systems, that is to say, the general problem of the SIGN: sign as a generic notion with respect to the particular classes of signs.

The question of the sign and of signs was approached several times by the thinkers of Antiquity, of the Middle Ages and of the Renaissance. Around the end of the seventeenth century, John Locke's famous essay, in its final chapter on the tripartite division of the sciences, promoted this complex problem to the level of the last of the "three great provinces of the intellectual world" and proposed to call it "σημειωτική or the 'Doctrine of signs', the most usual whereof being words", given that

to communicate our thoughts for our own use, signs of our ideas are also necessary. Those which men have found most convenient, and therefore generally make use of, are articulate sounds.[2]

It is to words, conceived of as "the great instruments of cognition", to their use and to their relation to ideas that Locke devotes the third book of his *Essay Concerning Humane Understanding* (1694).

---

[1] É. Benveniste, *Coup d'oeil sur le développement de la linguistique* (Paris: Académie des inscriptions et belles-lettres, 1963).
[2] John Locke, *Essay Concerning Humane Understanding* (London, 1694), Book IV, Ch. 21, sec. 4.

II

From the beginning of his scientific activities, Jean Henri Lambert took account of the *Essay* and, while working on the *Neues Organon* (1764),[3] which holds a pertinent spot in the development of phenomenological thought, he saw himself profoundly influenced by Locke's ideas, despite his taking a critical stance toward the sensualist doctrine of the English philosopher.[4] Each of the two volumes of the *Neues Organon* is divided into two parts and, among the four parts of this whole treatise, the third — *Semiotik oder Lehre von Bezeichnung der Gedanken und Dinge*, followed by the *Phänomenologie* — inaugurates the second volume (pp. 3–214) of the work and owes to Locke's thesis the term *semiotic* as well as the theme of research, "the investigation of the necessity of symbolic cognition in general and of language in particular" (paragraph 6), given that this symbolic cognition "is to us an indispensable adjunct to thought" (paragraph 12).

In the preface to his work, Lambert warns us that he is working on language in nine chapters of the *Semiotik* (2–10) but allows only one chapter to other types of signs, "because language is not only necessary in itself and extraordinarily diffuse, but occurs with all other types of signs". The author wishes to devote himself to language, "in order to get to know its structure more closely" (paragraph 70) and to approach "general linguistics, *Grammatica universalis*, which is still to be sought". He reminds us

that in our language the arbitrary, the natural and the necessary are blended. The primer of general linguistics should then mainly discuss the natural and the necessary, and the arbitrary, as far as is possible, sometimes on its own, sometimes in tight link with the natural and the necessary.

According to Lambert, the difference between these three elements which one finds in signs reveals a tight relationship with the decisive fact "that the first causes of language are in themselves already in human nature", and therefore this problem demands a meticulous examination (paragraph 13). The problem of algebra and of other systems of science's artificial languages with respect to natural languages (*wirkliche Spra-*

---

[3] J. H. Lambert, *Neues Organon, oder Gedanken über die Erforschung und Bezeichnung des Wahren und dessen Unterscheidung vom Irrthum und Schein* 1–2 (Leipzig: Johann Wendler, 1764). Reprint: *Philosophische Schriften* 1–2, ed. Hans-Werner Arndt (Hildesheim: Georg Olms, 1965).
[4] Cf. Max E. Eisenring, *Johann Heinrich Lambert und die wissenschaftliche Philosophie der Gegenwart* (Zürich: Muller and Werden, 1942), 7, 12, 48ff., 82.

'gedoppelte Aufmerksamkeit'

chen) is treated by Lambert (paragraph 55ff) as a sort of double translation (*gedoppelte Übersetzung*).

The book studies the difference in the use of natural and arbitrary signs (paragraphs 47 and 48); the natural signs of affects (*natürliche Zeichen von Affekten*) are those that first attract attention (paragraph 19). Lambert takes into account the significant role played by gestures, for example, "in order to enlighten the concept, which is dark in the soul [mind], *** or at least to give an indication of it to ourselves and to others", and he foresees the semiotic scope of *simulacra* (which reappear after a century in Peirce's list under the labels of *icons* or *likenesses*).[5] Lambert raises the question of signs whose internal structure is founded upon similarity relationships (*Ähnlichkeiten*) and, in interpreting signs of a metaphorical order, he evokes the effects of synesthesia (paragraph 18). Despite the summary character of his remarks on non-verbal communication, neither music, nor choreography, nor the blazon, nor the emblem, nor ceremonies escape the researcher's eye. The transformations of the signs (*Verwandlungen*) and the rules for their combination (*Verbindungskunst der Zeichen*) are placed on the agenda for further study.

III

It is because of Locke's and Lambert's creative initiative that the idea and the name of semiotics reappear at the beginning of the nineteenth century. In his early career, the young Joseph Marie Hoene-Wroński, familiar with Locke's work, sketched, among other speculative essays, a *Philosophie du language* which was not published until 1879.[6] The author, who is linked by his disciple Jerzy Braun to Husserl's phenomenology and who is presented as "the greatest of Polish thinkers",[7] examines "the faculty of signation (*facultas signatrix*)". The nature of signs (see p. 38) must be studied first of all with respect to the categories of existence, that is to say, to the MODALITY (proper/improper signs) and to the QUALITY (determined/undetermined signs), and secondly with respect to the categories of production, that is to say, to the QUANTITY

[5] Charles Sanders Peirce, *Collected Papers* I (Cambridge, Mass.: Harvard University Press, 1931), 588. In further references to *Collected Papers* I–VIII (1931–1958), the subdivisions of the text are indicated by Arabic numerals accompanied by the number of the volume in Roman numerals and separated by a period.

[6] J. M. Hoene-Wroński, "Philosophie du langage", *Septs manuscrits inédits écrits de 1803 à 1806* (Paris, 1897).

[7] Jerzy Bronisław Brau, *Aperçu de la philosophie de Wroński* (Rome: P.U.G., 1969).

(simple/composite signs), to the RELATION (natural/artificial signs) and the UNION (mediate/immediate signs). Following Hoene-Wroński's program, it is the "perfection of signs" ("perfection of language" in Locke's terms, "*Vollkommenheit der Zeichen*" according to Lambert) which forms "the object of *SÉMÉIOTIQUE*" (p. 41). One should note that this theory reduces the field of "signation" to acts of cognition: "This signation is possible, whether for sensory form or for sensory or intelligible content, of the objects of our knowledge", while "the signation of acts of will and feeling" seems to be "impossible" (p. 38ff.).

IV

The Prague philosopher, Bernard Bolzano, in his major work *The Theory of Science* (1837),[8] mainly in the last two of the four volumes, reserves much space for semiotics. The author frequently cites Locke's *Essay* and the *Neues Organon*, and discovers in Lambert's writings "on semiotics *** many very estimable remarks", though these are of little use "for the development of the most general rules of scientific discourse", one of the aims Balzano sets himself (paragraph 698).

The same chapter of *The Theory of Science* bears two titles, one of which — *Semiotik* — appears in the table of contents (vol. IV, p. xvi), the other of which — *Zeichenlehre* — heads the beginning of the text (p. 500); paragraph 637, which follows, identifies both designations — the theory of signs or semiotics (*Zeichenlehre oder Semiotik*). If, in this chapter and in several other parts of the work, the author's attention is held above all by the testing of the relative perfection of signs (*Vollkommenheit oder Zweckmässigkeit*) and particularly of signs serving logical thought, then it is in the beginning of the third volume that Bolzano tries to introduce the reader to the fundamental notions of the theory of signs throughout paragraph 285 (pp. 67–84) which overflows with ideas and is titled "the designation of our representations" (*Bezeichnung unserer Vorstellungen*).

This paragraph begins with a bilateral definition of the sign, "An object *** through whose conception we wish to know in a renewed fashion another conception connected therewith in a thinking being, is known to us as a *sign*". A whole chain of geminate concepts follows, some of which are very new, while others, referring back to their anterior

---

[8] Bernard Bolzano, *Wissenschaftslehre. Versuch einer ausführlichen und grösstentheils neuen Darstellung der Logik mit steter Rücksicht auf deren bisherige Bearbeiten 1–4* (Sulzbach: J. E. v. Seidel, 1837). Reprint ed. Wolfgang Schultz (Leipzig: Felix Meiner, 1930–1931).

sources, are newly specified and enlarged. Thus Bolzano's semiotic thoughts bring to the surface the difference between the meaning (*Bedeutung*) of a sign as such and the significance (*Sinn*) that this sign acquires in the context of the present circumstance, then the difference between the sign (1) produced by the addresser (*Urheber*) and (2) perceived by the addressee who, himself, oscillates between understanding and misunderstanding (*Verstehen und Missverstehen*). The author makes a distinction between the thought and expressed interpretation of the sign (*gedachte und sprachliche Auslegung*), between universal and particular signs, between natural and accidental signs (*natürlich und zufällig*), arbitrary and spontaneous (*willkürlich und unwillkürlich*), auditory and visual (*hörbar und sichtbar*), simple (*einzeln*) and composite (*zusammengesetzt*, which means "a whole whose parts are themselves signs"), between unisemic and polysemic, proper and figurative, metonymical and metaphorical, mediate and immediate signs; to this classification he adds lucid footnotes on the important distinction to be made between signs (*Zeichen*) and indices (*Kennzeichen*) which are devoid of an addresser, and finally on another pressing theme, the question of the relationship between interpersonal (*an Andere*) and internal (*Sprechen mit sich selbst*) communication.

v

The young Edmund Husserl's study, "*Zur Logik der Zeichen (Semiotik)*", written in 1890, but not published until 1970,[9] is an attempt to organize the sign categories and to answer the question of knowing in which sense language, that is, our most important system of signs, "furthers and, on the other hand, once again inhibits thinking". Criticism of signs and their improvement are conceived of as an urgent task which confronts *logic*:

A deeper insight into the nature of signs and of arts will rather enable [logic] to devise additionally such symbolic procedural methods upon which the human mind has not yet come, that is, to lay down the rules for their invention.

The 1890 manuscript contains a reference to the "*Semiotik*" chapter of *The Theory of Science* which is said to be *wichtig* (p. 530): in aiming at two targets in this essay, one structural and the other regulative, Husserl

---

[9] E. Husserl, "Zur Logik der Zeichen (Semiotik)", *Gesammelte Werke* 12 (The Hague: Nijhoff, 1970).

does in fact follow the example of Bolzano, whom he will later call one of the greatest logicians of all time. In the semiotic ideas of the *Logical Investigations* one can find "decisive instigations from Bolzano" as the phenomenologist acknowledges; and the second volume of the *Investigations*, with its important treatise on general semiotics set up as a system, exerted a profound influence on the beginnings of structural linguistics. As Elmar Holenstein indicates, Husserl made several notes in the margins of paragraph 285 in his own copy of Bolzano's *The Theory of Science III* and he underlined the term *Semiotik* and its definition in Locke's *Essay* in its German translation, *Über den menschlichen Verstand* (Leipzig, 1897).[10]

VI

For Charles Sanders Peirce (1839–1914), the nature of signs remained a favorite subject of study since 1863 (cf. V.488 and VIII.376) and especially from the time of his magnificent profession of faith — "On a New List of Categories" — which was published in 1867 by the American Academy of Arts and Sciences (cf. 1.545–559); thereupon followed two ingenious contributions to the *Journal of Speculative Philosophy* in 1868 (cf. V.213–317), and finally, materials collected in 1909–10 for his unfinished volume *Essays on Meaning* (cf. II.230–32; VIII.300).[11]

It is notable that, throughout the thinker's whole life, the conception which underlies his continual efforts to establish a science of signs gained in depth and in breadth, and simultaneously remained firm and unified. As for the "semiotic", "semeiotic", or "semeotic", it only surfaces in Peirce's manuscripts at the turn of the century; it is at this time that the theory "of the essential nature and fundamental varieties of possible semiosis" captures the attention of this great researcher (I.444; V. 488). His insertion of the Greek σημειωτική, as well as the concise definition "doctrine of signs" (II.277) — puts us on the track of Locke, whose celebrated *Essay* was often referred to and cited by the doctrine's partisan. In spite of the marvelous profusion of original and salutary finds in Peirce's semiotics, the latter nonetheless remains tightly linked to his precursors — Lambert, "the greatest formal logician of those days" (II.346), whose *Neues Organon* is cited (IV.353), and Bolzano, whom he

---

[10] E. Holenstein, *Linguistik, Semiotik, Hermeneutik: Plädoyers für eine strukturale Phänomenologie* (Frankfurt am Main: Suhrkamp, 1976), 206, fn. 9.

[11] Cf. Irwin C. Lieb, ed., *Charles S. Peirce's Letters to Lady Welby* (New Haven, Conn.: Whitlocks, 1953), 40.

knows from the latter's "valuable contribution to the lucidity of human concepts" and his "work on logic in four volumes" (IV.651).

Still, Peirce declared rightly: "I am, as far as I know, a pioneer, or rather a backwoodsman, in the work of clearing and opening up what I call *semiotic*, *** and I find the field too vast, the labor too great, for a first-comer" (V.488). It is he who is "the most inventive and the most universal of American thinkers",[12] who knew how to draw up conclusive arguments and to clear the ground in order to erect at his own risk the framework of the science which two centuries of European philosophical thought had anticipated and foreseen.

Peirce's semiotic edifice encloses the whole multiplicity of significative phenomena, whether a knock at the door, a footprint, a spontaneous cry, a painting or a musical score, a conversation, a silent meditation, a piece of writing, a syllogism, an algebraic equation, a geometric diagram, a weather vane, or a simple bookmark. The comparative study of several sign systems carried out by the researcher revealed the fundamental convergences and divergences which had as yet remained unnoticed. Peirce's works demonstrate a particular perspicacity when he deals with the categoric nature of language in the phonic, grammatical and lexical aspects of words as well as in their arrangement within clauses, and in the implementation of the clauses with respect to the utterances. At the same time, the author realizes that his research "must extend over the whole of general Semeiotic", and warns his epistolary interlocutor, Lady Welby: "Perhaps you are in danger of falling into some error in consequence of limiting your studies so much to Language."[13]

Unfortunately, most of Peirce's semiotic writings were only published during the fourth decade of our century, i.e. around twenty years after the author's death. Nearly a century was needed to print some of his texts; thus the amazing fragment of one of Peirce's courses given in 1866-67 — "Consciousness and Language" — first appeared in 1958 (VII.579-96); let us note too that there remains in Peirce's heritage numerous unpublished pieces. The tardy publication of his works, which appeared dispersed and in fragments in the maze of the *Collected Papers of Charles Sanders Peirce*, vol. I-VIII, for a long time hampered a complete and exact understanding of his precepts and unfortunately delayed their effective influence on the science of language and the harmonious development of semiotics.

---

[12] Cf. R. Jakobson, "Quest for the Essence of Language", *Selected Writings* II (The Hague-Paris: Mouton, 1971), 345ff.
[13] I. C. Lieb, ed., *op. cit.*, 39.

Readers and commentators of these works have often been mistaken about the fundamental terms introduced by Peirce, although they are indispensable to an understanding of his theory of signs and although these terms, even if forced occasionally, nonetheless receive a definition that is always very clear in the author's text. Thus the *interpreter* and the *interpretant* designations have given rise to an unfortunate confusion, in spite of the distinction Peirce makes between the term *interpreter*, which designates the receiver and decoder of a message, and *interpretant*, that is, the key which the receiver uses to understand the message he receives. According to popularizers, the sole role attributed to the *interpretant* in Peirce's doctrine consists in clarifying each sign by the mediating context, while in fact the brave "pioneer" of semiotics asks rather "to distinguish, in the first place, the Immediate Interpretant, which is the interpretant as it is revealed in the right understanding of the sign itself, and is ordinarily called the *meaning* of the sign" (IV.536). In other words, it is "all that is explicit in the sign itself, apart from its context and circumstances of utterance" (V.473); all signification is but the "translation of a sign into another system of signs" (IV.127). Peirce casts light upon the ability of every sign to be translatable into an infinite series of other signs which, in some regards, are always mutually equivalent (II.293).

According to this theory, the sign demands nothing more than the possibility of being interpreted, even in the absence of an addresser. The symptoms of illnesses are therefore also considered signs (VIII.185, 335) and at a certain point, medical semiology neighbors semiotics, the science of signs.

In spite of all the differences in the presentation's details, the bipartition of the sign into two conjoined facets and, in particular, the Stoic tradition, which conceives of the sign (σημεῖον) as a referral on the part of the *signans* (σημαῖνον) to the *signatum* (σημαινόμενον), remains strong in Peirce's doctrine. In conformity with his trichotomy of semiotic modes and with the rather vague names that he gives them, (1) the *index* is a referral from the *signans* to the *signatum* by virtue of an effective contiguity; (2) the *icon* is a referral from the *signans* to the *signatum* by virtue of an effective similarity; (3) the *symbol* is a referral from the *signans* to the *signatum* by virtue of an "imputed", conventional, habitual contiguity. Accordingly (cf. in particular II.249, 292ff., 301, and IV.447ff., 537), "the mode of being of the symbol is different from that of the icon and from that of the index". In contradistinction to these two categories, the symbol as such is not an object; it is nothing but a frame-rule which must clearly be distinguished from its functioning in the form of "replicas" or "instances", as Peirce tries to define them. The elucidation of the generic character which qualifies both the *signantia* and the *signata* in the code of language (each of these aspects "is a kind and not a single thing") has opened new perspectives on the semiotic study of language.

Now, the trichotomy in question has also given rise to erroneous views. Attempts have been made to attribute to Peirce the idea of the division of all human signs into three rigorously separate classes, while the author only considers three modes, one of which "is predominant over the others" and, in a given system, finds itself often linked to the other two modes or to either of them. For example,

a symbol may have an icon or an index incorporated into it (IV.447). It is frequently desirable that a representamen should exercise one of those three functions to the exclusion of the other two, or two of them to the exclusion of the third; but the most perfect of signs are those in which the iconic, indicative, and symbolic characters are blended as equally as possible (IV.448). It would be difficult if not impossible, to instance an absolutely pure index, or to find any sign absolutely devoid of the indexical quality (II.306). A diagram, though it will ordinarily have Symbolide Features, as well as features approaching the nature of Indices, it is nevertheless in the main an Icon (IV.531).

In his successive attempts to establish a complete classification of semiotic phenomena, Peirce ended up outlining a table consisting of 66 divisions and subdivisions,[14] which embraces the action "of almost any kind of sign" — action known under the ancient name of σημείωσις. Ordinary language and the diverse types of formalized languages find their place in Peirce's semiotics which emphasizes not only the primacy of the symbolic relationship between the *signans* and the *signatum* in the linguistic data but at the same time, the co-presence of the iconic and indexical relationship.

VII

Ferdinand de Saussure's contribution to the progress of semiotic studies is evidently more modest and more restricted. His attitude toward the *science de signes* and the name *sémiologie* (or sporadically *signologie*),[15] which he imposed on it immediately, remains, it seems, completely

---

[14] Cf. *ibid.*, 51–53.
[15] Cf. F. de Saussure, *Cours de linguistique générale*, critical edition prepared by Rudolf Engler, 2 (Wiesbaden: Otto Harrassowitz, 1974), 47ff. Further references to this edition (vol. 1, 1967; vol. 2, 1974) are given in the text with volume and page number in parentheses.

outside of the current created by such names as Locke, Lambert, Bolzano, Peirce and Husserl. One can surmise that he did not even know of their research in semiotics. Nonetheless, in his lessons he asks: "Why hasn't semiotics existed until now?" (1:52). The question of the precedent which might have inspired the program constructed by Saussure remains unanswered. His ideas on the science of signs have only come to us in the form of sparse notes, the oldest of which date back to the 1890's,[16] and in the last two of his three courses in general linguistics (1:33, 45–52, 153–55, 170ff.).

From the end of the century, Saussure tried to get, according to his own terms, "a correct idea of what a semiological system is"[17] and to discover the traits "of language, as of the entire general semiologic system",[18] while having in mind mainly systems of "conventional signs". The oldest of Saussure's remarks on the theory of signs try to apply it to the phonic level of language; with a clarity superior to the treatment of the same matter in his later teachings, these theses allow for the emergence of

the relationship between sound and idea, the semiological value of the phenomenon [which] can and should be studied outside all historical preoccupations, [since] study of the state of language on the same level is perfectly justified (and even necessary, although neglected and poorly understood) insofar as we are dealing with semiologic facts.[19]

The equation *Phonème = Valeur sémiologique* is placed at the head of the *phonétique sémiologique*, the new discipline foreseen by Saussure at the beginning of his activities at the University of Geneva.[20]

The only mention of Saussure's semiological ideas that appeared during his lifetime is a brief summary which his relative and colleague, A. Naville, gives in a book in 1901.[21] The text of the *Cours de linguistique générale*, published in 1916 by Charles Bally and Albert Sechehaye from notes taken by members of Saussure's audience, is so reworked and touched up by the editors that it causes quite a number of errors in the master's teachings. At present, thanks to the beautiful

---

[16] Cf. Robert Godel, *Les sources manuscrites du "Cours de linguistique générale" de F. de Saussure* (Geneva: Librairie E. Droz, 1957), 275.
[17] Cf. *ibid.*, 49.
[18] F. de Saussure, "Notes inédites", *Cahiers Ferdinand de Saussure* 12 (1954), 71.
[19] Cited by R. Jakobson in "World Response to Whitney's Principles of Linguistic Science" (1971); reprinted in the present volume, *infra*, 228ff.
[20] *Ibid.*
[21] Adrien Naville, *Nouvelle classification des sciences. Étude philosophique* (Paris: Alcan, 1901), chapter 5.

critical edition by Rudolf Engler (cf. fn. 15 above), we are able to compare the direct accounts of Saussure's students and to get a far truer and far more precise idea of the original text of his talks.

Unlike Peirce and Husserl, who were both conscious of having laid the foundations of semiotics, Saussure speaks of semiotics in the future only. According to the notes on Saussure's courses between 1908 and 1911 which were collected by several students (cf. 1:xi), language is above all a system of signs, and therefore it must be classified as a science of signs (1:47). This science has hardly developed. Saussure proposes to call it *sémiologie* (from the Greek σημεῖον, sign). One cannot say what this science of signs will be, but it is our task to say that it is worthy of existence and that linguistics will occupy the principal compartment of this science: "this will be one particular case of the great semiological fact" (1:48). Linguists will have to distinguish the semiological characteristics of language in order to place it properly among systems of signs (1:49); the task of the new science will be to bring out the differences between these diverse systems as well as their common characteristics — "There will be general laws of semiology" (1:47).

Saussure underlines the fact that language is far from being the only system of signs. There are many others: writing, visual nautical signals, military trumpet signals, gestures of politeness, ceremonies, sets of rites (1:46ff.); in the eyes of Saussure, "Customs have a semiological character" (1:154). The laws of transformation of the systems of signs will have completely topical analogies with language's laws of transformation; and, on the other hand, these laws will reveal enormous differences (1:45, 49). Saussure envisions certain dissimilarities in the nature of different signs and in their social value: the personal or impersonal factor, a thought-out act or an unconscious one, dependence or independence vis-à-vis the individual or social will, ubiquity or limitedness. If one compares the different systems of signs with language, one will witness, according to Saussure, the surfacing of aspects which one had not suspected; in studying rites or any other system separately, one will notice that all of these systems yield a common study — that of the specific life of signs, semiology (1:51).

According to the thesis Saussure maintained from the time of his preparation in 1894 of an unfinished study on William Dwight Whitney, "language is nothing more than one *particular case* of the Theory of Signs", and

this will be the major reaction of the study of language in the theory of signs, this will be the ever new horizon which it will have opened — to have taught and revealed to the theory of signs *a whole other and new side of the sign*, that is to say that the sign does not begin to be really known until we have seen that it is not only a transmissible thing but by its very nature a thing *destined to be transmitted*.[22]

(Therefore, in Peirce's terms, the sign demands the participation of an "interpreter".)

Now, at the same time, Saussure puts the "particularly complex nature of the semiology of spoken language" (*loc. cit.*) in opposition to the other semiological systems. According to the Saussurean doctrine, these systems use signs which have at least a basic link of reference between the *signatum* and the *signans*, *icons* in Peirce's terminology, *symbols* as Saussure's *Course* will call them later: "The symbol is a sign, but not always completely arbitrary" (1:155). On the contrary, language is "a system of independent symbols". Thus, in 1894, purely conventional and, as such "arbitrary", signs are those which Peirce called *symbols* (or *legisigns*). "The independent symbols", according to the old notes of Saussure, "possess the particular major characteristic of not having any sort of perceivable connection with the object to be designated". The result is that "whoever sets foot on the terrain of language may say to himself that he is abandoned by all the analogies of heaven and earth".[23]

Although Saussure is inclined to see the primary concerns of semiology in "arbitrary systems", this science, he affirms, will always see its field grow, and it is difficult to predict where semiology will stop (1:153ff.). The "grammar" of the game of chess, with the respective value of its pieces, authorizes Saussure to compare the game and language and to conclude that in these semiological systems "the notion of identity meshes with that of value, and vice versa" (1:249).

It is precisely questions linked to identities and values which, according to an astute note made by Saussure at the beginning of the century, appear to be decisive in mythical studies, as in the "parental domain of linguistics": on the level of semiology

all the incongruities of thought stem from insufficient reflection about what *identity* is, or what the characteristics of identity are, when we talk about a nonexistent being, like a *word*, or a *mythic person*, or *a letter of the alphabet*, which are only different forms of the sign in a philosophical sense.

---

[22] Cited *infra*, 228.
[23] *Ibid.*

"These symbols, without realizing it, are subject to the same vicissitudes and to the same laws as are all the other series of symbols *** — They are all part of semiology."[24] The idea of this semiological being which does not exist *in itself*, "at any time" (*à nul moment*) (2:277) is adopted by Saussure in his 1908–09 course where he proclaims "the reciprocal determination of values by their very coexistence", while adding that there are no isolated semiological beings, and that such a determination can occur only on a synchronic level, "for a system of values cannot stay astride a succession of epochs" (2:304).

Saussure's semiotic principles during the last twenty years of his life demonstrate his striking tenacity. The 1894 sketches, cited above, open with an inflexible assertion:

The object that serves as sign is never "the same" (*le même*) twice: one immediately needs an examination or an initial convention to know within what limits and in the name of what we have the right to call it the same; therein lies its fundamental difference from an ordinary object.

These notes insist on the decisive role of the "plexus of eternally negative differences", the ultimate principle of non-coincidence in the world of semiological values. In approaching semiological systems, Saussure tries to "take exception to what preceded", and as of 1894 he gladly refers to comparisons between the synchronic states in language and the chessboard. The question of the "antihistoric character of language" will even serve as title to Saussure's last notes in 1894 (2:282), and, one could add, to all of his thoughts on the semiological aspects of language and of all the *créations symboliques*.[25] These are the two intertwined principles of Saussurean linguistics — *l'arbitraire du signe* and the obstinately "static" conception of the system — which nearly blocked the development of the *sémiologie générale* that the master had foreseen and hoped for (cf. Saussure, 1:170ff.).

Now, the vital idea of semiological invariance which remains valid throughout all of its circumstantial and individual variations is clarified by Saussure thanks to a felicitous comparison of language to the symphony: the musical work is a reality existing independently of the variety of performances made of it; "the performances do not attain

---

[24] Cf. Jean Starobinski, *Les mots sous les mots. Les anagrammes de Ferdinand de Saussure* (Paris: Gallimard, 1971), 15.
[25] Cf. his notes published by D'Arco Silvio Avalle, "Noto sul 'segno'", *Strumenti critici* 19 (1972), 28–38; cf. also D. S. Avalle, "La sémiologie de la narrativité chez Saussure", in *Essais de la théorie du texte*, ed. C. Bouazis (Paris: Éditions Galilée, 1973).

the status of the work itself". "The execution of a sign is not its essential characteristic", as Saussure points out; "the performance of a Beethoven sonata is not the sonata itself" (1:50, 53ff.). We are dealing with the relationship between *langue* and *parole* and with the analogous link between the "univocality" (*univocité*) of the work and the multiplicity of its individual interpretations. Mistakenly, in the text arranged by Bally and Sechehaye, these interpretations are represented as "errors that [the performers] might commit".

Saussure must have thought that in semiology the "arbitrary" signs were going to occupy a fundamental place, but it would be useless to look in his students' notes for the assertion that the Bally-Sechehaye text gives, that is: "signs that are entirely arbitrary actualize the ideal of semiological process better than other signs" (1:154).

In his expansionist view of the science in the process of becoming (*science en devenir*) Saussure goes as far as to admit that "everything comprising forms must enter into semiology" (*loc. cit.*). This suggestion seems to anticipate the current idea of the topologist Réné Thom, who wonders if one must not immediately attempt to develop a "general theory of forms, independent of the specific nature of substratum space".[26]

VIII

The relationship of the science of language and languages with that of the sign and of different signs was defined briefly and explicitly by the philosopher Ernst Cassirer in his address to the New York Linguistic Circle, pointing out that "linguistics is a part of semiotics".[27]

There is no doubt that signs belong to a field which is distinguishable in certain respects from all the other facets of our environment. All of the sectors of this field need to be explored, taking into account the generic characteristics and the convergences and divergences among the various types of signs. Any attempt to tighten the limits of semiotic research and to exclude from it certain types of signs threatens to divide the science of signs into two homonymous disciplines, namely *semiotics* in its largest sense and another province, identically named, but taken in its narrower sense. For example, one might want to promote to a specific science the study of signs we call "arbitrary", such as those of language

---

[26] R. Thom, "La linguistique, discipline morphologique exemplaire", *Critique* 30 (1974), 244ff.
[27] E. Cassirer, "Structuralism in Modern Linguistics", *Word* 1 (1945), 115.

(so it is presumed), even though linguistic symbols, as Peirce demonstrated, can easily be related to the *icon* and to the *index*.

Those who consider the system of language signs as the only set worthy of being the object of the science of signs engage in circular reasoning (*petitio principii*). The egocentrism of linguists who insist on excluding from the sphere of semiotics signs which are organized in a different manner than those of language, in fact reduces semiotics to a simple synonym for linguistics. However, the efforts to restrict the breadth of semiotics sometimes go even further.

At all levels and in all aspects of language, the reciprocal relationship between the two facets of the sign, the *signans* and the *signatum*, remains strong, but it is evident that the character of the *signatum* and the structuring of the *signans* change according to the level of linguistic phenomenon. The privileged role of the right ear (and, more properly, that of the left hemisphere of the brain) solely in the perception of language sounds is a primary manifestation of their semiotic value, and all the phonic components (whether they are distinctive features, or demarcational, or stylistic, or even strictly redundant elements) function as pertinent signs, each equipped with its own *signatum*. Each higher level brings new particularities of meaning: they change substantially by climbing the ladder which leads from the phoneme to the morpheme and from there to words (with all their grammatical and lexical hierarchy), then go through various levels of syntactic structures to the sentence, then to the groupings of sentences into the utterance and finally to the sequences of utterances in dialogue. *Each one* of these successive stages is characterized by its own clear and specific properties and by its own degree of submission to the rules of the code and to the requirements of the context. At the same time, each part participates, to the extent possible, in the meaning of the whole. The question of knowing what a morpheme means, or what a word, a sentence or a given utterance means, is equally valid for all of these units. The relative complexity of signs such as a syntactic period, a monologue or an interlocution, does not change the fact that in any phenomenon of language everything is a sign. The distinctive features or the whole of a discourse, the linguistic entities, in spite of the structural differences in function and in breadth, all are subject to one common science, the science of signs.

The comparative study of natural and formalized languages, and above all those of logic and mathematics, also belongs to semiotics. Here the analysis of the various relationships between code and context has already opened broad perspectives. In addition, the confrontation of language with "secondary modeling structures" and with mythology particularly points to a rich harvest and calls upon able minds to undertake an analogous type of work which attempts to embrace the semiotics of culture.

In semiotic research touching upon the question of language, one will have to guard against the imprudent application of the special characteristics of language to other semiotic systems. At the same time, one must avoid denying to semiotics the study of systems of signs which have little resemblance to language and following this ostracizing activity to the point of revealing a presumably "non-semiotic" layer in language itself.

IX

Art has long escaped semiotic analysis. Still there is no doubt that all of the arts, whether essentially temporal like music or poetry, or basically spatial like painting or sculpture, or syncretic, spatio-temporal, like theater or circus performances or film showings, are linked to the sign. To speak of the "grammar" of an art is not to employ a useless metaphor: the point is that all art implies an organization of polar and significant categories that are based on the opposition of marked and unmarked terms. All art is linked to a set of artistic conventions. Some are general, for example, let us say that we may take the number of coordinates which serve as a basis for plastic arts and create a consequential distinction between a painting and a piece of statuary. Other conventions, influential ones or even mandatory ones for the artist and for the immediate receivers of his work, are imposed by the style of the nation and of the time. The originality of the work finds itself restricted by the artistic code which dominates during a given epoch and in a given society. The artist's revolt, no less than his faithfulness to certain required rules, is conceived of by contemporaries with respect to the code that the innovator wants to shatter.

The attempted confrontation between arts and language may fail if this comparative study relates to ordinary language and not directly to verbal art, which is a transformed system of the former.

The signs of a given art can carry the imprint of each of the three semiotic modes described by Peirce; thus, they can come near to the *symbol*, to the *icon*, and to the *index*, but it is obviously above all in their artistic character that their significance ($\sigma\eta\mu\varepsilon\iota\omega\sigma\iota\varsigma$) is lodged. What does this particular character consist of? The clearest answer to this question was given in 1885 by a young college student, Gerald Manley Hopkins:

The artificial part of poetry, perhaps we shall be right to say all artifice, reduces itself to the principle of parallelism. The structure of poetry is that of continuous parallelism.[28]

The "artifice" is to be added to the triad of semiotic modes established by Peirce. This triad is based on two binary oppositions: contiguous/similar and factual/imputed. The contiguity of the two components of the sign is factual in the *index* but imputed in the *symbol*. Now, the factual similarity which typifies *icon* finds its logically foreseeable correlative in the imputed similarity which specifies the *artifice*, and it is precisely for this reason that the latter fits into the whole which is now forever a four-part entity of semiotic modes.

Each and every sign is a *referral* (*renvoi*) (following the famous *aliquid stat pro aliquo*). The parallelism alluded to by the master and theoretician of poetry, Gerard Manley Hopkins, is a referral from one sign to a similar one in its totality or at least in one of its two facets (the *signans* or the *signatum*). One of the two "correspective" signs, as Saussure designates them,[29] refers back to another, present or implied in the same context, as we can see in the case of a metaphor where only the "vehicle" is *in presentia*. Saussure's only finished writing during his professorship in Geneva, a clairvoyant work on the concern for repetition in ancient literatures, would have innovated the world-wide science of poetics, but it was unduly hidden, and even today the notebooks, which are quite old, are only known to us through Jean Starobinski's fascinating quotations. This work brings out "the 'coupling', that is, the repetition in even numbers" in Indo-European poetry, which allows for the analysis of "the phonic substance of words whether to construct an acoustical series (e.g. a vowel which requires its 'counter-vowel'), or to make of them a significative series".[30] In trying hard to couple signs which "find themselves naturally evoking each other",[31] poets had to control the traditional "skeleton of the code", namely, first the strict rules of approved similarity, including accepted license (or, as Saussure puts it, the "transaction" on certain variables), then the laws prescribed for the even (*paire*) distribution of corresponding units throughout the text and, finally, the order (*consecutivité* or *non-consecutivité*) imposed on reiterative elements with respect to the march of time.[32]

---

[28] G. M. Hopkins, "Poetic Diction" (1865), in *The Journals and Papers*, ed. H. House (London: Oxford University Press, 1959), 84.
[29] Cf. J. Starobinski, *op. cit.*, 34.
[30] *Ibid.*, 21, 31ff.
[31] *Ibid.*, 55.
[32] *Ibid.*, 47.

"Parallelism" as a characteristic feature of all artifice is the referral of a semiotic fact to an equivalent fact inside the same context, including the case where the aim of the referral is only an elliptic implication. This infallible belonging of the two parallels to the same context allows us to complement the system of times which Peirce includes in his semiotic triad: "An icon has such being as belongs to past experience *** An index has the being of present experience. The being of a symbol *** is *esse in futuro*" (IV.447; II.148). The artifice retains the *atemporal* interconnection of the two parallels within their common context.

Stravinsky never tired of repeating that "music is dominated by the principle of similarity".[33] In the musical art the correspondences of elements that are recognized, in a given convention, as mutually equivalent or in opposition to each other, constitute the principal, if not the only, semiotic value — "intramusical embodied meaning", according to the description by the musicologist Leonard Meyer:

Within the context of a particular musical style one tone or group of tones indicates — leads the practiced listener to expect — that another tone or group of tones will be forthcoming at some more or less specified point in the musical continuum.[34]

The referral to what follows is felt by composers as the essence of the musical sign. In the eyes of Arnold Schönberg, "to compose is to cast a glance upon the theme's future".[35] The three fundamental operations of the musical "artifice" — anticipation, retrospection and integration — remind us of the fact that it is the study of melodic phrase undertaken in 1890 by Ehrenfels which suggested to him not only the notion of "Gestalt", but also of a precise introduction to the analysis of musical signs:

In temporal formal qualities only *one* element can, logically, be given in [acts of] perceptual representations, while the rest are available as images of memory (or as images of expectation projected into the future).[36]

If in music the questions of intrinsic relationships prevail over the

---

[33] Igor Stravinsky, *Poetics of Music in the Form of Six Lessons* (Cambridge, Mass.: Harvard University Press, 1942).
[34] Leonard B. Meyer, *Music, the Arts, and Ideas* (Chicago: University of Chicago Press, 1967), 6ff.
[35] Jan Maegaard, *Studien zur Entwicklung des dodekaphonen Satzes bei Arnold Schönberg* (Copenhagen: W. Hansen, 1974).
[36] Christian von Ehrenfels, "Über 'Gestaltqualitäten'", *Vierteljahrsschrift für wissenschaftliche Philosophie* 14: 3 (1890), 263ff.

tendencies of an iconic order and are capable of reducing them to nothingness, the representational function, on the other hand, easily comes to the fore in the history of the necessarily spatial visual arts.[37] Nonetheless, the existence and the great successes of abstract painting are incontrovertible facts. The *"responsions"* between the various chromatic and geometric categories which, it goes without saying, play a non-prescriptive role in representational painting, become the only semiotic value in abstract painting. The laws of opposition and equivalence which govern the system of the spatial categories that are at work in a painting offer an eloquent example of similarities imputed by the code of the school, of the epoch, of the nation. Now, here, clearly, as is the case in all semiotic systems, the convention is founded on the use and the choice of universally perceptible potentialities.

Instead of the temporal succession which inspires the anticipations and retrospections of the listener of musical phrases, abstract painting makes us aware of a simultaneity of conjoined and intertwined "correspectives". The musical referral which leads us from the present tone to the anticipated or remembered tone is replaced in abstract painting by a reciprocal referral of the factors in question. Here the relationship of the parts and the whole acquires a particular significance, although the idea of the entire work is emphasized in all arts. The manner of being of the parts reveals their solidarity with the whole and it is according to this whole that each of its component parts emerge. This interdependence between the whole and the parts creates a patent referral from the parts to the whole and vice versa. One might recognize in this reciprocal referral a synecdochic procedure, following the traditional definitions of the trope, like that of Isidorus Hispalensis: *"Synecdoche est conceptio, cum a parte totum vel a toto pars intellegitur."*[38] In short, significance underlies all the manifestations of the "artifice".

X

By way of concluding, we can propose a tautological formula: Semiotics or, put otherwise, *la science du signe et des signes*, the science of signs, *Zeichenlehre*, has the right and the duty to study the structure of all of the types and systems of signs and to elucidate their various hierarchical

---

[37] Cf. R. Jakobson, "On Visual and Auditory Signs" and "About the Relation between Visual and Auditory Signs", *Selected Writings* II (The Hague-Paris: Mouton, 1971), 334–344.
[38] Cf. Heinrich Lausberg, *Handbuch der literarischen Rhetorik* (Munich: Max Hueber, 1960), paragraph 572.

relationships, the network of their functions and the common or differing properties of *all* systems. The diversity of the relationships between the code and the message, or between the *signans* and the *signatum*, in no way justifies arbitrary and individual attempts to exclude certain classes of signs from semiotic study, as for example non-arbitrary signs as well as those which, having avoided "the test of socialization", remain individual to a certain degree. Semiotics, by virtue of the fact that it is the science of signs, is called upon to encompass *all* the varieties of the *signum*.

Opening report at the First International Congress of Semiotics, Milan, June 2, 1974; first published, in French, by Indiana University Press under the title *Coup d'œil sur le développement de la sémiotique* (Bloomington, Indiana, 1975). Translated from the French by Patricia Baudoin.

THE WORLD RESPONSE TO WHITNEY'S PRINCIPLES OF LINGUISTIC SCIENCE

To the account of Whitney's Indological studies his Autobiographical Sketch adds that "he has also produced a couple of volumes on the general science of language". When the first of these two fundamental contributions appeared in 1867 both in London and New York, under the title *Language and the Study of Language* (*Twelve Lectures on the Principles of Linguistic Science*), two learned German reviewers — Heyman Steinthal in the *Zeitschrift für Völkerpsychologie und Sprachwissenschaft*, vol. 5 (1868), and Wilhelm Clemm in *Kuhns Zeitschrift für vergleichende Sprachforschung*, vol. 18 (1869) — warmly welcomed this comprehensive volume, and both of them emphasized its American background. As Steinthal (1823–1899), the noted promoter of ethnic and linguistic psychology, believed, one had to remember that "the author is a North American and writes for North Americans; what he says and also how he says it is conditioned by the readership for which he writes and in the author's views certain features of his people could even probably be detected." Steinthal alluded to the "different education, different inclination, and different demands" of German readership. According to the classical philologist Clemm (1843–1883), the primary orientation of Whitney's work toward American readers might seriously impede its translation.

Nevertheless, Whitney's compendium was soon translated into German and Dutch, and his second book of general linguistics, *The Life and Growth of Language* (London and New York, 1875), immediately gave rise to three translations: French (Paris, 1875), Italian (Milan, 1876), and German (Leipzig, 1876). A Swedish version followed in 1880. These writings entered at once into international circulation. Thus the London publication of 1867, jointly with its German version, and likewise the English original of 1875, with its three translations of 1875 and 1876, figure among the chief references in the first pages of the *Comprehensive Program* which Jan Baudouin de Courtenay (1845–1929) published as an appendix to his trailblazing lectures of 1876–1877 at Kazan' University.

The relevance of these sources persisted, and in the *General Course* of comparative linguistics, read at Moscow University in 1901–1902 by the head of the Moscow linguistic school, F. F. Fortunatov (1848–1914), the first place among the few recommended manuals belongs to *The Life and Growth of Language* in the original, or in translation, preferably German. In agreement with the American scholar, Fortunatov pointed out the close relationship between language and society. His critical attitude toward August Schleicher's (1821–1868) oversimplified and mechanistic view of the Indo-European ancestor language also links him with Whitney's severe revision of the Schleicherian tenet.

A session of the First American Congress of Philologists held at Philadelphia, December 27–28, 1894, shortly after the death of W. D. Whitney (1827–June 7, 1894), was dedicated to his memory. The *Report* of that Whitney Memorial Meeting (published in Boston, 1897) bears vivid testimony to the unforeseen difference between the American and European reactions to Whitney's attainments in general linguistics. This aspect of his activities was set aside by the domestic scholars who took part in the commemoration, whereas the responses from Europe received by the organizers of the memorial meeting rendered homage to Whitney's historic role in the astounding growth of linguistic science.

In particular, the co-founders and leaders of the influential Neogrammarian school and of its capital base in Leipzig University, the creative spirit of the new current, August Leskien (1840–1916), and his persistent disciple, the famous Indo-Europeanist Karl Brugmann (1849–1919), acknowledge the decisive impetus which the American's ideas gave to this trend from its beginning.

According to Leskien's letter,

> Whitney's views, particularly most recently, have effected far more in linguistics than one at first realizes. The work of the linguist proceeds for the most part in particulars, in which there is little opportunity to refer directly to Whitney. But during the last decades, even in specialized studies, and much more naturally in questions of general principles, a methodological path has been cleared that seeks to approach the true nature of things, in this case the real makeup of language; and certainly a large part of the inspiration for this comes, indirectly or directly, from Whitney.[1]

---

[1] "Whitney's Anschauungen haben, namentlich in neuster Zeit, in der Sprachwissenschaft weit mehr gewirkt, als man auf den ersten Blick bemerkt. Die Arbeit der Sprachforscher bewegt sich ja zum grossen Theil in Detailfragen, bei denen weniger Gelegenheit ist sich unmittelbar auf Whitney zu beziehen, aber selbst bei Specialuntersuchungen, noch mehr natürlich bei allgemeineren und prinzipiellen Fragen, hat sich in den letzten Jahrzehnten immer mehr eine Behandlungsweise Bahn gebrochen, die der wirklichen Natur der Dinge, d.h. hier den realen Verhältnissen der Sprache, gerecht zu werden sucht, und sicher geht ein grosser Theil der Anregung dazu mittelbar oder unmittelbar von Whitney aus."

Brugmann insisted on the thorough indebtedness of Indo-European comparative study to Whitney's activities in Indic philology, and especially to his "indeed epoch-making" *Sanskrit Grammar*, but even more to the immense stimulations "that his consideration of the principles of language history gave to Indogermanists" (*die seine Behandlung der Principienfragen der Sprachgeschichte den Indogermanisten gegeben hat*). In Brugmann's evaluation, "Whitney was, among the Indogermanists, the first to promulgate really sound essentials of language history free of any fanciful and disturbing pretense". It is significant that the champion of the Neogrammarian school assails its narrow-minded followers for their blind empiricism and aversion to theoretical questions: "Even the most gifted, if he wants to speculate on the individual events of a linguistic development, needs a knowledge of the essence of the forces by which the historical facts are produced. Only the self-control and self-criticism made possible by this more general training save him from the arbitrariness and error to which a crude empiricism is everywhere exposed." [2]

Brugmann opens his Leipzig message of November 25, 1894, "Zum Gedächtniss W. D. Whitneys", by recalling the years of initial quest for the new linguistic doctrine: "In the years when, in the homeland of Indo-European studies, we were pressing for a fundamental revision of research method and the establishment of a proper reciprocity between linguistic philosophy and specialized studies, Whitney was for me, as for other younger scholars, a guide in the contest of ideas, whose reliability was beyond cavil and whose hints could always be followed with much profit. And in the course of time the high opinion that I got of Whitney in my student days has only become more firmly established." [3]

When discussing the history of linguistics in a lecture of 1909, Ferdinand de Saussure (1857–1913) mentioned the date 1875 as a turning point. First, he said, Whitney's *Life and Growth of Language*, which appeared at that time in English and French, "gave the impetus".

---

[2] "Auch der Begabteste bedarf, wenn er über die einzelnen Ereignisse einer Sprachentwicklung speculieren will, einer Kenntniss des Wesens der Kräfte, durch die die geschichtlichen Thatsachen geschaffen sind. Nur die durch diese allgemeinere Bildung ermöglichte Selbstcontrole und Selbstkritik bewahrt ihn vor den Willkürlichkeiten und Irrtümern, denen eine rohe Empirie allenthalben ausgesetzt ist."

[3] "War doch in jenen Jahren, da man im Mutterlande der Indogermanistik auf eine gründliche Revision der Forschungsmethode und auf die Herstellung einer angemessenen Wechselwirkung zwischen Sprachphilosophie und Specialforschung drang, mir wie anderen jüngeren Gelehrten Whitney in Streit der Meinungen ein Wegweiser, dessen Zuverlässigkeit ausser Frage stand und dessen Winken man stets mit reichem Nutzen folgte, und hat sich mir doch die hohe Meinung, die ich von Whitney in meinen Lehrjahren gewann, im Lauf der Zeit nur befestigt."

Then we witnessed the birth of "a new school", or in terms preferred by Saussure, "there arose the Neogrammarian trend" (*Cours de linguistique générale*, in R. Engler's critical edition, p. 16). Saussure spent 1876 and 1877 in Leipzig, which in those years was, in his judgment, "the principal center" of this "scientific movement" (see *Cahiers F. de Saussure*, vol. 17, 1960, p. 15). He audited Leskien's lectures and, at least through the mediation of Leskien, whose German translation of Whitney's *Leben und Wachstum der Sprache* was printed in Leipzig in 1876, he must have become familiar with this *Wegweiser* of the Neogrammarian pioneers.

When asked by the organizers of the Philadelphia Memorial Meeting for his appraisal of Whitney's life work, Saussure, with his usual "epistolophobia" and his growing disgust at the difficulty of writing "ten lines concerned with the facts of language and having any common sense" (letter to A. Meillet of January 4, 1894), endeavored to acknowledge and answer the invitation, and covered a notebook of some forty sheets with the draft for a reply which, however, was never finished and never sent. The notebook quoted here is kept in the Public and University Library of Geneva (Ms fr. 3951:10); only fragments were published by Engler, *op. cit.*, and by R. Godel in *Cahiers F. de Saussure*, vol. 12 (1954), pp. 59ff., and in his valuable monograph *Les sources manuscrites du Cours de linguistique générale de F. de Saussure* (1957), pp. 43–46.

The rough version of Saussure's answer reads: "The thought which inspired the American Philological Association, in asking a number of [scholars], American and [European], to summarize their own opinions of the role that Whitney played in the different areas of science of their concern, seems to me a most fortunate one. Only by the comparison of opinions reached in complete freedom in absolutely different quarters will there emerge a notion of — and at the same time a full tribute to the memory of — him whose recent loss we lament along with you."[4] Saussure feels, however, overwhelmed by the task of summarizing "the work accomplished by Whitney" and ventures to open a free discussion, since "it is easier under the circumstances to give free rein to the pen" (*Il est plus facile dans ces conditions de laisser courir la plume*). He begins with stressing the peculiar facets in Whitney's "role and destiny":

---

[4] "La pensée dont s'est inspirée l'American Philological Association, en demandant à un grand nombre de [savants], américains et [européens], de résumer selon leur propre opinion le rôle qu'a rempli Whitney dans les différents départements de la science qui les regarde, me semble une pensée des plus heureuses. De la seule comparaison de jugements portés en toute liberté de côtés absolument différents se dégagera un enseignement, en même temps qu'un hommage plus complet à la mémoire de celui dont nous avons déploré avec vous la perte récente."

1st. Though never having himself written a single page that one might say was intended by him to do comparative grammar, he exerted an influence on all study of comparative grammar; and this is not the case with anyone else. He is chronologically the first preceptor in the principles which will serve when applying the method in the future.

2nd. Of the different attempts between the years 1860 and 1870, which *for the first time* began to extract from the mass of results accumulated by comparative grammar some generalizations about language, all were frustrated or without general value, except that of Whitney, which from the very first was on the right track, and which today need only be patiently carried on.

Let us consider first of all this second role, for it is evident that in this way — that is to say because he showed linguists a sounder view of what was generally the object treated under the rubric of language — he induced them to use slightly different methods in the laboratory of their day-to-day comparative work. The two things, a good generalization about language, which can interest just about anyone, or a sound method to propose to comparative grammar toward the precise operations of [?], are actually the same thing.[5]

Saussure sets off Whitney's performance against the desolate state of the extant linguistic tradition similarly despised by both scholars:

For all time it will be a subject for philosophical reflection that during a period of fifty years linguistic science, born in Germany, developed in Germany, cherished in Germany by innumerable people, has never had the slightest inclination to reach the degree of abstraction which is necessary in order to master on the one hand *what one is doing*, on the other hand why what one is doing has a legitimacy and a *raison d'être* in the totality of sciences; but a second subject of astonishment is to see that when at last this science seems to triumph over her torpor, she winds up with the ludicrous attempt of Schleicher, which totters under its own preposterousness. Such was the prestige of Schleicher for simply having *tried* to say something general about language, that even today he

---

[5] "1° Que n'ayant jamais écrit une seule page qu'on puisse dire dans son intention destinée à faire de la grammaire comparée, il a exercé une influence sur toutes les études de grammaire comparée; et que ce n'est pas le cas d'aucun autre. Il est en date le premier moniteur dans les principes qui serviront en pratique de méthode à l'avenir.

"2° Que des différentes tentatives qui *pour la première fois* tendaient, entre les années 1860 et 1870, à dégager de la somme des résultats accumulés par la grammaire comparée, quelque chose de général sur le langage, toutes étaient avortées ou sans valeur d'ensemble, sauf celle de Whitney, qui du premier coup était dans la direction juste, et n'a besoin aujourd'hui que d'être patiemment poursuivie.

"Considérons avant tout ce second rôle, car il est évident que c'est par là, c'est-à-dire parce qu'il avait inculqué aux linguistes une plus saine vue de ce qu'était en général l'objet traité sous le nom de langage, qu'il les déterminait à se servir de procédés un peu différents dans le laboratoire de leur comparaisons journalières. Les deux choses, une bonne généralisation sur le langage, qui peut intéresser qui que ce soit, ou une saine méthode à proposer à la grammaire comparée pour les opérations précises de [?], sont en réalité la même chose."

seems an unrivaled figure in the history of linguistics, and one sees linguists putting on comically grave airs when dealing with this great figure. *** From everything that we can check, it is apparent that he was a complete mediocrity, not without pretensions.[6]

After some critical reflections upon the late American linguist, the letter of praise sketched by Saussure yields to a second, antithetic draft.

Upon receiving your esteemed letter, dated at Bryn Mawr on the 29th of October and which reached me on the 10th of Nov., I would have immediately to answer you this:

1st. You give me great honor in asking me to appraise Whitney *as a comparative philologist*. But Whitney never was a *comparative philologist*. He has left us not a single page allowing us to appraise him as a comparative philologist. He has left us only works which deduce from the results of comparative grammar a higher and general view of language: that being exactly his great originality since 1867. ***

2nd. As soon as it is no longer a question of mere universal statements that one can make about language, I am in agreement with no one school in general, no more with the reasonable doctrine of Whitney than with the unreasonable doctrines that he victoriously [fought]. And this disagreement is such that it admits of no compromise or shading, under penalty of finding myself obliged to write things that make no sense to me.

I would consequently have to beg you to release me immediately from the task of speaking about the oeuvre of Whitney in linguistics, even though this oeuvre is by far [the best].[7]

---

[6] "Ce sera pour tous les temps un sujet de réflexion philosophique, que pendant une période de cinquante ans, la science linguistique née en Allemagne, développée en Allemagne, chérie en Allemagne par une innombrable catégorie d'individus, n'ait jamais eu même la velléité de s'élever à ce degré d'abstraction qui est nécessaire pour dominer d'une part *ce qu'on fait*, d'autre part en quoi *ce qu'on fait* a une légitimité et une raison d'être dans l'ensemble des sciences; mais un second sujet d'étonnement sera de voir que lorsqu'enfin cette science semble triompher de sa torpeur, elle aboutisse à l'essai risible de Schleicher, qui croule sous son propre ridicule. Tel a été le prestige de Schleicher pour avoir simplement *essayé* de dire quelque chose de général sur la langue, qu'il semble que ce soit une figure hors pair encore aujourd'hui dans l'histoire des études linguistiques, et qu'on voit des linguistes prendre des airs comiquement graves, lorsqu'il est question de cette grande figure. *** Par tout ce que nous pouvons contrôler, il est apparent que c'était la plus complète médiocrité, ce qui n'exclut pas les prétentions."

[7] "A la réception de votre très honorée lettre, datée de Bryn Mawr 29 Octobre et qui m'est parvenue le 10 nov., j'aurais dû immédiatement vous répondre ceci:

"1° Vous me faites le haut honneur de me demander d'apprécier Whitney *as a comparative philologist*. Mais jamais Whitney n'a voulu être un *comparative philologist*. Il ne nous a pas laissé une seule page permettant de l'apprécier comme comparative philologist. Il ne nous a laissé que des travaux qui déduisent des résultats de la grammaire comparée une vue supérieure et générale sur le langage: cela étant justement sa haute originalité dès 1867. ***

Finally, on the last page of his notes, the Swiss scholar outlines the third version of his planned but never accomplished reply to the American invitation to give his view on the deceased linguist, and this new variant is concentrated upon the historic significance of the latter's work: "I believe that it would be the best and the simplest homage to bestow on the oeuvre of Whitney to state how little this oeuvre has suffered from the injuries of time."[8] Such a eulogy, as Saussure underlines,

> would be extraordinary in linguistics itself. Of all the specialized or general books which today are 30 years old is there one in linguistics that has not become irreparably obsolete for us? I look and find no other. — By which we do not dream of saying in any way that Whitney's book is definitive, or that it contains everything that one might want; that is something the author himself would have rejected; but what it does contain, and what Whitney first said in 1867, as it is universally recognized, has not been rendered void in 1894. That is a fact more instructive than much commentary, one to serve as a touchstone in the appraisal of a thinker.[9]

Saussure was pondering an extensive essayistic reply in which he could "give free rein to his pen" and which would contain such sections as "Comparative Grammar; Comparative Grammar and Linguistics; Language, a human institution (*or* Whitney and institutions); Linguistics, a twofold science; Whitney and the Neogrammarian school; Whitney as a phonologist".[10] The final chapter — "Definitive value" — was to have

---

"2° Du moment qu'il ne s'agit plus que des choses universelles qu'on peut dire sur le langage, je ne me sens d'accord avec aucune école en général, pas plus avec la doctrine raisonnable de Whitney qu'avec les doctrines déraisonnables qu'il a victorieusement [combattues]. Et ce désaccord est tel qu'il ne comporte aucune transaction ni nuance, sous peine de me voir obligé d'écrire des choses n'ayant aucun sens à mes yeux.

"J'aurais dû dès lors vous prier de me décharger immédiatement du devoir de parler de l'œuvre de Whitney en linguistique, alors même que cette œuvre est de beaucoup [la meilleure]."

[8] "Je crois que ce sera le meilleur et le plus simple hommage à décerner à l'œuvre de Whitney que de constater à quel point cette œuvre a peu souffert de l'injure du temps."

[9] "Un éloge de ce genre devient extraordinaire dans la linguistique proprement dite. De tous les livres, spéciaux ou généraux, qui ont aujourd'hui 30 ans de date, quel est celui qui en linguistique n'ait pas irrémédiablement vieilli à nos yeux? Je le cherche et n'en trouve pas d'autre. — En quoi, nous ne songeons à dire aucunement que le livre de Whitney soit définitif, ou qu'il contienne tout ce qu'on pourrait désirer; c'est là ce que l'auteur lui-même eût repoussé; mais ce qu'il contient, et ce que Whitney disait le premier en 1867, n'est pas encore frappé de nullité en 1894, de l'aveu universel. C'est là un fait plus instructif que beaucoup de commentaires pour servir de pierre de touche dans l'appréciation d'un esprit."

[10] "La Grammaire Comparée; La Grammaire Comparée et la Linguistique; Le langage, institution humaine (*or* Whitney et l'institution); La linguistique, science double; Whitney et l'école des néo-grammairiens; Whitney phonologiste."

been a recognition of Whitney's merit "in having made himself sufficiently independent of comparative grammar to have taken the first philosophical view of it".[11]

Saussure's notebook of 1894 is packed with exciting, challenging preliminaries to this literary plan, abandoned as usual in his Geneva practice, and thus the Whitney Memorial Meeting impelled the eternal seeker to think over his own linguistic program and to lay it down, for the first time, in a written and perhaps most radical form.

These tentative items begin with a brief reference to Whitney's inquiry into speech sounds: "Insofar, I say, as phonology concerns linguistics, it is to be noted in this letter that several positive contributions were made to it on different occasions by Whitney, who, moreover, from the very first through his studies on the Prātiçākhyas of the different Vedas, was attentive to the details which can elucidate pronunciation."[12] From this "auxiliary science" Saussure proceeds to Whitney's endeavor to solve "a question of greater interest for linguistics. And without solving the problem (simply because he forgot *one* element, indeed the most decisive one, of which I cannot speak here), he made what is still by far the most reasonable statement about this question."

The essence of this striking innovation rests upon Whitney's thesis that language is a human institution: "that changed the axis of linguistics."[13] The substantial particularity of this institution consists in the fact that "language and writing are *not founded on a natural connection of things*. There is no connection at any time between a certain sibilant sound and the form of the letter *S*, and likewise it is no more difficult for the word *cow* than for the word *vacca* to designate a *vache* ['cow']. It is this which Whitney never tired of repeating, in order

---

[11] "*** de s'être rendu assez indépendant de la grammaire comparée, tout pour en avoir tiré le premier une vue philosophique."

[12] "Pour autant, dis-je, que la phonologie touche à la linguistique, il est à remarquer dans cette lettre que plusieurs contributions positives y ont été apportées à différentes reprises par Whitney, d'ailleurs attentif depuis le premier moment en raison de ses études sur les Prātiçākhyas de différents Véda, à tous les détails qui peuvent éclairer la prononciation."

[13] "Mais il y a une tentative de Whitney de résoudre une question autrement intéressante pour la linguistique. Et sans résoudre le problème (simplement parce qu'il a oublié *un* élément, il est vrai le plus décisif, dont je n'aurais pas le loisir de parler ici), il a dit, de beaucoup, ce qu'il y a encore de plus raisonnable sur cette question.

"Whitney a dit: le langage est une *Institution* humaine. Cela a changé l'axe de la linguistique."

better to make understood the fact that language is a pure institution."[14]

Saussure notes the American's belief that in language "there is never a trace of internal correlation between vocal signs and the idea" and underscores that "in his whole oeuvre, Whitney did not cease to take his position on these grounds". Saussure feels particularly impressed by the passage in *The Life and Growth of Language* in which Whitney stated that

> men used their voices to give signs to their ideas as they would have used gesture or anything else, and because it seemed to them *more convenient* to use their voices. We consider that here, in these few lines, which seem to be a great paradox, is the most precise philosophical idea ever given about language; moreover our more day-to-day practice with the things submitted to our analysis would have everything to gain by starting from this given. For it establishes the fact that language is nothing more than a particular case of the sign, unable to be judged by itself.[15]

In his courses on general linguistics Saussure still agrees with Whitney's emphasis on the conventional character of language but admits a certain predisposition toward the use of vocal organs for human language.

In the shrewd reasonings of Whitney on language as an institution, Saussure detects a shortcoming to be straightened out. "The continuation would say, we believe: it is a human institution without analogue." The main reservation made by the critic is directed against the general impression one gains from Whitney's writings that "common sense were enough" to eliminate all the phantoms and to grasp the essence of linguistic phenomena: "Now this conviction is not ours. On the contrary, we are profoundly convinced that whosoever sets foot on the field of *language* can say to himself that he is abandoned by all the analogies in heaven and [earth]. That is precisely why there could be built upon language such fantastic constructions as that which Whitney demol-

---

[14] "Mais le langage et l'écriture ne sont *pas fondés sur un rapport naturel des choses*. Il n'y a aucun rapport à aucun moment entre un certain son sifflant et la forme de la lettre *S*, et de même il n'est pas plus difficile au mot *cow* qu'au mot *vacca* de désigner une vache. C'est ce que Whitney ne s'est jamais lassé de répéter, pour mieux faire sentir que le langage est une institution pure."

[15] "Whitney dit que les hommes se sont servis de la voix pour donner des signes à leurs idées comme ils se seraient servis du geste ou d'autre chose, et parce que cela leur a semblé *plus commode* de se servir de la voix. Nous estimons que c'est là, en ces deux lignes, qui ressemblent à un gros paradoxe, la plus juste idée philosophique qui ait jamais été donnée du langage; mais en outre que notre plus journalière pratique des objets soumis à notre analyse aurait tout à gagner à partir de cette donnée. Car elle établit ce fait que le langage n'est rien de plus qu'un cas particulier du signe, hors d'état d'être jugé en lui-même."

ishes, but also why there remains much to be said in another sense."[16]

Saussure answers by tracing the features which distinguish sign systems, that is, semiotic institutions, from all other human institutions, and particularly those features which specify language and writing in comparison with other semiotic patterns and thus exhibit

the very complex nature of the particular semiology called language. Language is nothing more than a *special case* of the Theory of Signs. But precisely by this fact alone it is absolutely impossible that it be a simple thing (or a thing directly perceivable by our minds in its mode of being).

The chief effect of the study of language on the theory of signs, the forever-new horizon it will have opened up, will be to have taught and revealed *a whole new aspect of the sign*; namely, that the latter begins to be really understood only when it is seen to be a thing which is not only transmittable but by its nature *destined to be transmitted* [and] modifiable. But for anyone who wants to work on the theory of language this is a hundred-fold complication.

Philosophers, logicians, psychologists have perhaps been able to teach us what is the fundamental bond between the idea and its symbol, in particular an *independent symbol* which represents it. By *independent* symbol we understand those categories of symbols whose chief character is to have visibly *no manner of connection* with the thing designated and to be no longer able to depend on it even indirectly in the course of their fortunes.[17]

Other semiotic institutions, such as rituals or fashions, imply a certain inner connection between the two aspects, *signifiant* and *signifié* (to use the terms which later, in 1911, Saussure took over from the Stoic tradition), and therefore "remain *simple* in their complications; on the

---

[16] "Or cette conviction n'est pas la nôtre. Nous sommes au contraire profondément convaincus que quiconque pose le pied sur le terrain de la *langue* peut se dire qu'il est abandonné par toutes les analogies du ciel et de la [terre]. C'est précisément pourquoi on a pu faire sur la langue d'aussi fantaisistes constructions que celle que démolit Whitney, mais aussi pourquoi il reste beaucoup à dire dans un autre sens."

[17] "*** la si complexe nature de la sémiologie particulière dite langage.

Le langage n'est rien de plus qu'un *cas particulier* de la Théorie des Signes. Mais précisément par ce seul fait, il se trouve déjà dans l'impossibilité absolue d'être une chose simple (ni une chose directement saisissable à notre esprit dans sa façon d'être).

"Ce sera la réaction capitale de l'étude du langage sur la théorie des signes, ce sera l'horizon à jamais nouveau qu'elle aura ouvert, que de lui avoir appris et révélé *tout un côté nouveau du signe*, à savoir que celui-ci ne commence à être réellement connu, que quand on a vu qu'il est une chose non-seulement transmissible, mais de sa nature *destiné à être transmis* [et] modifiable. — Seulement, pour celui qui veut faire la théorie du langage, c'est la complication centuplée.

"Des philosophes, des logiciens, des psychologues, ont peut-être pu nous apprendre quel était le contrat fondamental entre l'idée et le symbole, en particulier un *symbole indépendant* qui la représente. Par symbole *indépendant*, nous entendons les catégories de symboles qui ont ce caractère capital de n'avoir *aucune espèce de lien* visible avec l'objet à désigner, et de ne plus pouvoir en dépendre même indirectement dans la suite de leurs destinées."

contrary, it is fundamentally impossible that a single entity of language *be simple* since it presupposes the combination of two things *without connection*, an idea and a symbolic object devoid of any internal bond with this idea".

"It is exactly to the extent that the external object is a sign" and thus, implicitly, "is perceived as a sign [= *signifiant*] that it is by any right a part of language."[18]

Saussure's Whitney notebook opens with a fundamental semiotic statement: "The object which serves as a sign is never '*the same*' twice: from the first we need an investigation or an initial convention in order to know for what reason [and] within what limits we have the right to call it the same; there is its fundamental difference with any other object."[19]

This assertion displays a close correspondence with the continual inquiry of Charles Sanders Peirce into the relationship between *Legisigns* and *Replicas* (or *Instances*). In general Saussure's remarks on *sémiologie*, inspired by his meditations on Whitney, are essentially akin to the *semiotic* ideas of Peirce who, however, nowhere refers to his New England countryman.

Prompted by A. Sechehaye's *Programme et méthodes de la linguistique théorique* (1908), Saussure returned to the cardinal questions of language. He asserted in his notes, as we know from R. Godel's quotations, that two Poles, Baudouin de Courtenay and M. Kruszewski (1851-1887), both still disregarded by the bulk of Western scholars, "were nearer than anyone else to a theoretical view of language". He felt it necessary to adduce a third name: "The American Whitney, whom I revere, never said a single word on the same subjects which was not right; but like all the others, he does not dream that language needs systematics."[20] Saussure's notes of 1894 tried to explain this alleged lack of systematization with the help of a comparison, pursued later, between

---

[18] "Les autres institutions demeurent *simples* dans leurs complications: au contraire il est fondamentalement impossible qu'une seule entité de langage soit *simple*, puisqu'il suppose la combinaison de deux choses *privées de rapport*, une idée et un objet symbolique dépourvu de tout lien avec cette idée.

"Ce n'est que dans la mesure exacte où l'objet extérieur est signe (est aperçu comme signe [= *signifiant*]) qu'il fait partie du langage à un titre quelconque."

[19] "L'objet qui sert de signe n'est jamais '*le même*' deux fois: il faut dès le premier moment un examen ou une convention initiale, pour savoir au nom de quoi [et] dans quelles limites nous avons le droit de l'appeler le même; là est la fondamentale différence avec un objet quelconque."

[20] "Baudouin de Courtenay et Kruszewski ont été plus près que personne d'une vue théorique de la langue, cela sans sortir des considérations linguistiques pures; ils sont d'ailleurs ignorés de la généralité des savants occidentaux. — L'Américain Whitney, que je révère, n'a jamais dit un seul mot sur les mêmes sujets, qui ne fût juste; mais comme tous les autres, il ne songe pas que la langue ait besoin d'une systématique."

language and the game of chess: the necessity of a clear-cut distinction between two aspects of the game, namely, the simultaneous positions of the figures and the temporal sequence of their moves. This distinction is then said to be particularly important for the science of language: among human institutions language is the only one which is not submitted "to continuous mental correction, because from the outset it does not proceed with any visible agreement between the idea and the means of expression".[21] The interconnection of these two facets is viewed by the scholar as merely conventional (Whitney's term *arbitrary*, later adopted by Saussure, was used only once and crossed out in his notebook). Consequently,

it would be truly presumptuous, from that, to believe that the history of language should resemble even distantly that of any other institution.

That language is, at every moment of its existence, *a historical product* — that much is evident. But that at no point of language does this historical product represent anything other than the compromise (the ultimate compromise) with certain symbols that the mind accepts — this is a truth even more absolute, for without this last circumstance there would be no language. Now the manner in which the mind may employ a symbol (*if we first admit that the symbol remains unchanged*) is a whole science which has nothing to do with historical considerations. Moreover, [if the] symbol changes, then immediately there arises a new state, necessitating a new application of universal laws.[22]

As to the changes themselves, Saussure insists on their merely fortuitous character: "Everything goes on outside the mind." And above all, "in its *genesis* a process arises from some accident". If one were to cling to the comparison with a chess game, then — in Saussure's dogma

nothing prevents us from assuming that the player is completely absurd, as is the randomness of phonetic and other events.

For many years we have maintained the conviction that linguistics is a *split*

---

[21] "La différence de l'institution du langage d'avec les autres institutions humaines; à savoir celle-ci n'est pas soumise à la correction continuelle de l'esprit, parce qu'elle ne découle pas, depuis l'origine, d'une harmonie visible entre l'idée et le moyen d'expression."
[22] "Il serait vraiment présomptueux de croire que l'histoire du langage doive ressembler même de loin, après cela, à celle d'une autre institution.

"Que le langage soit, à chaque moment de son existence, *un produit historique*, c'est ce qui est évident. Mais qu'à aucun moment du langage, ce produit historique représente autre chose que le compromis (le dernier compromis) qu'accepte l'esprit avec certains symboles, c'est là une vérité plus absolue encore, car sans ce dernier fait il n'y aurait pas de langage. Or la façon dont l'esprit peut se servir d'un symbole (*étant donné d'abord que le symbole ne change pas*) est toute une science, laquelle n'a rien à voir avec les considérations historiques. De plus, [si le] symbole change, immédiatement après, il y a un nouvel état, nécessitant une nouvelle application des lois universelles."

science, and so profoundly, irreparably split that one might indeed ask if there is sufficient reason to maintain under the name linguistics an artificial unity, giving rise precisely to all the errors, all the inextricable snares we are struggling against.[23]

Saussure entitled his final remarks to this question "On the Antihistoricalness of Language". He ventured to corroborate this headline:

There is no "language" and no science of language except on the prior condition of abstracting from what has gone before, from what interconnects the periods. *** It is the absolute condition for understanding what takes place — or simply what *is* — in a given state that one abstracts from what is not of that state — for example, from what preceded — especially from what preceded. But what is the result of this for generalization? Generalization is impossible. *** To conceive of a generalization which would manage equally both of these things is to ask for the absurd. It is this kind of absurdity that linguistics, from its birth, has wanted to impose on the mind. Consequently, it would be impossible to discuss a single term used in linguistics in its daily work without taking up *ab ovo* the entire question of language,[24] still less to formulate an appraisal of a doctrine which, as rational as it was, did not take account [?].[25]

It is an evident allusion to Whitney's doctrine. But, on the other hand, Saussure's belief in the preponderance or even hegemony of "nonhistorical" linguistics expressed in his notebook with such an intransigence was, nonetheless, subject throughout the nineties to recurrent and

---

[23] "Tout se passe hors de l'esprit."
"Par sa génèse un procédé provient de n'importe quel hasard."
"*** rien n'empêche de supposer le joueur tout-à-fait absurde comme c'est le hasard des événements phonétiques et autres."
"Nous nourrissons depuis bien des années cette conviction que la linguistique est une science *double*, et si profondément, irrémédiablement double qu'on peut à vrai dire se demander s'il y a une raison suffisante pour maintenir sous ce nom de linguistique une unité factice, génératrice précisément de toutes les erreurs, de tous les inextricables pièges contre lesquels nous nous débattons."
[24] "Il n'y a pas un seul terme employé en linguistique auquel j'accorde un sens quelconque," said Saussure in his letter to Meillet quoted earlier.
[25] "Il n'y a de 'langue' et de science de la langue, qu'à la condition initiale de faire abstraction de ce qui a précédé, de ce qui relie entre elles les époques. *** C'est la condition absolue pour comprendre ce qui se passe, ou seulement ce qui *est*, dans un état que de faire abstraction de ce qui n'est pas de cet état, par exemple de ce qui a précédé; surtout de ce qui a précédé. Mais que résulte-t-il de là pour la généralisation? La généralisation est impossible. *** Concevoir une généralisation qui mènerait de front ces deux choses est demander l'absurde. C'est ce genre d'absurde que la linguistique, depuis sa naissance, veut imposer à l'esprit. Il serait, par suite, impossible soit de discourir sur un seul des termes usités en linguistique dans la pratique de chaque jour sans reprendre *ab ovo* la question totale du langage, soit encore moins de formuler une appréciation sur une doctrine qui n'a pas tenu compte, si rationnelle qu'elle fût, [?]."

pungent hesitations. Thus even in his Whitney notebook we run into expressions of uncertainty:

It is extremely uncertain and difficult to say if it is a historical entity or rather something else, but in the current stage of trends, there is no danger in especially stressing its nonhistorical side.[26]

In the same notebook "the real question" (*la vraie question*) was propounded but struck out by Saussure himself:

Can one "force" language to become historical subject matter, appropriately historical? — But inversely, will it for an instant be possible to forget the historical side?[27]

One may, moreover, recall that Baudouin de Courtenay, in his Polish monograph of 1894 on phonetic alternations, blamed Saussure for a unilateral historicism and for a disregard of coexistent elements in language. The latter's introductory lectures of 1891 at the University of Geneva claimed that "everything in language is *history*, that is to say that it is an object for historical analysis, and not for abstract analysis",[28] and even when reviewing J. Schmidt's monograph of 1895 — *Kritik der Sonantentheorie* — for the *Indogermanische Forschungen* of 1897, Saussure affirmed that

when true linguistic theory is first done, one of the very first principles which will be set down is that never, in any case, can a rule whose characteristic it is to operate in a *state of language* (= between 2 contemporaneous terms) and not in a *phonetic event* (= 2 successive terms) have more than a fortuitous validity. *** And in any case, in order to put forth the rule in a true sense, one must recapture the anterior item in place of the contemporaneous one. ***[29]

---

[26] "Il est extrêmement douteux et délicat de dire si c'est plutôt un objet historique ou plutôt autre chose, mais dans l'état actuel des tendances, il n'y a aucun danger à insister surtout sur le côté non-historique."
[27] "Peut on 'forcer' le langage jusqu'à devenir une matière historique, proprement historique? — Mais inversement, sera-t-il un seul instant possible d'oublier le côté historique?"
[28] "Tout dans la langue est *histoire*, c'est à dire qu'elle est un objet d'analyse historique, et non d'analyse abstraite."
[29] "Quand on fera pour la première fois une théorie vraie de la langue, un des tout premiers principes qu'on y inscrira est que jamais, en aucun cas, une règle qui a pour caractère de se mouvoir dans un *état de langue* (= entre 2 termes contemporains) et non dans un *événement phonétique* (= 2 termes successifs) ne peut avoir plus qu'une validité de hasard. *** Et dans tous les cas, pour poser la règle sous un vrai sens, il faudra reprendre le terme antérieur au lieu d'un terme contemporain ***"

Saussure's focusing upon "states of language" alienates him from Whitney's principles of linguistic science and draws his designs and propositions nearer to Peirce's semiotic quest:

The altogether ultimate law of language is, by what we venture to say, that there is never anything which can consist in one item (as a direct consequence of the fact that linguistic symbols are without connection to what they must designate), thus that two such have their value only by their reciprocal *difference*, or that none has any value, even through a part of itself (I assume "the root," etc.) other than by this same network of eternally negative differences.[30]

Side by side with *différences*, the notebook uses also the term *oppositions*, most probably modeled upon Baudouin's example (*protivopoložnosti*) and later promoted as a basic concept of Saussurian doctrine. The kernel of this doctrine emerges in the notebook: "The a priori absolute evidence that there will never be a single fragment of language which can be founded on anything, as an ultimate principle, other than its noncoincidence with the remainder; positive form being irrelevant, to a degree to which we have no idea ***; for this degree is tantamount to zero."[31]

Saussure's approach to the systems of correlative linguistic values permitted him to re-evaluate the achievements of such distinguished scholars as Whitney in the light of the anticipated future: "Besides, we should have no illusions. There will arrive a day where it will be recognized that the quanta of language and their relations are in their essence consistently expressible through mathematical formulas."[32] Otherwise one would have to renounce any comprehension of linguistic facts: "This is what, despite ourselves, deeply changes our point of view on the worth of everything which has been said, even by very eminent men."[33]

---

[30] "La loi tout à fait finale du langage est à ce que nous osons dire qu'il n'y a jamais rien qui puisse résider dans un terme (par suite directe de ce que les symboles linguistiques sont sans relation avec ce qu'ils doivent désigner), donc que tous deux ne valent que par leur réciproque *différence*, ou qu'aucun ne vaut, même par une partie quelconque de soi (je suppose 'la racine' etc.), autrement que par ce même plexus de différences éternellement négatives."

[31] "*** l'évidence absolue, même à priori, qu'il n'y aura jamais un seul fragment de langue qui puisse être fondé sur autre chose, comme principe ultime, que sa non-coïncidence, ou sur le degré de sa non-coïncidence, avec le reste; la forme positive étant indifférente, jusqu'à un degré dont nous n'avons encore aucune idée ***; car ce degré est entièrement égal à zéro."

[32] "Au reste, ne nous faisons pas d'illusions. Il arrivera un jour où on reconnaîtra que les quantités du langage et leurs rapports sont régulièrement exprimables de leur nature fondamentale par des formules mathématiques."

[33] "C'est ce qui change beaucoup, malgré nous, notre point de vue sur la valeur de tout ce qui a été dit, même par des hommes très éminents."

Both Saussure's requirement of autonomy for linguistics and his criticism of Whitney's view of this question had been anticipated one decade earlier by the paramount Czech philosopher T. G. Masaryk (1850–1937), whose treatise *Základové konkretné logiky* ("Fundamentals of Concrete Logic", 1885) tended to draft a rational systematics of sciences. Masaryk's discussion of the relation between linguistics and neighboring disciplines borders upon Whitney's "couple of volumes" which inaugurate the selection of sources recommended in the Czech treatise. Its author adheres to Whitney's view of language as a social institution but essentially modifies the latter's thesis:

> The question arises whether linguistics is an independent science, and especially one might argue whether in some way it does not pertain to sociology. I think, however, that linguistics is an independent science, in view of its own particular subject matter, namely language, which both in its being and buildup is distinct from the phenomena treated by sociology. However close may be the connection which ties the development of speech and writing to the genesis and development of the inner life, nonetheless it is an entirely separate theme and has to be investigated by its own science.

In his book of 1885 Masaryk condemned any superficial imitation of extraneous methods by linguists. He assailed logical incongruity and fear of theory as handicaps to the development of linguistics. In the author's vision, principles of linguistic science were to be systematically elaborated as a necessary theoretical basis of concrete linguistics — *special*, oriented toward single languages and language families, and *general*, destined to elicit and sum up the experience from the whole universe of languages. It was Whitney's latent intuition which must have furthered the thought of the twofold subdivision of the study of language — both abstract and concrete — into its synchronic (fundamental) and historical (secondary) aspects, that thought which haunted Masaryk in the eighties and Saussure in the nineties and was fraught with serious consequences for the further development of linguistic science.

The most comprehensive essay devoted to Whitney's initiatory attainments in the theory of language and to their place in the world history of ideas was written by the prominent Italian linguist Benvenuto Terracini (1886–1968). It was published, on the occasion of the fiftieth anniversary of Whitney's death, in *Revista de Filologia Hispanica*, vol. 5 (1943) under the title "W. D. Whitney y la lingüistica general". In its Italian version, "Le origini della linguistica generale", which was included in Terracini's *Guida allo studio della linguistica storica* (Rome, 1949), Whitney is portrayed as the "initiator of general linguistics built upon historical empiricism" who still endows his readers with a feeling of "a particular charm". Especially, pervasive European discussions on the "institutionalism" and "conventionalism" of language never fail to bring forward again and again Whitney's name and creed.

In his native country, the immediate impact of Whitney's contributions to the general science of language was far weaker. For long years it looked as if students "absorbed in particulars" disregarded his prefatory warning of 1867 not to lose "sight of the grand truths and principles which underlie and give significance to their work, and the recognition of which ought to govern its course throughout". American academic publications confined their occasional tributes of respect to cursory remarks that Whitney's theoretical studies "cannot have remained wholly without effect" and that they "helped chase many a goblin from the sky" (Benjamin Ide Wheeler). New linguistic ideas which began to sprout here, mainly towards the threshold of our century, were tied to the advance of anthropology and to the methodological questions stirred by the developing research in American Indian languages, their structure, and interrelation.

If, according to Brugmann's letter, cited earlier, "a German colleague" felt the great indebtedness of European science to the New Englander Whitney, "the great departed scholar", now it was the Westphalia-born Franz Boas (1858–1942) who in 1886 transferred his versatile scientific activities from Germany to America and initiated vast descriptive, anthropologically oriented linguistic fieldwork which involved a wide team of explorers and revealed a vital need of new methods and theoretical inferences. As Leonard Bloomfield (1887–1949) wrote in his obituary of Boas, "the progress which has since been made in the recording and description of human speech has merely grown forth from the roots, stem, and mighty branches of Boas' life work".

In the succeeding generation of American scholars, the scope of linguistic interests has embraced the local native languages and the Indo-European world as well. Significantly enough, Whitney's legacy was deliberately restored by Leonard Bloomfield, whose first outline, *An Introduction to the Study of Language* (New York, 1914), is, even in its title, associated precisely with Whitney's tradition. The initial lines of Bloomfield's Preface announce that the purpose of the new publication is the same "as that of Whitney's *Language and the Study of Language* and *The Life and Growth of Language*, books which fifty years ago represented the attainments of linguistic science and, owing to their author's clearness of view and conscientious discrimination between ascertained fact and mere surmise, contain little to which we cannot today subscribe. The great progress of our science in the last half-century is, I believe, nevertheless sufficient excuse for my attempt to give a summary of what is now known about language."

Bloomfield retained his admiration for Whitney's linguistic essentials and once, in the early 1940's, he said that his first guide to a synchronic study of languages was Whitney's *Sanskrit Grammar* of 1879. It is worthy of note that A. Hillebrandt's review of 1880 recognized the novelty of this grammar in its inquiry into a state of language (*Erforschung des Sprachzustandes*), and the best translator and commentator of Saussure's *Corso di linguistica generale* (Bari, 1967), Tullio De Mauro, compared this feature of Whitney's textbook with Saussure's synchronic approach to language.

Linguistic structures are "context-sensitive": they shift their meaning correspondingly to their variable surroundings. In a similar way linguistic theories undergo modifications according to the historical environment and personal ideology of their interpreters. Thus Whitney's doctrine is differently viewed and treated by Brugmann, by Saussure, by Terracini, by Bloomfield, and presumably also by the present-day critical readers. Hitherto in all interpretations of Whitney's contributions to general linguistics, the invariant idea is that on the subjects he discussed, he made no fallacious statements, and thus in questions of general linguistics, he remarkably surpassed his predecessors and contemporaries. The variables in the appraisal of Whitney's legacy concern not so much what he said as what and how much remains to be said "dans un autre sens" and what is the relative pertinence for the science of language of that which was revealed in comparison with that which remained unvoiced.

Written as a preface to *Whitney on Language: Selected Writings of William Dwight Whitney*, ed. M. Silverstein (Cambridge, Mass.: M.I.T. Press, 1971).

LA PREMIÈRE LETTRE DE FERDINAND DE SAUSSURE À ANTOINE MEILLET SUR LES ANAGRAMMES

PUBLIÉE ET COMMENTÉE PAR
ROMAN JAKOBSON

Genève, 12 nov. 06

Mon cher ami
Avant même de répondre à vos lignes, permettez-moi un remerciement rétrospectif. Il continue d'être très actuel pour moi. Je veux parler du témoignage affectueux que vous m'avez donné voici quelques mois dans l'enceinte du Collège de France en mêlant mon nom à un passage de votre discours d'ouverture, et en en faisant une mention qui devait être sensible à mon amitié. C'est de ces paroles plus qu'aimables, mais c'est aussi de tout le contenu de votre beau morceau [d'ouverture], qui est si riche d'idées, et si bien choisi comme leçon d'ouverture, que je voulais vous parler, dans une lettre dont je ne vous dirai point le sort: il fut analogue à celui d'autres que vous connaissez! — C'est par une nouvelle pensée tout aussi amicale pour moi que vous songeriez à mettre en avant mon nom pour les Conférences étrangères qui ont lieu au Collège de France, et c'est un honneur qui se refuse difficilement dès qu'il est offert. Je l'accepte en principe. Je tiens seulement, et au cas où la proposition prendrait un corps, à ce que les personnes qui ont à décider, sachent que je ne me reconnais aucune espèce de talent de parole; en sorte que dans une alternative où le Collège aurait à se diriger d'après cette considération, je vous prie de retrancher d'avance mon nom.
En tout état de cause ou de choses, je pense que c'est seulement pour 1908 que la question se proposerait pour moi, déjà par le fait qu'un savant suisse, M. Naville, a eu les honneurs du début.
Je vois, par parenthèse (qui ne regarde plus directement[1] le Collège de France), que vous mentionnez les Nibelungen comme un de mes sujets d'étude. C'est exact! Mais vous en ai-je écrit? Je ne crois pas l'avoir fait, cela eût comporté, vis-à-vis de vous, un minimum de 25 pages dont je n'ai pas le souvenir. Assurément si le temps m'est donné de reprendre cette étude, j'aimerais autant avoir une fois à parler à Paris de cette légende que des principes de la linguistique. Mais l'étude n'a rien à faire, d'autre part,

---

[1] Le mot "directement" est ajouté en marge par F. de Saussure.

avec l'*Histoire des religions; à moins que la* légende, *comme telle, même sans intervention d'êtres divins, soit comprise dans l'histoire des religions?? On sait que la version allemande des Nibelungen ne comporte pas de personnes divines. La version norroise les laisse apparaître uniquement dans les parties qui sont surajoutées, et personnellement je combats toute origine mythologique; en sorte que s'il s'agit de religion, j'aurais les mains vides, au moins à mon point de vue personnel, s'il faut parler des Nibelungen.*

Je crois que ma dernière lettre était de Rome. Je ne sais si c'est par inspiration des tombeaux des Scipions ou autrement que j'ai passé ensuite mon temps à [traiter] creuser le vers saturnien, sur lequel j'arrive à des conclusions tout-à-fait différentes de celles de Louis Havet.

Mais je vais d'emblée joindre à ceci une demande que j'avais le projet de vous faire, et à propos duquel vous auriez reçu une lettre si vous ne m'aviez prévenu [,] à propos d'autre chose:

*Me rendriez-vous le service, d'amitié, de lire des notes sur l'*Anagramme *dans les poèmes homériques que j'ai consignées, entre autres études, au cours des recherches sur le vers Saturnien; et à propos desquelles je vous consulte[rais, si vous] confidentiellement, parce qu'il est presque impossible à celui [qu'il] qui en a l'idée de savoir s'il est victime d'une illusion, ou si quelque chose de vrai est à la base de son idée, ou s'il n'y a que moitié vrai. En cherchant partout quelqu'un qui puisse être le contrôleur de mon hypothèse, je ne vois depuis longtemps que vous; [mais] et comme je lui demanderais en même temps de me garder toute discrétion vis-à-vis de cette hypothèse, peut-être illusoire, c'est encore à vous que je m'adresserais pour avoir toute confiance de ce côté-là. Je ne vous cache pas que, si vous acceptez, le prochain courrier vous apportera douze ou quinze cahiers de notes. Toutefois ces notes sont rédigées comme en vue d'un lecteur, loi que je me suis imposée afin d'avoir pour ainsi dire un premier contrôle[, et] vis-à-vis de moi-même, — et elles n'offrent donc pas de difficulté de lecture. En second lieu je puis dire qu'il n'est pas nécessaire de lire le tout, et que comme tout se compose d'articles séparés, dont le plus long ne dépasse pas 8–10 pages, cette lecture n'impose aucun effort continu. Voyez si vous avez le temps pour cela, et répondez-moi très franchement au cas où vous seriez [au contraire] surchargé en ce moment, comme c'est presque à prévoir à l'instant où s'ouvrent vos nombreux cours du Collège de France et des autres Écoles. Sur la question que vous me posiez, je ne puis que confirmer, avec remerciements, la réponse que je vous donnais en commençant, acceptation pour 1908 à part mes scrupules de conférencier.*

Votre affect^t dévoué
F. DE SAUSSURE

* * *

Les lettres de F. de Saussure à A. Meillet, parues dans les *Cahiers Ferdinand de Saussure* (cité *infra: CFS*) (1964, XXI:89–130), ont été remises par Madame Meillet à Émile Benveniste qui note dans le bref Avant-propos de cette importante publication (p. 91) que quelques lettres de cette série semblent manquer, en particulier celle où Saussure "faisait la première annonce de ses recherches sur le saturnien". Il s'agit de la lettre que Madame Meillet a découverte par hasard, au cours de l'été 1970, dans un livre de la bibliothèque de son mari et que nous publions ci-dessus.

Le "remerciement rétrospectif", exprimé par Saussure au début de cette lettre, se rapporte à la *Leçon d'ouverture du cours de Grammaire comparée au Collège de France*, lue par Meillet le mardi 13 février 1906 sous le titre "L'État actuel des études de linguistique générale". En parlant des maîtres auxquels il doit beaucoup pour sa formation intellectuelle, le successeur de Michel Bréal y rappelle, à côté de James Darmesteter mort prématurément, encore "un autre nom: après avoir donné à notre pays dix ans d'un enseignement lumineux et avoir suscité autour de lui les vocations scientifiques, M. Ferdinand de Saussure est rentré dans sa patrie pour y occuper la chaire de grammaire comparée à la belle Université de Genève. Aucun de ceux qui ont eu le bonheur de les entendre n'oubliera jamais ces leçons familières de l'École des hautes études où l'élégance discrète de la forme dissimulait si bien la sûreté impeccable et l'étendue de l'information, et où la précision d'une méthode inflexiblement rigoureuse ne laissait qu'à peine entrevoir la génialité de l'intuition."

Saussure, accoutumé à mettre en cause son "épistolophobie" afin de justifier les intervalles fréquents et prolongés dans sa correspondance, l'invoque une fois de plus pour motiver son intention inaccomplie de discuter le contenu du discours de Meillet, mais en fait, c'est la divergence des vues qui a dû contribuer à l'abstention. L'idée de l'impossibilité d'aborder un changement linguistique "en dehors de la considération du système général de la langue où il apparaît" et l'appel à la recherche des lois générales, tant morphologiques que phonétiques, "qui ne valent pas pour un seul moment du développement d'une langue, qui au contraire sont de tous les temps; qui ne sont pas limitées à une langue donnée, qui au contraire s'étendent à toutes les langues" et donc "s'appliquent à l'humanité entière", cette recherche qui, d'après le discours de Meillet, "doit être désormais l'un des principaux objets de la linguistique", se trouvait nettement incompatible avec la rupture complète entre l'idée du système et celle des changements fortuits et aveugles, professée ensuite par Saussure dans ses cours de linguistique générale.

Les premières six conférences étrangères de la Fondation Michonis ont été faites au Collège de France, du 4 au 22 novembre 1905, par l'égyptologue genevois Édouard Naville, un parent de F. de Saussure, et publiées ensuite dans les *Annales du Musée Guimet*, 1906, XXIII. C'est par lui que Saussure avait eu "quelques nouvelles (fort bonnes)" concernant l'élection de Meillet au Collège de France (cf. *CFS* XXI:105). Finalement, dans une lettre de Rome datée du 23 janvier 1906, Saussure remercie Meillet de lui avoir fait apprendre sa nomination officielle et lui adresse tous les "bons souhaits pour la nouvelle carrière d'activité" (*ibid*.: 106).

Suivant les renseignements des archives du Collège de France, qui nous sont parvenus par l'intermédiaire complaisant de Claude Lévi-Strauss, c'est à l'Assemblée du 6 novembre 1906 que le nom de Saussure fut mis en avant par Meillet pour les conférences de la Fondation Michonis en 1907, tandis que Paul Foucart, professeur d'épigraphie et antiquités grecques, lors de la même Assemblée, proposa Charles Michel, l'auteur des travaux sur Jamblique et les Évangiles apocryphes. Meillet a dû informer immédiatement Saussure de son projet. La prompte réponse de Saussure, datée du 12 novembre 1906 (cf. *supra*) et remettant la question jusqu'à l'année 1908, paraît avoir ajourné la proposition de Meillet, et finalement le philologue Charles Michel, de Liège, et l'historien Alexandru Xenopol, de l'Université de Jassy, furent désignés conjointement.

Il est véritablement difficile de s'expliquer pourquoi la question d'inviter au Collège Ferdinand de Saussure ne s'est plus jamais posée en dépit de son "acceptation pour 1908". Ses "scrupules de conférencier" ne pouvaient être guère pris au sérieux, puisque ses leçons, comme l'avait dit Meillet, manifestaient au contraire une "élégance discrète de la forme". Nous ne possédons malheureusement aucune lettre de Saussure à Meillet entre celle du 12 novembre 1906 et le message commencé le 23 septembre 1907 et terminé "quelque quinze jours" plus tard, un texte où l'on trouve plusieurs allusions difficiles à déchiffrer. Comme l'a vu Benveniste (*ibid*.: 107), elles "supposent une lettre antérieure [et même, pourrait-on ajouter: un échange de lettres] que nous n'avons pas". Saussure commence ce message de 1907 ainsi: "Votre lettre m'a causé avant tout *une déception* [la différence d'écriture ici et dans le reste des citations provient de l'original], mais elle contient une promesse, et cette promesse, quand même vous en mettez l'échéance à un nombre assez vague de mois, je la retiens avec précision, et j'en fais dès à présent ma fiche de consolation" (*ibid*.). Cette allusion permet de se demander s'il ne s'agit pas là de l'invitation au Collège, ajournée mais toujours envisagée pour l'avenir: "Rien ne pouvait me faire plaisir comme la perspective sérieuse que vous me donnez de vous voir" (*ibid.*).

Notons que, d'après les données des archives du Collège de France, Ferdinand de Saussure n'y a jamais professé, bien que deux fois la question ait été posée: déjà à l'Assemblée du 18 mars 1888, le prédécesseur de Meillet au Collège, Michel Bréal, a proposé Saussure pour son "remplacement conditionnel" au cours du second semestre; mais cette proposition, comme plus tard celle de Meillet, ne s'est pas réalisée.

C'est en réfléchissant sur les thèmes appropriés pour les conférences parisiennes que Meillet a dû questionner Saussure sur les *Nibelungen* comme un de ses "sujets d'étude". La réponse de Saussure, dans sa lettre du 12 novembre 1906 publiée ci-dessus, nous permet, entre autres, de dater de plus près son travail inédit sur les *Nibelungen* gardé dans la Bibliothèque publique et universitaire de Genève (cf. R. Godel, *Les sources manuscrites du Cours de linguistique générale de F. de Saussure*, Paris, 1957:136): "Assurément, si le temps m'est donné de reprendre cette étude, j'aimerais autant avoir une fois à parler à Paris de cette légende que des principes de la linguistique. — Mais l'étude n'a rien à faire, d'autre part, avec l'Histoire des religions; *** en sorte que s'il s'agit de religion, j'aurais les mains vides, au moins à mon point de vue personnel, s'il faut parler des Nibelungen." A ce qu'il paraît, Meillet avait en vue l'intérêt manifesté au Collège pour des conférences de caractère interdisciplinaire qui toucheraient non seulement à la philologie, mais aussi à l'histoire des religions, comme l'a fait Édouard Naville en discutant dans ses leçons la civilisation des anciens Égyptiens, leurs mythes et divinités, *Le Livre des Morts*, etc.

Cette réponse de Saussure vient nous renseigner une fois de plus sur le rôle opportun qu'a pris dans sa recherche, au début de notre siècle, la poésie de pair avec les "principes de la linguistique". En réfléchissant sur les thèmes à traiter dans les conférences parisiennes, Saussure confie à Meillet un nouveau problème de poétique en train de devenir, sous l'étiquette d'*anagramme*, le point crucial et l'objet favori de son examen; peut-être espère-t-il employer ses notes là-dessus, "rédigées comme en vue d'un lecteur", pour en faire un exposé au Collège de France. En tout cas, la lettre du 12 novembre 1906 nous informe sur les débuts des études assidues du linguiste concernant la "poétique phonisante, et spécialement l'anagramme".

Ayant pris la décision "de mettre une interruption" dans ses "occupations et préoccupations habituelles", Saussure écrit à Meillet le 10 janvier 1906 qu'à cause "de fatigue et de surmenage", il a dû se faire octroyer un congé à l'Université de Genève, et qu'après avoir passé le mois de décembre à Naples, il réside avec sa femme à Rome (Hôtel Pincio, Via Gregoriana) "pour un séjour prolongé" (*CFS* XXI: 105). " Je m'en trouve fort bien", ajoute-t-il, et ses lignes du 23 janvier 1906 apportent quelques détails sur le passe-temps du savant en "repos nécessaire": "Inutile de vous dire que je ne fais pas grand chose ici. L'inscription archaïque du Forum est un amusement tout indiqué lorsque j'éprouve le besoin de me casser la tête" (*ibid.*: 106). Un renvoi à ces lignes dans la lettre du 12 novembre (cf. *supra*) est suivi d'un rapport sur un nouveau casse-tête trouvé par le visiteur de Rome: "Je ne sais si c'est par inspiration des tombeaux des Scipions ou autrement que j'ai passé ensuite mon temps à creuser le vers saturnien sur lequel j'arrive à des conclusions tout à fait différentes de celles de Louis Havet", le célèbre auteur du traité *De Saturnio, Latinorum versu inest reliquiarum quotquot supersunt sylloge* (Paris, 1880). Cf. la lettre du 14 juillet 1906 où Saussure résume les résultats de ses recherches sur le vers saturnien: J. Starobinski, "Le texte dans le texte. Extraits inédits des Cahiers d'anagrammes de F. de Saussure", *Tel Quel* (Paris, 1969, XXXVII: 3–33), pp. 7–10.

Nous apprenons en même temps que c'est "au cours des recherches sur le vers saturnien" que Saussure, "entre autres études", a consigné "des notes sur l'*Anagramme dans les poèmes homériques*". Et puisqu'il est "presque impossible à celui qui en a l'idée de savoir s'il est victime d'une illusion, ou si quelque chose de vrai est à la base de son idée, ou s'il n'y a que moitié vrai", Saussure tient à consulter Meillet comme le seul contrôleur possible en lui demandant de garder toute discrétion vis-à-vis d'une hypothèse "peut-être illusoire". Si le destinataire le veut bien, douze ou quinze cahiers d'articles "dont le plus long ne dépasse pas 8–10 pages", lui seront apportés par le "prochain courrier".

Or, malgré l'offre de lire ces "feuilles sur l'anagramme homérique", faite et réitérée par Meillet, Saussure lui communique le 23 septembre 1907 qu'il se trouve décidé à lui envoyer plutôt un aperçu des résultats auxquels il arrive "pour le Saturnien latin". Ce chapitre lui semble "plus capital que celui d'Homère": "Je laisse la question ouverte provisoirement pour les dits poèmes homériques, et je reviens à ce que je disais être mon point de départ — que j'aurais peut-être mieux fait d'explorer à fond dès l'année dernière au lieu de partir par la tangente sur Homère: *** le Saturnien latin m'eût offert, je crois, un champ plus sûr, si je l'avais tout de suite fouillé à fond sans sortir de ce cercle" (*ibid.*: 108 *sq.*). Saussure ajoute un bel exposé des conclusions auxquelles il avait été conduit "par l'examen des restes de la poésie saturnienne" et entrevoit résolument la même "forme *anagrammatique* du phonisme" dans le vers germanique et védique (*ibid.*: 109–114).

Après avoir reçu d'abord cette longue lettre et ensuite, sous un autre pli, un manuscrit "un peu grossi" avec des notes sur le saturnien, Meillet répondit à Saussure par une lettre dont la date exacte reste peu claire: "Sur les faits relativement troubles qu'apporte le saturnien, j'avais été déjà très frappé par la netteté des coïncidences. Avec les précisions nouvelles que vous apportez, il me semble qu'on aura peine à nier la doctrine en son ensemble. On pourra naturellement épiloguer sur telle ou telle anagramme; mais sur l'ensemble de la théorie, je ne crois pas." Et avec sa perspicacité habituelle il pronostique: "Je vois bien qu'on aura un doute pour ainsi dire a priori. Mais il tient à notre conception moderne d'un art rationaliste." C'est grâce à la publication étoffée de Jean Starobinski, *Les Anagrammes de Ferdinand de Saussure: textes inédits* (Paris, Mercure de France [cité *infra*: MF], 1964), que nous avons pu prendre connaissance de ce remarquable document (p. 261).

Saussure, qui avait attendu avec angoisse "l'opinion d'un confrère non prévenu, et jugeant froidement" (*CFS* XXI:112), réagit vivement dans sa lettre du 8 janvier à l'adhésion sincère de Meillet: "Je me souviens avec une bien véritable gratitude du concours amical que vous m'avez donné au début de cette recherche, lorsque nous parlions du vers saturnien, et que vous m'avez donné un appui précieux par votre critique; car je crois bien que si vous ne m'aviez pas confirmé que l'idée de l'anagramme ne vous semblait pas fausse, d'après les exemples saturniens, je n'aurais pas eu l'idée de poursuivre une recherche qui se trouve solutionnée complètement en dehors du Saturnien et de mon objet primitif" (*ibid.*: 119).

Notons que, précisément dans la même lettre, le linguiste genevois attachant "l'importance de premier ordre" à la réaction de son élève parisien aux "cahiers d'anagrammes" qu'il lui envoyait graduellement, confesse qu'il a cessé tout à fait "de douter, non seulement quant à l'anagramme en général, mais sur les principaux points qui en forment l'organisme, et qui pouvaient sembler nébuleux" (*ibid.*: 118). "Je ne vois décidément plus — se croit-il en droit de dire — la possibilité, pour ce qui me concerne, de garder un doute"; et sa conclusion lui paraît "absolument certaine pour tout le monde, dès qu'on verra le caractère tout à fait illimité du fait et de ses exemples" (*ibid.*: 119). Dans une carte postale du 10 février 1908, Meillet ajoute à la collection de son maître un bel exemple anagrammatique qu'il dit avoir trouvé en ouvrant Horace "exactement au hasard" (*Tel Quel*, 1969, XXXVII: 32).

Il est véritablement surprenant que les 99 cahiers manuscrits de Saussure, consacrés à la "poétique phonisante" et en particulier au "principe de l'anagramme", aient pu rester plus d'un demi-siècle dissimulés aux lecteurs, jusqu'à ce que Jean Starobinski ait eu l'heureuse idée d'en publier plusieurs échantillons soigneusement choisis et commentés (MF: 242–262). Comme nous nous sommes permis d'observer à leur apparition (*Selected Writings*, 1966, IV:685): "In the last years of his scientific activity, F. de Saussure fully realized how unexplored and obscure are the general questions of language and the problems of poetic texture as well. The theory and analysis of the sound figures [jeux phoniques], particularly anagrams, and their role in the diverse poetic traditions as elaborated by him simultaneously with his renowned courses of general linguistics may certainly be counted among Saussure's most daring and lucid discoveries." Les mêmes oscillations continuelles entre la vision d'une voie ouverte sur les phénomènes qu'il tient pour incontestables, et la peur d'être "victime d'une illusion", caractérisent les recherches faites par Saussure dans les deux domaines. Ses études sur l'anagramme ont été au moins "rédigées comme en vue d'un lecteur" et considérées par leur auteur comme parties "du livre" en préparation (cf. MF: 261), tandis qu'en matière de théorie linguistique, il se dit constamment dégoûté "de la difficulté qu'il y a en général à écrire seulement dix lignes ayant le sens commun" (*CFS* XXI:95) et ne griffonne que des ébauches éparses, en rejetant de plus en plus l'idée d'un cours publié. Quant à la prétendue décision prise finalement par Saussure de ne pas publier ses études sur les anagrammes, faut-il rappeler ce qu'il dit lui-même sur son "talent" d'interrompre la publication de ses articles linguistiques "non seulement écrits, mais en grande partie composés" (*ibid.*: 108)?

Giuseppe Nava note la "particulière lucidité" avec laquelle ce chercheur sut affronter "les aspects antinomiques" que sa théorie de la structure poétique lui présentait (*CFS*, 1968, XXIV:76), mais on pourrait employer une formule tout à fait analogue à propos des "antinomies" traitées dans son *Cours* (ou plutôt dans ses cours) *de linguistique générale*. Dans les deux cas, Saussure met en relief des contradictions irréconciliables en pressentant la synthèse avec une clairvoyance extraordinaire, mais reste en même temps enchaîné par les préjugés de son ambiance idéologique, qui l'empêchent de tirer parti de ses propres intuitions.

Ainsi, la première des deux lettres de Saussure à Giovanni Pascoli, découvertes, publiées et commentées par Giuseppe Nava — celle du 9 mars 1909 — nous montre leur auteur vivement tourmenté par la question de savoir si "certains détails techniques qui semblent observés dans la versification" sont "purement fortuits, ou sont-ils voulus, et appliqués de manière consciente?" (*ibid.*: 79). La seconde lettre de

Saussure au poète Pascoli, datée du 6 avril 1909, pose à plusieurs reprises la même question inquiète, s'agit-il ou non de "simples coïncidences fortuites":
1. "Est-ce par hasard ou avec intention" ***?
2. "Est-ce encore par hasard" ***?
3. "Est-il également fortuit" ***? (*ibid.*: 80–81).

Cependant le besoin de ces tentatives appelées à "vérifier l'intention" se trouve aboli par les remarques brèves, mais pertinentes, qu'on découvre subitement dans les Cahiers d'anagrammes. "La matérialité du fait", dont le poète lui-même peut se rendre compte ou non, reste en vigueur quel que soit le dessein conscient de l'auteur et le jugement du critique. "Que le critique d'une part, et que le versificateur d'autre part, le veuille ou non", comme le dit Saussure: cf. J. Starobinski, "Les mots sous les mots: textes inédits des Cahiers d'anagrammes de F. de Saussure", in *To Honor Roman Jakobson* (The Hague-Paris, 1967: 1906–1917), p. 1907. Mais, en dépit de ces écarts sporadiques, d'ordinaire la dichotomie factice du fortuit et du prémédité pesait sur le réseau conceptuel du chercheur, et entravait l'édification de sa doctrine linguistique ainsi que le fondement théorique de ses découvertes pénétrantes dans les régions inexplorées de la poésie. Découvertes d'autant plus saisissantes que, sur cette voie, Saussure n'a pas rencontré de jalons à suivre, tandis que dans les thèses de son *Cours de linguistique générale*, il se trouve inspiré par la quête de quelques précurseurs.

La reconnaissance du rôle décisif de l'intention latente et subliminale, dans la création et dans le maintien des structures poétiques, rendrait plus que superflue toute "hypothèse d'une tradition *occulte* et d'un secret soigneusement préservé" (cf. J. Starobinski, MF: 256). Il nous suffit de rappeler les devinettes russes qui, comme on l'a maintes fois démontré dans les études de folklore, renferment souvent dans leur texte le mot d'énigme sous forme d'anagramme, sans que ceux qui les proposent ou les résolvent, soupçonnent le fait de l'anagramme.

L'hypothèse de travail, dont Saussure fait usage en déterrant l'anagramme dans les littératures anciennes, fut l'idée que "depuis les temps indo-européens *** celui qui composait un carmen avait à se préoccuper ainsi, d'une manière *réfléchie*, des syllabes qui entraient dans ce carmen, et des rimes qu'elles formaient entre elles ou avec un mot donné" (*CFS* XXI: 114). Or, précisément pour éviter le problème épineux que nous pose la prétendue "manière *réfléchie*", Saussure lui-même est tenté d'envisager la "coutume poétique" des anagrammes sans avoir à décider "quel en devait être le *but* ou le *rôle* dans la poésie" (MF: 256). "Ce n'est pas seulement la *fonction de l'anagramme* (comme telle) qui peut s'entendre, sans contradiction, de manière diverse; c'est aussi son rapport avec les formes plus générales du jeu sur les phonèmes; et ainsi la question admet de tous les côtés des solutions diverses *** Ce ne sont pas, évidemment, les interprétations, les justifications imaginables pour un tel fait qui manquent: mais pourquoi en choisir une et la donner comme par évidence pour la bonne, alors que je suis bien persuadé d'avance que chaque époque pouvait y voir ce qu'elle voulait, et n'y a pas toujours vu la même chose" (*ibid.*: 257). "La raison *peut avoir été* *** purement poétique: du même ordre que celle qui préside ailleurs aux rimes, aux assonances, etc. Ainsi de suite. De sorte que la prétention de vouloir dire à aucune époque *pourquoi* la chose existe va au-delà du fait": J. Starobinski, "La puissance d'Aphrodite et le mensonge des coulisses" (*Change*, 1970, VI:91–118), p. 92.

Par conséquent, aussi paradoxal que cela peut paraître, ce sont les cahiers inédits en question qui, tout en devant leur origine à l'intérêt du comparatiste pour "le principe indo-européen de poésie", présentent ses premières et presque seules tentatives d'un travail de description concrète sur le plan de la synchronie linguistique. Parmi les autres échantillons splendides, citons ses remarques sur le premier hymne du *Rg-Véda* qui se résout en nombres pairs pour toutes les consonnes et en des multiples de trois pour les voyelles, et qui surajoute à cette "analyse phonico-poétique" une véritable analyse "grammatico-poétique" (*ibid.*: 250 *sq.*). Dans ces recherches, Saussure ouvre des perspectives inouïes à l'étude linguistique de la poésie. Il démontre la nécessité d'aborder les questions de détail, telles que l'allitération proprement dite, par rapport au cadre "d'un phénomène autrement vaste et important" (*CFS* XXI: 109), étant donné que "*toutes* les syllabes allitèrent, ou assonent, ou sont comprises dans une harmonie phonique quelconque" (MF: 245). Les groupes phoniques "se font écho"; "des vers entiers semblent une anagramme d'autres vers précédents, même à grande distance dans le texte" et "les polyphones reproduisent visiblement, dès que l'occasion en est donnée, les syllabes d'un mot ou d'un nom important" qui soit figure dans le texte, soit "se présente naturellement à l'esprit par le contexte" (*CFS* XXI: 110 *sq.*). La poésie "analyse la substance phonique des mots soit pour en faire des séries acoustiques, soit pour en faire des séries significatives lorsqu'on allude à un certain nom", ou "mot anagrammisé" selon le terme saussurien. Bref, "tout se répond d'une manière ou d'une autre dans les vers" (MF: 252, 255), et suivant le schéma et les termes des Stoïciens empruntés par Saussure pour son cours de 1911, dans le premier cas, celui d'une "corrélation de phonèmes" considérée d'une manière indépendante, il s'agit d'une correspondance sur le plan des signifiants, et dans l'autre, celui des "polyphones anagrammatiques", les signifiants font dédoubler leurs signifiés.

L'anagramme poétique franchit les deux "lois fondamentales du mot humain" proclamées par Saussure, celle du lien codifié entre le signifiant et son signifié, et celle de la linéarité des signifiants. Les moyens du langage poétique sont à même de nous faire sortir "hors de l'ordre linéaire" (MF: 255) ou, comme le résume Starobinski, "l'on sort du temps de la 'consécutivité' propre au langage habituel" (*ibid.*: 254).

L'analyse linguistique des vers latins, grecs, védiques et germaniques esquissée par Saussure est, sans aucun doute, bienfaisante non seulement pour la poétique, mais aussi, selon l'expression de l'auteur, "pour la linguistique elle-même". "La génialité de l'intuition" du chercheur met au jour la nature essentiellement et, faut-il ajouter, universellement polyphonique et polysémique du langage poétique et défie, comme Meillet l'a bien vu, la conception ambiante "d'un art rationaliste", autrement dit l'idée creuse et importune d'une poésie infailliblement rationnelle.

A présent, cette œuvre nous devient peu à peu accessible grâce aux quatre précieuses publications de Jean Starobinski citées ci-dessus. Or la lecture de ces beaux fragments nous fait attendre avec d'autant plus d'impatience la parution finale de l'ensemble des quatre-vingt-dix-neuf cahiers — demeurés malheureusement inédits depuis une soixantaine d'années — qui "forment la partie la plus considérable des manuscrits" que Saussure a laissés (cf. R. Godel, "Inventaire des manuscrits de F. de Saussure remis à la Bibliothèque publique et universitaire de Genève", *CFS*, 1960, XVII), et qu'on avait pris à tort pour des recherches singulières et stériles.

Originally published in *L'Homme* XI, 2 (1971).

A FEW REMARKS ON PEIRCE, PATHFINDER IN THE SCIENCE OF LANGUAGE

ROMAN JAKOBSON

When pondering a statement by Peirce, one is constantly surprised. What are the roots of his thought? When another's opinion is quoted and reinterpreted by Peirce, it becomes quite original and innovative. And even when Peirce cites himself, he often creates a new idea and he never ceases to strike his reader. I used to say he was so great that no university found a place for him. There was, however, one dramatic exception — the few semesters of Lecturership in Logic at Johns Hopkins — and I am happy to be able to speak on Peirce at the University where he spent five years. During this period the scholar launched outstanding semiotic ideas in the volume of *Studies in Logic*, edited by him in 1883. There begins his fruitful discussion on the "universe of discourse", a notion introduced by A. De Morgan and revised and made by Peirce into a gratifying problem for the science of language (see now his *Collected Papers*, 2.517ff.).[1] The same *Studies in Logic* also carried novel views on predication in Peirce's note "The Logic of Relatives" (3.328ff.), in which he wrote:

A dual relative term, such as "lover" *** is a common name signifying a pair of objects *** Every relative has also a *converse* produced by reversing the order of the members of the pair. Thus, the converse of "lover" is "loved".

It is to the same question of duality, which still preoccupies linguists and semioticians, that Peirce returned in 1899 in discussing with William James the dyadic category of action: "This has two aspects, the Active and the Passive, which are not merely opposite aspects, but make relative contrasts between different influences of this Category as More Active and More Passive" (8.315).

At the conclusion of the Bloomington Joint Conference of Anthropologists and Linguists in July 1952 it was said that "one of the greatest

---

[1] References to C. S. Peirce's *Collected Papers* 1–8 (Cambridge, Mass.: Harvard University Press, 1938–1952) are given directly in the text, with volume number followed by a period and the subsection (not page) cited.

pioneers of structural linguistic analysis", Charles Sanders Peirce, not only stated the need for semiotics, but moreover drafted its basic lines. It is his "life-long study of the nature of signs, *** the work of clearing and opening up" the science of semiotics, "the doctrine of the essential nature and fundamental varieties of possible semiosis" (5.488), and in this connection his life-long "careful study of language" (8.287) which enable us to regard Peirce "as a genuine and bold forerunner of structural linguistics". The essential topics of signs in general and verbal signs in particular permeate Peirce's life work.

In a letter of 1905 (8.213), Peirce says:

On May 14, 1867, after three years of almost insanely concentrated thought, hardly interrupted even by sleep, I produced my one contribution to philosophy in the "New List of Categories" in the Proceedings of the American Academy of Arts and Sciences, Volume VII, pp. 287–298 [see 1.545ff.] *** We may classify objects according to their matter; as wooden things, iron things, silver things, ivory things, etc. But classification according to STRUCTURE is generally more important and it is the same with ideas. I hold that a classification of the elements of thought and consciousness according to their formal structure is more important *** I examine the phaneron and I endeavor to sort out its elements according to the complexity of their structure.

Here from the start we face a clearly structural approach to problems of phenomenology, or in Peirce's terms, "phaneroscopy" (cf. 1.284ff.). In the letter quoted above Peirce adds, "I thus reached my three categories [of signs]". The editor accompanies these words with a footnote: "Peirce then begins a long discussion of the categories and signs", but unfortunately this discussion remains unpublished.

We should not forget that Peirce's life was a most unhappy one. Terrible external conditions, a daily struggle to stay alive, and the lack of a congenial milieu impeded the development of his scientific activities. He died on the eve of the First World War, but only in the early 1930's did his main writings begin to be published. Before then only a few of Peirce's drafts on semiotics were known — the first sketch of 1867, a few ideas outlined during the Baltimore period, and some cursory passages in his mathematical studies — and for the most part, his semiotic and linguistic views, elaborated through several decades, especially around the turn of the century, remained completely hidden. It is unfortunate that in the great years of scientific fermentation which followed World War I the newly appeared Saussurian *Cours de linguistique générale* could not be confronted with Peirce's arguments: such a match of ideas, both concordant and rival, would perhaps have altered the history of general linguistics and the beginnings of semiotics.

Even when the volumes of Peirce's writings began to appear, between the thirties and the fifties, there remained a number of obstacles to a reader's making a close acquaintance with his scientific thought. The "collected papers" contain too many serious omissions. The capricious intermixture of fragments belonging to different periods at times bewilders the reader, especially since Peirce's reflections developed and changed and one would like to follow and delineate the transition of his concepts from the 1860's to our century. The reader is obliged to rework assiduously for himself the whole plan of these volumes in order to get a perspective and to master the whole of Peirce's legacy.

One may quote, for instance, the greatest French linguist of our time, Émile Benveniste, a remarkable theoretician of language. In his paper of 1969, "Sémiologie de la langue", which opened the review *Semiotica*, Benveniste attempted a comparative evaluation of Saussure and Peirce, the latter of whom he knew only from his *Selected Writings*, a non-semiotic anthology compiled by P. P. Wiener in 1958: "En ce qui concerne la langue, Peirce ne formule rien de précis ni de spécifique *** La langue se réduit pour lui aux mots." However, in reality Peirce spoke on the "impotence of mere words" (3.419), and for him the importance of words arose from their arrangement in the sentence (4.544) and from the build-up of propositions. To exemplify the novelty of his approaches, let us quote at least Peirce's bold reminder that in the syntax of every language there are logical icons of mimetic kind "that are aided by conventional rules" (2.281). Admiring "the vast and splendidly developed science of linguistics" (1.271), Peirce embraced all the levels of language from discourse to the ultimate distinctive units and he grasped the necessity of treating the latter with respect to the relation between sound and meaning (1.243).

In Peirce's response of 1892 to the English translation of Lobačevsky's *Geometrical Researches*, which "mark an epoch in the history of thought" and which entail "undoubtedly momentous" philosophical consequences, an autobiographical allusion is obviously hidden: "So long does it take a pure idea to make its way, unbacked by any interest more aggressive than the love of truth" (8.91). Precisely the same may be said about Peirce; many things could have been understood earlier and more clearly if one had really known Peirce's landmarks. I must confess that for years I felt bitterness at being among linguists perhaps the sole student of Peirce's views. Even the brief remark on semiotics in Leonard Bloomfield's *Linguistic Aspects of Science* seems to go back to Charles Morris' commentaries rather than to Peirce himself.

It should not be forgotten that in Peirce's basic project, his *System of*

Logic, from the point of view of Semiotic (8.302), he attempted to show "that a Concept is a Sign" and to define a sign and resolve it "into its ultimate *elements*" (8.302, 305). For him, semiotics involved a treatment "of the general conditions of signs being signs" and in Peirce's view it was wrong both to confine semiotic work to language and, on the other hand, to exclude language from this work. His program was to study the particular features of language in comparison with the specifics of other sign systems and to define the common features that characterize signs in general. For Peirce, "natural classification takes place by dichotomies" (1.438) and "there is an element of twoness in every set" (1.446). "A *dyad* consists of two *subjects* brought into oneness" (1.326), and Peirce defines the present inquiry as "a study of dyads in the necessary forms of signs" (1.444). He sees language in its formal, grammatical structure as a system of "relational dyads". The essential dyadic relation for Peirce is in opposition; he insisted on "the manifest truth that existence lies in opposition" and declared that "a thing without oppositions *ipso facto* does not exist". According to Peirce, the primary task is to master "the conception of being through opposition" (1.457).

One of the most felicitous, brilliant ideas which general linguistics and semiotics gained from the American thinker is his definition of meaning as "the translation of a sign into another system of signs" (4.127). How many fruitless discussions about mentalism and anti-mentalism would be avoided if one approached the notion of meaning in terms of translation, which no mentalist and no behaviorist could reject. The problem of translation is indeed fundamental in Peirce's views and can and must be utilized systematically. Notwithstanding all the disagreements, misunderstandings, and confusions which have arisen from Peirce's concept of "interpretants", I would like to state that the set of interpretants is one of the most ingenious findings and effective devices received from Peirce by semiotics in general and by the linguistic analysis of grammatical and lexical meanings in particular. The only difficulty in the use of these tools lies in the obvious need to follow Peirce's careful delimitation of their different types and "to distinguish, in the first place, the Immediate Interpretant, which is the interpretant as it is revealed in the right understanding of the Sign itself, and is ordinarily called the *meaning* of the sign" (4.536): such an interpretant of a sign "is all that is explicit in the sign itself apart from its context and circumstances of utterance" (5.474). I do not know of a better definition. This "selective" interpretant, as distinguished from the "environmental" one, is an indispensable but all too frequently overlooked key for the solution of the vital question of general meanings in the various aspects of verbal and other sign systems.

Peirce belonged to the great generation that broadly developed one of the most salient concepts and terms for geometry, physics, linguistics, psychology, and many other sciences. This is the seminal idea of INVARIANCE. The rational necessity of discovering the invariant behind the numerous variables, the question of the assignment of all these variants to relational constants unaffected by transformations underlies the whole of Peirce's science of signs. The question of invariance appears from the late 1860's in Peirce's semiotic sketches and he ends by showing that on no level is it possible to deal with a sign without considering both an invariant and a transformational variation. Invariance was the main topic of Felix Klein's *Erlanger Program* of 1872 ("Man soll die der Mannigfaltigkeit angehörigen Gebilde hinsichtlich solcher Eigenschaften untersuchen, die durch die Transformationen der Gruppe nicht geändert werden"), and at the same time the necessity of replacing the accidental variants by their "common denominators" was defended by Baudouin de Courtenay in his Kazan lectures. Thus, convergent ideas destined to transform our science, and sciences in general, emerged almost simultaneously. No matter where the model came from, these were timely pursuits for a wide field of research and they are still able to engender new, fruitful interactions between diverse disciplines. In particular, linguistics has very much to learn both from modern topology and from one of Peirce's most fertile semiotic formulations replying to the question of invariance: a symbol "cannot indicate any particular thing; it denotes a kind of thing. Not only that, but it is itself a kind, and not a single thing" (2.301); consequently, "the word and its meaning are both general rules" (2.292).

Peirce asks, "How is it possible for an indecomposable element to have any differences of structure?" and answers, "Of internal logical structure it would be clearly impossible", but as to the structure of its possible compounds, "limited differences of structure are possible". He refers to the *groups*, or vertical columns of Mendeleev's table, which "are universally and justly recognized as ever so much more important than the *series*, or horizontal ranks in the same table" (1.289). Thus, in the question of the relation between the components and the compound, Peirce denies (in the same way as the Gestalt psychologists) the possibility of speaking about constituents without analyzing the structural relation between the constituents and the whole. Far from being a mere conglomerate, which Gestaltists labeled *Und-Verbindung*, any whole is conceived of by Peirce as an integral structure. This model remains valid in its dynamic perspective as well. According to fragments of his *Minute Logic*, sketched in 1902 but never completed, "To say that the future does not influence the present is untenable doctrine" (2.86). Here two aspects of causes are distinguished by Peirce: "Efficient causation is that kind of causation whereby the parts compose the whole; final causation is that kind of causation whereby the whole calls out its parts. Final causation without efficient causation is helpless *** Efficient causation without final causation, however, is worse than helpless, by far; *** it is blank nothing" (1.220). No structural classification is possible without taking into account these two copresent and interacting causations.

The most widely known of Peirce's general assertions is that three kinds of signs exist. Yet the things which are the best known quite easily undergo various distortions. Peirce does not at all shut signs up in one of these three classes. These divisions are merely three poles, all of which can coexist within the same sign. The symbol, as he emphasized, may have an icon and/or an index incorporated into it, and "the most perfect of signs are those in which the iconic, indicative, and symbolic characters are blended as equally as possible" (4.448).

Peirce's definition of the three semiotic "tenses" was recently brought to the attention of the astute French topologist René Thom, who was happy to find here the solution he himself had strenuously sought for years. Thus, permit me to conclude my few remarks with this seemingly entangled, but essentially lucid formula whereby at the turn of the century Charles Sanders Peirce succeeded in bridging the chief problems of semiotics and grammar:

Thus the mode of being of the symbol is different from that of the icon and from that of the index. An icon has such being as belongs to PAST experience *** An index has the being of PRESENT experience. The being of a symbol consists in the real fact that something will be experienced if certain conditions be satisfied [4.447]. — It is a potentiality; and its mode of being is *esse in futuro*. The FUTURE is potential not actual [2.148]. — The value of an icon consists in its exhibiting the features of a state of things regarded as if it were purely imaginary. The value of an index is that it assures us of positive fact. The value of a symbol is that it serves to make thought and conduct rational and enables us to predict the future [4.448].

The predominant task of symbols in our verbal (and not only verbal) creativity could be considered the mainspring of Peirce's doctrine, but I hate to use the label "doctrine", for the thinker himself categorically declared that for him science was not doctrine, but inquiry.

First presented as a lecture at the Charles Sanders Peirce Symposium, Johns Hopkins University, September 26, 1975, and published in *Modern Language Notes* 92 (1977).

EINSTEIN AND THE SCIENCE OF LANGUAGE

In an address broadcast in September 1941 to a meeting of the British Association for the Advancement of Sciences and entitled "The Common Language of Science",[1] Einstein reminded his listeners that at a most advanced stage of development language, despite all its deficiencies, "becomes an instrument of reasoning in the true sense of the word". One may add that for Einstein himself language, from its rudiments to the various stages of increased development, became, especially during the American, the most retrospective, period of his life, a favorite theme of intense metalinguistic reasoning. The scientist's heightened attention to these questions and his startling gift for thoughtful, eloquent testimonials on the different topics of this area should be confronted with the data conveyed about Einstein's childhood by his biographers.

Thus, for instance, the lines devoted to "little Albert" in Philipp Frank's most instructive volume assert: "Indeed, it was a very long time before he learned to speak, and his parents began to be afraid that he was abnormal. Finally the child did begin to speak, but he was always taciturn. ***" Even when nine years old and in the last grade of elementary school, "he still lacked fluency of speech, and everything he said was expressed only after thorough consideration and reflection".[2]

A number of biographers have commented on Einstein's incapacity or reluctance to talk until the age of three and on his lifelong difficulties in learning and mastering foreign languages. In addition, Gerald Holton first published the written assertion of Einstein's sister, Maja, that in his childhood the acquisition of speech "proceeded slowly, and spoken language came with such difficulty that those around him were afraid he would never learn to talk".[3]

---

[1] Published in *Advancement of Science* 2, no. 5 (1941), pp. 109–110.
[2] P. Frank, *Einstein: His Life and Times,* trans. George Rosen, ed. and rev. Shuichi Kusaka (New York: Alfred A. Knopf, 1947), pp. 8, 10.
[3] G. Holton, *Thematic Origins of Scientific Thought: Kepler to Einstein* (Cambridge, Mass.: Harvard University Press, 1973), p. 367.

The prominent mathematician Jacques Hadamard — at the time, dean of sciences in the École Libre des Hautes Études, created in New York by French refugees, and a visiting professor at several American universities — pursued his inquiry into the process of mathematical discovery, research he had begun in Paris and developed during 1943–1944 in connection with his extensive course of lectures at the École Libre. His systematic work on this subject resulted in a book published in 1945. On various occasions he approached me to discuss problems linking this attractive project with the science of verbal and other signs. In accordance with Hadamard's proposal, I sketched, and he inserted into his study, my brief linguistic outlook of those days on the puzzle of wordless deliberations:

Signs are a necessary support of thought. For socialized thought (stage of communication) and for the thought which is being socialized (stage of formulation), the most usual system of signs is language properly called; but internal thought, especially when creative, willingly uses other systems of signs which are more flexible, less standardized than language and leave more liberty, more dynamism to creative thought. *** Amongst all these signs or symbols, one must distinguish between conventional signs, borrowed from social convention and, on the other hand, personal signs which, in their turn, can be subdivided into constant signs, belonging to general habits, to the individual pattern of the person considered and into episodical signs, which are established ad hoc and only participate in a single creative act.[4]

At the very moment of sending his book to the printer, Hadamard received, as he states in a footnote, "a letter from Professor Einstein *** containing information of capital interest". This late "Testimonial" was adjoined to the volume as its second appendix. Both of us subjected the "circumstantial and thorough" answers of Einstein's message to a close examination and confronted his introspection with the aforementioned linguistic summary. The innermost and nearly wordless character of Einstein's creative process was described in his replies to the questions about the kinds of signs that emerge in his mind when absorbed in scientific discoveries: "The words or the language, as they are written or spoken, do not seem to play any role in my mechanism of thought."

The psychologist Max Wertheimer narrates how he used to sit for hours alone with Einstein while the latter disclosed to him "the story of the dramatic development which culminated in the theory of relativity".

---

[4] J. Hadamard, *An Essay on the Psychology of Invention in the Mathematical Field* (Princeton, N.J.: Princeton University Press, 1945), pp. 96–97.

Einstein affirmed here (decades before his letter to Hadamard!) that his thoughts on this subject did not arise in any verbal formulation: "I very rarely think in words at all. A thought comes, and I may try to express it in words *afterward*." The belief of certain people that "their thinking is always in words" made him laugh.[5] Evidently, the development of Einstein's thought forestalled the consolidation of his language.

As Einstein testified in the letter appended to Hadamard's book, "certain *signs* and more or less clear *images*" (italics added), the two kinds of "psychical entities which seem to serve as elements in thought", can be — already in this preverbal period — deliberately reiterated and reordered and thus become a personal repertory of significative devices. The question of joint reproduction and recombination indicates that the identification and rearrangement of components, or, in other terms, the complementary ideas of invariance and contextual variability, actually obsessed Einstein with regard to a prelinguistic, individually semiotic stage. For him, as he states in his "Testimonial", it was evident that the "desire to arrive finally at logically connected concepts is the emotional basis of this rather vague play with the above mentioned elements".

Three subjective factors — desire, emotion, and "pure intuition" — underlie Einstein's conception of creative thought as selective, assertive, and combinatory play. His repeated reference to "this rather vague play" is connected with his *profession de foi* launched at the conclusion of the same testimonial: "what you call full consciousness is a limit case which can never be fully accomplished."

It is quite symptomatic for Einstein's mentality and for his acute memory of a child's lingering struggle with the unassailable language that in the replies he offered to Hadamard's and Wertheimer's astute questions, both the laborious search for "conventional words" and their interference with the original "associative play" are relegated — whether by unwillingness or by inability — to an evidently later, "afterward" stage, a "secondary" phase aimed at a "sufficiently established" system of standardized words and regular constructions, namely, words and constructions capable of being reproduced at will and, above all, "communicated to others". Einstein's testimony that "in a stage when words intervene at all, they are", in his case, passive — that is, "*purely auditive*" — fully corresponds to the child's correct perception of environmental speech paired with the still defective production of his own utterances.

Similar evidence appears in "Conversations with Albert Einstein",

---

[5] M. Wertheimer, *Productive Thinking* (New York: Harper, 1959), pp. 213–228.

recorded by the physicist R. S. Shankland: "When I read, I *hear* the words. Writing is difficult, and I communicate this way very badly."[6] It is notable that in Einstein's case, as elucidated by Hadamard, the primordial elements of usual thought, "before the words intervene", seem to be of the visual, as well as of the muscular, apparently gesticulatory type.

In his "Autobiographical Notes", Einstein draws a distinct line of demarcation between personal thinking and interpersonal *communication*.[7] In the latter process, by means of verbalization and syntactic rules, the conceptual systems become "communicable", whereas the process of *thinking* itself creates what he calls "a free play with concepts", which may even develop for the most part without the use of sensorily cognizable and reproducible signs, and beyond that may develop "to a considerable degree unconsciously". As Einstein had posited a decade earlier, all that is necessary is to fix a set of rules, comparable with the arbitrary rules of a game, whose rigidity alone makes the game possible, whereas "the fixation will never be final".[8]

The relation between "the concepts which arise in our thought and in our linguistic expressions" acquires two disparate treatments in Einstein's writings. In his "Remarks on Bertrand Russell's Theory of Knowledge", he insists on the impossibility of either the conceptual or the verbal "free creations of thought" being inductively gained from sense experiences: "we do not become conscious of the gulf — logically unbridgeable — which separates the world of sensory experiences from the world of concepts and propositions"[9] — briefly, the raw empirics from the theory of science. On the other hand, Einstein repeatedly assailed language for compelling us to work with words importunately tied to inadequate, prescientific concepts and for turning our conventional instrument of reasoning "into a dangerous source of error and deception". For instance, the essential equivalence of two concepts is easily hidden when use is made of disconnecting misnomers.

With regard to Einstein's personal and primary inclination to attribute to the act of thinking complete independence from language, it is evident from his own testimony that emotional yearnings not only are at

---

[6] In *American Journal of Physics* 31 (1963), p. 50.
[7] A. Einstein, "Autobiographical Notes", trans. P. A. Schilpp, in Schilpp, ed., *Albert Einstein: Philosopher-Scientist* (Evanston, Ill.: Library of Living Philosophers, 1949).
[8] A. Einstein, "Physics and Reality", trans. J. Piccard, *Journal of the Franklin Institute* 221 (1936), pp. 349–382.
[9] A. Einstein, "Remarks on Bertrand Russell's Theory of Knowledge," trans. P. A. Schilpp, in Schilpp, ed., *The Philosophy of Bertrand Russell* (Evanston, Ill.: Library of Living Philosophers, 1946), pp. 277–291, esp. p. 287.

work in guiding inventive thought in his role as philosopher-scientist but also underlie — in such tragic experiences as the events of the Second World War — his "passionate striving for clear understanding" of mankind and for supernational "general truths". At such moments "the words of the language" suddenly emerge to the foreground. In his broadcast of 1941, quoted above, Einstein concluded: "the mental development of the individual and his way of forming concepts depend to a high degree upon language" and upon "the verbal guidance of his environment". The discoverer still insists, however, that scientific concepts "have been set up by the best brains of all countries and all times", and, *of course*, as he remembers to add, it is done in the *solitude* of the creative process. Yet this time he takes into account also the "*cooperative* effort as regards the final effect", a joint effort that "in the long run" may overcome the contemporary "confusion of goals".

Aside from Einstein's intimate, one might even say innate, conversance with the fundamental questions of the place assigned to language in the human mind, deep spiritual bonds tied the physicist to a remarkable forerunner of modern linguistics, the Swiss scholar Jost Winteler (1846–1929). Winteler's dissertation, issued in 1876, displays a challenging methodological novelty and acuity in his approach to the sound system of languages, with his fundamental distinction between its "accidental features" (variations) and "essential properties" (invariants).[10] But the author's theoretical fundamentals were received among academic bureaucrats with biased distrust. Hence the courageous seeker was doomed to sacrifice his far-sighted scientific plans for the gloomy lot of a lifelong, first active but early retired schoolmaster.

In 1895 the adolescent Albert Einstein, having failed the entrance examination to the Federal Institute of Technology in Zurich, took a year's refuge in the cantonal school at Aarau and there became a student, boarder, and young friend of Jost Winteler, who later also was to be the father-in-law of Albert's sister, Maja. A good deal of evidence shows how auspicious this sojourn turned out to be. Thus, Miss Helen Dukas has kindly supplied a quotation from the short biographical memoir written by Maja Winteler in 1924:

In the family of a teacher of the [Aarau] school and scholar in the linguistic-historical field, [Einstein] found acceptance and sympathy for his manner, and he therefore felt at once very much at home. *** Thus the time in Aarau became for him in many ways significant, and one of the best of his whole life.

[10] Jost Winteler, *Die Kerenzer Mundart des Kantons Glarus, in ihren Grundzügen dargestellt* (Leipzig and Heidelberg, 1876).

The young student and the older man evidently saw political matters in a similar light. Professor Elmar Holenstein of Ruhr-Universität Bochum refers in his comprehensive paper, "Albert Einsteins Hausvater in Aarau: Der Linguist Jost Winteler",[11] to an unpublished letter by Einstein to Winteler of 1901, condemning the German "worship of authorities" (*Authoritätendusel*) as "the greatest enemy of truth". A month before his death Einstein continued to praise his Aarau teachers, "who based themselves on no external authority".

The daily conversations with the lucid preceptor probably acquainted the responsive teenager with the essential principle and term of Winteler's dissertation — the "situational relativity" (*Relativität der Verhältnisse*)[12] — and with the indissoluble interconnection of the concepts *relativity* and *invariance*, which underlie Winteler's linguistic theory and which competed for a while as tentative names of Einstein's primary discovery. Particularly instructive among Holenstein's unpublished sources is the letter written 10 April 1942 to the director of the Swiss Landesbibliothek about Jost Winteler, the Aarau teacher, by one of the latter's sons, Dr. Jost Fridolin Winteler, seeking to demonstrate how steadfast remained the memory of the relations between the teacher and his students and the appreciation of the former's clear and perspicacious judgment:

Von ihm habe ich auch erstmalig Ausführungen über Relativität gehört, die dann Einstein, der die Kantonschule in Aarau Besuchte, da die Matura bestand und bei uns wohnte, mathematisch entwickelt hat (1895–96) [It is from him (Jost Fridolin's father) that I heard for the first time statements about relativity, which then were developed mathematically by Einstein (1895–96), who studied at and graduated from the Aarau canton school and stayed as a boarder in our house].

According to Einstein's own acknowledgment, "the germ of the special relativity theory" was already contained in those paradoxical reflections (*Gendankenexperiment*) that first inspired him throughout his Aarau school year and appeared to him "intuitively clear".[13]

Winteler's empathic style strikes the readers of the preface to his doctoral thesis:

My work in its essence is addressed solely to those who are able to grasp the verbal form as that revelation of the human mind which stands to the mind itself in much more inner and sweeping relations than even the best products of a most

---

[11] In *Schweizer Monatshefte* 59 (March 1979), pp. 221–233.
[12] Winteler, *Die Kerenzer Mundart*, p. 27.
[13] "Autobiographical Notes", p. 53.

consumate literature. Thus the addressees of my work must conceive of the inquiry into the latent powers which determine the continual motion of the verbal form as a task which, in its interest and relevance, competes with any other field of knowledge.[14]

A thorough affinity seems to link this passage with the fervent lines of the address that Einstein delivered in 1918 in honor of Max Planck: "The supreme task of the physicist is to arrive at those universal elementary laws from which the cosmos can be built up by pure deduction. There is no logical path to these laws; only intuition, resting on sympathetic understanding of experience, can reach them."[15]

The Aarau disciple preserved forever an exalted memory of Winteler's "clairvoyant mind". Among the numerous precious letters exchanged between 1903 and 1955 by the two eternal friends, Albert Einstein and Michele Besso,[16] one encounters a staggering message sent 16 February 1936 from Princeton to Bern with feverish images, such as "a tormenting mathematical demon", "the desperate state of human affairs", and "die Narren in Deutschland". The dramatic message bears a momentous reference to "Professor Winteler's prophetic spirit, who recognized the imminent danger so early and so thoroughly". The whole letter abruptly concludes with words of hope that the transient autarchy of bare statistical physics will finally be overcome by the universal speculative mind.

* * *

We examined Einstein's ideas on language in light of his diverging attitudes toward cognition, on the one hand, and toward communication, on the other. We also touched upon the question of Einstein's boyhood proximity to an outstanding linguistic pathfinder of that epoch. Let us turn to the question of Einsteinian impulses reflected in contemporary linguistic theories, or at least to analogies between modern physics and linguistic trends.

Despite the variety of relativistic ideologies in the diverse provinces of artistic and scholarly activities, the common denominator of their main slogans, devices, and attainments is beyond doubt. I quote a nearly

---

[14] Winteler, *Die Kerenzer Mundart*, p. viii.
[15] A. Einstein, "Principles of Research", in Einstein, *Ideas and Opinions* (based on *Mein Weltbild*, ed. Carl Seelig), new trans. and rev. Sonja Bargmann (New York: Crown Publishers, Inc., 1954), pp. 224–227.
[16] Albert Einstein and Michele Besso, *Correspondance 1903–1955*, ed. P. Speziali (Paris, 1972).

twenty-year-old attempt to delineate the international strivings that have animated our generation:

> Those of us who were concerned with language learned to apply the principle of relativity in linguistic operations; we were consistently drawn in this direction by the spectacular development of modern physics and by the pictorial theory and practice of cubism, where everything "is based on relationship" and interaction between parts and wholes, between color and shape, between the representation and the represented. "I do not believe in things," Braque declared, "I believe only in their relationship."[17]

Notwithstanding the somewhat different forms that the notion of "fundamental affinities" takes in the arts and in the sciences, the dominance of the search for relationship over that for the related items themselves knits together the topological nucleus of this century's art and Einsteinian science. Whatever private alienation the revolutionary scientist may feel toward some forms of artistic innovation, one cannot bypass eloquent documents of solidarity, such as the professions of faith of the great modern seekers in art — for example, Piet Mondrian's declaration of 1920, published in *Néo-plasticisme* (Paris): "Les plans colorés, tant par position et dimension que par la valorisation de la couleur n'expriment plastiquement que *des rapports* et non des formes."

When recollecting and rereading the various evidence of the close intertwining among the Moscovite artistic, literary, and scientific avant-garde of the 1910's and 1920's, I realize how great and productive the fascinated acquaintance with the writings of Einstein and his adherents was. Both the Moscow Linguistic Circle, a young experimental association struggling for a revised theory of language and poetry, as well as the later historic ramification of the same trend, the so-called Prague structural school, explicitly referred to Einsteinian methodological endeavors in attempting to link the focal problems of relativity and invariance. One of the examples illustrating the professed relationship is the Project of Standardized Terminology, prepared and published by the Prague Linguistic Circle for the Phonological Conference of 1930.[18] In the list of "fundamental notions", the first place belonged to the *phonological opposition*, and this entry was followed by a reference to the opposites themselves, termed *phonological units*. This architectonic hierarchy became ever closer to "the new physical view" insofar as the

---

[17] These lines were written on the threshold of the 1960's for the conclusion to my *Selected Writings* I (The Hague: Mouton, 1962), p. 632.
[18] In *Travaux du Cercle Linguistique de Prague* 4 (1931), pp. 309–323, esp. p. 311.

structural analysis of the verbal universe superseded the previous mechanical approach. In "Einstein's Theory of Relativity" as conceived by the philosopher Ernst Cassirer, "there exists only the unity of certain *functional relations*, which are differently designated according to the system of references in which we express them".[19]

The appreciation of the relativity of the form of thought attempted by two of the most original American linguists, Edward Sapir (1884–1939) and Benjamin Lee Whorf (1897–1941), and in particular the former's direct reference to "the physical relativity of Einstein",[20] offer another significant example of a daring linguistic initiative that purposely bordered upon Einstein's conceptual framework and upon the direct, albeit restrictive, question posed in Einstein's broadcast of 1941: "to what extent the same language meant the same mentality". Any impact necessarily implies not only similarities but also instructive cleavages of opinion.

Perhaps the most telling concordances between innovation in physics and that in contemporary linguistics are those coincidences that seem to be due to purely convergent, independent development. Such latent correspondences reveal a substantially parallel course in these different sciences. Both Einstein's demand of the theoretical physicist to strive for the highest possible standard of rigorous precision in the description of pure *relations*, as in his address at Max Planck's sixtieth birthday (1918), quoted above, and the close counterpart of this demand — namely, the ever stricter inquiry into the physical world as a network of interrelated components— stand in eloquent correspondence with the tasks of advanced linguistics. Careful comparisons between the fundamental concepts of relativistic physics and the constituents of language as analyzed and defined by contemporary linguists disclose a salient isomorphism that could be easily exemplified on the different levels of verbal structure.

A few widespread phonological cases may suffice to reveal the generality of the problem. The *distinctive features* that fulfill the main task of speech sounds are, as Einstein would term them, rigorously relational ideas, intuited as binary oppositions. Thus, for instance, in those consonantal systems that make sense-discriminative use of the so-called "flatness" feature, flat consonants are phenomenologically equivalent; in our perception they are mainly distinguished by a particular

---

[19] E. Cassirer, *Substance and Function & Einstein's Theory of Relativity* (New York: Dover, 1923), p. 398.
[20] E. Sapir, *Selected Writings* (Berkeley: University of California Press, 1949), p. 159.

lowering of their inferior formant. In diverse languages we observe certain differences in the sensorimotor modalities of this process. For example, a fairly similar auditory effect is obtainable by labialization and by pharyngealization, or, in other terms, by the narrowing of the frontal or of the buccal ends of the mouth cavity. But since the difference between these two special cases is never used for sense-discriminative purposes, the common denominator outweighs the difference (as well as some other, likewise superficial modalities). The typology of languages asserts the structural invariance of the feature in question, and the universal laws of language prove to admit no more than one single opposition of present and absent flatness.[21] In linguistics the principle of equivalence (instead of mechanical sameness) puts limits on the significance one can expect from a search for separate, uncoordinated particulars of experience and yields instead the gradual discovery of law-governed paucity in the fundamental relationships that underlie the verbal (as well as the physical) universe.

"Nun fiel mir ein" (Now it came to me) — that is the item from Einstein's "Autobiographical Notes"[22] that sounds like a first glimpse of the general theory of relativity and like a joint slogan of the contemporary sciences, all tending to transform an abundance of raw stuff into a parsimony of general laws. The problem of *equivalence* proved to be as pertinent for the principle of relativity as for the discovery of linguistic universals. A substantial revision of the time-space model, notwithstanding the differences in the statement of these questions with respect to diverse sciences, leads us far from the previous mechanical routine. Among such new linguistic vistas calling for a vital interdisciplinary discussion, one may bring to the foreground the notion of dynamic synchrony, the reversible course of current events, and the conception of any change in progress as an intrinsic simultaneity of sensible *oscillations*. Niels Bohr repeatedly insisted on the deep links that at present tie together physics and linguistics, to whose interrelation both of us devoted a joint MIT seminar at the end of the 1950's. The "exigencies of relativistic invariance", in Bohr's favored term,[23] were intently discussed with respect to the search for and structure of the ultimate constituents of both the physical and the linguistic universe, the "elementary quanta", as they were termed in physics and were picked up from physics by linguists. The endeavor of our linguistic generation to

---

[21] Cf. R. Jakobson and L. Waugh, *The Sound Shape of Language* (Bloomington, Ind.: Indiana University Press, 1979), pp. 113ff.
[22] "Autobiographical Notes", pp. 64–65.
[23] N. Bohr, *Atomic Physics and Human Knowledge* (New York: Wiley, 1958), pp. 71–72.

conceive of the verbal mass as a "discontinuous" matter, which is composed of elementary quanta and hence reveals a "granular" structure, partly continues an older set of efforts. At the same time, however, it exhibits an evident dependence on the development of the exact sciences, which was, I testify, a genuine source of inspiration for the linguistic avant-garde of the first third of our century, both in the Western and the Eastern scientific centers.[24]

Let us finally mention that two polar and inseparable problems — namely, symmetry (with its various transformations) and asymmetry, on the one hand, and the breaking of symmetry, on the other — permeate the diverse sciences. In his *Thematic Origins of Scientific Thought* Gerald Holton pointed out the initiative, vital role that symmetry arguments have acquired in Einsteinian physics. Substantially analogous concepts find an ever wider application in the analysis of any linguistic structure. Yet the entire symmetry-asymmetry complex in linguistic research, both in its ontological commitment and in the role of a pure formal device, must be seen to belong more to the victories of tomorrow rather than to the solutions of yesterday and today. However, we may perhaps console ourselves on that point with a thought that Einstein wrote down only four weeks before his death: "For us *** the distinction between past, present, and future is only an illusion, albeit a stubborn one."[25]

An epochal scientific theory may regenerate in contemporaneous poetry into an elemental myth. Thus, for instance, Vladimir Majakovskij, the Russian avant-garde poet, from his first, anxious glimpses of 1920 into the theory of relativity and until the eve of his suicide in 1930,[26] praised "the futurist brain of Einstein" and devoted his ultimate drama of 1929, *Banja* (Bathhouse), to the crushing victory of such an unusual brain over the alleged absolute of time.[27]

Presented at the Einstein Centennial Symposium in Jerusalem, March 16, 1979, and published in *Albert Einstein: Historical and Cultural Perspectives*, ed. G. Holton and Y. Elkana (Princeton, 1982).

---

[24] A. Einstein and L. Infeld, *The Evolution of Physics* (New York: Simon and Schuster, 1942), pp. 263–313.
[25] Einstein and Besso, *Correspondance*, p. 537.
[26] See my essay "On a Generation that Squandered Its Poets", in *Twentieth-Century Russian Literary Criticism*, ed. V. Erlich (New Haven: Yale Univ. Press, 1975), p. 151.
[27] For her critical remarks on several passages of this paper, the author's deep gratitude is due to Dr. Amelia Rechel-Cohn of Harvard University.

THE TWENTIETH CENTURY IN EUROPEAN AND AMERICAN LINGUISTICS: MOVEMENTS AND CONTINUITY

Dear friends! I was asked to speak at the present Symposium devoted to the European background of American linguistics about the science of language in America and in Europe in the twentieth century. Apparently this topic was suggested because I witnessed the international development of linguistic thought through the long period of six decades — I followed this development first in the upper classes of the Lazarev Institute of Oriental Languages, afterwards as a student of linguistics and subsequently as a research fellow at Moscow University, then from 1920 in Prague and in other Western-European, especially Scandinavian, centers of linguistic thought, and since the forties in America, with frequent visits to other areas of intense linguistic research.

As my eminent colleague Einar Haugen said in his recent paper "Half a Century of the Linguistic Society", "each of us treasures his own memories".[1] Thus, may I refer to my first, though indirect, acquaintance with the LSA. In March of 1925, the pioneering Czech scholar expert in both English and general linguistics, Vilém Mathesius, together with his younger, devoted collaborator in these two fields, Bohumil Trnka, invited Sergej Karcevskij and me to a consultative meeting. Mathesius began by citing two events. The first of them was the tenth anniversary of the Moscow Linguistic Circle, which, let us add, was already dissolved at that time, yet whose creation in 1915 and whose vital activities were a durable stimulus in the Russian and international development of linguistics and poetics. On my arrival in Prague in 1920, Mathesius questioned me about the make-up and work of the Moscow Circle and said, "We will need such a team here also, but now it is still too early. We must wait for further advances." At the outset of our debates in 1925, he announced the most recent and impelling news — the formation of the Linguistic Society of America. Mathesius was one of those European linguists who followed with rapt attention and

---

[1] *Language* 50 (1974), 619–621.

sympathy the impressive rise of American research in the science of language.

In October 1926, the Prague Linguistic Circle had its first meeting. It is well-known that this Prague association, which, strange as it seems at first glance, has also been dissolved, gave in turn a powerful and lasting impetus to linguistic thought in Europe and elsewhere. From the beginning, there was a close connection between the Linguistic Society of America and the Prague Linguistic Circle. I don't know whether the young generation of scholars realizes how strong these relations were. N. S. Trubetzkoy's letters reveal some new data on the manifold ties between American linguistics and the "École de Prague".[2] At the end of 1931, Trubetzkoy, at the time immersed in the study of American Indian languages, emphasized that "most of the American Indianists perfectly describe the sound systems, so that their outlines yield all the essentials for the phonological characteristics of any given language, including an explicit survey of the extant consonantal clusters with respect to the different positions within or between the morphemes". Trubetzkoy had a very high opinion of the American linguist whom he called "my Leipzig comrade". This was Leonard Bloomfield, who in 1913 shared a bench with Trubetzkoy and Lucien Tesnière at Leskien's and Brugmann's lectures. Bloomfield praised "Trubetzkoy's excellent article on vowel systems" of 1929 and devoted his sagacious 1939 study on "Menomini Morphophonemics" to N. S. Trubetzkoy's memory.[3]

The Prague Circle had very close ties with Edward Sapir. When we held the International Phonological Conference of 1930, Sapir, though unable to attend, kept up a lively correspondence with Trubetzkoy about his Prague assembly and the development of the inquiry into linguistic, especially phonological, structure. Almost nothing remains of this exchange. Those of Sapir's messages which had not been seized by the Gestapo were lost when the Viennese home of Trubetzkoy's widow was demolished by an air raid. In their turn, Trubetzkoy's letters perished when Sapir, at the end of his life, destroyed his entire epistolary archive. However, some quotations from Sapir's letters have survived in Trubetzkoy's correspondence, and others were cited by Trubetzkoy at our meetings. It is noteworthy that Sapir underscored the similarity of his and our approaches to the basic phonological problems.

These are not the only cases of the transoceanic propinquity between

---

[2] R. Jakobson, ed., *N. S. Trubetzkoy's Letters and Notes* (The Hague: Mouton, 1975).
[3] See C. F. Hockett, ed., *A Leonard Bloomfield Anthology* (Bloomington-London: Indiana University Press, 1970), 247, 351–362.

linguists of the American and of the Continental avant-garde. We may recollect and cite a remarkable document published in *Language* (vol. 18, 307–9). In August 1942 the Linguistic Society of America received a cable forwarded by the Soviet Scientists' Anti-Fascist Committee. This was a telegraphic letter of more than 4,000 words sent from Moscow and signed by a prominent Russian linguist, Grigorij Vinokur, the former secretary of the Moscow Linguistic Circle. In this cabled report Vinokur emphasized the particular affinity of the young Russian linguists, especially the Moscow phonologists, with the pursuits and strivings of the LSA. He noted how profoundly Sapir was valued by the linguists of the USSR. Apparently the first foreign version of Sapir's *Language* was an excellent Russian translation of this historic handbook by the Russian linguist A. M. Suxotin, with interesting editorial notes about the parallel paths in international linguistics.[4]

In the light of all these and many other interconnections, the question of purported hostility between American and European linguists comes to naught. Any actual contact puts an end to the belief that these were two separate and impervious scientific worlds with two different, irreconcilable ideologies. Sometimes we hear allegations that American linguists repudiated their European colleagues, particularly those who sought refuge in this country. I was one of those whom the Second World War brought to the Western hemisphere, and I must state that the true scholars, the outstanding American linguists, met me with a fraternal hospitality and with a sincere readiness for scientific cooperation. If there were signs of hostility and repudiation — and they were indeed evident — they occurred solely on the side of a few inveterate administrators and narrow-minded, ingrained academic bureaucrats and operators, and I am happy to acknowledge the unanimous moral support and defence which came from such genuine men of science as Charles Fries, Zellig Harris, Charles Morris, Kenneth Pike, Meyer Schapiro, Morris Swadesh, Stith Thompson, Harry V. Velten, Charles F. Voegelin, and many others.

One of the first American linguists whom I met on my arrival in this country and who became a true friend of mine was Leonard Bloomfield. Both orally and in writing, he repeatedly expressed his aversion to any intolerance, and he struggled against "the blight of the odium theologicum" and against "denouncing all persons who disagree" with one's interest or opinion or "who merely choose to talk about something else"

---

[4] *Jazyk: Vvedenie v izučenie reči* (Moscow-Leningrad: Gos. Social'no-Èkonomičeskoe izdatel'stvo, 1934).

(in 1946). The fact that one, Bloomfield wrote, "disagrees with others, including me, in methods and theories does not matter; it would be deadly to have one accepted doctrine" (in 1945). I recollect our cordial and vivid debates; Bloomfield wanted me to stay and work with him at Yale, and assured me that he would be happy to have someone with whom he could have real discussions. The great linguist severely repudiated any selfish and complacent parochialism.

From my first days in this country in June 1941 I experienced the deep truth in Bloomfield's later obituary judgment on Franz Boas: "His kindness and generosity knew no bounds".[5] The fundamental role in American linguistics played by this German-born scholar, 28 years old at his arrival in the United States, was wisely appraised by Bloomfield: "The progress which has since been made in the recording and description of human speech has merely grown from the roots, stem, and mighty branches of Boas' life-work." As to the founder and skillful director of the *Handbook of American Indian Languages* himself, I recall his amiable, congenial house in Grantwood, New Jersey, where the host, with his keen sense of humor, used to say to his sister in my presence: "Jakobson *ist ein seltsamer Mann*! He thinks that I am an American linguist!"

Boas strongly believed in the international character of linguistics and of any genuine science and would never have agreed with an obstinate demand for a regional confinement of scientific theories and research. He professed that any analogy to a struggle for national interests in politics and economics was superficial and far-fetched. In the science of language there are no patented discoveries and no problems of inter-tribal or interpersonal competition, of regulations for imported and exported merchandise or dogma. The greater and closer the cooperation between linguists of the world, the vaster are the vistas of our science. Not only in the universe of languages, but also throughout the world of convergent development of bilateral diffusion.

One may add that isolationist tendencies in the scientific life of the two hemispheres were mere transient and insignificant episodes and that the international role of American linguistics and, in particular, the transoceanic influence of the American achievements in the theory of language appear as early as the European models do in American linguistics.

During the second half of the past century it was Germany which witnessed the widest progress and expansion of comparative Indo-European studies. Yet the new and fecund ideas in general linguistics

---

[5] *A Leonard Bloomfield Anthology*, 408.

emerged outside the German scholarly world. Toward the end of the nineteenth century Karl Brugmann and August Leskien, the two leading German comparatists and proponents of the world-famed Leipzig school of Neogrammarians, emphatically acknowledged the immense stimulation which the American linguist William Dwight Whitney gave to the European research in the history of languages by his original treatment of general principles and methods. At the same time, Ferdinand de Saussure stated that Whitney, without having himself written a single page of comparative philology, was the only one "to exert an influence on all study of comparative grammar", whereas in Germany linguistic science, which was allegedly born, developed, and cherished there by innumerable people, in Saussure's (as also in Whitney's) opinion never manifested "the slightest inclination to reach the degree of abstraction necessary to master what one is actually doing and why all that is done has its justification in the totality of sciences".[6] Having returned at the end of his scholarly activities to the "theoretical view of language", Saussure repeatedly expressed his reverence for "the American Whitney, who never said a single word on these topics which was not right". Whitney's books on general linguistics were immediately translated into French, Italian, German, Dutch, and Swedish and had a far wider and stronger scientific influence in Europe than in his homeland.

For many years American students of language, absorbed in particulars, seemed to disregard Whitney's old warning to linguists in which he adjured them not to lose "sight of the grand truths and principles which underlie and give significance to their work, and the recognition of which ought to govern its course throughout" (1867).[7] Leonard Bloomfield was actually the first American scholar who from his early steps in linguistic theory endeavored to revive Whitney's legacy in the study of language.

As a parallel to the earlier and deeper naturalization of Whitney's *Principles of Linguistic Science* in the Old World one may cite the reception of Saussure's *Cours de linguistique générale* in the New World. Although it opened a new epoch in the history of linguistics, the appearance of this posthumous publication found, at first, only a few linguists ready to accept the basic lessons of the late Genevan teacher. Originally most of the Western-European specialists outside of his native Switzerland showed restraint toward Saussure's conception, and, strange

---

[6] See R. Jakobson, "The World Response to Whitney's *Principles of Linguistic Science*", reprinted *supra*, 219–236.
[7] W. D. Whitney, *Language and the Study of Language. Twelve Lectures on the Principles of Linguistics* (N.Y.: Scribner, 1867).

to say, France was one of the countries particularly slow in assimilating his theory. One of the earliest open-minded appraisers and adherents of the *Cours* was an American scholar. Its first two editions were commented on by Bloomfield not only in the separate review of the *Cours* for the *Modern Language Journal* (1923–24), but also in Bloomfield's critiques of Sapir's *Language* (1922) and of Jespersen's *Philosophy of Grammar* (1927), and in a few further texts, all of them made easily available by Charles F. Hockett in his magnificent anthology.[8]

According to the aforesaid review, the nineteenth century "took little or no interest in the general aspects of human speech", so that Saussure in his lectures on general linguistics "stood very nearly alone", and his posthumous work "has given us the theoretical basis for a science of human speech". In reviewing Sapir's *Language*, Bloomfield realizes that the question of influence or simply convergent innovations is "of no scientific moment", but in passing he notes the probability of Sapir's acquaintance with Saussure's "book, which gives a theoretical foundation to the newer trend of linguistic study". In particular, he is glad to see that Sapir "deals with synchronic matters (to use de Saussure's terminology) before he deals with diachronic, and gives to the former as much space as to the latter".

Bloomfield subscribes not only to the sharp Saussurian distinction between synchronic and diachronic linguistics, but also to the further dichotomy advocated by the *Cours*, namely a rigorous bifurcation of human speech (*langage*) into a perfectly uniform system (*langue*) and the actual speech-utterance (*parole*). He professess full accord with the "fundamental principles" of the *Cours*:

For me, as for de Saussure *** and, in a sense, for Sapir ***, all this, de Saussure's *la parole*, lies beyond the power of our science. *** Our science can deal only with those features of language, de Saussure's *la langue*, which are common to all speakers of a community, — the phonemes, grammatical categories, lexicon, and so on. *** A grammatical or lexical statement is at bottom an abstraction.[9]

But in Bloomfield's opinion, Saussure "proves intentionally and in all due form: that psychology and phonetics do not matter at all and are, in principle, irrelevant to the study of language". The abstract features of Saussure's *la langue* form a "system, — so rigid that without any adequate physiologic information and with psychology in a state of

---

[8] *A Leonard Bloomfield Anthology*, 106–109, 91–94, 141–143.
[9] *Ibid.*, 141–142, 107.

chaos, we are", Bloomfield asserts, "nevertheless able to subject it to scientific treatment".

According to Bloomfield's programmatic writings of the twenties, the "newer trend" with its Saussurian theoretical foundation "affects two critical points". First, and once more he underscores this point in his paper of 1927 "On Recent Work in General Linguistics",[10] Saussure's outline of the relation between "synchronic" and "diachronic" science of language has given a "theoretical justification" to the present recognition of descriptive linguistics "beside historical, or rather as precedent to it".[11] In this connection it is worth mentioning that even the striking divergence between the search for new ways in Saussure's synchronic linguistics and his stationary, nearly Neogrammarian attitude toward "linguistic history", was adopted by Bloomfield, who was disposed to believe that here one could hardly learn "anything of a fundamental sort that Leskien didn't know".[12]

Referring to the second critical point of the "modern trend" in linguistics, Bloomfield commends two restrictive definitions of its sole attainable goal: he cites the Saussurian argument for "*la langue*, the socially uniform language pattern"[13] and Sapir's request for "an inquiry into the function and form of the arbitrary systems of symbolism that we term languages".[14]

When maintaining that this subject matter must be studied "in and for itself", Bloomfield literally reproduces the final words of the *Cours*. Strange as it seems, here he shows a closer adherence to the text of Saussure's published lectures than the lecturer himself. As has since been revealed, the final, italicized sentence of the *Cours* — "*la linguistique a pour unique et véritable objet la langue envisagée en elle-même et pour elle-même*" — though never uttered by the late teacher, was appended to the posthumous book by the editors-restorers of Saussure's lectures as "*l'idée fondamentale de ce cours*". According to Saussure's genuine notes and lectures, language must not be viewed in isolation, but as a particular case among other systems of signs in the frame of a general science of signs which he terms *sémiologie*.

The close connection between Bloomfield's (and, one may add, Sapir's) initial steps in general linguistics and the European science of language, as well as Whitney's significance in the Old World, exemplify

---

[10] *Ibid.*, 173–190.
[11] *Ibid.*, 179.
[12] *Ibid.*, 177–178, 542.
[13] *Ibid.*, 177.
[14] *Ibid.*, 92–93, 143.

the continuous reciprocity between the linguists of the two hemispheres.

In his first approach to the "principle of the phoneme" Bloomfield pondered over the concepts developed by the school of Sweet, Passy, and Daniel Jones, and when we met, he cited his particular indebtedness to Henry Sweet's "classical treatise" on *The Practical Study of Languages* (1900).[15] From the very outset of his concern for phonemic problems, Bloomfield confronted the difference between the discreteness of phonemes and "the actual continuum of speech sound" and Saussure's opposition of *langue/parole*,[16] and he found "explicit formulations" in Baudouin de Courtenay's *Versuch einer Theorie der phonetischen Alternationen* of 1895.[17] From this book he also got the fruitful concept and term *morpheme*, coined by Baudouin.[18] Upon the same label, likewise borrowed from Baudouin's terminology, French linguistic literature mistakenly imposed the meaning "affix".

There are certain classical works in the European linguistic tradition which have constantly attracted special attention and recognition in the American science of language. Thus, the two books which so captivated Noam Chomsky, one by Humboldt and one by Otto Jespersen, have more than once since their appearance evoked lively and laudatory responses from American linguists: thus, in Sapir's estimation, "the new vistas of linguistic thought opened up by the work of Karl Wilhelm von Humboldt", and the latter's treatise *Über die Verschiedenheit des menschlichen Sprachbaues* compelled Bloomfield to admire "this great scholar's intuition"; as to Jespersen's masterpiece, Bernard Bloch in 1941 praised "the greatness of the *Philosophy of Grammar*", and Bloomfield's review of 1927 pointed out that by this book "English grammar will be forever enriched".[19]

---

[15] In *Cahiers Ferdinand de Saussure* 32 (1978, p. 69) Calvert Watkins published remarkable excerpts from Bloomfield's letter of December 23, 1919 to the specialist in Algonquin languages at the Smithsonian, Truman Michelson: "My models are Pāṇini and the kind of work done in I.-E. by my teacher, Professor Wackernagel. No preconceptions; find out which sound variations are distinctive (as to meaning), and then analyze morphology and syntax by putting together everything that is alike." Bloomfield asks whether Michelson has got hold of de Saussure's *Cours de linguistique générale*: "I have not yet seen it, but Professor Wackernagel mentioned it in a letter and I have ordered it and am anxious to see it." The European and especially Swiss roots of Bloomfield's innovative search — Jakob Wackernagel and Ferdinand de Saussure — become still clearer.
[16] *A Leonard Bloomfield Anthology*, 179.
[17] *Ibid.*, 248.
[18] *Ibid.*, 130.
[19] B. Bloch, review of Jespersen's *Efficiency in Linguistic Change*, *Language* 17 (1941), 350–353; *A Leonard Bloomfield Anthology*, 143, 180.

The wide-spread myth of a sole and uniform American linguistic school and of its exclusive control throughout the country, at least during certain periods in the development of the science of language in the United States, is at variance with the actual situation. Neither the geographical nor the historical significance of one or another scientific trend can be based on the excessive number of students who, as Martin Joos neatly remarked (1957:v), "accept the current techniques without inquiring into what lay behind them".[20] What really counts is the quality alone, both of theoretical and of empirical attainments.

In America, as well as in Europe, there has fortunately always been an imposing variety of approaches to the foundations, methods, and tasks of linguistics. In its initial output, the Linguistic Society of America displayed a remarkable diversity of views. Its first president, Hermann Collitz of the Johns Hopkins University, in his inaugural address (December 28, 1924) on "The Scope and Aims of Linguistic Science", spoke about the rapidly improving conditions for a new advancement of "general or 'philosophical' grammar", which for a while "had to be satisfied with a back seat in linguistics".[21] Collitz laid stress on the principal problems of general linguistics, one of which concerns "the relation between grammatical forms and mental categories". He referred in this connection to "an able study written by an American scholar, namely: *Grammar and Thinking*, by Albert D. Sheffield" (New York: 1912), a book, let us add, "heartily welcomed" in Bloomfield's review of 1912 as "a sensible volume on the larger aspects of language".[22] The other concern of general linguistics was defined by Collitz as "uniformities and permanent or steadily recurring conditions in human speech generally". The latter item shortly thereafter became a subject of controversy in the gatherings and publications of the LSA: skeptics were disposed to deny the existence of general categories, as long as no linguist can know which of them, if any, exist in all languages of the world, whereas Sapir with an ever growing persistence worked on a series of preliminaries to his *Foundations of Language*, a wide-ranging program of universal grammar that he cherished till the end of his life.

The passage of the aforementioned inaugural address on the "mental categories" as correlates of external forms hinted at a question about to become for decades an enduring *casus belli* between two linguistic currents in America, where they have been nicknamed respectively

---

[20] M. Joos, ed., *Readings in Linguistics* 1 (Washington: American Council of Learned Societies, 1957), v.
[21] *Language* 1 (1925), 14–16.
[22] *A Leonard Bloomfield Anthology*, 34.

"mentalism" and "mechanism" or "physicalism". With regard to the pivotal problems of general linguistics touched upon by Collitz, Bloomfield's prefatory article — "Why a Linguistic Society?" — for the first issue of the Society's journal *Language* adopted a conciliatory tone: "The science of language, dealing with the most basic and simplest of human social institutions, is a human (or mental or, as they used to say, moral) science. *** It remains for linguists to determine what is widespread and what little is common to all human speech."[23] Yet the two integral theoretical articles which made up the second issue of the same volume — Sapir's "Sound Patterns in Language" and "Linguistics and Psychology" by A. P. Weiss — brought to light a major scientific dissent. Sapir's epochal essay (1925), one of the most farsighted American contributions to the apprehension and advance of linguistic methodology, asserts from its first lines that no linguistic phenomena or processes, in particular neither sound patterns nor sound processes of speech (for instance "umlaut" or "Grimm's law", so-called), can be properly understood in simple mechanical, sensorimotor terms. The dominant role was said to pertain to the "intuitive pattern alignment" proper to all speakers of a given language. According to the author's conclusion, the whole aim and spirit of the paper was to show that phonetic phenomena are not physical phenomena *per se* and to offer "a special illustration of the necessity of getting behind the sense data of any type of expression in order to grasp the intuitively felt and communicated forms which alone give significance to such expression".

Sapir's assaults against mechanistic approaches to language run counter to the radical behaviorism of the psychologist Albert Paul Weiss. The latter's article appeared in *Language* thanks to the sponsorship of Bloomfield, who taught with Weiss at Ohio State University, 1921–27, and who was increasingly influenced by his doctrine. In this paper of 1925 Weiss envisions a "compound multicellular type of organization" produced by language behavior, and he assigns to written language the rise of an even "more effective sensorimotor interchangeability between the living and the dead". Bloomfield's wide-scale outline of 1939, *Linguistic Aspects of Science*, with its numerous references to Weiss, picks up and develops this image: "Language bridges the gap between the individual nervous systems. *** Much as single cells are combined in a many-celled animal, separate persons are

---

[23] *Ibid.*, 109–112.

combined in a speech community. *** We may speak here, without metaphor, of a social organism."[24]

What, however, most intimately fastens Bloomfield to the works of Weiss is the latter's demand that human behavior be discussed in physical terms only. "The relation between structural and behavior psychology", examined by Weiss in the *Psychological Review* (1917), rejects the structuralist's aim "to describe the structure of the mind or consciousness" and denies the possibility of cooperation between structuralism and behaviorism, so far as the fundamental conceptions underlying both methods and the theoretical implications of either method are subjected to a close scrutiny.[25]

In conformity with these suggestions, any "mentalistic view" was proscribed by Bloomfield as a "prescientific approach to human things" or even a "primeval drug of animism" with its "teleologic and animistic verbiage": will, wish, desire, volition, emotion, sensation, perception, mind, idea, totality, consciousness, subconsciousness, belief, and the other "elusive spiritistic-teleologic words of our tribal speech". In the mentioned *Linguistic Aspects of Science* one chances to come across a paradoxically phrased confession: "It is the belief [!] of the present writer that the scientific description of the universe *** requires none of the mentalistic terms."[26] Bloomfield's presidential address to the Linguistic Society of America in 1935 prophesied that "within the next generations" the terminology of mentalism and animism "will be discarded, much as we have discarded Ptolemaic astronomy".[27]

It is this drastic dissimilarity between the two leading spirits of the Linguistic Society in the very essence of their scientific creeds which found its plain expression in Sapir's oral remarks on "Bloomfield's sophomoric psychology" and in Bloomfield's sobriquet for Sapir, "medicine man".[28] A diametrical opposition between both of them with regard to such matters as "the synthesis of linguistics with other sciences" was deliberately pointed to in Bloomfield's writings.[29]

This difference between two methods of approach deepened with the years and greatly affected the course and fortunes of semantic research in American linguistics. On the one hand, the inquiry into the "commu-

---

[24] L. Bloomfield, "Linguistic Aspects of Science", *International Encyclopedia of Unified Science* 1:4 (Chicago: University of Chicago, 1939).
[25] A. P. Weiss, "The Relation Between Structural and Behavioral Psychology", *Psychological Review* 24 (1917), 301–317.
[26] "Linguistic Aspects ...", 13.
[27] *A Leonard Bloomfield Anthology*, 322.
[28] *Ibid.*, 540.
[29] *Ibid.*, 227, 249.

nicative symbolism" of language in all its degrees and on all its levels, from the sound pattern through the grammatical and lexical concepts, to the "integrated meaning of continuous discourse", was becoming of still higher import in the work of Sapir, and with an avowed reference to his enlightening teaching, it was said in 1937 by Benjamin L. Whorf that "the very essence of linguistics is the quest for meaning".[30] On the other hand, Bloomfield, though realizing perfectly that the treatment of speech-forms and even of their phonemic components "involves the consideration of meanings", admitted at the same time in his paper "Meaning" of 1943 that "the management of meanings is bound to give trouble" as long as one refuses to adopt "the popular (*mentalistic*) view" and to say "that speech forms reflect unobservable, non-physical events in the *minds* of speakers and hearers".[31]

The difficulty in considering meaning while negating any "mental events" provoked repeated efforts by some younger language students to analyze linguistic structure without any reference to semantics, in contradistinction to Bloomfield's invocation of meaning as an inevitable criterion. Bloomfield himself was ready to deny not only the validity of such claims, but even the possibility of their existence.[32] Nonetheless, experiments in antisemantic linguistics became widespread toward the late forties. I was invited in the summer of 1945 to give a series of lectures at the University of Chicago. When I informed the University of my title for the planned cycle — "Meaning as the Pivotal Problem of Linguistics" — there came a benevolent warning from the faculty that the topic was risky.

It would be fallacious, however, to view the avoidance of semantic interpretation as a general and specific feature of the American linguistic methodology even for a brief stretch of time. This tentative ostracism was an interesting and fruitful trial accompanied by simultaneous and instructive criticism, and it has been superseded by an equally passionate and acclaimed striving for the promotion of semantic analysis first in vocabulary, then also in grammar.

Yet, finally, what bears a stamp of American origin is the semiotic science built by Charles Sanders Peirce from the 1860's throughout the late nineteenth and early twentieth centuries, a theory of signs to which, as was justly acknowledged (under Charles Morris' influence) by

---

[30] B. L. Whorf, *Language, Thought and Reality* (Cambridge, Mass. — London: M.I.T. Press, 1956), 79.
[31] *A Leonard Bloomfield Anthology*, 401.
[32] Cf. Charles C. Fries, "Meaning and Linguistic Analysis", *Language* 30 (1954), 57–68.

Bloomfield, "linguistics is the chief contributor", and which in turn has prepared the foundations for a true linguistic semantics. But in spite of this, Peirce's *semiotic* remained for many decades fatally unknown to the linguists of both the New and the Old World.

Now to sum up. In America the science of language produced several remarkable, prominent, internationally influential thinkers — to mention only some of those who are no longer with us, Whitney, Peirce, Boas, Sapir, Bloomfield, Whorf. What we observe at present, and what proves to be timely indeed, is an ever higher internationalization of linguistic science, without a ludicrous fear of foreign models and of "intellectual free trade".

One can still reproach American students and scholars, as well as those in diverse European countries, for a frequent inclination to confine the range of their scientific reading to books and papers issued in their native language and homeland and particularly to refer chiefly to local publications. In some cases this propensity results merely from an insufficient acquaintance with foreign languages, which is a debility widely spread among linguists. It is for this reason that important studies written in Russian and other Slavic languages have remained unknown, although some of them provide new and suggestive approaches.

One should finally mention the most negative phenomenon of American linguistic life. Bloomfield, who in 1912 had expressed "a modest hope *** that the science of language may in time come to hold in America also its proper place among sciences",[33] returned to this question in his notable survey, "Twenty-one Years of the Linguistic Society", shortly before the end of his scholarly activity. He was certainly right in concluding that "the external status of our science leaves much to be desired though there has been some improvement".[34] Now, however, this improvement is rapidly vanishing. Once again we observe that the blame does not lie with linguists, but with those bureaucrats who, under the pretext of scarcity and restraint, are prone to abolish or reduce departments and chairs of general linguistics, of comparative Indo-European studies, of Romance, Scandinavian, Slavic and other languages. In Sapir's pointed parlance, efforts are being made to establish and perpetuate the "very pallid status of linguistics in America", because this science seems to be hardly "convertible into cash

---

[33] *A Leonard Bloomfield Anthology*, 33.
[34] *Ibid.*, 493.

value".³⁵ Such antiscientific measures are most deplorable. In spite of the present crisis, America still remains more prosperous than most of the European countries, but even under their economic recession, none of them has dismantled its graduate schools and their linguistic programs. Nevertheless, permit me, in conclusion, once more to quote Leonard Bloomfield. The forecast made 45 years ago (December 30, 1929) in his address before a joint meeting of the Linguistic Society of America and the Modern Languages Associations reads:

I believe that in the near future — in the next few generations, let us say — linguistics will be one of the main sectors of scientific advance.³⁶

Do not all of us here share this belief?

First presented as the opening paper at the Golden Anniversary Symposium of the Linguistic Society of America, New York, Dec. 27, 1974. Elaborated in Peacham, Vermont, summer of 1975, and published in *The European Background of American Linguistics*, ed. H. M. Hoenigswald (Dordrecht, 1979).

---

[35] E. Sapir, "The Grammarian and His Language", *American Mercury* 1 (1924), 149–155.
[36] *A Leonard Bloomfield Anthology*, 227.

TOWARD THE HISTORY OF THE MOSCOW
LINGUISTIC CIRCLE

A brief historical survey of the Moscow Linguistic Circle (MLC) is of importance not only in view of its significant role in the development of Russian linguistics, but also because this Circle served as a model for the creation of avant-garde linguistic associations which arose in diverse countries and which took over the design of the name and some of the inner structure, as well as certain thoughts and intentions of the MLC. In particular, the MLC had a direct and decisive influence on the formation of the Prague Linguistic Circle in 1926, on the latter's organization and program, as has been repeatedly pointed out by the founder and president of the Prague Circle, Vilém Mathesius. The principles elaborated by the Prague Circle entered into international linguistic life under the label "Prague School", and were linked by many threads to the seeking and striving of MLC.

The following outline is based 1) on the mimeographed "Materials toward the History of MLC" prepared on the basis of its archives by three active representatives of the Circle, A. A. Buslaev, B. V. Hornung, and V. I. Nejštadt on January 6, 1956; 2) on letters about the history of the MLC which were exchanged in the mid-70's between R. Jakobson and the late A. A. Reformatskij, a distinguished linguist devoted to the Moscow cultural tradition and especially to the memory of MLC; and 3) on the few scattered, printed sources (among them my paper "An Example of Migratory Terms and Institutional Models", in *Selected Writings* II [The Hague, 1971], 527ff.). As the only one who remains of the seven founding members of the Circle (F. N. Afremov, P. G. Bogatyrev, A. A. Buslaev, S. I. Ragozin, P. P. Svešnikov, N. F. Jakovlev), and with hardly even a handful of survivors from the fifty active members the Circle numbered in 1923, I feel it appropriate to write down my chronicler's note and to dedicate it to the expert in world history of linguistics, Eugenio Coseriu.

The Moscow Linguistic Circle was an association of young explorers founded in March 1915 on the initiative of a group of students from the

Historico-Philological Faculty of Moscow University, with the active support of the Moscow Professor and leading Russian dialectologist D. N. Ušakov and two famous members of the Russian Academy of Sciences, F. E. Korš and A. A. Šaxmatov. From its first steps, the Circle took for its task the inquiry into the burning questions of linguistics, conceived as the science devoted to language in its various functions, including first and foremost the analysis of poetic language. The comprehensive investigation of poetics, and particularly of metrics and the interrelation between the written and oral varieties of verbal art and of language in general, entered into the basic program of our preoccupations; and from studies in folklore the way naturally led to an ethnological research of wider radius.

According to an early report of the first secretary of the MLC, G. O. Vinokur, the activity of the Circle consisted "both in adducing new materials and in the interpretation of old ones yet from a new standpoint". The work in the Circle had a laboratory character and ready-made academic lectures played a smaller role than debates where methods and approaches were developed in a joint collective exchange of opinions. An important place in the Circle's activities was given to the summer expeditions of its members according to programs coordinated beforehand. Most of this field work combined dialectological material with an exact notation of folklore texts and with ethnological observations, and a new attitude to theoretical questions such as the close coexistence, interplay, and blend of dialects or languages gradually found an ever clearer expression. The increasing interest of the observers was concentrated on the distinctive properties of folklore creativity connected with the character of interrelations between the narrator and the collective body.

The field work of 1915 was chiefly devoted to the study of areas near Moscow which formerly were believed to be deprived of their original features by the influence of the industrial center and new cultural standards, yet actually proved to preserve many archaic dialectal peculiarities and folklore survivals. The expeditions organized in 1916 gave convincing answers to some obscure questions of how to classify South Russian dialects, particularly their vowel patterns: former annoying misunderstandings disappeared in the light of a rudimentary phonological treatment. Also the question of a connection between the epic tradition and the boundaries of North Russian dialects was clarified by the Circle's field workers. The detailed investigation of the North Caucasian linguistic and ethnic area in 1921–22, led by N. F. Jakovlev, E. M. Šilling, and L. I. Žirkov, used new methodological devices of sound and form analysis and in this way reached results important both for the study of Caucasian languages and for general linguistics.

From 1918 the meetings of MLC became particularly frequent and the number of its members and visitors increased and encompassed a considerable part of the younger generation of Moscow researchers in the varied questions of language, literature, and folklore. It was to the discussions of MLC that studies on formerly unsolved and controversial questions of verse and its theory were particularly indebted, namely writings by B. V. Tomaševskij, O. M. Brik, R. O. Jakobson, B. I. Jarxo, and others. Communications and debates in MLC gave the first impetus to the development of phonological problems and stimulated a due attention to the questions of linguistic culture. Such fundamental questions of oral creations as a typological classification of popular anecdotes, the magic of spells, and the reconstruction of folklore texts received new methodological interpretations and solutions from P. G. Bogatyrev and N. F. Jakovlev in the Circle's meetings of 1918–20. The foundations of a phenomenology of language in the arresting treatment by Husserl's disciple G. G. Špet left a notable imprint on the development of MCL in its final period and provoked heated arguments about the place and limits of empiricism and about the role of semantics in the science of language. The problems of "inner form" launched by Humboldt and the criteria of delimiting poetic and usual language were among the points at issue.

In 1924, after hardly ten years of lasting activities, MLC was liquidated. Its premature end was caused partly by outer and partly by inner factors. Yet the contribution of the Circle both to Russian and to international linguistics should not be minimized. One should likewise mention the deep, organic ties of this short-lived experiment with its temporal and spatial environment.

Two important environmental factors must be taken into account as a beneficial background which stimulated the rise and astounding growth of MLC. First, it was the contagious force of the Russian cultural, in particular literary, avant-garde, with which the most active of the young Russian linguists were closely connected, and one may note that the militant poet Vladimir Majakovskij (1893–1930) joined the Circle in 1919, and a few months later his first public reading and discussion of the poem "150.000.000" took place in a special meeting of MLC. The latter counted the poets Boris Pasternak (1890–1960), Nikolaj Aseev (1889–1963), and Osip Mandel'štam (1891–1938) among its members and active debaters of poetic language and theory.

The second significant contribution to the effective initiative of a Circle called upon to develop an accurate approach to joint problems of linguistics and poetics was the specific tradition of Moscow University which linked these tasks and attributed a truly scientific essence and primary importance to the scrutiny of language. The fundamental writings in this direction by the founder of Moscow University, M. V. Lomonosov (1711–1765), an original, versatile savant and poet, are but one and the first of characteristic examples.

Testimonies made by two students of the Historico-Philological Faculty of Moscow University, representatives of quite different generations, and who later became famed political historians, merit adduction. V. O. Ključevskij (1841–1911) refers in his student letters of the early sixties to the leading role of the renowned scholar F. I. Buslaev (1818–1897), who served at Moscow University from 1848 to 1881 and upheld both as an explorer and instructor the substantial connection of language and poetry, as well as the urgency of their concerted interpretation. "There is nothing better", the student asserts, "than the Sunday courses in comparative and general linguistics gladly given by Buslaev at his home for a few volunteers". Not long after, Ključevskij's letters report that "essentials of comparative philology and, so to say, the philosophy of linguistics have assumed enormous proportions. *** Each of us raves about roots and suffixes, and to plunge into this world of microscopical infusorians, termed roots and prefixes, — means to detect many things of interest."

When twenty-five years later P. N. Miljukov (1859–1943) entered Moscow University, at once his attention was attracted to and impressed by the common predilection for linguistics, "reputed to be among sciences the second in exactitude after mathematics". In an epoch of passion for "exact" sciences, this reputation seemed to justify, as Miljukov's memoirs affirm, his preference for the Philological Faculty to the Faculty of the Natural Sciences. Hence, before concentrating his studies on Russian cultural and political history, the final field of his scholarly activities, Miljukov endeavored to familiarize himself with comparative linguistics and mythology in F. F. Fortunatov's (1848–1914) and V. F. Miller's (1848–1913) classes. Fortunatov, who was then at the beginning of his teaching career, grew into the originator and spiritual head of the Moscow Linguistic School, with its paramount insistence on the search for general laws, for the problems of mind and language, and for the interrelations between verbal form and function. These may be seen as historical prerequisites for a further and wider development and revision, tasks which excited the seekers grouped around the newborn linguistic circle.

Written in Peacham, Vermont, August 1979, for the Eugenio Coseriu Festschrift, *Logos Semantikos* 1: *Geschichte der Sprachphilosophie und der Sprachwissenschaft* (Madrid: Gredos-Berlin: de Gruyter, 1981).

ОЧЕРЕДНЫЕ ЗАДАЧИ ОБЩЕЙ ЛИНГВИСТИКИ

Мне очень радостно говорить в Московском университете. Я последние дни много размышлял на одну тему: беседы с московскими лингвистами разных поколений, чтение их работ — все это меня снова и снова заставляет задуматься над тем, что за удивительное явление — ведь и в стиле, и в содержании мысли здесь чувствуется могучая традиция — традиция Московского университета при всех разительных отличиях его отдельных этапов. Когда я говорю "традиция", я не хочу быть нисколько односторонним. Нельзя не согласиться с композитором Стравинским, когда он говорит, что новаторство и традиция — два неразрывно связанных понятия. И вот факт этой самой традиции и ее связанности с новизной исканий — явление воистину замечательное.

Тут есть еще один факт, которого мы, москвичи, бывшие в Московском университете в какой-либо момент его истории, не замечали — он был для нас слишком естественным — это громадная роль лингвистики в жизни Московского университета, его тяга к языкознанию, сказавшаяся с самого начала давно минувших дней. Нелегко найти в XVIII веке более яркого лингвиста, совмещающего наблюдательную практику с острой теорией, большего в своих догадках, чем основатель Московского университета Ломоносов. А первый профессор русского языка в Московском университете, тот ученый конца XVIII века, труды которого в будущем году здесь наконец будут изданы, Барсов, о котором нынешние немецкие лингвисты недаром говорят, что его понимание теоретических принципов совмещается с тщательной разработкой самых мелких лингвистических фактов, к которым он относится с такой же любовью, как к отвлеченным теоретическим проблемам лингвистики.

Если мы перейдем разом во вторую половину XIX века, я позволю себе для примера обратиться к эпистолярной и мемуарной литературе тех лет и сослаться на показания двух известных московских историков-бывших студентов Московского университета 60–70 годов. И Ключевский, и Милюков поступили в университет, совершенно не думая о языкознании. И вдруг оба пишут, в разное время: не могли мы себе представить, что главный нерв жизни историко-филологического факультета — это наука о языке. Один из них пишет: поразительно до чего это увлекательно заниматься наукой, которая оказалась самой точной из всех наук, после математики. Это оправдывает в их глазах самый выбор филологического факультета и зовет к посильным занятиям наукой о слове. А другой из них восхищается тем стихийным потоком тех мельчайших инфузорий, из которых слагается язык, и в которых наука вскрывает замечательные закономерности. И вот эти студенты, которым потом было суждено стать историками, были призваны осознать, что лингвистика — истинная школа научного мышления.

Я перехожу к той эпохе, которая наложила отпечаток и на русскую, и на мировую науку о языке. Это — московская лингвистическая школа Филиппа Федоровича Фортунатова. Речь идет о конце прошлого века и о самом начале века нынешнего, как эпохе создания целого ряда больших лингвистов и ученых трудов, которые до сих пор не устарели и все еще свежи и новы в своих теоретических положениях.

Фортунатов был ученый, который при жизни почти ничего не напечатал. Список его работ такой маленький, что трудно было бы его предложить бюрократам американских университетов в профессора: недостаточно мол опубликовано. Может быть, такова практика не только в американских университетах. Но надо сказать, что когда теперь Академия Наук СССР напечатала его литографированные курсы, там находится понимание соотношения лингвистических фактов, понимание языка во всем богатстве его функций.

Помнится, в мои чуть ли не первые студенческие дни, осенью 1914 года, заседание памяти только что почившего Фортунатова прозвучало всем нам, университетским юнцам, внятным призывом к научному подвигу. Так был задуман, а в 1915 году основан Московский Лингвистический Кружок, которым сейчас вдруг заинтересовались во всем ученом мире. У меня спрашивают: расскажите его историю, вы единственный, вероятно, кто её еще помнит не по протоколам, а по живому участию. Московский кружок искал нового в лингвистике, он искал новых связей этой дисциплины в узком смысле слова с учением о различных функциях языка и особенно о поэтической функции. И когда мы теперь смотрим на расстоянии шести с лишним десятков лет на работы этого кружка, охватывавшего почти всех молодых московских лингвистов того времени, что же мы видим. Мы замечаем необыкновенное уважение к существовавшей тогда традиции и в тоже время твердое понимание необходимости превзойти её, преодолеть в ней всяческий застой и сыскать новые пути.

Когда я читаю нынешние работы московских лингвистов и не только московских, а подвергшихся влиянию московской лингвистической школы и её развития, я особенно отчетливо вижу, какую роль сыграл этот самый кружок в своей борьбе, в своих дискуссиях, в своих исканиях новых лингвистических положений, новых методов, новых подходов, новых принципов и новых технических средств, как изучать язык.

Мне хотелось бы, не оставаясь дольше в области истории, поставить несколько вопросов в связи с сегодняшним этапом лингвистических исследований. Что для них наиболее характерно, что обещает новое развитие, что здесь плодотворно, что влияет на другие научные области и что оказывается под влиянием других областей.

И тут я должен сказать, что́ для нынешнего состояния лингвистики особенно характерно понимание вреда сепаратизма. Нельзя отделять одни слои, одни уровни языковой системы от других уровней, части и целое, которые глубоко сопряжены, нельзя говорить о целом, не учитывая влияния частей на целое, как нельзя говорить о частях, не понимая, что части существуют только в пределах данного целого. Мало того, нельзя говорить о языке, отрывая его от окружающей системы культурных факторов. Сейчас лингвистика тесно сплетается с целым рядом этнологических наук, сейчас лингвистика тесно связана с историей языка, а история языка и история культуры оказываются неразрывным целым. Причем, было бы самым зловредным фактом, если бы мы рассматривали одну плоскость, одну область как диктующую другим областям. Тут есть соотношение, закономерность, и есть более широкая система, по отношению к которой язык только законная часть.

Сейчас любопытно, что дело уже не ограничивается одними лишь науками о культуре. В настоящее время такие проблемы, которые казались совершенно непонятными многим лингвистам прошлого, оказываются на очереди. Так сейчас на очереди исключительно интересная проблема нейролингвистики, а именно изучение соотношения между речью и мозгом. Я должен признаться, что редко какая-нибудь научная работа производила на меня такое впечатление, как недавно прочитанная и изученная мною книга здешних ученых, русских нейрологов Балонова и Деглина, трактующая именно отношение между речью и мозгом. Эти крупнейшие открытия советской науки взаправду сенсационны в самом лучшем смысле этого слова. Они действительно показывают, что можно понять отношение между структурой мозга и структурой речи, и что можно на основании структуры речи понять многое в деятельности мозга, до недавнего времени остававшееся просто неизвестным.

Замечательные международные открытия в области патологии речи, включая сюда и афазию, и нарушения речи у психических больных, открывают ряд дверей: двери для понимания лингвистики и двери для понимания патологии. Это сейчас признают глубочайшие психиатры и психологи; и всё это — только блестящее начало, и каждый шаг обещает новые плодотворные выводы.

Когда я сегодня настаивал на важности соотношения между целым и частями, а именно на взаимоотношении частей и на влиянии целого на части и частей на целое, я конечно не думал открыть неведомый мир; конечно, в научной традиции эти идеи уже существовали. Мы страдаем слишком суженным подходом к лингвистическим заветам прошлого века, особенно его последней половины. На поверхностный взгляд, в то время блистала одна лишь школа, притом школа, для которой не существовало вот этих общих проблем, и которая была занята одной только историей отдельных языковых изменений.

Это была так называемая младограмматическая немецкая школа, с главным своим центром в Лейпциге, и она действительно была необычайно сильна и влиятельна, её влияние простиралось на различные научные центры мира, но притом это было бы крайне упрощенным взглядом видеть одни только официальные верхи тогдашней науки, потому, что рядом с этой школой было большое лингвистическое движение международного масштаба, и такое движение существовало и в Англии, и в Швейцарии, и в самой Германии и в различных русских центрах, доходя до Казани. Казанская школа, созданная двумя гениальными польскими лингвистами конца XIX века Яном Бодуэном де Куртэне и Миколаем Крушевским — это одно из самых ярких явлений в истории лингвистики. И там уже намечались и ставились все те проблемы, которые сейчас становятся самыми насущными вопросами.

Я говорил об отношении частей и целого. Что с этим неразрывно связано? Вопрос, который для нынешней лингвистики является, я бы сказал, основным, центральным пунктом. Это вопрос, который в математике называется вопросом инвариантности, инвариантов и вариаций.

Отношение между инвариантностью и вариациями было темой неслучайно назревавшей и в математике, и в лингвистике век тому назад, на протяжении 70-ых годов прошлого столетия. То, что мы в настоящее время наблюдаем в лингвистике в этом отношении, находит себе в математике особенно близкую параллель. Нельзя говорить об одних лишь влияниях, но нельзя разрывать целостность явлений. То, что в математике делает топология, особенно близко лингвистическим исканиям. Это именно поиски инвариантов в условиях разнообразных трансформаций. Это сейчас для лингвистики важно на каждом шагу. И, как правильно отмечают историки математической науки, этот вопрос об инвариантности в математике стал особенно плодотворным, когда была выдвинута на первый план проблема, в свою очередь давно находившая своих искателей, а именно проблема относительности. Принцип релятивизма. И тут историю различных наук в свою очередь сопрягает направление, а именно все поиски междупредметных отношений, которые позволяют понять самые предметы через их многообразие и закономерные отношения.

Был швейцарский лингвист Jost Winteler, который в 1876 году написал диссертацию о своем родном швейцарско — немецком говоре и в этой своей диссертации выдвинул пункт: необходимо прежде всего анализировать законы внутриязыковых отношений. Он преподавал в средней школе и среди его учеников был подрастающий Эйнштейн, который от него услыхал впервые — теперь нам об этом говорят все архивные данные — впервые услыхал, что такое относительность. Эта мысль, это понятие попало на продуктивную почву. Так называемый принцип относительности получил право гражданства. Но конечно вопрос не во влияниях, а во внутренних связях, обнаруживающихся между различными областями.

Между прочим этот ученый Винтелер так и не попал ни в какой университет, чему удивляться отнюдь не приходится. Недаром журил его один из коллег: "Почему ты не написал на банальную тему? Ты сегодня уж был бы ординарным профессором." А дальше преподавателя в средней школе он так никогда и не пошел. Винтелер горевал, что его идеи упали на камень и не дадут плодов. Однако они дали плоды, правда, не в лингвистике, а в физике. Эйнштейн его слушал и в американской эмиграции незадолго до своей смерти повторял: это был мудрый человек, он все предвидел.

Теория относительности, т.е. тот принцип, что надо рассматривать прежде всего отношения, что именно отношения определяют предмет, что без этой самой характеристики отношений ничего нельзя объяснить, этот подход находит себе все новое применение в культурной жизни нашего века и быть может особенно отчетливо в современной лингвистике.

Между прочим, я тут говорил о соотношении между языкознанием и другими науками, о соотношении между различными уровнями языковой системы, но нельзя забывать еще об одном немаловажном расширении горизонта. Надо помнить, что хотя существуют плодотворные местные, областные, национальные черты наук в различных странах, но ничто не наделено таким большим плодотворным значением, как международные связи в науке. И конечно в лингвистике международная работа показывала, показывает и чем дальше, тем еще больше будет показывать необходимость интерпретации лингвистики всего мира как единого целого.

Мне хотелось бы только наметить, иначе пришлось бы развернуть здесь целый курс, хотелось бы по крайней мере упомянуть те признаки, которые на указанном фоне особенно четко характеризуют сегодняшнюю, а может быть, еще больше, поскольку можно предсказывать, то завтрашнюю науку о языке.

Это — вопрос о диалектическом синтезе. Диалектический синтез для очередного этапа науки особенно существен. Если на склоне XIX-ого века превалировали чисто аналитические проблемы, то вскоре стало ясно, что этот односторонний анализ не дает возможности понять целостные задачи языка. Скажем, рассматривался язык в пределах одной функции, а именно ежедневный бытовой язык, язык сообщений о предметном мире, и не учитывалось в достаточной степени многообразие речевых функций.

Теперь мы преодолеваем такую ущербленную трактовку языка, и в частности учтена наконец та языковая функция, которая долго оставалась недостаточно освещенной. Мы имеем в виду поэтическую функцию, которая своеобразными путями преобразует речь. И сейчас мы знаем, что эта самая поэтическая функция живет в каждом человеке, независимо от того, разговаривает ли он, читает ли он лекцию или пишет стихи. В различных степенях она всегда участвует. И лингвистика призвана осветить это участие.

Не забудем одного. Не так уж много существует универсалий в области культуры, не так уж много универсальных явлений, которые характеризуют человечество во всей его истории. Это во-первых — язык, факт его наличия, ибо нет человеческих общин без речи. Это языковые коллективы, и каждый член таковых кроме решительно патологических казусов, усваивает речь, слушает, говорит, понимает что-то, и если его соседи говорят на другом, ему непонятном языке, это только другая разновидность человеческой речи.

С другой стороны, какой еще рядом с языком существует универсальный факт? Повидимому, нет ни одного человеческого общества, ни одного племени, у которого бы не было поэзии. Поэтическая функция в её крайнем проявлении — опять-таки универсальный феномен. И вот соотношение этих двух универсальных явлений требует очень тщательного разбора.

Есть еще одна функция, о которой я больше постараюсь сказать не сегодня в Москве, а в Тбилиси, где на днях открывается важная конференция, посвященная роли бессознательного в человеческой жизни, и я позван говорить там о бессознательном в языке, при чем, разумеется, на первый план попадает и вопрос о функции, ограничивающей самостоятельность бессознательного фактора в речевых процессах. Это так называемая "метаязыковая" функция, соответственно окрыленному термину "метаязык", лансированному знаменитым польским логиком Тарским. Если в отвлеченных логических операциях вопросы метаязыка нашли себе широкое и продуктивное приложение, то их значимость в речевом обиходе оставалась до самого последнего времени недостаточно освещена лингвистами. Понятие метаязыка покрывает тот округ речевой деятельности, где предметом сообщения служит язык как таковой и его составные элементы. Стремясь определить, что такое метаязык, я тем самым даю металингвистическое высказывание, потому что говорю о языке.

Если иностранец, недостаточно владеющий русским языком, спросит, что такое "ослица", то вы либо переведете это слово на другой язык, или скажете "ослица — это самка осла". Это опять-таки метаязыковая операция. Мы мыслим метаязыковыми операциями, мы пользуемся метаязыком, когда говорим о языке, и эти процессы занимают громадную роль в нашей языковой жизни.

Начиная с раннего детства мы параллельно усваиваем и язык, и метаязык, стремясь понять, чем отличается один языковой знак от другого языкового знака, что в них общего и что отличного. Если младенец на своих первых языковых шагах говорит: "бабочка" обо всем, что летает, то следующим шагом будет усилие понять: какая разница между словами "самолет" и "бабочка". Он не ошибался, когда называл самолет бабочкой — просто значение этого слога в той стадии его языковой практики было: "бабочка" — летающий предмет. А на второй стадии происходит различение этих предметов, и так далее и так далее.

Роль метаязыка колоссальна и без последовательного существенного внимания к метаязыку мы не в силах понять язык. В конце концов, то что делают лингвисты — это метаязыковые операции. Примерно со второго года жизни дети овладевают подобными операциями, не умея однако абстрагировать и назвать самоё операцию. Детское усвоение метаязыка — преддверие овладения речью, так же, как утрата метаязыка в афазических заболеваниях — это одно из самых сокрушительных явлений речевой патологии.

На пути к охвату языка во всех его внутренних, неизбывных рычагах, мы должны до конца осознать внутриязыковую принадлежность двух основных рычагов — времени и пространства. Таковые представляются часто лингвистам "внешними факторами", но на самом деле — это внутренние элементы языковой системы. Как известно, вообще нет системы, которая бы не изменялась. Система и изменение — это явления, глубоко сопряженные, как мы знаем из кибернетики и из многих других областей науки. И это особенно касается языка. Представлялось, будто можно давать описание языка, говоря только о статических факторах, о неизменных компонентах, а с другой стороны делать историю языка, где бы говорилось об одних только изменениях. На самом деле то, что нужно — это динамическое описание системы, динамическая синхрония. Ведь нет таких явлений в языке, как изменение, которое происходит в течение суток. Изменения — медлительный процесс, и вот в этих-то изменениях, которыми полон язык, постоянно наблюдается сожительство начала и конца: старт, исходный пункт, с одной стороны, и результат, финиш, с другой стороны.

В том же обществе, в течение некоторого времени, и притом нередко продолжительного времени, существуют в качестве двух стилистических эквивалентов и начальная форма, и последующая форма — и то, с чего изменение начинается, и то, чем оно заканчивается. Этот факт подлежит учету. Это сожительство обнаруживаться не только у молодежи, которая ближе к концу изменения, или у старого поколения, которое более традиционно, нет, даже один и тот же человек варьирует постоянно формы то более, то менее архаичные, и притом сознает, что одни из них более архаичны, а другие — менее, и соответственно чувствует, когда который из двух вариантов надо употреблять. Это все равно, сказал я в одной из своих ранних работ, как с галстуками: если у вас есть два галстука, один — более консервативный, а другой — более модный, то вот мы присутствуем при двух этапах изменения и мы пользуемся обоими этапами как разнофункциональными вариантами. Очень многое меняется в интерпретации изменений при подходе ко времени как внутреннему фактору. При этом, конечно, необходимо считаться и с другим, противоположным аспектом. Конечно, важно, когда мы говорим о московском наречии сегодняшнего дня, знать, что в нем существует целая гамма временных вариаций. Но с другой стороны, если мы говорим об истории русского языка с IX до XX века, надо помнить, что дело не в одних изменениях. Тут налицо диахрония статических форм. Что сохранилось, что осталось от раннего русского языка в дальнейшем ходе развития, и что переменилось, что появилось нового оттого, что канва неизменного контекста такова — вот тематика для описательной лингвистики в ее историческом разрезе.

И наконец, mutatis mutandis, то же самое имеет место по отношению к пространству. Живут рядом разные диалекты и эти диалекты характеризуются сходствами и различиями. Эти сходства и эти различия требуют от нас учета инвариантов. Что именно не подлежит вариации, сохраняется неизменным, и что изменчиво. Каждый из нас говорит в своей семье несколько иначе, хотя бы в интонации, хотя бы в расстановке пауз, чем когда выходит на улицу. Когда же выходит на улицу, снова иначе, чем когда он в своем квартале. Здесь поиски инвариантов и вариаций становятся еще важнее, потому что все развитие лингвистики нынешнего века показывает, что даже там, где нет исторического родства, наблюдаются общие зуковые явления и общие грамматические явления у соседних языков. Вначале этот факт особенно поражал: почему? каким образом? Однако надо помнить, что соседи не только воюют, но и разговаривают, хотя бы и враждебно, и что развертываются, распространяются, движутся в пространстве языковые черты. Часто они даже покрывают целый ряд языков. Например, далеко не случайно, что почти все языки Советского Союза характеризуются различием между твердыми и мягкими согласными и что наблюдаются лингвистические особенности, характерные для целого ряда азиатских языков, не связанных между собою генетически.

Иными словами, здесь имеет место диффузия, т.е. происходит распространение речевых явлений, не останавливающееся на языковых границах. Это очень важно, и зловредное отсутствие достаточного международного сотрудничества привело к тому, что до сих пор не существует атласов, регистрирующих пределы языковых явлений, например всё еще отсутствуют атласы звуковой структуры языков целого материка; нет и в помине мировых лингвистических атласов. И когда набрасываются пробные эскизы в этом направлении, то неизменно падает новый свет на вопросы, требующие вразумительного решения.

Проблематика так называемых "языковых союзов" нераз удивляла наблюдателей, но следует учесть, что всякое языковое изменение оказывается неизбежно сопряжено с той или иной степенью диффузии, и что таковая находит себе максимальное проявление именно в языковых союзах.

Если кто-либо просто поскользнулся в речи, его уклон от нормы остается бесследной обмолвкой, если он не будет повторен самим автором невпопадицы и затем подхвачен его семьей и дальнейшим окружением. Если даже в основе диффузии лежит не единичная модель, а серия взаимно независимых конвергентных новшеств, все же между возникновением и экспансией изменения тесная связь остается в силе, и между очагом новшества и его диффузией нет принципиальной границы. Только следует помнить, что диффузия это творческий, целестремительный процесс.

На очереди стоит живо дебатируемый в сегодняшней науке вопрос о сходстве и смежности, как двух классах сочетаний между внутриязыковыми единицами. Но всего не охватишь, и доклад на эту — ответственную и, мне кажется, увлекательную — тему я откладываю до следующего раза.

A hitherto unpublished lecture delivered at Moscow University on September 29, 1979.

PËTR BOGATYRËV (29.I.93–18.VIII.71): EXPERT IN TRANSFIGURATION

To the lasting memory of Konstantin Bogatyrëv

On the threshold of our century, in Saratov, a pupil of the primary school, Pëtr Grigor'evič Bogatyrëv, was — because of his unusual declamatory ability and passion — elected to recite Puškin's "Hussar" at a public educational gathering. In a presumptuous chat with a green youth, the title hero of the facetious poem recounts the metamorphosis of his Kievan landlady into a witch, flying off astride a broom, and quotes the angry retorts of the exposed sorceress. The poet's embodiment of the whole whimsical conversation was in turn recreated by the inspired and inspiring schoolboy. This performance so impressed a stately auditor that it unexpectedly opened up successive steps for the fledgling reciter toward high school and university studies.

Bogatyrëv's first monograph on Russian literature, printed in Berlin in 1923, is entitled "Puškin's Poem 'The Hussar', Its Sources and Its Influence on Folk Poetry", and throughout the thirties the author of this study repeatedly returned to the same double topic — Puškin's recreation of folklore stimuli and the new transformations of the poet's "Hussar" at its reverse penetration into folk tales and plays. The multilayered composition and history of Puškin's grotesque attracted the student's curiosity: the witch's squabble with the Hussar, taken over by Puškin from the oral tradition; the Hussar's boasting to the green youth, borrowed by the poet from a recently published story; Puškin's creative recasting of these sources and its reflections in the peasant milieu, which radically reshaped the classic's heritage and used it both in prose and in jocular folk verse for pageants at country fairs.

The variegated combinations and collisions of tradition and improvisation fascinated Bogatyrëv, as they appeared and merged both in written and oral literature, and even more so in theatrical life. Thus, at the VIIth International Congress of Anthropologists and Ethnologists (Moscow, 1964), he concluded his report on tradition and improvisation in folk art with the thesis that "in folk art tradition and improvisation form a dialectical unity".

In high school and later at the university, Bogatyrëv oscillated between two prospects, that of becoming himself an actor or an explorer of the theatre, and both of these approaches to scenic art pertained to the essence of his inner life. The stage was the greatest fascination of the boy's student years, and he used to stand in line throughout the long, freezing Moscow winter nights in order to obtain the cheap theatre tickets. The author's statement in the preface to the Russian edition of his selected writings, *Questions in the Theory of Folk Art* (Moscow, 1971), that "most of the works in this collection are concentrated around one single theme and relate to one sphere of popular culture, the folkloric act (*dejstvo*)", accurately characterizes Bogatyrëv's quest, particularly during the freest and strongest period of his research, which was progressively connected with Czechoslovakia of the twenties and thirties. One can see the summit of this period in his book *Czech and Slovak Folk Theatre* (published in Prague, 1940, before his return to Moscow). It is a work of remarkable depth and scope, despite the tragic events of the late thirties, which prevented the full development and complete realization of the scholar's planned investigations.

In the introductory chapter the author himself evaluates his book as "the first modest attempt at a general inquiry into the form and function of the folk theatre as a structured art". With such men of the stage as Evreinov, Bogatyrëv shares the view that our entire life is saturated with theatrical elements and that now and again we are transfigured and play out in our lives various roles, sometimes quite unexpected and unusual ones. Transfiguration appears as a fundamental feature that distinguishes drama from lyric and epic. The dualism of the actor and his role is experienced by the spectator and carries a relevant value. This dualism, implemented not only by the artists on stage but by each of us in the diverse social situations we find ourselves in, has been carefully examined by Bogatyrëv, and this scrutiny may be considered an acute and spontaneous realization of the program launched by Charles Sanders Peirce over a century ago under the slogan "Man, A Sign", calling for a systematic inquiry both into "the meaning of the human sign" and into "the material quality of the man-sign" (*Collected Papers*, V, §5). The problem of the "man-sign" is investigated by the Moscow-Prague scholar, especially as applied to folklore in its two specific domains, properly theatrical acts, with their predominance of the aesthetic function, and magic acts, as they were labeled and discussed primarily in the author's French book, *Actes magiques: rites et croyances en Russie Subcarpathique* (Paris, 1929). This book is an important stage in Bogatyrëv's field work, which was conducted first in Russian areas —

the districts of Serpuxov (1914), Vereja (1915) and Šenkursk (1916) — and then among the Carpathian Ukrainians (1923–26). From the very beginning, folk rituals and beliefs were at the center of Bogatyrëv's observation and description, as is apparent already in the first of his lengthier studies (published in *Ètnografičeskoe Obozrenie*, in which diverse students of our generation made their début). This study described the Russian beliefs of the Šenkursk district (1918).

In our scholar's conviction, the dramatic obstacles and dangers accompanying field work were an inherent part of an intent folklore research — such natural occurrences as the "impossible mud in the mountains, the wild animals, and the typhus" which he mentions in a letter sent in 1923 from the Carpathian Verxovina to the benevolent Prague professor Jiří Polívka, or as the events recounted in his quiet report on how he and his fellow travellers narrowly escaped being lynched in 1915 by the peasants of the Vereja district, who suspected them of being German agents sent to poison the wells (cf. my account in the "Retrospect" to *Selected Writings* IV, 643f.). Despite all these difficulties he fought, as he states in a letter, for "that friendly atmosphere when the wall between the urban folklorist and the guardians of folklore unnoticeably dissolves". In his approach, the necessity for collectors of folklore to engage in severe and varied field-work training was unquestionable. The ethnographer had to examine the folk tradition and its transformations in the remote backwoods of places like the Carpathian mountains or the Archangel tundra and, on the other hand, in the environs and outskirts of big cities like Moscow among peasants and factory workers.

From the early twenties on, Bogatyrëv was strongly influenced by Saussure's emphasis on synchronic linguistic descriptions, but at the same time — and the more his work progressed, the more strongly — dynamic elements in the synchronic view of folklore played the decisive role in his observations and conclusions. What he saw with particular clarity was the competition between different, even opposite functions attached to one and the same folklore act, especially conflicts between the aesthetic and magical functions, both in folk theatre and in religious ritual. In this respect his French paper on jocular and erotic plays in the funerary rites of Carpathian Rus' (1926) contains immensely rich material and comments. The proximities and distances between the play (*jeu*) and the magical act (*acte magique*) led Bogatyrëv to look for the theatrical element in the performance of ritual and for the magical aspects of the theatrical realm, and he even devoted a special paper to "the superstitions of actors" (1927).

The study of functional hierarchy, namely of the dominant and secondary functions and the laws of their changes, is among the strongest attainments of Bogatyrëv's research, as is shown for instance in his study "The Christmas Tree in Eastern Slovakia" (*Germanoslavica*, 1932–33), where he demonstrates how a folk borrowing lost its aesthetic character and took on instead a magic-religious function. As another example of borrowings with a change in the dominant function, he cites galoshes, which when adopted by the Russian peasantry lost their original function of guarding one's feet against rain and mud and became instead purely decorative footwear which had itself to be protected from the elements. (Incidentally, a Russian satirical ditty [*častuška*] goes as follows: "I have galoshes and I'm saving them for the summer weather, but, as a matter of fact, I don't have them at all"; here the alleged change in function becomes a disguise for the actual lack of galoshes.)

The changeability and variety of functions attributed to a ritual, and its frequent obligatoriness, coupled with a complete lack of motivation or a subconscious one, compel Bogatyrëv to warn against oversimplified historical or synchronic interpretations. From this point of view, his richest collection and discussion of material is found in his monograph *Polaznik* (Kraków, 1933–34), where the South Slavic, Hungarian, Slovak, Polish, and Ukrainian beliefs concerning the earliest Christmas visitor to the house are examined and the whimsical metaphoric and metonymic connections of the visitor's person and conduct with the omen he brings to the house for the forthcoming year are attentively catalogued and interpreted.

The folk theatre, which Bogatyrëv studied from his youngest years until his last writings, was for him marked by the greatest multiplicity of meanings, by the greatest variability of constituents taken over from diverse arts, and was believed to exhibit the highest syncretism. In this connection the inquirer disclosed the greatest divergences between the director, the actors and the spectators, and at the same time the convergences of their roles. Here the attention of the analyst was focused on "the dialectical opposition of the stage and the audience" and on its removal. Such typical phenomena of the folk theatre as the lack of the three classical unities or the substitution of gestures for decorations and the interweaving of buffoonery and tragedy led Bogatyrëv to interesting juxtapositions of the folk drama with the medieval stage and with Chaplin's films, a topic he first approached as early as 1923 and to which he returned in 1938. Bogatyrëv's intensive cooperation with such outstanding representatives of the avant-garde Czech theatre as J. F.

Burian and Jindřich Honzl were most fruitful, both for the scholar and for Czech theatrical life, especially for Burian's remarkable experiments in staging Czech folk plays. This collaboration also resulted in several instructive essays which Bogatyrëv wrote especially for the Programs of Burian's theatre from 1936 through 1939, with one more after the war, in 1946.

The theme of the interconnections between closed semiotic systems and the danger of misinterpreting any one such system from the standpoint of another was a topic which went through Bogatyrëv's entire scientific career. His first book, *The Czech Puppet Theatre and the Russian Folk Theatre* (Berlin-Moscow, 1923), written in the spirit of the earliest Russian formalist papers, was chiefly preoccupied with single verbal devices (*lazzi*) but the mutual relation of "the puppet theatre and the theatre of live actors" continued to intrigue the author and became the captivating topic of one of his last expositions, a strictly semiotic study posthumously published in Tartu in 1973. The theatrical tendency to bring human actors closer to puppets or, on the contrary, puppets to human actors, the intermediary position of puppets between theatrical and figurative art, and finally the joint play of the puppets with the puppeteer and accordion player are vividly approached by the analyst.

The semiotic problems of the relations between folklore and written literature were the subject of heated debates in the Moscow Linguistic Circle in 1919–20, and it was there that Bogatyrëv first insisted on the possibility of a rigorous typology of narrative plots used in folklore and proposed along these lines an unfortunately never published classification of folk anecdotes (*fabliaux*), a task realized a few years later by V. Propp in application to fairy tales. Bogatyrëv's lecture on "Folk Tales about Fools", delivered in the Circle in 1919, deeply impressed the audience and was supplemented by some seemingly close and, as the speaker himself noted, at the same time distant parallels in literature proper. Thus in Bogatyrëv's scheme, "fools of the second category" were those who do standard things, but in inappropriate situations, e.g. use the proper funeral formulas but at weddings and vice versa. The joke he added was: "Eugene Onegin is a typical fool of the second category who rejected Tat'jana at the wrong moment and then, again in the wrong moment, declared his love for her."

The necessity for a clear-cut delimitation between literary history and folkloristics and the need to rehabilitate the autonomy of the latter were for both of us, from the days of the Moscow Linguistic Circle on, a burning topic of discussion, which in 1929 found its final expression in our joint essay for the Festschrift in honor of the Dutch philologist and folklorist J. Schrijnen, later followed by a condensed program in the Slavic ethnographic periodical *Lud Słowiański* (1931). Schrijnen devoted a supportive review article to this essay and deliberately followed its principles in his treatise *Nederlandische Volkskunde* (1930–33), but at the time the idea of "collective creation" and "preliminary censorship" underlying the oral tradition was for the most part either rejected or ignored, whereas in recent years our joint essay has been translated into half a dozen languages and has provoked new comments and lively discussions.

Bogatyrëv fully recognized the strong and frequent mutual influences of oral and written verbal art and of folk arts and "high art" in general. At the same time he stressed the reciprocal ties, and to mere mechanical imitations he opposed the phenomenon of a creative transformation, "a dialectical struggle between the borrowing artist and the borrowed matter", and insisted, particularly in his papers of the mid-thirties, on this quite substantial difference. He cited such genuinely creative instances of inspiring folklore models as the work of the Czech Romantics Erben and Mácha, such painters as Picasso in his borrowings from African art, such musicians as Janáček, Musorgskij, and Stravinskij, and such great men of the theatre as Meyerhold. The surprisingly strong penetration of folklore forms into the art of advertisements and of the urban fairs was Bogatyrëv's topic of the sixties, especially in Steinitz's Festschrift of 1965 and in the paper presented to the Prague Slavistic Congress of 1968.

The recognition of interrelationship and mutual exchange never weakened Bogatyrëv's awareness of impassable boundaries. Thus, for instance, he carefully recorded dreams of peasants, especially of storytellers, and came to the conclusion that there were no mutual influences between dreams and Russian fairy tales, just as in Russian tradition there appeared to be no means or features common both to fairy tales and to the mythological data attested in local historical documents or folk beliefs.

In 1915 Bogatyrëv was one of the co-founders of the Moscow Linguistic Circle and in the late twenties and thirties he took an effective part in the activities of the Prague Linguistic Circle as lecturer, discussant, and contributor to its periodicals. His cooperation with the linguistic nucleus of both associations furthered his close acquaintance with the development of structural linguistic thought, just as, on the other hand, Bogatyrëv's ethnological considerations and reflections widened the semiotic scope of his fellow linguists, especially during the thirties, when linguistic methods were extended in the Prague Linguistic Circle into an all-embracing semiotic program. The relevance of the linguistic model for cultural anthropology and in particular for the science of folklore was insistently emphasized by Bogatyrëv at all the international congresses and conferences of anthropologists, ethnologists, and linguists to which he contributed in oral and written form, and from the beginning of the 1930's he insisted on a systematic application of "functional structuralism" to ethnographic studies and in particular on what he called the "structural inquiry into the functional transformation of ethnographic phenomena". Achievements in linguistic description, geography, typology, structural and functional analysis, and the distinctions between productive and ossified forms were extended by Bogatyrëv for wider ethnological application. At the same time he was remarkably able to grasp not only the analogies between language and popular traditions, but also the differential features that had to be taken into account.

In insisting once more on the study of the "man-sign" as the focal point of Bogatyrëv's semiotic quest, one has to pay attention to the semiotic pertinence of etiquette and in particular to deal with the semantics of peasant etiquette. It was this complex of research tasks that he advanced as an urgent program at the Tartu semiotic meeting of 1970, the last one that he attended.

In Bogatyrëv's studies on "theatrical signs", the actor is a sign and his costume or mask is "a sign of a sign". The chapter entitled "Theatrical Costume and Mask" in his book *Czech and Slovak Folk Theatre* (1940) is full of stimulating remarks on the multiple functions played by these attributes of the actor. In his outline "Costume as Sign — a Functional and Structural Conception in Ethnography", published by the Prague Linguistic Circle in its Czech journal of 1936, and in his book *The Functions of Folk Costume in Moravian Slovakia*, Bogatyrëv distinguishes two functional varieties proper to the costume: the latter functions simultaneously as a thing and as a sign. These semiotic contributors to the sign values of the human being found in Bogatyrëv's research the first draft for their elucidation, as was immediately noted by such linguistic theoreticians as Trubetzkoy and Hjelmslev.

Bogatyrëv keenly sensed the fluctuating boundaries between the theatre and everyday life, and his amazing sense of humor enlivened the merging of the two. He was able to change spontaneously into an actor. According to Bogatyrëv's description of folk theatre the actors, when representing dignitaries, would speak with a solemn, ceremonial diction. When he was looking for a job in 1919 and was interrogated by the incredulous officials as to whether he was not of bourgeois origins, Bogatyrëv abruptly answered the question "Your father?" in the stentorian voice of the folkloric dignitary: "Craftsman!" As the questioning continued — "And your grandfather?" — he came out with the even more thunderous reply, "Serf!", which had a theatrically staggering effect on the pompous examiners. Soon after, he was mobilized in the Civil War and succeeded in obtaining the position of director in a Red Army Theatre Group. The detachment stopped in the village (*aul*) of a Caucasian mountain tribe and was refused a place for the night. During the Red officer's discussion on the right to a night's lodging, Bogatyrëv surreptitiously sat down by the family bonfire, knowing full well that once he had done so, the local etiquette imperatively dictated that he be taken for a ritual friend (*kunaq*) deserving full hospitality. Back in Moscow, he taught on the Workers' Faculty (*rabfak*) of the Technical School, where in a lecture to an audience of Komsomol youths on pagan survivals he touched upon the superstitious belief in water spirits (*vodjanye*). One of the auditors suddenly interrupted him: "I myself saw one!" Bogatyrëv began to answer, "It must have been your imagination ...," when the youth broke out, "Oh no, my mother was with me and also saw him clearly!" Such a typical topsy-turvy inversion of tutorship and pupilage did not disturb the young but experienced ethnographer.

From 1958 Bogatyrëv worked as a Senior Research Associate at the Moscow Institute of World Literature, but was constantly hounded by a quasi-academic administrator who in 1963 finally succeeded in having him dismissed. But the victim of this crying injustice had a true gift for stage impersonation and was too much aware of the double nature of any primitive spectacle — drama and buffoonery walking hand in hand — to be seriously upset about it. With a gentle raillery he viewed his oppressor as a rather obtuse farcical villain and awaited the intervention of a good spirit. Actually, the renowned literary historian N. K. Gudzij played such a role and in 1964 contrived to have Bogatyrëv restored as a teacher at Moscow University after some fifteen years of ostracism; Bogatyrëv's commemoration of Gudzij was simply but eloquently entitled "A Friend of Folklorists" (1968).

D. S. Lixačev, the distinguished reviewer of Bogatyrëv's selected writings, which were published in Moscow a few months before the author's death, states that the great scholar remained almost unknown to readers in his homeland before the appearance of the book reviewed. Even since its appearance, most of the articles published by Bogatyrëv in Czechoslovakia and other Western countries before the last war have not yet become known to Soviet readers. It was indeed in Czechoslovakia that he played the greatest role as author and teacher both through the language in which he wrote and through the regional examples he used. In the Western world, he is still practically unknown. Only a scant part of his work has yet become available in Western languages.

The enormous amount of Russian and Ukrainian folklore materials collected through the decades by the indefatigable field worker have never been published and mostly disappeared in the historical turmoil of our epoch. Despite his and his colleagues' repeated efforts, the unprecedented volume, his Moscow University thesis of 1918 containing an exhaustive survey of Russian facetiae of the seventeenth and eighteenth centuries, remains unpublished; and how many sketches of works were lost, uncompleted, as for instance his critical edition of our joint collection of plentiful folklore records from the Vereja district, in preparation for the Moscow Ethnographical Society. The same fate overtook the manual of Russian folk theatre on which we assiduously worked together during the winter months of 1919 at a temperature of 24°F in our room on Lubjanskij Thruway, with ice in our inkwell instead of ink, to the accompaniment of the sound of gun-fire from the neighboring street.

The historical turmoil of the times has been to a great degree responsible for the sad fact that all we possess of Bogatyrëv's writings is but a preliminary to his broad and wide outlook on the rural world of semiotic values and its central figure, the rustic "man-sign". Thus, for instance, in the special preface to the English edition of his monograph on the functions of the folk costume (1971), he cautions "those who want to develop the science of signs" that, properly speaking, his essay written years earlier (in 1937) only "borders upon the now rapidly expanding field of semiotics".

In August 1914 I met Bogatyrëv for the first time by chance as we stood in line waiting to register for classes, he in the third and I in the first year of our university studies. As strange as it may seem, the conversation immediately centered on our envisaged future research. He proposed a joint fieldwork project in folklore and dialectology (which we carried out a few months later in the Vereja district of the Moscow province). Our roles of ethnographer and linguist were already fixed, yet the critical feature was that the idea of a significant whole as the immediate aim of research stood before and at once united us. The complex and unitarian character of any integral structure was a permanent guiding concept in Bogatyrëv's scientific vistas, and it is indicative that in his doctoral orals of 1930 at Bratislava University, when confronted with the examiners' skepticism, he pointed to Ehrenfels' idea of *Gestaltqualität* as the chief attainment of modern psychology. In essence he remained the same, and the letters he wrote shortly before his death were reports on further work and plans for the urgent development of what had not yet been achieved.

The *Bulletin* of Moscow University states in an obituary that "Pëtr Grigor'evič lived through a great, complex, and beautiful life". It was beautiful indeed through his inflexible will power in achieving his magnificent purposes in spite of all the hideous menaces and obstacles which were constantly in wait for him, but the phrase "beautiful life" in regard to Bogatyrëv's curriculum vitae becomes a dramatic *oxymoron*, that ambiguous device on which he liked to base his study of folk plays and satires.

What would Bogatyrëv himself say to the epithet "beautiful"? Would he not recollect the apt reference in his Copenhagen Congress paper of 1939 to the "taboo of silence": the Carpathian plowman must remain speechless throughout the whole day of the first tillage.

Written in Peacham, Vermont, in the summer of 1975 and published in *Sound, Sign and Meaning: Quinquagenary of the Prague Linguistic Circle*, ed. L. Matejka (Ann Arbor: Michigan Slavic Publications, 1976).

SELECTED LIST OF P. G. BOGATYRËV'S WRITINGS

1. "Verovanija velikorussov Šenkurskogo uezda (Iz letnej èkskursii 1916 g.)", *Ètnografičeskoe obozrenie* 28 (Moscow, 1918), 42–80.
2. *Češskij kukol'nyj i russkij narodnyj teatr* (Berlin-Petersburg, 1923), 124 pp.
3. "Stixotvorenie Puškina 'Gusar', ego istočniki i ego vlijanie na narodnuju slovesnost'", *Očerki po poètike Puškina* (Berlin, 1923), 147–195.
4. "Les apparitions et les êtres surnaturels dans les croyances populaires de la Russie Subcarpathique", *Le Monde Slave* 3 (Paris, 1926), 34–55.
5. "Les jeux dans les rites funèbres en Russie Subcarpathique", *ibid.*, 196–224.
6. *Actes magiques, rites et croyances en Russie Subcarpathique* (Travaux publiés par l'Institut d'études slaves 9, Paris, 1929), 162 pp.
7. "Die Folklore als eine besondere Form des Schaffens" (with R. Jakobson), *Donum natalicium Schrijnen* (Nijmegen-Utrecht, 1929), 900–913.
8. "K probleme razmeževanija fol'kloristiki i literaturovedenija" (with R. Jakobson), *Lud Słowiański* 2 (Kraków, 1931), 229–233. — English translation: "Folklore and Literature", *Readings in Russian Poetics: Formalist and Structuralist Views*, ed. by L. Matejka and K. Pomorska (Cambridge, Mass., 1971), 91–93.
9. "Der Weihnachtsbaum in der Ostslowakei (Zur Frage der strukturellen Erforschung des Funktionswandels ethnographischer Fakten", *Germanoslavica* 2 (Prague, 1932–33), 254–258.
10. "Märchen und Buch", *Sbornik v čest' na prof. L. Miletič* (Sofia, 1933), 479–489.
11. "Was ist Folklore?", *Slavische Rundschau* 5 (Prague, 1933), 183–186.
12. "'Polaznik' u južnyx slavjan, mad'jar, slovakov, poljakov i ukraincev", *Lud Słowiański* 3 (Kraków, 1933–34), 107–114 and 212–273.
13. "La chanson populaire du point de vue fonctionnel", *Travaux du Cercle Linguistique de Prague* 6 (1936), 222–234.
14. *Funkcie kroja na Moravskom Slovensku* (Turč. sv. Martin, 1937), 76 pp. — English translation, with a preface by B. L. Ogibenin, *The Functions of Folk Costume in Moravian Slovakia* (Approaches to Semiotics 5, The Hague-Paris, 1971), 107 pp.
15. "Zur Frage der gemeinsamen Kunstgriffe im alttschechischen und im volkstümlichen Theater", *Slavische Rundschau* 10 (Prague, 1938), 154–161.
16. "Die aktiv-kollektiven, passiv-kollektiven, produktiven und unproduktiven ethnographischen Tatsachen", *II. Congrès international des sciences anthropologiques et ethnologiques* (Copenhagen, 1939), 343–345.
17. "Le folklore de la construction rurale en Slovaquie orientale et en Russie Subcarpathique", *Revue de Synthèse* XVII (Paris, 1939), 105–108.
18. *Lidové divadlo české a slovenské* (Prague, 1940), 314 pp.
19. "Der slowakische Volksheld Jánošík in Volksdichtung und bildender Volkskunst (Hinterglasmalerei), Zur Frage des vergleichenden Studiums von Volksdichtung und bildender Volkskunst", *Zwischen Kunstgeschichte und Volkskunde. Festschrift fur Wilhelm Fraenger* (Berlin, 1960), 105–126.
20. "Ausrufe von Austrägern und wandernden Handwerkern als Reklamzei-

chen", *Beiträge zur Sprachwissenschaft, Volkskunde und Literaturforschung Wolfgang Steinitz zum 60. Geburtstag* (Berlin, 1965), 61–73.
21. "Semantika i funkcija sel'skogo ètiketa", *Semeiotiké. Tezisy dokladov IV letnej školy po vtoričnym modelirujuščim sistemam 17-24 avg. 1970 g.* (Tartu, 1970), 67–71.
22. *Voprosy teorii narodnogo iskusstva* (Moscow, 1971), 543 pp., with an introduction by the author. Russian versions of 6, 7, 9, 14, 16, 18 and five later papers written in Moscow, with a Bibliography of Bogatyrëv's publications. — Rev. by D. S. Lixačev in *Izvestija AN SSSR, Serija literatury i jazyka* 31 (1972), 76–79.
23. *Souvislosti tvorby* (Prague, 1971), 210 pp., edited and commented by J. Kolár. Czech anthology of 26 papers written by Bogatyrëv through his "Czechoslovak years" from 1923 to 1939, reprinted in Czech (one in Slovak) or translated into Czech from other languages, and followed by B. Beneš's Bibliography of Bogatyrëv's publications.
24. "O vzaimosvjazi dvux blizkix semiotičeskix sistem", *Semeiotiké. Trudy po znakovym sistemam* 6 (Tartu State University, 1973), 306–329.
25. *Semiotics of Art* (Cambridge, Mass.: M.I.T., 1976), ed. by L. Matejka and I. R. Titunik, with an English translation of four of Bogatyrëv's papers published in Prague from 1936 to 1940.

ПО ПОВОДУ КНИГИ Н. С. ТРУБЕЦКОГО "ЕВРОПА И ЧЕЛОВЕЧЕСТВО"

Князь Сергей Трубецкой, выдающийся философ, общественный деятель и ректор Московского университета (1862–1905) счел для сына Николая (1890–1938) домашнее образование с ежегодной сдачей гимназических экзаменов более плодотворным путем по сравнению с школьной учебой, и в 1908 г. испытания на аттестат зрелости нашли его ученым широких познаний и глубоких интересов, успевшим с пятнадцатилетнего возраста, т.е. между 1905 и 1908 годом, опубликовать в *Этнографическом Обозрении* несколько ценных самостоятельных работ по финно-угорскому и кавказскому народоведению. Николай Сергеевич поступил на философско-психологический отдел историко-филологического факультета Московского университета, надеясь заняться там в первую очередь психологией народов, историей философии и методологическими проблемами. Однако в скором времени, — как отметил в своей автобиографической записке сам Трубецкой (*Grundzüge der Phonologie*, Göttingen, 1962 г., 274–5), — он убедился, что философско-психологический отдел отнюдь не связан с его кругом интересов и в третьем семестре он перешел в языковедческий отдел. Но хотя ни объем, ни направление в языковедческом отделе не удовлетворяли юного искателя, он предпочел работать на этом поприще, придя к убеждению, что "лингвистика — единственная ветвь гуманитарных дисциплин, располагающая научным методом, в то время как другие отрасли (народоведение, история религий, история культуры и др.), лишь последовав опыту языкознания, окажутся в состоянии перейти с алхимической ступени развития на более высокий уровень". Именно в то время, в 1909–10 г., студент Трубецкой задумал книгу, в последствии прозванную *Европа и человечество*, а первоначально носившую более отвлеченное заглавие *Об эгоцентризме*. Мысли об этом труде тесно связаны с той дискуссией, которой тщетно добивался Трубецкой у тогдашних философов и психологов Московского университета, а именно дискуссией по насущным вопросам психологии народов, историософии и методологии гуманитарных наук. Эта книга владела помыслами стремительно росшего языковеда в довоенные, согласно его отзыву, неслыханно напряженные годы, а затем в годы войны, и нам обоим явственно запомнилось, как мы поочередно провожали друг друга пешеходом домой после заседаний Комиссии по народной словесности или же Московской диалектологической комиссии, живо беседуя о теоретических основаниях национализма. И несмотря на то, что в 1921 году наши головы были полны лингвистических исканий, Трубецкой был прав, когда рисовал мне названную проблематику, как "то, что, повидимому Вас наиболее интересует и что для меня тоже всего важнее".

В ранних размышлениях Трубецкого его труд *Европа и человечество* выступал как первая часть трилогии *Оправдание национализма*. Эту первую часть он предполагал посвятить памяти Коперника. Вторая, как писал мне Трубецкой в марте 1921 года из Софии в Прагу, должна была называться *Об истинном и ложном национализме* с посвящением памяти Сократа; а третью, под заглавием *О русской стихии*, автор думал посвятить памяти Стеньки Разина или Емельки Пугачева. Посвящения решено было опустить во избежание упреков в претенциозности.

В самом начале книги *Европа и человечество*, выпущенной в свет в 1920 году Российско-Болгарским Издательством, Трубецкой, в то время доцент Софийского университета, поверенный курсом введения в сравнительное языковедение, стремился объяснить позднее появление издавна задуманного труда: в свое время он встречал исключительно непонимание своих мыслей и не считал своевременным их обнародование, выжидая более благоприятного момента. "Если же теперь я все-таки решился выступать печатно, то это потому что за последнее время я, среди своих собеседников, встречаю не только понимание, но и согласие с моими основными положениями." Те огромные мировые сдвиги, которыми ознаменовались заключительные годы войны и последующий ход событий, показали неумолимому критику эгоцентризма, что многие уже пришли к его же выводам "совершенно самостоятельно", хотя в суровых отзывах авторитетов о "вредном направлении" всё еще не было недостатка.

Непосредственно после выхода этой книги ее автор определял ее назначение как чисто отрицательное: "Никаких положительных, конкретных руководящих принципов она давать не собирается. Она должна только свергнуть известные идолы и, поставив читателя перед опустевшими пьедесталами этих идолов, заставить его самого пошевелить мозгами, ища выхода. Выход должен быть указан в последующих частях трилогии. В первой же части я предполагал только намекнуть на это направление, в котором следует искать выхода." (См. *N. S. Trubetzkoy's Letters and Notes*, prepared for publication by R. Jakobson, The Hague: Mouton, 1975, стр. 12.)

Отрицательной установке этой вступительной платформы к дальнейшей разработке авторской идеологии существенно соответствует пафос капитального пересмотра основ традиционной лингвистики, над которым с 1917 года вопреки всем внешним помехам лихорадочно трудился Трубецкой.

Поскольку наиболее содержательным источником, несомненно, являются суждения самого автора вслед за выходом *Европы и человечества*, привожу их в пространном извлечении.

"Существенное в книге — это отвержение эгоцентризма и 'эксцентризма' (полагания центра вне себя, в данном случае, — на западе). И главное требование, вытекающее из этого, единственный возможный выход (точнее: направление к выходу) мною указан: это — революция в сознании, в мировоззрении интеллигенции нероманогерманских народов. Без этой революции никакой выход невозможен, то, что происходит сейчас не есть выход, пока революции в сознании не произошло. Сущность революции в сознании состоит в полном преодолении эгоцентризма и эксцентризма, в переходе от абсолютизма к релятивизму. Это есть единственная надежная преграда на пути захватных стремлений романогерманской цивилизации. Понять, что ни 'я', ни кто другой не есть пуп земли, что все народы и культуры равноценны, что высших и низших нет, — вот всё, что требует моя книга от читателя. Но, как сказано, это мало понять, это надо прочувствовать, выстрадать, этим надо вполне проникнуться. 'Наказ ученику учиться у учителя, но критически к нему относиться', как выражаетесь Вы, — конечно, плод неудачной формулировки и того, что я вдался в ненужную деталь. Собственно, я только хотел указать на то, что никакая культура невозможна без заимствований извне, но что заимствование не предполагает непременно эксцентризма. Конечно этого можно было и не говорить, и жалко, что я это сказал, ибо это ослабило основную мысль, породив впечатление, будто кроме революции в сознании я указываю еще какие-то практические выводы. С этой стороны я сам неудовлетворен концом своей книги, написанным наскоро и при том значительно позднее всей книги. Я хотел, чтобы моя книга поставила читателя перед пустым местом и заставила его поразмыслить над тем, чем эту пустоту наполнить. А создалось впечатление, что я сам пытаюсь наполнить эту пустоту туманным суррогатом. Между тем, наполнение пустоты предполагалось в последующих частях трилогии, причем это наполнение возможно лишь при условии полного проникновения читателя в реальность пустоты, полной революции в сознании, о которой я говорю. — Чем же наполнить пустоту? Я говорю в своей книге, что всякая оценка основана на эгоцентризме, и что поэтому *из науки* всякая оценка должна быть изгнана. Но в культурном творчестве, в искусстве, в политике, вообще во всяком роде *деятельности* (а не *теории*, каковою является наука) без оценки обойтись невозможно. Следовательно, известный эгоцентризм всё таки необходим. Но это должен быть эгоцентризм облагороженный, не бессознательный, а сознательный, связанный с релятивизмом, а не с абсолютизмом. Я нахожу его в сократовском принципе 'познай самого себя' или — что то же — 'будь самим собой'. Всякое стремление быть не тем, чем я есмь на самом деле, всякое 'желание быть испанцем', как говорит Козьма Прутков [коллективный псевдоним в сатирической деятельности нескольких русских писателей прошлого века], ложно и пагубно. Познай самого себя есть принцип универсальный, абсолютный и вместе с тем относительный. Этим принципом и надо руководиться при оценке, безразлично — идет ли дело об отдельном человеке или о народе. Всё, что дает человеку или народу возможность быть самим собой, — хорошо, всё, что мешает этому, — дурно. Отсюда вытекает требование самобытной национальной культуры. Это в свою очередь обусловливает различие между истинным и ложным национализмом. Национализм хорош, когда он вытекает из самобытной культуры и направлен к этой культуре. Он ложен, когда он не вытекает из такой культуры и направлен к тому, чтобы маленький по существу неевропейский (нероманогерманский) народ разыгрывал из себя великую державу, в которой всё 'как у господ'. Он ложен и тогда, когда мешает другим народам быть самими собой и хочет принудить их принять чуждую для них культуру. 'Национальное самоопределение', как его понимают бывший президент Вильсон и разные самостийники вроде грузин, эстонцев, латышей и проч., есть типичный вид ложного национализма первого рода. Немецкий шовинизм или англоамериканское культуртрегерство — вид ложного национализма второго рода. Наш русский 'национализм' дореволюционного периода есть и то и другое. Истинный национализм предстоит создать. Это и есть выход. Направление к нему, — сначала упомянутая революция в сознании, затем творческая работа самопознания и самобытной культуры. Практически, разумеется, путь лежит через физическую борьбу, восстание 'стонущих племён' и т.под. Но без революции в сознании и без сознательного облагороженного эгоцентризма, словом, без истинного национализма — всё это ни к чему не приведет.

Вы спрашиваете: Разве то, что происходит сейчас, не есть огромное восстание России, влекущей за собою остальные 'племена, стонущие под игом без различия цвета кожи' против романогерманцев? — Инстинктивная, подсознательная сущность *народного* 'большевизма', разумеется, в этом и состоит. Как я выражаюсь в предисловии к русскому переводу Уэльсовой *Russia in the Shadows* у нас в России и в Азии *народный* большевизм есть восстание не бедных против богатых, а презираемых против презирающих [H. G. Wells, *Россия во мгле*, Российско-Болгарское издательство, София, 1920, p. III–XV]. Для русского 'народа' слово 'буржуй' обозначает не богача, а человека иной культуры, мнящего себя высшим в силу именно своей принадлежности к этой культуре. У азиатов это еще ярче. Всё это так. Но восставшим народом руководят вожди, интеллигенты. И вот, в сознании этих-то интеллигентов и не произошла та революция, которую я считаю необходимой. Они продолжают пребывать во власти европейских предрассудков, базироваться на эволюционной науке, на учении о прогрессе и на всем порождении романогерманского эгоцентризма. Они социалисты, а социализм и коммунизм — законные дети европейской цивилизации: тот факт, что Маркс по происхождению не романогерманец, конечно, этому ничуть не противоречит. Коммунистическое государство, как его понимают и хотят строить наши большевики, есть наиболее законченная 'обнаженная' форма романогерманской государственности. Эти вожди восстания 'стонущих племен' не только не дают отдельным людям или народам познать самих себя и стать самими собой, но даже наоборот, заставляют их быть не тем, что они есть, и затемняют их сознание. При таких условиях весь истинный смысл народного движения извращается. Никакого освобождения от морального гнета романогерманской цивилизации не получается. Освобождение от гнета физического — эфемерно и к тому же чисто временно. Представьте себе на минуту, что красной армии удастся прорваться в Германию, и что в этой последней произойдет коммунистический переворот. Какие практические последствия будет иметь этот факт? Ось мира немедленно переместится из Москвы в Берлин. Настоящее коммунистическое государство, как порождение романогерманской цивилизации, предполагает известные культурные, социальные, экономические, психологические и т.д. условия, существующие в Германии, но несуществующие в России. Пользуясь этими преимуществами и отрицательными уроками русского большевизма, немцы создадут образцовое социалистическое государство, и Берлин сделается столицей все-европейской или даже всемирной федеративной советской республики. Господа и рабы всегда были, есть и будут. Они существуют и при советском строе у нас в России. Во всемирной советской республике господами будут немцы, вообще романогерманцы, а рабами — мы, т.е. все остальные. И степень рабства будет прямо пропорциональна 'культурному уровню', т.е. отдалению от романогерманского образца. Это — в плоскости так сказать материальной. В области же духовной культуры зависимость от романогерманской цивилизации будет еще сильней, ибо социализм не может допустить других идеологий, кроме определенно канонизированных. Значит, ничто не изменится. Не надо забывать, что хищничество и поработительство не есть свойство каких либо классов европейского общества, а всей романогерманской цивилизации как таковой. Я постарался развить это в V-й главе своей книги. При таких условиях большевизм не только не есть восстание против романогерманцев, но наоборот, самое мощное средство европеизации даже таких народов, которые до сих пор от европеизации уклонялись. Вы говорите о романогерманских низах. Эти низы во первых так и останутся низами, точно также, как у нас в России, ведь не рабочие же и крестьяне в самом деле управляют. А те, кто из низов пролезет в верх, сами сделаются такими же, как те, кто сейчас на верху. Но и по существу Вы слишком преувеличиваете психологическое различие между низами и верхами в романогерманском обществе. Различие, конечно, есть, но оно совсем другого порядка, чем различие между 'Европой и Человечеством'. Нероманогерманским народам нужна новая, нероманогерманская культура. Романогерманским же низам никакой принципиально-новой культуры не нужно, а хочется лишь поменяться местами с правящими классами с тем, чтобы продолжать всё то, что делали до сих пор эти классы: заправлять фабриками и наемными 'цветными' войсками, угнетать 'черных' и 'желтых', заставляя их подражать европейцам, покупать европейские товары и поставлять в Европу сырье. Нам с ними не по пути. Если они, не дай Бог, захватят власть, то всеобщая европеизация неизбежна. Это — 'последняя ставка', только не для 'Человечества', а для 'Европы'. Это — грозная опасность, только не для 'Европы', а для 'Человечества'.

Вот почему я всё таки настаиваю на том, что переворот в сознании интеллигенции нероманогерманских народов есть единственный выход. Без этого всё сейчас происходящее приведет лишь к усилению зла. Способны ли правители Советской России к такому перевороту — сомневаюсь. А потому смотрю на дело пессимистически. Самое худшее, что может произойти, это — преждевременное восстание низов романогерманского мира, связанное с перемещением мировой оси в Берлин, вообще на запад: после этого переворот в сознании, скорее всего, совсем не произойдет, а если и произойдет, то будет уже поздно. Но возможно, конечно, что романогерманские низы ничего не предпримут, и тогда Россия, предоставленная на долгое время самой себе и азиатской ориентации, либо принудит своих вождей произвести переворот, либо стихийно заменит их другими, к этому перевороту более способными. Что будет, — сказать трудно: боюсь, что — самое худшее …

Если когда-нибудь мои заветные мечты осуществятся, то я представляю себе, что в мире будет несколько больших культур с 'диалектными', так сказать, вариантами. Но отличие от европейского идеала состоит в том, что во первых этих больших культур всё таки будет несколько, а не одна, а во вторых их диалектические варианты будут более яркими и свободными. Главное, при наличности истинного национализма, основанного на самопознании, и при отсутствии эксцентризма, каждый народ будет принадлежать к данной культуре не случайно, а потому, что она гармонирует с его внутренней сущностью, и что эта внутренняя сущность именно в данной культуре может находить себе наиболее полное и яркое выражение."

О том, "чем именно должна отличаться от европейской цивилизации та культура, к которой принадлежит Россия, и какие именно народы, кроме русских, могут принять участие в этой культуре", Трубецкой собирался говорить в третьей части своей трилогии (*О русской стихии*), однако сетовал сперва на библиотечные пробелы, а затем на издательские трудности, но вскоре в Софии вышел русский сборник *Исход к Востоку* (Российско-Болгарское издательство, 1921), в котором Трубецкой опубликовал краткое изложение обеих последних частей своей трилогии, II. *Об истинном и ложном национализме*, стр. 71–85, и III. *Верхи и низы русской культуры*, стр. 86–103, жалуясь однако, что "третью часть, по существу этнографическую, пришлось сильно скомкать и смазать" ввиду невозможности достать в Софии нужную литературу. Согласно тогдашнему объяснению Трубецкого, он и другие участники сборника (Г. В. Флоровский, П. Н. Савицкий и П. П. Сувчинский) "объединились на некотором настроении и мироощущении, несмотря на то, что у каждого свой подход и свои убеждения". Сущность сборника Трубецкой усматривал "в нащупывании и прокладывании путей для некоторого нового направления, которое носится в воздухе", и которое, отмечал он именем всей группы, "мы называем термином *евразийство*, может быть и не очень удачным, но бьющим в глаза, вызывающим, а потому — подходящим для агитационных целей" (*Letters and Notes* ..., стр. 21). Идея Евразии, географического целого, более или менее совпадающего по своим пределам с границами России и многочисленными внешними и культурными особенностями отличающегося от обеих смежных областей, Европы и Азии в собственном смысле последнего имени, легла в основу евразийского направления. Когда это движение, в основе своей выросшее на исходных взглядах автора *Европы и человечества*, вошло, на рубеже двадцатых и тридцатых годов, в полосу затяжного кризиса, Трубецкой, заживо задетый наступившими раздорами, охладел к участию в евразийской политике, хотя и вернулся в *Евразийскую Хронику* 1935 года (стр. 29–37) для опубликования краткой вводной заметки *Об идее-правительнице идеократического государства*. Поднятая Трубецким тема грядущей идеократии, пришлась ему глубоко по сердцу, и последние годы жизни он, несмотря на физические нелады, одновременно без устали работал над книгой об идеократии и над томом *Grundzüge der Phonologie*, подводившим итоги всем его исследованиям звуков речи. Последний труд смерть оборвала на одной из последних страниц и он был издан по рукописи Пражским Лингвистическим Кружком в 1939 году, тогда как объемистая рукопись *Истинной идеократии как единственно желанной и жизнеспособной формы правления*, законченная в рукописи автором незадолго до кончины, оказалась, как ни горестно об этом рассказывать, непоправимо уничтожена.

Уже в последние годы своей жизни Трубецкой знал, что многие диагнозы и прогнозы как отечественных, так и мировых дел, напечатанные им в 1920 году, оказались опровергнуты историей, но в то же время и критический автор, и непредубежденный читатель не могли не сознать полноценного ядра книги, и читателю с каждым годом и десятилетием становилось всё яснее, сколько пылкой юношеской мудрости лежит в неумолимом и при этом на редкость человечном разоблачении того, как писал Трубецкой в своей книге (стр. 13), "гипноза слов", который всё беспощаднее держит в тисках наше и мировое бытие. Искусное сочетание убедительных антропологических экскурсов с гениальным языковым чутьем сказалось в авторе *Европы и человечества* еще до появления его первых лингвистических разысканий и даже на расстоянии шестидесяти с лишним лет, отделяющих нас от скромной софийской публикации, не может оставить безразличным мыслящего читателя.

Written in Cambridge, Mass., February-March 1982, as an introduction to the Italian edition of Trubetzkoy's book, *L'Europa e l'umanità* (Turin: Einaudi, 1982). The title has been supplied by the editor.

THE IMMEDIATE QUESTS AND ACCOMPLISHMENTS OF COMPARATIVE LINGUISTICS

Among the favorite themes and main tasks of linguistics from the last century to the early years of the present century were the questions of the reconstruction of Proto-Indo-European. In international university practice the basic and often the sole linguistic faculty went under the name of the faculty of comparative Indo-European linguistics. The epoch in question summed up in the classic manuals the results of its constant efforts to discover the heterogeneous particularities of the common proto-language from which the genetically related members of the Indo-European language family derive.

At the height of the twentieth century the change in the tasks confronting linguistics was expressed in two ways. On the one hand, experiments in applying the technical devices and practices elaborated by Indo-European studies to other language families of both the Old and New Worlds became ever more frequent; on the other hand, linguists became fascinated with the methods of the strictly descriptive approach to individual languages at a given stage of their development, irrespective of questions of historical comparison with other stages and with related languages. Both circles of pressing quests inescapably led to the verification and critical re-examination of the inherited methodology.

On the one hand, the application of the comparative-historical method to the question of the ancestors and kinship ties of diverse and heterogeneous families deepened and enriched the problematics of language reconstruction; on the other hand, it was precisely descriptive linguistics that advanced the fundamental questions of the linguistic system and its law-governed structure and in particular laid the foundations for a systematic inquiry into the interrelation of sound form and meaning.

Between the above-noted widening of the comparative-historical problematic and the clear orientation of descriptive linguistics toward the discovery of systemic structure a process of integration naturally occurs: the compulsion to limit the tasks of comparative linguistics to merely *genetic* comparison vanishes, and at the same time questions of systemic structure finally go beyond the borders of *descriptive* linguistics and find fruitful application to the historical past of the language being studied and reconstructed.

For the first time the indissolubility of the notions of a law-governed system and its changes, in turn of a regular nature, is realized. The boundaries of linguistic comparison widen in an essential way; new tasks are added to the study of the common legacy of language families. First, the common features acquired by the phonological and grammatical structure of languages contiguous in space are subjected to clarification, and thus enter, as it were, into relations of alliance. Second, the possibility and even necessity of juxtaposing diverse language (above all, phonological) systems, irrespective of the question of the presence or absence of genetic relationship or geographical propinquity, becomes an established fact.

As a result of the comparative analysis of such systems there arises in turn the possibility of their consistent typological classification and its theoretical grounding. With such prerequisites the data of living languages, supported by the documentation of historical languages, make it possible to verify the probability of the proto-language systems reconstructed by the comparative method and convincingly prompt the most plausible solution of difficult problems in reconstruction. In a word, typological comparison proves to be a beneficial tool in comparative-historical procedures.

All these principles of general linguistics, newly discovered or at least conceived anew, now present every concrete investigative work with inescapable and pressing demands. The collective work of Tomaz Valer'janovič Gamkrelidze and Vjačeslav Vsevolodovič Ivanov, *Indoevropejskij jazyk i indoevropejcy* ("Indo-European and the Indo-Europeans"), completely fulfills the mission formulated by the authors in the subtitle: "A Reconstruction and Historical-Typological Analysis of the Proto-Language and Proto-Culture". Those deep shifts and transformations which characterize the stage now attained in the development of linguistic science, and in which a considerable creative role fell to the lot of both mentioned investigators, lay at the methodological base of their searches. Here the early approaches of international seekers to all the particular questions of Proto-Indo-European linguistic antiquity are taken into account, and a fascinating reply is given to the theses which gained scientific currency on the border of the two centuries. This stage in the scientific work of Ivanov and Gamkrelidze is marked not only by the unusual answers they offer to the given questions, but also by their very formulation of such questions and by their unprecedentedly wide thematic horizon.

In correspondence with the dialectical reduction of the dichotomy of the temporal progression and the cross-section (diachrony and synchrony) and with the parallel inclusion of temporal diffusion into the number of internal linguistic factors, the book naturally transforms the scheme of Common Indo-European, viewed by the scholarly tradition as static and uniform in time and space, and creates a model of dynamic synchrony with an integral grasp of the foundations of the proto-language, its evolutionary shifts, its internal, regional differentiation, and its sequential crossing with neighboring language areas. Precisely in light of questions about the mutual relations of dialects of the Indo-European proto-language and about its interrelations with adjacent proto-languages arises the promising work of the two linguists on the geographical determination of the primordial Indo-European homeland (evidently Asia Minor) and on the proposed paths of the initial migrations undergone by the different branches of the common Indo-European territory.

The broad interpretation of two concepts — *comparison* and *system* — in contemporary linguistics is attended by the steadfastly progressing relativization of the entire linguistic structure and an ever more consistent transformation of linguistics into a science of intralinguistic relations. Moreover, the attention of linguists, especially Ivanov and Gamkrelidze, is held in the first place by the indissoluble interconnection between the parts and the whole. The main key point of this complex problematics is the interrelation of the *invariant* and *variation*, that vital theme of all contemporary scientific thought. The dependence of variation on the diversity of contexts becomes ever more clear in harmony with the development of the thesis of linguistics of our day which opposes natural language, adjusting itself to the context (context-sensitive), to languages irrespective of the changing context (context-free), i.e., artificial, formalized systems. Here, of course, variations of form and meaning play an essential role: both on the level of sound, as well as the various levels of grammatical meanings, the systematic extraction of invariants becomes the central linguistic task.

This entire methodological program is widely developed on the example of the reconstruction of Proto-Indo-European. With the decomposition of the phoneme into minimal sense-discriminative components, the concept of *context*, which earlier had been limited to the temporal sequence of combinations of phonemes, has been expanded to include combinations of simultaneous components, and the twofold dimension of phonological combinations reveals step by step new, uninvestigated typological regularities in the interrelation between both classes of combinations and within each class. See, for example, the remarkable typological works of Ivanov and Gamkrelidze on preferred or, on the contrary, avoided combinations of differential components "on the axis of simultaneity" (cf. T. V. Gamkrelidze's theses in the collection *Problemy lingvističeskoj tipologii i struktury jazyka*, Institut jazykoznanija AN SSSR, 1977) and on the principal varieties of symmetrical relations, which, as V. V. Ivanov has shown, form the basis of linguistic structure.

With the development of the problematics of context, the simplistic interpretation of stylistic variants as "free" variations gives way to an understanding of style as a distinctive context, and the conditions offered to language by the different speech functions enter clearly into the circle of the general conceptions of contextuality. We are indebted to the correct initiative of Ivanov and Gamkrelidze in including Indo-European poetics, in particular metrics and the question of the anagrammatic tradition, first raised by Saussure, within the number of pressing tasks of linguistic reconstruction.

The questions of restoring the proto-language and the proto-culture are not without reason raised in conjunction with one another as connected parts of a single whole; a consistently integral approach requires that one have at one's disposal a lexicon of the reconstructed proto-language arranged according to semantic families and that one discover the corresponding prehistoric realia through the prism of the Common Indo-European lexicon. The notion of the lexicon as a structural system, usually left unelaborated in comparison to the phonological and grammatical levels, acquires a reliable foundation, and in such areas as, for example, mythology and ritual, it opens the way for a systematic application of the comparative method.

Written in February 1979 as a preface to *Indroevropejskij jazyk i indoevropejcy* by V. V. Ivanov and T. V. Gamkrelidze. Translated into English for the present volume by Stephen Rudy.

D

PHILOLOGICAL GLEANINGS

WHEN A FALCON HAS MOLTED

The first fruit of the three-year international seminar in New York (1943–1945) dedicated to a systematic and comprehensive analysis of the *Igor' Tale* was a thorough critical edition of the text. According to the division of the text proposed in that edition,[1] it contains 218 versets distributed among thirty chapters. The speech of Grand Prince Svjatoslav, the "golden oration mingled with tears" (*zlato slovo slьzami sъměšeno*) which extends from the 111th through the 119th verset, constitutes the sixteenth of thirty chapters and thus begins the second half of the entire composition. Of a total of 218 versets, the second half comprises 109 versets, from the 110th to the 218th. With its second verse the "golden oration", the central and pivotal moment in the dramatic development of the entire narration, begins.

Svjatoslav, grand prince of Kiev, son of the elder of Oleg's sons, Vsevolod, and in the year of Igor's campaign the eldest of the Russian princes, turns to Igor' and Vsevolod, the sons of his uncle and namesake Svjatoslav, the younger of Oleg's sons (i.e. to his younger and lower-ranking cousins), and addresses them as nephews (112 *synovьcja*). The author of the *Igor' Tale* himself extols the international "glory of Svjatoslav" (90 *slavu Svjatoslavlju*), and in praising the Grand Prince calls him "the father" of Igor' and Vsevolod (88) as vassals of the Kievan

---

[1] *La Geste du Prince Igor — épopée russe du douzième siècle*. Texte établi, traduit et commenté sous la direction d'H. Grégoire, R. Jakobson et M. Szeftel = *Annuaire de l'Institut de Philologie et d'Histoire Orientales et Slaves* 8 (École Libre des Hautes Études à New York, L'Université Libre de Bruxelles, 1948; photo-reproduction: Kraus Reprint, Nendeln, Liechtenstein, 1971). The "Essai de reconstruction du *Slovo* dans sa langue originale" (150–178) included there is the basis for the citations in the present article. Cf. R. Jakobson, *Selected Writings*, IV: Slavic Epic Studies (The Hague-Paris, 1966), which includes a critical text of the *Tale* (133–160) with a reconstruction of the original and a translation into modern Russian (164–191). This translation, with the same division into versets, is reprinted in *Trudy Otdela drevnerusskoj literatury AN SSSR* 14 (1958), 116–121.

suzerain.² Accordingly, in interpreting Svjatoslav's "troubled dream", the Kievan boyars speak of two falcons who have flown off "the golden paternal throne" (102 *dъva sokola sъletěsta sъ otьnja stola zlata*), and with similar terms the author later begins his concluding story of Igor's return from captivity "to the paternal golden throne" (184 *kъ otьnju zlatu stolu*).

The "golden oration" of the suzerain condemns the younger princes' self-serving and reckless pursuit of glory (112) and recalls as an example for them their "ancestral glory" (115 *vъ pradědьnjuju slavu*), i.e. the glory of the ancestors of the "powerful, wealthy, most militant" Jaroslav Vsevolodovič, to which his Černigov dignitaries and steppe allies were faithful, especially the victorious Olbers, identified by O. O. Pritsak as the Mongolian suzerains of the entire Qipčak domain.³ Of Oleg's four grandsons the two sons of his elder son, the older Svjatoslav Vsevolodovič, prince of Kiev, and the younger Jaroslav Vsevolodovič, prince of Černigov, are compared and contrasted to the two sons of Oleg's younger son, Igor' Svjatoslavič, prince of Novgorod-Seversk, and his younger brother Vsevolod Svjatoslavič, prince of Trubačevsk.

The Kievan prince, the head of the family, accuses both younger princes of attempting unauthorized military activities (116) and, as D. S. Lixačev correctly noted, of desiring to acquire the glory for the successful battle that the older princes conducted against the Polovcians the preceding year, as well as to keep for themselves alone the glory of the subsequent campaign (116 "*Nъ rekosta: mužjaimъ sja sami, prědьnjuju slavu sami poxytimъ, a zadьnjuju si sami podělimъ*" "But you [both] said: let us ourselves be heroes, let us gain the past glory ourselves, and divide the future [glory] between ourselves").⁴ In these words, ascribed by Svjatoslav to Igor' and his brother, according to Ju. M. Lotman's apt interpretation, "the aspiration to glory is combined with an unauthorized deviation from the system of hierarchic feudal subordination, i.e., with independence of activity", whereas "Igor', who has arrogated to himself the behavioral norms of the suzerain ('glory'), is, in fact, a vassal of the Kievan prince".⁵

---

² B. A. Rybakov, "*Slovo o polku Igoreve*" *i ego sovremenniki* (Moscow, 1971), 87ff.; Rybakov, "Knjaz' Svjatoslav Vsevolodovič (opyt istoričeskoj xarakteristiki)", *Materialy i issledovanija po arxeologii SSSR* 11 (1949), 93–99.
³ R. Jakobson, *Selected Writings* IV, 698.
⁴ D. S. Lixačev, "Iz nabljudenij nad leksikoj *Slova o polku Igoreve*", *Izvestija Otd. Lit. i Jaz. AN SSSR* 8,6 (1949), 552ff.
⁵ Ju. M. Lotman, "Ob oppozicii čest'–slava v svetskix tekstax kievskogo perioda", *Trudy po znakovym sistemam* 3 = *Učenye zapiski Tartuskogo gos. universiteta* 198 (Tartu, 1967), 109. Cf. Lotman, "Ešče raz o ponjatijax slava i čest' v tekstax kievskogo perioda", *Trudy po znakovym sistemam* 5 = *Učenye zapiski Tartuskogo gos. universiteta* 284 (Tartu, 1971).

To the self-assurance of the young princes and their deliberate separation from those who are their elders in rank and age, the "golden oration" responds with the persistent question — 117 "*A či divo sja, bratie, staru pomoloditi?*" "And is it really a marvel, brethren, for an old man to grow young?" — and in response falls back on a metaphoric allusion to the valor of old, experienced warriors, including the "awesome, great" Svjatoslav of Kiev himself, who had earlier been glorified (versets 88–90) precisely for his mighty destruction of the enemy's power. Thus after the elder prince's question "And is it really a marvel, brethren, for an old man to grow young?", there follows an oratorical, figurative image of this same Svjatoslav: 118 "*Koli sokolъ vъ mytъxъ byvaetь, vysoko pъtičь vъzbivaetь: ne dastь gnězda svoego vъ obidu*" "When a falcon has molted [a number of times] it drives birds upwards: it will not permit its nest to be offended."

The meaning of the phrase *sokolъ vъ mytъxъ* is unambiguous and clear. V. L. Vinogradova, in her rich lexicological guide to the *Tale*,[6] recalled the old evidence of the lexicographer Burnašev: "*Mytь*. The molting of hunting birds. A molted gerfalcon or hawk, i.e., one which has molted, and the age of which is designated by the number of molts, e.g., a falcon of two molts, three molts, etc."[7] Dal's dictionary, I (1880²), 365, notes that in relation to falcons "molt" serves as a synonym for "year". A. A. Potebnja's commentary to the above-mentioned verset showed the indisputably obvious: "'a falcon of two or three molts', which has molted two or three times, is two or three years old, and consequently a 'falcon that has molted [a number of times]' (*sokol v mytex*) is of advanced age (*v letax*), is old. This is a proverb of the same type as Polish 'old but hale' (*stary ale jary*), Ukrainian 'an old ox doesn't spoil the furrows' (*staryj vil borozny nepsue*)".[8] The phrase *sokolъ vъ mytъxъ* "a falcon that has molted [a number of times]" clearly corresponds in form and meaning to such popular expressions as Russian "a man of years" (*čelovek v letax*), "aged, not young".[9] Cf. the synonymous forms: Russian *v godax*, Ukrainian *v litax*, Polish *w leciech*, Czech *v letech*, Slovak *v rokach*, Serbian *u godinama*. According to V. N.

---

[6] V. L. Vinogradova, *Slovar'-spravočnik "Slova o polku Igoreve"* 3 (Leningrad, 1969), 127ff.
[7] V. P. Burnašev, *Opyt terminologičeskogo slovarja sel'skogo xozjastva, fabričnosti, promyslov i byta narodnogo* 1 (SPb., 1843), 410ff.
[8] A. A. Potebnja, *Slovo o polku Igoreve* (Voronež, 1878), 104.
[9] See *Slovar' sovremennogo russkogo literaturnogo jazyka*, AN SSSR 6 (1957), 191, with the following examples: *Nu, už čelovek v letax: emu ved' pod sorok budet* (Suxovo-Kobylin); *Ušakov byl uže v letax, — nedavno pered tem emu ispolnilos' pjat'desjat četyre goda* (Sergeev-Censkij).

Peretc, summing up the interpretations of his predecessors, "obviously a word for a falcon that has molted many times and is most terrible to enemies of its nest, which emphasizes the success of Svjatoslav's campaign".[10]

Thus verset 118 in a modern English translation would be: "When a falcon has molted a number of times [i.e., if a falcon is old] it drives birds [cf. the opposition of a falcon and a hostile flock of birds: 79 *daleče zaide sokolъ, pъtičъ bija* 'The falcon has gone far, slaying birds'] upward [chases further upward]; it will not permit its nest to be offended." The 118th verset is translated similarly in *La Geste du Prince Igor*: "Lors qu'un faucon a déjà mué plusieurs fois, il chasse les oiseaux très haut dans la nue et ne laisse pas sa couvée exposée à l'outrage" (H. Grégoire); "If a falcon has had his molts, high does he smite the birds" (S. H. Cross).

N. F. Grammatin had already realized that a connection between the two contiguous images "for an old man to grow young" and "a falcon that has molted [a number of times]" is most convincing since "a falcon, having molted, clothes itself in young feathers",[11] in other words, grows young.

The terms *trex mytej* "of three molts" and *v mytex* "having molted [a number of times]" are related to each other exactly as the terms *stol'kix-to let* "of so many years" and *v letax* "having [a number of] years". V. P. Petrus' reasonably objects to the possibility of ascribing an image of power and strength to a period of temporary weakness for a fighting bird, the time when it "'molts', i.e., is ailing".[12] But his attempt to avoid this apparent difficulty by reconstructing a reading *mytъ* "duty, assessment, tax" in the given context instead of the term *mytъ* is inappropriate, devoid of the slightest probability, and, most importantly, completely superfluous, since his article did not allow for the chronological calendrical meaning inherent in the plural forms *myti, mytej, mytex* "molts".

It is obvious that V. P. Petrus's ornithological observations are the source of the following allegation by A. A. Zimin: "According to the *Tale* a falcon 'having molted', i.e., in a period of molting, displays particularly militant tendencies. This, of course, is an error."[13] The

---

[10] V. N. Peretc, *Slovo o polku Igorevim* (Kiev, 1926), 270.
[11] N. F. Grammatin, *Slovo o polku Igorevom*, istoričeskaja poèma, pisannaja v načale XIII v. (Moscow, 1823).
[12] V. P. Petrus', "Sokol v mytex", *Učenye zapiski Kirovskogo pedagogičeskogo instituta* 11 (1957), 103ff.
[13] A. A. Zimin, "Kogda bylo napisano *Slovo?*", *Voprosy literatury* 11,3 (1967), 145.

error, however, turns out to be not in the text of the 118th verset of the *Tale* but in the critic's confidence that *v mytex* here means "in a period of molting", one of the numerous examples of A. A. Zimin's lack of understanding of Old Russian texts and his notorious inattention to the results of half a century of investigative work on the *Tale*.

To the 118th verset of the *Tale* is juxtaposed, as Peretc has already indicated, a phrase that is included in a late redaction of the *Povest' ob Akire* ("Tale of Akir"). According to O. V. Tvorogov's interesting study,[14] the mention of a falcon of three molts "occurs only in the third redaction of the story": the older copies of this redaction date to the middle of the seventeenth century, and "it is obvious that the archetype of the third redaction already included the phrase, the distorted variants of which are preserved in twenty of the thirty-six copies we examined". The reading of the archetype as reconstructed by the investigator is totally convincing: *koli, sokol trex mytej, togda ne dast v obidu gnezda svoego* "When a falcon has reached its third molt, it does not permit its nest to be offended", or more accurately *gnezda svoego* ız *obidu*, according to the GBL copy, coll. Muz, F. 29, 1567, which in all likelihood "goes back directly to the archetype". Copies that preserve the verb in the subordinate clause are instructive: *koli byl sokol trex mytej* "when the falcon was of three molts" and especially *egda bo sokol trex mytej byvaet* "but when the falcon is of three molts".[15] The epithet "golden", which is added to the substantive "nest" in one group of copies, elicits a conjecture about the borrowing of the adjective from the phrases *sedъla zlata* "golden saddle", *stola zlata* "golden throne" (abandoned by the young falcons!), and *zlato slovo* "golden oration" in earlier lines of the *Tale* (91, 102, 111). As Tvorogov noted, in the archetype of another group of copies the phrase "to be offended" (*vъ obidu*) is distorted: in these manuscripts we read *vabiši, vabiššsja, vybitsja, vospiti* (!). Here one should not exclude contamination of similar sounding words at the ends of two contiguous sentences of the 118th verset: *vъzbivaetь* "drive up" and *vъ obidu* "to offense".

The sentence about the adult, full-grown falcon clearly passed into the *Povest' ob Akire* from the *Tale*. In the latter it is inseparably connected

---

[14] O. B. Tvorogov, "'Sokol trex mytej' v povesti ob Akire premudrom", *Voprosy teorii i istorii jazyka — Sbornik statej, posvjaščennyj pamjati B. A. Larina* (Leningrad, 1969), 111–114.

[15] *Pamjatniki starinnoj russkoj literatury*, izd. gr. G. Kuševelymy-Bezborodko, 2 (SPb., 1860), 368. Cf. V. P. Adrianova-Peretc, "Frazeologija i leksika Slova o polku Igoreve", *Slovo o polku Igoreve i pamjatniki Kulikovskogo cikla*, ed. D. S. Lixačev and L. A. Dmitriev (Moscow-Leningrad, 1966), 90.

to the preceding sentence (117), which the subsequent one (118) complements and explains: it is not a marvel for an old man to grow young, and when a falcon's nest comes under threat an old falcon, having grown young, chases away the raiders. On the other hand, in the response of Akir the Most Wise to Emperor Sinograf, who has been frightened by the Egyptian pharaoh's threats, the introductory sentence — "*vъverzi na gospoda pečalъ svoju, i toi tja prepitaet, ne dast v věku molitvy pravedniku*" "throw your sorrow onto the Lord and he will strengthen you; he will not give prayer to a righteous man forever" — provides no clue to understanding the following aphorism about a falcon of three molts.

In the copies of the *Povest' ob Akire* one is struck by the distortions in the sentence about the defender-falcon, partially or even entirely depriving it of meaning and attesting a failure to understand the image. "A falcon of three molts" deteriorates into an empty, petrified formula, inserted by individual scribes into various passages of the text they were copying; thus, in the collection of examples assembled by Tvorogov, we encounter Akir *na carevu službu, aki sokol trex mytej* "at the emperor's service, like a falcon of three molts".

Compared to the sentence about a falcon "that has molted [a number of times]" ("is old", *v mytex* = *v letax*), firmly fused with the theme of the "golden oration" and the entire composition of the "grave stories about Igor's campaign", the "gloss about the falcon 'of three molts' (three years)", included in a late version of *Akir* without any thematic or compositional justification, gives, in A. A. Zimin's opinion, "the best reading of this fragment", another claim that is without any justification whatsoever.

The first part of the question-answer construction, the 117th verset of the *Tale of Igor''s Campaign,* finds a close correspondent in the first parts of two versets of the *Pisanija Sofonii Rjazancja,* the so-called *Zadonščina.* By comparing their variants these two versets, 86 and 123, can be easily reconstructed.[16] Monk Peresvet 84 *poskakivaet na svoem borzě koni, zlačenym dospěxom posvěčivajuči, a inii ležatъ posěčeni u Donu na brezě* "gallops about on his fleet-footed steed, shining in his gilded armor, while the others lie dead on the bank of the Don". Either Peresvet, doomed to imminent death (cf. verset 81), or the author after him exclaims: 86 "*Či ne lěpo bylo by tu, brat'e, staru pomoloditisja a molodomu pleč' svoix popytati*" "Would it not now be fitting, brethren,

---

[16] See R. Jakobson and D. S. Worth, *Sofonija's Tale of the Russian-Tatar Battle on the Kulikovo Field* (The Hague, 1963), 28–39, or *Selected Writings,* IV, 560–571.

for the old man to grow young [i.e., Peresvet himself and his brother Osljabja or Oslebja] and for the young man to put his shoulders to the test [i.e., Jakov, Oslebja's child]?". Oslebja announces the death of Peresvet and Jakov (87-89). A similar military slogan concludes the final appeal of Prince Dmitrij 119 *svoimъ bojaromъ* "to his boyars": 122 *"To ti, brat'e, ne naši medi sladcii Moskovьstii"* "These are not, brethren, our sweet meads of Moscow." 123 *"Tuto, bratьe, staru pomoloditisja, a molodu čьsti dobyti"* "Here, brethren, the old man will grow young and the young must obtain honor."

The internal antithetic parallelism of the adjectives *staru* "old" — *molodu* "young" in combination with infinitives and paregmenon at the junction of the parallel constructions *pomoloditisja* "to grow younger" — *molodu* "young" give, without doubt, a new semantic coloration to the question that introduces the *Tale's* edifying parable of the falcon that has molted. However, a genetic relation between the 117th verset of the *Tale* and a similar formula that appears twice in the *Zadonščina* is unquestionable, and it remains for us merely to repeat[17] that the *Igor' Tale*, although it survived to modern times only in a single copy of the sixteenth century, nonetheless contains numerous examples that preserve in combinations of verbs with the reflexive particle *sja* the original grammatical order, characteristic of Russian writings of the pre-Mongol era; specifically, in eight instances the enclitic *sja* is separated from the verb and follows the first stressed word of the syntactic unit, e.g. 117 *"A či divo sja, bratie, staru pomoloditi"* "And is it really a marvel, brethren, for an old man to grow young", or 71 *Tu sja brata razlučista* "There the [two] brothers separated." On the other hand there is no copy of the *Zadonščina* where the early word order is preserved; the form *sja* always follows the verb by itself or as the second of two postpositive particles. In versets 86 and 123, there is *pomoloditisja* "to grow younger" or *pomoloditsja* "he will grow younger" (e.g., in the fifteenth century Kirillo-Belozerskij copy *Togo daže bylo nelěpo staru pomoloditisja*[18] "Would it not even be fitting, brethren, for the old man to grow young"), and in 140 *Tuto poganii razlučišasja* "There the pagans scattered", or,

---

[17] *Selected Writings*, IV, 152, 159, and 690ff.; A. N. Kotljarenko, "Sravnitel'nyj analiz nekotoryx osobennostej grammatičeskogo stroja Zadonščiny i *Slova o polku Igoreve*", *Slovo o polku Igoreve i pamjatniki Kulikovskogo cikla*, 143ff.; F. P. Filin, "Starye mysli, ustarelye metody (otvet A. Ziminu)", *Voprosy literatury* 11,3 (1967), 170.

[18] And similarly in the printed variant of the *Narration of Mamai's Defeat*, which copied this formula: "*Lepo bo est' v to vremja staru pomoloditisja*" "For it is befitting at this time for an old man to grow young": see L. A. Dmitriev, "Vstavki iz *Zadonščiny* v *Skazanii o Mamaevom poboišče* kak pokazateli po istorii teksta ètix proizvedenij", *Slovo o polku Igoreve i pamjatniki Kulikovskogo cikla*, 417.

with the characteristic contamination of the old order, which goes back to the *Tale*, and a new order, in the Museum copy No. 2060 *Tuto sja poganii razlučišasja* "There the pagans scattered."

Let us recall that the placement of enclitics after the first word of the syntactic unit in the archaic type of Indo-European languages was first considered by Jacob Wackernagel, who published this discovery in 1891, and E. Berneker's attempt to apply this law of Wackernagel's to the earliest stage of the Russian language dates only to 1900.[19] If, in the case of textual coincidences between the *Tale* and the *Zadonščina*, a significant difference is found in the treatment of the pronominal form *sja*, this once again indisputably proves that in a general literary inventory of the two texts it is to the *Tale* that historical primacy belongs and that this military story of appanage Rus' must have served as a model for Sofonija of Rjazan'. The historical-grammatical argument presented here would be adequate to refute the arbitrary thesis insistently reiterated by A. A. Zimin that "the author of the *Tale of Igor's Campaign* had available the *Zadonščina* in its expanded redaction".[20] If one is to believe this thesis, it would then have to be proposed that the author of the *Tale* skilfully translated the *Zadonščina* into the language of pre-Mongol Rus', that before the beginning of historical linguistics he divined Wackernagel's Law, having outstripped by at least a century the noteworthy discoveries facilitated by the development in the nineteenth century of the comparative-historical method in linguistics.

If one is to believe the aforementioned article, then it would further have to be proposed that the author of the *Tale* happened upon the migratory aphorism of the old falcon in a late version of the *Povest' ob Akire*, selected the inflammatory words about the second youth of an old warrior from the *Zadonščina*, and then melded both fragments into an integral thought about the salutary protection of the younger knights of a family by their elders. And finally it would have to be proposed that this entire thought in turn organically penetrated the "golden oration", an inspired appeal to conquer the fateful sickness of appanage Rus' — "the princes do not help" — an appeal ideologically similar to another brilliant monument of the same epoch, the *Slovo o Knjazex* ("Tale of the Princes").

The deep artistic and logical interrelation of both versets 117 and 118,

---

[19] Cf. B. Havránek, *Genera verbi v slovanských jazycích* 1 (Prague, 1928); R. Jakobson, "Les enclitiques slaves", *Atti del Congresso di Linguistica tenuto in Roma il 19–26 Settembre 1933* (Florence, 1935) — cf. *Selected Writings* II, 16–22.
[20] A. A. Zimin, *op. cit.*, 141. We have given a detailed response to his other arguments in *Selected Writings* IV, 656–704.

striving to smooth out the dissension between the "silver gray hair" of the old princes and the "foolish daring" (*buestьju*) of the young, compels one finally to doubt the miraculous combination of two citations from different sources. This doubt becomes a conclusive impossibility if one considers that the 118th verset of the *Tale*, the promise of Svjatoslav, the old falcon, not to allow "his nest to be offended" is obviously related to references in the 40th and 41st versets of the same text to the danger threatening the far-flown "brave nest of Oleg" (*Olьgovo xorobroe gnězdo*), which was not "born to be offended". In the *Tale*, yet another image connects the two narrations about the nest and offense — the head of the family and the protector of the nest (cf. the possessive forms 40 *Olьgovo*, 118 *svoego* and the final reference to the family's protection from offense: 41 *ne bylo ono obidě poroženo* "it was not born to be offended", 118 *ne dastь gnězda svoego vъ obidu* "it will not permit its nest to be offended"). The motif of determined flight away or upward that occurs throughout the *Tale* occupies a central place in both frames (40 *zaletělo* "it flew away", 118 *vysoko pъtičь vъzbivaetь* "drives birds upward"), and in both instances similar constructions follow: the negation *ne*, a verb in the third person (*bylo ono poroženo, dastь*) and a modifier indicating the goal (*obidě, vъ obidu*).

A conjecture that the images under consideration — nest, offense, head of the family — traveled from the *Povest' ob Akire* to the 118th verset of the *Tale*, and from there to the 40th and 41st versets, is implausible, since the motif of offense (*obida*) runs throughout the text of the *Tale*: 62 *za obidu Olьgovu* "for the offense against Oleg", 76 *vъstala obida* "There arose offense", 129 *za obidu sego vrěmene* "for the offense of this time". And finally, the 28th and 29th versets of the *Zadonščina*, the former in part and the latter entirely, coincide with the 40th and 41st versets of the *Tale*: 28 "*Gnězdo esmja velikogo knjazja Volodimera Kievьskogo*" "We are the nest of Grand Prince Volodimer of Kiev", 29 "*Ne vъ obidě esmja byli poroženi*" "We were not born to be offended", etc. (in the Undol'skij copy "*Ne v obide esmi byli po roženiju*" "we were not by birth [destined] to be offended").[21] We should mention in passing that the triple assonance of initial vowels characteristic of the *Tale* — 30 *Ol'govo* "of Oleg", 41 *ono obidě* "it", "to be offended" — has come to naught in the *Zadonščina*.

Thus the dramatic combination of the images of "nest" and "offense" appears in two thematically and compositionally related sections of the *Tale*, one of which is unquestionably reflected in the *Zadonščina* and the

---

[21] Cf. *Selected Writings* IV, 553, 562.

other in the late redaction of the *Povest' ob Akire*; these correspondences can be explained only by the influence of the *Tale* in the first instance on the *Zadonščina* and in the second on a late text of the *Povest' ob Akire*.

The primordial relationship of the 117th and 118th versets of the *Tale* to one another and to the surrounding versets is further supported by the sound symbolism of the text. As we have had more than one occasion to observe, the *Igor' Tale* is saturated with diverse sound repetitions, a peculiarity it shares with various fragments of epic composition interspersed in the chronicles of pre-Mongol Rus'.[22]

The internal structure alone of each of the two aforementioned versets reveals a considerable emphasis on repeated sound combinations which unite the lexical components of the utterance: 117 *a či* DI*vo sja* (*Zadonščina*: *či ne lěpo*) *** *pomolo*DI*ti* "and is it really a marvel", *Zadonščina*: "would it not be fitting" *** "to grow young", 118 KOL*i* SOKOL*ъ* *** *vy*SOKO "when a falcon *** on high" — the last word is lacking in the *Povest' ob Akire* — V*ъ myть*X*ъ* BYVAETь *** V*ъ*ZBIVAETь *** V*ъ o*BI*du* "has molted [a number of times] *** drives upward *** to be offended" — this repetition is lacking in the *Povest' ob Akire*). Cf. in the 116th verset *mužja*IM*ъ* SJA SAMI "let us ourselves be heroes" and the repeated alliteration of the sibilants foregrounding and connecting the key words: S*ami* "ourselves" and S*lavu* "glory".

Still more significant are the repetitions that connect the motto of the young princes (116) with both halves of the Grand Prince's response (117, 118): 116 POXYTIM*ъ* *** PODĚLIM*ъ* "let us gain *** and divide" — 117 POM*o*L*o*DITI "to grow young" — 118 MYTь*X*ъ "has molted [a number of times]". The younger princes' encroachment on former (*prě*Dь*NJUJU*) and subsequent (*za*Dь*NJUJU*) glory evokes successively the ancestral associations in the elder prince's exhortation, which are conveyed by striking paronomasia: 115 PR*ad*ĚDь*NJUJU* SLAVU "ancestral glory" — 116 PRĚDь*NJUJU* SLAVU "past glory"; *reko*STA *** ZADь*Njuju* "you [both] said *** future" — 118 N*e* DASTь *g*NĚZDA "[he] will not permit [his] nest".

The phonetically similar beginning and ending (117 *a či* DI*vo* SJA "and is it really a marvel" — 118 *g*NĚ*z*DA SVO*ego* "his nest" delimit Svjatoslav's response from the speech put into the mouths of the obstinate brothers. The grand prince's rebuke is particularly emphasized by the symmetrical distribution of stressed vowels with the inversion of *A* in the last section of the verset: 117 *I – A* || *A – I*, 118 *O – Y – A* || *O – I – A* || *A –*

---

[22] *Selected Writings* IV, 234, 303, 328ff., 603, 606ff., 662ff. and 680–686. Cf. D. I. Čiževskij, "On Alliteration in Ancient Russian Literature", *Russian Epic Studies*, ed. by R. Jakobson and E. J. Simmons = *Memoirs of the American Folklore Society* 42 (1949).

O – I. The "other voice" of the verset is fundamentally distinguished from the two following sentences by its own symmetrically oriented distribution of stressed vowels, where a pair of contiguous stressed *A*'s appears in each of the three grammatically parallel sections of the sentence and where *Ě* occupies the first position in the second section and the final position in the third: *mužjAimъ sja sAmi, prĚdъnjuju slAvu sAmi *** zAdъnjuju si sAmi podĚlim* "Let us ourselves be heroes, ‖ the past glory ourselves *** | divide the future [glory] between ourselves".

In a word, no matter from what perspective one approaches Svjatoslav's colorful tirade about the old becoming young and about the victorious "help" (*posobii*) of the old for the young, its two halves display a striking reciprocal coordination and a natural connection of both versets with the context. This clearly disproves the idle conjectures about the borrowing by the author of the *Igor' Tale* of both sentences, each separately, from two separate and varied written sources. The attempt to disprove the antiquity of the text, which A. A. Zimin has rightly recognized as "one of the most significant works of world culture", by appeal to the expression *sokol v mytex* "falcon who has molted [a number of times]" shares the fate of all previous arguments advanced by Soviet and non-Soviet investigators: a careful examination turns any of these pieces of evidence into incontrovertible proof of the fact that the *Tale* belongs to the times of "Igor', Svjatoslav's son, Oleg's grandson". Such proofs continue to persuade one that the text does not contain a single feature that might permit one to doubt its age of nearly eight hundred years and that, furthermore, every attempt at a different, later dating inevitably encounters insoluble contradictions that one cannot brush off with a premature, precipitate verdict against the *Tale* for its supposed "errors".[23]

Written in August 1972 for the Festschrift in honor of Mihailo Stevanović (*Južnoslovenski filolog* 30, 1973). Translated from Russian for the present volume by David Birnbaum.

---

[23] We have evaluated here versets 40, 41, 111–119 of the *Tale* (and also 62, 71, 76, 79, 88–91, 102, 129, 184 in passing) and versets 28, 29, 84–86, 123 of the *Zadonščina*.

GOROUN'S URN

The "fragments of a clay urn (amphora) with an inscription written in Cyrillic letters" during, or more precisely, toward the end of, the tenth century,[1] which were found during the 1949 excavations in one of the tumuli of the Gnezdovo burial grounds near Smolensk, attracted the attention not only of archeologists and historians, but also of linguists, being the oldest extant specimens of East Slavic writing, with the possible exception of certain coins of Prince Vladimir. Already in the first philological article devoted to the inscribed vessel from tumulus No. 13,[2] the initial conjectural and thoroughly unacceptable reading of the inscription, *gorouxšča*,[3] was subjected to scathing criticism. However *goroušna*, proposed by the critic, in turn occasioned weighty objections to such dubious features for the turn of the millenium as the omission of the front jer in the word *goroušьna* and the use of a ligature in inscribing the cluster *šn*, with the unusual metathesis *nš* (in the ligature the letter *š* is placed on the *right* vertical stroke of the letter *n*).

The attempt one year later at a new interpretation — *gorouxpsa*, i.e., *gorouxъ pьsa* "Goruxъ wrote"[4] — again raised doubts: the personal name Goruxъ is unattested in Slavic texts. The omission of both the front and back jers is more than dubious. The ligature *xps*, especially at the border of two words (subject and predicate), is most unusual, and furthermore, the sentence itself scarcely corresponds to the structure of ancient inscriptions on domestic objects. Finally, the form of the letter

---

[1] Cf. G. F. Korzuxina, "O gnezdovskoj amfore i ee nadpisi", *Issledovanija po arxeologii SSSR* (Leningrad State University, 1961), 226ff.; D. A. Avdusin, "Tainstvenny 9-j vek", *Znanie–sila*, 1969, No. 1, p. 74.
[2] P. Ja. Černyx, "K voprosu o gnezdovskoj nadpisi", *Izvestija AN SSSR, Otd. lit. i jaz.*, 1950, No. 9, 398ff.
[3] M. N. Tixomirov, "Drevnejšaja russkaja nadpis'", *Literaturnaja gazeta*, May 20, 1950; D. A. Avdusin and M. N. Tixomirov, "Drevnejšaja russkaja nadpis'", *Vestnik AN SSSR*, 1950, No. 4, 74ff.
[4] F. V. Mareš, "Dva objevy starých slovanských nápisů (v SSSR u Smolenska a v Rumunsku)", *Slavia* 20 (1951), 497ff.

ps, which the interpreter perceived in the text of the inscription, has no parallel in Cyrillic writing.

The recently expressed proposal that "originally the Gnezdovo inscription read *goroušča*, which was altered [!] to *gorounšča*",[5] calls for serious reservations. A form *goroušča* could only be a contamination of East Slavic *gorouča* or *gorjuča* by Church Slavonic *gorǫšta*. The author of the article under consideration recalls that the neuter plural participle was used "with the meaning of an abstract noun", and cites G. F. Korzuxina's conjecture that the Gnezdovo urn, like the amphorae from the North Shore of the Black Sea which preserve traces of oil, might have served for the transportation of oil from the south to the Smolensk region and the inscription, accordingly, would signify *gorjučee* "fuel". It is difficult to believe in the use of merchandise labels on the urns of Krivič *družina*-men or Taman' oil merchants at the end of this last millenium and to find in the Gnezdovo inscription a close likeness to the present-day technical term *gorjučee*, i.e., fuel for engines.[6] It is even more difficult to accept the Gnezdovo inscription as an example of the Church Slavonic substantivization of neuter plural participles, calqued from Greek, for bookish abstractions. On the other hand, A. S. L'vov is inclined to construe from the spelling *goroušča* the meaning *gorčica* "mustard". Alongside the Church Slavonic adjectives *goroušьnъ*, *gorjušьnъ*, texts in the Russian recension also include the spellings *gorouščьnъ*, *gorjuščьnъ* as a result of contamination by the Church Slavonic participle in its Russian sound-form *goroušč*-. However, such a literary contamination could not have led to the replacement of the Old Russian nominal form *gorjuxa* "mustard" by the neologism *goroušča*, which contradicts all laws of Slavic word derivation and sound changes. It is impossible to propose that the word *gorjuxa* "was reinterpreted as *goroušča* apparently due to mustard's property of burning in one's mouth", as if the term *gorjuxa* with its active and productive suffix evokes any less of a burning association (cf. *sinjuxa* "cyanosis" — *sinet'* "become blue", *vertuška* "revolving object, top" — *vertet'* "twirl").

In any case, the distinct letter *n* remains without any real explanation despite all paleographic tricks. This letter, according to the impression

---

[5] A. C. L'vov, "Ešče raz o drevnejšej russkoj nadpisi iz Gnezdova", *Izvestija AN SSSR, Serija lit. i jaz.* 30 (1971), 47ff. The reading *gorounšča* was prompted by a note in Olga Nedeljković's article "Poluglasovi u staroslovenskim epigrafskim spomenicima", *Slovo* 17 (1967), 5ff.

[6] See *Slovar' sovremennogo russkogo jazyka* (AN SSSR) 3 (1954), 288. As G. F. Korzuxina (p. 229) noted, "one can hardly admit the existence in the tenth century of the term '*gorjučee*', which we use at the present time".

of the investigator cited above, was drawn in and attached to the letter *šč* "when the inscription was already completed". The supposed reason for this insertion was that "the spelling *gorousča* could be interpreted either as *fuel* or as *mustard*. *** For the purpose of clarifying the meaning the original inscription *gorousča* was altered to *gorounšča*, to reproduce Old Church Slavonic *gorǫšte*" and in this way to unambiguously signify "combustible liquid". The scribe "was, in all probability, a Russian, since scarcely anyone else could have altered *gorousča* to *gorounšča* to clarify the meaning". If the composer of the Gnezdovo inscription had "a knowledge of Old Church Slavonic", then one is forced to ask why he replaced the usual *ǫ* (Ѫ) with the peculiar trigraph *oun* (OYH). Latin and Greek reproductions of South Slavic nasals as *in* or *on* cannot, of course, serve as a parallel. There inevitably arises the natural question: for whom were these three syllables, scratched out in the clay of the urn with a dubious differentiation of imaginary homonyms, intended? Even if one believes in the actual existence of these fictitious forms, it is difficult to imagine a person in the years of Svjatoslav's or Vladimir's reign confronted with the difficult choice between mustard and combustible liquid. And finally, no matter to whom one ascribes authorship of the inscription, to a local *družina*-man or a supplier of urns from another city,[7] doubt remains as to where one could find a secular circle of people who, before the beginning of literary activity in Rus', were acquainted with both the vernacular language and Church Slavonic, and, furthermore, not only with the written structure of the latter, but also with its sound structure.

It seems that for an interpretation of the Gnezdovo inscription there is no need to resort either to conjectures about digraphs such as *šn*, *xps*, *nšč*, or to the invention of imaginary words such as *Gorux* or *gorušča* "mustard", or to hypotheses about the unusual content of an ancient inscription on an everyday object. The reading offered for discussion twenty years ago — *gorouňa*[8] — still remains graphically, lexically, and thematically the simplest and most well-founded solution.

In Old Church Slavonic Cyrillic texts a combination of a palatal *l* and *n* with vowels is conveyed in three ways: by a superscript diacritic, a jotated vowel letter, or a combination of both devices. The independent use of the first method is illustrated by the following examples from the Codex Supraliensis: *moľaaxx*, *ľoutosti*, *pokloňo*, cf. *ogňou* alongside

---

[7] Cf. D. A. Avdusin, "Otčet o raskopkax Gnezdovskix kurganov v 1949 g.", *Materialy po izučeniju Smolenskoj oblasti* 1 (Smolensk, 1952), 334ff.
[8] R. Jakobson, "Vestiges of the Earliest Russian Vernacular", *Word* 8 (1952), 350ff.; reprinted in *Selected Writings* II (The Hague, 1971), 611ff.

*ognju.*⁹ An arc is often written directly over the consonant letter: *vol̂a*, *voña.*¹⁰ A superscript diacritic takes the form of "an arc curved sometimes upward and sometimes downward (thus ⌢ or ⌣)."¹¹ Examples of direct contact of an arc with a vertical stroke of a consonant are not rare, and the penultimate letter in the inscription *gorouña*, with the connection of the inverted arc to the second vertical stroke of the letter *n* (н), is precisely such an example.

The personal name *Gorun* is known to early Slavic onomastics, and the feminine possessive form obviously serves as a modifier of the understood substantive *kъrčaga* "urn". The Slavic Middle Ages has abundant recordings of the name of the owner on his household articles, often in a possessive form. In all probability, *gorounъ* was the name of a *družina*-man cremated in a boat and buried in Gnezdovo tumulus No. 13 with the ritual smashing "into little pieces" of the deceased's amphora, inscribed with his name.

Written in Cambridge, Mass. in spring of 1972 for *Ezikovedski izsledvanija v pamet na Prof. St. Stojkov* (Sofia, 1974). Translated from Russian for the present volume by David Birnbaum.

---

[9] A. Marguliés, *Der altkirchenslavische Codex Suprasliensis* (Heidelberg, 1927), §21.
[10] M. Weingart, *Rukovět' jazyka staroslovĕnského* (Prague, 1937), 115.
[11] N. S. Trubetzkoy, *Altkirchenslavische Grammatik* (Vienna, 1954), 50ff.

THE ETYMOLOGY OF *GRIB* (E. SL. FUNGUS, W. SL. BOLETUS)

A series of my critical notes on Max Vasmer's *Russisches etymologisches Wörterbuch* appeared in the journal *Word* (1951, 1952, 1955) and in the *International Journal of Slavic Linguistics and Poetics* (1959). The last link of a multi-nuclear sentence was devoted to the origin of the mushroom name *grib*. Hitherto, we still meet with the view that for the origin of this word "no single etymological solution" has been found and that my above-mentioned etymology "is solved on a purely formal level" (see V. A. Merkulova, *Očerki po russkoj narodnoj nomenklature rastenij*, M., 1967, 167). Yet, if presented less concisely, the proposed hypothesis offers also a substantial semantic motivation.

In listing the onomatopoeic vocalic alternants /G R vowel B/ expert etymologists, and among them Vasmer, object with full right against the attempts to separate the morpheme *greb* in its meaning "row" from the same form when it designates the process "dig". The meanings "dig", "scratch", "scrape", "poke around", "grab at" emerge as a feature common to all the Slavic onomatopoeic alternants with an initial *G R* followed by *E* or *O* or *A* and subsequent *B* (cf. *Gráblju zémlju grábljami* "I rake the ground with a rake"). One must acknowledge the same semantic feature in the morpheme *GRIB* within South Slavic verbal forms such as Serbo-Croation *gribati* "to scratch", "to scrape" and *griblja* "furrow", Bulgarian dialectal *gríbvam* and *gríbam* derived from *grebá* and the alternating verbal forms *grebá/gríba* with the meaning "to dig" (see V. Georgiev et al., *B"lgarski etimologičen rečnik*, IV, 1965, 276, 280) and finally, *grib*, fungus, properly, "what pushes out of the earth": cf. the Russian dialectal idiom linking together the roots *grib* and *greb*: *grib podgrëb* (V. Dal', *Tolkovyj slovar' živogo velikorusskogo jazyka* I [second edition], 83). This semantic value closely corresponds with the meaning of the verbal root *greb* and especially with its uses in reflexive forms such as *grestis'* = "to strive after", "to grab": *Kuda ty grebëš'sja* = "where are you striving for?" This value stands in association with that of *GREB*, *GROB*, *GRAB* morphemes. The pushing from under the earth with the shoving of the latter is an apt representation of mushrooms, and in particular, of their cryptogamous multiplication. The age-old connection of the whole surveyed onomatopoeic set with chthonic imagery is quite typical of the Slavic mushroom name, *grib*, and *gǫba* as well. This connection in diverse Slavic languages finds its striking expression in the frequent application of *grib* and *gǫba* as nominal roots to various types of excrescences or of protuberances on the earth, on the human or animal body, or on the water's floor (cf. Russian dialectal *gríba* "alluvium").

Written in Cambridge, Mass., 1980, for the journal *Semiotica*.

E
POETICS

ANDREW MARVELL'S POEM *TO HIS COY MISTRESS*

I   Had we but World enough, and Time,
        This coyness Lady were no crime.
        We would sit down, and think which way
        To walk, and pass our long Loves Day.
   5 Thou by the *Indian Ganges* side
      Should'st Rubies find: I by the tide
      Of *Humber* would complain. I would
      Love you ten years before the Flood:
      And you should if you please refuse
 10 Till the Conversion of the *Jews*.
      My vegetable Love should grow
      Vaster than Empires, and more slow.
      An hundred years should go to praise
      Thine Eyes, and on thy Forehead Gaze.
 15 Two hundred to adore each Breast:
      But thirty thousand to the rest.
      An Age at least to every part,
      And the last Age should show your Heart.
      For Lady you deserve this State;
 20 Nor would I love at lower rate.

II   But at my back I alwaies hear
      Times winged Charriot hurrying near:
      And yonder all before us lye
      Desarts of vast Eternity.
  5 Thy Beauty shall no more be found;
      Nor, in thy marble Vault, shall sound
      My ecchoing Song: then Worms shall try
      That long preserv'd Virginity:
      And your quaint Honour turn to dust;
 10 And into ashes all my Lust.
      The Grave's a fine and private place,
      But none I think do there embrace.

III   Now therefore, while the youthful hew
      Sits on thy skin like morning <dew>
      And while thy willing Soul transpires

>   At every pore with instant Fires,
> 5   Now let us sport us while we may;
>   And now, like am'rous birds of prey,
>   Rather at once our Time devour,
>   Than languish in his slow-chapt pow'r.
>   Let us roll all our Strength, and all
> 10 Our sweetness, up into one Ball:
>   And tear our Pleasures with rough strife,
>   Thorough the Iron gates of Life.
>   Thus, though we cannot make our Sun
>   Stand still, yet we will make him run.[1]

Perhaps the most interesting pages in *Poet's Grammar* by Francis Berry are devoted to English poetry of the seventeenth century, especially to the Metaphysicals. This keen observer has noticed the conspicuous difference in the verbal pattern of the three parts of Marvell's poem *To his Coy Mistress* (published in 1681): the initial paragraph of ten distichs, the medial one of six, and the final of seven. "As the subjunctive 'would's' and 'should's' ruled the first paragraph, and as the auxiliary 'shall' denoting future certainty ruled the second paragraph, so does the adverb of time 'now' followed by a First Person plural 'let us' (for to *enjoy* love, the choice must be mutual) of the Imperative rule the last paragraph."[2]

An inquirer into the grammar of this poem could, however, obtain more instructive data if, instead of singling out a few features, he were to submit the whole selection and arrangement of grammatical categories in Marvell's poem to a consistent analysis and if, in his search and approach to linguistic facts, he were to turn to the methods and descriptions of the modern science of language, rather than to the outdated dogma of "Classical Grammarians".

The poem, with its numerous verbs, at the same time shows radical restrictions in its conjugational pattern, some of them general but others confined to certain parts of the text. Each paragraph of the poem consists in its turn of three sections: a core (*2*), and two marginals — an entry (*1*) and a close (*3*). All three are quite different in their grammatical make-up, with a particularly salient contrast between the core and the marginals.

---

[1] The text used here is that of Herbert J. C. Grierson (ed.), *Metaphysical Lyrics and Poems of the Seventeenth Century* (Oxford, 1921), p. 73f.
[2] F. Berry, *Poet's Grammar* (London, 1958), p. 109f.

Sections	§ I	§ II	§ III
1	Initial entry	Medial entry	Final entry
2	Initial core	Medial core	Final core
3	Initial close	Medial close	Final close

The initial entry differs from the two other entries and may be labeled "external entry" in contradistinction to both "internal entries". Likewise the final close is an "external close" of the poem to be distinguished from the two other "internal closes". The two "external marginals" of the poem, the first entry and the last close, are noticeably different from the "internal marginals" which delimit the medial paragraph from the other two.

The close covers the final two-line sentence of each paragraph. The entry fills the first four lines of the second and third paragraphs but is confined in the first paragraph to its initial distich, while the second distich presents a kind of transition from the entry to the core (it is akin to the core by its verbs but to the entry by its pronouns).

While those auxiliaries which are used with infinitives, as *shall/should*, *will/would*, *may*, *can*, *let* and *do*, all occur in the poem, there are no auxiliaries combined with participles as *have* and *be* (except the negative construction II $_5$*shall no more be found*). In other functions both verbs occur, but only in the marginals of the poem. The subjunctive forms of these so-called "substantive" verbs open the composition (I $_1$*Had we* *** I $_2$*This* *** *were no crime*), and the latter verb reappears as a copula also in the penultimate line of the second paragraph: II $_{11}$*The Grave's a fine and private place*. Except for one negated passive quoted above, all the verbal phrases of the poem are active.

In contradistinction to the entries, which all are deprived of infinitives, both other sections contain infinitives, 29 in all (15 in the first, 5 in the second and 9 in the third paragraph). In fact all the full, lexical verbs occur only in their infinitive form, and the final line of the poem accumulates three such forms: III $_{13}$*Thus, though we cannot make our Sun* $_{14}$*Stand still, yet we will make him run*. Any simple infinitive presents the action in its fullness without any quantification imposed by the verbal aspects: such oppositions as "perfect" *vs.* "non-perfect" or "progressive" *vs.* "non-progressive" are entirely suppressed in the poem. No characterized aspects (traditionally labeled "durative tenses") figure in this work.

The entries contain only simple finite verbs — two in each entry: I $_1$*had we*, I $_2$*this* *** *were*: II $_1$*I* *** *hear*, II $_3$*lye* $_4$*Desarts*: III $_2$*sits*, III

₃*transpires*. Also both internal closes carry a simple finite verb in their penultimate line (I $_{19}$*you deserve*; II $_{11}$*the Grave's a* *** *place*), and the second of these closes also in the parenthesis of its last line (II $_{20}$*I think*). Throughout the rest of the poem the finite forms are auxiliary components of verb phrases (with the exception of a stereotyped locution in a subordinated clause — I $_9$*if you please*.)

There is no indicative in the external marginals of the poem, and the simple finite verbs of the initial entry are subjunctives, whereas in the internal marginals all the simple finite verbs are indicative present forms.

The cores of the three paragraphs are ruled by verb phrases with the auxiliaries *should/would* in the first paragraph, *shall* in the second, and *let* in the third. The form *let us* signals the hortative mood, the verb phrases with *shall* (or *will*) and the corresponding preterit forms *should/would* may be characterized as an "expective" mood, an actual expectation in the present form, while in the preterit the expectation appears to be removed.

The indicative forms of the internal marginals serve as a neutral background; they separate the three cores of the poem from each other and bring out the three contrasting modal strings which specify each of these cores: the actual expectation of the second paragraph as a perpetual antithesis (II $_1$*But at my back I alwaies hear*) to the dismissed expectation of the first paragraph, and on the other side the imperative call of the third paragraph (III $_1$*Now therefore* ***) for immediate action as a synthesizing answer both to the frustrated and to the frustrating expectancy.

Time is the only noun repeated in all three paragraphs (I_1, II_2, III_7). Marvell utilizes three faded, idiomatic metaphors combined with time in a slightly figurative meaning and revives all three of them, transforming them into leading motifs of the three parts of the triptych. The stereotyped expression "if we have time" changes into an image of fictitious proprietors of time, and the initial *we* (I_1, I_3) splits into the pronouns of the addresser and addressee, greatly distant from each other: I $_5$*Thou by the Indian Ganges side* $_6$*Should'st Rubies find*; *I by the Tide* $_7$*Of Humber would complain*.

There seems to transpire in this poem a stylistic distinction between *thou* and *you* and between the corresponding possessive pronouns; *you* and *your* are apparently used with an ironically tinged reverence and exaltation: I $_9$*And you should if you please refuse* $_{10}$*Till the Conversion of the Jews* *** I $_{18}$*And the last Age should show your Heart*. $_{19}$*For Lady you deserve this State* *** II $_9$*And your quaint Honour turn to dust* ***.

The addresser's *I* merges in metonymic subjects, expressing either the addresser's activities or their duration: I $_{11}$*My vegetable Love should grow* *** I $_{13}$*An hundred years should go to praise* ***. These metonymic subjects and second person pronouns require a different variety of the expective mood than that required in the poem by first person pronouns; the latter forms consistently require (in Twaddell's terminology)[3] the "absolute" *would*, whereas the "contingent" *should* is combined with the other subjects. When, after the sententious indicative of the penultimate line (I $_{19}$*For Lady you deserve this State*), there reappears for the last time a *would*-phrase, the negation clamps down the modal string of the first paragraph (I $_{20}$*Nor would I love at lower rate*).

The locution "time hurries on" (cf. *Oxford English Dictionary*, X, 39), supplied with the mythological imagery of the *winged Charriot* (II$_2$), evokes the traditional argument "memento mori" with the inevitable worms, wedged, however, into a sarcastic erotico-nutritional pun: II $_7$*then Worms shall try* $_8$*That long preserv'd Virginity*. The pronouns of the first and second person disappear, replaced by metonymic abstracts with possessive *my* and *thy* or *your* as attributes and constantly with a "contingent" *shall*.

The medial close contrasts with the core of the same second paragraph, and in fact with all the cores of the poem, by its indicative present forms, by an equational preposition (II$_{11}$) like that of the initial entry (I$_2$), and by new grammatical categories which occur nowhere else in the poem. These are, on the one hand, the negative pronominal totalizer *none*, deliberately opposed to the adjacent parenthetic *I* and both contrasting with the substantival subjects of the foregoing core and, on the other hand, the "assertorial" or "verdictive" modality[4] of the predicate — II $_{12}$*But none I think do there embrace* — with a return to the adversative conjunction which opens the entry of the same paragraph.

The current figurative expression "to consume time" is vivified by the substitution of a more expressive, though synonymous, verb "to devour". The final paragraph inverts the agent-goal relation of the preceding part. The virtual victims of voracious worms are themselves called to devour all-devouring time: III $_6$*And now, like am'rous birds of prey*, $_7$*Rather at once our Time devour*, $_8$*Than languish in his slow-chapt pow'r*. The obliterated metaphoric value of the possessive pronoun in the cliché *our time* is restored, and thus the inaugural image of the poem — I

---

[3] See W. F. Twaddell, *The English Verb Auxiliaries* (Mimeogr., Providence, R.I., 1959).
[4] Cf. R. Jakobson, *Selected Writings* II (The Hague-Paris, 1971), p. 490f.

$_1$*Had we but World enough, and Time* — is reaffirmed. In III $_{13}$*Our Sun*, the final symbolic substitute for *our Time*, the same pronoun reappears with the identical connotation of real possession, and the customary application of the sexual pronoun *he* to *time* (III$_8$) and *sun* (III$_{14}$) actually becomes in the poem a personifying device along with the striking hypallage — *his slow-chapt pow'r*. The call for devouring time is accompanied by the simile — III $_6$*like am'rous birds of prey* — which again (like II$_7$, II$_8$) combines erotic and nutritional imagery. These two animal tropes — one superimposed upon the *dramatis personae* (*worms*) and the other identified with them (*am'rous birds*) — are opposed to the botanic nature of the previous metaphoric epithet: I $_{11}$*My vegetable love should grow*.

In the entry of the second paragraph the grammatical subject was the singular personal pronoun *I*, designating the author who foresees *Desarts of vast Eternity* lying *before us* (II$_3$, II$_4$). The core section displayed a string of desolating *shall*'s and merely substantivized subjects, still connected with the author and his addressee by possessive pronouns *my* and *thy* or *your*; the verdictive statement of the close with the negative universal pronoun in plural puts an end to any personal, private, erotic motifs: II $_{12}$*But none I think do there embrace*.

On the contrary, the final paragraph passes from figurative substantival subjects, connected through the possessive *thy* with the addressee, to a string of *let us* clauses. The pronoun encompassing the addresser and the addressee, which inaugurated the poem (*Had we*, etc.) before setting both of them apart, is reinstated, and even the individual properties of each of the two participants become their common attributes: III $_9$*Let us roll all our Strength, and all* $_{10}$*Our sweetness, up into one Ball*. The objective form *us* yields to the subjective *we* in the finale of the paragraph and of the entire poem, and correspondingly there emerges the absolute expective, the only variety of the expective mood which the poem admits after first person pronouns. The auxiliary *will* regains its proper semantic load under the impetus of the cognate epithet in the entry: III $_3$*And while thy willing Soul transpires*. After having opened the medial paragraph, the first person pronoun, *I*, is suppressed in its further development, whereas in the final paragraph the order is quite the opposite; the pronoun *we* sets in toward the end. This personal plural form impressively contrasts with the depersonalized plural *none* of the medial close. The poem begins and finishes with *we* sentences, but to the removed, frustrated expectancy which marked the beginning (I $_3$*We would sit down, and think which way*) there corresponds an actual anticipation at the end. The leitmotif of the first paragraph — I $_1$*Had we*

*** *Time* — is alluded to in the final close by an absolute potential, negated in favor of an absolute expective: III $_{13}$*Thus, though we cannot make our Sun* $_{14}$*Stand still, yet we will make him run*. This negation of the absolute potential (*we cannot*) contrasts at the same time with the contingent potential used in the core: III $_5$*Now let us sport us while we may*.

The distribution of negatives reveals their constructive role in the poem. All the three closes include a negation, the two internal closes in their last line (I $_{20}$*Nor*, II $_{12}$*But none*), and the external close in the first of its two lines (III $_{13}$*Thus, though we cannot*). There is furthermore a negation in the second line of the initial entry (I $_2$*This coyness Lady were no crime*), and a paired negation inaugurates and characterizes the medial core: II $_5$*Thy Beauty shall no more be found*; $_6$*Nor, in thy marble Vault, shall sound*, II $_7$*My ecchoing song* ***. Briefly, the paragraphs are divided from each other by a negation at the end of the internal closes; on the other hand, the external marginals both contain a negation in the second line from the border, and thus negatives link together the initial entry, the medial core and the final close of the poem. The pattern of negatives in the poem may be schematically represented as a combination of a falling diagonal with a ground horizontal:

	§I	§II	§III
1	no		
2		no	
3	no	no	no

In the initial sentence of the poem a negative inference from a nullified premise is likewise nullified. The central section of the whole piece replies with a repeatedly negative anticipation. In its final sentence Marvell's message recalls the initial fiction, denies its possibility (*cannot*), but surmounts this negation by expressing a mutual willingness for an active dynamic solution: III $_{14}$*yet we will make him run*.

Beside the characteristic grammatical features of each of the three cores (*should* phrases do not appear outside of the initial core, *shall* phrases outside of the medial, and *let us* outside of the final), the striking grammatical differentiation of three kinds of compositional units — entries, cores and closes — and the grammatical split of the entries and closes into internal and external marginals are of great importance for the whole structure of the poem: the absence of infinitives in all the entries and their occurrence in all the other sections; the occurrence of simple finite verbs in all the entries and their general absence in the cores; the occurrence of present indicative verbs in all the internal marginals and their absence elsewhere; the co-occurrence of simple verbs and auxiliaries only in closes and/or a solitary appearance of auxiliary forms absent elsewhere (*do, can, will*). The balanced interplay of all these grammatical features performs significant functions in the semantic texture of Marvell's poem.

Written in 1959 as an "illustration" to the paper "Poetry of Grammar and Grammar of Poetry" (cf. *Selected Writings* III, 63–97); published here for the first time.

DERŽAVIN'S LAST POEM AND M. HALLE'S FIRST LITERARY ESSAY

Three days before his death, the great master of Russian poetic art Gavrila Romanovič Deržavin (1743–1816) wrote his brief parting message, an octet entitled *Na tlennost'* ("On Perishability"), which appeared for the first time in the periodical *Syn Otečestva*, XXXI, a few months after the author's decease.

The following transliteration of these eight lines, in agreement with standard phonetics at the transition from the XVIII to the XIX century, cancels the distinction between *jat'* and *e*. The conservative rule which rejects the change of /é/ to /ó/ must be followed in the recitation of Deržavin's lines and even more so in their analysis.

1. Reká vremén v svoém stremlén'i
2. Unósit vsé delá ljudéj
3. I tópit v própasti zabvén'ja
4. Naródy, cárstva i caréj.
5. A ésli čtó i ostaétsja
6. Črez zvúki líry i trubý,
7. To véčnosti žerlóm požrétsja
8. I óbščej ne ujdét sud'bý.

(1. The river of times in its stream
2. Washes away all deeds of humans
3. And drowns in the abyss of oblivion
4. Peoples, kingdoms, and kings.
5. And if even something remains
6. Through the sounds of lyre and trumpet,
7. It will be devoured by the muzzle of eternity
8. And will not escape the common destiny.)

In my Harvard seminar on Russian poetics in 1951, Morris Halle observed that the initial, capital letters of each of the eight lines of this poem form an acrostic which underscores the theme of the poem as expressed by its title. This acrostic consists of two words — RUINA ČTI "the ruin of glory" — one a gallicism and the other an Old Russian relic, both of which were familiar to the Russian readership of that epoch. Halle published his discovery and comments in the *International Journal of Slavic Linguistics and Poetics*, I (1958), pp. 232–236, under the title "O nezamečennom akrostixe Deržavina" ("On an unnoticed acrostic of Deržavin").

An attentive insight into the make-up of this concise meditative miniature shows the enormous filigree elaboration applied to all levels of its constituents, from the one-sentence quatrains and the couplets to the lines, feet, syllables, phonemes, and their components. Whatever the level of these constituents, they are always endowed with a semantic value.

The single subject of the first quatrain, the destructive power of the times, is metaphorically depicted as *reka vremen*, with the two transitive verbs, 2. *unosit* and 3. *topit*, as predicates, governing a double series of plural accusatives, 2. *dela*, 4. *narody, carstva i carej*. This first quatrain represents the dramatic events from the standpoint of their unnamed victim. The two pronominal subjects of this stanza, the indefinite 5. *čto* and the anaphoric 7. *to*, refer to any victim by using the most generalized form, the singular neuter, accompanied by three intransitive verbal predicates (5. *ostaetsja*, 7. *žerlom požretsja*, 8. *ne ujdet*), two of which are reflexive forms and the second of which is, moreover, a passive construction.

The dynamic image in the first stanza of time rapidly carrying away things and beings and dooming them to oblivion yields in the second stanza to the static image of everything sharing its common and inevitable destiny of disappearance, or in other, again metaphoric terms, of being swallowed by the muzzle of eternity (7. *večnosti žerlom*).

The active mind of the first quatrain is paralleled by the enriched intervals between the syllabic summits of the line, namely the disposition of the verses toward plentiful consonantal clusters, in particular four groups of four asyllabics (1. vreme*n v sv*oem *str*emlen'i; 3. topi*t v pr*opasti; 4. ca*rstv*a), whereas the second quatrain lacks such clusters. On the other hand, the passive mind of the latter stanza seems to be paralleled by the phonemic scarcity of intervals between the syllabic summits of the line, namely a predilection for hiatus (5. čt*o i o*staetsja; 6. lir*y i*; 8. *i o*bščej n*e u*jdet), whereas the first quatrain admits a hiatus solely at its end, in the transition to the next stanza (4. carstva *i*).

While the inclination toward clusters is attached to the first, and hiatus to the second, quatrain of the poem, the acrostic inverts this distribution: the vertical hiatus of r*ui*na corresponds to the middle lines, 2.–3., of the first quatrain, and the cluster *čti* to the middle lines, 6.–7., of the second quatrain. The dissimilarity between the two nouns of the acrostic is significant: the first noun contains a pair of vowels (*ui*) framed by two sonorants (*r—n*), and the second is an inflectional stem confined to voiceless plosives (*čt*). It is just this striking morphophonemic contrast of a vocalic preponderance syntactically superimposed upon bare consonantism which must have motivated the joint emergence of two unwonted vocables.

The concentration of attention in the first quatrain upon the consonantal pattern also finds its expression in abundant paronomasias (1. re*ká* v*remén* *** st*remlén*'i; 1. *svoém* 2. *v*se; 2. *del*á *l*judéj; 3. tópit — própasti; 4. na*ródy*, *cár*stva i *car*éj), as compared to the single sample of poetic etymology in the second quatrain (7. *žer*lom *požr*etsja).

In the iambic tetrameters of the octet either all four even syllables (ictuses) are stressed, or one of the two inner ictuses (the second or third of the even syllables) is unstressed. In the penultimate line of each quatrain the unstressed ictus falls on the final syllable *sti* of a trisyllabic noun (3. *v propasti*; 7. *večnosti*); in all other cases the unstressed ictus indicates either an initial antepretonic syllable (5. *ostaetsja*) or — in the even (masculine) lines — a proclitic (4. *i carej*; 6. *i truby*; 8. *ne ujdet*).

Both of the two lines within a couplet display an identical relationship between stress and ictus. All even syllables are stressed in the two expressly scanned lines of the first couplet (1.-2.), and this severe scanning style is enhanced by the oxytonic phrasing of the entire line (1. Reká/ vremén/ v svoém/ stremlén'i) and by beginning only one line of the whole poem with an oxytone. Cf. *Glagól vremén* at the beginning of the epitaph *Na smert' knjazja Meščerskogo* written by Deržavin in 1779.

The two lines of the octet's final couplet disclose the solemn style of classical tetrameters by leaving the fourth syllable unstressed (7. *To véčnosti*; 8. *I óbščej ne ujdét*). The specificity of this couplet which substitutes the motionless image of eternity for the initial dynamic picture of flowing times finds its expression in the sudden perfectivization of the finites: 7. *požretsja*; 8. *ne ujdet*. The latter form is supplied with a negation, the only one in the poem, and is followed by the concluding adverbal genitive, which contrasts with the six adnominal genitives in the octet. The sole adjective of the poem (8. *obščej*) functions as an attribute to this adverbal genitive. Rhymes such as 5. impf. *ostaetsja* — 7. pf. *pozretsja*, and 6. *zvuki* *** *truby* — 8. *ne ujdet sud'by*, underscore the grammatical divergence of the confronted words. Cf. 1. loc. *stremlen'i* — 3. gen. *zabven'ja*; 2. gen. *ljudej* — 4. acc. *carej*.

The four lines of the two inner couplets of the poem (3.-4. and 5.-6.) omit the stress on their sixth syllable, which is a characteristic of the narrative, colloquially-oriented variety of the iambic tetrameter. These couplets also show certain syntactic similarities: the first line of the couplet contains the predicate, while the subsequent line is occupied by secondary parts of the sentence in the form of fused phrases (4. *Narody, carstva i carej*; 6. *Črez zvuki liry i truby*).

The pattern of stressed vowels in the even syllables corroborates the poetic unity of the octet and its significant division into a pair of stanzas. The "moderate" vowels, flat (rounded) *O* and non-flat (unrounded) *E*, occur in both quatrains. The compact (open) *A* is found only in the even lines of the first quatrain and at the beginning of the poem (*Reká*). The diffuse (closed) vowels, the flat (rounded) *U* and the non-flat (unrounded) *I*, along with back *Y*, the contextual variant of the same phoneme, occur only in the even lines of the second quatrain. Moreover, the occurrence of *A* is limited to a position before a stressed *E* in the following word, and *U* requires a subsequent *I*. The last stressed vowel of any line is the non-flat member of the pair *O-E* or *U-I*. Thus the octet shows a general motion toward lower sonority and higher tonality. The words of the diiambic acrostic which sums up the plot of the octet, *ruina čti*, echo with their reiterated *I* the vocalic trend of the poem.

The limitations imposed by the octet on the admissible concurrences of grammatical categories for the sake of their higher semantic expressivity may be exemplified by the use of feminines (all inanimate) only in singular and masculines solely in plural: 1. *reka*, 3. *v propasti*, 6. *liry i truby*, 7. *večnosti*, 8. *sud'by*; but 2. *ljudej*, 4. *narody, carej*, 6. *zvuki*. The feminine singular forms in the acrostic (*ruina, čti*) show once more the close connection between the acrostic detected by Morris Halle and the poetics of Deržavin's octet.

The discoverer of *ruina čti* is correct in connecting the protracted inattention to this acrostic with the old surmise of viewing Deržavin's octet as merely an uncompleted fragment (232f.). This surmise in turn is based on the unusualness of short poems in Deržavin's legacy. Yet it must be taken into account that it is precisely the singular brevity of Deržavin's farewell poem which explains and expiates its extraordinary condensation of artistic devices.

Written in Cambridge, Mass., January 1982, for the Festschrift in honor of Morris Halle on his sixtieth birthday, *Language, Sound, Structure*, ed. M. Aronoff, R. T. Oehrle et al. (Cambridge, Mass., 1984).

ИГРА В АДУ У ПУШКИНА И ХЛЕБНИКОВА

Велимир Хлебников, завзятый, внимательный читатель, был, разумеется, знаком с популярнейшим в те времена брокгаузовским изданием сочинений Пушкина, выходившим под редакцией С. А. Венгерова, и в частности с отрывками из неосуществленной "Адской поэмы" (т. II, СПб., 1908, с. 85),[1] а также с "адскими" рисунками кишиневской тетради поэта, воспроизведенными на двух последующих страницах того же тома.[2] В редакторском комментарии эти рисунки были оценены как существенное дополнение к тексту отрывков: "В творческом воображении Пушкина несомненно бродило много отдельных деталей будущей поэмы, часть которых он зарисовал." Сопоставление иллюстраций с литературными фрагментами привело Венгерова к заключению, что замысел поэмы "был большой и сложный".

В работе над поэмой "Игра в аду" (1912) Хлебников и его сотрудник А. Е. Крученых явно отталкивались от пушкинских словесных и графических мотивов. Мотив вечной игры, приписанной кромешным картежникам в пушкинских строках, — "*Ведь мы играем не [из] денег, / А только б вечность проводить!*" — вызывает у Хлебникова отклики: "Приникли у стола. / Сражаться вечно"; "Кружатся вечно близ стола"; "И стол вовек не будет пуст. / Игра пошла", "Промчатся годы — карты те же".[3] Возможно, что и в "разговоре Маяковского с Александром Сергеевичем" ("Юби-

---

[1] Впоследствии конгломерат, составленный Венгеровым, текстологи разъяснили как наброски к двум замыслам, относящимся к разным творческим периодам. См. об этом: Д. Д. Благой, "Фауст в аду (об одном неизученном замысле Пушкина)", в кн.: Д. Д. Благой, *От Кантемира до наших дней* 1 (Москва, 1972), 286–303.
[2] Новую репродукцию рисунков см.: Т. Г. Цявловская, "'Влюбленный бес' (неосуществленный замысел Пушкина)", в кн.: *Пушкин. Исследования и материалы* 3 (Москва-Ленинград, 1960), 103, 107.
[3] См.: Велимир Хлебников, *Собрание произведений* 2 (Ленинград, 1930), 119–135. Ср. также: Велимир Хлебников, *Неизданные произведения*, ред. и коммент. Н. Харджиева (Москва, 1940), 226–230; 438–440. Для удобства сопоставления пушкинские строки здесь и ниже набираются курсивом.

лейное") посреди парафразированных пушкинских стихов мотив располагающих вечностью собеседников восходит к тому же пушкинскому материалу. Схож в обеих адских поэмах словарный обиход бесовской игры. Игрецкие возгласы в пушкинских набросках "*Что козырь? — Черви — Мне ходить. / Я бью*" и "*Я дамой *** Крой! Я бью тузом. / Позвольте, козырь. — Ну, пойдем*" подхвачены Хлебниковым: "Какова? / Его семерка туз взяла! / Перебивают как умело"; "И взвился вверх веселый туз"; "И режет всех без козырей". У Пушкина: "*Беру. — Кругом нас обыграла. / Ей, смерть! Ты право сплутовала; Уж не тебе меня ловить*", а у Хлебникова: "Он, чудилося, скоро / Всех обыграет"; "Затрепетал *** Меня бы не надули!"; "Все мечут банк и, загибая, / Забыли путь ловца".

"Земные сыны" "Игры в аду" разделяют *детей земных изгнанье*, подсказанное Пушкиным. "(*Во тьме кромешной / Есть отдаленный уголок*) / *Где слез во мраке льются реки*" — так начинается в пушкинском черновике описание Геенны, "*Откуда изгнаны навеки / Надежда, мир, любовь и сон*". Соответственно в поэме Хлебникова "Из слез, что когда-либо лились, / Утесы стоят и столбы"; "Надежды луч не трепетал"; скрылись "И мир любви и мир убогий". "*Где свищут адские бичи*", — там, согласно пушкинской версии, "(*грешника) внимая стон / Ужасный Сатана хохочет*", а в хлебниковской интерпретации "Свист, крики, плач чуть слышны, / Им внемлет, дремля, властелин. / Он спит сам князь — под кровлей — / Когда же и поспать? / В железных лапах крикнут кролики, / Их стон баюкает, как мать ***".

"Тех властелинов весел сброд", повествует "Игра в аду", и вот невнятность человечьих стонов беспечным бесам-игрокам находит себе на протяжении четвертого из пушкинских пяти отрывков исчерпывающее объяснение:

> *Какой порядок и молчанье!*
> *Каков огромный сводов ряд,*
> *Но где же грешников варят?*
> *Все тихо. — Там, гораздо дале.*
> *— Где мы теперь? — В парадной зале.*

Уже у Пушкина параллелизмом словосочетаний ("*Какой порядок — Какой *** сводов ряд*") и словообразовательной связью *порядка* и *ряда* подсказано каламбурное сближение архитектурного свода со сводом законов, обнаженное в хлебниковских строках "И своды надменные взвились — / Законы подземной гурьбы", а вслед за тем повторенное в "Гимне судье" Маяковского. Дрожь и вытье уставших мучиться рабов, сурово покаранных дьявольскими судьями и обреченных на варку в меди, заостряют контраст хлебниковских двустиший:

> Разятся черные средь плена
> И злата круглых зал,
> И здесь вокруг дрожат полена,
> Чей души пламень сжал.

Насмешливое изображение чертей в свою очередь примечательно в обоих сравниваемых произведениях. Пушкин: "*А этот бес — как важен он, / Как чинно выметает вон / Опилки, серу, пыль и кости*". У Хлебникова "мрачный бес, с венцом кудрей", даже лежа на полу, "все ж кудри чешет гребешком".

Не ограничиваясь гротескной парафразой пушкинских набросков, "Игра в аду" пародирует строки сна Татьяны, а также произведения других поэтов-классиков, начиная с Ломоносова. Особенно любопытно отметить, что поэма Хлебникова соприкасается с адскими рисунками кишиневских тетрадей даже в мотивах, которым нет параллелей в пушкинских стихотворных отрывках. Среди способов и орудий мучительства и казни, наряду с варкой грешников, сближающей и стихи, и рисунки Пушкина с "Игрой в аду", "визг верховный колеса" связывает поэму Хлебникова не с пушкинским текстом, а лишь с изображением палаческого колеса в правом нижнем углу его рисунка, воспроизведенного Венгеровым на с. 87. В пушкинских строках нет ни ведьм, ни эротических образов, в противоположность изобилующей таковыми "Игре в аду" и адским рисункам Пушкина.

В комментарии Венгеров цитирует критический отзыв Анненкова о сатанинских эскизах поэта ("Пушкин в Александровскую эпоху", с. 174). Анненков усматривает в рисовальщике "дикую изобретательность" и "горячечное, свирепое состояние" фантазии, схожее с "душевной болезнью", тогда как самому Венгерову эти рисунки представляются веселыми, забавными и "вольтериански-фривольными". Оба суждения друг другу отнюдь не противоречат. Стремительная, сгущенная, лихорадочная фантасмагория графических дерзаний бурной кишиневской эпохи в творческой жизни Пушкина, с их полными лукавого юмора, порой саркастическими, фривольными, кощунственными нотками встречает близкое соответствие в технике и тематике хлебниковской "Игры в аду" и в то же время нежданно перекликается с боем быков в силуэтных рисунках Пикассо. Композиция адских эскизов Пушкина своевольно громоздит и переплетает разнородные образы и, к примеру сказать, вклинивает в набросок ушастой человеческой головы вместо органов зрения и обоняния огромный профиль черта, раздувающего ногою огонь для расправы над жертвами и подремывающего, опершись на правую руку. Вся эта затейливая, ничему, кроме авторской прихоти, не подвластная композиция как бы предвещала причудливый, бредовый, горячечный склад "Игры в аду", где — по словам ее эпилога — "тихо вьется небылица".

Written in Cambridge, Mass., May–June 1974, for *Sravnitel'noe izučenie literatur: Sbornik statej k 80-letiju Akademika M. P. Alekseeva* (Leningrad, 1976).

FROM ALJAGROV'S LETTERS

It was in 1914–15 that the seventeen-year-old R. Aljagrov showed his verbal experiments to a few men of the Russian literary and artistic avant-garde such as Velimir Xlebnikov (1885–1922), A. E. Kručenyx (1886–1971), Mixail Matjušin (1861–1934), Kazimir Malevič (1878–1935), and Pavel Filonov (1883–1941) and enjoyed their approval. These included, in particular, his attempts at supraconscious poetry (*zaumnaja poèzija*) built of invented words. In literary history it was apparently the first endeavor to construct in this way longer, connected texts alien in their sounds and sequences to those of the given language and free of any inserted traces of verbal motivation such as references to dreams, zoological sound emissions, or machine noises.

A typical example of such innovations was the first of the two Aljagrov compositions included in his and Kručenyx's joint booklet prepared in 1914 but carrying the date 1916. This early test of the pen is transliterated here, with the "soft" and "hard" signs of the Cyrillic original rendered by single and double apostrophes respectively:

> mzglýbžvuo jix"jan'dr'jú čtlěsčk
> xn fja s"p skypolzá
> avtábdlkni t'japrá kakájzčdi

Aljagrov accompanied his supraconscious artifacts with theoretical reasonings about this ultimate goal of poetry, but at the same time he agreed with Aleksej Eliseevič Kručenyx, who was in 1914 his closest interlocutor in talks and letters. One could not but accept the latter's claim that supraconscious language is a powerful constituent of verbal art, but like mustard it cannot be the sole item of a dish or of a diet. Aside from unusual words, unusual sequences of traditional lexical entities were used in the poetic experiments of Kručenyx's correspondent, as for instance an inner fragment of a multifarious poem he worked on in June, 1914.

V èlektro ty v kostjumce èlektrik
Tak siluètna v takt mig glaz tam tem' son bra
Derzka ruka soseda èkran bystrostr vsjak štrix
Kol' rezv sportsmen xvat' julkij mjač i rad ljub trjuk.

Aljagrov's messages were preserved by Kručenyx, and some of these letters are still extant. Here appears in translation, supplemented with a few bracketed annotations, the following one sent from Moscow to Petersburg in February, 1914.[1]

"I am granting your request in full, Aleksej Eliseevič, and am

---

[1] The original Russian text of the letter, hitherto unpublished, reads as follows:
"Исполняю сугубо вашу просьбу, Алексей Елисеевич, и посылаю вам в некотором роде словесное стихотворение, написанное три недели тому назад. В нем слово не самовитое, но гибнущее от разрыва сердца в устремлении к лаконизму и аритмичности. Все слова в нем мужского рода (вы так просили). Слово у меня не самовитое, ибо самовитое слово подразумевает известную статичность в авторе, впрочем вполне и недостижимо (элементарные истины). Стихотворение это пустите пожалуйста под Алягровым с следующим заглавием 'Пругвачу будетлянину Алексею Крученых'. Пругва = буква, острый неологизм душевнобольного Платона Лукашевича (из книжки Радина 'Футуризм и безумие'). Там много интересных цитат. Впрочем, вы хорошо знакомы с поэзией сумасшедших, и бесконечно правы в утверждениях касательно их. Если возможно, напечатайте пожалуйста прозаическими строками без опечаток, особенно в пунктуации. Кстати, пожалуйста напишите мне, когда выйдет наш сборник и все прочее и заодно пришлите мои заметки, а главное 'Рыкающий Парнас'. Между прочим газеты, журналы, витрины магазинов наводнены статьями о футуризме, иные с претензией на серьез. Взялись за футуризм мусагетцы: на днях посвятит ему пол-лекцию Степун; Вячеслав Иванов читал лекцию якобы о Чурлянисе, в действительности о будетлянах. Я не был, но вот приблизительно содержание части лекции: симпатичнейшие из юношей, иррациональные бродяги, блудные сыны, покинувши отчий дом, остались одиноки на высокой горе, отвергнув гармонию. Не высмеивать должны мы их, а памятник поставить за их безумно дерзкий подвиг; однако воспоем гимн божественной гармонии и т. д. Никто не пророк в своем отечестве, но они нигде не найдут себе отечества, пристанища; они единственные истинные русские анархисты ... Вы спрашивали меня, где приходилось мне встречать стихи из гласных. Как образцы таковых, интересны магические формулы гностиков.
Помните, вы говорили, что любой ряд букв в прямом и обратном порядке — есть поэзия, и называли это демонической или подпольной точкой зрения.
Ведь до сих пор поэзия была цветными стеклами (*Glasbilder*), как стеклам солнечный свет, ей романтический демонизм придавал живописность сквозя [сквозь стекла].
Но вот победа над солнцем и эф-луч (из ваших же произведений). Стекло взорвано, из осколков иначе льдышек (это из сказки Андерсена) создаем узоры ради освобождения. Из демонизма, нуля творим любую условность, и в ее интенсивности, силе залог аристократизма в поэзии (это я в пику вам). А вы смеетесь, говорите: прекрасная греза и пр. Не греза, а то дыхание, о котором говорит Мартынов, та радость творчества, о которой пишете вы, та способность к окрашиванью, на которую указывает Маринети. А на человеческую точку наплевать. Маринети между прочим жаждет встречи с вами будетлянами и дебата, хотя бы при посредстве переводчика. Разбейте его с его рухлядью и дешевкой, это так легко вам. А это будет очень важно. Между прочим, *очень, очень прошу* вас на все предыдущее ответить, это мне очень важно, ведь никто так далеко не зашел, как мы

sending you a poem 'in words' of a sort [using habitual words], written three weeks ago. In it the word is not 'selfsome' [*samovityj*, 'self-centered', according to Xlebnikov's terminology], but has perished from an explosion of the heart in a striving for laconism and arhythmicality. All the words in it are of masculine gender (as you requested). My language is not selfsome, for the selfsome word presupposes a certain stasis on the part of the author, which is, incidentally, unrealizable (elementary truths). Please publish the poem under the name Aljagrov with the following title: 'To the Futurist *prugvač* Aleksej Kručenyx'. *Prugva-bukva* [*prugva* is from Old Russian *prug* 'locust' by analogy with *bukva* 'letter'] is the clever neologism of the mentally ill Platon Lukaševič [who in 1846 published his numerous bold fantasies on language] from Radin's book *Futurism and Madness* [Petersburg, 1914]. There are many interesting quotations there. By the way, you are well acquainted with the verses of madmen and endlessly correct in what you say about them. If possible, please print [the poem sent] in prose lines without misprints, especially in the punctuation. Incidentally, please write me as to when our collection will appear, etc. [This planned publication was never realized. Of all the joint literary projects only one booklet written by Kručenyx and Aljagrov, daringly and opulently decorated by Olga Rozanova (1886–1918), and cited at the beginning of this article, was published in 1915 (though dated 1916). The title of this booklet, *Zaumnaja gniga*, jokingly blends *kniga* 'book' with *gnida* 'nit'. The collage of the cover alluding to a buttoned heart consists of a red colored heart with a genuine white button affixed to it. The catalogue of the Exhibition, *Paris-Moscou 1900–1930*, at the Centre Georges Pompidou, 1979 (pp. 425, 428) appraises the book as 'l'un des plus beaux du futurisme russe.' In 1976 the published catalogue of the Ex Libris Bookstore, New York, fixed for this 'milestone of Russian futurism' a price of $8,000.]

At the same time send my remarks and especially a copy of *Roaring*

с вами, к чему ж нам терять из виду друг друга. Если передернетесь, если не ответите, ведь мне остается ваши же слова повторить: Ух старая рефлексия проклятая!

В Москве никто не знает о существовании новых ваших книжек, я указывал приказчику Образования на это, просил выставить в окне, он отвечает: 'И слава Богу, что не знают'. Что делать? Мои предыдущие построения относительны, не забывайте же, что я оперирую со словами.

К чему идет Хлебников? кланяюсь ему.

Всего лазоревого (так, говорят, И. Северянин письма заканчивает). Ответьте пожалуйста поскорей."

Parnassus [a one-volume series of futurist texts published in Petersburg, January, 1914, and prohibited by the censorship as 'amoral']. By the way, the newspapers, magazines, store windows are flooded with articles on futurism, some of which have pretensions to seriousness. The Musagetes [symbolists grouped around the publishing center Musaget] have taken to futurism — in a few days Stepun [Russian philosopher and critic (1884–1965)] is devoting half a lecture to it. Vjačeslav Ivanov [1866–1949] delivered a lecture, supposedly on Čiurlionis [the Lithuanian symbolist painter Mikalojus Čiurlionis (1875–1911)] but actually on the futurists. I didn't go, but here's the approximate content of part of the lecture: the most sympathetic of youths, irrational tramps, prodigal sons who, after abandoning the paternal home, remained on the mountain top, rejecting harmony. We shouldn't poke fun at them, but erect a monument to their madly bold feat; nevertheless, let us raise a hymn to divine harmony, etc., etc. No one is a prophet in his own country, but they won't find themselves a fatherland or a refuge anywhere; they are the sole true Russian anarchists ...

You asked me where I happened to come across poems composed of vowels. The magical formulae of the gnostics are interesting as models of such.

Remember, you said that poetry is any sequence of letters in direct or inverted order, and called this a demonic or 'underground' point of view.

You know, poetry up to now was a stained-glass window (*Glasbilder*), and like the sun's rays passing through the panes, romantic demonism imparted picturesqueness to it.

But here's victory over the sun and the f-ray (from your own works) [cf. Gisela Erbslöh, *Pobeda nad solncem, ein futuristisches Drama von Kručenych*, (played in Petersburg, Dec. 1913), Munich, 1976]. The glass is blown up, from the fragments — in other words, pieces of ice (this is from Andersen's fairytale ['The Snow Queen']) — we create designs for the sake of liberation. From demonism, from null, we create any convention whatsoever, and in its intensity, its force, is the pledge of aristocratism in poetry (here I'm at my peak). But you laugh and say: a fine dream, etc. It's not a dream, but the breath of which [D. P.] Martynov speaks [Russian provincial school principal, author of the book *Revelation of the Mystery of Human Language*, 1898, with innumerable delirious etymologies referred to in Radin's book cited above], the joy of creation of which you write, the ability to color that Marinetti points out. And as to the human speck, I spit on it! Marinetti, by the way, craves a meeting with you futurists [*budetljanin*, Xlebnikov's term corresponding to 'futurist'] and a debate, even if through the medium of a translator. [Written during Marinetti's Russian sojourn in February 1914]. Smash him and his junk and trash to bits — you're so good at it! And it's most important. Incidentally, I very, very much ask you to answer all the above, it's very important to me: no one's gone as far [particularly in questions of poetic language] as you and me, how can we lose sight of one another? If you flinch, if you don't answer, all I can do is repeat your own words: oh, damned old reflex!

In Moscow no one knows of the existence of your new books. I pointed this out to the clerk at Obrazovanie [large Moscow bookstore on Kuzneckij Most], asked him to put them in the window. He answers: 'Thank God no one knows!' What's one to do?

The above phrases are relative: don't forget that I'm using words.

What's Xlebnikov up to? Give him my best.

I wish you the very azure (thus, they say, I. Severjanin [the ego-futurist poet, (1887–1942)] closes his letters). Please answer as soon as you can."

The rendered document of February 1914 may be of interest as depicting the reflections and fermentation of a teen-ager, one of many attached to the vast avant-garde movement of Russia's prerevolutionary years.

Written in 1979 for the Festschrift in honor of Victor Erlich, *Russian Formalism in Retrospect*, ed. R. L. Jackson and S. Rudy (New Haven, 1984).

ИЗ КОММЕНТАРИЯ К СТИХАМ МАЯКОВСКОГО "ТОВАРИЩУ НЕТТЕ — ПАРОХОДУ И ЧЕЛОВЕКУ"

Прозорливый до ясновидения Ю. И. Лотман дал в своем недавнем труде — *Роман А. С. Пушкина "Евгений Онегин"* — образцовый комментарий не только к сложнейшему из пушкинских творений, но за одно и в первую очередь к методам и задачам комментатора.

Стихи "Товарищу Нетте — пароходу и человеку", написанные Маяковским в Ялте 15 июля 1926 года, напечатанные в московских *Известиях* 22 августа и многократно читанные автором в различных лекционных выступлениях, снискали себе широкую популярность в русском читательском мире, особенно среди советской учащейся молодежи. Центральная часть стихотворения, повествующая о прижизненной близости дипкурьера Нетте к Маяковскому, вызывала в разнообразных кругах немало недоуменных вопросов. "Помнишь, Нетте, в бытность человеком, / Ты пивал чаи со мною в дип-купе?", и в завершение ночной строфы, "напролет болтал о Ромке Якобсоне и смешно потел, стихи уча".

В пересказе П. И. Лавута, устроителя гастролей Маяковского, авторское предуведомление при чтении стихотворного обращения было подхвачено примечанием к тем же стихам в его *Собрании сочинений*. Оно сообщало, что "здесь встречается фамилия Якобсон, Ромка — это наш общий знакомый, ученый, филолог", познакомивший автора с героем этих стихов. Названное примечание не могло рассеять недоумения слушателей и читателей: почему вся ночь нежданной дорожной встречи или встреч Маяковского с Нетте оказалась посвящена болтовне об общем знакомом, почему этот ученый филолог, некогда познакомивший поэта с дипкурьером, выступает под эмфатической кличкой, и почему с памятью о нем оказывается связано напряженное учение стихов сосредоточенным стражем дипломатической почты. Почему, наконец, именно эти детали "отстоялись словом" и следственно приобрели, согласно автобиографическому лозунгу Маяковского

(*Я сам*), жизненный интерес в творчестве поэта?

Среди общих поисков ответа отмечу присланный мне запрос из восточных округов РСФСР по поручению вдовы Теодора Нетте через множество долгих лет после его смерти. Думаю, кажущиеся неясности исчезают в свете показаний моего ответного письма. Поэтому цитирую его сохранившуюся в моем архиве копию, пополняя эти извлечения некоторыми опущенными в письме подробностями, заключенными здесь в квадратные скобки.

"С Теодором Нетте я встретился впервые в конце июня 1920 г. в Таллине, где мы ждали из Москвы д-ра Гиллерсона, чтобы ехать с ним в составе миссии Красного Креста в Прагу. Задачей миссии была репатриация бывших русских военнопленных, остававшихся в Чехии с австровенгерских времен, а также установление первых шагов к дипломатическим сношениям с Чехословакией. Гиллерсон был главой миссии, я как славист был приглашен в роли переводчика, а Нетте был временно прикомандирован к миссии как дипкурьер. Мы выехали из Таллина в первых числах июля морским путем на Штетин, а оттуда поездом в Прагу с остановкой и пересадкой в Берлине. Нетте и я ехали в одной каюте и как то сразу очень подружились. Он рассказал про свою жизнь: работал сыздетства в сапожной мастерской вместе с отцом, не помню, в котором латвийском городе, и еще подростком вместе с отцом попал в тюрьму за участие в революционном движении. После революции он принимал деятельное участие в борьбе за Советскую Латвию. Мужественный боевой закал сочетался в нем с редкой добротой, сердечностью и душевной чистотой. Горячо любил поэзию, и латышскую, и русскую, и могу сказать — русским владел он превосходно. Ночью в каюте он читал мне наизусть и излагал своего любимого латышского поэта Яна Райниса [1865–1929], а я [ночь напролет] читал ему Маяковского. Нетте не знал его стихов и только слыхал о нем неприязненно критические отзывы.

Перед майским отъездом из Москвы мне не раз довелось слышать авторскую читку *Ста пятидесяти миллионов* [в частности его читку публичную — одну перед Луначарским со товарищи, другую в Московском Лингвистическом Кружке]. У меня на глазах работал Маяковский над этой поэмой с лета 1919 г., которое мы вместе проводили в одной даче в Пушкине, потом осенью и зимой, когда мы жили дверь в дверь в Лубянском проезде — д.3, кв. 11 и 12 — и нераз сообща обсуждали всё новые страницы. Маяковский сдавал написанное машинистке, снова правил ее машинопись, вычеркивал, вписывал вставки, менял текст, опять давал его перепечатать, а после перепечатки выбрасывал оригинал в корзину. Одну из этих промежуточных версий, которую как раз он собирался выкинуть, я попросил его подарить мне. [Поэма была едва дописана, а враждебная кампания против нее уже подымалась и в Госиздате, и еще в других советских учреждениях, и Маяковский, опасаясь, что рукопись будут морить, просил меня попытаться выпустить у чехов ее спешное предварительное издание. Напомним, что еще в 1926 г. Маяковский говорил, что 'написать стихи трудно, напечатать еще трудней'. План срочного пражского выпуска оказался неосуществим, но зато удалось найти в чешских писателях увлеченный интерес к поэме, приведший к ее успешному стихотворному переводу. Запись поэмы, подаренная мне Маяковским покоится в ЦГАЛИ под пометкой — Машинопись 1920 г., с авторскими пометками и вставками, и все найденные в ней варианты текста вошли в *Собрание сочинений* Маяковского, т. II, 1957]. Я бережно хранил ее, она ехала со мной, в моем портфеле, и я прочел Теодору всю поэму. Он был в необычайном восторге, говорил, что это первые стихи революционных лет, которые не могут не задеть за живое, возмущался, что могут осуждать поэта, [готовился по мере сил бороться против этих козней], и я должен был свято обещать Теодору, что когда он поедет обратно в Москву, я дам ему письмо, которое он лично вручит Маяковскому. [Нежданная связь ученого филолога с революцией в поэзии изумляла Теодора и пришлась ему по душе.]

В Праге Нетте пробыл до конца лета, мы бродили с ним по городу, он восхищался красотой и величием его зодческой старины, вспоминал попутно живописную старую Ригу. Однажды он убедил меня поехать с ним в далекую от центра, небольшую кофейную, где бедняк-тапер очаровал его своей игрой. Музыку Теодор и любил, и понимал. Чех, которого он открыл и обласкал, оказался действительно чутким пианистом. Впоследствии я случайно поселился по близости этого кафе [называвшегося *Дерби*, *Bělského třída*] и за одним из его столиков написал почти все свои работы двадцатых годов [привлек туда же членов президиума Пражского Лингвистического Кружка, и именно там были написаны в 1928 году прославившиеся 'Тезисы' Кружка]. Там же я вспоминал и Теодора, и пропавшего бесследно музыканта.

Обещание Теодору я исполнил, послал через него и со строками о нем письмо Маяковскому. В мае или в июне 1921 г. мы с Нетте в одно и то же время оказались в Берлине. Он рассказывал, как полюбился ему Маяковский, как радушно тот его встретил, и как

I. From left to right: L. JU. Brik, O. M. Brik, R. O. Jakobson, V. V. Majakovskij. Bad Flinsberg, July 1923.

II. From top to bottom: R. Jakobson, T. Nette, Zemit-Zimin. Prague, summer 1920.

они оба 'болтали о Ромке Якобсоне'. [Разумеется, Нетте поведал Маяковскому нашу ночную беседу в каюте, восторг слушателя поэмы и решение бороться против хулителей поэта.] Нетте порадовал меня новостью о выходе *Ста пятидесяти миллионов* и подарил мне эту анонимную книжку. Я настрочил о ней первое оповещение для берлинской газеты *Накануне*. А когда в октябре 1922 года я еще раз попал в Берлин и едва ли не прямо на вечер стихов только что прибывшего в Берлин Маяковского, мы затем сидели впятером — Владимир Владимирович, Лиля Юрьевна, О. М. Брик, [только что приехавший со мной из Праги], Виктор Шкловский и я — за бутылкой вина, Маяковский с ласковой усмешкой напомнил мне: 'А твой Нетте с письмом, он — чудак и очень мил.' [Тот же сердечный отзыв был повторен Маяковским, когда я свиделся с ним и с обоими Бриками летом 1923 года во Флинцберге (см. приложение 1 с тамошним уличным снимком всех нас четверых) и слушал захватывающее исполнение Маяковским поэмы *Про это*.]

С тех пор только раза два я виделся с Нетте, когда он привозил диппочту в Прагу. Мы попрежнему были связаны крепкой дружбой, конечно вспоминали Маяковского, стихи которого он знал уже от доски до доски. Нетте еще в двадцатом году пытался уйти со службы и вовсю приняться за учение, и говорил об этом плане всё более настойчиво. [Посетивший Прагу в апреле 1927 года Маяковский после чтения стихов о Нетте сотрудникам полпредства рассказал мне, что того] всё просили повременить с уже решенным уходом и согласиться на столько-то сверхсрочных поездок. Нетте нехотя уступил, и ненароком пришел конец."

В заключение своего письма я отвечал приветом на привет вдовы Теодора и просил передать ей, что в день нашей последней встречи он с нежностью говорил о ней. А по поводу дошедшей до нее его фотографической карточки, с которой у меня сохранилась копия (см. приложение 2), я отвечал: "Снята она в конце лета 1920 г. в Ростоках под Прагой, перед жилищем д-ра Гиллерсона. Снимал нас, если не изменяет память, секретарь миссии — Левин. Посередине фотографии — Нетте, поверх его — я, а третий — приятель Теодора, тоже дипкурьер — Земит-Зимин. До революции он работал грузчиком в архангельском порту. Добродушный крепыш, он славился и смешил Теодора и всех нас богатырским аппетитом — он в один присест десятками уплетал смачные пражские сосиски."

"Тебе, Ромка, хвали громко" — гласил эмфатический призыв старому другу, вписанный в 1918 году Маяковским в его только что вышедший том стихов. Приобщение товарища Теодора к новой русской поэзии — его ознакомление со стихами Маяковского, а затем с самим стихотворцем и лозунг борьбы с ненавистниками нового слова, внушенный тем же Ромкой филологом тому же товарищу Нетте в пароходной каюте, связываются цепкой ассоциацией сызнова ночной беседой в дип-купе между тем же Теодором и на этот раз Владимиром Маяковским.

По дороге опять из Москвы в Берлин, необычная память Маяковского на всё, что он читал или слышал, уточнила и обогатила воспоминание о чаях, пивавшихся в дип-купе.

"Оды торжественное О" соседит в творчестве Маяковского, мечтателя о грядущей мастерской человечьих воскрешений, с пародийным подступом к одной и той же теме, в данном случае с воскрешением замороженного клопа. Так и за посланием "Товарищу Нетте — пароходу и человеку", воспевающим перевоплощение погибшего дипкурьера в прозванный его именем пароход ("Здравствуй, Нетте, как я рад, что ты живой дымной жизнью труб, канатов и крюков"), непосредственно следуют в цикле стихотворений Маяковского за 1926 год его сатирические стихи под заглавием "Ужасающая фамильярность", едко осуждающие развязное присвоение героических имен вещевому миру. "Есть Марксов проспект и улица Розы", а про Мейерхольда скоро будут спрашивать: "Это тот, который гребешок."

В цикле 1926 года массе злободневных сатир противостоят два лирических послания только что погибшим — Сергею Есенину и Теодору Нетте — с дательной формой адресата в обоих заглавиях и вторым лицом на протяжении обоих текстов. Стихи "Товарищу Нетте" написаны через три месяца после выхода стихов "Сергею Есенину" (16 апр. 1926), и еще в афише кавказской лекции поэта летом 1929 года непосредственно выступает смежность — *Нетте; Есенин* (см. В. Катанян, Москва, 1956, стр. 379). Из двух насильных смертей — одна, от собственной руки, другая от руки пересилившего убийцы, обе издавна знакомы стихам Маяковского. Первая, есенинская, в 1930 году пресекшая бытие самого Маяковского, повторно выступает в его стихах с заклинательным отказом (*Про это*: "Не доставлю радости видеть, что сам от заряда стих"). Вторая — в неравной борьбе с насильниками, в свою очередь сродни поэме *Про это*, и ее разделом "Последняя смерть" ("Со всех винтовок, со всех батарей, с каждого маузера и браунинга *** в упор — за зарядом заряд ***").

Покорное зрелище мирного ложа смерти ненавистно поэту. Он стоит перед выбором: либо смерть "последняя", в терминах поэмы

Про это, т. е., гибель от несчетного врага, или же — "стоит только руку протянуть", — легкий путь самоубийцы.

Даже благочестивое уподобление "на крест" промелькнуло в стихах "Товарищу Нетте", убитому 5 февраля 1926 г. при попытке защиты диппочты от ринувшейся на него шайки налетчиков, а согласно фабуле поэта, растерзанному, но ожившему. (В поэме *Про Это* "последняя смерть" поэта влечет за собой прошение: "воскреси!")

В эпилоге стихов *** *пароходу и человеку* — мученический конец неравной борьбы возведен в единственный вожделенный удел:

> Но в конце хочу —
>   других желаний нету —
> встретить я хочу
>   мой смертный час
> так,
>   как встретил смерть
>   товарищ Нетте.

Сопряжение неминуемой "последней смерти" ("Но у меня выходов нет") и добровольного "расчета с жизнью" объявилось Маяковскому и отстоялось словом и делом в роковом апреле тридцатого года.

Written on Ossabaw Island, Georgia, January 1982, for *Semiosis: In honorem Georgii Lotman*, edited by M. Halle, L. Matejka, K. Pomorska, and B. Uspenskij (Ann Arbor, 1984).

PART THREE

RETROSPECTIONS

MY FAVORITE TOPICS

The question of invariance in the midst of variation has been the dominant topic and methodological device underlying my diversified yet homogeneous research work since my undergraduate attempt of 1911 to outline the formal properties of the earliest Russian iambs. The interplay of invariance and variation continued to attract my attention ever more insistently. Versification, with its diaphonous dichotomies of downbeat–upbeat, break–bridge, and with its correlation of two fundamental metrical concepts, namely design and instance, offered the self-evident possibility of determining the relational invariance that the verse retains across its fluctuations, and of defining and interpreting the scale of the latter.

A monograph of 1923, *On Czech Verse, Primarily in Comparison with Russian*, which was later included, together with a few subsequent papers on metrics, in my *Selected Writings* (henceforth abbreviated as *SW*), vol. V/1979 (pp. 3–223, 570–601), initiated a long and detailed discussion about the relationship between poetic forms and language. This investigation required a careful delineation of the diverse functions assigned by a given language to its prosodic elements, a delineation that plays a substantial role in the relative application of those elements in the corresponding system of versification.

The continued inquiry into this problem, which ties together metrics and linguistics, impelled me to elucidate and exemplify such essentially topological questions as, for instance, the invariants retained and the variations experienced throughout the diverse works of one and the same poet or of different poets within the same literary school, as well as the question of the metrical cleavage between single literary genres. The transformation undergone by certain verse types all along the history of a given poetic language called for the same kind of treatment. I used chiefly Slavic, especially Czech, verse types as experimental material.

The convergent and divergent metrical rules in a set of similar languages, whether cognate or remote, brought me within the reach of comparative metrics in its two aspects, the historical and the typological. By collating the oral traditions of the different Slavic peoples I ventured to uncover the rudiments of Proto-Slavic versification (*Oxford Slavonic Papers* III/1952, pp. 21–66, re-edited in *Selected Writings* IV/1966, pp. 414–463), thereby contributing to Meillet's search for Indo-European verse. Concurrently, advances in metrical typology led me to an ever more detailed extraction of invariants and thus towards a closer insight into metrical universals, as was emphasized in my study "Linguistics and Poetics" (*SW* III/1981, pp. 18–51). An examination of distant metrical phenomena, such as Germanic alliteration, the admissive rules of Mordvinian meters, or the modular design of Chinese regulated verse, enhanced my search for the universal foundations of versification (see *SW* V: *On Verse, Its Masters and Explorers*).

It was the difference between the two classes of prosodic elements, the sense-discriminative function on the one hand, and the delimitative one on the other, that naturally became a topic of discussion in my metrical monograph of 1923, along with the simultaneous application of the same functional approach to the entire sound pattern of language. The book in question proposed the name "phonology" for the study of speech sounds with regard to meaning and asserted the strictly relational character of the sense-discriminative entities, linked to each other by binary oppositions as components of the ever hierarchical phonological systems. Since my first steps in phonology I have been continuously attracted to the search for the ultimate constituents of language and the powerful structural laws of the network they comprise. I endeavored to trace the allusions to the existence of such ultimate entities in the wisdom of antiquity and the emergence one century ago of the concept "phoneme" in the perspicacious works of a few bold linguistic pioneers (see *SW* II/1971: "Toward a Nomothetic Science of Language", pp. 369–602).

The breaking-down of the phoneme into "distinctive features" as the actually ultimate components of the phonological system suggested itself and was achieved toward the end of the 1930's (cf. *SW* I/1962: *Phonological Studies*, 221–223, 272–316, 418–434, and *Six leçons sur le son et le sens*, 1976). This task demanded a rigorous insight into the common denominator of multiple variables; the notion of contextual variants gradually became more pertinent and more precisely elaborated, and the consistent segmentation of speech proved to be feasible (cf. Jakobson & Linda Waugh, *The Sound Shape of Language*, 1979).

The structure of phonological systems is of great linguistic interest; the typological comparison of such systems reveals significant underlying laws and prompts the final conclusion that "the sound patterns of single languages are varying implementations of universal invariants" (*ibid.*, p. 234). Through the argument of the incompatibility and equivalence of certain distinctions we arrived at the conclusion of the highly limited number of valid distinctive features.

The phonological quest for relational invariants proved to be applicable to the other levels of language as well, and especially to the fundamental question of the interconnection between general and particular (more properly speaking, contextual) meanings of the grammatical categories. This is apparent, e.g., in my treatment of grammatical cases and of the duplex overlapping structures labeled "shifters", which separate verbs and pronouns from nouns (*SW* II, section A, pp. 3–208). In my paper "Russian Conjugation" (*ibid.*, pp. 119–129), the same criterion of invariance is seen to underlie the grammatical form and makes it possible to predict the entire paradigm. The entangled morphonology of Gilyak required a similar treatment (*ibid.*, 72–102).

Similar to the way in which the realization of the intimate relation between the sound level of language and verse led to new insights in the field of metrics, the new approach to grammatical categories enabled me and my collaborators of the last two decades to outline the significant, but until recently underrated, role of grammatical tropes in poetry. Cf. *SW* III/1981: *Poetry of Grammar and Grammar of Poetry*, with many analyzed ("parsed") poems of varied tongues and centuries.

The grammatical parallelism widespread in world poetry (*ibid.*, pp. 98–135) consists in a combination of invariants and variables that speaks eloquently to the users of the given poetic canon but that still demands closer scientific analysis, a technique that should prove equally fruitful for both linguistics and poetics, particularly as regards the intricate syntactic questions involved.

The elaboration of a linguistically oriented inquiry into verbal art necessitated a wide adoption of the invariance test. It was with this in mind that I tentatively approached the question of poets' myths, e.g. "The Statue in Puškin's Poetic Mythology" and the monolithic buildup of Majakovskij's mythic imagery (see *SW* V, pp. 237–281 and 355–413).

In defiance of the accustomed mechanistic effacement of the boundary between the writer's individualized production and the collectivistic orientation of oral traditions, P. Bogatyrev's and my lengthy fieldwork in folklore led us to insist on the different correlation of invariance and variability in oral tradition as the latter's specific feature, fraught with consequences. It was precisely this point of departure that gave the impetus to my volume of studies prepared for the most part during the

1940's and devoted to the Slavic, especially Russian, oral and written epic tradition (*SW* IV/1966: *Slavic Epic Studies*; cf. *Premesse di storia letteraria slava*, Milano, 1975), as well as to my deliberations on comparative Slavic and Indo-European mythology (cf. *SW* VII/1984) and especially on its vestiges in languages and folklore.

Returning to the inferences I have made on the basis of my phonological and grammatical research, I should like merely to list several further areas that belong among my favorite themes of investigation.

Time and space, usually regarded as extrinsic factors in relation to the verbal code, prove to be veritable constituents of the latter. In the speakers' and listeners' code any change in progress is simultaneously present in its initial and final forms as stylistic variants, one more archaic and the other more advanced, both being mutually interchangeable in the speech community and even in the use of its individual members (as I remarked, e.g., about the Common Slavic accentual evolution in my three essays included in the expanded edition of *SW* I/1971, 664–699). Since my earliest report of 1927 to the newborn Prague Linguistic Circle I have pleaded for the removal of the alleged antinomy synchrony/diachrony and have propounded instead the idea of permanently dynamic synchrony, at the same time underscoring the presence of static invariants in the diachronic cut of language (cf. *SW* I, 1–116, 202–220).

The verbal code is convertible also with respect to the factor of space. It contains a set of variants serving for different degrees of adaptation to interlocutors of diverse dialectal and social distance. Diffusion of linguistic characters results from such variations, and during the 1930's I devoted several essays (reproduced in *SW* I, 137–201, 234–246) to one of the extreme manifestations of the space factor in the life of languages, the interlingual rapprochement termed *Sprachbund* by N. Trubetzkoy; and later I repeatedly, though so far in vain, appealed for phonological atlases of vast territories, a task with undoubtedly surprising vistas.

A concentration on questions of the hitherto neglected, ontogenetic aspect of our science occupied my sojourn of 1939–1941 in three Scandinavian countries and resulted in the book *Kindersprache, Aphasie und allgemeine Lautgesetze* (Uppsala, 1941; cf. *SW* I, pp. 328–401), as well as in many later observations and reflections on the nearly regular order of children's verbal acquisitions and of aphasic losses (see *Studies on Child Language and Aphasia*, 1971). The intimate connection between mastering language and metalanguage was for me an instructive conclusion from observations of children's linguistic development, observations which induced me to propose a revision in the network of verbal functions (cf. my Presidential Address of 1956 to the Linguistic Society of America, "Metalanguage as a Linguistic Problem", reproduced above, p. 113ff.).

My continuous studies in aphasia can be summed up as follows: "The basic binary concepts viewed in the linguistic quest as the key to understanding the obvious dichotomy of aphasic disturbances, namely dyads such as Encoding/Decoding, Syntagmatic/Paradigmatic, and Contiguity/Similarity, gradually found access to the advanced neuropsychological treatment of aphasic enigmas" ("Brain and Language", reprinted above, p. 163ff.). The multifarious linguistic and poetic manifestations of the last dyad, which may be outlined as Metonymy/Metaphor (cf. *SW* II, pp. 239–259), urgently demand a deeper and wider scrutiny.

The ever increasing recognition of the biological roots of *language* does not cancel out the equally relevant social premises of *languages* — the coaction of an interlocutor and the indispensability of learning. Since the 1920's, spent in Prague, I have perused one of the most impressive displays of the creative power of language, the history of Slavic self-determination, which was supported from the beginning by linguistic incentives such as the Pentecostal miracle and the vernacularization of the Holy Communion. (My various contributions to this topic are collected in *SW* VI/1984: *Early Slavic Paths and Crossroads*.)

I have actively looked forward to the development of semiotics, which helps to delineate the specificity of language among all the various systems of signs, as well as the invariants binding language to related sign systems (cf. the present volume, p. 199ff.).

To conclude, I avow that binary solutions attract me, and I believe in the mutual salutory influence of *linguistics and philology*. No doubt, my linguistic reasonings often profited from my painstaking philological excurses treating such intricate sources as Old Church Slavonic songs and poems, both related to and autonomous from their Byzantine models. The interplay of linguistic theory and philological art proved helpful in treating the most peculiar displays of Slavic verbal culture, such as vestiges of the earliest Russian vernacular, or the *ornatus dificilis* of the Old Russian *Igor' Tale*, or the Czech (labeled "Canaan") glosses in early medieval Hebrew texts, or the Czech mock mystery of the XIVth century with its daring interlacing of sacred, secular, and lascivious motifs, or the Hanseatic manual of colloquial Russian compiled in Pskov on the threshold of the Times of Trouble.

Yet what must have primarily influenced my approach to poetics and linguistics was my proximity to the poets and painters of the avant-garde. Thus, my programmatic monograph on Xlebnikov's verbal art, written in 1919 and printed in 1921 (see *SW* V, pp. 299–354), owes certain of its arguments to my meetings with this unparalleled poet, which began on the eve of 1914. A few weeks later, in a Moscow cafe, the "Alpine Rose" I endeavored to elucidate the essentials of Xlebnikov's poetics to the unyielding Italian guest Filippo Tommaso Marinetti. I would like to add that my article "Futurism" (cf. *SW* III, p. 717f.), published August 2, 1919 in the Moscow newspaper *Iskusstvo*, praised the Italian painters of that trend for their expulsion of absolutes and for dispensing once and for all with one-way static perception: the paths leading toward experimental art and toward the new science appealed to us precisely because of their common invariants.

Written in Peacham, Vermont, August 1980, and first published in Italian in *Premi "Antonio Feltrinelli" 1980* (Rome: Accademia Nazionale dei Lincei) on the occasion of the author having been awarded the Premio Internazionale per la Filologia e Linguistica.

ON THE DIALECTICS OF LANGUAGE

The 1982 Hegel-Preis was for me not only a most high honor, but also a quite unexpected and total surprise. I tried and tried to find an explanation for the Society's apparent view that my immersion in Hegel went beyond personal criteria and touched upon present general, acute interests in the history of science. Hence I was led to realize that my lifelong tendency to overcome in scholarship mere short-sighted empiricism on the one hand and abstract speculative dogmatism on the other has become a vital component of today's scientific exploits. The recent declaration by Ernst Mayr of his great attraction to Hegel's scheme of thesis-antithesis-synthesis (*The Growth of Biological Thought*, 1982, p. 9) is a telling example.

The *hic et nunc* of linguistic reality brings every human being face to face with a multitude of spatial fields and temporal moments, and any production or perception of language reaches its steady manifestation through the selection and combination of suitable entities from within this double multitude. Our selective and combinatory verbal activities are generally restrained and directed by a system of acting rules. It has frequently occurred to linguistic interpreters that the use of language was being conceived without respect to these rules. Speech production and perception in their temporal changes remained the only focus of scholarly observation. The opposite trend was the view that *rules* confine the production and perception of language at any given stage, and these rules, promoted as the chief subject of linguistic study, were termed *langue* versus *parole*, or "code" versus "message", or "competence" versus "performance". A singleness was attributed to the rules of competence, and this was resolutely superposed on the plurality of performances. I have objected to this strict mechanistic rupture between invariant and variants: no speaker appears to be limited to one single code. In essence he holds to the same language with the closest and most distant members of his environment, yet constantly modifies his manifold code and thus adapts his competence to diverse interlocutors, different topics, and his own ceaselessly varying verbal styles. There is, as in any system, an incessant linkage of variants and invariance, a permanent unity and diversity of phonological, morphological, syntactic, lexical, and variational means. The universal phenomenon of dynamic synchrony points to a constant interchange of the code.

Both in various self-adaptations to the interlocutor (verbal conformisms) and in different degrees of mutual repulsions (verbal nonconformisms), we submit our code to a maximal variability, an inconstancy both in space and in time. Such has been my recognition of the inseparability between invariance and variability. This thesis appeals to me as the *conditio sine qua non* of scientific analysis from the early steps of Hegel's dialectics to the present-day sciences, especially linguistics, and our indebtedness to the Master's inspirations is far from exhausted. In particular, time and space are two mutually inseparable, inner factors of language, and the latter and its interpretation remain inalienable from these factors. Every verbal activity implies incessant selections and decisions between locomotor opportunities which suggest themselves, regardless of whether it concerns an intimately merged idiom or a distant coincidence, as well as which stage of the mutation in progress — an imminent archaism or the final phase of innovation.

Written in June, 1982, on the occasion of the author's having been awarded the Hegel Prize of the city of Stuttgart. First published in R. Jakobson, H.-G. Gadamer, E. Holenstein, *Das Erbe Hegels* II (Frankfurt am Main: Suhrkamp, 1984), 8–10.

LIST OF ILLUSTRATIONS

Between pages 364 and 365:

I. From left to right: L. JU. Brik, O. M. Brik, R. O. Jakobson, V. V. Majakovskij. Bad Flinsberg, July 1923.

II. From top to bottom: R. Jakobson, T. Nette, Zemit-Zimin. Prague, summer 1920.

INDEX OF NAMES

Aarsleff, H. 198
Abbott, G. F. 22
Adam of Bremen 3
Adrianova-Peretc, V. P. 325
Afremov, F. N. 279
Alajouanine, Th. 137
Albrecht, C. 10
Alcman 31
Alekseev, M. P. 356
Aljagrov, R. (pseudonym of R. Jakobson) 358f.
Andersen, H. C. 64, 358, 360
Anderson, J. M. 196
Angelergues, R. 129
Aničkov, E. 33
Annenkov, P. V. 355
Anučin, D. 36
Aquinas, Thomas, St. 192
Armstrong, D. 179
Arnaudov, M. 21
Arnauld, A. 197
Arndt, H. W. 200
Arnold, E. 194f.
Aronoff, M. 352
Aseev, N. 281
Augustine, St. 88, 99
Aureuga, R. d' 193
Avalle, D. S. 211
Avdusin, D. A. 332, 334
Avraamij, St. 33

Bally, C. 208, 212
Balonov, L. J. 59, 166ff., 170, 172, 176, 178, 286
Baranovskaya, S. A. 64

Bargmann, S. 260
Baric, H. 21
Barinova, G. A. 64
Barkau, D. 178
Barous, K. 38
Barrado Sánchez, M. 196
Barsov, A. A. 283
Bartholomae, C. 20
Baru, A. 166, 178
Basanavičius, J. 37
Bassin, F. V. 162
Baudoin, P. 218
Baudoin de Courtenay, J. 43, 82, 126, 128f., 131, 148ff., 151f., 156, 219, 229, 232f., 252, 272, 286
Beethoven, L. von 212
Békésy, G. von 104
Bel, A. F. G. 196
Beneš, B. 304
Bentham, J. 117
Benveniste, É. 27, 29, 31, 39, 49f., 85, 99, 128, 130, 140, 185, 198f., 239f., 250
Berko, J. 134
Berneker, E. 328
Berry, F. 342
Beševliev, I. 10
Besso, M. 260, 264
Bever, T. G. 173, 178
Beyn, E. S. 136
Biegeleisen, H. 11
Bierwisch, M. 139
Birnbaum, D. 331, 335
Blagoj, D. D. 353
Blasius, St. 8

INDEX OF NAMES

Bloch, B. 272
Bloomfield, L. 90, 118f., 122, 235f., 250, 266ff., 269ff., 272ff., 275ff., 278
Blumstein, S. 131, 137, 139
Boas, F. 110, 153f., 156, 235, 268, 277
Bocheński, J. M. 188f., 195
Boehner, P. 192, 195
Boethius Dacus 192, 193f.
Bogatyrëv, K. P. 293
Bogatyrëv, P. G. 10, 279, 281, 293–302, 373
Bohnenberger, K. 48
Bohr, N. 111, 161, 263
Boisacq, E. 42
Bolzano, B. 202ff., 208
Bonfante, G. 13, 72
Bouazis, C. 211
Bradke, P. von 42
Bradshaw, J. L. 173, 178
Bragina, N. N. 165, 174, 178
Braine, M. 145
Braque, G. 125, 261
Braun, J. 201
Bréal, M. 239, 241
Brekle, H. H. 198
Brender, F. 23
Brik, L. JU. 365
Brik, O. M. 281, 365
Broadbent, D. E. 164, 178
Broca, P. 175, 178
Browne, M. W. 179
Brückner, A. 10, 18, 25f., 29, 37, 42f., 45ff.
Brugmann, K. 81, 131, 220f., 235f., 266, 269
Bruner, J. S. 86
Būga, K. 39
Bühler, G. 20
Bühler, K. 115
Bulaxovskij, L. 17
Bultaxe, C. A. M. 180
Burian, J. F. 297
Burks, A. W. 179
Burnašev, V. P. 323
Bursill-Hall, G. L. 187, 190, 195
Buslaev, A. A. 279

Buslaev, F. I. 282
Bystron, J. 10f.

Caesar, Gaius Julius 89
Campbell, B. G. 103
Candrea, I. 22, 24, 26
Cannicott, S. M. 165, 178
Caraman, P. 47
Cassirer, E. 212, 262
Catherine II 146
Chadwick, H. M. 19
Chaplin, C. 296
Chiarello, R. 173, 178
Chomsky, N. 89, 198, 272
Cjavlovskaja, T. G. 353
Clark, H. H. 71
Clemm, W. 219
Collitz, H. 273f.
Copernicus, N. 306
Coseriu, E. 187, 279, 282
Critchley, M. 178
Croce, B. 197
Cross, S. H. 18, 35, 324
Cvetkova, L. S. 137
Čajkanović, V. 30
Černý, F. 46
Černyx, P. JA. 332
Čiurlionis, M. 358, 360
Čiževskij, D. I. 330
Čukovskij, K. I. 120, 157f.
Čulnović-Konstantinović, V. 21
Čurmaeva, N. V. 21

Dal', V. I. 18, 323, 336
Damásio, A. R. 172f., 178
Damasio, H. 172f., 178
Dante, A. 103
Darmesteter, A. 150, 239
Davidson, K. 179
Deglin, V. L. 59, 166ff., 170, 172, 176, 178, 286
De Morgon, A. 120, 248
Deržavin, G. R. 349–352
Descartes, R. 197
Dickenmann, E. 30
Diels, P. 17

INDEX OF NAMES

Dittrich, Z. R. 12
Dmitriev, L. A. 325, 327
Dmitrij, Prince 327
Dobrovský, J. 37
Dobroxotova, T. A. 165, 174, 178
Dobrynja 18
Donaldson, M. 71
Donatus 196
Dostál, A. 45
Doyle, A. C. 114
Dubois, J. 136
Duchesne-Guillemin, J. 27, 29
Duclos, C. P. 197
Dukas, H. 258
Dumézil, G. 15, 27, 31, 40ff., 43, 49
Duns Scotus, John 190
Duridanov, I. 16

Eckert, G. 21
Eggert, G. H. 175, 178
Ehrenfels, C. von 216, 301
Einstein, A. 83f., 92, 105, 254, 264, 287f.
Eisenring, M. E. 200
Eliade, M. 42
Elijah 6
Elkana, Y. 100
Emin, N. O. 27
Engler, R. 129, 148, 152, 207, 209, 222
Erben, K. J. 298
Erbslöh, G. 360
Èrdedi, I. 13
Erdmann, K. O. 194
Erlich, V. 264, 361
Ernout, A. 42
Esenin, S. 366
Es'kova, N. A. 64
Estal Fuentes, E. del 196
Evreinov, N. 294

Fant, C. G. M. 59ff.
Feuchtwanger, E. 140
Filin, F. P. 22, 327
Filipović, M. S. 16f., 21, 24
Flajšhans, V. 38

Florovskij, G. V. 312
Formozis, P. E. 21
Fortunatov, F. F. 91, 157, 220, 282, 284
Foucart, P. 240
Foucault, M. 197
Fraenger, W. 303
Fraenkel, F. 37
Frank, P. 254
Franz, L. 14
Frege, G. 119
Friedrich, J. 23, 39
Fries, C. 267, 276
Frinta, A. 46

Gainotti, G. 174, 178
Galaburda, A. M. 166, 178
Gal'kovskij, N. M. 10, 23
Gamkrelidze, T. V. 315ff.
Garcia, C. 196
Gates, A. 173, 178
Gazzaniga, M. S. 137, 164, 178
Gelb, A. 128
Georgiev, V. 336
Gerov, N. 19
Geschwind, N. 165f., 169, 174f., 177f.
Gillerson, Dr. 363, 365
Gimbutas, M. 48
Glinka, G. 92
Godel, R. 129, 208, 222, 229, 241, 247
Goethe, J. W. von 143, 160
Gogol', N. V. 70
Goldstein, K. 128
Golling, J. 197
Gonda, J. 40
Goodglass, H. 131, 134, 137ff.
Gorodcov, V. 11
Grabmann, M. 189
Grammatin, N. F. 324
Grégoire, A. 141, 321, 324
Gregory (of Nazianzus) the Theologian, St. 23
Greimas, A. J. 32
Grierson, H. J. C. 342
Grimm, The Brothers 109
Grimm, J. 274

INDEX OF NAMES 383

Griswold, H. D. 41
Gross, M. 138
Gudzij, N. K. 300
Guillelmus Occam: see *Occam, William of*
Guillelmus de Shyreswoode: see *William of Sherwood*
Gvozdev, A. N. 120, 141, 157ff.

Haase, F. 10
Hadamard, J. 255f.
Hájek, T. 36
Hajný, A. 27, 52
Hall, R. A., Jr. 198
Halle, M. 60f., 138, 349ff., 352, 367
Halliday, A. M. 165, 179
Hamilton, Allan McLane 139
Hanako 101
Harris, Z. S. 267
Hartmann, E. von 149
Hattori, S. 101f.
Haugen, E. 265
Havers, W. 13
Havet, L. 238, 242
Havranek, B. 328
Hayes, J. R. 71
Hécaen, H. 129f., 134, 136
Heidegger, M. 190
Heine, H. 109
Helmold 3, 5, 17f., 30
Hesiod 20, 31
Hillebrandt, A. 40ff., 46, 236
Hills, E. C. 13
Hirt, H. 20
Hitler, A. 14
Hjemslev, L. 299
Hockett, C. F. 266, 270
Hoene-Wroński, J. M. 201f.
Hoenigswald, H. M. 278
Holenstein, E. 204, 259
Holton, G. 83, 254, 264
Honzl, J. 297
Hoops, J. 44, 48
Hopkins, G. M. 214f.
Hora, J. 109
Horace 243

Hornung, B. V. 279
House, H. 215
Huberin, K. 36
Hugo de Sancto Victore 192
Humboldt, W. von 107, 197, 272, 281
Hunt, J. 134
Hunt, R. W. 192, 195
Husserl, E. 189f., 203f., 208f., 281
Hymes, D. H. 186

Igor', son of Svjatoslav 33, 321f., 331
Infeld, L. 264
Ingalls, D. H. H. 48
Isidorus Hispalensis (Isidore of Saville) 217
Isserlin, M. 128, 134
Istrin, V. 35
Ivanov, I. 16, 19
Ivanov, V. V. 19f., 34, 44, 59, 70, 165, 169, 174f., 179, 315ff., 358, 360

Jackson, J. H. 95, 139, 169f., 175, 179
Jackson, R. L. 361
Jagić, V. 29, 37
Jakobsen, T. 186
Jakobson, R. 29f., 36f., 39, 45, 59ff., 64, 101, 113, 123, 126ff., 132, 136, 160, 163, 166, 168, 172ff., 176f., 179, 191, 193, 205, 208, 217, 237, 245, 263, 266, 269, 281, 307, 321f., 326, 328, 330, 334, 345, 362, 365, 372
Jakovlev, N. F. 279ff.
Jakubinskij, L. P. 17
James, H. 117
James, W. 248
Jan of Holešov 46
Janáček, L. 298
Jánošik, J. 303
Jaroslav, son of Vsevolod 322
Jarxo, B. I. 281
Jensen, S. S. 192
Jespersen, O. 60, 186, 270, 272
Jireček, J. 36f.
Johannes de Rus 189
Johannis Dacus 192

INDEX OF NAMES

Johansson, K. F. 44
John the Exarch 69
John of Salisbury 90, 190, 195
Jones, D. 272
Joos, M. 273
Jordanes 4
Jordanes von Sachsen 189

Kaegi, A. 20
Kakuberi, T. D. 179
Kalima, J. 31
Kantemir, A. D. 353
Kaper, W. 157
Karačić, V. 22
Karcevskij, S. 265
Katanjan, V. 366
Kawamoto, S. 107
Keiler, A. 177
Kemp, P. 11
Kemper, T. L. 178
Kepler, J. 254
Khagani 9
Kiefer, F. 196
Kimura, D. 164, 168, 172, 179
Kind, T. 22
King, F. L. 168, 179
Kirša Danilov 70
Kirsanov, S. 92
Klein, F. 82, 252
Kleinschmidt, G. 20
Ključevskij, V. O. 282, 284
Kluckhohn, C. 102
Knox, C. 168, 179
Köhler, W. 145
Koff, E. 172, 180
Kolár, J. 304
Kořinek, J. M. 26, 51
Korš, F. E. 280
Korzuxina, G. F. 332f.
Kotljarenko, A. N. 327
Kreeger, L. C. 179
Kretschmer, P. 42
Kristeva, J. 140
Kroeber, A. L. 102
Kručenyx, A. 353, 358ff.
Krueger, F. 144

Kruszewski, M. (Kruševskij, N.) 30, 82, 148ff., 151f., 156, 229, 286
Kuiper, F. B. J. 38
Kukenheim, L. 190
Kuroda, S.-Y. 190
Kusaka, S. 254
Kušelevym-Bezborodko, G. 325

Laguna, G. A. de 67
Lakoff, R. 198
Lamanskij, V. I. 33
Lambert, J. H. 200ff., 204, 208
Lancelot, C. 197f.
Landgraf, G. 197
Lange-Stender 37
Laroche, E. 42
Lausberg, H. 217
Lavut, P. I. 362
Lázaro Carreter, C. F. 196
Lazicius, J. 22
Laziczius, Gy. 121
Lecours, A. R. 131
Leibniz, G. W. 190
Leicht, P.-S. 10
LeMay, M. 178
Lermontov, M. 109
Leskien, A. 20, 37, 220, 222, 266, 269, 271
Lévi-Strauss, C. 32, 118, 240
Levin 365
Lhermitte, F. 131
Liaño Pacheco, J. M. 196
Lidén, E. 19
Lieb, I. C. 204f.
Linacer, T. 196
Lindblom, B. 61
Lixačev, D. S. 300, 304, 322, 325
Lobačevskij, N. 250
Locke, J. 190f., 199ff., 202, 204, 208
Lomonosov, M. V. 282, 355
Lotman, JU. M. 322, 362, 367
Ludwig, A. 20
Lüders, H. 42
Lukaševič, P. 358f.
Lullus, R. 193
Lunačarskij, A. V. 363

INDEX OF NAMES

Luria, A. R. 132, 137, 163, 176, 179
L'vov, A. S. 333

Macdonell, A. A. 20, 29, 40, 42, 48
Mácha, K. H. 298
Máchal, H. 19
Máchal, J. 10
Machek, V. 10, 25, 38, 47, 51
Macůrek, J. 17
Maegaard, J. 216
Magdeburg, Archbishop of 24
Maikov, L. 38
Majakovskij, V. V. 264, 281, 353, 355, 362–367, 373
Malinowski, B. 115
Malmberg, B. 60
Mandelbaum, D. G. 64f., 71
Mandel'štam, O. 281
Mannhardt, J. W. E. 22, 37
Mansikka, V. J. 10, 47
Manthey, F. 192
Mareš, F. V. 332
Marguliés, A. 335
Marinetti, F. T. 358, 360, 376
Marinov, D. 11, 21, 23
Martin, R. J. 192
Martin de Dacia 192
Marty, A. 114, 190
Martynov, D. P. 358, 360
Maruszewski, M. 163, 179
Marvell, A. 341–348
Marx, K. 309
Masaryk, T. G. 234
Matejka, L. 302ff., 367
Mathesius, V. 265, 279
Mauro, T. de 236
Mayrhofer, M. 40
Meillet, A. 10, 14, 19
Mažiulis, A. 37
Meillet, A. 39, 42f., 131, 222, 231, 239ff., 242f., 247
Mel'čuk, I. I. 71
Menasce, P. J. de 27
Mencken, H. L. 13
Mendeleev, D. I. 252
Merkulova, V. A. 336

Meščerskij, Prince A. I. 351
Meyer, K. H. 10
Meyer, L. B. 216
Meyerhold, V. E. 298, 366
Michel, C. 240
Michelsen, C. 197
Michelson, T. 272
Mikkola, J. J. 45
Miklosich, F. 24, 45, 47, 197
Miljukov, P. N. 282, 284
Miller, V. F. 34, 282
Milner, B. 164f., 172, 177, 179f.
Milner, J. C. 140
Mindadze, A. A. 172, 179
Mladenov, S. 17, 22
Molière, J.-B. 117
Mondrian, P. 261
Monrad-Krohn, G. H. 177, 179
Moody, E. A. 195
Morris, C. 250, 267, 276
Mosidze, V. M. 179
Moszyński, K. 10
Moses of Xoren 27
Mountcastle, V. B. 179
Mullally, J. P. 188
Musorgskij, M. 298

Napoleon 118
Nasonov, A. N. 17
Nava, G. 244
Navarro Funes, A. 196
Naville, A. 208
Naville, É. 240f.
Naville, M. 237.
Nejedlý, Z. 46
Nejštadt, V. I. 279
Nette, T. 362–367
Nicolaus de Bohemia 189
Nicolaus de Parisiis 191
Niederle, L. 10, 17, 23f., 26, 29f., 37, 46
Niedermann, M. 23
Nikolaenko, N. 178
Nikol'skij, N. 11
Nyberg, H. S. 29

Occam (Okham), William of 192, 195
O'Davoren 40
Öhman, S. 61
Oehrle, R. T. 352
Ogibenin, B. L. 303
Oldenberg, H. 41f.
Oleg 33, 321f., 329, 331
Olsen, M. 48
O'Mahony, B. E. 187
O'Neill, E. 114
Onishi, Dr. 124
O'Rahilly, T. F. 40
Osljabja 327
Osolsobě, I. 171, 179
Otto, A. 188, 192
Otto of Bamberg 3

Padučeva, E. V. 76
Palm, T. 10
Palmer, L. R. 8, 31, 51
Pāṇini 272
Panov, M. V. 65
Parker, D. 115
Pascoli, G. 244f.
Passy, P. 272
Pasternak, B. L. 109, 281
Patera, A. 45
Peirce, C. S. 81, 87, 90, 103, 117f., 120, 133, 147, 174, 179, 190f., 195, 201, 204ff., 207ff., 210, 213ff., 216, 229, 233, 248, 276f., 294
Peisker, J. 49
Peresvet, Monk 326f.
Peretc, V. N. 324f.
Petrus Abaelardus 188, 190, 195
Petrus Helias 195
Petrus Hispanus 188ff., 195
Petrus de Limoges 185
Petrus, V. P. 324
Pettazoni, R. 40
Peuser, G. 164, 179
Picasso, P. 125, 298, 356
Piccard, J. 257
Pick, A. 128, 134
Pike, K. 267

Pinborg, J. 185, 187, 189ff., 192f.
Pipping, H. 60
Pisani, V. 15, 17, 33, 37, 42f., 48f.
Planck, M. 260, 262
Pogodin, A. 34, 43
Pokorny, J. 20, 25, 40, 44
Polivanov, E. 126
Polivka, J. 295
Pomorska, K. 303, 367
Pompidou, G. 359
Ponomarev, A. 34
Pos, H. 122, 144
Potebnja, A. A. 47, 111, 323
Prangišvili, A. S. 161f
Priscian (Priscianus) 195f.
Pritsak, O. O. 322
Prokopios 4
Propp, V. JA. 32, 297
Prutkov, K. 308
Pugačev, E. 306
Puhvel, J. 41
Puškin, A. S. 120, 293, 353–356, 362, 373

Quine, W. V. O. 118

Radin, E. P. 358ff.
Ragozin, S. I. 279
Rainis, J. 363
Razin, S. 306
Rechel-Cohn, A. 264
Rees, A. 40
Rees, B. 40
Reformatskij, A. A. 63, 65, 279
Renou, L. 27, 29, 49
Rešel, T. 36
Ribérac, A. D. de 193
Rijk, L. M. de 188, 194f.
Robertus Kilwardby 191
Robins, R. H. 187
Roos, H. 192
Rosen, G. 254
Ross, A. S. C. 134
Roth, R. 48
Rotta, P. 187
Rozanova, O. 359

INDEX OF NAMES

Rozwadowski, J. 10, 14
Rudy, S. 32, 317, 361
Russel, B. 257
Ruwet, N. 140, 196
Rybakov, B. A. 322

Salomon, E. 134
Sanctis, F. de 197
Sanctius Brocensis (Sánchez de las Brozas), F. 100, 196f.
Sapir, E. 64f., 71, 85, 90, 98, 122, 154ff., 161f., 167f., 180, 188, 262, 266f., 270ff., 273ff., 276f., 278
Saussure, F. de 39, 82, 99, 125, 129, 148, 152f., 156, 194, 198, 207ff., 210ff., 215, 221f., 224ff., 227ff., 230ff., 233f., 236ff., 239ff., 242ff., 245ff., 249, 269ff., 272, 295, 317
Savickij, P. N. 312
Saxo Grammaticus 3, 6, 17
Schapiro, M. 267
Schiller, F. von 160
Schilpp, P. A. 257
Schleicher, A. 220, 223f.
Schmaus, A. 12
Schmidt, J. 20, 232
Schneeweis, E. 11, 21
Schönberg, A. 216
Schooneveld, C. H. van 179
Schrijnen, J. 298
Schroeder, L. von 20
Schütz, J. 45
Schützenberger, M. P. 138
Schultz, W. 202
Scioppius, G. 197
Sealey, R. 37
Sechehaye, A. 125f., 129, 148, 208, 212, 229
Seelig, C. 260
Seiler, H. 67
Senn, A. 23
Sergeev-Censkij, S. I. 323
Seržputovskij, A. 10
Severjanin, I. 359
Shakespeare, W. 115, 117
Shankland, R. S. 257

Shapiro, S. 65
Shaw, G. B. 117
Sheffield, A. D. 273
Sherbowitz-Wetzor, O. P. 18, 35
Sherozia, A. E. 161f.
Sievers, E. 60
Siger de Cortraco 188
Silverstein, M. 236
Simmons, E. J. 330
Simon Dacus 188, 192
Simpson, G. G. 97
Skok, P. 22f.
Sobolevskij, A. 10, 17, 23, 34
Sofonija of Rjazan' 326, 328
Sovijärvi, A. 182
Sperry, R. W. 137, 164, 169, 178, 180
Speziali, P. 260
Sreznevskij, I. 24, 30, 33, 45
Starobinski, J. 194, 211, 215, 242ff., 245ff.
Stéfanini, J. 187
Steinitz, W. 298, 304
Steinthal, H. 219
Stender-Petersen, A. 12, 16, 18
Stepun, F. 358, 360
Stevanović, M. 331
Stojkov, S. 335
Stoilov, A. P. 21
Stradivarius 104
Stravinsky, I. 186, 198, 216, 283, 298
Stumpf, C. 145
Suvčinskij, P. P. 312
Suxotin, A. M. 267
Suxovo-Kobylin, A. V. 323
Svešnikov, P. P. 279
Svjatoslav (Grand Prince) 33, 321ff., 329ff., 334
Swadesh, M. 267
Sweet, H. 272
Syrku, P. 27, 53
Szeftel, M. 321
Szemerényi, O. 42
Šaxmatov, A. A. 33, 280
Ščerba, L. V. 126
Ševoroškin, V. V. 64f.
Šilling, E. M. 280

Šklovskij, V. 365
Špet, G. G. 281
Švačkin, N. X. 157f.
Švedova, N. JU. 76

Tacitus 40
Tarski, A. 117, 289
Taszychi, W. 30
Taylor, J. 179
Tedesko, P. 50
Terracini, B. 234, 236
Tesnière, L. 132, 266
Thietmar of Merseburg 3
Thom, R. 138, 212, 253
Thomas de Erfordia (Thomas of Erfurt) 190
Thompson, S. 267
Thorpe, W. H. 106
Thurot, C. 188, 191
Tiktin, H. 24, 26
Titunik, I. R. 304
Tixomirov, M. N. 332
Tixonravov, N. 33
Tobolka, Z. V. 36
Tolstoy, L. N. 147
Tomaševskij, B. V. 281
Toporov, V. N. 34
Trautmann, R. 30
Trnka, B. 265
Trojanović, S. 16
Trubetzkoy, N. S. 69, 82f., 105, 123, 127, 169, 180, 266, 299, 305–313, 335
Tsurumi, Shunsuke 101, 103
Tvorogov, O. V. 325f.
Twaddell, W. F. 345

Ujváry, Z. 21
Unbegaun, B. 10, 12, 21
Urbańczyk, S. 10
Ušakov, D. N. 280
Usener, H. 46
Uspenskij, V. 367
Uznadze, D. N. 160f.

Václavik, A. 17

Vaillant, A. 68, 70
Vasmer, M. 65, 336
Velten, H. V. 267
Vendryès, J. 20, 40, 42
Vengerov, S. A. 353, 355
Venturi, P. T. 15, 33
Verburg, P. A. 187, 193
Vine, B. 147
Vinogradova, V. L. 34, 323
Vinokur, G. O. 267, 280
Vinosalvo, G. de 193
Vitus, St. 7
Vladimir, Prince 18, 30, 33f., 329, 332, 334
Voegelin, C. F. 267
Voznesenskij, A. 92
Vries, J. de 40, 43ff., 48
Vsevolod, son of Svjatoslav 321f.
Vyncke, F. 12

Wackernagel, J. 20, 42, 272, 328
Walde, A. 20, 42
Wales, R. 71
Wallerand, G. 188
Wallon, H. 144
Walters, D. A. 89
Watkins, C. W. 41, 48, 272
Waugh, L. R. 59, 166, 168, 177, 179, 263, 372
Webb, C. C. J. 195
Weigl, E. 139
Weingart, M. 335
Weir, R. H. 157
Weiss, A. P. 274f.
Welby, Lady 204f.
Wells, H. 309
Wepman, J. 137
Werner, K. 190
Wernicke, C. 175, 178
Wertheimer, M. 255f.
Wessén, E. 44
Wheeler, B. I. 235
Whitney, W. D. 48, 208f., 219ff., 222ff., 225ff., 229ff., 232ff., 235f., 269, 271, 277

Whorf, B. L. 107f., 161f., 262, 276f.
Wienecke, E. 10, 14
Wikander, S. 27
William of Occam. See: *Occam, William of*
William of Sherwood 189f., 195
Wilson, W. 308
Winteler, J. F. 82ff., 85, 258ff., 287
Winteler, M. 254, 258
Wolf, C. G. 172, 180
Wolfram 193
Worth, D. S. 326

Xardžiev, N. 353
Xenopol, A. 240
Xlebnikov, V. 126, 359ff., 375f.

Zaliznjak, A. A. 65
Zámrský, M. 36
Zarębina, M. 140
Zelenin, D. 10, 13, 46
Zemit-Zimin 365
Zibrt, Č. 10f., 36, 47
Zimin, A. A. 324ff., 327f., 331
Žirkov, L. I. 280

INDEX OF LANGUAGES DISCUSSED

Albanian 6, 20, 22, 25, 36, 39
American Indian languages 153, 266, 268
Anatolian 44
Anglo-Saxon 31
Arabic 196
Armenian 7, 19, 27, 49f., 52
Arumanian 22
Avestan 14, 25, 38, 42, 50

Baltic languages, Balts 4ff., 9, 14, 19, 32, 37, 39, 42, 44
Baltic Slavs (Balto-Slavic) 15ff., 23
Bantu 107
Bulgarian, Bulgarians 4, 6, 17, 19, 21f., 336
Bushmen languages 105

Caucasian languages 280f., 300, 305
Celtic, Celts 6, 8, 21, 25, 31f., 40, 42ff.
Celtic-Latin 21
Chinese 120
Church Slavonic 3, 13ff., 29, 31f., 68, 333ff., 375
Croatian, Croats 27
Czech, Czechs 4, 7f., 25ff., 30, 36f., 42, 46, 48, 51ff., 70f., 109, 114, 181, 265, 296ff., 299, 323, 371, 375

Danish 192
Dutch 269

East Slavic languages 3, 7f., 16, 37, 50, 53, 332f.

Egyptian 241
English 13, 60, 71, 90, 104, 109ff., 114, 117, 119, 122f., 132, 134f., 138, 145f., 168, 181, 265, 272, 341
Estonian 45

Finnish 45
Finno-Ugric 305
French 12, 89, 99 109f., 122f., 131f., 137, 141, 181, 193, 269, 294

German, Germans 3, 14, 16, 71, 109ff., 122, 129, 131, 143, 181, 193, 242, 269
Germanic languages 6, 22, 32, 48, 247, 372
Gilyak 105, 373
Gothic 4, 6, 21
Greek, Greeks 3f., 6, 20ff., 25, 30, 32, 34ff., 38, 42, 51, 81, 99, 111, 116, 195, 209, 247, 333f.

Hebrew 182, 375
Hittite 20, 25, 39, 42, 44
Hungarian 296

Icelandic 3
Indic 7, 32, 42, 49, 81, 116
Indo-European 4ff., 12ff., 15, 19f., 23, 25, 28, 30ff., 39, 41ff., 44f., 47f., 51, 215, 220f., 235, 245f., 272, 277, 314ff., 317, 328, 372, 374
Indo-Iranian 5, 8f., 28f., 39, 44, 47, 49
Iranian, Iranians 4f., 7ff., 15, 25, 27ff., 30, 32, 42, 49ff., 52

INDEX OF LANGUAGES DISCUSSED

Irish 21, 40, 193
Italian 12, 103, 269, 376

Japanese 101, 107, 110f.

Kafirs, Pamirian 20
Karelian 31
Kashubian 26

Latin 3f., 6, 8, 17, 20, 25, 30f., 39, 42, 81, 100, 193, 195ff., 242, 247, 334
Latvian 19, 23, 37ff., 46, 48, 363
Lekhitic 17
Lithuanian, Lithuanians 5ff., 19, 22, 23, 25, 27, 37ff., 41ff., 46, 48, 115, 360

Macedonian, Macedonians 21f., 25, 36
Mitannian 47
Mongolian 322
Mordvinian 372
Moravians 17, 38

Norwegian 101, 107, 177

Old Church Slavonic: see *Church Slavonic*
Old High German 21
Old Indic 8, 20, 25, 27, 31, 194
Old Irish 19, 24, 40
Old Norse 39, 44

Pashto 20
Persian 9
Phrygian 7, 9
Polabian 6, 16
Polish, Poles 3f., 6, 8, 21, 23, 26, 29f., 47, 51, 68, 71, 116, 149, 181, 296, 323
Pomeranian 17
Provençal 193

Romance languages 32, 277
Rumanian 7, 22, 24, 26f., 53
Russian 3, 6ff., 8f., 12, 15ff., 18, 21ff., 24ff., 29ff., 33f., 37f., 42ff., 46ff., 50, 62ff., 65, 68ff., 71f., 73ff., 76f., 92, 101f., 108, 110f., 115, 120, 122f., 125f., 138, 141, 157ff., 168, 173, 175, 181, 193, 245, 265, 267, 277, 279ff., 289ff., 293ff., 296ff., 301, 321, 323, 327f., 333, 336f., 349, 353ff., 356, 359, 371, 373ff.

Samoyed languages 104
Sanskrit 38, 43, 194, 221, 236
Scandinavian languages 277
Serbian, Serbs 6, 8, 13, 18, 22, 29, 323
Serbocroatian 8, 23, 38, 68f., 71, 336
Slavic languages and Common Slavic 3ff., 6f., 8f., 12ff., 15f., 18f., 22, 25f., 28ff., 30ff., 37, 39, 43f., 46ff., 50ff., 68f., 126, 277, 328, 332, 335f., 371f., 374f.
Slovak 7, 17, 27, 38, 53, 296, 299, 323
Slovenian 4, 8, 27, 51
South Slavic languages 4, 6, 16, 21, 23, 36, 51
Sumerian 81, 186
Swedish 269
Swiss-German 83

Thraco-Phrygian 4f.

Ukrainian 26, 295f., 301, 323
Umbrian 8, 41
Uralic languages 13

Vagrian 30
Varangians 6, 18
Vedic 5, 7f., 38ff., 42, 46, 48, 51f., 194, 242, 247
Vepsian, Veps 31, 45

Welsh 21
West Slavic languages 4, 6f., 16, 26, 43, 51, 280, 296, 334, 336

INDEX OF SUBJECTS

Abrupt: see *Continuant*.
Abstraction 151
Acquisition of language: see *Language, acquisition of*.
Acrostic 249, 351f.
Action, dyadic category of 248
Active mood 90, 138, 248
Actor 294, 297, 299
Acute: see *Grave*.
Adaptation 106
Addition 71
Addresser/addressee 67, 75, 88, 96, 113ff., 117, 133, 139, 203, 206, 347
Adjective 68, 70, 137f., 145, 188; diminutive 71; possessive 76
Adverb 69
Advertisement 298
Affective expressions 168
Affix 73
Affricate 61
Agent 90, 138
Agrammatism 134ff., 137
Agraphia 139, 181
Alexia 139
Algebra 200
Alliteration 116, 330, 372
Ambiguity 133
Amusia 140, 173
Anagram 237–247 *passim*, 317
Animal communication 93ff., 97, 147
Anthropology 235, 298f.
Antonym 69f., 172
Aphasia 67, 121, 128–140 *passim*, 146, 163–182 *passim*, 286, 374; agrammatical 136; sensory 136f.; temporal 138; topographic syndromes of 132
Appellative 96
Apperception 150f.
Arabic linguistic thought 191
Arbitrariness 200
Aristotelianism 196
Ars poetica 193
Art 103f., 214, 217
Artifice 215
Asemasia 139
Aspect, verbal 110, 158, 343
Assimilation 62ff.
Atlases, linguistic 292
Autonomy 96, 102, 129
Avant-garde 357, 361, 375

Bedeutung 203
Behaviorism 147, 275
Bilingualism 88, 100f.
Binary opposition 86, 88, 144, 262, 372
Biology 143, 150
Brain 106; and language 59, 163–180 *passim*, 286; cerebral hemispheres 165, 168, 177; cortex 132; functional asymmetry of 165, 174; left hemisphere 164, 166ff., 170ff., 173ff., 176f., 213; lesions 132, 163, 165, 169, 176; right hemisphere 137f., 164, 166ff., 170f., 173, 175, 177; split brain research 86, 130, 137, 164, 166; topography of 163
Byword 70
Byzantine literature 193

Carol, Christmas 46f.
Case 188
Censorship 298
Ceremony 201, 206
Change, linguistic 160, 239, 286, 290f., 315f., 374
Chess, game of 210, 230
Child language 129; sequence of phonological acquisition 141, 144; child's view of language 157ff. See also *Language, acquisition of.*
Choreography 201
Cinema 66, 214
Circumlocution 92, 100, 117
Circus 214
Clause 95f., 132, 135, 205
Code, verbal 86ff., 90, 95f., 117, 133, 157, 172, 213, 215, 217f.
Code-switching 88
Collective 143; creation 298
Colonialism 102, 129
Communication 81, 87, 98, 101, 113, 115; ostensive 171
Communism 310
Compact/diffuse 167
Comparative method 15
Competence 87, 133, 139
Complementarity 111, 161
Concurrence 59, 61
Conjunction 104, 118
Conscious/unconscious 143, 148–162 *passim*, 256, 289
Consonant 60, 89, 166f., 191; plosive 60
Context 89f., 95f., 99, 113, 118, 136, 195, 213, 316f.
Context-free 89, 99, 316
Context-sensitivity 59, 89, 95, 99, 236, 316
Contextual meaning 89, 118f., 194f., 373
Contextual variation 87, 256, 372
Contiguity/similarity 171f., 174, 176, 201, 203, 206, 215f., 292, 315, 375
Continuant/abrupt 60f., 123
Contradictories 71, 85, 89

Constrictive 60
Convention, linguistic 206, 211, 235; artistic 214
Convertibility 88
Correlation 127
Costume 299, 301
Creativity 92, 95f. 99, 106, 121, 142, 147, 193, 375
Cubism 125, 261
Cultivators 8
Culture 102f., 106f., 111, 285
Customs 209
Cybernetics 143
Cyrillic script 332f.

Declension 69, 73
Decoding: see Encoding
Decoration 296
Deixis 95f.
Demarcational elements 213
Depth 71
Design, verbal 95, 371
Desinence 73f.
Diachrony 142, 151, 213, 234, 270f., 285, 291, 296, 316, 374. See also *Synchrony.*
Dialectics 186f., 198
Dialectology 280, 301
Dialogue 143, 213
Dichotic hearing 164, 166, 170, 173, 177
Dichotomy 97, 375; dichotomous constructions 66
Difference: see *Sameness.*
Diffusion 292
Diminutive 69, 71, 158
Diphthong 25, 43
Discontinuous matter 264
Discourse 86, 120, 250
Discovery 187
Distance 71
Distinctive features 59ff., 74, 86ff., 93, 106, 122f., 125, 127, 130f., 159, 166f., 213, 262, 372
Double articulation 189
Dream 298

Dualism, religious 5
Dvoevěrie (Double faith) 3, 31
Dyad 251, 375; relational 251
Dynamics 88, 97, 142f., 151, 263, 290, 295, 316, 374. See also *Statics*.

Egocentrism 306ff., 309
Ejaculations 168f.
Electroconvulsive therapy (ECT) 164ff., 167f., 170f., 173, 175ff.
Ellipsis 87, 100, 117, 120, 139, 157, 160, 182, 196f.
Emblem 201
Emission 132
Empiricism 81, 221, 235, 281
Enclitic 64, 327
Encoding/decoding 59, 117, 133, 176, 375
Epic tradition 70, 280, 294, 374
Epilepsy 164, 173
Epithet 17, 20, 325, 346
Equivalence 85, 91, 117, 263
Erotic symbolism 109
Ethnology 153f., 280, 285, 299
Etiquette 299f.
Etymology 13, 28, 30f.
Eurasian movement 312
Excentrism 307, 311
Exclamation 93, 168
Existence, categories of 201
Explicitness 87, 100, 117, 139, 157, 160
Extension 69, 195

Fabliaux 297
Facetiae 301
Factual/imputed 215
Faith 5, 15
Fairy tales 297
Family rites 4
Fashion 228
Feudalism 322
Fictions 66, 95, 120, 135
Field work, folkloric 295
Flat/non-flat 74f., 262f.
Folk riddle 17

Folk ritual 295
Folk song 17, 38, 46, 70
Folk theatre 294ff., 297, 299, 302
Folklore 6ff., 15, 17, 24, 26f., 29f., 32, 36ff., 41, 125, 159, 245, 280f., 293ff., 297, 301, 373f.
Folklore, literary transformations of 293
Folkloric act 294
Folkloristics 297
Form 126; inner 281; overlapping 87
Functions, linguistic 91, 93, 113, 284, 288, 296; aesthetic 295f.; cognitive 114; conative 91ff., 96, 113ff.; denotative 113; emotive 87, 91, 93, 96, 109, 113ff.; expressive 114; incantatory 115; magical 295; metalingual 91, 113, 117, 156, 160, 289; phatic 91, 113, 115; poetic 87, 91f., 109, 113, 115f., 126, 174, 285, 288; referential 91ff., 96, 113, 115; representational 217
Funerary rites 295
Future 66, 92, 135, 147, 174f., 216, 252f., 264
Futurism 357–361 *passim*, 376

Gender 108f., 158f.
Genetics 81, 105
Geneva school 142
Genre 371
Geometry 82, 252
Geographical propinquity 315
German view of Slavs 14, 16
Germanic verse 242, 247
Gestalt 145, 216, 252, 301
Gesture 201, 209, 296
Gift of tongues 81, 97
Glory (*slava*) 322, 330f.
Glossematics 191
Glottogony 97
Gnezdovo inscription 332–335 *passim*
Gnosticism 360
Goal 90
God, gods 4ff., 14f.
Grammar 86, 100, 129, 133, 186,

INDEX OF SUBJECTS

189f., 192, 210, 213, 253, 272; comparative 223ff., 226, 239, 269; development of 145; philosophical 197, 273; spatial relations in 68–72; speculative 191; universal 190f.
Grammar of poetry 342, 373
Grammatical categories 88, 110, 124, 138, 154, 172, 270, 352, 373
Grammatical concepts 188, 193, 276
Grammatical meaning 73, 89, 99, 110, 119, 121, 154, 187, 193f., 251, 316
Grave/acute 60, 74f.
Greek verse 247
Grimm's law 274
Grotesque 293, 355

Habit 150
Height 71
Heredity 106
Heteronomy 102, 129
Hiatus 350
Hic et nunc 90, 94, 106, 135
Hierarchy, linguistic 85, 87, 94ff., 106, 113, 127, 130, 134, 138, 140, 145, 167, 213, 296, 372
History 232, 234
Holophrase 60, 90, 135, 145
Holophrastic stage 66
Homeric poems 238, 242
Homonymy 31, 37, 87, 121, 133f., 172
Humanism 187
Hypocorisms 45

Icon 174, 201, 206f., 210, 213ff., 216, 250, 253
Ideocracy 312
Imitation 142
Immediacy 167, 170ff., 173f., 177
Imperative 92, 114, 136
Implicational laws 59, 87, 93, 97, 106, 142
Improvisation 293
Index (indexical sign) 203, 206f., 213ff., 216, 253
Idols 7f., 15, 17f., 33ff.

Indic poetry 194
Indo-European poetry 215, 246, 317
Igor' Tale 321–331 *passim*
Innovation 283
Input 88
Internal (inner) speech 91, 98, 192, 203
Instances 207, 229, 371
Insulin shocks 166
Integration 96, 102, 129
Intention 195, 245
Interdictions, verbal 13
Interjections 114, 168f.
Interpreter/interpretant 118, 206, 210, 251
Intonation 170
Intuition 155
Invariance 59, 82, 84, 87, 89f., 99, 114, 127, 191, 199, 211, 252, 256, 258f., 263, 287, 291, 316, 371ff. See also *Variation*.
Invariants, relational 85f., 88
Irish poetry 193
Isolationism 15, 37, 101f., 108, 129

Jers 332

Kinship terminology 118

Labial 74, 263
Language 81, 85, 98, 101, 103f., 111, 228, 271; acquisition of 60, 66, 71, 90, 93ff., 96f., 103, 120, 128, 134, 136, 138 141–148 *passim*, 157, 163, 166, 186, 290, 374; alliance 315; and culture 285; and thought 203, 255ff., 258, 282; as human (social) institution 226, 234f., 274; families 314; object 116f., 195; origin of 97
Languages, artificial 90, 200, 316; formalized 99, 112, 213; inflectional 136; natural 213, 316; topology of 263
Langue/parole 212, 270ff.
Latin verse 193, 247
Lazzi 297

Learning 143, 155
Legisigns 210, 229
Levels, linguistic 88f., 129f., 144, 171
Lexical meaning 90, 99, 119, 121, 187, 193f., 213, 251, 276
Lexicon 270, 317
License 215
Linguistic Society of America 265, 267, 273
Linguistics 84, 99, 131, 252, 263; comparative 16, 21, 32, 81, 85, 314ff., 317, 328; comparative Indo-European 12; descriptive 271, 291, 314ff.; diachronic 221; general 85; historical 15; history of 82, 185f., 198, 221, 271; structural 127
Literacy 91
Literary history 297
Logic 116, 118, 192, 202f., 213, 248
Long/short 122f.
Lyric 294

Magic 8, 25, 45, 50, 115, 294ff.
Man-sign 294, 299, 301
Mark 122f.
Marked/unmarked 59ff., 69ff, 85f., 88, 90, 122f., 127, 131, 138, 145
Mask 299
Mathematics 82, 84, 164, 172, 213, 282, 287
Matrices 89, 95
Meaning 85f., 88, 99, 118, 130, 189, 203, 206, 213, 236, 251, 276; central 118; contextual: see *Contextual meaning*; figurative 95, 120; general 89f., 99, 118, 194; grammatical: see *Grammatical meaning*; inherent 195; lexical: see *Lexical meaning*; marginal 90, 95, 118; normal 118; transferred 90, 118f.; widened 119
Mechanism 92, 274
Mediacy 167, 177
Medieval stage 296
Medieval theory of language 81, 99, 104, 116, 185–198 *passim*

Memory 150, 187
Mendeleev's table 252
Mentalism 251, 274ff.
Message, verbal 67, 95ff., 113, 115, 133, 136, 172, 218
Metalanguage 90f., 96, 100, 113, 116f., 118ff., 121, 127, 157f., 186, 195, 374
Metaphor 95, 118f., 201, 215, 296, 375. See also *Metonymy*.
Metathesis 13, 28, 30
Metonymy 95, 119, 296, 344f., 375. See also *Metaphor*.
Metrics 280, 371, 373; comparative 372
Middle Ages 199
Modistae 187, 192f.
Mood 67
Morpheme 73, 88, 99, 106, 131f., 213, 266, 272
Morphological categories 137
Morphology 88f., 94, 105, 131, 239
Moscow Linguistic Circle 265, 267, 279–282, 284f.
Moscow linguistic school 220, 282, 284f.
Moscow University 281ff.
Mushroom 336f.
Music 40, 173f., 201, 211, 214, 216f.; fundamental operations of 216
Mutation 82
Myth, poetic 373
Mythology 3–53 *passim*, 213, 317, 374; comparative 12, 15; comparative Indo-European 12, 32; Slavic 12. See also Index of Mythological Names and Index of Mythological Motifs.

Name, bipartite 44f.; personal 8, 16, 24, 29, 34; proper 96, 118; mythological 13; mythological, Indo-European 39; theophoric 45
Narrative plots, typology of 297
Narrated event 66, 89
Nasalized/non-nasalized 74f., 89

INDEX OF SUBJECTS

Nationalism 308f., 311
Natural selection 97
Nature 106f.
Negation 95
Neogrammarians 81, 85, 142, 186, 198, 220ff., 225, 269, 271, 286
Neologism 147, 158
Neurolinguistics 132, 176f., 285
Neurology 131
Nibelungen 237f., 241
Noises 167f.
Nomina actionis/nomina actoris 137
Noun 67, 136ff., 172, 188, 373; concrete 137

Obstruent 59, 62f., 74
Occult tradition 245
Onomastics 20, 24, 32, 45, 335
Ontogeny 93, 160
Opposition, linguistic 89, 122, 125, 127, 131, 233, 248, 251, 261
Oral tradition 70, 91, 293, 298, 373; Slavic 15
Originality 214
Output 88
Oxytone 74

Paganism 3, 24, 26, 31, 33
Painting 214; abstract 217
Palatalization 62, 75
Paradigmatics 73, 188
Paraphrase 157
Parallelism 215f., 327, 354, 373
Paregmenon 327
Paronomasia 17, 38, 116
Pars pro toto 171
Part and whole 94, 129, 144, 217, 252f., 261, 285ff., 316
Patristic philosophy 192
Patronymic 15, 29
Parts of speech 188, 193
Passive mood 90, 138, 248
Past 66, 92, 135, 147, 174, 216, 253, 264
Performance/work 138f., 211f.
Person 67

Pharyngealization 263
Phenomenology 125, 190, 200f., 204, 249, 281
Philology 224, 282, 375
Phoneme 59f., 64, 73, 93, 99, 106, 126f., 131, 155, 166f., 208, 213, 246, 270, 272, 316, 372
Phonetics 239
Phonological opposition 261; system 59, 167; units 261
Phonology 105, 122, 125f., 131, 133, 155, 169, 225, 266, 281, 372
Phrase 94, 132, 135, 146
Phraseology 104
Phylogeny 160
Physics 82, 111, 252, 260f., 288
Pitch 177
Play 256, 295; eternal, motif of 353
Pleophonic form 24, 37
Poésie recluse 193
Poetic language 280f.; texture 244
Poetics 375
Poetry 99, 108f., 111, 116, 125f., 214f., 241, 246, 261, 282
Polysemy 247
Port Royal grammar 197f.
Prague Linguistic Circle 261, 266, 279, 312, 364
Predicate 66, 94, 135f., 145f.; psychological 94
Prefix 62f.
Preposition 62f., 95
Present 92, 216, 252f., 264
Preterit 89
Preverb 137
Probability 59
Production 256; categories of 256
Productivity 69
Progress 103f.
Pronoun 67, 73, 76, 137, 188, 373; personal 75, 96, 136; reflexive 75
Prosody 371f.
Proverb 70
Psychology 129, 219, 252, 301; of peoples 306
Puppet theatre 297

Quantity, vocalic 122
Quantum theory 105
Quanta, elementary 263
Question 95

Radio 91
Rationalism 196
Reading 91, 139, 182
Reconstruction 12, 314, 317
Redundancy 167, 213
Reduplication 22, 24
Referent 96, 113
Relativity (relativism) 84, 259, 261, 287, 307f.; configurational 84; situational 259; theory of 83, 255, 262f.
Religion, history of 238, 241
Religious terminology 13
Religious vocabulary, Slavic 14
Renaissance 199
Repetition, sound 330
Reported speech 96
Rhetoric 91, 99, 196
Ritual 13, 15, 228, 295f., 317, 335
Ritual implements 5
Root 136
Rural world 301

Sameness/difference 211, 229, 233, 263
Sandhi 64
Sanskrit poetics and linguistics 194
Sapir-Whorf hypothesis 107f., 161f.
Saturnine verse 238, 242f.
Schizophrenia 164, 172
Scholastics 186, 190, 194, 196
Schoolmen 81, 187, 195
Scipions, tomb of 238, 242
Sculpture 214
Selection 89, 93, 95, 121, 142
Self-determination 308
Self-motion 143
"Selfsome" word (*samovitoe slovo*) 359
Semantics 86, 90, 99, 104, 118, 120, 194f., 281

Semiology 206, 212
Semiotics 87, 98f., 118, 140, 171, 176, 191, 199–218 *passim*, 228, 249, 251, 271, 276f., 297ff., 301, 375; of culture 214; relation of linguistics to 212ff.
Sense-discrimination 60, 169, 263, 316, 372
Sensory impairment 121
Sentence 99, 106, 132, 145ff., 189, 213, 250; declarative 92, 114f., 136; dyadic 146; elliptic 137; impersonal 197; interrogative 177; subject/predicate 66f., 90, 145
Sequence 60, 316
Set 160f.
Sharp/non-sharp 74f., 123, 262f.
Shifters 67, 96, 136, 172, 373
Sign 118, 140, 174, 190f., 193, 199, 203, 227, 229, 249, 255f., 276, 299; arbitrary and spontaneous 203, 210ff., 230; auditory and visual 203; bilateral definition of 202; classification of 203, 206; conventional 208, 230, 255; determined/undetermined 201; dichotomy of, with objects 116; mediate/immediate 202f.; metonymical and metaphorical 203; modality of 201; natural and accidental 203; natural and arbitrary 200f.; nature of 201; personal 255; proper and figurative 203; proper/improper 201; simple/composite 202f.; systems 89ff., 98, 106, 205, 211, 228, 239, 251, 375; translatability of 86, 118, 206; unisemic and polysemic 203; universal and particular 203
Signal 94, 97, 168, 170. See also *Immediacy*.
Signans/Signatum 99, 206f., 210, 213, 214, 218
Signifiant/signifié 89, 228f., 247
Signifier, linearity of 247
Signification 195, 203
Signum 99

Similarity: see *Contiguity/Similarity*
Simultaneity 82, 217, 263, 316f.
Sinn 203
Skaldic poetry 193
Slavic-Iranian affinities 4, 14f., 29; religious vocabulary 5
Slavic deities 5
Slavs, Christianization of 3, 9
Sociologism 142
Sociology 234
Sodium Anytal injections 165
Sonority 60, 62
Sound 189; and meaning 250, 314; figures 244; pattern 276
Space 66, 68, 81, 88, 90f., 98, 101, 103, 106, 135, 143, 147, 172, 199, 291, 315f., 374
Spatial hearing 171
Speech 167; conditioned 133; displaced 90, 95, 147; emotive 169f., 173; event 66f., 75, 89, 96; perception of 130, 139; production 139; sounds 86, 130, 145, 155; spontaneous 133f.
Sprachbünde 291f., 374
Statics 88, 97, 142, 151, 211, 291, 316, 374. See also *Dynamics*.
Stoics 190, 196, 206, 228, 246
Stops 60f.
Strident/nonstrident (mellow) 60f.
Structural analysis 32, 85
Structuralism 125ff., 275, 299
Structure 125, 249; deep 191; duplex 96f., 136; secondary modeling 213; syntactic: see *Syntactic structures*.
Style, parabolic-figurative 193; verbal 96, 104
Stylistic variation 74, 87, 160, 169, 213, 290, 317, 374
Subject 66, 94, 135ff., 138, 146f.
Subjunctive 342ff.
Subliminal verbal patterning 244f.
Substantive 188, 193
Suffix 68f., 145f.; diminutive 69, 158; inflectional 138; *-n-* 20, 39, 43ff.;

-unъ 16, 19, 24; *-una, -uga* 22; *-unni, -ŭnas* 39; *-ut-* 24; *-yn-* 19
Suicide 366f.
Supposition 194f.
Suppositiones 194
Supraconscious poetry (*zaumnaja poèzija*) 357
Symbol 118, 174f., 190, 207, 210f., 213ff., 216, 228ff., 253
Symbolism 193, 276
Symmetry/asymmetry 84, 264, 317
Synchrony 32, 88, 142, 151, 211, 231, 234, 236, 263, 270f., 295f., 316, 374. See also *Diachrony*.
Syncretism 296
Synecdoche 171, 217
Synesthesia 201
Synonymy 20, 23, 28, 31, 117, 119, 121, 157, 172
Syntagmatic/paradigmatic 172, 176, 375
Syntax 90, 94, 105, 137f., 147, 196, 250; syntactic structures 89, 99, 132, 135, 188f., 191, 213
Systems 314ff.; self-regulating 87. See also *Sign, systems*.

Teaching 143
Teleology 125ff., 275
Television 91
Tense 67, 96, 188
Textual criticism 21
Theatre 66, 214, 294. See also *Folk theatre*
Time 8, 66, 81, 88, 90f., 95, 98, 101, 103, 106, 135, 138, 143, 147, 175, 199, 316, 374
Token, verbal 95
Tonality 167
Topology 84f., 125, 127, 212, 252f.
Toponymy 7, 9, 13, 16f., 19, 21, 25f., 34, 36f., 44, 49
Tradition 186, 198, 283, 293
Transfiguration 294
Transformation 85ff., 89ff., 92, 150, 209, 252, 264, 287

Translation 88, 91, 100, 107, 109, 111, 117, 121, 201, 251
Transposition 91, 111
Trier bas-relief 42
Tropes and figures 92, 99
Truth test 92, 95, 114
Typology 32, 59, 85, 87, 299, 315, 317, 372

Unity/diversity 81, 130
Unities, classical 296
Universals 59, 61, 87, 97, 105f., 142, 191, 263, 289, 372f.; and particulars 90
Universe of discourse 120, 248
Univocality 212
Unmarked: see *Marked/unmarked*
Utterance 205, 213

Value 126, 208, 211, 216, 233, 253
Variation 82, 84f., 87, 99, 114, 211, 252, 258, 287, 291, 316, 371. See also *Invariance*.
Vedic verse 226, 242, 247

Verb 67, 137f., 172, 188, 373
Verbal noun 137f., 172
Versification 244, 371
Victorian era 82
Vocabulary 100, 104f., 147
Vocalic/non-vocalic 60, 167
Vocalism/consonantism 145
Vocative 114
Voiced/voiceless 62ff., 123
Vowel 60, 191; nasal 89; plain 74; rounded 74; supporting 60

Wackernagel's law 328
Width 71
Will 153
Word 88ff., 94f., 99, 106, 131, 134, 145f., 161, 189, 199, 213; auxiliary 172; main/accessory 145
Writing 91, 139, 164, 172, 182, 186, 209, 223, 234

Zoomorphic style 36
Zoroastrian cosmology 29

INDEX OF MYTHOLOGICAL NAMES*

Āditya (Vedic) 39
Agni (Indo-Iran.) 29
Ahura-Mazdā (Avestan) 42
Aĩsa (Greek) 31, 51
Aṁśa (Vedic) 8, 31, 51
Apollo (Greek) 8
Ardvī Sūrā Anāhitā (Iran.) 9
Artemis (Greek) 8
Asura (Vedic) 25, 42, 45, 47

Bacchus (Greek) 22
Bakxēbakxon (Greek) 22
Băbărútă (Rum.) 24
Bhaga (Vedic) 8, 31, 51
Belías, Bẽlos (Greek) 33
Bojan (Rus.) 24, 36, 40
Bussumarus (Celtic) 43

Dabogъ (Slavic) 30
Daímones ploutodótai (Greek) 31
Dažьbogъ (Slavic) 8, 29, 50f.
Dažbogovičь (Ukr.) 29
Daždьbogъ (Slavic) 29
Didjul (Bulg.) 22
Didjulja (Bulg.) 22
Djudjul (Bulg.) 22
Dodola, Dudula (South Slavic) 7, 22f.
Dodólă (Rum.) 22
Dudola (South Slavic) 22
Dudolă, Dudulă (Rum.) 22
Dudule (Alb.) 22
Dudulejka (Serb.) 22

Dudutis, Dundutis (Lith.) 23
Dundùlis (Lith.) 23
Dundusėlis (Lith.) 23
Dzidziela (Polish) 23

Esus (Celtic) 25, 42f.

Fjǫrgyn (Norse) 6, 22, 39
Fjǫrgynn (Norse) 6, 20, 22, 39, 48
Fortūna (Latin) 39

Helios (Greek) 8
Hephaestus (Greek) 7, 26
Hercules (Greek) 29

Indra (Vedic) 47
Indra Vṛtrahan. See: *Vṛtrahan*

Jarilo (Rus.) 7, 18
Jarog (Polish) 7, 28f., 51
Járog (Slovenian) 7, 51
Jarovit (Baltic) 7, 18
Járožica (Slovenian) 51
Jols (Rus.) 45f., 48
Jupiter (Latin) 7, 23. Epithets of: Elicius 7, 23; Pluvius 23

Mamercus (Latin) 22
Mamurins (Latin) 22
Marmar, Mamers (Latin) 22
Mars (Latin) 22
Mithra (Iranian) 5, 39
Mokošь (Slavic) 8f.

*Variant forms of primary names are listed in alphabetical order with the language given in parentheses; for filiation, refer to the text.

INDEX OF MYTHOLOGICAL NAMES

Óðinn (Norse) 44
Óðr (Norse) 44
Oùranós (Greek) 39

Papalúdă, Papalúgă (Rum.) 24
Papir (Ukr.) 26
Parjánya (Vedic) 5, 7, 20f., 39, 48
Parom (Slovak) 17
Pemperuga (South Slavic) 22
Pepereda (South Slavic) 22
Peperunga (South Slavic) 22
Perëndi (Alb.) 6, 20, 39
Pereplut (Old Rus.) 23f.
Pȩ̃rkuôns (Latvian) 19, 39
Perkúna, Percuna (Lith.) 6, 22, 39
Perkúnas (Lith.) 6f., 19, 22
Peron (Slovak) 17
Perperona (Bulg.) 22
Perperoûna (Greek) 22
Perperuna (Slavic) 6, 22f., 39
Perudi (Alb.) 20
Perun (Pamirifian Kafirs) 20
Perunъ (Slavic) 5f., 8, 16–24, 33ff., 39, 44, 48
Peruna- (Hittite) 20, 39, 44
Perúnas (Lith.) 7, 19
Perynъ (Slavic) 39
Piorunic, Pioruniec, Poruniec (Baltic) 17
Pirpirúnă (Arumanian) 22
Póros (Greek) 31, 51
Porovitъ (Baltic) 7, 18
Prepeluga (Old Rus.) 24
Preperuda, Peperuda (South Slavic) 22, 24
Preperuga, Peperuga (South Slavic) 22
Preperuna (South Slavic) 22
Pripegala (Old Rus.) 6, 24
Pŕ̥poruša (Dalmatian) 23

Quirinus (Latin) 8, 31

Radášek (Cz.) 26, 51
Rárach, Rarách (Cz.) 26, 51f.
Raráš (Cz.) 26, 51

Raráščata (Cz.) 51
Rarášek (Cz.) 26, 51f.
Rarašik (Slovak) 51
Raroch (Cz.) 51
Raróg (Pol.) 26
Rárog (Slovenian) 51
Rarogъ (Slavic) 7, 26, 28f., 51
Raroh (Cz.) 26, 51
Rároh (Slovenian) 51
Rároh (Slovak) 26, 51
Rárohy (Cz.) 51
Rárož (Cz.) 51
Rodjenica (Srb.-Cr.) 8
Rodъ (Old Rus.) 8, 31
Rojenica (Slovenian) 8
Rožanica (Slavic) 8
Rjujevit (Baltic) 18
Ruevitъ (West Slavic)

Sabadios (Phrygian) 7
Sъlnьce (Slavic) 50
Simarglъ (Slavic) 9
Sīmorg (Iran.) 9
Stribogъ (Slavic) 8, 30, 50f.
Sucellos (Celtic) 43
Sünd (Vepse) 31
Svarogъ (Slavic) 7f., 25–31, 49f.
Svarožičь (Rus.) 7, 49f.
Svętovitъ (Baltic) 7, 18
Šüntü (Karelian) 31

Taranis (Celtic) 43
Tarḫunnaš (Hittite) 39
Teutates (Celtic) 8, 31
Thor (Norse) 6, 18f., 48

Ull (Norse) 44, 48
Ullinn (Norse) 44f., 48
Ullr (Norse) 25, 44f., 48

Vaha (Avestan) 50
Vahagn (Armenian) 7, 22, 27, 49f., 52
Vahēvahē (Armenian) 22
Vahram (Armenian) 27
Vala (Vedic) 46f.

INDEX OF MYTHOLOGICAL NAMES

Varagn (Iran.) 50
Vāragna (Iran.) 7, 50f.
Varhragn (Armenian) 50
Varhran (Zoroastrian) 28
Varuṇa (Vedic) 39–48 *passim*
Vāta- (Indo-Iran.) 8
Vayu (Iran.) 30
Vėlė (Lith.) 37, 46
Veleda (Celtic) 25, 40
Veles (Cz.) 8, 25, 36f., 42, 45ff., 48
Vẽlės, Vẽlės (Lith.) 25, 37ff.
Velesъ/Volosъ (Slavic) 8, 24f., 33–48 *passim*
Veḷi (Latvian) 38
Velionìs, Veliónis (Lith.) 37, 39
Vẽlinas (Lith.) 25, 37, 39, 41f., 44f., 48
Veliuonà (Lith.) 25, 37, 39
Velis (Latvian) 46
Vellaunus (Gaul.) 43ff.
Veļ̃ls (Latvian) 37
Vélnias (Lith.) 37
Veḷ̃ns (Latvian) 37, 45f., 48
Vels (Latvian) 37

Véls (Lith.) 37
Větrъ (Slavic) 8, 50
Vještica (Serb.) 22
Vofionus (Umbrian) 8, 31
Volosъ. See: *Velesъ*
Vram (Armenian) 27
Vr̥θra (Iran.) 50
Vrthragna, Vr̥θragna, Vərəθraɣna (Iran.) 7f., 27ff., 49ff., 52
Vr̥tra (Indic) 49
Vr̥trahan, epithet of Indra (Indic) 7f., 27, 29, 49f., 52

Wališ- (Anatolian) 44f.
*Wulpuz (Norse) 25, 44

Xъrsъ (Old Rus.) 8, 29, 50
Xursīd (Persian) 8
Xvarənah (Avestan) 50

Zeus (Greek) 6f., 17, 20, 26. Epithets of: Dodōnē 7, 23; Keraunós 6, 20, 39; Naíos 7, 23; Phēgōnaîos 20
Žvoruna (Lith.) 39

INDEX OF MYTHOLOGICAL MOTIFS

Animal realm (kingdom) 7, 27f., 35, 37, 44f.
Arrow 30
Aurochs, gold-horned 7
Autumn 7, 18
Ax 43

Binding (fettering) 44
Bird 27f.
Bright 7, 18
Bull 38, 43
Butterfly 22

Calendrical rites 4, 7, 18
Cattle 8, 24f., 34f., 37, 41f., 47
Chief 25, 42
Child-bearing 9
Chthonic imagery 39, 337
Cloud 4, 15
Courtyard 47
Cow 38, 41, 46f.

Demonology 4, 7, 9, 14, 23, 26, 29, 31, 36f., 42, 47
Disease 5, 38, 41
Divination 8, 18, 40
Dragon 27f., 36
Druid 21
Dwarf, fiery: see Gnome

Egg of black hen 27
Evil spirits 5, 36
Exorcism 38
Eyes 28, 39, 50

Falcon 7, 27f., 50f., 323–330 *passim*.
Female deities 8ff.
Female demons 4f.
Fire 7f., 26ff., 29, 52
Fire-worshippers 26
Fortune-telling 18
Four-faced 7

Gnome 7, 26ff.
God, gods 4ff., 14f.
Gold 35
Good 5, 25, 42

Health 5, 43
Hill 6, 21
Holy 5
Horse 7f., 14
Hunter 37, 39, 44

Incantation 17, 21
Idols 7f., 15, 17f., 33ff.

Lightning 6
Lotus 28

Magician (magus) 24f., 40, 44f.
Marsh 39
Masculine force 18
Master 25, 42f.
Metamorphoses 27f.
Moist 8, 9
Mountain 30, 49

Oak 6, 20f., 47

Oaths 44f.; infringement of 35, 41f. 45. Also see *Treaties*.
Omniscience 40, 42, 45

Pairs, mythological 31
Paradise 5
Poet 24, 40f.
Procreation 31

Radiance (halo) 29, 50
Rain charms 6, 21ff.
Right, guardian of 41
Ring 6, 44
Ritual implements 5
River-spirits 21

Sacrifice 4, 13, 17
Sanctuaries 14
Seer 8, 24f., 36, 40, 42, 44
Semen 9
Seven 50
Sheep 9, 41
Singer 44
Sky 4, 6, 21
Smithery 7
Soothsayer 25
Spreading, dispersing 30, 51

Spring 7, 18
Striking, beating 6, 19, 22f., 43f.
Summer 18
Sun 8, 26, 29f., 49ff.

Taboo 6f., 13, 17, 23, 26, 28, 31, 44, 46
Thunder 6, 16, 19f., 22f., 43f.
Treaties, peace 3, 5, 8, 24, 33f., 38, 44; guarantor of 41f.
Tree 21, 43, 47

Victory 48
Vigilance 40, 42
Virgin 6, 21
Virility 7, 18
Vision 43, 50

War 20, 50
Water-spirits 21
Waters 38, 42
Wealth 5, 8, 25, 30f., 48, 51
Weapons 26, 29, 35
Whirling 6, 23
Whirlwind 7, 27
Wind 7f., 28, 30, 50ff.
Winter 18